PROSELYTIZATION REVISITED

LONDON   OAKVILLE

PROSELYTIZATION REVISITED

Rights Talk, Free Markets and Culture Wars

Edited by

Rosalind I.J. Hackett

3|10

Published by Equinox Publishing Ltd.
UK: Unit 6, The Village, 101 Amies St.,London SW11 2JW
USA: DBBC, 28 Main Street, Oakville, CT 06779
www.equinoxpub.com

First published 2008

British Library Cataloguing-in-Publication Data
A catalogue record for this book is available from the British Library.

Library of Congress Cataloging-in-Publication Data
Proselytization revisited : rights talk, free markets, and culture wars
/ edited by Rosalind I.J. Hackett.
    p. cm.
Includes bibliographical references and index.
ISBN-13: 978-1-84553-227-7 (hb)
ISBN-13: 978-1-84553-228-4 (pbk.)
1. Proselytizing. I. Hackett, Rosalind I. J. BL637.P76 2008
207'.2—dc22
                    2007046731

Typeset and edited by Queenston Publishing, Hamilton, Canada.

Printed in the United States of America by The Maple-Vail Book Manufacturing Group, Lakeville, MA.

Proselytization Revisited
Rights Talk, Free Markets and Culture Wars

Contents

Revisiting Proselytization in the Context of Rights Talk,   1
Free Markets and Culture Wars

Rosalind I. J. Hackett

Section I

Conflicts over Proselytism - An Overview and   35
Comparative Perspectivective

Jean-François Mayer

Conversion of the World: Proselytization in India and   53
the Universalization of Christianity

Jacob De Roover and Sarah Claerhout

The Logic of Anti-Proselytization, Revisited   77

Grace Kao

Section II

The Changing Face of Christian Proselytization: New   109
Actors from the Global South

Paul Freston

Muslim Apostasy, Christian Conversion, and Religious   139
Freedom in Egypt

Heather J. Sharkey

Seeing is More Than Believing: Posters and   167
  Proselytization in Nigeria
F.-K. Asonzeh Ukah

Section III

Buddhism and the Politics of Conversion in Sri Lanka   199
Steve C. Berkwitz

Merit and the Search for Inner Peace: the Discourses   231
  and Technologies of Dhammakaya Proselytization
Rachelle M. Scott

Asia's Antioch: Evangelical Christianity and   253
  Proselytism in Singapore
Jean DeBernardi

False Consciousness and the Jargon of Authenticity: 283
  Religion and Nationalism in the Christianised
  Lowland Philippines

Paul-François Tremlett

Salvation through Secular Protest: the Development of   301
  Falun Gong Proselytization
Patsy Rahn

The Social and Legal Context of Proselytization in   321
  Contemporary Japanese Religions
Mark Mullins

Section IV

Negotiating Proselytism in 21st Century Russia   339
Olga Kazmina

Between Da'wa and Mission: Turkish Islamic   365
    Movements in the Turkic World (Central Asia and
    the Caucasus)

Bayram Balci

Spiritual Wars in the 10-40 Window: Korean   389
    Proselytism among Russia's Asian Minorities

Julia S. Kovalchuk

SECTION V

Proselytization or Information? Wicca and the Internet   409

Shawn Arthur

You Can't Talk to an Empty Stomach: Faith-based   431
    Activism, Holistic Evangelism, and the Publicity of
    Evangelical Engagement

Omri Elisha

Proselytization: Closing Thoughts from a Sociologist   455
James T. Richardson

Index   465

Preface and acknowledgements

For several years I vowed never to do an edited book again. But the experience of this project compelled me to break that vow. It began with the urge to write something on the changing face of proselytization in our globalizing world, accompanied by the realization that I could not do it alone. So I decided to organize a symposium on the topic for the International Association for the History of Religion's nineteenth World Congress in Tokyo in March 2005. Several of the authors traveled from around the world to participate in this most stimulating academic encounter, and we followed up with more sessions at the 2007 American Academy of Religion and American Anthropological Association meetings in San Diego and Washington, DC respectively. In the interim, the academic *communitas* was nurtured by various exchanges within the group and among authors, as well as by internet and media postings of stories relating to controversial aspects of proselytizing (Jean-François Mayer and his www.Proselytism.info website were an invaluable resource in this regard).

I am especially gratified that this volume contains chapters from several younger scholars from around the globe. Their work reflects intimate knowledge of the various localities where they reside and/or have conducted recent fieldwork. The project is also enriched by the contributions of several seasoned scholars who have been able to provide analyses of larger social and religious fields. My own interests in religious change and (re)affiliation in Africa date back three decades, but, like many of the authors in the collection, I am struck by how the legal and mass-mediated dimensions of these issues have increased. This is why we chose to focus more on the *processes*, such as how religious groups and individuals propagate their messages, with a view to implementing their goals and attracting new followers, rather than the end *product* of actual "conversion" (which some of our authors argue is a very individualized, Western Christian concept). Transnational religious movements are a popular topic with researchers, journalists and public analysts these days and the case studies herein offer local, regional, national, and transnational perspectives on new strategies of representing and transmitting religious ideas and identities.

This project germinated and took shape while I was enjoying first-class academic support as a Rockefeller Fellow at the Joan B. Kroc Institute for International Peace Studies at the University of Notre Dame in 2003–04. Work on the chapter drafts was also facilitated by a non-teaching semester kindly granted to me in spring 2006 by my home institution, the University of Tennessee. I was aided in the task of editing the manuscript in the early stages by my then graduate assistant, Peter Kraslawsky. In the latter phase, Caroline Straight helped turn my roughshod index into a polished reality, with the assistance of Jonathan Kenigson on the sudoku aspects of index generation. Janet Joyce was my editor in a former life for another project, so I am more than happy that she and her fine Equinox team are the publishers of the current book. Finally, the book is dedicated to Professor Andrew F. Walls, not just because he set me on the high road to an academic career, but also for all the fresh thinking and ideas he has brought to the study of missionary activity in Africa and beyond.

Rosalind I. J. Hackett
Knoxville, Tennessee
January 27, 2008

Contributors

Shawn Arthur is an Assistant Professor of Religion at Appalachian State University in Boone, North Carolina. He received his Ph.D. from Boston University specializing in Daoism and Chinese Medicine, and he continues to author articles in his secondary field of interest: Contemporary Paganism.

Bayram C. Balci is the Director of the Institut Français d'Etudes sur l'Asie Centrale (IFEAC) in Tashkent, French Research Institute on Central Asia. He is the author of *Entre Islam et laïcité, les missionnaires de l'Islam en Asie Centrale, les Ecoles turques de Fethullah Gülen,* (Paris: Maisonneuve et Larose, 2003) and, with Raoul Motika, *Religion et politique dans le Caucase post soviétique* (Paris: Maisonneuve et Larose, 2007).

Stephen C. Berkwitz is an Associate Professor of Religious Studies at Missouri State University. He is the author of *Buddhist History in the Vernacular: The Power of the Past in Late Medieval Sri Lanka* (Brill, 2004) and *The History of the Buddha's Relic Shrine: A Translation of the* Sinhala Thupavamsa (Oxford University Press, 2007). He received a Fulbright Senior Scholar Award for Sri Lanka in 2006.

Sarah Claerhout is a research and teaching assistant at the Research Centre *Vergelijkende Cultuurwetenschap*, Ghent University, Belgium. The focus of the Research Centre is on the study of the Western culture through its understanding of other cultures and on the cultural differences between Asia and the West. She is currently working on a doctoral thesis on the Western understanding of religious conversion since the Reformation and the implications of this understanding for the debates on religious conversion in colonial and postcolonial India.

Jean DeBernardi is Professor of Anthropology at the University of Alberta. She is the author of *Rites of Belonging: Memory, Modernity and Identity in a Malaysian Chinese Community* (Stanford University Press, 2004) and *The Way that Lives in the Heart: Chinese Popular Religion and Spirit Mediums in Penang, Malaysia* (Stanford University Press, 2006). With funding from the Chiang Ching-kuo foundation and the Social Science and Humanities Research Council of Canada she is now doing research on the modernization of Daoism in Southeast Asia and China.

Omri Elisha is a cultural anthropologist and Resident Scholar at the School for Advanced Research, Santa Fe, NM. He has received research awards from the Social Science Research Council and Louisville Institute, and was a Post-doctoral Fellow at Fordham University. He has published in scholarly as well as journalistic venues, and is currently writing a book on conservative evangelical activism and US megachurches for University of California Press.

Jakob De Roover is a Postdoctoral Fellow of the Research Foundation (FWO) Flanders at the Research Centre *Vergelijkende Cultuurwetenschap*, Ghent University, Belgium. His research concerns the cultural history of liberal toleration and secularism in Europe and its impact on colonial and postcolonial India. In spring 2007 he was a visiting research scholar at the Department of Philosophy, Columbia University, New York, followed by a semester as Visiting Assistant Professor at the Department of Philosophy and Religion and as Research Scholar at the Mahatma Gandhi Center for Global Nonviolence, both at James Madison University in Virginia.

Paul Freston is Byker Chair in Sociology at Calvin College, Michigan and professor of sociology on the post-graduate programme in social sciences at the Universidade Federal de Sao Carlos, Brazil. He is the author of several books, including *Evangelicals and Politics in Asia, Africa and Latin America* (Cambridge University Press, 2001).

Rosalind I. J. Hackett is a Distinguished Professor in the Humanities at the University of Tennessee, Knoxville, where she teaches Religious Studies and Anthropology. She has published widely on religion in Africa, notably on new religious movements, as well as on art, media, gender, conflict, and religious freedom in the African context. In 2005 she was elected as President of the International Association for the History of Religions (until 2010). She is currently bringing to completion a co-edited volume *Religious Dimensions of Conflict and Peace in Neoliberal Africa* (Univ. of Notre Dame Press) and *Nigeria: Religion in the Balance* (US Institute of Peace).

Grace Y. Kao is Assistant Professor of Religious Studies in the Department of Interdisciplinary Studies at Virginia Tech. Her book, *Grounding Human Rights in a Pluralist World: Between Minimalist and Maximalist Approaches*, is currently under contract with Georgetown University Press. Her work has also appeared in a number of other outlets, including the *Journal of the American Academy of Religion* and the *Journal of the Society of Christian Ethics*. In 2005-2006, she was awarded an American Fellowship by the American Academy of University Women (AAUW).

Olga Kazmina is an Associate Professor of Ethnology at Moscow State University. She is the author of more than 150 publications. Her most recent articles (in Russian) are "Orthodox Religiosity in Contemporary Russia: Historical Problem of the Correlation of Religious Identity and Religious Practice" in the *Bulletin of Peoples' Friendship University of Russia* and "The Problem of Proselytism and the Formation of New Religious Situation in Russia" in the *Bulletin of Moscow University*. She has been a member of the editorial board of the *Journal of the American Academy of Religion* since 2004.

Julia S. Kovalchuk (PhD, 2006) is a researcher in the Institute of Archaeology and Ethnography Siberian Branch of the Russian Academy of Science (Sector of Ethnology). Her research interests focus on Pentecostalism, the history of Christianity in Asia, the contemporary religious situation in Siberia, Protestant missions in Russian Federation, and religious and ethnic identity.

Jean-François Mayer is the editor of the website Religioscope (www.religion.info) and the director of the newly-founded Institut Religioscope (www.religioscope.org). From 1998 to 2007, he taught at the University of Fribourg, Switzerland. He is the author of several books and numerous articles on new religious movements and other developments in the field of contemporary religion. List of publications: www.mayer.info.

Mark R. Mullins is Professor in the Graduate School of Global Studies and Faculty of Liberal Arts, Sophia University, Tokyo, where his teaching and research focuses on religion in modern societies. He is the author and co-editor of a number of works, including *Religion and Society in Modern Japan* (1993), *Christianity Made in Japan* (1998), and *Religion and Social Crisis in Japan* (2001). His current research focuses on neo-nationalism and contemporary Japanese religions.

Patsy Rahn works in the Education Department of the Indiana University Art Museum. She has published several articles including: "Media as a means for the Falun Gong movement" (*Asia Media*, 2005) and "The Chemistry of a Conflict: The Chinese Government and the Falun Gong" (*Terrorism and Political Violence*, 2002). She has also published several book reviews in *Nova Religio: The Journal of Alternative and Emergent Religion.*

James T. Richardson, Professor of Sociology and Judicial Studies at the University of Nevada, is Director of the Grant Sawyer Center for Justice Studies at the University, where he also directs the graduate degree programs for trial judges offered in conjunction with the National Judicial College and the National Council of Juvenile and Family Court Judges, both of which are headquartered on the university campus. His current research interests focus on the interface of law and religion, especially how legal systems are used as social control devices for minority religions. His latest book is *Regulating Religion: Case Studies from Around the Globe* (Kluwer, 2004).

Rachelle M. Scott is an Assistant Professor of Religious Studies at the University of Tennessee – Knoxville. She is the author of *Nirvana for Sale?: Buddhism, Wealth, and the Dhammakaya Temple in Contemporary Thailand* (SUNY, forthcoming) and "A New Buddhist Sect?: The Dhammakaya Temple and the Politics of Difference" (*Religion*, December 2006). She received a NEH summer grant to study religion and mediation in Thailand in 2005.

Heather J. Sharkey is Assistant Professor of Middle Eastern and Islamic Studies in the Department of Near Eastern Languages and Civilizations at the University of Pennsylvania. She is the author of *Living with Colonialism: Nationalism and Culture in the Anglo-Egyptian Sudan* (University of California Press, 2003) and *American Evangelicals in Egypt: Missionary Encounters in an Age of Empire* (Princeton University Press, forthcoming, 2008). The Carnegie Corporation of New York selected her as a Carnegie Scholar in 2006.

Paul-François Tremlett is a Research Associate in the Study of Religions at the School of Oriental and African Studies in London. He is also a Visiting Lecturer at the Institute of Ismaili Studies. He is assistant editor of *Culture and Religion* and a co-editor of *Taiwan in Comparative Perspective*. He has published essays on theory and method in the study of religions and on aspects of religion and culture in the Philippines and Taiwan. Two books: *Lévi-Strauss on Religion* (Equinox, 2008) and *Religion and the Discourse on Modernity* (Continuum, 2008) are forthcoming. He is also co-editor, with Fang-long Shih and Stuart Thompson of *Re-Writing Culture in Taiwan* (Routledge, 2008).

Asonzeh Ukah is a lecturer and Research Fellow in the Department for the History of Religions, University of Bayreuth, Germany. He has published widely in learned journals, notably on new religious media and visual culture in Africa. He is the author is *A New Paradigm of Pentecostal Power: A Study of the Redeemed Christian Church of God in Nigeria* (New Jersey/Asmara: Africa World Press, 2008).

CHAPTER 1

Revisiting Proselytization in the Twenty-first Century[1]

Rosalind I. J. Hackett

Contrary to the hopes and expectations of many, the neo-liberal trends of our global era have neither led to free markets for religion everywhere nor always to civility between religions in modern pluralistic states. In fact, the human rights revolution has arguably engendered new conflicts between local and foreign religious groups in a range of settings, not least Russia and India (Witte 2007). One of the most noticeable areas of contention pertains to the propagation of one's religion with the intent to convert others.[2] From French schools to tsunami-affected areas, in Turkish streets and Indian state legislatures, accusations of aggressive or improper proselytizing activity now make global news. Legal scholar John Witte trenchantly describes the problem of proselytizing as "one of the great ironies of the democratic revolution of the modern world" (Witte 2007, 13).

The problems arising over proselytism were significant enough in the late 1990s that the Center for the Study of Law and Religion at Emory University —under the leadership of the aforementioned John Witte—embarked on a major project known as the "The Problem and Promise of Proselytism in the New Democratic World Order (1995–2000)." It was described as "an empirical and normative study of the new war for souls breaking out in various new democracies of the world between and among indigenous faiths and foreign proselytizing faiths."[3] After a series of international conferences, the resulting four volumes explored this new battleground of local and foreign religions, and between religions and the state, in a range of contexts and traditions, against the backdrop of democratization and the human rights revolution (An-Na'im 1999; Witte and Bourdeaux 1999; Witte and Martin 1999; Sigmund 1999; see also Witte 2007).

Nearly a decade later, in light of even greater intensification of this "war for souls" and heightened global insecurity and terrorism, a new project was envisaged by this editor: to assemble a wide-ranging group of scholars—all well positioned, by virtue of recent field research or location in the actual regions under study—to expand and update the earlier studies, and provide new conceptual focus.[4] Several of the contributors agreed on "proselytization" as the primary operational concept, rather than on proselytism or conversion. Despite the interconnections,[5] it was felt that the emphasis on "proselytiza-tion" called for greater attention to the *process* rather than the *product*, the *means* more than the *end*. In other words, the possible religious conversion (an event of personal, spiritual transformation) was often less important for generating conflict than the *forms of expression, transmission, and behavior* deployed to this end.[6] We considered that the latter was the area where more changes and backlash were observable.

"Proselytization" also lends itself to a less negative reading than "proselyt-ism" (often interpreted as unethical, coercive, or fraudulent), and allows for greater comparison of changing strategies amidst ever more competitive pub-lic spheres. Moreover, the term clearly connotes the instrumentalist side of transmitting one's religion—comprising a range of acts and forms of com-munication (such as "witnessing," "professing," "advocating") which, taken alone, do not convey the significance, nor the problematic, of the broader concept.[7] It also has the capacity, as some of the authors demonstrate, to comprise not just actions intended to effect religious (re)orientation, but also efforts to bring about a change in attitude toward the source group.[8]

While social, cultural, and historical interpretations characterize this collec-tion of essays, media and legal issues stand out in several of the contributions. This is because law and the mass media represent the new interface for rela-tions between and within religions, as well as between religions and the state.[9] Together with the discursive strategies of marketing and growth from the modern business world, they can radically influence the key factors of public recognition and representation. As anthropologists and sociologists remind us, context is all-important in understanding how and why individuals and communities decide to change their religious affiliation and/or persuade oth-ers to do likewise (Hefner 1993; Austin-Broos 2003). Nowadays that context is as much translocal as local, transnational as well as national, due to new trends in migration, travel, communication, and trade (on West Africa, see Fourchard *et al.* 2005). It is also historical, with current dispensations often influenced by previous patterns of inclusion and exclusion, together with other manipulations of religion, whether feudal, colonialist, or nationalist.

As communal rights rise to the fore in this era of global religious resurgence, challenging the post-Enlightenment individualistic, secular ideal, it seems more relevant to analyze proselytization as a salient aspect of heightened forms of religious activism, competition, and conflict. In fact, human rights scholar Abdullahi An-Na'im argues that an individualized conception of freedom of religion "cannot adequately address the concerns of communities about proselytization, and its consequences"; it must be balanced by "a dynamic and creative understanding of *collective* rights" (An-Na'im 1999, 15–16, emphasis in original). Hence, we pay less attention in this volume to the individualistic, experiential dimension. The nature and experience of conversion, notably of the individual, have been extensively treated in a range of works, notably by Lewis Rambo (1995; 1999; see also Nock 1933 and Leone 2003). There is also a sense in which "conversion" is more closely identified with the Christian tradition (Asad 1996, De Roover and Claerhout this volume), than modern forms of proselytizing and anti-proselytizing.[10]

A controversial freedom

Legal scholar Johan van der Vyver describes the right to engage in missionary activity as "perhaps the most controversial component of religious freedom" (van der Vyver 1999, 128). He further states that the disagreements over the right to spread and convert others to one's religion "remain a stumbling block in efforts to establish universal respect for and adherence to the vital components of religious freedom as contemplated by the founders of the United Nations" (van der Vyver 1998, 420). Legal scholars who specialize in religious freedom issues all link proselytizing activities with the freedom to change one's religion (Lerner 2000, 81). Natan Lerner notes the "considerable controversy" generated by issues relating to change of religion during the drafting of the Universal Declaration of Human Rights in 1948 (Lerner 2000, 80). In fact, he talks of a "downward or deteriorating trend" in the recognition of both the right to proselytize and to change one's religion (Lerner 2000, 118). M. Abdelfattah Amor, the former UN Special Rapporteur on Freedom of Religion or Belief, noted in one of his reports that the major violations of Article 1 of the 1981 UN Declaration on the Elimination of All Forms of Intolerance and of Discrimination Based on Religion or Belief came from restrictions on proselytizing, and forced conversions.[11] John Witte reminds us that the "right to choose or change religion" only attained that status after what he terms "centuries of cruel experience" (Witte and Martin 1999, xvi).

Fomenting religious hatred is prohibited in international law, so too is forced conversion, yet there are considered to be ambiguities and gaps in the standards with regard to proselytizing (Boyle and Sheen 1997, 12). There is virtually no explicit mention of the freedom to disseminate a religion or belief in international human rights instruments (Stahnke 2004, 626). What are sometimes referred to as "religious rights" are fundamental, but not absolute (Stahnke 1999, 261, 269–70; Lerner 2000, 126). In other words, the right to express and practice one's religion is subject to restrictions that can be imposed by the state in the interests of public order, security, and decency. This is where discrimination and abuses can occur, with minority groups being the most affected (Adams 2000; Richardson 2000, 2004; Lerner 2000, 125; Stahnke 2004, 623).

Clearly some form of regulation is required by public authorities to mediate between competing groups over the right to proselytize, especially when conflicts arise (An-Na'im 1999; Martin and Winter 1999; Stahnke 2004), and to prevent excessive collusion between local religions and political leaders intent on keeping out their foreign religious rivals (Witte 2007, 14). The state is not supposed to be the arbiter of the validity of religious beliefs and practices, but employ international human rights standards in trying to strike "a peaceful balance between the interests of those holding different beliefs on proselytism, as well as the interests of those holding no religious beliefs" (Stahnke 2004, 622). In similar vein, Elizabeth Prodromou points to the dangers of both defensive states responding to religious pluralization and proponents of unnecessarily "dogmatic secularism" (Prodromou 2006). The challenge for the modern state is how to craft a general rule which balances the multiple legal and theological understandings of proselytizing and conversion (Witte 2007, 14). Moderation rather than a moratorium on proselytizing activities is the answer in John Witte's estimation (Witte 2007, 17–18: see also van der Vyver 1998).

Concept and conflict

One of the most helpful sources for analyzing the concept and understanding the conflicts, past and present, arising over the right to proselytize is Tad Stahnke's "Proselytism and the Freedom to Change Religion in International Human Rights Law" (1999; see also 2004).[12] In his view, proselytism—whether viewed as an exercise of expression or a manifestation of religious belief—*is not inherently problematic*, it is the difficulty of "finding the proper balance between the freedom to proselytize and the multitude of rights, duties, and interests of religious groups, individuals, and the state that may conflict with that freedom" (Stahnke 1999, 252).[13] As he rightly states, given the variables at play in each context, there are *no general solutions* to the problems posed by proselytism. However, he does suggest that societies open to religious change and exchange tend to be more accommodating of the freedom to proselytize (Stahnke 1999, 253). When the need to resolve conflict arises, states must be aware of the rights and interests at stake in each case, and any regulation—direct or indirect—must be consistent with international human rights standards (Stahnke 1999, 253–54). Stahnke demonstrates that discrimination—intentional or unintentional—may result from restrictions on proselytism, particularly if missionizing and conversion are integral to the religious group's orientation. He identifies four primary factors that states employ to distinguish between "proper" and "improper" proselytism, namely 1) the characteristics of the source; 2) the characteristics of the target; 3) where the proselytism takes place; and 4) the nature of the exchange between the source and the target (Stahnke 1999, 254). Coercion is a central variable in this framework, but Stahnke underscores the variability of interpretations between the two poles of acceptable and unacceptable forms of proselytization (Stahnke 2004, 645). He even suggests that the widely divergent practices of states may account for the reluctance of international bodies to tackle proselytism issues (Stahnke 2004, 648). Some aspects of proselytizing are particularly challenging to delineate, such as blasphemy and injury to religious feelings (Stahnke 2004). He also shows how the protection of the rights and interests of the source, target, and state may support both the freedom to proselytize and its restriction.

Stahnke defines "proselytism" as "expressive conduct undertaken with the purpose of trying to change the religious beliefs, affiliation, or identity of another" (Stahnke 2004, 256). Under the rubric of proselytism, he includes a range of forms of expression and activity, such as "religious discussions; preaching; teaching; the publication, distribution or sale of printed and electronic works; broadcasting; solicitation of funds; or provision of humanitarian or social services"—as long as they are intended to convert others (Stahnke 2004, 262). As he himself states, his definition avoids negative connotations—a position that we endorse, and conveys the intentionality of the conduct. It is for the latter reason that he avoids the suggestion of "process" in the term "proselytization," an aspect, in contrast, that we prefer to emphasize, without diminishing that proselytizing is "purposeful human action" (Stahnke 2004, 255).

In this critical and comparative overview of proselytism, Stahnke rightly emphasizes the variability in perception and understanding across and within religious traditions. A lot will depend on whether a group is the source or the target of proselytism, whether the targets are within or outside the tradition (Stahnke 2004, 256), and whether the sources are majority or minority religions, and hold to exclusivist or inclusivist beliefs (Stahnke 2004, 257). While he wishes to eschew "the intricacies of theological disputes and intra or interreligious relations," he rightly notes that these different religious positions influence state policies (Stahnke 2004).

A particularly potent example of majoritarian religious influence can be found in the writings of Makau Mutua on African and other indigenous religions. Mutua, who writes both as legal scholar and African, has been particularly vocal about the plight of indigenous religions in the face of "imperial religions" and a human rights corpus which discriminates against non-proselytizing and non-competitive religious systems (Mutua 2004; see also 1999). The consequences in his estimation have been disastrous for Africans, nothing short of "cultural genocide" (2004, 652). Africans had no choice in whether they wanted to compete or not in the marketplace of ideas— "[u]niversalist religions were either introduced or forcibly imposed as part of the colonial cultural package" (Mutua 2004, 652). Moreover, "salvation" was frequently a "precondition for services in education and health" (Mutua 2004, 652). Challenging the assumption of the rights regime that a "level playing field" existed under such conditions, or indeed for other indigenous peoples today, Mutua explores human rights notions that are more conducive to indigenous beliefs having the right to be respected and left alone by more dominant exogenous traditions.

Mutua suggests that there are possible contradictions between proselytization and the human rights corpus in terms of the former's emphasis on demonizing, displacing or destroying other groups and the latter's ideal of promoting diversity and the right to advocate different beliefs. In his words, "it seems inconceivable that the human rights movement would have intended to protect the right of certain religions to destroy others" (Mutua 2004, 653). Part of the problem, in his estimation, is that article 18 of the International Covenant on Civil and Political Rights (ICCPR) guarantees the right to freedom of thought, conscience, and religion and provides for certain limitations, but it fails to delineate the duties that should be borne by proselytizing religions (Mutua 2004, 654).[14] In both the ICCPR and article 18 of the Universal Declaration of Human Rights references to indigenous religions, let alone their rights, are absent. However, the use of force and state resources to make converts are both prohibited. Are not missionaries who worked against other religions, with the support of the colonialists, in violation of such provisions, asks Mutua? (Mutua 2004, 661).

For Mutua the most fundamental of all human rights is the self-determination principle which, he argues, should be expanded from its more political meaning to include cultural survival (Mutua 2004, 666). He contends that this should trump other human rights principles of free speech, assembly, and association. This has been the position of those who have been advocating for greater UN recognition of the rights of indigenous peoples in the form of the Draft Declaration on the Rights of Indigenous Peoples (Mutua 2004, 662). It builds on the General Comment of the Human Rights Committee on Article 27 of the ICCPR, providing that states are under an obligation to protect the cultural, linguistic, and religious rights of minorities, not just as individuals but as groups (Mutua 2004, 661–62). These positive developments, along with the 1981 African Charter of Human and People's Rights, notes Mutua, are undermined by the "general disregard of the African past" by contemporary African governments—predicated on modernization and haunted by demonization (Mutua 2004, 663).

While some argue that Mutua's protectionist approach to indigenous religions is paternalism in another guise, and that the business of cultural (self-)determination is prone to essentialism and out of step with post-colonial realities (and, as Kao argues in this volume, pre-colonial also), he certainly succeeds in turning the spotlight on some of the paradoxes and imbalances in the human rights corpus. His focus on the rights pertaining to cultural diversity and religious freedom, notably the right to persuade or proselytize others, is particularly salient for several of the cases discussed in this book.

Evaluation and comparison

Turning to other disciplinary perspectives on the question of proselytization and its attendant conflicts, it behooves us to begin with those whose business it is to analyze and evaluate Christian missionary activity on a global scale. Church historians and missiologists tend to be more focused on the propriety of witnessing and disseminating their faith in a pluralistic world (see e.g., Bonk 2000; Oladipo 2005). As noted astutely by church historian Cecil Robeck, "one group's evangelization is another group's proselytism" (Robeck 1996, 2). For the most part these scholars operate with a negative understanding of proselytism as a type of "evangelistic malpractice" or "sheep-stealing," even though the original biblical meaning of a proselyte as convert was more neutral (Robeck 1996, 2; see also Beach 1999, 3). The opening up of new missionary fields in Eastern Europe, for example, has reactivated old concerns about legitimate targets and territories, and sparked new complaints about the cultural insensitivities of some of the younger evangelical and Pentecostal groups. The World Council of Churches (WCC) has moved to more of a dialogical relationship with other religions,[15] rather than direct missionary effort, and the Roman Catholic Church forbids force or enticement in missionary activity.[16] Most evangelicals, according to Robeck, still view persons of other religious communities and denominations, whose commitment or affiliation is only nominal, as legitimate targets of evangelism (1999, 3). It is noteworthy that a landmark study process, "An Interreligious Reflection on Conversion: From Controversy to Shared Code of Conduct" began in 2006 between the Vatican, the World Council of Churches and evangelical and

Pentecostal representatives.[17] Seeking to affirm freedom of religion as a "non-negotiable" human right valid for everyone everywhere and to cure the "obsession of converting others," its goal is to produce a joint code of conduct on religious conversion for Christians by 2010.[18] Christian and Muslim groups in Norway believe that they have signed the first joint declaration in 2007 supporting the right to convert between religions without fear of harassment as a basic religious freedom.[19]

While the bulk of missiological scholarship addresses intra-Christian relations, and evaluates Christian missionary efforts, a few authors have opted for more comparative analysis, particularly those interested in Christian-Muslim relations. The comparison of Christian mission and Muslim *da'wah* features prominently in these writings (Scantlebury 1996, 31; Wagner 2003).[20] For example, David Kerr contrasts the "centrifugal" tendencies of Christianity's "sending" mission and the "centripetal" or "calling notion" of Islamic *da'wah* (Kerr 2000). Rashied Omar, a scholar of Islam who writes from the perspective of interreligious relations, notes that non-Muslim scholars prefer to emphasize the similarities between *da'wah* and Christian mission, while Muslim scholars are more keen to point out the differences (Omar 2006, 5). Omar is above all interested in the "reemergence of the themes of religious conversion and the ethics of mission as critical issues for interreligious dialogue" (Omar 2006, 8). He links this renewed "interest" to the new "belligerent environment" generated by the 9/11 terrorist attacks, and the subsequent "war on terrorism" launched by the Bush administration (Omar 2006, 9). He notes that some evangelical leaders talked openly about how the American invasions of Afghanistan and Iraq offered "exciting new prospects for proselytizing Muslims" (Omar 2006, 10). But it is the "aid evangelism" of some Christian humanitarian organizations in these contexts (i.e. promoting Christianity under cover of relief efforts) that has proved so problematic in his view—serving to reinforce hardline Muslim views on apostasy (cf. Dixon 2005).

Some of the most thorough analysis of Christian missionary activity on a global scale has been done by missiologists.[21] The latter are interested in the new demographics and patterns of missionary activity, and how to define a contemporary missionary, given the increase in the numbers of short-term (i.e. two-week) mission trips. Widely reported figures reveal that of the more than 400,000 Christian missionaries worldwide only 2–3% work among unreached peoples.[22] The work of church historian Andrew Walls (2001a; 2001b), in particular, has spearheaded an important reorientation in the field of mission studies. He has argued over several years that Christianity's center of gravity was shifting from the Western industrialized nations to Asia, Africa, and Latin America.[23] Each year there are fewer Christians in the West and more Christians in the rest of the world.[24] Historian of religion Philip Jenkins, who has also written extensively on the rise of Christianity in the southern hemisphere, predicts in his much-cited *The Next Christendom: the Coming of Global Christianity* (2002) that by the year 2050 only one Christian in five will be a non-Latino white person.[25]

So in a relatively brief amount of time, Christianity has been transformed from a European to a global religion (Sanneh 1989; Sanneh and Carpenter 2005; Bediako 1999, 1995; 2000; and Freston, this volume). Mission theologian Christopher J.H. Wright talks of "an upside-down world" where distinguishing between home and mission field no longer makes sense and where what was considered "normal" before in terms of Christian demographics now has to be "unlearned."[26] Lamin Sanneh's latest book examines the roots of this "post-Western awakening" of world Christianity, as well the challenges and implications of this new religious resurgence (Sanneh 2007). Jenkins contends that the churches that grow most rapidly in the global south are far more traditional, morally conservative, evangelical, and apocalyptic than their northern counterparts. He considers that this will lead to increased interreligious conflict and challenges to the secularist paradigms of modern nation-states worldwide.

This now burgeoning field of "World Christianity," shaped by the work of scholars such as Andrew Walls, Lamin Sanneh, Kwame Bediako, Dana Robert, and Jon Bonk,[27] and their respective centers and institutes,[28] has been instrumental in advocating a more multilateral and polycentric perspective on conversion and missionary activity,[29] and one which factors in the broad spectrum of agency, such as that of women (Robert 2002; Bowie *et al.* 1993; Kulp 1987), and indigenes (Brock 2005; Kaplan [ed.] 1995; Kaplan 2004).[30] One of the most influential publications has been Lamin Sanneh's *Translating the Message: the Missionary Impact on Culture* (1989) where he argued that, in contrast to Islam and contrary to a lot of academic and popular thinking, Christianity has served to preserve indigenous life and culture, because of its strong emphasis on mother-tongue translation. Likewise, where indigenous culture has been strong, it has absorbed Christian life and worship, thereby sustaining and even increasing its vitality. In contrast, where conversion has been to Islam, indigenous cultures have tended to be weak, and soon lose entirely the capacity to think religiously in their mother tongue.[31] Interestingly, Michael McGinnis suggests that today's "secular missionaries," namely those international non-governmental and inter-governmental organizations seeking to propagate their programs of development, democracy, and peace-building, could take a leaf out of the book of Protestant missionaries who have devoted extensive efforts to the translation of the biblical message into local languages and "symbolic repertoires" (McGinnis 2007).

Newer studies are characterized by an emphasis on the complexities and sometimes unintended consequences of missionary activities. For example, historian of religion Paul Kollman's "The Evangelization of Slaves and Catholic Origins in East Africa" (2005) examines how the 19th century missionary practices of the Congregation of the Holy Ghost or Spiritans—such as making converts out of ransomed slaves—met with mixed success, yet shaped the origins of East African Catholicism. Brian Stanley's edited work, *Missions, Nationalism, and the End of Empire* (2003) looks at some of the paradoxical outcomes of Christian missions, such as their roles in the promotion of nationalism and the dissolution of colonialism in Asia and Africa (see also Meyer 2002). Dorothy Hodgson explores why Maasai Catholicism ended up attracting more women converts than men, when the latter had been targeted by the Spiritan fathers (Hodgson 2005).

The predominance of resources and research on Christian missions leads some scholars to call for investigation of the missionary impulse in other traditions, both religious and non-religious, and more comparative studies in evangelism and proselytism. Such is the objective of Jamie Scott and Gareth Griffiths in their book, *Mixed Messages: Materiality, Textuality, Missions* (Scott and Griffiths 2005; cf. Bryant and Lamb eds. 1999). They also advocate more synergy between the fields of mission studies, cultural studies, and postcolonial studies, as well more attention to the material as well as the textual cultures of missions (cf. Rambo 1999). Two recent volumes by mainly European scholars emphasize the language, discourse and narratives of conversion on a more comparative and historical basis (Bremmer *et al.* eds. 2006a, 2006b; see also Viswanathan 1998).

The historically negative relationship between missionaries and anthropologists has shaped much of the academic output and lack of research interest by (relativist) anthropologists on the (universalizing) activities of missionaries. Robert Priest claims that the stereotypical notion of the "missionary position"—which he finds recycled in numerous writings, stemming it seems from Kinsey's (mis)reading of Malinowski—not only jeopardizes serious research on missionary activity and indigenous responses, but also silences and excludes the voice of Christian scholars in the field of anthropology and the academy more generally (Priest 2001). He examines the way the expression has found symbolic and moral resonance at the dialectical intersections of modernist and postmodernist discourses.

The set of responses following Priest's article provides a rich array of anthropological reflections on missionary activity, and their complex history of entanglements and divergences. The hostility to Christian moralism and intolerant evangelism invoked through the enduring and multivalent metaphor of the "missionary position" is not, in James Clifford's estimation, just an outmoded, colonialist phenomenon (Clifford 2001, 48). In line with the orientation of the present text, he opines:

> but what if, instead of missionary positions, we focused on insistent radio messages or intrusive airplanes? There are probably more well-funded missionaries preaching today in remote, powerless places than in Kinsey's time. And the articulation of their message with global American power has obvious neocolonial importance. (Clifford 2001, 48)

This pointer to the political economy of present-day evangelization, and new strategies instead of old messages, informs a number of the chapters in this volume. Other respondents to the Priest article, such as Michèle Dominy, prefer to remind readers of those anthropologists whose research advocates less polarized interpretations and better reflect the complexity of agency and reception in multiple contexts (Comaroff and Comaroff 1991; see also Etherington 2005). Again, this more multilateral approach can be discerned in several of the contributions in the present work.

Despite this "distaste for evangelical Christianity," anthropologists, according to Jeremy Benthall (2001), are good at making up for their blind spots (he cites the instances of tourism and the mass media). He notes with appreciation the emergence of "more serious ethnographies of Christian groups and missionary activities" (Benthall 2001, 46). From the earlier emphasis on the association of Christian missions with empire-building and colonialism (Beidelman 1982), there is now more interest in the impact of religious conversion on questions of local, national, and transnational identity, modernity, materiality, agency, cultural continuity/discontinuity, inculturation, and cultural transformation (J. Comaroff 1985; J.L. Comaroff and J. Comaroff 1991, 1992; J.L. Comaroff and J. Comaroff 1997; Van der Veer [ed.] 1996; Asad 1996; Meyer 1999; Hefner 1993; Buckser and Glazier eds. 2003; Orta 2004; Engelke 2004; Keane 2007). Dorothy Hodgson's study of Maasai Catholicism (2005) makes a cogent case for according gender a central place in any mission history or ethnography. In a special issue of *Missiology,* several anthropologists assess the complex relationship between missionaries, anthropologists, and human rights.[32] Joel Robbins, in particular, has been at the theoretical and empirical forefront of this new wave of insightful anthropological studies of Christianity in both non-Western and Western contexts (Robbins 2003, 2004; see also Cannell 2006).

Sociologists have not displayed the same reticence to analyzing proselytization and conversion because of their longstanding interests in alternative or new religions. In fact, a good portion of the sociological literature has centered on the so-called "brainwashing theory" (Snow and Machalek 1984; Machalek and Snow 1993; Richardson 1998; see also Bruce 2006). Several scholars have challenged, through empirical research, the popular notion that recruitment to new religious movements has been involuntary, through the use of coercive mind-control techniques (Barker 1984; Richardson 1991; Bromley and Robbins 1992; Richardson and Introvigne 2001; Anthony and Robbins 2004). The "world-saver" conversion/recruitment model developed by Lofland in conjunction with Stark (1965) has proved influential in being able to combine psychological and sociological explanations, and to move from deterministic to more activist and interactionist approaches (Richardson 1998).[33] Bainbridge (1992), for example, proposes a model of conversion that unites the traditions of strain theory (i.e. people join religious sects in the hope of transforming their frustrated and deprived lives) and social influence theory (i.e. people are drawn to religious sects for social reasons) (on the latter, see Kent 2001).

For others, the attraction of the newer rational choice theory is that it gives agency to the individual seeker in a competitive public sphere (Finke and Stark 2003; Stark and Finke 2000; Hak 2006; Kosmin and Keysar 2006). Anthony Gill's analysis of the "economics of evangelization" in Latin America is a good illustration of this type of approach (Gill 1999). Also of import to the subject of proselytization is the analysis of the social control and regulation of religious groups (see especially, Richardson 2004). Some sociologists, such as Paul Freston, are exploring these questions of recruitment and conversion within the context of transnational religious movements, such as Brazilian Pentecostal and evangelical churches (Freston 2001, and this volume), and proffering more varied conceptualizations of the phenomenon of conversion (Ireland 1995). Freston considers that more attention should be devoted by sociologists of religion to the switching of religious identities in the current phase of globalization, and the impact of expansionist religions, such as evangelical Christianity, on conflict situations (Freston 2002).

Steve Bruce suggests that there is a certain "weariness" with the topic of conversion among present-day sociologists (Bruce 2006, 6). He attributes this in part to the fact that the literature on conversion is linked to new religious movements which, in his estimation, "have turned out to be fairly trivial" (Bruce 2006, 9) and to greater social scientific interest in more large-scale religious change such as fundamentalism and Pentecostalism. Yet, he argues, there are fewer areas of inquiry better suited for balancing explanations of people's behavior between structural forces and individual agency (Bruce 2006, 11). The same case could be made, we propose, for the topic of proselytization.

Orientation and significance of this book

While some of the authors in this volume indeed draw on the vast body of scholarship on conversion alluded to above, our overall emphasis is on the changing profile, if you will, of twenty-first century proselytization. Our primary concern is to identify the new actors/sources, areas, strategies, media, challenges, as well as new conflicts stemming from proselytizing activity in our globalizing world.

This work also aims to provide both empirical data and analytical reflection on how proselytization is implicated in broader questions of religious resurgence and conflict. The clash of civilizations thesis advocated by Samuel Huntington (1996), which continues to resonate in policy and media circles, appears less plausible, for example, when one tracks the proselytizing initiatives of Nigerian and Brazilian Pentecostals among nominal Christians in the United States, or Roman Catholics among Russian Orthodox believers in Russia. Moreover, focusing on proselytizing activities leads right into public debates about the appropriate place of religion in changing public spheres (Hackett 2005), and new forms of religious activism, as stated earlier. These debates are increasingly articulated in the language of constitutional and human rights law. Recognition of the right to proselytize in any particular context is a good indicator of respect for the range of rights related to freedom of religion and belief, i.e. not just freedom of worship, but also freedom of expression and association. As noted above, it is often the minority or sectarian groups that are the litmus test in this regard. A U.S.-based study of proselytization notes that most case law that restricts the free exercise of religion pertaining to proselytizing activity in the United States has developed "in response to groups or individuals that are outside the mainstream" (Hunter and Price 2001, 539).

For those interested in the transnationalization of religion, attention to some of the more innovative forms of religious activism discussed in this book and beyond should prove revealing. The networks established by some of the younger Pentecostal organizations from the global South, such as the (Brazilian) Universal Church of the Kingdom of God or the (Nigerian) Redeemed Christian Church of God, would be the envy of many a CEO.[34] The non-denominational para-church agencies, such as the Full Gospel Business Men's Fellowship International and the Haggai Institute, have devised creative means for engaging educated elites and mission-oriented publics through an emphasis on leadership development and religious entrepreneurism. Such trends are imbricated with global market forces, whether directly or indirectly (Fourchard *et al.* eds. 2005). They may also generate international economic and political capital for emerging democracies (Strandsbjerg 2005;

van der Veer 1996, 19). Many proselytizers take advantage of deregulation and liberalization, just as they may adopt the styles of new entrepreneurs in quest of profit and markets. Public places, as in Africa's streets and market-places, as well as convention centers, can provide a location for the adop-tion and cross-fertilization of transnational preaching styles (Mary 2005; Ojo 2005, cf. Mullins on Japan, this volume).

For the burgeoning sub-field of media and religion studies, a focus on pros-elytization yields rich results.[35] It not only demonstrates how modern media technologies empower religious organizations to disseminate their messages on ever-larger scales, but also how these new forms of communication may also occasion new forms of self-representation in competitive marketplaces (on Nigerian Pentecostalism, see Ukah 2005 and this volume). In fact it may be argued that media presence and media practice are increasingly integral to a religious group's self-fashioning and functioning. Negotiating religious dif-ference is conducted increasingly via the interface of chat rooms, blogs, and websites than in more conventional forms of face-to-face dialogue, although the relationship between online and offline religion is a complex issue and in need of further research (Dawson and Cowan [eds.] 2004).

Whatever the long-term implications may be for political and religious landscapes of changing patterns and more competitive forms of religious expansionism, the ongoing challenge to prevailing models of secularism, notably those predicated on Western relegations of religion to the private realm, seems assured (Hackett 2005). Proselytic activity interrogates unre-alistic distinctions between the public and private. Targeting for the most part individual religious (re)affiliation, but with hopes of collective transfor-mation, proselytization resorts to very public strategies to achieve its goals. In the process of assuming even greater global outreach, some of the new agents of proselytization contribute (directly or indirectly) to the much-need-ed de-Westernizing of the renewed debates on secularism and secularization (Madan 2006; Casanova 2006; Asad 2003; Jakobsen and Pellegrini 2000; Keddie 1997).[36] As several of the examples discussed in this text cogently illustrate, proselytization often functions as the thorn in the flesh of the secular state. In fact, its effects may be so feared or negatively perceived that they may be projected onto religious behavior not intended as such. The re-cent controversies over religious dress and symbols in a number of European and Middle Eastern countries are a pertinent illustration of this (McGoldrick 2006; Gunn 2004).

Overview of chapters

The first three chapters of the book's first section cast the net widely in their efforts to revisit the phenomenon of proselytization both theoretically and empirically. Based on more than twenty years of research on new religious movements around the world, **Jean-François Mayer** provides a general over-view of some of the conflicts surrounding proselytization. He draws up six theses based on the recurring patterns he discerns in responses to proselyt-izing activities: namely, there will be increasing conflicts, but greater accept-ance of pluralism in long term; there will be reinforcement of images of civilizational clashes; proselytism is often perceived as an attempt to extend ideological influence and political dominance; threats to national interests are more feared than to religion; critics of proselytism often try to have their objections conform to principles of religious freedom; and proselytic activity often fosters change and creation of new strategies and organizations among religious groups targeted by missionaries. Mayer predicts that missionary ac-tivities will become more diversified and more subject to accountability. In contrast, **Jakob De Roover and Sarah Claerhout** assert that the problems relating to proselytization and religious conversion are overstated. Informed by their studies of the Indian religious scene they argue that the generaliza-tion about an inherent religious rivalry in cultural diversity, and religions as belief systems to which truth predicates apply, stems from "a predicament that exists predominantly in Christianity and Islam." They further contend that by presupposing this "self-evident" understanding of religion, the cur-rent principle of religious freedom has transposed a theological problem into a universalistic, secular notion. In this way, it privileges the religions of Chris-tianity and Islam. Hence, in the Indian context at very least, they propose that religious human rights, notably pertaining to propagation and manifes-tation, aggravate, rather than alleviate, the tensions.[37] **Grace Kao** pursues the issue of accountability with regard to proselytizing in greater depth, suggest-ing that there is a trend among academics and religious practitioners alike to tolerate religious differences or at least preclude what has been called "evan-gelistic malpractice." Usinga a rich array of recent examples, she provides a typology of five types of anti-proselytization discourse: (1) appropriate targets and tactics, (2) substitution, (3) non-recruitment, (4) group protection, and (5) anti-imperialism. Several of the authors make use of this template in their own chapters. In critically assessing each of the positions in her typology, Kao concludes that the logic of anti-proselytization might be better served if it directly responded to and accordingly interrogated the logic of proselytiza-tion itself. This could generate, in her view, much-needed self-critique and dialogue.

The second section begins with a chapter by **Paul Freston** which also has broad implications as it examines the under-researched phenomenon of Christian missions originating from the global South. He provides salient examples of how Brazilian missionaries can experience more legitimacy than their Western counterparts in a range of settings. As a sociologist, he is particularly interested in how this "changing face" of Christian proselytizing affects the debates over the rights and wrongs of proselytization in a globalizing world. Most proselytizing today, he argues, occurs from the periphery to the center of world power (in keeping with the shift in the center of Christianity), and mainly between so-called world religions. **Heather J. Sharkey** reminds us that an historical dimension can be salutary in understanding present tensions and negotiations over the right to proselytize. In her case study of the American Presbyterian mission in early twentieth century Egypt, she examines how Christian missionary attitudes towards proselytism, religious choice, and conversion clashed with prevailing Muslim beliefs about apostasy and communal allegiance, serving to galvanize the country's Islamist and nationalist movements. She discusses how negotiations over religious freedom were embedded in local, national, and international politics. Sharkey further argues that, in similarity to the Indian and Sri Lankan contexts, resistance to proselytization—then as now—can derive as much from nationalist and anti-imperialist/anti-colonialist sentiments as from religious teachings and values (such as apostasy). Moving to another influential African country, **Asonzeh Ukah's** analysis of the rise of poster proselytization in the pluralistic and competitive religious scene that is Nigeria today reveals the dominance of the Pentecostal churches in the marketing sector. However, the fact that these advertising campaigns tend to encourage "church-switching" rather than the conversion of non-Christians has provoked criticism of Pentecostal leaders for unethical practices and overly entrepreneurial approaches to religion. Ukah's account provides rich evidence of how particular modern media are being creatively adapted to specific contexts for religious propaganda, and of the merits of considering marketing and advertising theory when analyzing such modern forms of religious expression.

The southern and eastern regions of Asia covered in the third section of the book, offer some highly illuminating and topical examples of how proselytization and religious conversion have assumed central importance in public debates. **Stephen Berkwitz** traces the historical roots of the current controversy in Sri Lanka and the recent efforts by some Sinhala Buddhist nationalists to limit the activities of evangelical Christian communities (and by extension, global forces) using "anti-conversion" legislation. He discusses the "high stakes" involved as proselytizing and conversion are connected not just to disputes over religious and national identities and questions of religious freedom and cultural sovereignty but to the very identity of the state itself. **Rachelle Scott's** work complements this focus well by showing what difference the modern media make. She shows that not only are the discourses of proselytization increasingly mediatized, but so too are the debates surrounding them. She analyzes recent controversies over the marketing techniques of the Dhammakāya temple in Bangkok, one of Thailand's most progressive temples. She shows how the Dhammakāya's proselytic message is adapted to reach both local and global audiences, and must be interpreted within broader debates concerning modernity, authenticity, and Buddhist missionary activity.

Singapore represents one of Asia's primary hubs for shopping, tourism, and transportation, but this multi-ethnic, multi-religious metropolis has also become an important regional center for Asian Christian missions. **Jean DeBernardi's** account sheds light on the multilateral complexity of Singapore's missionary enterprise. She also discusses how Singaporean evangelicals use popular forms of intercessory prayer and rituals of deliverance as part of the practice of proselytism. As these forms of prayer involve deviant labeling of non-Christian groups, evangelicals find themselves in tension with their government and its social engineering projects, notably the promotion of religious harmony. Similar nationalist forces also shape a less urban site of proselytization in the Philippines. **Paul-François Tremlett** is interested in the proselytizing strategies of state and religious agents and agencies in and around Mount Banahaw among Tagálog-speaking peoples of central-southern Luzón in the Philippines. He also suggests that these proselytizing discourses and practices integrate with wider discourses in the Philippines about national identity and culture, and articulate new relations between nation and locality. Tremlett demonstrates that the complex discursive and material production of Mount Banahaw as a site of nationalist inculcation serves to de-legitimize other ideologies and theologies—whether, Protestant, Catholic, or Rizalist religio-nationalist movements. However, if there is conversion, Tremlett claims, it is of Mount Banahaw as touristic and new age mecca for middle-class Filipinos from the capital.

In East Asia, two religious movements have come to world attention because of their well publicized propagation efforts and resultant bans on their activities. **Patsy Rahn's** study of the controversial Chinese spiritual movement, Falun Gong, reveals how the group has made proactive use of the local and international media to protest being banned by the Chinese government in 1999. She shows how they have linked their secular goal of counteracting the Chinese government's negative portrayal of their activities, and ending the ban and alleged mistreatment of its members within China, to their higher spiritual goal of personal and universal salvation. In this way, they have creatively turned the dispute into their main means of proselytization. Rahn's case study is a prime example of how the modern mass media can become the primary interface for proselytic activity. The media have also helped shape the legal standing of newer religious movements in the case of Japan.

Proselytization activities have flourished in Japan's post-war free-market religious economy, but, as **Mark Mullins** proposes, they are often a source of social conflict and widespread media coverage. The majority of Japanese people today hold negative attitudes towards the activities of religious groups, and an increasing number consider that proselytization should be restricted by law. Mullins links this gap between constitutional ideals and social reality to Japanese disapproval of exclusivist religions—whether early mission Christianity or new religions such as Soka Gakkai, and extremist groups such as Aum Shinrikyo which attacked the Tokyo subway in 1995.

The fourth section of the book begins with **Olga Kazmina's** study of the rise of proselytism as a politically contentious issue in contemporary Russia. Her account further underscores the importance of understanding the historical dimension of interreligious tensions. She traces the current anxieties of the Russian Orthodox Church to the 1990s when newer Christian movements began arriving in Russia. Attempts to restrict the "missionary field" were also heightened by the politicization of religion into the early 2000s. These debates have now appropriately shifted into the sphere of inter-denominational relations and religious education, according to Kazmina. Her analysis also highlights the changing roles of the state, the media and academics, as well as the interplay of local and global forces, in negotiating the stakes of religious competition and co-existence in Russia today. The next two chapters both describe regions that are in cultural and political formation, and have only recently opened up to exogenous missionary activity. **Bayram Balci** describes how the modern Turkish missionary movement led by Fetullah Gülen —seeking to re-Islamize Central Asia and the Caucasus—has had to develop a range of new proselytic strategies and discourses, namely educational and business development, in the post-Soviet context. He argues that this form of "hidden" or "indirect" proselytization, notably through a successful private school system that appeals to emerging national elites, is the most expedient in the various Turkic Republics with their different historical, geographical, cultural, and political configurations. In Turkey, Gülen has been accused of trying to undermine the secular state. **Julia Kovalchuk's** chapter provides important new findings on the proselytizing activities of Korean Protestants (predominantly Pentecostal) in the new mission field known as the "10–40 window." This is a term that Christians use to refer to an area stretching from West Africa to East Asia that falls from 10 to 40 degrees north of the equator whose populations encompass the majority of the world's Muslims, Hindus, and Buddhists. Using interviews, field observation, and analysis of media sources, her research focuses on Siberia and the far eastern parts of Russia where the large numbers of non-Christian ethnic populations attract the new Korean missionaries. Kovalchuk evaluates the varying strategies of the missionaries, and discusses responses to their efforts by both urban and ethnic populations in republics seeking to forge new ethno-political and religious identities.[38]

The two final chapters discuss two very different groups in the contemporary U.S. context, Wiccans and evangelicals, as they rethink their outreach and influence in increasingly competitive religious public spheres. In his research on Wiccans and contemporary Pagans and their use of the Internet, **Shawn Arthur** has identified a new trend in their self-representation and self-promotion. While the Wiccan ethos is not to proselytize or seek converts, Arthur finds evidence in the majority of Wiccan websites of both explicit and implicit proselytizing, i.e. attempts to attract new members, as well as to persuade outsiders to adopt a more positive view of Wiccan beliefs and practices. He calls this new initiative to combat misinformation "online apologetics," and links this cyber-activism to offline activities which seek to gain public legitimacy, such as Pagan Pride Day. American evangelicals are renowned the world over for their missionary efforts. **Omri Elisha's** account identifies new strategies and concerns in the way they approach proselytism. Against the backdrop of welfare reform initiatives in the United States in the 1990s, socially engaged Christian conservatives in particular have come to see the politics of faith-based activism as an opportunity to mobilize congregations around refined notions of evangelism. Examining ethnographic data, theology, and "mobilization literature," Elisha discusses the new structures, networks, and partnerships that have been established to not just promote the gospel through charity and social action but also to advance conservative Christian values and norms of moral governance—a process that he terms "cultural Christianization."

Concluding observations

While the majority of the authors have operated with a shared notion of proselytization as the initiatives, practices, discourses intended to effect, in Grace Kao's phrasing, "a significant change in the pre-existing religious commitments, identity, membership, or lack thereof of others" (and some, such as Rahn, Arthur, and Tremlett would add "attitudes" to the list), more diversity obtains in the empirical details. One size no longer fits all for the modern missionary. Missionary flows are increasingly multi-directional and multilateral. As Paul Freston tellingly states in his chapter, proselytizing now occurs mainly between so-called world religions (whether conversionist in orientation or not) and less between "traditional" and "world" religions—which was the focus of earlier works on conversion by van der Veer (1996) and Hefner (1993). Christian missionaries still dominate the global field of missionary activity, but there is more and more cross-fertilization in the practice of proselytization, notably given the powerful mediation of modern mass media.

If our book has invited a rethinking of the mediation of proselytization in what Manuel Castells calls our "global network society" (1997), then we must also hope that the concept of agency calls for similar re-examination in light of post-colonial and global developments. As argued by Talal Asad, the concept—as it relates to issues of conversion—is often tinged with "ideological assumptions in and about our modern condition" (Asad 1996, 272; cf. van der Veer 2006, 12–13). The freedom to act renders the act of conversion "rational." In the case of proselytization (where the emphasis tends to be more on the proselytizer and proselytizing than proselytized), the "paradigmatic agent" is not so much the "human individual" (Asad 1996, 271), as collectivities—local, national, multi- and trans-national. Poststructuralist approaches can also miss the mark. In his study of CBN (Christian Broadcast Network) WorldReach and its highly successful orchestration of "media, money, technology, and ideology" for harvesting souls,[39] M. Scott Rubenberg chides Arjun Appadurai (1996) for failing to incorporate "volitional agency" as a "viable cultural flow" in his analysis of the cultural dimensions of globalization (Rubenberg 2000).[40]

However, the capacity to act is affected by the reconfigurations of freedoms and restrictions of a late capitalist, security-conscious world, as well as attendant changes in the relations of power within and between religious communities. This complex nexus of cultural, religious, political and legal factors—Peter van der Veer talks of a "field of power" (2006, 10)—influences both the practice of proselytization, and its interpretation and reception, in diverse ways.[41] In the post-colonial world, territories and peoples—whether far-flung or proximate—are no longer just available targets for proselytizing groups. Access has to be granted, assembly has to be approved, and legitimacy has to be established for proselytic activity. While it was not uncommon for missionaries to deploy a "language of freedom versus coercion" (van der Veer 2006, 12), the politics of proselytizing has become increasingly legalized in the modern democratic sphere.

Beyond or in conjunction with that, as several of the contributions have admirably illustrated, newer missionary groups have to negotiate their niche in longstanding dispensations between historic religious organizations and state authorities. As we have seen, they draw on local and global discourses in numerous ways. Much research remains to be done, for instance, on how the U.S. International Religious Freedom Act may be serving as a powerful resource—symbolic, political, and/or legal—for local or international religious groups seeking to proselytize and establish themselves in unreceptive, if not outwardly hostile, political environments.[42] It will also be important to assess the short- and long-term impact of the new code of conduct on religious conversion among Christians planned for 2010, currently being negotiated by a wide spectrum of Christian groups.

In addition to this ethical revisiting of proselytization in some camps, it also remains to be seen whether the critique leveled at human rights norms pertaining to religion and belief for their privileging of major missionary religions, or Christianity more specifically, is sustained and leads to any significant legal or policy changes. This may depend in part on whether anti-proselytization discourse becomes more inscribed into the global South critiques of Western bias or partial universalism in human rights interpretation (see for example Santos and Rodríguez-Garavito 2005; Santos 2003; An-Na'im 2002). It seems unlikely, however, given historical and current trends in this post 9/11 era, as well as the continuing talk of culture wars, media coverage of religious militancy,[43] and the hegemony of free market logic, that issues surrounding proselytization, proselytism, or religious conversion will disappear from academic or public attention in the foreseeable future.

Notes

1. An early version of this text was presented at a University of Alberta, Canada lecture, March 6, 2007, and the South and Southeast Asian Association for the Study of Culture and Religion (SSEASR) conference, Bangkok, Thailand, May 24–27, 2007. I wish to express my appreciation for the questions and comments received.

2. One of the first texts to explore this tension between proselytism and pluralism was that of (Marty and Greenspahn 1988).

3. http://www.law.emory.edu/cms/site/index.php?id=1786 [accessed May 11, 2007].

4. The genesis of the present volume dates back to a symposium on the topic organized for the 19th World Congress of the International Association for the History of Religions in Tokyo, Japan in March 2005.

5. John Witte talks of the problem of proselytism as the "corollary" to the problem of conversion (2007, 17), and George Thomas describes proselytizing as being a "natural accompaniment to conversion" (Thomas 2001). While the Indian government does make a distinction (from 1977 onwards) between the right to propagate religion and the right to convert (Viswanathan 2000), labeling the more "intransitive" activity of proselytizing as less problematic, it is clear that any form of missionary presence is an anathema to Hindu activists. Peter van der Veer writes of how the Hindu nationalist press defended attacks against Christian missionaries "as justifiable anger *against foreign attempts* to convert the Hindu nation" (van der Veer 2006, 3 [my emphasis]).

6. Jean DeBernardi observes that in Singapore both terms—"proselytism" and "proselytization" are associated with the negative practice of trying to convert others, as too is "evangelical." Personal communication, September 15, 2007.

7. A similar rationale is laid out in Martin and Winter (1999). This is also a useful account

of how Christian evangelism came to be interpreted as witness and dialogue, displacing the increasingly negative understanding of "proselytism." Cf. John Witte's definition, deriving from the 1966 International Covenant on Civil and Political Rights, "...understood as the right to 'manifest,' 'teach,' 'express,' and 'impart' religious ideas for the sake, among other things, of seeking the conversion of another" (2007, 17).

8. We are here focusing on the more prevalent meaning of "proselytization" as a religious practice, without excluding more secular interpretations, as does Talal Asad with his definition of conversion narratives (Asad 1996, 266).

9. For some discussion of the significance of the rise of the legal and human rights interface for religious studies, see Hackett and Sullivan (2005); Hackett (2004) and Sullivan (2005).

10. On Arabic anti-missionizing texts, see Sharkey (2004).

11. See U.N. Doc. E/CN.4/1996/95 (cited in Lerner 2000, 102, 171, n.83). For the declaration, see http://www.ohchr.org/english/law/religion.htm [accessed May 6, 2007].
    Article 1 reads:
    "1. Everyone shall have the right to freedom of thought, conscience and religion.
    This right shall include freedom to have a religion or whatever belief of his choice,
    and freedom, either individually or in community with others and in public or
    private, to manifest his religion or belief in worship, observance, practice and
    teaching."

12. Also available at http://www.irla.org/documents/articles/stahnke-proselytism.html [accessed May 6, 2007].

13. Stahnke notes that there can be practical ramifications to the choice of designation. For instance, some international legal instruments recognize that the protection of national security can be a valid reason for limitations on the freedom of expression, whereas this is not listed as a justification for limitations on the freedom to *manifest* religion or belief (Stahnke 2004, 627).

14. In discussing the work of the European Commission and Court of Human Rights, Malcolm D. Evans talks of a concern to reconcile competing interests and ensure respect for everyone's beliefs. However, Evans considers that the relativizing of the voice of religion to the demands of human rights is a "dangerous conflation of roles and debates" (Evans 2000, 190), resulting in an "impoverished, or negative, vision of religious liberty" (Evans 2000, 191).

15. World Council of Churches and the Roman Catholic Church, 1995. *The Challenge of Proselytism and the Calling to Common Witness*

    http://www.oikoumene.org/en/resources/documents/wcc-commissions/joint-working-group-between-the-roman-catholic-church-and-the-wcc/25-09-95-challenge-of-proselytism.html [accessed June 30, 2007].

16. Decree *Ad Gentes* On The Mission Activity Of The Church http://www.vatican.va/archive/hist_councils/ii_vatican_council/documents/vat-ii_decree_19651207_ad-gentes_en.html [accessed June 30, 2007]. For more discussion of "false evangelism," see Beach (1999).

17. See http://www.oikoumene.org August 6, 2007.

18. Cf. also efforts by Orthodox Christianity to reconceptualize proselytism and rediscover evangelism (Prodromou forthcoming).

19. "Norway: Christians, Muslims defend right to convert." *The Jerusalem Post,* Aug 22, 2007, www.jpost.com [accessed August 31, 2007].

20. Cited in Omar 2006.

21. See especially, http://www.library.yale.edu/div/MissionsResources.htm.

22. See for example, http://www.uscwm.org/mobilization_division/pastors_web_folder/ global_mission_statistics.html [accessed May 5, 2007]. See also http://www.lausanne-worldpulse.com/ and http://bgc.gospelcom.net/worldpulseonline/missionhandbook/ [accessed May 6, 2007].

23. See Tim Stafford, "Historian Ahead of His Time." *Christianity Today*, February 5, 2007 http://www.christianitytoday.com/ct/2007/february/34.87.html [accessed May 6, 2007].

24. For a global snapshot of statistical trends, see the work of David Barrett and Todd John-son at the Center for the Study of Global Christianity, Gordon-Conwell Theological Seminary http://www.gordonconwell.edu/ockenga/globalchristianity/resources.php, as well as the comprehensive *World Christian Encyclopaedia* 2nd ed. (Barrett *et al.* [eds.] 2001) and World Christian Database http://worldchristiandatabase.org/wcd/ [accessed May 6, 2007]. See also *World Christian Trends AD 30–AD 2200: Interpreting the Annual Christian Megacensus* (Barrett *et al.* [eds.] 2001).

25. For a summary, see his "Christianity's New Center" *The Atlantic,* September 12, 2002 http://www.theatlantic.com/doc/prem/200209u/int2002-09-12 [accessed May 6, 2007].

26. Christopher J.H. Wright, "An Upside-Down World: Distinguishing between home and mission field no longer makes sense." *Christianity Today* posted January 18, 2007.

27. Jon Bonk is Project Director of the electronic resource, *Dictionary of African Christian Biography* http://www.dacb.org.

28. Lamin Sanneh is Professor of Missions and World Christianity at Yale University, An-drew F. Walls is the ex-founding director of the Centre for the Study of Christianity in the Non-Western World at Edinburgh University and Professor of World Christianity at Princeton Theological Seminary, Kwame Bediako is Founder/Director of the Akrofi-Christaller Institute for Mission Research and Applied Theology, Akropong-Akuapem, Ghana, Dana L. Robert is Co-Director of the Center for Global Christianity and Mis-sion, Boston University, and Jonathan Bonk is Executive Director of the Overseas Min-istries Study Center in New Haven, Connecticut.

29. The new *Encyclopedia of Missions and Missionaries* (Bonk [ed.] 2007)includes other "ma-jor religions" in addition to Christianity, such as Buddhism and Islam.

30. See the *Journal of African Christian Thought* (published by the Akrofi-Christaller Insti-tute), and especially the December 2006 issue (vol. 9, no. 2) issue entitled "Christian Mission and Scholarship" in appreciation of Emeritus Professor Andrew F. Walls.

31. For a critique of this interpretation, see Hock (2006).

32. See *Missiology: An International Review* 24(2): 1996, guest edited by Thomas N. Headland.

33. For a good overview of scholarly trends on the sociology of conversion, see Richardson 1998. Lofland's 1966 study of a "doomsday cult" was one of the earliest to distinguish between different strategies employed by the group to promote conversion: overt and covert, embodied and disembodied (Lofland 1977).

34. On transnational religion, see Robertson and Garrett (1991); Rudolph and Piscatori eds. (1997); Corten and Marshall-Fratani (2001); Juergensmeyer (2005) and Beyer (2001).

35. Recent publications of importance in this area include: Hoover and Clark eds. (2002); Mitchell and Marriage (2003); Meyer and Moors (2006) and Hoover (2006).

36. For helpful critical overviews, see "Who Is Secular in the World Today?" a special insert in *Religion in the News*, Fall 2006, by Ariela Keysar and Barry Kosmin; a special double issue of the *Hedgehog Review* "After Secularization," vol. 8, nos. 1–2 (Spring/Summer 2006).

37. See the critique articulated by some Hindu activists and scholars of Hinduism that the Hindu view of religious freedom is not based on the freedom to proselytize but to retain one's religion and not be subject to the proselytization of others (e.g. Sharma 2004, 2000/01).

38. Proselytization can be a marker of a nation (as in the case of Nigeria) and not just a group (Fourchard *et al.* 2005). Korea and the U.S. would also be current examples of this (Brouwer *et. al.* 1996).

39. CBN claims that since 1995 they have brought 222 million people to Christianity through their media outreach http://www.cbnafrica.com/outreach/affiliates/CBN-WorldReach.asp [accessed September 2, 2007].

40. This would resonate with Asad's notion of the "transitive" in the Christian conversion process (Asad 1996, 266).

41. Cf. Asad's insistence on the historical and non-universalist properties of the concept of agency (1996, 271).

42. In fact, in his book on the rise of the evangelical-led campaign for international religious freedom, Allen Hertzke notes the missionary character of this new area of religious activism (Hertzke 2004). See also Doris Buss and Didi Herman's study of the Christian Right's efforts to establish a role for conservative Christianity in international law and politics (Buss and Herman 2003).

43. See, especially, CNN's much hyped worldwide documentary, "God's Warriors" aired in August 2007 http://www.hvc-inc.com/clients/cnn/warriors/index.html [accessed August 24, 2007].

References

Adams, IV, Nathan A. 2000. A Human Rights Imperative: Extending Religious Liberty Beyond the Border. *Cornell International Law Journal* 33(1): 1–66.

An-Na'im, Abdullahi A. 1999. Competing Claims to Religious Freedom and Communal Self-Determination in Africa. In *Proselytization and Communal Self-Determination in Africa*, ed. A.A. An-Na'im. Maryknoll, 1–28. New York: Orbis.

———. 2002. Redressing Universal Ambivalence about the Universality of Human Rights. *Journal of Human Rights* 1(4): 607–09.

———, ed. 1999. *Proselytization and Communal Self-Determination in Africa*. Maryknoll, NY: Orbis Books.

Anthony, Dick, and Thomas Robbins. 2004. Conversion and "Brainwashing" in New Religious Movements. In *The Oxford Handbook of New Religious Movements*, ed. J.R. Lewis, 243–97. New York: Oxford University Press.

Appadurai, Arjun. 1996. *Modernity at Large: Cultural Dimensions of Globalization*. Minneapolis: University of Minnesota Press.

Asad, Talal. 1996. Comments on Conversion. In *Conversion to Modernities: The Globalization of Christianity*, ed. P. van der Veer, 263–73. New York: Routledge.

———. 2003. *Formations of the Secular: Christianity, Islam, Modernity*. Stanford: Stanford University Press.

Austin-Broos, Diane. 2003. The Anthropology of Conversion: An Introduction. In *The Anthropology of Religious Conversion*, ed. A. Buckser and S.D. Glazier, 1–12. Lanham, MD: Rowman and Littlefield.

Bainbridge, William Sims. 1992. The Sociology of Conversion. In *Handbook of Religious Conversion*, ed. H.N. Malony and S. Southard, 178–91. Birmingham, AL: Religious Education Press.

Barker, Eileen. 1984. *The Making of a Moonie*. Oxford: Blackwell.

Barrett, David B., George T. Kurian and Todd M. Johnson, eds. 2001. *World Christian Encyclopaedia*, 2nd ed. Oxford: Oxford University Press.

Barrett, David B., Todd M. Johnson, Christopher Guidry, and Peter Crossing, eds. 2001. *World Christian Trends AD 30–AD 2200: Interpreting the Annual Christian Megacensus*. Pasadena, CA: William Carey Library.

Beach, B.B. 1999. *Evangelism and Proselytism: Religious Liberty and Ecumenical Challenges*: International Religious Liberty Association.

Bediako, Kwame. 1995. *Christianity in Africa: the Renewal of a non-Western Religion*. Maryknoll, NY: Orbis.

———. 1999. Africa and Christianity on the Threshold of the Third Millennium: the Religious Dimension. *African Affairs* Centenary Edition.

———. 2000. *Jesus in Africa: The Christian Gospel in African History and Experience*.

Akropong-Akuapem, Ghana: Regnum Africa.

Beidelman, T.O. 1982. *Colonial Evangelism: A Socio-Historical Study of an East African Mission at the Grassroots.* Bloomington: Indiana University Press.

Benthall, Jonathan. 2001. Comment. *Current Anthropology* 42(1): 46.

Beyer, Peter, ed. 2001. *Religion in the Process of Globalization.* Wurzburg: Ergon Verlag.

Bonk, Jonathan. 2000. Missionary Activities: Minimizing Adverse Reactions Without Sacrificing Rights to Manifestation. *Fides et Libertas. The Journal of the International Religious Liberty Association.* (2000): 89–94.

———, ed. 2007. *Encyclopedia of Missions and Missionaries.* New York: Routledge.

Bowie, Fiona, Deborah Kirkwood, and Shirley Ardener, eds. 1993. *Women and Missions: Past and Present. Anthropological and Historical Perceptions.* Providence, RI: Berg.

Boyle, Kevin, and Juliet Sheen, eds. 1997. *Freedom of Religion and Belief: A World Report.* London: Routledge.

Bremmer, J.N., W.J. van Bekkum, and A.L Molendijk, eds. 2006. *Cultures of Conversions.* Vol. 1, *Groningen Studies in Cultural Change,* 18. Amsterdam: Peeters.

———, eds. 2006. *Paradigms, Poetics and Politics of Conversion,* vol. 2, *Groningen Studies in Cultural Change,* 19. Amsterdam: Peeters.

Brock, Peggy, ed. 2005. *Indigenous Peoples and Religious Change.* Leiden: Brill.

Bromley, David. G. and Thomas Robbins. 1992. The Role of Government in Regulating New and Unconventional Religions. In *Government Monitoring of Religions,* ed. J. Wood, 205–240. Waco, TX: Baylor University Press.

Brouwer, Steve, Paul Gifford and Susan D. Rose. 1996. *Exporting the American Gospel: Global Christian Fundamentalism.* New York: Routledge.

Bruce, Steve. 2006. Sociology of Conversion: the Last Twenty-five Years. In *Paradigms, Poetics and Politics of Conversion,* ed. J.N. Bremmer, A.L. Molendijk and W.J. Bekkum, 1–12. Amsterdam: Peeters.

Bryant, M. Darrol , and Christopher Lamb, eds. 1999. *Religious Conversion: Contemporary Practices and Controversies.* New York: Continuum.

Buckser, Andrew, and Stephen D. Glazier, eds. 2003. *The Anthropology of Religious Conversion.* Lanham, MD: Rowman and Littlefield.

Buss, Doris, and Didi Herman. 2003. *Globalizing Family Values: The Christian Right in International Politics.* Minneapolis: University of Minnesota Press.

Cannell, Fenella, ed. 2006. *The Anthropology of Christianity.* Durham, NC: Duke University Press.

Casanova, Jose. 2006. Secularization Revisited: A Reply to Talal Asad. In *Powers of the Secular Modern: Talal Asad And His Interlocutors,* ed. D. Scott and C. Hirschkind, 12–30. Stanford, CA: Stanford University Press.

Castells, Manuell. 1997. *The Information Age: Economy, Society and Culture.* Vol. I:

The Rise of the Network Society; Vol. II The Power of Identity; Vol. III End of Millennium. Oxford: Blackwell.

Clifford, James. 2001. Comment. *Current Anthropology* 42 (1):47–48.

Comaroff, Jean. 1985. *Body of Power, Spirit of Resistance*. Chicago: University of Chicago.

Comaroff, Jean, and John L. Comaroff. 1991. *Of Revelation and Revolution: Christianity, Colonialism, and Consciousness in South Africa*, vol. 1. Chicago: University of Chicago Press.

———. 1992. *Ethnography and the Historical Imagination*. Boulder, CO: Westview.

Comaroff, John L., and Jean Comaroff. 1997. *Of Revelation and Revolution: The Dialectics of Modernity on a South African Frontier*, vol. 2. Chicago: University of Chicago Press.

Corten, André, and Ruth Marshall-Fratani, eds. 2001. *Between Babel and Pentecost: Transnational Pentecostalism in Africa and Latin America*. Bloomington: Indiana University Press.

Dawson, Lorne L., and Douglas E. Cowan, eds. 2004. *Religion Online: Finding Faith on the Internet*. New York: Routledge.

Dixon, David N. 2005. Aid Workers or Evangelists, Charity or Conspiracy: Framing of Missionary Activity as a Function of International Political Alliances. *Journal of Media and Religion* 4(1): 13–25.

Engelke, Matthew. 2004. Discontinuity and the Discourse of Conversion. *Journal of Religion in Africa* 34(1–2): 82–109.

Etherington, Norman, ed. 2005. *Missions and Empire, Oxford History of the British Empire Companion Series*. New York: Oxford University Press.

Evans, Malcolm D. 2000. Religion, Law and Human Rights: Locating the Debate. In *Law and Religion in Contemporary Society: Communalism, Individualism and the State*, ed. P.W. Edge and G. Harvey, 177–197. Aldershot, UK: Ashgate.

Finke, Roger, and Rodney Stark. 2003. The Dynamics of Religious Economies. In *Handbook for the Sociology of Religion*, ed. M. Dillon, 96–109. New York: Cambridge University Press.

Fourchard, Laurent, André Mary, and René Otayek, eds. 2005. *Entreprises Religieuses Transnationales en Afrique de l'Ouest*. Paris: Karthala.

Freston, Paul. 2001. The Transnationalization of Brazilian Pentecostalism: the Universal Church of the Kingdom of God. In *Between Babel and Pentecost: Transnational Pentecostalism in Africa and Latin America*, ed. A. Corten and R. Marshall-Fratani, 196–215. Bloomington: Indiana University Press.

———. 2002. Globalisation, Religion and Evangelical Christianity: A Sociological Meditation from the Third World. In *Currents in World Christianity*. Pretoria: UNISA Press.

———. The Changing Face of Christian Proselytization: New Actors from the

Global South. In *Proselytization Revisited: Rights Talk, Free Markets and Culture Wars*, ed. Rosalind I.J. Hackett, 109–38. London: Equinox.

Gill, Anthony. 1999. The Economics of Evangelization. In *Religious Freedom and Evangelization in Latin America*, ed. P. Sigmund, 72–84. Maryknoll. NY: Orbis Books.

Gunn, T. Jeremy. 2004. Under God but Not the Scarf: The Founding Myths of Religious Freedom in the United States and Laïcité in France. *Journal of Church and State* 46(1): 7–24.

Hackett, Rosalind I.J. 2004. Human Rights: An Important and Challenging New Field for the Study of Religion. In *New Approaches to the Study of Religion*, ed. A. Geertz, P. Antes and R. Warne, 165–191. Berlin: Verlag de Gruyter.

———. 2005. Rethinking the Role of Religion in Changing Public Spheres: Some Comparative Perspectives. *Brigham Young University Law Review* 3: 659–82.

Hackett, Rosalind I.J., and Winnifred Fallers Sullivan. 2005. Introduction: A Curvature of Social Space. *Culture and Religion* 6(1): 1–15.

Hak, Durk. 2006. Conversion as a Rational Choice: An Evaluation of the Stark-Finke-Model of Conversion and (Re-)affiliation. In *Paradigms, Poetics and Politics of Conversion*, ed. J.N. Bremmer, W.J. van Bekkum and A.L. Molendijk, 13–24. Amsterdam: Peeters.

Hefner, Robert W. 1993. Introduction: World Building and the Rationality of Conversion. In *Conversion to Christianity: Historical and Anthropological Perspectives on a Great Transformation*, ed. R. W. Hefner, 3–43. Berkeley and Los Angeles: University of California Press.

Hertzke, Allen. 2004. *Freeing God's Children: The Unlikely Alliance for Global Human Rights*. Lanham, MD: Rowman and Littlefield.

Hock, Klaus. 2006. Translated Messages? The Construction of Religious Identities as Translatory Process. *Mission Studies: Journal of the International Association for Mission Studies* 23(2): 261–78.

Hodgson, Dorothy L. 2005. *The Church of Women: Gendered Encounters between Maasai and Missionaries*. Bloomington: Indiana University Press.

Hoover, Stewart M. 2006. *Religion in the Media Age, Religion, Media and Culture*. New York: Routledge.

Hoover, Stewart M., and Lynn Schofield Clark, eds. 2002. *Practicing Religion in the Age of the Media*. New York: Columbia University Press.

Hunter, Howard O., and Polly J. Price. 2001. Regulation of Religious Proselytism in the United States. *Brigham Young University Law Review* 2: 537–74.

Huntington, Samuel. 1996. *The Clash of Civilizations and the Remaking of World Order*. New York: Simon and Schuster.

Ireland, Rowan. 1995. Pentecostalism, Conversions, and Politics in Brazil. *Religion* 25(2): 135–45.

Jakobsen, Janet R., and Ann Pellegrini. 2000. World Secularism at the Millennium: Introduction. *Social Text* 18(2): 1–27.

Jenkins, Philip. 2002. *The Next Christendom: The Coming of Global Christianity*. New York: Oxford University Press.

Juergensmeyer, Mark, ed. 2005. *Religion and Global Civil Society*. New York: Oxford University Press.

Kaplan, Steven. 2004. Themes and Methods in the Study of Conversion in Ethiopia: A Review Essay. *Journal of Religion in Africa* 34(3): 372–89.

———, ed. 1995. *Indigenous Responses to Western Christianity*. New York: New York University Press.

Keane, Webb. 2007. *Christian Moderns: Freedom and Fetish in the Mission Encounter*. Berkeley and Los Angeles: University of California Press.

Keddie, Nikki. 1997. Secularism and the State: Towards Clarity and Global Comparison. *New Left Review* 226: 21–40.

Kent, Stephen A. 2001. *From Slogans to Mantras: Social Protest and Religious Conversion in the Late Vietnam Era*. Syracuse, NY: Syracuse University Press.

Kerr, David A. 2000. Islamic Da'wa and Christian Mission: Towards a Comparative Analysis. *International Review of Mission* 89(353): 150–71.

Kollman, Paul V. 2005. *Evangelization of Slaves and Catholic Origins in East Africa*. Maryknoll, NY: Orbis Books.

Kosmin, Barry A., and Ariela Keysar. 2006. *Religion in a Free Market Religious and Non-Religious Americans: Who, What, Why, Where*. Ithaca, NY: Paramount Market Publishing.

Kulp, P. M., ed. 1987. *Women Missionaries and Cultural Change*, vol. 40. Studies in Third World Societies. Williamsburg, VA: Department of Anthropology, College of William and Mary.

Leone, Massimo, ed. 2003. *Religious Conversion and Identity—The Semiotic Analysis of Texts*. New York: Routledge.

Lerner, Natan. 2000. *Religion, Beliefs, and International Human Rights*. Maryknoll, NY: Orbis.

Lofland, J., and Rodney Stark. 1965. Becoming a World-Saver. *American Sociological Review* 30: 863–74.

Lofland, John. 1977. *Doomsday Cult: A Study of Conversion, Proselytization, and Maintenance of Faith*. New York: Irvington Publishers.

Machalek, Richard , and David A. Snow. 1993. Conversion to New Religious Movements. In *Handbook of Cults and Sects in America*, ed. D.G. Bromley and J.K. Hadden. Greenwich, Conn: JAI.

Madan, T. N. 2006. *Images of the World: Essays on Religion, Secularism and Culture*. New York: Oxford University Press.

Martin, J. Paul, and Harry Winter. 1999. Religious Proselytization: Historical and Theological Perspectives at the End of the Twentieth Century. In *Proselyti-*

zation and Communal Self-Determination in Africa, ed. A.A. An-Na'im, 29–50. Maryknoll, NY: Orbis.

Marty, Martin E., and Frederick E. Greenspahn, eds. 1988. *Pushing the Faith: Proselytism and Civility in a Pluralistic World*. New York: Crossroad.

Mary, André. 2005. Introduction. In *Entreprises Religieuses Transnationales en Afrique de l'Ouest*, ed. L. Fourchard, A. Mary and R. Otayek, 37–42. Paris: Karthala.

McGinnis, Michael D. 2007. From Self-reliant Churches to Self-governing Communities: Comparing the Indigenization of Christianity and Democracy in sub-Saharan Africa. *Cambridge Review of International Affairs* 20, 3 September 2007, 401–416.

McGoldrick, Dominic. 2006. *Human Rights and Religion: The Islamic Headscarf Debate in Europe*. Oxford and Portland, OR: Hart Publishing.

Meyer, Birgit. 1999. *Translating the Devil: Religion and Modernity among the Ewe in Ghana*. Edinburgh: Edinburgh University Press.

———. 2002. Christianity and the Ewe Nation: German Pietist Missionaries, Ewe Converts and the Politics of Culture. *Journal of Religion in Africa* 32(2): 166–99.

Meyer, Birgit, and Annelies Moors, eds. 2006. *Religion, Media, and the Public Sphere*. Bloomington: Indiana University Press.

Mitchell, Jolyon, and Sophia Marriage, eds. 2003. *Mediating Religion: Conversations in Media, Religion, and Culture*. Edinburgh: T. and T. Clark.

Mutua, Makau. 1999. Returning to My Roots: African 'Religions' and the State. In *Proselytization and Communal Self-Determination in Africa*, ed. A.A. An-Na'im, 169–190. Maryknoll, NY: Orbis.

———. 2004. Proselytism and Cultural Integrity. In *Facilitating Freedom of Religion or Belief: A Deskbook*, ed. T. Lindhom, J.W.C. Durham and B.G. Tahzib-Lie, 651–668. Leiden: Martinus Nijhof.

Nock, A.D. 1933. *Conversion*. Oxford: Oxford University Press.

Ojo, Matthews A. 2005. Nigerian Pentecostalism and Transnational Religious Networks in West African Coast Regions. In *Entreprises Religieuses Transnationales en Afrique de l'Ouest*, ed. L. Fourchard, A. Mary and R. Otayek, 395–416. Paris: Karthala.

Oladipo, Caleb O. 2005. An Epistemological Defense of Religious Tolerance: Faith, Citizenship, and Crises of Religious and Cultural Identities in Post-Western Missionary Africa. *Philosophia Africana* 8(1): 21–35.

Omar, A. Rashied. 2006. The Right to Religious Conversion: Between Apostasy and Proselytization. Occasional Paper 27. South Bend, IN: Joan B. Kroc Institute of International Peace Studies, University of Notre Dame.

Orta, Andrew. 2004. *Catechizing Culture : Missionaries, Aymara, and the "New Evangelization"*. New York: Columbia University Press.

Priest, Robert J. 2001. Missionary Positions: Christian, Modernist, Postmodernist. *Current Anthropology* 42(1): 29–68.

Prodromou, Elizabeth. forthcoming. Beyond the Dickensian Paradoxes of Human Rights: Reconceptualizing Proselytism, Rediscovering Evangelism. In *Religion and Violence*, ed. E. Clapsis.

Rambo, Lewis. 1995. *Understanding Religious Conversion.* New Haven, CT: Yale University Press.

———. 1999. Theories of Conversion: Understanding and Interpreting Religious Change. *Social Compass* 46(3): 259–71.

Richardson, James T. 1991. Cult/Brainwashing Cases and the Freedom of Religion. *Journal of Church and State* 33: 55–74.

———. 1998. Conversion. In *Encyclopedia of Religion and Society*, ed. J.W.H. Swatos, 119–121. Walnut Creek, CA: Altamira Press.

———. 2000. Discretion and Discrimination in Legal Cases involving Controversial Religious Groups and Allegations of Ritual Abuse. In *Law and Religion*, ed. R.J. Ahdar, 111–132. Aldershot, UK: Ashgate.

———. 2004. Regulating Religion: A Sociological and Historical Introduction. In *Regulating Religion: Case Studies from Around the Globe*, ed. J.T. Richardson, 1–22. New York: Kluwer.

Richardson, James T., and Massimo Introvigne. 2001. "Brainwashing" Theories in European Parliamentary and Administrative Reports on "Cults" and "Sects." *Journal for the Scientific Study of Religion* 40(2): 143–68.

Robbins, Joel. 2003. What is a Christian? Notes Toward an Anthropology of Christianity. *Religion* 33(3): 191–291.

———. 2004. The Globalization of Pentecostal and Charismatic Christianity. *Annual Review of Anthropology* 33: 117–43.

Robeck, Jr., Cecil M. 1996. Mission and the Issue of Proselytism. *International Bulletin of Missionary Research* 20(1): 2–8.

Robert, Dana L., ed. 2002. *Gospel Bearers, Gender Barriers: Missionary Women in the Twentieth Century.* Maryknoll, NY: Orbis Press.

Robertson, Roland, and W. Garrett, eds. 1991. *Religion and Global Order.* New York: Paragon.

Rubenberg, M. Scott. 2000. The Christian Broadcast Network and Worldreach. *Polygraph: An International Journal of Culture and Politics* 12: 121–135.

Rudolph, Susanne Hoeber and James Piscatori, ed. 1997. *Transnational Religion and Fading States.* Boulder, CO: Westview Press.

Sanneh, Lamin. 1989. *Translating the Message: The Missionary Impact on Culture.* Maryknoll, NY: Orbis.

———. 2007. *Disciples of All Nations: Pillars of World Christianity.* New York: Oxford Univesity Press.

Sanneh, Lamin, and Joel Carpenter, eds. 2005. *The Changing Face of Christianity:*

Africa, the West and the World. New York: Oxford Univesity Press.

Santos, Boaventura Sousa de. 2003. *Toward a New Legal Common Sense: Law, Globalization, and Emancipation.* Evanston, IL: Northwestern University Press.

Santos, Boaventura de Sousa, and César A. Rodríguez-Garavito, eds. 2005. *Law and Globalization from Below: Towards a Cosmopolitan Legality.* New York: Cambridge University Press.

Scantlebury, Elizabeth. 1996. Islamic Da'wah and Christian Mission: Positive and Negative Models of Interaction between Muslims and Christians. *Islam and Christian-Muslim Relations* 7(3): 253–69.

Scott, Jamie S. and Gareth Griffiths, eds. 2005. *Mixed Messages : Materiality, Textuality, Missions.* New York: Palgrave Macmillan.

Sharkey, Heather J. 2004. Arabic Antimissionary Treatises: Muslim Responses to Christian Evangelism in the Modern Middle East. *International Bulletin of Missionary Research* 28: 98–102, 104.

Sharma, Arvind. 2000/01. Measuring the Reach of a Universal Right: From West to East, "Freedom of Religion" is Never a Simple Concept. *Religion and Values in Public Life* 8(4): 10–12.

———. 2004. *Hinduism and Human Rights: A Conceptual Approach (Law in India).* New York: Oxford University Press.

Sigmund, Paul E., ed. 1999. *Religious Freedom and Evangelization in Latin America.* Maryknoll, NY: Orbis.

Snow, David A., and Richard Machalek. 1984. The Sociology of Conversion. *Annual Review of Sociology* 10: 167–90.

Stahnke, Tad. 1999. Proselytism and the Freedom to Change Religion in International Human Rights Law. *Brigham Young University Law Review* 1: 251–350.

———. 2004. The Right to Engage in Religious Persuasion. In *Facilitating Freedom of Religion or Belief: A Deskbook,* ed. T. Lindholm, W. C. Durham and B. Tahzib-Lie, 619–649. The Hague: Konninklijke Brill NV.

Stanley, Brian. 2003. *Missions, Nationalism, and the End of Empire.* Grand Rapids, MI: Eerdmans.

Stark, Rodney, and Roger Finke, eds. 2000. *Acts of Faith: Explaining the Human Side of Religion.* Berkeley and Los Angeles: University of California Press.

Strandsbjerg, Camilla. 2005. Les Nouveaux Réseaux Evangéliques au Bénin. In *Entreprises Religieuses Transnationales en Afrique de l'Ouest,* ed. L. Fourchard, A. Mary and R. Otayek, 223–241. Paris: Karthala.

Sullivan, Winnfred Fallers. 2005. *The Impossibility of Religious Freedom.* Princeton, NJ: Princeton University Press.

Thomas, George. 2001. Religions in Global Civil Society. *Sociology of Religion* 62(4): 515–533.

Ukah, Asonzeh F.K. 2005. The Local and the Global in the Media and Material Culture of Nigerian Pentecostalism. In *Entreprises religieuses transnationales en Afrique de l'Ouest*, ed. L. Fourchard, A. Mary and R. Otayer, 285–313. Paris: Karthala.

———. Seeing is More Than Believing: Posters and Proselytization in Nigeria. In *Proselytization Revisited: Rights Talk, Free Markets and Culture Wars*, ed. Rosalind I.J. Hackett, 167–198. London: Equinox.

van der Veer, Peter. 2006. Conversion and Coercion: The Politics of Sincerity and Authenticity. In *Cultures of Conversion*, ed. J.N. Bremmer, W.J. van Bekkum and A.L. Molendijk, 1–14. Amsterdam: Peeters.

———, ed. 1996. *Conversion to Modernities: the Globalization of Christianity*. New York: Routledge.

van der Vyver, Johan D. 1998. Religious Freedom and Proselytism: Ethical, Political and Legal Aspects. *The Ecumenical Review* 50(4): 419–29.

———. 1999. Religious Freedom in African Constitutions. In *Proselytization and Communal Self-Determination in Africa*, ed. A.A. An-Na'im, 109–143. Maryknoll, NY: Orbis.

Viswanathan, Gauri. 1998. *Outside the Fold: Conversion, Modernity, and Belief*. Princeton, NJ: Princeton University Press.

———. 2000. Literacy in the Eye of the Conversion Storm. *Polygraph: An International Journal of Culture and Politics* 12: 13–26.

Wagner, William. 2003. A Comparison of Christian Mission and Islamic Da'wah. *Missiology* 31(3): 339–47.

Walls, Andrew F. 2001a. *The Cross Cultural Process in Christian History*. Maryknoll, NY: Orbis.

———. 2001b. *The Missionary Movement in Christian History: Studies in Transmission of Faith*. Maryknoll, NY: Orbis.

Witte, Jr. John. 2007. Soul Wars: New Battles, New Norms. *The Review of Faith and International Affairs* 5(1): 13–19.

Witte, John, and Michael Bourdeaux, eds. 1999. *Proselytism and Orthodoxy in Russia*. Maryknoll, NY: Orbis.

Witte, John, and Richard C. Martin, eds. 1999. *Sharing the Book: Religious Perspectives on the Rights and Wrongs of Proselytism*. Maryknoll, NY: Orbis.

CHAPTER 2

Conflicts over Proselytism: An Overview and Comparative Perspective

Jean-François Mayer

"Missionaries are missionaries!" Such was the instant reaction of an Indian police official, speaking of missionary activities in his area, and whom I had asked to tell more precisely *which* missionaries he had in mind. Similar reactions can be observed in many places around the world. Whether it be Hindus, Buddhists, Muslims, Christians, or secularists, there are people of all persuasions who harbour suspicions about missionaries.

Conflicts over proselytism are not just an issue for non-Western countries. They are, in effect, a widespread phenomenon, the only difference being that people react in the name of their various ideologies or beliefs. In a number of Western countries, scholars have documented and analyzed over the past three decades a number of "cult" controversies. Those controversies—justified or not—represent reactions against missionary activities associated with non-conventional groups. Cults do not typically come under fire just because they propagate bizarre ideas, but because they *convert* people; parents worry about their sons and daughters choosing new lifestyles and orientations. The proselytizing activities and methods of cults are considered to be dishonest and subversive. They are often accused of making individuals into obedient zombies through mind control.

Another conflict over proselytism in the Western world has been the Islamic scarf controversy in France. Before the country decided to completely ban religious emblems, such as Islamic scarves and Sikh turbans, in French schools in 2004 (not in universities, however), there had been an initial decision to ban the scarf (in 1989) in cases where wearing it would "constitute an act of pressure, provocation, proselytism or propaganda."[1] It proved, however, quite difficult for school directors to assess what the intent was in each case, hence the law banning the headscarf entirely was instituted. When introducing to the French Parliament the bill on implementing the principles of secularity in state schools on 3 February 2004, French Prime Minister, Jean-Pierre Raffarin, commented:

> Because the State is the protector of the freedom of conscience, it has a duty to intervene when **proselytism**, a withdrawal into a community, or a refusal to recognize the equality of the sexes threaten that fundamental liberty at the heart of our Republican pact. ...
>
> School is a place of Republican neutrality and must remain so because it is above all else the place where minds are formed, where knowledge is passed on and where children learn to live as citizens—all concepts incompatible with **proselytism**.[2]

Thus proselytism is problematic in the eyes of secularists, as well as believers, who feel threatened by missions. There are those who see proselytism as a threat. Years ago, Martin Marty adequately summarized the issues at stake:

> When people proselytize, they represent not just an impulse or an emotion but a world. Through their agency, one world advances and encroaches upon another. An embodiment of one world invites or urges others to become part of it, to see things in a new way, to be uprooted from old communities and contexts and to find new ones. (Marty 1988, 155)

My original interest in this question of proselytism was awakened by the research which I have been conducting on new religious movements since the 1980s. I could observe at that time methods used by movements to recruit new members, but also concerns expressed by relatives, representatives of mainline religions and officials. It was remarkable to see the variety of conversion types, ranging from the "Paul on the road to Damascus model" which is expressed in the following pattern: I entered the room, I saw the guru, and I knew immediately I had to follow him, to a trial and error model where people would convert after a long time of experimentation and trials. This made me aware of the reality of a religious market, but also of the need for smaller religious movements to proselytize not only in order to grow, but also just to survive, due to turnover. As an historian, I occasionally did research on groups across several decades, and it became clear that persistent missionary efforts sometimes yielded only modest results such as merely keeping a group from declining in numbers, despite the many hours spent each week disseminating its message.

I also paid attention early on to conversions and missionary activities in the context of mainline religions. In the 1980s, I participated in a French project, initiated by the Centre de Recherche et d'Etude sur la Diffusion et l'Inculturation du Christianisme (CREDIC), consisting of interviews with returned missionaries (mostly Roman Catholic and Reformed ministers). Listening to people who had sometimes spent twenty years or more in mission fields, it was fascinating to hear them reflecting on their perceptions of missionary work in retrospect: most of them felt that they had gone abroad in the hope of changing people, but had come back quite changed themselves by their experiences.

During the 1990s, I focused increasingly on religious factors in international developments, which led to the launching of my bilingual (French-English) website Religioscope—www.religion.info—in January 2002. During travels in various parts of the world, or through material collected on areas which I have not been able to visit myself, I have encountered again and again hotly debated issues pertaining to missionary activities. In 1999, in South India, I even had the unexpected experience of being mistaken for a missionary by a group of Hindu activists who surrounded me and threatened me: "We don't like missionaries here!" It took a long discussion to calm them down. Such events taught me further about the resentment which missionary activities can generate.

Whatever our personal beliefs, as scholars we are faced with this challenge: we need to understand and analyze in a dispassionate way the issue of proselytism. We must produce case studies and reconstruct carefully the details of specific situations and encounters. But we also need to attempt to see if common—or at least frequent—patterns emerge when we look at cases in range of places, religious environments, and political contexts. Based upon observations by other scholars, as well as myself, in several parts of the world, this is what I will attempt to do here. I will present my observations in the form of six theses, each of which will be briefly explicated and discussed.

1. **Conflicts over missionary activities are likely to increase, due to the current forces of globalization. In the long term, however, missionary activities might also lead to an increased acceptance of pluralism.**

In September 2003, during a walk with a group of young Muslims in mountains not very far from Dushanbe, Tajikistan, we entered a camp formerly used by Communist Youth, and now made available for rental to any organization willing to pay for it. The camp was used at that time during an entire month by about a hundred local evangelicals, being trained by Korean missionaries. Interestingly, one of the Muslims walking with me was a Turkish follower of Fetullah Gülen—and the *Fetullahci* have been described by some experts, such as Bayram Balci (see Chapter 15, this volume), as a missionary

Muslim movement in Central Asia (even if followers of Fetullah Gülen do not see themselves in such a light).

In San Cristobal de las Casas, in Chiapas, Mexico, two hundred Mexicans, many of them formerly Protestant, who had been expelled from their homes by local Catholics, converted to Islam and formed a small commune of their own. They were converted by Spanish missionaries of the Murabitun movement, an Islamic group founded in the 1970s by a Scotsman (Garvin 2005).

It is remarkable that in the same place in Central Asia, one can find Muslim and Christian missionaries, Tajiks, Russians, Turks and Koreans competing. Similarly, in Chiapas, where indigenous practices are common, Roman Catholicism and various Protestant organizations already compete with one another (beside Zapatista insurgents), alongside Muslim missionaries. This is increasingly bound to become the case. Travelling has become easy, missionaries are no longer supposed to leave their home country for life or many years, instead they are able just to fly somewhere for the duration of a seminar, before reporting back to headquarters. There have actually been some recent discussions among US evangelicals on the implications and consequences of sending short-term missionaries. This is a trend that is likely to increase with improved travel.

The impact of the Internet should also be kept in mind: beliefs can spread even without the physical presence of a missionary. In New Orleans, a colleague, Cathy Wessinger, took me to a local Voodoo priestess, who was proud to tell me she had followers in Russia who had found her on the Web!

The availability of many messages and easy access to a variety of groups means that the 21st century could be an age of unprecedented proselytism. This will lead to conflicts and tensions. In the long term, however, consequences cannot be foreseen with certainty. It might also lead to an increasing acceptance of pluralism, once the fact of competing religions in a worldwide religious market becomes accepted (at least in some parts of the world).

Yet we can still expect many Muslims to uphold the doctrine according to which a Muslim should not be allowed to leave the tradition, and any attempt to do so should be punishable by death. Many Russian Orthodox Christians will continue to resent the missionary activities of other Christians in what they consider the "canonical territory" of the Russian Orthodox Church (see Kazmina, Chapter 14, this volume). But we would be well served to beware of approaches which consider the attitudes of believers to be fixed forever—since change is a permanent feature of our human existence. A recent survey conducted on Muslims in Switzerland on behalf of the Swiss weekly *L'Hebdo* (9 December 2004) revealed that 54.6% of Muslims living in Switzerland considered it "perfectly acceptable" for a Muslim to leave

Islam in order to join another religion. Similarly, a recent book authored by two Muslims comes to the conclusion that, from the most reliable religious sources, there are several possible interpretations in Islam regarding apostates, including the view that one should have the freedom to choose one's own religion. This approach, the authors claim, would be appropriate for a multi-religious and multicultural world, while punishment for apostasy by death is seen as untenable in the modern period (Saeed *et al.* 2004).

Forecasts should however remain cautious: we do not yet know which new groups might begin to proselytize, and which impact and consequences such activities might have in the future.

2. Proselytism can reinforce images of a clash of civilizations.

Reactions against Christian proselytizing activities in Iraq have illustrated this phenomenon. While proselytism is obviously only part of a wider picture, it has been perceived as one more piece of evidence of a crusade against Islam. It has also made local Christians—with a history in those areas—nervous about the image it projects to their Muslim neighbors.

Swiss journalist Christoph Zürcher followed a caravan of Overland Missions in Zambia and published an article in the newspaper *NZZ am Sonntag* (20 June 2004) describing what he saw: evangelists working with military know-how (the leader of the Overland Missions team had worked in Angola with the Unita guerilla group) and believing themselves to be on the frontline of the war of civilizations. In all countries, where Overland Missions is active, missionaries are provided with maps dividing villages to be visited into three categories: "unreached," "neglected" and "in danger." The first group consists of those people who have never been visited by missionaries before, the second group includes those who had converted, but may have lost touch with Christianity in the meantime. The third category—"in danger"—applies to places where Islam has already reached.

One should not underestimate the impact of victorious reports and missionary plans written in the style of a planned military offensive and sent back to headquarters by enthusiastic missionaries anxious to improve fundraising! Needless to say, in the age of the Internet, they are not only read by intended recipients, but also used as evidence of a conspiracy by members of targeted religious groups.

One should also remember that reactions to missionary activities have for a long time contributed to the emergence of revivalist and militant movements in a variety of cultural contexts. One of the two original goals of the Muslim Brotherhood, when it was founded in Egypt in 1928, was to counteract Christian missionary propaganda. Its first congress, in 1933, was devoted to this topic. There are also indications that the Brotherhood originally developed in areas where missionary activities happened to be strong (Ternisien 2005, 30–33).

In areas of Africa, and possibly other places around the world as well, it is obvious that Christians and Muslims will increasingly compete over the conversion of souls. According to German scholar Frieder Ludwig, Tanzania would be one instance of a country where Christian activism (following Pentecostal impetus) and Islamic revivalism seem to be increasingly clashing (Ludwig 1996). Interestingly, on both sides, the role of outside factors and groups is not insignificant, since, according to Ludwig, Christian-Muslim coexistence had long been peaceful in Tanzania.

Of course, it would be an exaggeration to claim that proselytism has such an impact everywhere, or that missionary work is the only root of such religious developments. It should always be considered in a specific context. However, since civilizations tend to be associated with beliefs, it is quite understandable that propagation of other beliefs may exacerbate clashes, or be used as the basis for an argument.

3. **Proselytism is not just seen as a way of spreading religious ideas: it is often perceived as an attempt to extend ideological influence and political dominance.**

On a well-known Indian website for political analysis, a Hindu intellectual based in America (and a nuclear physicist by training), Moorthy Muthuswamy, published the following remarks:

> For any nation that wants to project its power and achieve prosperity, it makes sense to have its dominant ideology be a dominant one also in countries around the world. It creates a sense of commonality and help build relationships that are beneficial. In the past, even Christian dominated, officially "democratic and secular" nations have given official backing to spreading of Christian ideology around the world. Nowadays, unofficial and indirect backing is the norm. In addition these countries have demanded and obtained, "religious freedom" in less developed countries such as India, so that their missionaries can use modern marketing tools and wealth to convert the local population to their ideology. The fact that the United States' "Religious Freedom Commission" [sic] has until recently, downplayed religious abuses by Saudi Arabia (its ally) and highlighted China's (a competitor) protection of its population from proselytizers, including ones from America, should give away the strategic nature of the Commission reports. The Chinese leadership has clearly understood this strategic game and has worked successfully to shield its populations from either Christian or Muslim missionaries. (Muthuswamy 2004)

Roman Catholic clergy, leftist militants, and activists for indigenous rights have frequently expressed the same views regarding evangelicals in South America. They have been seen as agents of US imperialism, and as conduits of foreign influence and money. "Fundamentalist missionaries" in South America have been blamed for "infringing upon national sovereignty;" they have sometimes been accused of being "CIA agents" in religious garb (Gros 1992). According to Frigerio's analysis of Argentinian cult controversies (which included evangelicals/Pentecostals) from 1985–1992, a major issue during the first period was that cults were "groups financed from abroad" (Frigerio 1993). Additionally, journalist Alfredo Silletta warned that "[c]ults are invading Argentina." Such a militant vocabulary was not just used for sensationalist purposes. Silletta was convinced that confrontation "is not only a military one, but an ideological one too," and implicated cults (including evangelicals) as being a part of a US strategy to make people lose interest in the fight for social justice (Silletta 1991, 151). Such theories do not only find an audience in Latin America—on the front page of the May 2001 issue of the French monthly *Le Monde diplomatique*, one could read an article titled: "Cults: Trojan horse of the United States in Europe." Where proselytism is seen as a strategic threat, efforts by superpowers such as the United States to promote international religious freedom may in some cases confirm suspicions. In Vietnam, the government reacts harshly against the evangelical movement among Hmong tribals, because it is afraid that the United States, after being unable to defeat the Vietnamese militarily, is now attempting to reach the same goal through alternative, somewhat more peaceful ways. It is also afraid that religion will encourage separatist aspirations (Lewis 2002, 104–05). In a completely different ideological context, identical fears are expressed by Hindu activists in areas such as North-East India: Christians there are often accused of promoting separatism. To some extent, there may indeed be a relation between separatist trends and religious changes. But it is usually a consequence of a variety of factors, and not merely the turning to new beliefs.

A common concern about proselytism as a tool for subverting a society can even unite different religions. In the former Soviet Union, "traditional religions" often join in a common cause against competitors in a religious market they would prefer to keep unchanged. On 23 December 1997, members of a joint commission of the Moscow Patriarchate and of the Islamic Republic of Iran signed a joint declaration which, besides emphasizing "the closeness of their understanding of some aspects of the relations between religion, state and society," stated:

> The Commission condemned proselytism, promotion of religion by means
> of violence, pressure, threatening and dishonesty which ruin inter-religious
> peace and contradict human freedom. Both sides rejected use of pseudo-

missionary activities in service of political, economic and cultural domination.[2]

Clearly, fears about proselytism as an ideological strategy also relate to concerns about its impact on national interests.

4. **Where there are conflicts over proselytism, missionary activities are often understood or presented as a threat not so much to religion as to national interests.**

When I met Dr. Mete Gündogan, one of the leaders of the Saadet Party (i.e. the smaller party which continues to follow the line of veteran Islamic Turkish politican Erbakan in the Milli Görüs tradition), at the headquarters of the Party in Ankara, in September 2004, he was open about his views regarding missionaries:

> I thought you would be bewildered why we are against missionaries in this country. We are against missionaries because missionaries are used by modern imperialists for their capital or industrial exploitation. So nobody can come to this country as an agent of any imperialistic or capitalistic ideas. This is considered as double agenda. All over the world, nobody likes people who have double agenda [sic]. So missionaries are seen in this country as the people who have double agenda [sic]. Practicing their religious beliefs is quite welcome and quite normal.
>
> Islam is a strong religion in this land or this region.... We do not hold inside antagonism against Christianity, we are not antagonists. But if a bunch of people comes to us as something on behalf of some other circles, this is not liked. Missionaries in Turkey are not a threat to our religion. Missionaries in Turkey are a threat to the unity of the Turkish Republic and to Turkish Republic's industrial and economic sovereignties, because they have a double agenda.[3]

One can hear similar statements from other countries in the Muslim world, as well as from Hindus. Muslim and Christian agencies present "a source of grave threat to our national security and integrity," writes Rashtriya Swayamsevak Sangh (RSS) ideologue H.V. Seshadri (1998, 58). Another Hindutva thinker, Sita Ram Goel, situates it into a wider historical context:

> Hindu society has to understand very clearly that what it is faced with in the form of Christianity and Islam is not religions but imperialist ideologies whose appetite has been whetted by conquest of a large part of the world.... There is little chance that Hindu society will ever be able to contain Christianity and Islam if Hindus continue to regard these imperialist ideologies as religions. (Goel 1987, 75)

"Ban proselytisation and avert disintegration" warned a pamphlet published by the Vishva Hindu Parishad (VHP) (Manian n.d.). The question asked to people converting is: "Where do you belong? Whom do you side with?" As Bhatt has observed, the VHP and RSS attitudes toward Christians are based on "a narrative of a global Christian conspiracy," attempting to promote an "alien" religion (Bhatt 2001, 198–99). Hindu activists claim that India (Bharat) is holy land, but Christians and Muslims have their holy land elsewhere, and for this reason hold dual loyalties, unable to relate fully to Bharat as a holy land. A few years ago, the leader of the RSS suggested there should be an Indian "national church," immune from foreign interferences, quoting China as an example of the course which should be followed—an unusual positive reference to India's big neighbour from the mouth of an Indian nationalist!

As it is often the case in such controversies, critics of proselytism indeed raise some issues which are not unsubstantiated, even if in reality they are more complex. It may be that proselytism and subsequent conversions sometimes lead to an estrangement, and it cannot be denied that they have an impact on cultures, positive or not—one remembers accusations of "ethnocide" launched by some anthropologists. Antony Copley has remarked that, for a Hindu in South India in the mid-19th century, conversion would imply converting "both to Christianity and to western culture" (Copley 1999, 180). However, this is not a general rule, more often conversions lead to a rearrangement of identities and affiliations, which by definition are multidimensional. When speaking with converts to a variety of religious paths, one constantly comes across such cases: religious identity forms one layer among others.

It is also not wrong that conversion can have a political impact. In Tripura, North-East India, where Christian missions were only allowed from 1938 onwards, and the development of Christianity has been a relatively recent phenomenon, clearly Christianity has helped disseminate liberal ideas among the younger generation. According to Debbarma, Christianity has also been instrumental in arousing a sense of national consciousness among the indigenous (tribal) population, which forms today a minority in Tripura (Debbarma 1996, 102). Conversion not unfrequently accompanies social mobility and access to education, often through mission schools. Undoubtedly, there will be political consequences, and an impact on social structures as well.

Reducing conflicts over proselytism to hostile encounters between religions offers an overly reductionist perspective. Some of the advocates of "religious nationalism" are not actually strong believers. Shiv Sena's charismatic leader, Bal Thackeray, became an agnostic after his pious wife passed away because she had forgotten to take a medicine with her and God didn't remind her.

This does not prevent him from continuing to describe himself as Hindu: "My Hinduism is nationalism. ... I am proud of being a Hindu" (*India Today*, 15 December 1995).

Regarding the statements which have been quoted, there is no reason to doubt the sincerity of people claiming to see missionaries as a threat to national security. However, it may also be in part a rationalization of a clash of beliefs in a modern context in which people are aware that it is not "politically correct" to criticize change of religion in itself. There is certainly a combination of both dimensions.

5. **Groups and people critical of proselytism tend to distinguish the issue from religious freedom, which they usually profess to accept in principle.**

Human rights can sometimes turn into an argument *against* proselytism. Article 13 of the Greek Constitution of 1975 expressly forbids proselytism, but the same article states also that any "known religion" can be freely practiced. Greek laws do not forbid conversions—otherwise Greece could not be a member of the European Union, but undue influence in attempting to convince a person to change his or her religion. Interestingly, the European Court of Human Rights has never condemned the constitutional principle banning proselytism in itself, although some judges have been of the opinion that it represents a limitation of religious freedom *de facto* (Öktem 2002).

In a book published on human rights in Islamic law, a Muslim expert from the United Arab Emirates—holding a Ph.D in International Law of Human Rights from Exeter University—has attempted to explain that not allowing a Muslim to change his religion is in fact compatible with international principles regarding religious freedom:

> since it does not interfere with the rights of non-Muslims to freedom of religion or belief, it may be considered as a sort of internal domestic affair which only concerns Muslims. Namely, all religions, moral and legal systems stipulate certain conditions which are applicable only to their adherents or to people under their jurisdictions. (Al-Marzouqi 2001, 437–38)

It is unlikely that this will sound convincing to many advocates of religious freedom, but it demonstrates how many people feel regarding the pressing need for restrictions on proselytism into some form of agreement with widely acknowledged international principles. Today, conflicts involving proselytism rarely deny the basic principle of religious freedom. Instead, reactions against missionary activities attempt to show that conversions have been performed in an unacceptable, unethical way, and that people have been pressured or lured through promises of material gain. In Bangladesh, Christian missions are accused by some people of "seriously disturbing communal harmony" and of "exploiting both the ignorance and poverty of the people" (Islam n.d.). It would be fairly simple to gather dozens of similar quotes from a variety of Hindu, Muslim, Buddhist and Christian sources.

Some thinkers have argued that proselytism should be condemned from the perspective of human rights. Such were the remarks of a Hindu living in the United States at a conference on "Human Rights and Religion" at Cornell University in November 2000:

> The following phrases are commonly used by proselytizers in describing their non-Christian target prospects: "sinners," "condemned," "damned," "heathen," "pagan," etc. If it were not done under the cover of religion, would this not have been declared as hate speech? Does such speech, even if disguised, generate communal tensions? Is this responsible for negative episodes in India between Hindus and Christians who coexisted peacefully for centuries before the arrival of the proselytizers? ... Does it violate the UN Human Rights provision that guarantees "dignity" to all people as a basic human right? (Malhotra 2001)

Italian scholar Silvio Ferrari has accurately remarked that proselytism is coming increasingly under attack: it is seen more and more as an infringement upon rights to private life and religious identity. While there was an earlier a debate on "illegitimate" proselytism, it is now proselytism per se which is seen as questionable, even by legal experts. Ferrari comes to the conclusion that only self-limitation by proselytizing groups and stronger sensitivity toward targets of missionary activities can prevent conflicts over proselytism, otherwise states might increasingly intervene for the sake of peace within societies (Ferrari 2000).

The conflicts generated over proselytizing activities should be considered in this new context, where freedom to proselytize and freedom to worship are no longer necessarily seen as complementary. In a long article on issues of proselytism, Natan Lerner emphasizes the need to protect "the right to convert and the right to proselytize," but also observes that these are "not absolute rights." He suggests one limitation related to the (controversial) emergence of group rights in addition to individual rights:

> One of the limits of the right to proselytism is the protection of communal or collective identities. Minority rights are relevant to this concept. The international community has been reluctant to abandon the individualistic approach followed since the establishment of the United Nations. A change in this approach seems necessary since group rights deserve to be protected. (Lerner 1998, 559)

Amidst a changing geo-political environment, conflicts over proselytism are becoming a more complex issue with the debate moving toward a focus on competing rights. At least in words, opponents of proselytism avoid being seen as enemies of religious freedom, but as helpers of victims. The website www.christianaggression.org emphasizes: "This website holds the Christian faith in high regard and is in no way anti-Christian. Rather this website is opposed to the aggression practiced under the name of Christianity."[4]

6. Conflicts over proselytism foster change and encourage the creation of new strategies and organizations among religious groups targeted by missionaries.

A look at the history of neo-Hinduism[5] shows how its emergence and development were closely connected with issues raised by the challenge of Christian and—sometimes—Muslim missions. Observers have interpreted the appearance of groups with new organizational features (and some level of missionary impetus) within Hinduism as "counter-missions." Indeed, a number of such groups adopted structures mimetic of their (Christian) competitors, beginning with the use of the label "mission" (from the already old Ramakrishna Mission to more recent groups such as Mata Amritanandamayi Mission).

Missionary activities have also contributed to the emergence of activist organizations intended to counter the actions of particular missionaries, and to promote the interest of the former's religious groups. In Sri Lanka, Buddhist revival cannot be separated from reactions against missionary activities. A victorious debate by a well-known monk with a Methodist missionary in 1873 "symbolized the beginning of the Buddhist revival in Sri Lanka" (Little 1994, 18). The more recent trends of Buddhist activism stemmed from reactions in the 1950s against the prominent positions occupied by Christians in economic and political spheres, as well as the role of Christian schools (Tambiah 1993, 593–95). A key issue which led to the founding of the VHP in 1964 was the International Eucharistic Congress in Bombay that same year, with the announcement that it would be marked by the conversion to Christianity of 250 Hindus. This convinced a number of Hindus that the only appropriate line of defence would be the creation of a pan-Hindu, "ecclesiastical" organization, assembling on the same platform all sections of Hinduism. (Jaffrelot 1994, 187–88).

One of the most significant consequences is that reacting to proselytism has led some non-proselytizing religions to proselytize. An interesting exemple is provided by "reconversions" to Hinduism in India. The practice of *shuddhi* (Ghai 1990)—which existed already as a process of purification—was developed as a reaction both to Muslim and to Christian conversions. Originally, it was used by the Arya Samaj for reconverting individuals—including individuals who were not born Hindus, but whose ancestors had been Hindus (Jordens 1991). At first, it was not widely accepted. But the Muslim Moplah insurgency on the Malabar Coast in 1921, during which many Hindus had forcefully been converted to Islam, made *shuddhi* a convenient and more widely accepted tool in order to reintegrate those people into the Hindu fold. Today, one can read regularly in Indian media reports regarding reconversions of groups (usually in rural areas). However, the acceptance of *shuddhi* has also paved the road for receiving into Hinduism people without any Hindu lineage, e.g. Westerners. In this way, *shuddhi*—originally a defensive strategy against conversions—has played a role in universalizing Hinduism.

Even more striking—and much remains to be studied here—is the way in which reactions to proselytism have led tribal religious groups to organize and restructure, in order to counter the threat of proselytism. Such groups are reported to exist today in six of the seven states of North-East India, the oldest one being the Seng Khasi, founded in Meghalya in 1899. Incidentally, this organization is also one of the founding members of the Indian chapter of the Unitarian-inspired International Association for Religious Freedom (IARF). Referring to such attempts to organize traditional religions, Samir Kumar Das remarks that, "[f]or them, it is like founding a new religion seen as a cementing force in the face of a Christian or Hindu onslaught" (Kumar Das 2004, 249). Indeed, Hindu missions also bring changes to traditional religions, which can lead to tensions, although there are also cases of cooperation between revivalist organizations of tribal religions and Hindu activists.

One of the most extraordinary attempts to coordinate resistance to proselytism has been provided by a group of people belonging to the RSS, who have launched a World Council of Elders of Ancient Traditions and Cultures. They organized in Mumbai in February 2003 the First International Conference and Gathering of the Elders. Participants adopted the Mumbai Manifesto, which states:

> We have inherited from our ancestors rites and rituals to invoke Divinity, by different names and different forms. ... We declare that we will work together towards ... [h]ighlighting the pains and trauma of religious conversions made on the presumption that others' traditions, cultures or religions are inferior, and thus create an awareness to stop any religious conversions.[6]

According to a report circulated by a Western Neo-Pagan who attended, half of the participants were of non-Indian origin, including African-American women representing the Yoruba tradition, Native Americans, a Zoroastrian, two Orthodox Jewish rabbis (since they do not proselytize), a Unitarian Universalist, and two leaders of the Pagan Lithuanian organization Romuva.

The report stated that

> the Zulu tradition was represented by two white South African men and
> two white American nurses currently staying in South Africa. We also had
> a real black Zulu but he practises Hinduism and was preparing to visit Sai
> Baba after the Council.[7]

This is revealing of the globalized context within which conflicts over proselytism may take place today.

Conclusion

The various situations presented in the previous pages illustrate how conflicts over proselytism are multifaceted, and not only a matter of conflicting religious beliefs. There are:

1) *Religious* dimensions: religious monopolies or a religious balance between various groups are put into question by newly introduced religious beliefs or revivalist movements within already existing traditions. Such developments lead established religious bodies to react in the name of religion, heritage, and nationalism or ethnicity.

2) *Political* dimensions: the introduction of new beliefs can be perceived as a threat to national integrity or as a tool in the hands of foreign powers for spreading their influence. Those feelings can also be shared by people who are not believers or adherents.

3) *Social* dimensions: the diffusion of alternative beliefs is seen as destructive to the heritage of a group, its way of life, or even its survival. This may lead not only to reactions, but also to innovations within a religious tradition, as it adjusts itself to new challenges. It may even absorb some of the ideas or strategies of the invading groups in the process.

Researching conflicts involving proselytism requires an historical perspective: no-one could properly analyze the current controversies in India without taking a look first at nineteenth-century debates, which have been influencing up to now the perception of missionary activities. Furthermore, one should also be aware of changing global contexts.

There are undoubtedly commonalities between reactions against proselytism in various cultures: for example, "cults" are the Trojan horse of the United States in Europe, according to some French observers. Islam and Christianity are a means of fulfilling imperialist ambitions in India, Christian missions are the equivalent of Western imperialism in the Middle East, etc. A number of quotations from primary sources have been provided here as they highlight the similarities apparent between various contexts. This does not lessen the significance of particular local factors. For instance, a colonial past seems to have exacerbated conflicts surrounding the issue of proselytism in several cases, since foreign religions may then be seen as components of a colonialist legacy. Religious nationalist groups, claiming that decolonization is an unfinished business and that minds remain enslaved by foreign ideologies, quite often see missionary activities as part of the wider problem.

A comparative perspective, such as the one adopted here, helps to understand that reactions against proselytism represent a more widespread phenomenon. Far from disappearing, they may take new forms. Besides the defensive postures of religious activists within various traditions, liberals are also suspicious of proselytism, which is hardly compatible with relativism. Proselytism also comes under attack from people who associate proselytizers with people infringing upon individual freedom.

With or without proselytism, a dynamic multireligious environment means that it cannot be taken for granted that everyone will stay within their respective traditions. Intermarriage is often perceived as a serious threat as proselytism (or even more so). Instead of fighting a losing battle, there are representatives of less missionary-minded traditions who see it as a good argument for converting prospective spouses to one's own religious tradition. An editorial in *Hinduism Today* (July-September 2005) commented: "If there is no channel for the non-Hindu partner to become a Hindu, the likelihood increases that the Hindu will convert to the spouse's religion or fall away from religion altogether." Demographic challenges—including consequences of intermarriages—have led some groups in modern Judaism to advocate a return to the proselytism which existed in ancient times (Rosenbloom 1978, 123–37). It is not only proselytism which has led to such reactions, but the experience of a climate favourable to individual religious choices. Even non-missionary religions may become more open to potential converts, if not actively seeking them.

Few religions, however, will be eager to adopt direct proselytizing strategies. Proselytism tends to be associated today with an alleged dark side of missionary work—even when missions in themselves are not considered as undesirable. "Sharing the Good News is not a hate crime", protested *Christianity Today* in its February 2003 issue. Maybe, but religious groups with a missionary tradition (mostly Christians) have felt the need to distinguish between (bad) proselytism and (legitate) sharing of the message. We have seen that proselytism has also become questioned by legal experts. Secular questioning of proselytism will continue, for a variety of reasons. For example *Frontline,* a respected, leftist Indian news magazine, also very critical of Hindu nationalism, declares, "U.S. evangelicalism does not represent Christianity but does represent the Bush administration's agenda for global hegemony" (25 February 2005).

However so designated, proselytizing looks set to continue, although it will likely become more diversified. The logic of the religious market implies the freedom to convince people to change their minds and choose new options; moreover, missionary religions have tools and access that they have never enjoyed before in world history. But proselytizers of any stripe will be increasingly asked to be accountable, and field criticism issued from various corners. Proselytism may not be advocated as such to avoid confrontation however, since proselytism and conflict seem to have become almost synonymous in our globalizing, increasingly interconnected, world.

Notes

1. Quoted from an English translation published by the French Ministry of Foreign Affairs and available online: http://www.diplomatie.gouv.fr/actu/bulletin.gb.asp?liste=20040216. gb.html [cited 27 August 2005]. For the French version, see http://www.conseil-etat.fr/ce/missio/index_mi_cg03_01.shtml

2. See note 1, above.

3. *Communique* <http://www.russian-orthodox-church.org.ru/ne231273.htm> [cited 27 August 2005].

4. Interview with Dr. Mete Gündogan, Saadet Party, Ankara, 8 September 2004.

5. Cited 27 August 2005.

6. "Neo-Hinduism" describes reform as well as modern movements within Hinduism, appearing since the 19th century and frequently including new organizational structures. Neo-Hindu groups often show nationalist, universalizing and missionary impulses.

7. In order to dispel any possible misunderstanding, it may be useful to mention that my name was added to the list of signatories without my knowledge or permission (as representative of the... "multicultural" tradition!), although I had not attended. I had planned to attend and had clearly stated that it would be as an academic observer—but I was finally unable to be present.

8. Frederic Lamond, "India Offers Pagan Leadership", privately circulated report, 2003.

References

Al-Marzouqi, Ibrahim Abdulla. 2001. *Human Rights in Islamic Law*. 2nd ed. Abu Dhabi: n.p.

Bhatt, Chetan. 2001. *Hindu Nationalism: Origins, Ideologies and Modern Myths*. Oxford and New York: Berg.

Copley, Antony. 1999. *Religions in Conflict: Ideology, Cultural Contact and Conversion in Late Colonial India*. New Delhi: Oxford India.

Debbarma, Sukhendu. 1996. *Origin and Growth of Christianity in Tripura*. New Delhi: Indus Publishing Company.

Ferrari, Silvio. 2000. La liberté religieuse à l'époque de la globalisation et du posto-modernisme: la question du prosélytisme. *Conscience et Liberté* 60: 9–23.

Frigerio, Alejandro. 1993. "La invasion de las sectas:" el debate sobre nuevos movimientos religiosos en los medios de comunicacion en Argentina. *Sociedad y Religion* 10/11: 28–30.

Garvin, Natascha. 2005. Conversion and Conflict: Muslims in Mexico. *ISIM Review* 15: 18–19.

Ghai, R.K. 1990. *Shuddhi Movement in India: A Study of Its Socio-Political Dimensions*. New Delhi: Commonwealth Publishers.

Goel, Sita Ram. 1987. *Defence of Hindu Society*. Rev. ed. New Delhi: Voice of India.

Gros, Christian. 1992. Fondamentalisme protestant et populations indiennes: quelques hypothèses. *Cahiers des Amériques latines* 13: 119–134.

Islam, Md. Saidul. n.d. The Creeping March of Christianity: The Widespread Evangelization in Bangladesh. Available from http://www.islam-bd.org/articles/Creeping_March_of_Christianity.pdf_ [cited 27 August 2005].

Jaffrelot, Christophe. 1994. La Vishva Hindu Parishad: structures et stratégies. *Purusartha* 17: 183–217

Jordens, J.T.F. 1991. Reconversion to Hinduism: The *Shuddhi* of the Arya Sama. In *Religion in South Asia: Religious Conversion and Revical Movements in South Asia in Medieval and Modern Times*, ed. G.A. Oddie. 2nd ed, 215–230. New Delhi: Manohar.

Kumar Das, Samir. 2004. Ethnicity and the Rise of Religious Radicalism: The Security Scenario in Contemporary Northeastern India. In *Religious Radicalism and Security in South Asia*, ed. S.P. Limaye, M. Malik and R.G. Wirsing, 245–72. Honolulu: Asia-Pacific Center for Security Studies.

Lerner, Natan. 1998. Proselytism, Change of Religion, and International Human Rights. *Emory International Law Review* 12(1): 477–561.

Lewis, James. 2002. The Evangelical Religious Movement Among the *Hmông* of Northern Vietnam and the Government's Response: 1989-2000. *Crossroads: An Interdisiciplinary Journal of Southeast Asian Studies* 16(2): 79–112.

Little, David. 1994. *Sri Lanka: The Invention of Ethnicity*, Washington, DC: United States Institute of Peace Press.

Ludwig, Frieder. 1996. After Ujamaa: Is Religious Revivalism a Threat to Tanzania's Stability? In *Questioning the Secular State: The Worldwide Resurgence of Religion in Politics*, ed. David Westerlund, 216–236. London: Hurst.

Malhotra, Rajiv. 2001. An Unholy Business. *Hinduism Today* July-August: 27.

Manian, R.B.V.S. n.d. *Ban Proselytisation and Avert Desintegration*. Chennai: Vishva Hindu Parishad.

Marty, Martin E. 1988. Proselytism in a Pluralistic World. In *Pushing the Faith: Proselytism and Civility in a Pluralistic World*, ed. Martin E. Marty and Frederick E. Greenspahn, 155–163. New York: Crossroad.

Muthuswamy, Moorthy. 2004. *Dynamics of Proselytizing: Implications for India.* Available from http://www.southasiaanalysis.org/papers12/paper1131.html [cited 27 August 2005].

Öktem, Emre. 2002. Les affaires de prosélytisme dans les Balkans portées devant la Cour européenne des droits de l'homme. *Turkish Review of Balkan Studies* 7: 79–105.

Rosenbloom, Joseph R. 1978. *Conversion to Judaism: From the Biblical Period to the Present.* Cincinnati: Hebrew Union Colleage Press.

Saeed, Abdullah, and Hassan Saeed. 2004. *Freedom of Religion, Apostasy and Islam.* Aldershot-Burlington: Ashgate.

Seshadri, H.V. 1998. *RSS: A Vision in Action.* 2nd ed. Bangalore: Sahitya Sindhu Prakashana.

Silletta, Alfredo. 1991. *Las sectas invaden la Argentina.* 7th ed. Buenos Aires: Punto-sur Editores.

Tambiah, Stanley J. 1993. Buddhism, Politics, and Violence in Sri Lanka. In *Fundamentalisms and the State: Remaking Polities, Economies, and Militance,* ed. Martin E. Marty and R. Scott Appleby, 589–619. Chicago and London: University of Chicago Press.

Ternisien, Xavier. 2005. *Les Frères Musulmans.* Paris: Fayard.

CHAPTER 3

Conversion of the World: Proselytization in India and the Universalization of Christianity

Sarah Claerhout and Jakob De Roover[1]

Religious conversion and proselytization are taken to be general problems of plural societies today. The basic structure of these problems seems so self-evident that it is rarely stated explicitly: the encounter between different religions gives rise to competition regarding the gain and loss of adherents. Some of the followers of one religion reject its teachings and accept those of another. This competition in its turn generates tension, conflict and violence between the religious groups in question. Such is the tacit consensus on the nature of the predicament. The common solution is as clear: the principle of freedom of religion should be respected in all societies. Each citizen has the right to choose freely between religions and a liberal neutral state ought to safeguard this freedom.

We will argue the consensus is mistaken. First, it is impossible to speak of one problem and process of religious conversion as though it were shared by various religions and societies. One does not possess any theoretical criteria today to distinguish religious conversion from other processes of change. Therefore, one is unable to identify this process and the related problems across different societies. Second, we will argue that religious conversion is commonly held to be omnipresent, because of three underlying assumptions. These assumptions view the cultural diversity of humanity as a religious rivalry and religions as belief systems to which truth predicates apply. Third, we will take the Indian case to show that religious conversion is a predicament that exists predominantly in Christianity and Islam. Once one travels beyond the worlds of these religions—into the Hindu, Jain and Buddhist traditions for instance—the basic structure of the predicament disappears, because such traditions do not conceive of religions as rival doctrines.

Finally, we trace some of the implications of the argument for the principle of religious freedom. It turns out that this principle is not as neutral and universal as it is claimed to be. In fact, by presupposing a particular understanding of religion, the current principle of religious freedom privileges the religions of Christianity and Islam. The universal declaration of a right to religious freedom is part of the problem in India, rather than providing a solution. To really grasp the Indian problems of religious conversion and freedom, we conclude, the international community will have to let go of some of its common-sense assumptions, normative judgments and cultural intuitions about religion and freedom.

The problem of religious conversion

Good reasons appear to exist to present religious proselytization as an issue of growing import in world politics. In the standard view, the problem is common to all societies where two or more religions coexist. In such plural societies, competition arises between the different religions or religious groups. This may take many different forms. Recent studies on "the controversial issue" of conversion stress the variety of the problem (Bryant and Lamb 1999; Buckser and Glazier 2003; Robinson and Clarke 2003). Israel and several Muslim nations have put legal restrictions on conversion. In Sri Lanka, Buddhist *bhikkhus* and laymen show a strong hostility towards Christian missionary activities in their society. The *Hindutva* movement and traditional Hindus do the same in India. Both in Russia and Latin America, the dominant churches are dismayed at the arrival of U.S.-based evangelicals on a mission to bring all peoples of the world to true faith. These are but a few cases, but the general picture is clear: "Conversion is the troubling issue underlying these discordant voices. And it is at the very heart of the new religious pluralism that is sweeping the planet" (Bryant and Lamb 1999, 11). In all plural societies, the consensus suggests, we encounter variants of one problem, namely, that of religious conversion.

This consensus involves a difficulty. In order to see the problem of religious conversion in all these different societies and situations, we should know what the problem *is*, *i.e.* how to identify it. Any change in the life of an individual cannot be an instance of religious conversion. A firm decision to stop having fast food could hardly be that. Neither could any movement of an individual (or of a group) between two communities, organizations or systems. A scientist's rejection of one hypothesis about the nature of quarks and his acceptance of another does not embody the problem of conversion.

Unless we are to trivialize the notion, we should be able to distinguish between such events and cases of conversion. Still, there is great difficulty in deciding *what makes some event or process into a religious conversion*. This creates confusion and ambiguity throughout the contemporary debate.

Take the following point, often made in the literature on the subject: the narrow concept of conversion, based in the Christian religion, should be extended so that other aspects and kinds of conversion can be included. The editors of a recent volume, *The Anthropology of Religious Conversion*, argue along these lines:

> Cross-cultural analyses of conversion inevitably encounter difficulties when they try to define their subject. Academic models of conversion tend to draw heavily on Christian imagery, particularly on such dramatic scenes as Paul's vision on the road to Damascus. These images construct conversion as a radical, sudden change of belief, one in which old ways and associations are left behind as a result of a new theological outlook. How can such models encompass non-Christian religions, which often regard belief as less important than religious practice? How can they accommodate the slow and partial stages through which conversion often takes place? Even more difficult, how can they accurately describe cultures for which belief, practice and membership have profoundly different meanings than they do in Western society? (Buckser and Glazier 2003, xvi)

Indeed, scholars studying the Indian traditions face this difficulty. The editors of *Religious Conversion in India* stress that their volume "invokes the idea of conversion as a terrain of multiple and diverse possibilities, rather than restricting it to the assumed rigidity of Islamic or Christian conversion" (Robinson and Clarke 2003, 13). It brings together "on the same ground multiple contexts—ancient Jain and Buddhist conversions, conversion to varied varieties of Islam or Christianity or even Sikhism at different points of time and through differing modes and motivations as well as tribal conversions and transformations of sect and caste," but this "is not the yoking of a series of incompatibles" (Robinson and Clarke 2003, 13). Others state that "the authoritative understandings of conversion…remain rooted in common sense European connotations of the category" and that conversion "is, of course, a Western idea" (Dube and Dube 2003, 222–23; Brekke 2003, 182). Or they point out "not only is the concept of conversion which we understand today a category which emerges out of the Semitic religious traditions but it is also a product of modernity" (Fenech 2003, 149). The difficulty is profound: the current model of religious conversion is limited to a Western and Christian understanding. At most, it can include Islamic conversion, but other instances are excluded.

We have to spell out clearly what this situation could imply. It could entail that conversion is a process and a problem *internal to* Christianity and Islam. The model cannot be extended because the phenomenon under analysis exists only in these religions. It may also imply that conversion is a general phenomenon and that until today the Western model constricts our understanding. To show this is the case, one would have to identify the common structure or the characteristic properties of this phenomenon, which differentiate it from other processes of change. Next, one could consistently extend the understanding of religious conversion so as to analyze the relevant processes. There is a third possibility also: one *presupposes* that a series of events are instances of religious conversion; one notes no theoretical model is available that allows one to make sense of these events *as* conversions; one suggests the current model or concept should be extended. In this case, one has no way of being sure that one is not yoking together "a series of incompatibles." If one is not able to identify the basic structure of the phenomenon, how does one know one is studying religious conversion and not entirely different processes?

This last presupposition often surfaces in the literature on conversion. To take one example, Dube and Dube are critical of the concept of conversion, because it is at once "too constrained a concept and too grand an arena" (2003, 223). They suggest their study of the "transformations of caste and sect" in India indicates "the importance of understanding conversion less as unremitting rupture and more as the fashioning of novel practices, beliefs, identities, visions, and boundaries of discrete religiosities—often vernacular, distinctly Indian" (Dube and Dube 2003, 249–50). However, it remains unclear what makes these various "transformations" and "fashionings" into the same kind of event as Islamic and Christian conversion. One could always extend one's definition of the word "conversion" so as to include these processes, but this does not increase our understanding. On the one hand, the obscurity of a term—religious conversion—has increased. On the other, the nature of cultural processes of change continues to escape us, because we classify them as conversions.

Remarkably, this approach has become a theoretical guideline. Thus, the editors of the same volume discuss "the many meanings of religious conversion" on the Indian subcontinent:

> Our understanding of the processes of conversion should be broad enough
> to capture…variations across time and complexities across denomination
> and region. There does not seem to be a good enough reason to abandon the
> term conversion, for there are few others to replace it without difficulty…
> It appears much more exciting and relevant to speak of a range of situations
> and meanings that are a part of the field of conversion, with "conversion"

requiring a proper initiation ritual, exclusive adherence to a set of dogmas and abandonment of all other beliefs and practices being only one possibility and, perhaps, lying at one extreme. (Robinson and Clarke 2003, 10)

The formulation is as striking as it is confusing. First, it is not clear whether the authors desire to capture a *general process* of conversion across time, region and denomination or different kinds of processes they call "conversion." The difficulty, they suggest, is to make our understanding *broad enough*. The question whether a general process of conversion actually exists across the various cultural and religious traditions in India does not seem legitimate. One has to extend one's theorizing until it encompasses all cases of what one presupposes to be religious conversions. Second, the authors confuse the use of a term ("conversion") with the understanding of a process (conversion). The problem is not what word we use, but whether or not we are actually studying the same object, the same kind of process, the same human phenomenon in different situations and societies. Third, this problem cannot be resolved by talking about "a field of conversion" containing "a range of situations and meanings," unless it is clear *which* range of situations exemplifies religious conversion. One pole may be exclusive adherence to a particular set of dogmas and abandonment of all others, but what does the other pole consist of and what lies in between?

To sum up, the following puzzle haunts the study of religious conversion: it is assumed to be a problem challenging all plural societies and common to most religious traditions, but there is no clarity whatsoever on how to distinguish religious conversion from other processes of change.

Conversion and religious rivalry

What makes one perceive the predicament of conversion as "at the very heart of the new religious pluralism that is sweeping the planet?" Where originates the certainty that religious conversion is a general problem of the modern world, in spite of the inability to identify its characteristic structure? To solve this puzzle, we shall have a closer look at some of the ambiguous cases in India, which have been identified as instances of religious conversion.

Today, scholars conceive of many shifts between communities and traditions in India as conversions. A typical proposal is that changes within and among the various Hindu traditions, castes and sects should be understood as instances of religious conversion (Dube and Dube 2003; Hardiman 2003). The Buddhist, Jain and Sikh traditions are also included (Brekke 2003; Dundas 2003; Fenech 2003). Even the shifts among the tribal peoples of India are counted as conversions. David Hardiman makes the point as follows:

Although studies of the process of conversion in India tend to focus on the change from one religious category to another, e.g. from Hinduism to Islam, or Hinduism to Christianity, it can be argued that many internal "conversions" have also occurred, e.g. from Shaivism to Vaishnavism, or from one Bhakti sect to another. This rule may be seen to apply similarly in the case of transformations amongst the so-called "tribals" of India. (Hardiman 2003, 255)

Hardiman himself raises the question whether or not we can define such movements as conversions. Even though there "was no talk of any 'conversion' to 'Hinduism'," he suggests, "systems of belief and practice that were carried on within India frequently competed with each other to attract followers" (Hardiman 2003, 277). This may have been the case. However, the same is also true about different scientific theories and research traditions in the West from the seventeenth century onwards. The philosophical schools of Ancient Greece and Rome were equally involved in a competition to attract followers. Yet, no one thinks of studying those cases of competition as religious conversion. Why, on the contrary, is this so self-evident where it concerns shifts among Indian traditions?

The facile way out is to suggest that it must be religious conversion in the Indian case, because different religious traditions are involved. However, this presupposes that the traditions or groups involved *are religions* indeed. Bringing into play the word "religious" does not help us to grasp what is happening. The theoretical difficulties still remain in place. Most would agree that movements between the different denominations of Christianity—*e.g.* from Catholicism to Protestantism—are religious conversions. The question, then, is how shifts among the different Hindu traditions could be instances of the same process as a conversion experience within the Christian fold or shifts of believers among Christianity and Islam. The import of such theoretical questions is ignored, precisely because of the assumption that the Hindu, Buddhist and Jain traditions are also religions. They are taken to be variants of the same phenomenon as Christianity and Islam. Therefore, it has become self-evident that changes and competition among these traditions revolve around the issue of religious conversion.

This background assumption becomes even more significant when we consider a typical explanation of the Indian clash over conversion: it is not so much a religious issue, but one related to political dynamics, the contest for power and the struggle for social equality. On the one hand, it is argued that the dominant Hindu community or the *Hindutva* movement fears it will lose power because of conversion. As the *Secular Perspective* puts it:

In practice all religious communities want to add to their numbers to enhance their political weight. In this case every conversion to Islam or

Christianity is strongly resented by the rightists in the majority community as it amounts to loss of numbers and hence loss of political weightage. It was for this reason that the conversion of a few Dalits to Islam in Meenak-shipuram caused such furore in 1981. (Ashgar Ali Engineer 1999)

Some say that high caste Hindus oppose the conversion of the lower castes away from Hinduism, because it would diminish their grip on Indian society (Vyas 2002). Others suggest that the assault on conversion is but a pretext of the *Hindutva* movement to promote its goal of a Hindu nation: "Conversion to Christianity threatens the construction of India as a nation for Hindus" (Menon 2003, 50; Sarkar 1999). These accounts of "the politics of conversion" are increasingly popular, but they make one wonder *which* problem is being examined (e.g. Viswanathan 1998). How is the problem different from the contest between political parties in any democracy, trying to gain voters or to prevent losing them? Such a contest may also involve threats to one ideology by another. It often concerns parties with some religious affiliation, which try to win votes. It is a contest for political power. As a consequence, certain communities will fear a decline of their grasp on society.

On the other hand, there is the question of the religious conversion of *Dalits* in modern India—the famous case being B.R. Ambedkar's "conversion to equality" (Viswanathan 1998, 211–39). His rejection of the Hindu caste system took the form of an initiation into Buddhism. This gave rise to a new Buddhist movement in India:

> The Navayana Diksha, India's twentieth-century Buddhist conversion movement, has been more of a communal, social action than a personal or ideological one. Its intended goals have been more material and psychological than metaphysical or spiritual; its visible effects have been more political than ritual. Rather than being focused upon some sort of personal transcendence or salvation, Navayana Buddhism is focused on the achievement of social equality in modern society. Before it was a conversion *to* a different ideology, the Navayana Diksha was proposed and engaged as a conversion *from* India's ruling communal ideology, of Hinduism. It continues to be primarily a rational, political choice with psychological and spiritual consequences, more than a theological or metaphysical choice, or a leap of soteriological faith. (Tartakov 2003, 194)

Brojendra Banerjee states that the *Dalit* conversions

> represent a social stirring, and are not a political or, paradoxically, even a religious problem... The harijans and the dalits are in revolt against deep-seated and humiliating social inequality, upon which the exploitation and oppression they suffer is founded. (1983, 393)

The main issue in these shifts is the rejection of an inegalitarian ideology in favor of a message of social equality. How do we know this is an issue of religious conversion? It appears to stand closer to the decision of a European laborer to join the socialist party because he prefers its program of social equality, than to John Henry Newman's conversion to Catholicism. If these shifts in India represent a social stirring or a political choice, why not study them as such? If they exemplify the struggle for political power or similar processes in the Indian society, why theorize them in terms of religious conversion?

Again, certain background assumptions make this step self-evident: the Hindu caste system is taken to represent a religious ideology of inequality; while Buddhism is its egalitarian counterpart. The two entities are religious rivals with conflicting messages. These claims would help if only it were clear what renders the entities in question *religious* and what makes a shift between them into a conversion. When one invokes the suitable terms, even the French Revolution could be described as an expression of the predicament of religious conversion. One could describe the shift of an individual from the *Ancien Régime* ideology to egalitarian Enlightenment philosophy as a conversion, if only one proposed that these two represent distinct religious systems. However, one's understanding of these historical situations does not grow by attaching these labels. The same appears to be true of the Indian case.

Taken together, three background assumptions serve to identify these and other cases in India (and elsewhere) as questions of religious conversion. The same set of underlying assumptions, we propose, sustains the contemporary understanding of conversion as a world problem.

1. The first assumption is that a variety of cultural traditions must be understood *as religions*. Hence, religious conversion becomes the common problem we confront at their encounter. Take the movement of a Christian into Hinduism. Why should this be a religious conversion? Why is this not the same kind of event as a scientist rejecting one theory to accept another? After all, the person in question also seems to reject a particular set of propositions (e.g. that a righteous soul will obtain eternal life in heaven through God's grace) and accept another (e.g. that of the transmigration of souls). Why should a Christian becoming Hindu not be described as a radical change of dietary habits instead of a conversion? The change often involves a shift towards a vegetarian diet. Or why is it not equivalent to a swap of one's favorite pop star or actor—the pictures being replaced and the reverence being redirected? The obvious answer to such questions (which makes the questions seem absurd) lies in the presumed fact that Hinduism and Christianity are phenomena of the same kind: they are both *religions*. Therefore, a

movement from one to the other is a religious conversion.

2. The second assumption is that these different religions are rivals. The common structure attributed to the problem of conversion becomes clearest when it is described in minimal terms. As the legal scholar Moshe Hirsch puts it in his reflections on the freedom of proselytism in international law:

> Conversion is a dynamic dimension in the life of every religion. Through this process religions acquire new believers and lose existing ones. It is generally safe to assume that every religion is interested in increasing the number of its adherents and avoiding as much as possible the conversions of its believers to other religions. The predominant motivation behind these complementary aims is the metaphysical moral conception of contemporary world religions, which generates the desire to bring about universal acceptance and application of the particular religious vision which one holds to be universally true...The basic setting in which the process of conversion takes place has strong features of a zero-sum game, in which anything that one player wins the other loses. In inter-religious conversions, every new convert to a particular religion is also an apostate from the other religion. The preferences of the two religions are thus opposed, and they are considered rivals.
>
> (Hirsch 1998, 441)

What Hirsch states explicitly, is most often assumed implicitly: the problem of conversion revolves around the rivalry between religions. This does not concern just any kind of rivalry. For instance, two groups or organizations with different religious affiliations may compete economically or socially, while there is no relation to the rivalry between religions. This could be free market competition between two capitalist companies, which happen to be run by different religious groups. Or the kind of social competition one finds among Protestant churches in the United States.[2] The kind of rivalry involved in conversion, however, is *religious* rivalry: a competition between the teachings, doctrines or belief systems of the two religions in question.

3. The third assumption concerns the origin of this rivalry: different religions are rivals, because truth predicates apply to them. That is, competition exists between the teachings, doctrines or belief systems of religions, because they make *rival truth claims*. Could *orthopraxy* not cause rivalry between religions in the same way as orthodoxy? Generally, this has not been the case. In so far as religious conflicts seemed to revolve around practices, this happened because these were seen as the embodiments of incompatible doctrines. One need think only of the clashes between Catholics, Lutherans and Calvinists about the liturgy of the mass, the *fractio panis* and the relation to the doctrine of transubstantiation. Where it is not based in orthodoxy, *orthopraxy* is directed only at those who belong to a particular tradition.

The strictness of ritual might generate temporary conflicts within traditions, but it does not transform different religions into rivals. Truth claims do so. An illustration is found in the account about the conversion of *Dalits* from Hinduism into Buddhism or Christianity. The *Dalits* are taken to reject the Hindu doctrine of the caste system and its four *varnas* in favor of Buddhism's or Christianity's message of human equality. These are viewed as competing religious doctrines about the nature of humanity; hence the possibility to convert from one to the other.

The theology of conversion

What is the problem in these assumptions? *Prima facie*, they appear trivial: the cultural universality of religion and the rivalry between different religions are common-sense facts about the human condition. However, we think they are wrongly taken to be so: in reality, these "facts" are a set of theological claims of Christianity, which have shaped today's received view of the cultural diversity of humanity. Again, the situation in India will serve as the starting-point of our argument.

In Indian society, two groups of cultural traditions coexist that seem to be of a very different nature: the Hindu, Buddhist and Jain traditions on the one hand, and Christianity and Islam on the other. Conversion has become a bone of contention between these two groups. Christians, Muslims and secularists claim the right to propagate and change one's religion is part of the freedom of religion. This freedom, they argue, is a basic human right, which ought to be protected by any democracy. In contrast, a strong aversion towards Christian and Islamic proselytization prevails among most Hindu, Buddhist and Jain groups. They claim conversion violates the Indian social fabric at its heart. Some plead for a constitutional ban. Recently, the *Rajasthan Dharma Swatantrik Bill* (Freedom of Religion Bill) (2008) stirred up the polemics and revealed that the question of conversion in India is more controversial than ever.[3] Two opposite ways of looking at the diversity of the Indian society can be contrasted along the dividing line between these two groups of traditions. We will do so only briefly, because it has been done elaborately elsewhere (Balagangadhara and De Roover 2007).

1. A notorious difficulty in the study of religion is to show how both the Hindu, Buddhist, Jain and other Asian, African and Ancient Greek and Roman traditions on the one hand, and Christianity, Judaism and Islam on the other, could possibly be variants of the same kind of phenomenon, namely, religion. Often, for instance, one notes that Hinduism lacks all the characteristics that allow us to recognize and differentiate the latter three *as* religions: a fixed body of doctrine, an ecclesiastical organization or central

authority, a holy book, *etc.* (e.g. Dandekar 1969, 237; Knott 2000, v; Weightman 1984, 191–92). This gives rise to doubting whether it could be a religion at all. In other words, the contemporary literature offers reasonable grounds to suspect that the Hindu, Jain and Buddhist traditions and the religions of Christianity and Islam are *phenomena of different kinds.*

In contrast, if we look at Indian diversity from the viewpoint of Christianity and Islam, we get the following picture. It is obvious to them that all the cultural traditions in Indian society are phenomena of the same kind, namely, religion. The universality of religion has always been an unquestionable truth to the religions of the Book. They share an account of the history of humanity, which incorporates all other human traditions and makes them into false religions. In the words of a critic, the theological account goes as follows:

> There was once a religion, the true and universal one, which was the divine gift to all humankind. A sense or spark of divinity is installed in all races (and individuals) of humanity by the creator God himself. During the course of human history, this sense did not quite erode as it was corrupted. Idolatry and worship of the Devil—the false God and his minions—were to be the lot of humankind until God spoke to Abraham, Isaac and Jacob, and led their tribe back onto the true path. (Balagangadhara 1994, 57)

The true religion has existed since the creation of man, but degenerated everywhere until it was restored to its pristine purity in Christianity or in Islam, so these two tell us respectively. Even when the traditions they encountered were of a totally different nature, it was obvious to them that (false) religion would be present everywhere.

In his *"The Heathen in His Blindness..."* (1994), S.N. Balagangadhara shows how this belief in the cultural universality of religion still precedes all theory formation and empirical research on religion. That is, neither empirical nor theoretical grounds have been given for the universality of religion. The problem was never even addressed. This could happen, because Christian theology has remained the underlying framework of the contemporary study of culture and religion. Its theological truths have become the "facts" of the western common sense and the scholarly consensus. Among these is the cultural universality of religion. Theology provides the only conceptual ground for the belief that the native traditions of India and the three Semitic religions are variants of the same phenomenon—religion. Once we discard the theology, scientific theorizing shows that they are *not* (Balagangadhara 1994, 289–389).

2. Turn back to the account of Christianity and Islam. Their view makes all cultural traditions in the Indian society into *each other's rivals.* As religions, they must necessarily be competitors. One of them is the biblical God's gift

to humanity, while all others are the devil's corruptions. Islam and Christianity are each other's rivals in the restoration of divine truth, while the Hindu, Buddhist and Jain traditions are idolatry or false religion. Consequently, it is clear that different traditions confront each other as rival religions in India. As it was put by a missionary scholar in the early twentieth century:

> ...[I]t will be seen at a glance that the Indian Empire is remarkable...as a meeting-place and arena of conflict for all the great religions of the world. For example, in most non-Christian countries the chief opponent of Christianity is either Buddhism alone or Islam alone, but in the Indian Empire Christianity is confronted at once by Hinduism, Islam, and Buddhism, the three strongest non-Christian religions (Griswold 1912, 163–64).

Even though the explicitly theological framework has shifted into the background, the following step makes clear how it sustains the background assumption that different religions are competitors.

If we look at the diversity in India from the perspective of Hindu, Jain and Buddhist traditions, it turns out the assumption is alien to them. These traditions do *not* see the cultural diversity as a rivalry of religions. Historically, when they came into contact with Christianity and Islam, they expressed *incomprehension* towards the presumed rivalry. An excellent early illustration is to be found in a seventeenth-century dialogue between the French traveler François Bernier and some Brahmins:

> When I told them that in cold Countries it would not be possible to observe that Law of theirs in Winter (which was a sign of its being a meer human invention) they gave this pleasant answer: That they pretended not their Law was universal; that God had only made it for them, and it was therefore they could not receive a Stranger into their Religion: that they thought not our Religion was therefore false, but that it might be it was good for us, and that God might have appointed several different ways to go to Heaven; but they will not hear that our Religion should be the general Religion for the whole earth; and theirs a fable and pure device. (Bernier 1671, 149–50).

The reaction was similar when the evangelical missionary Bartholomaeus Ziegenbalg tried to convince the Malabarian Brahmins of the truth of Christianity in the eighteenth century. These Brahmins maintained that "every one may be saved by his own Religion, if he does what is Good, and shuns Evil" (Ziegenbalg 1719, 15). Today, the Hindu view still obtains that different human traditions co-exist without competing as rivals. Even those most critical of Christianity agree on this: "We have three thousand rishis in Hinduism and we feel that Jesus would merit being added to that revered galaxy. We do not hate Christ or Christians. We leave them alone. We respect Jesus as the founder of a great religion. We wish all religions well" (Srinivasan 2000, i).

3. In the view of Christianity and Islam, religions are competitors because they revolve around doctrines, which can be either true or false. Since such truth predicates apply to them, they are engaged in a perpetual competition over religious truth. Christianity and Islam claim that—because they are the unique revelations of the biblical God to humankind—they are true. They believe there is one true God, who is the Creator and Sovereign of the world. The world (everything that has ever happened, happens, and will happen) expresses His will or purpose. According to each of these religions, their respective doctrine is the true revelation in which the biblical God discloses His will to humanity. The only road to salvation lies in a genuine belief in this doctrine and submission to the divine will. This self-image also entails a description of the other as a rival religion. Other traditions are either heresies, deficient worship, or false religions. The different traditions in the Indian society are the result of the devil's work to seduce humanity into his worship. In this way, Christianity and Islam take religion to revolve around the question of the truth and falsity of a set of doctrines.

From the Hindu, Buddhist and Jain perspective, on the contrary, the different cultural traditions could never be religious rivals, because truth predicates do *not* apply to them. The various traditions are part of a human search for truth and the different practices are paths in this ongoing quest. As Gandhi writes: "Religions are different roads converging to the same point. What does it matter that we take different roads so long as we reach the same goal?" (Gandhi 1942, 2). The idea that a certain religion is true, while others are false, is improper. In the view of these traditions, there is no one true God who has revealed His will, which should be accepted by humankind. There are many different deities and different stories about them. Different traditions differentiate communities from one another. Richard Zaehner puts the issue as follows in his classic introduction to *Hinduism* (1966):

> Hindus sometimes pride themselves, with some truth, that their religion
> is free from dogmatic assumptions, and that, this being so, their record in
> the matter of religious persecution is relatively clear. They do not think of
> religious truth in dogmatic terms: dogmas cannot be eternal but only the
> transitory, distorting, and distorted images of a truth that transcends not
> only them but all verbal definition. For the passion for dogmatic certainty
> that has racked the religions of Semitic origin from Judaism itself, through
> Christianity and Islam, to the Marxism of our day, they feel nothing but
> shocked incomprehension. (Zaehner 1966, 3–4)

Given this incomprehension towards dogmatic truth claims, it is often said that Hindus look at the truth of religions in a different way—"a pluralistic conception of religious truth," it is sometimes called. Indeed, one option is to say that the Hindu view *does* entail the ascription of truth-predicates to religions, but in a pluralistic manner: all religions are true. However, not only is it unclear what it means for truth to be conceived pluralistically, the attribution of this notion of religious truth to Hindus also threatens to turn them into beings who do not possess the basic capacity of consistent reasoning. If all religions are true, both Christian and Islamic doctrine have to be true at the same time. The implication would be that Hindus fail to see that one religious doctrine which claims that Jesus is God and the son of God stands in contradiction to another which asserts that God is one and cannot have a son.

The alternate option avoids denying the capacity of logical reasoning to Hindus. It agrees that, today, English-educated Indians have learnt to talk in terms of "religion" and "truth." Historically, the Hindu traditions have generally tried to make sense of the Christian claims about religion and truth from their traditional perspective, which cannot assign truth predicates to traditional practices. The result is the often-repeated claim that all religions are true. This does not reflect a pluralistic notion of religious truth, but an attempt to translate the attitude of one culture into the language of another. The Hindu view does not see the different traditions of humanity as either true or false. Consequently, the belief that the diversity of traditions reflects a rivalry over religious truth is confined to religions like Christianity and Islam.

The significance of the three assumptions becomes clear when we realize they are mutually exclusive: either one looks at the diversity of the Indian society (or of humanity in general) as a rivalry of religions or one sees it as a co-existence of traditions. In each of the assumptions, one side is the logical negation of the other: (1) The Hindu traditions and Islam and Christianity are phenomena of the same kind, or they are not. (2) As such, they are religious rivals, or they are not. (3) As rivals, they compete with each other regarding truth or falsity, or they do not. They can do so because *some* religion is false, but they never could if *no* religion is false. In each case, the positive statement corresponds to the Christian and Islamic theological view of the cultural diversity of humanity. It also coincides with the three assumptions shaping today's view of religious conversion as a universal problem. The negations fall together with the view of the Hindu, Jain and Buddhist traditions. The conclusion is inevitable: conversion becomes a vital problem of religious diversity, *if and only if one looks at the world the way Christianity and Islam do*. In other words, the problem of religious conversion exists only within the experiential world of these religions.

At the explicit theological level this is clear. As a consequence of the universal truth claims these religions make, a dynamic of proselytization is intrinsic to Christianity and Islam. When the biblical God reveals His will, it covers the whole of humankind. It cannot be confined to any one group of people. Those who receive this revelation have a duty to convert the others into accepting the biblical God's message. As Bede Griffiths put it in the twentieth century:

> When one lives in a country of nearly 450,000,000 inhabitants, of whom
> not more than 2 per cent are Christians and 1 per cent Catholics, the
> problem of the salvation of the unbeliever is something which is continu-
> ally before one's eyes. But it is not only in India, or the Far East as a whole
> (where the proportion of Christians is even less), that this question is forced
> upon the mind. It seems to me that it is one of the most urgent problems, if
> not *the* most urgent problem, which faces a Christian everywhere today.
>
> (Griffiths 1966, 191)

In Christ, the biblical God has disclosed His will to humanity. This is the one and only truth. It is only through belief in it that human beings can be saved from eternal damnation. All other religions are false. Under these conditions, it is immoral not to try and convert others. The cultural traditions of these others become obstacles to conversion to the true God.

To summarize, this theology of the problem of conversion has received its "secular" translation in the three background assumptions. When all religions are rivals, conversion indeed becomes the predicament at their encounter. In this image, the rivalry over doctrinal truth lies at the heart of the diversity of the Indian society and the world at large. As long as this theology remains the background that sustains and constrains one's understanding of cultural diversity, one is bound to see religious conversion as a universal predicament and religious liberty as its solution. The further the theology shifts into the background, the vaguer one's understanding of the problem of conversion will become. Today scholars are no longer able to identify its structure. Nevertheless, the background assumptions inherited from the Christian theological framework compel one to see the problem of religious conversion at the heart of the pluralism of our planet.

Conversion, religious freedom and cultural alienation

The conflict between these two views of religious diversity gives rise to a clash over the principle of religious freedom. When religion is viewed as a matter of doctrinal truth and different religions are rivals, then the freedom to convert from one religion to another becomes of the greatest importance to humanity. It is a question of eternal life and death: either one remains caught in the snares of false religion or one is free to convert to the true religion. The question is also about one's ethical life here on earth. Since false religion always implies immoral and unjust practices according to the Christian and Islamic viewpoints, conversion entails the escape from immorality and injustice. After the secularization of Christian theology, this is translated into the importance of the absolute right to profess, propagate and change one's religion. In other words, the dominant principle of religious freedom reproduces theological assumptions about the nature of religion.

This can be shown by returning to the view of the Hindu, Buddhist and Jain traditions. Where religion is conceived as the ancestral tradition of a community, the significance shifts to the freedom to continue one's tradition without aggressive interference from the outside. That is, the integrity of the ritual and narrative traditions of a community becomes central here. This does not entail that any criticism of these traditions is unwelcome. Both insiders and outsiders are free to proffer reasons to end a practice. Responses will be varied. The conservative followers of the tradition in question may react negatively, while the more progressive ones might listen to the voice of reason. However, both feel violated by the onslaught of Christianity or Islam on their traditions.

The charges of falsity and idolatry and the attempts to proselytize are experienced as violations of the integrity of a community. Since ancestral practices are considered to be the common inheritance that holds a community together, any denunciation of these as false religion and idolatry is viewed as an attempt to destroy the social fabric. From this perspective, successful conversions to Christianity and Islam create tears in this social fabric. Religious conversions disintegrate communities and families by drawing individuals away from the ancestral traditions. In other words, a stance of non-interference is central to these traditions.

These two viewpoints generate different interpretations of the freedom of religion. For Christians, Muslims and secularists in India, the principle revolves around the freedom to convert and proselytize. For Hindus, Buddhists and Jains, it revolves around freedom from the intrusion of proselytization. There is no neutral position between these two interpretations of religious freedom. Either one accepts that some religions are false or one believes that no religion is false. One cannot have both, since these are contradictory propositions. In the same way, there is no neutral ground between the claim that religion revolves around doctrinal truth or that it does not. Since the interpretations of religious freedom derive from these contradictory propositions, they are also mutually exclusive. Therefore, with regards to the problem of proselytization, it seems *logically impossible* to interpret the principle of religious freedom in a way that is neutral between religions like Islam and Christianity and the traditions of Hindus, Buddhists and Jains.

The dominant principle of religious freedom, then, must necessarily favor one of the two sides of the Indian equation. It does. The liberal principle of religious freedom, as enshrined in the Universal Declaration of Human Rights *and* in the Indian Constitution, privileges Christianity and Islam, because it involves the freedom to propagate or manifest one's religion and to proselytize. It implicitly endorses the assumption that religion revolves around doctrines and truth claims. Therefore, each citizen ought always to be free to decide about the truth or falsity of religion and one should also be free to persuade followers of other religions of the unique truth of one's own. This is not a scientific or neutral claim about the nature of religion, but a proposition from the theologies of Christianity and Islam.

In an important essay, Makau Mutua takes the dominant principle of religious freedom to task for its intrinsic inequity:

> Since the right to freedom of religion or belief includes the right to be left alone—to choose freely whether and what to believe—the rights regime incorrectly assumes a level playing field by requiring that African religions compete in the marketplace of ideas. The rights corpus not only forcibly imposes on African religions the obligation to compete—a task for which as nonproselytizing, noncompetitive creeds they are not historically fashioned—but also protects evangelizing religions in their march towards universalization. In the context of freedom of religion or belief, the privileging by the rights regime of the competition of ideas over the right against cultural invasion, in a skewed contest, amounts to condoning the dismantling of African religions. (Mutua 2004, 652)

We contend that the same is true for the Indian situation. The dominance of the framework that construes religions as rival belief systems has produced a skewed contest. It has perhaps not succeeded at dismantling the Hindu, Buddhist and Jain traditions, but has another pernicious consequence. During colonialism, Indian intellectuals have adopted this perspective as a self-description. Consequently, both secularists and Hindu nationalists in India are trapped in an intellectual stalemate.

These claims are in need of explanation. Firstly, what do we mean by the secularization of Christian theology? Conceptually, it refers to a dynamic, intrinsic to the Christian religion, in which this religion de-Christianizes itself. Christian theological schemes spread in society by casting off some of their explicitly theological features. They retain their basic conceptual structure, but the content becomes ever more variable (Balagangadhara 1994). Thus, ever more individuals begin to adopt and reproduce Christian viewpoints, without explicit conversion to Christianity and without awareness of the theological nature of these viewpoints. Christianity gradually universalizes itself, not only through proselytization, but also through its own secularization.

Historically, this internal religious dynamic of secularization can be illustrated in terms of conversion and religious freedom. Originally, freedom of religion in Christianity referred to the freedom to choose between God and the Devil, between true and false religion. Augustine and other church fathers conceived of freedom as the ability to resist the seduction of sin, which God's grace in Christ gives to the true believers. One was truly free, only if one submitted oneself to the biblical God's will. Thus one escaped from the grip of Satan.[4] This idea of freedom as subjection to God was further developed throughout the Middle Ages and achieved one of its vital manifestations in the *libertas ecclesiae* of the Investiture Contest (Berman 1983; Tellenbach 1936). Christian freedom was closely related to the original understanding of *conversion* as a lifelong process in which one turns to God and gradually submits one's own will to the divine will (Morrison 1992a, 1992b).

During the Protestant Reformation, these notions of conversion and Christian liberty underwent a crucial transformation. Luther and Calvin began to argue that the soul ought to be free from human authority while converting towards God and subjecting the human will to His divine will (Citron 1951; Harran 1983). Since this process was the work of the Spirit in the soul, it would be blasphemous to subordinate it to human laws. In other words, Christian freedom implied that each individual ought at all times to be free to choose between true and false religion, between conversion or damnation, between obedience to God or Satan's seduction.

It is our contention that this notion of Christian freedom was secularized in the subsequent centuries. In the European Enlightenment, this notion took the shape of the contemporary principle of religious freedom: the universal and individual right to accept any religious belief as true and to profess, propagate and change one's religion. Even in its minimal legal form, this principle reproduces the background theology by its inclusion of the freedom of conversion. The link between conversion and freedom of religion, then, is a theological legacy from the Christian West.

What happens when intellectuals from a non-Western culture begin to adopt secularized theology? More research is needed to grasp the mechanism behind this process. Today, we can only note some of its consequences. The secular intelligentsia of the subcontinent defends a theological perspective as though it were a neutral scientific truth. These thinkers propagate normative theories and principles, without having access to the cultural and historical experiences that are presupposed (Mitra 1997; De Roover 2002; Balagangadhara and De Roover 2007). Moreover, they do so while failing to appreciate the theological assumptions behind these same theories and principles. They advocate the link between conversion and religious freedom as an inviolable human right, while unaware of its theological nature. As a consequence, these secularists are unable to fulfill their intellectual duty to society. They cannot develop creative solutions for a problem like that of proselytization in India. Instead the dominant paradigm compels them to take sides and intensify the clash over conversion.

In what sense is the *Hindutva* movement part of the same development? Its advocates have tried to transform certain attitudes and practices of these traditions into proper doctrines. During the seventeenth and eighteenth centuries, Hindus reacted with incomprehension to the missionary claim that their religion was false doctrine, while Christianity was the truth. They pointed out that all religions may be good for their followers and that it all depends on one's inclinations and circumstances. Moreover, they said, it does not become a holy man to denounce other people's traditions in this way (Ziegenbalg 1719, 107; Fox Young 1981). During the nineteenth century, however, the reactions changed radically. Adopting the Christian and Islamic view that religion revolved around the truth of doctrines, certain Hindu groups began to defend the supposed doctrines they found in "the sacred books of the East." They claimed the Vedas and certain *dharmashastras* contained religious truth, rather than the Bible or the Koran. This tendency emerged in the Arya Samaj and similar organizations (Dayananda Saraswati 1875; Jones 1976), but soon engulfed many Hindu movements, including most precursors of the present-day *Hindutva*.

Perhaps the best illustration lies in the stance of non-interference. This was an attitude originally expressed in stories and aphorisms, and gave rise to specific practices. During the nineteenth century, however, the attitude was transformed into a doctrine of Hindu tolerance or the equality of all religions. Later, the *Hindutva* movement invoked this doctrine to show the superiority of Hinduism over Islam and Christianity (Mathur 1996, 65, 113, 131). Hinduism was tolerant and respectful of all religions, it was said, while Islam and Christianity were not. This exacerbated the conflict over issues like conversion.

When the stance of non-interference takes the form of a doctrine of equality of religions, it gives rise to a radical clash between the so-called Hindu doctrines and those of Islam and Christianity. For the latter religions, to say that all religions are equal countermands their imperative. The driving force behind Islam and Christianity is the conviction that they are the unique revelation of the biblical God, the true doctrine that conveys the divine will to humanity. The loss of this conviction entails the gradual dissolution of these religions.

In the last decade, however, the *Hindutva* movement has begun to insist that Muslims and Christians in India should adapt themselves to the Hindu ethos of tolerance and its doctrine of equality of religions. They have demanded the rewriting of the Koran and the Indianization of the Christian churches. The same doctrine allegedly inspires the anti-conversion laws that are popping up in ever more Indian states. All these steps have aggravated the conflict over religious conversion in contemporary India, rather than resolving it. They have transformed it into a deadlock. Secularists, Christians and Muslims insist that religious freedom entails *freedom of conversion*; the advocates of *Hindutva* maintain that it grants the *freedom from conversion*.

What is the way out of this deadlock? Neither anti-conversion laws nor the principle of religious freedom will do the job, since both privilege one of the two sides of the controversy. A facile majoritarianism would lead one to the suggestion that the Hindu position should be privileged. However, the anti-conversion laws are both reactionary and illiberal: they take away a freedom that is essential to Muslims and Christians.

What is the alternative? We can only be brief here. Looking into the history of the subcontinent, it is striking that, in several regions, the Hindu traditions and Indian Islam and Christianity succeeded at living together in a relatively stable manner. There is a risk of romanticizing the past here. Still, many scholars have pointed out that local Islamic and Christian traditions lost their aggressive proselytizing drive in India. Hindu attempts to impose anti-conversion legislation also seemed to be absent. The answer, then, consists of a question, or a set of research questions, to be precise: How have the Indian traditions succeeded at alleviating the problem of religious conversion in the past? Which mechanisms and dynamics were at play here? To what extent do these persist? How could they be rediscovered and revived in the interests of a vibrant pluralism in India today?

Conclusion

The universalization of Christianity has been far more successful than we are currently aware of. It operates not only through proselytization, but also through secularization. As a consequence of this second dynamic, the dominant epistemic, moral and legal frameworks, through which the international community addresses the problem of proselytization, reproduce theological assumptions in secular guise. These assumptions make one see religious conversion in all plural societies, without giving any clarity as to the distinct nature of the process. They also skew moral stands and legal solutions to the problem of proselytization in favor of religions like Christianity and Islam.

The same theologically inflected frameworks prevent the international community from appreciating the concerns of non-proselytizing ancestral traditions. Not only does Christian proselytization threaten to violate the integrity of these traditions, Christian secularization then robs them of their voice in the international debate. As a result, the traditional stance of non-interference is giving way for a shrill and increasingly aggressive voice: that of Hindu nationalism, which seeks to impose its own principles on all others.

We should not try to revive the past in order to resolve the present. Rather, we need to re-examine the nature of the Indian culture and its traditions, including Indian Islam and Indian Christianity. We require alternative frameworks that will reflect upon India's experiences of the last five centuries, the nonviolent as well as the violent experiences. These will try to move beyond the current deadlock. Most importantly, they should be humane towards all religions, all traditions and all human beings, so that the violence finally ends.

Notes

1. The authors would like to thank S.N. Balagangadhara, Rosalind Hackett and Grace Kao for their significant comments on earlier versions of this chapter.

2. In the United States today, the rivalry between different Protestant churches often takes a form very similar to any competition between social associations in general. They promise more facilities, more companionship, more care, etc. for their church members. This, however, does not express the religious rivalry between these churches, but rather social competition. Where a ecumenical mindset dominates among Protestant churches, as it does to a large extent in the contemporary U.S., they often no longer engage in explicit rivalry over the truth of doctrines.

3. See Kim 2003 for a general overview of the debate on religious conversion in India. See also Claerhout and De Roover 2005 for an analysis.

4. See especially Augustine's *Treatise on Rebuke and Grace*, one of his anti-pelagian writings.

References

Augustine. 1995. Treatise on Rebuke and Grace. In *Nicene and Post-Nicene Fathers, First Series, Volume 5: Augustin: Anti-Pelagian Writings*, ed. P. Schaff, 469–91. Peabody, MA: Hendrickson.

Balagangadhara, S.N. 1994. *"The Heathen in His Blindness…" Asia, the West and the Dynamic of Religion*. Second Edition. New Delhi: Manohar Publishers, 2005.

Balagangadhara, S.N., and Jakob De Roover. 2007. The Secular State and Religious Conflict: Liberal Neutrality and the Indian Case of Pluralism. *Journal of Political Philosophy* 15(1): 67–92.

Banerjee, Brojendra N. 1983. A Hindu Attitude to Conversion. *International Review of Mission* 72(287): 393–97.

Berman, Harold J. 1983. *Law and Revolution: The Formation of the Western Legal Tradition*. Cambridge, MA and London: Harvard University Press.

Bernier, François. 1671. *A Continuation of the Memoires of Monsieur Bernier concerning the Empire of the Great Mogol, Tome III and IV*. London.

Brekke, Torkel. 2003. Conversion in Buddhism? In *Religious Conversion in India: Modes, Motivations, and Meanings*, ed. R. Robinson and S. Clarke, 181–91. New Delhi: Oxford University Press.

Bryant, Darrol, and Christopher Lamb, eds. 1999. *Religious Conversion: Contemporary Practices and Controversies*. London: Cassell.

Buckser, Andrew, and Stephen D. Glazier, eds. 2003. *The Anthropology of Religious Conversion*. Oxford: Rowman and Littlefield.

Citron, Bernhard. 1951. *New Birth: A Study of the Evangelical Doctrine of Conversion in the Protestant Fathers*. Edinburgh: Edinburgh University Press.

Claerhout, Sarah, and Jakob De Roover. 2005. The Question of Conversion in India. *Economic and Political Weekly* 40(28): 3048–55.

Dandekar, R.N. 1969. Hinduism. In *Historia Religionum: Handbook for the History of Religions, Vol. 2, Religions of the Present*, ed. E. Jouco Bleeker and Geo Widengren, 237–345. Leiden: E. J. Brill.

Dayanand Saraswati, Swami. 1875. *Light of Truth or an English Translation of the Satyarth Prakash*, transl. by Chiranjiva Bharadwaja. New Delhi: Sarvadeshik Arya Pratinidhi Sabha. Repr. 1994.

De Roover, Jakob. 2002. The Vacuity of Secularism: On the Indian Debate and Its Western Origins. *Economic and Political Weekly* 37(39): 4047–53.

Dube, Saurabh, and Ishita Banerjee Dube. 2003. Spectres of Conversion: Transformations of Caste and Sect in India. In *Religious Conversion in India: Modes, Motivations, and Meanings*, ed. R. Robinson and S. Clarke, 222–54. New Delhi: Oxford University Press.

Dundas, Paul. 2003. Conversion to Jainism: Historical Perspectives. In *Religious Conversion in India: Modes, Motivations, and Meanings*, ed. R. Robinson and S. Clarke, 125–48. New Delhi: Oxford University Press.

Engineer, Ashgar Ali. 1999. Controversy on Conversion and Attacks on Christians. *Secular Perspective*, 16 January.

Fenech, Louis E. 2003. Conversion and Sikh Tradition. In *Religious Conversion in India: Modes, Motivations, and Meanings*, ed. R. Robinson and S. Clarke, 149–80. New Delhi: Oxford University Press.

Fox Young, Richard. 1981. *Resistant Hinduism: Sanskrit Sources on Anti-Christian Apologetics in Early Nineteenth-Century India*. Vienna: De Nobili Research Library.

Gandhi, Mohandas K. 1942. *To the Hindus and Muslims*, ed. Anand T. Hingorani. Karachi: Hingorani.

Griffiths, Bede. 1966. *Christ in India: Essays towards a Hindu-Christian Dialogue*. New York: Charles Scribner's Sons.

Griswold, Hervey. 1912. Some Characteristics of Hinduism as a Religion. *Biblical World* 40(3): 163–72.

Harran, M.J. 1983. *Luther on Conversion: The Early Years*. Ithaca and London: Cornell University Press.

Hardiman, David. 2003. Assertion, Conversion, and Indian Nationalism: Govind's Movement Amongst the Bhils. In *Religious Conversion in India: Modes, Motivations, and Meanings*, edited by R. Robinson and S. Clarke, 255–84. New Delhi: Oxford University Press.

Hirsch, Moshe. 1998. Freedom of Proselytism: Reflections on International and Israeli Law. *Ecumenical Review* 50(4): 441–49.

Jones, Kenneth W. 1976. *Arya Dharm: Hindu Consciousness in 19th-Century Punjab*. Berkeley: University of California Press.

Kim, Sebastian C.H. 2003. *In Search of Identity: Debates on Religious Conversion in India*. New Delhi: Oxford University Press.

Knott, Kim. 2000. *Hinduism: A Very Short Introduction*. Oxford: Oxford University Press.

Mathur, Sobhag. 1996. *Hindu Revivalism and the Indian National Movement: A Documentary Study of the Ideals and Policies of the Hindu Mahasabha, 1939–45*. Jodhpur: Kusumanjali Prakashan.

Menon, Kalyani. 2003. Converted innocents and their trickster heroes: the politics of proselytizing in India. In *The Anthropology of Religious Conversion*, ed. A. Buckser and S.D. Glazier, 43–53. Oxford: Rowman and Littlefield.

Mitra, Subrata. 1994. Flawed Paradigms: Some "Western" Representations of Indian Politics. In *State and Nation in the Context of Social Change*, ed. T.V. Sathyamurthy, 219–45. New Delhi: Oxford University Press.

Morrison, Karl F. 1992a. *Understanding Conversion*. Charlottesville: University Press of Virginia.

———. 1992b. *Conversion and Text: The Cases of Augustine of Hippo, Herman-Judah, and Constantine Tsatsos*. Charlottesville: University Press of Virginia.

Mutua, Makau. 2004. Proselytism and Cultural Integrity. In *Facilitating Freedom of Religion or Belief: A Deskbook*, ed. Tore Lindholm, W. Cole Durham Jr. and Bahia G. Tahzib-Lie, 651–68. Oslo Coalition on Freedom of Religion or Belief: Martinus Nijhoff.

Robinson, Rowena and Sathianathan Clarke, eds. 2003. *Religious Conversion in India: Modes, Motivations, and Meanings*. New Delhi: Oxford University Press.

Sarkar, Sumit. 1999. Conversions and Politics of Hindu Right. *Economical and Political Weekly*, 34(26), June 26.

Srinivasan, M.S. 2000. *Conversion to Christianity: Aggression in India*. Chennai: First Public Protection Trust.

Tartakov, Gary. 2003. B.R. Ambedkar and the Navayana Diksha. In *Religious Conversion in India: Modes, Motivations, and Meanings*, ed. R. Robinson and S. Clarke, 192–215. New Delhi: Oxford University Press.

Tellenbach, Gerd. 1936. *Church, State and Christian Society at the Time of the Investiture Contest*. Reprinted as Vol. 27 of Medieval Academy Reprints for Teaching. Toronto: Toronto University Press, 1991.

Viswanathan, Gauri. 1998. *Outside the Fold: Conversion, Modernity, and Belief*. Princeton, NJ: Princeton University Press.

Vyas, Neena. 2002. When Their Gods Failed them. *The Hindu*, Sunday October 20, 2002

Weightman, Simon. 1984. Hinduism. In *A Handbook of Living Religions*, ed. John R. Hinnells, 191–236. Harmondsworth: Penguin Books.

Zaehner, Richard C. 1966. *Hinduism*. Oxford: Oxford University Press.

Ziegenbalg, Bartholomeus. 1719. *Thirty Four Conferences Between the Danish Missionaries and the Malabarian Bramans…in the East Indies, Concerning the Truth of the Christian Religion*. London.

CHAPTER 4

The Logic of Anti-proselytization, Revisited[1]

Grace Y. Kao

Both the term and any activities associated with proselytization today have been cast in a pejorative light. This is not to suggest that proselytism is on a decline, but only that those who proselytize must now regularly defend the appropriateness of their intentions and actions. In short, a near consensus has emerged among scholars and practitioners of religion alike that genuine respect for the religiously *Other* must entail the toleration of religious differences or at least preclude what has been called "evangelistic malpractice." It remains to be seen, however, whether this view of respect upon which much contemporary anti-proselytization rests can itself be justified, and if so, how?

As a way of addressing this question, I will provide a typology of ways to argue for anti-proselytization. As will become clear, the plurality of these "ideal types" can be partially explained by the multiple, even if sometimes mutually opposing, accounts of what proselytism and its primary objective, conversion, even entail. To provide a working definition, then, the aim of proselytism is to bring about a significant change in the pre-existing religious commitments, identity, membership, or lack thereof of others. Those who respond positively to such recommendations might undergo one of several types of conversion, from intensifying their dedication to the religion with which they were only nominally affiliated, switching denominations to match that of the proselytizer, or beginning the process of adopting an entirely new religious tradition altogether (Rambo 1993, 12–14). The desired effect of proselytism in other cases might even turn more on apostasy, or the repudiation of a religious worldview and its way of life, than on its replacement with any given religious alternative. Such is the case when "cult deprogrammers" have the more limited—though still highly interventionist—objective of removing people from various new religious movements (NRMs) because of their perceived danger (Barker 2004).

In what follows, I will briefly describe and then critically assess the strengths and limitations of five distinct arguments against proselytism, or what I call *types of anti-proselytization*: (1) appropriate targets and tactics, (2) substitution, (3) non-recruitment, (4) group protection, and (5) anti-imperialism. Though I will make frequent references to the religious tradition with which I am most familiar and self-identify, Christianity, this typology actually cuts across religious traditions and denominations as opposed to divides neatly according to their visible boundaries. What is more, if all scholarship is "ultimately a projection of one's personal predicaments" as Lewis Rambo suggests (1993, xii), I should advise the reader at the outset of my own ambivalence. Put simply, I am troubled by some of the social, ethical, and theological problems that proselytism raises at the same time that I remain grateful for the past proselytizing work of others—British Presbyterian medical missionaries to Taiwan, to be exact—who were of great service to my great-grandparents and extended family.[2]

The anti-proselytization of appropriate targets and tactics

The first type of anti-proselytization under consideration does not so much take issue with any of the afore-mentioned aims of proselytism as it finds fault with certain strategies that are used to achieve them. Moral opprobrium is thereby not directed at the proselytizers' desire to counsel others either toward or away from any particular religious community, but at their targeting of particularly vulnerable populations for conversion or their offering of material inducements to bring about the same. Let us call this first type of anti-proselytization "appropriate targets and tactics."

One proselytizing tactic that is subject to considerable criticism is preaching to "captive audiences," whether by public school teachers to their students, prison guards to their prisoners, hospital staffs to their sick patients, military superiors to those they command, "cult deprogrammers" to those they have kidnapped or involuntarily medicated, or even Latter-day Saints (Mormons) to the dead whom they selectively baptize by proxy (Lynn *et. al.* 1995, 21–22; Goodstein 2005; Barker 2004, 579–80; Urbina 2003; Thiessen 2005).[3] Even if neither captive, nor officially subordinate, Article 10 of the Cairo Declaration on Human Rights in Islam (5 August 1990) suggests that the impoverished and the ignorant should be immune from the proselytizing reach of others. Additionally, the Interfaith Conference of Metropolitan

Washington (IFC)—the first staffed organization in the world to bring to-gether Protestant, Roman Catholic, Jewish, and Islamic communities for the purposes of dialogue and social action—would also protect "confused youth, [and] college students away from home" for similar reasons.[4]

This first type of anti-proselytization not only denounces the targeting of specific classes of people for proselytism, but also condemns the offering of material inducements (or else the threat of material deprivation for recalci-trance) for the same, especially when a significant disparity in wealth, power, or other resources exists between the proselytizer and the targeted audience.[5] The criticism becomes even more acute when proselytizers require partici-pation in a religious ritual or activity as a prerequisite for aid, as when an indigent population is forced to sit through a lengthy sermon or worship service before receiving much needed food, shelter, or medicine. Indeed, as the term "rice Christian" implies, many early modern converts to Christianity among African, Asian, and South American indigenous populations accepted baptism, together with European-style schooling and instruction in the lan-guages of their colonizers (*e.g.*, Dutch, English, French), primarily to gain access to the fruits of modern technology or upward social mobility (Car-mody 1988; Jordan 1993, 293; Pollack 1993, 167; Kipp 1995).[6]

While explicit bribery is to be shunned for obvious reasons, it remains to be seen whether the *conjoining* of aid with missionary outreach—with the stipu-lation that no religious confession or practice would serve as a prerequisite for aid—would be just as problematic. To be clear, the concern here would not be about religiously-affiliated humanitarian organizations such as Caritas Inter-nationalis, Church World Service (CWS), or Actions of Churches Together (ACT) that provide aid to those in need out of a sacramental understanding that God is disclosed in their actions, since such organizations specifically eschew conversion as a goal in their service to the common good. Rather, the questions would be whether and how the anti-proselytization of *appropri-ate targets and tactics* could account for organizations that understand their obligations to others in both spiritual and material terms and accordingly combine evangelistic outreach with the provision of material aid. For exam-ple, Operation Christmas Child, a ministry of the Rev. Franklin Graham's Samaritan's Purse, annually sends to millions of children worldwide shoe-box-gifts filled with school supplies, toys, games, hygiene products, and—where legal—colorful booklets about the Gospel in each child's own lan-guage. Perhaps the tactics of Operation Christmas Child pose no problems under this first type of anti-proselytization, since a child's receipt of a shoe-box-gift is not conditioned upon acceptance of any accompanying Gospel message. Others, however, might interpret Operation Christmas Child less charitably, as a clever pretext to "win souls," in light of its direct marketing to children and selection of the Christmas season to deliver gifts as a not-so-subtle reminder of its "true" Christian meaning (Fraser 2003).

Andrew Hewett, Executive Director of Oxfam Australia, contends that it is *always* problematic for relief agencies to bundle aid together with religious instruction, lest they compromise their ability to respond effectively to the most pressing needs at the time, exacerbate existing religious or ethnic conflict, and confuse potential beneficiaries into thinking that they must concur with the organization's creed in order to receive the aid (Heard 2003). To test the validity of Hewett's concerns, let us evaluate the disaster relief efforts that were administered by some religiously-affiliated organizations to the victims of the devastating Dec. 26, 2004 Indian Ocean earthquake-tsunami. It is worth underscoring that many of these groups did not proselytize, including Islamic Relief Worldwide (IRW) and the Church of Jesus Christ of Latter-day Saints, both of whom partnered together to deliver food, clothing, hygiene products, and body bags to tsunami-stricken areas (Casey 2005; Associated Press 2005). The Islamic Defenders Front and the Laskar Mujahidin likewise assisted relief efforts by removing corpses, bringing rice and sugar, and unloading supplies from cargo planes, though they also made their intentions known to preach *Shari'a* or Islamic law among the refugees as well as recruit new members (Casey 2005; Perlez 2005; Brummitt 2005).[7] Significantly more alarming was the plan by WorldHelp, a missionary organization founded in 1991 by a graduate of the Rev. Jerry Falwell's Liberty University. WorldHelp had originally hoped to place 300 newly orphaned Muslim children from the Indonesian province of Banda Aceh in a Christian orphanage in Jakarta, with the dual aim of "plant[ing] Christian principles as early as possible" and returning them to the region when grown to "reach the Aceh people" (Cooperman 2005; Sampson 2005). Though WorldHelp's plan was foiled and then abandoned entirely,[8] the incident apparently "sparked a furor" in Indonesia: one imam leading Friday prayers at a large downtown mosque in Jakarta had apparently heard of it when he warned the Muslim faithful to remain vigilant, since Christians and Jews would "never be satisfied until they had converted [us] all" (Sipress 2005).

A much more subtle, but still unscrupulous tactic in the eyes of critics involved the intermingling of disaster relief with religiously-infused grief counseling, especially to victims who were struggling with what philosophers and theologians have called the *problem of evil*. Evangelical Protestants from Antioch Community Church in Waco, Texas—the same church where two members were previously accused of and imprisoned for proselytizing by Taliban-controlled Afghanistan in August 2001—showered traumatized parents and children with gifts and attention as well as encouraged parents who had lost their children to persist in their faith in God (Rohde 2005). The conservative evangelical Christian organization Focus on the Family raised over two million dollars to deliver staples of food, water, and medicine, in addition to excerpts from Dr. James Dobson's *When God Doesn't Make Sense*—a book on theodicy written by the organization's founder and chairman (Dobson 2001; PR Newswire Association 2005; Focus on the Family 2005). Volunteer ministers from the Church of Scientology used a series of Scientology techniques (e.g., "nerve assists," "locational processing assists") on tsunami victims and distributed copies of L. Ron Hubbard's *The Way to Happiness*—a book authored by their founder that does not specifically extol Scientology by name, though espouses the philosophy of self-improvement that is nonetheless central to it (Stockman 2005; Goodman 2005; Hubbard 1981). The Scientologists further complicated the situation by stationing themselves under a banner that read "trauma center," thereby causing some locals to confuse them for medics or for Red Cross/Red Crescent personnel (Stockman 2005).

In sum, the relief efforts in the aftermath of the 2004 Indian Ocean tsunami not only disclose already controversial cases where humanitarianism was *coupled* with proselytism, but also even morally dubious situations where aid was *coterminous* with and virtually *indistinguishable* from religious instruction.[9] It is no wonder, then, why non-proselytizing relief agencies and critics like Hewett view the combining of preaching with aid with grave misgiving and even contempt.

However one evaluates the propriety of these and other relief efforts, the logic that undergirds this first type of anti-proselytization is arguably one of paternalistic concern, which in some cases is further intertwined with postcolonial resentment. What motivates "appropriate targets and tactics" is a mixture of fear and concern for all those whose poverty, lack of education or naivety, youth or old age, captivity or impaired movement, inferior status or subordinate role, material desperation or psychological duress as a result of a natural disaster, socio-political instability as a result of conflict or war, or any other vulnerability might be exploited by would-be proselytizers. We can even compare the rationale behind this first type of anti-proselytization with the World Health Organization's (WHO) position regarding human organ transplantation: the WHO condemns the commercial trade in human organs out of a dual concern that the poor will be unduly pressured into selling their organs and that such organs will go to the highest-bidders—not to the most medically deserving (1991, 2004). Lest the comparison be unclear, the analogous worry with proselytism is that the destitute might likewise "voluntarily" alter or even discard their current religious beliefs, practices, or identities in order to adopt—in whole or in part—those of the proselytizer in cases where the latter has significantly greater resources to offer.

While some measure of paternalistic concerns appears to be justifiable for these reasons, it would nevertheless be a mistake to regard *all* such targets of proselytism as totally passive or easily manipulatable. For there are even some cases where it is the proselytized recipients of the rites of conversion and not the agents of proselytism who are the ones taking advantage of the gross disparity in wealth and resources.[10] On a separate but related note, while it is obvious why preaching to "captive audiences" would constitute an abuse of power, it is less clear why proselytizing to other groups (such as the afore-mentioned "college students away from home") would invariably be prob-lematic, as well, particularly in cases where the proselytizers and their targeted audiences are drawn from the same peer group. Once we further acknowledge that motives for religious conversion are often over-determined, that converts can be rather selective in their performance of the requirements and rituals of their newly adopted religion, and that most individuals and societies *resist* conversion attempts, the paternalist's worst fears that vulnerable audiences will inevitably succumb to proselytizers' powers of persuasion should be suf-ficiently allayed (Carmody 1988; Keyes 1993; Pollack 1993; Rambo 1993, 35, 73, 90–91; Walls 1996, 89; Norris 2003, 171).

The anti-proselytization of substitution

Our second type of anti-proselytization seeks the substitution of all ethically unsound proselytism for activities believed to be more suitable. While much ink has been spilled over the question whether proselytism can be properly distinguished from its proposed alternatives—evangelism, invitation, dia-logue, mission, or common witness—this ongoing debate has not stopped many Christian ecumenicists from answering in the affirmative. To illustrate, the World Council of Churches (WCC) regards proselytism, the "encour-agement of Christians who belong to a church to change their denomina-tional allegiance," as a "scandal and a counter-witness" to Christian unity and accordingly promotes "responsible relationships in mission instead" (1997, sec. II, sec. III.2). The Pentecostals and Roman Catholics who are in dialogue with each other also reject proselytism, which they define as a "disrespectful, insensitive and uncharitable effort to transfer the allegiance of a Christian from one ecclesial body to another," in order to advance a "pure preaching of the Gospel" (Joint International Commission for Catholic–Pentecostal Dia-logue 1998, no. 83, 78). His Beatitude Teoctist, Patriarch of the Romanian Orthodox Church, has further called for the abolition of "any clear or hid-den manifestation of proselytism as well as disloyal confessional competition" in his address to Pope John Paul II and his entourage, so that all Christian churches might "undertake much more sustained efforts to offer a common witness to the world today" (2002). Beyond refraining from "sheep stealing," these Christian ecumenicists encourage each other to avoid undermining each other's legitimacy, whether by willfully misrepresenting differing beliefs and practices, invalidating the baptism that is offered in other churches, or presenting one's particular denomination or confession as the only authentic Christian witness and path to salvation.

While these proposals for tolerating intra-Christian doctrinal, ecclesiologi-cal, and liturgical differences advance the cause of anti-proselytization, it re-mains to be seen why such calls for mutual respect are to be restricted among Christians. Put differently, the major limitation of this anti-proselytization of substitution is its use of a double-standard, wherein the desire to change the institutional affiliation or denominational loyalty of other *Christians* is to be condemned as deplorable proselytism, while the intent to bring *non-Christians* into any given Christian fold is to be promoted as acceptable evan-gelism, witness, or invitation.

While some Christians would criticize this double-standard as a betrayal of inclusivist theology, others would retort that the inclusivist view that God has many children beyond the visible boundaries of the church neither abrogates, nor even tempers the duty of Christians to continue to proclaim the faith to outsiders. The Second Vatican Council's *Lumen Gentium* makes this latter point especially clear: the conviction that God's "plan of salvation" includes many who do not explicitly profess Jesus Christ must be held together with the Church's important mission to follow "the command of the Lord, 'Preach the Gospel to every creature'" (1964, para. 16). According to Cardinal Avery Dulles, S.J., the point can be put thus: "If we are convinced that baptism incorporates us into the body of Christ and that the Eucharist nourishes us with his flesh and blood, we will be eager to share these gifts as widely as pos-sible" (Dulles 2002). When seen in this light, perhaps the purpose of evange-lism even within a theologically inclusivist framework would be to draw what Catholic theologian and Vatican II (1964) *peritus* Karl Rahner has termed "anonymous Christians" into the explicit care of the Church.[11]

The anti-proselytization of non-recruitment

Our next type of anti-proselytization transcends the insights of the previous one by extending the "no poaching" agreement among Christians among Christians to cover adherents of other religions, as well. By relinquishing any and all desires to change the religious commitments of those who are not already fellow practitioners, this third type of anti-proselytization supports a goal of "non-recruitment."

It is here where Judaism provides an instructive example, since Judaism dif-fers markedly from other world religions in its traditional rejection of outreach

missionary activity and focus instead on "inreach," or the process of intensification of "Jews mak[ing] Jews into better Jews" (Broyde 1999, 45). Both the
Orthodox Jewish tradition of "rebuff[ing] initially potential converts" and
the formality of the conversion process itself—immersion in a ritual bath, acceptance by a proper Jewish court, and circumcision for males—are designed
to discourage impulsive and cavalier conversions (Broyde 1999, 52). While
the Torah itself contains tales of Gentiles joining the Jewish people, all such
conversions (whether recorded in sacred texts or drawn from contemporary
life) do not usually come as a result of any active Jewish encouragement (Novak 1999, 17). There is nevertheless today a growing interest in Gentile conversions to Judaism, attributable in part to the rise of interfaith relationships
and marriage (Buckser 2003, 72–73).

This longstanding Jewish disinterest in converting Gentiles to Judaism can
itself be explained by a host of historical, theological, and pragmatic reasons.
First, since membership in the Jewish community has primarily been transmitted matrilineally, Jews can "secure" successive generations of Jews without
even having to proselytize. Jews have also traditionally understood Jewishness
as a blessing with great responsibility that is not to be taken lightly. Moreover, since Orthodox Judaism teaches that (1) it is God, not humans, who
will ultimately bring the rest of the world into the covenant with Israel, and
that (2) there are, and always have been, at least two paths of righteousness:
a rigorous set of requirements for Jews and a less stringent set of expectations
for Gentiles, there is no pressing theological need to convert the latter (Novak
1999, 43–44). Finally, the historical fact that Jews were dominated politically
by either Christian or Muslim rulers for centuries, and thus could not actively
seek converts on pain of death or destruction to their communities, presented
Jews with very strong prudential reasons to delimit their religious instruction
amongst themselves.

While the above reasons for foregoing missionary outreach are largely
peculiar to Judaism itself, the anti-proselytization of non-recruitment need
not be confined to Judaism alone. Religious or theological pluralists could
undermine the desirability of proselytizing by affirming what is purportedly
"good" or "true" in all religions. Ironically, secularists could achieve similar
results by rehearsing their reasons for either indifference to religion or belief
in its marginal importance, at best. (Those who wish to protect the integrity
and cohesion of groups will be discussed in the fourth type of anti-proselytization, below).

It is worth noting that this third type of anti-proselytization has a much
higher standard of scrutiny than either of the first two types, since "non-
recruitment" renders problematic all actions with the intent to convert—
not simply those that involve illegitimate targets or tactics or occur in intra-

Christian contexts (Walls 1996, 119–20; Austin-Broos 2003, 1–2; Glazier 2003, 149–150, 158–65). For example, it is not uncommon for Mormons to seek out entire families for conversion by establishing friendships with non-Mormon families either through invitations to dinner, or by offering advice on how to improve their family life (Rambo 1993, 60). Thus, if some non-Mormons were to report feeling uneasy about how "nice" Mormons generally are to them, only the third but not the first type of anti-proselytization could account for suspicions of Mormon ulterior motives (since "niceness" is *prima facie* neither exploitative, nor inappropriate). Similarly, the type of massages (*e.g.*, "nerve assists") that Scientologists commonly offer to others would most likely pass muster under "appropriate targets and tactics," but not "non-recruitment." This is because a proselytizing intent could still be detected under the phenomenon of "experimental conversion," or the quasi-scientific stance that Scientologists and other groups actively encourage by asking outsiders to take nothing on faith, but to "try it" for themselves to see if it is not true, beneficial, or otherwise suitable (Rambo 1993, 15).

While this third type neither defines, nor denounces proselytism only when it is directed at other Christians, it succumbs to a partiality of its own. The anti-proselytization of non-recruitment singles out proselytism and not other forms of recruiting or advocacy for rebuke, even though the desire to persuade others to defect to one's position can be found among the religious and non-religious alike. According to Lawrence A. Uzzell, a self-professed proselytizer who has sponsored several American Protestants and Roman Catholics to Orthodox Christianity:

> We live in an age of persuasion, in which we are bombarded by political and commercial messages designed to change our thoughts and actions, but the unfavorable term "proselytism" is reserved for specifically religious persuaders. Phrases such as "feminist proselytism" or "environmentalist proselytism" are unknown; it is considered natural, even laudable, for adherents of those secular belief systems to seek converts all over the world, even in cultures where their beliefs are profoundly alien. (2004, 15)

Since secular forms of advocacy can, in some cases, be just offensive to and otherwise unwanted by their target audiences, perhaps the problem with this third type of anti-proselytization is that its very logic of non-interference compels it to go further than it already does.

Of course, those who wish defend their opposition to proselytism only might insist upon the special importance of religion in any given individual's life, the implication being that proselytism raises a set of delicate issues that secular advocacy does not. Indeed, some anthropologists have argued that "chang[ing] one's religion is to *change one's world*, to voluntarily shift the basic presuppositions upon which both self and others are understood (Buckser and Glazier 2003, xi, emphasis added). Other scholars have emphasized the psychological disorientation that normally accompanies religious conversion: there is grief over the loss of and deliberate break from past beliefs, priorities, rituals, and connections with families and friends (Rambo 1993, 53; Hefner 1993, 117–18). The overall point is that those who are successfully converted by proselytizers are likely to experience a major adjustment in personal and social identity, new kinds of moral authority, and thus, entirely new ways of relating to others (Austin-Broos 2003, 1–3; Hefner 1993, 17, 199).

These general features of religious conversion notwithstanding, the extent to which a convert will actually experience the kind of paradigm shift and radical social upheaval described above will depend upon many other considerations. Since religious communities understand the phenomenon of conversion differently, it is likely that conversion to a tradition that demands a repudiation of all past religious commitments and practices will be more disorienting and socially disruptive than converting to a tradition that permits hybridity (Rambo 1993, 34–35; Merrill 1993, 154).[12] In fact, those who are either able to fuse the "old" with the "new," or convert in an "additive" fashion by assimilating, subordinating, and re-interpreting old beliefs, the authority of previous scriptures, and prior ritual practices *instead of discarding them entirely* will most likely face a smoother transition to the newly adopted religion and less of a sense of total transformation (Jordan 2003, 285–286, 290). To be sure, the experience of conversion for either the convert or surrounding community will also vary according to factors beyond anyone's immediate control: whether the newly adopted religion enjoys a greater or lesser panoply of rights, privileges, or other resources than the previous one; is in the mainstream or on the margins of social approval; is supported or at least tolerated by local authorities rather than actively discriminated against; and could be adopted in an "ad hoc" fashion rather than being inextricably tied to other ethnic or political commitments.

Thus, once we acknowledge that generalizations about religious conversion can distort just as much as they can illuminate, we might be inclined to reassess our working assumptions about "conversions" in secular matters, as well. Admittedly, the most common forms of secular advocacy involve comparably limited and non-comprehensive demands: use *this* product, vote for *that* candidate, support *our* platform or cause. What's more, even secular calls for more substantial commitments tend to focus on practically-oriented matters of justice (*e.g.*, motivating people to take global warming seriously out of respect toward future generations) and do not generally aim to establish a new basis of external authority in their targeted audience's lives (*e.g.*, an especially revered set of texts, traditions, or persons).[13] Nevertheless, we must acknowledge that secular advocacy has the potential to induce comparable experiences of regret, social dislocation, and totally new ways of relating to others as can happen in religious conversion (e.g. members of a patriarchal society who have been persuaded by secular liberal feminists to reform their sexist ways, a family of cattle ranchers by vegan animal rights activists to abandon their traffic in meat, a cohort of soldiers by in-principle pacifists to repudiate militarism). These hypothetical examples aside, a former director of the Moscow office of the Keston Institute reports that many Russians are just as disturbed by the "democracy, capitalism, and Western way of life in general" that Protestant and Roman Catholic missionaries bring as they are with the latter's explicitly religious offerings (Uzzell 2002, 21–23, 2005).[14] Others have likewise regarded the religions preached by many American missionaries as one of several "appealing but ultimately shallow exports" in a long list of mostly non-religious items: "McDonald's, Coca-Cola, Disneyland, sneakers, blue jeans, rock music, [and] motion pictures" (Gunn 2000, 855). Thus, unless we are concerned with specific contexts where only proselytism is either expressly punishable by law or generating unique problems not unlike those caused by the introduction of secular imports, perhaps we should understand the differences between proselytism and secular advocacy as those of degree, rather than kind.

The anti-proselytization of group protection

The fourth type of anti-proselytization under consideration shifts its concern from the self-determination of individuals to that of entire groups or communities. Its basic assumption is that their collective identity and integrity need to be safeguarded from the corrosive influences of others—be they proselytizers from afar or dissidents from within.

A well-known example of this concern involves Minos Kokkinakis, a Greek Orthodox-turned-Jehovah's Witness from Crete who had been arrested more than sixty times and imprisoned repeatedly for violating a Greek law that made proselytism a criminal offense (Law No. 1363/1938, sec. 4). While the 1975 Greek Constitution grants the freedom to practice any "known religion" "without hindrance," it also regards the Christian Eastern Orthodox Church as the "dominant religion in Greece" and expressly prohibits proselytism (Art. 13, sec. 2; Art. 3, sec. 1). Law No. 1671/1939 further clarifies what is meant by proselytism:

> any direct or indirect attempt to intrude on the religious beliefs of a person
> of a different religious persuasion (*eterodoxos*), with the aim of undermining
> those beliefs, either by any kind of inducement or promise of an induce-

ment or moral support or material assistance, or by fraudulent means or by taking advantage of his inexperience, trust, need, low intellect or naivety (Sec. 2).

Despite its facially neutral character, there is evidence to suggest that the Greek anti-proselytism law was only being used against adherents of disfavored religions, not members of the Greek Orthodox Church (Gunn 1996, 323). For these and other reasons, the European Court for Human Rights eventually overturned Greece's ruling on May 25, 1993 and concluded that the human right to practice or manifest one's religion must encompass the freedom to try to convince one's neighbor of its validity (*Kokkinakis v. Greece*, 17 E.H.R.R. 397).

A similar concern for group protection can also be found in the contemporary Russian context, as members of the Russian Orthodox Church have repeatedly condemned both the influx and work of foreign missionaries who have come to regard Russia since the collapse of the Soviet Union as a new and exciting missions field. Such criticism of foreign missionaries is largely premised upon a belief that all ethnic Russians *are* already Orthodox whether or not they are particularly observant; thus, Russians must resist the temptation to either switch their allegiance to the Roman papacy, or succumb to the "simple evangelism" of instant rewards and immediate gratification that Pentecostals and other evangelicals puportedly bring (Berman 1996, 302–03; Uzzell 2002, 21; Uzzell 2005). The protectionist aims of the Moscow Patriarchate have even been helped in recent years by the secular arm of the state, as the Putin government has taken measures to suppress an activity "on which the written laws of the Russian Federation are silent: the religious offense of proselytism" (G. Fagan and L. Uzzell 2002, 7).

A comparable interest in protecting the integrity of a corporate body can be seen in the writings of Makua Mutua, a human rights scholar and Professor of Law at the University at Buffalo Law School. Mutua likewise interrogates the right to proselytize in the marketplace of religions, given its devastating effects on his particular area of concern—Africa. He finds that the impact of Christianity and Islam in Africa has been disastrous: indigenous religions have been delegitimized, locals have turned away from traditional healing, worship, and polygamy, and only a culturally disconnected people with a "colonized mindset" who are "neither African nor European nor Arab" now remain (1996, 430–34; 2004, 660–63).[15] Thus, after concluding that the right of self-determination is the most fundamental human right and invoking the United Nations Draft Declaration on the Rights of Indigenous Peoples, Mutua submits that certain groups must be protected from "cultural genocide" in their interactions with significantly more powerful entities (1996, 437; 2004, 652, 666). As in the Greek and Russian Orthodox cases discussed above, Mutua ultimately appeals to the prerogative that he believes history provides: indigenous African religions were the first on the scene, while both Christianity and Islam entered "not as guests but as masters" (1996, 438; 2004, 666; see also De Brennan 2005 for an insightful critique).

These three case-studies should not be taken as exhausting that which can be categorized under the anti-proselytization of group protection. For it is also not uncommon for *Hindutva* or Hindu nationalists to accuse Christian proselytism in India as being "part of a conspiracy to destroy 'Indian' culture and to destabilize the 'Indian' polity" (Menon 2003, 43–48). Moreover, some Islamic states either have formal bans against proselytism or prohibit apostasy and blasphemy in order to prevent conversions out of Islam and accordingly protect its dominant status (Stahnke 2004, 631–36; Ghanea 2004; Arzt 1999). Even France's anti-sect policies under the "About-Picard Law" and 2004 decision to prohibit children in public schools from wearing clothing or insignia that "conspicuously manifests a religious affiliation" (*e.g.,* the Muslim headscarf) have been justified on account of the "harm" that these so-called sects and ostentatious religious displays pose to human rights, public order (*l'ordre public*), and the French principle of secularity or *laïcité* (Judge 2004; Fautré, Garay, and Nidegger 2004; Gunn 2004; Barker 2004, 585).

Given these desires to preserve group identities, it seems appropriate to ask whether these "foreign" intrusions or "new" religious traditions are as polluting as is commonly alleged. It is here where we must concede that what historian of religion Bruce Lincoln calls "religions of resistance" or what Ernst Troeltsch earlier called "sects" can be highly subversive elements in any given society: they generally undercut conventional wisdom, oppose the *status quo*, and have the ability to attract the marginalized to their numbers who may, in turn, eventually revolt (Lincoln 2002). While the integrity and cohesiveness of groups can indeed be threatened by these elements,[16] it is also possible that these group identities are themselves premised upon historically dubious claims and ultimately indefensible presuppositions (Gunn 2003, 203).

We can, in fact, detect traces of the myth of a foregone era of religio-cultural homogeneity in all of the above examples. Taking these in turn, Article 14 of the 1975 Greek Constitution explicitly identifies Eastern Orthodoxy with Greekness:

> The Christian Eastern Orthodox Church, which during nearly four centuries of foreign occupation symbolised the maintenance of Greek culture and the Greek language, took an active part in the Greek people's struggle for emancipation, to such an extent that Hellenism is to some extent identified with the Orthodox faith.

In light of the pervasiveness of this myth, many members of the Russian Orthodox Church deliberately mischaracterize minority religions in Russia as "foreign," even though Lutheranism has been in St. Petersburg since it was founded
and the Baptists have been in the heartland of Russia since the mid-ninteenth
century (Uzzell 2005). Similarly, Mutua's invectives against the destructive
and foreign character of Islam and Christianity in Africa erroneously imply
that pre-colonial Africa possessed a "secure corporate identity" that was then
decimated by the afore-mentioned culprits, just as it ignores the facts that the
first Christian church in Africa was an African creation and that the history of
African Christianity stretches back to almost the apostolic age (Ranger 1993,
65–98; Walls 2002, 45, 89–91). Likewise, the *Hindutva* dual construction of
India as a "Hindu nation" and of Christianity as an *alien* religion that is seduc-
ing people away from their original faith is more ideological than descriptively
accurate, since Christianity has been part of the Indian religious landscape
since the fourth century (Menon 2003, 50). Finally, even the celebrated
French principle of *laïcité* to which the wearing of conspicuously religious
symbols in public schools was found to be in contradiction—in part for its
perceived proselytism—has mythic elements of its own. More specifically,
laïcité did not arise either as a pillar of the French Constitution or as a uni-
fying value shared by the French nation as much popular French rhetoric
suggests, but "grew out of periods that were filled with antagonism, conflict,
and prejudice" (Gunn 2004, 428–29, 432–42). It is arguable, then, that the
attitudes of the French secular republic as revealed in its anti-sect policies and
handling of the "headscarf affair" (*l'affaire du foulard*) are ultimately no different than those of dominant Orthodox and Catholic Churches in Central
and Eastern Europe, since "they all tend to act as watchdogs over their own
sphere of influence and serve as a bulwark against the invasion of cultural and
ideological pluralism" (Fautré, Garay, and Nidegger 2004, 617–18).

   What we have seen in these calls for "group protection" is a logic that combines ethnic essentialism with entitlements justified by ancestral precedence.
That is, once some sort of founding myth links ethnic or national identity
with either a religious tradition or a political ideology, it is then assumed
that Russians or Greeks who have "left" Orthodoxy, Africans who do not
practice indigenous religions, Indians who are not Hindu, and Muslims in
France who support the veiling of girls and women at all times while in public (or at least would grant them the right to decide the matter for themselves)
either have betrayed the essence of what it means to be Russian or Greek and
so forth, respectively, or were never fully-fledged members of those groups
to begin with. In addition, since religion has been conceptualized as more
of a corporate than individual affair in all of these afore-mentioned examples with the exception of the French case, religious diversity within these

groups can at most be tolerated, but not celebrated. In fact, so great is this desire to encourage adherence to and prevent defections away from the one, dominant religious or political tradition that both incentives and penalties for non-compliance are often placed in a single-direction. We have already briefly discussed the discriminatory application of the Greek anti-proselytism law. Elsewhere, some Islamic states prohibit proselytism (to Muslims) at the same time that they encourage missionary efforts to convert non-Muslims to Islam and even occasionally fund them. Similarly, the *Hindutva* see no contradiction in accusing Christian missionaries of using fraudulent means, they occasionally offer their own financial incentives to prevent such conversions, re-convert Christian tribals, or otherwise incorporate them into what Professor Menon has called the "metanarrative of the Hindu nation" (Stahnke 2004, 636–47; Menon 2004, 48–51).

By applying what Paul Ricoeur has called a "hermeneutics of suspicion" to these pleas for group protection, we can begin to reverse the assignment of criticism and blame. If uniformity is either only possible through the use of coercive state power or itself more imaginary than real, then the threatened or actual collapse of a group's cohesion and identity cannot be the principal fault of foreign missionaries. Those who object to proselytism for reasons of group protection can additionally be faulted for obscuring and granting *de facto* legitimacy to the past proselytizing efforts of their predecessors (*n.b.*, Greeks were "pagan" even before they largely became Orthodox Christian).[17] Finally, we can criticize the afore-mentioned constructions of corporate identity not only for consigning individuals to what their upbringing or socialization would enjoin, but also for denying groups the ability to experience authentic, internal change. Liberal-cosmopolitan philosopher Martha Nussbaum has noted, to the contrary, that most people are not rigid or xenophobic traditionalists, but instead "resourceful borrowers of ideas":

> The ideas of Marxism, which originated in the British Library, have influenced conduct in Cuba, China, and Cambodia. The ideas of democracy, which are not original to China, are by now extremely important ideas. The ideas of Christianity, which originated in a dissident sect of Judaism in a small part of Asia Minor, have by now influenced conduct in every region of the globe, as have the ideas of Islam. As Aristotle said, "In general, people seek not the way of their ancestors, but the good."
>
> (2001, 48–49; see also Appiah 2006)

The anti-proselytization of anti-imperialism

The final type of anti-proselytization that we will address regards those who proselytize as little more than tools or agents of imperialism. This ideal-type draws upon lessons learned from at least two different historical trajectories: (1) the military and political conquests of the early Islamic empire that facilitated conversions to Islam among the conquered peoples, especially in North Africa, the Middle East, and Persia and (2) both Christendom and modern European missions to parts of Africa, Asia, and the "New World" that combined a platform of socio-political hegemony with the spreading of the "good news" of Jesus Christ (Arzt 1999, 87–91; Stahnke 2004, 634–35; Sharkey 2005). In concentrating our analysis on the second of these for the present study, we note that the desire to inundate foreign lands with both Bibles and bombs still persists today. One extreme but contemporary example of this double intention involves conservative commentator Ann Coulter's shocking statements after the September 11, 2001 terrorist attacks on U.S. soil: "[The 'homicidal maniacs'] are the ones cheering and dancing right now. We should invade their countries, kill their leaders, and convert them to Christianity" (Coulter 2001).

While few can match Ann Coulter in the brazenness of her comments, she is certainly not alone in ruminating about combining American military action abroad with Christian proselytism. Samaritan's Purse once embarked on "Operation Desert Save" during the Persian Gulf War I (1990–1991) by sending thousands of Arabic-language New Testaments to U.S. troops in Saudi Arabia for distribution among the locals. This project not only violated a Saudi law that prohibited the dissemination of non-Islamic religious materials, but also—to the ire of General H. Norman Schwarzkopf, Commander in Chief of U.S. Forces in Operations Desert Shield and Desert Storm—compromised the understanding between the Saudi and U.S. governments that there would be no proselytizing (Graham 1997; Cooperman and Murphy 2003; Walsh 2003; Woodward 2003). What's more, the organization's long-standing president and CEO, the Rev. Franklin Graham, has since repeatedly called Islam a "very evil and a very wicked religion" and poised Samaritan's Purse to take advantage of the new opportunities for evangelism that Persian Gulf War II provides through relief work (Walsh 2003). The International Mission Board of the Southern Baptist Convention (SBC) announced similar intentions with respect to the 2003 invasion and occupation of Iraq, even as the SBC's former two-term president, Jerry Vines, incensed Muslims worldwide when he called the Prophet Mohammed a "demon-obsessed paedophile" at their annual pastors' conference in 2002. Both organizations have been joined, especially along the Iraqi-Jordanian border, by other Christian relief agencies and church groups, many of which proselytize discreetly under the cover of humanitarian aid, student visas, or other "tentmaking" vocations.

The Rev. Dr. Giles Fraser, vicar of Putney and lecturer in philosophy at

© Equinox Publishing Ltd. 2008

Wadham College, Oxford, is especially troubled by what he describes as a "toxic" form of Christianity—a theology that he finds popular among U.S. evangelicals that "systematically confuses the kingdom of God with the U.S. burgeoning empire" (Fraser 2003). According to Fraser and other critics, it is simply "no coincidence" that the mission fields that are most favored by American evangelicals are "also the targets of neo-conservative military ambition" (Fraser 2003; see also Walsh 2003). A version of Fraser's assessment can also be found among conservative Islamist discourse in Egypt, wherein the terms "the Crusaders, proselytizers, and Orientalists" are used nearly synonymously with "the West:" one conservative Islamist has even suggested that Christian missionaries bring *salibiyya* or "crusaderism" rather than *masihiyya* or "Christianity" (Ismail 1998, 204–06; Sharkey 2003; Sharkey 2004). Even more worrisome is the fact that many Muslims who are not Islamists have nevertheless come to regard the post-9/11 American-led "war on terror" as a war against Islam itself. The sheer popularity of this view, explains Malaysian political scientist and human rights scholar-activist Chandra Muzaffar, is a "perceived pattern of the Bush offensive. Afghanistan came before Iraq. Will it be Iran after this? You get the sense that Muslims are being targeted" (Elegant 2003).

Given the widespread suspicion that the undermining of Islam is part and parcel of the American agenda for reform in the Middle East, we should pause here to consider if there is anything that is fueling these fears beyond sheer speculation or historical mistrust. Admittedly, the Bush administration itself may have unwittingly fanned these rumors when President George W. Bush referred to the war on terrorism as a "crusade" within a week following the September 11, 2001 terrorist attacks and the Department of Defense initially gave a theologically-loaded code name, Operation Infinite Justice, to the escalation of military presence in the Persian Gulf region soon after. Moreover, Jerry Vines's and Franklin Graham's widely-publicized and inflammatory comments about Islam can neither be dismissed as the ravings of fringe extremists, nor regarded as politically inconsequential, given the strong political constituency that evangelical Christians in the U.S. possess.[18] While Franklin Graham may not have the stature of his father, Billy Graham, he still enjoys high visibility and ceremonial distinction in American public life: he was invited to preside over the interfaith prayer service for the victims of the Columbine High School massacre in 1999, issue the benediction at the Republican National Party convention in both 1996 and 2000, deliver the invocation at President Bush's first inaugural ceremony, and conduct services at the Pentagon on Good Friday in 2003—the last of these despite petitions by several Muslim office workers to the Pentagon chaplain's office that they replace Graham with a "more inclusive and honorable" leader (Woodward 2003, Cottle 2003). Further contributing to these widespread fears and concerns is the common perception of many outsiders to the American system that (1) religion and state form an integrated society in the U.S., (2) America is a "Christian nation," and (3) the afore-mentioned ministers who have made grossly insensitive comments about Islam are "spokespersons for the Christian Right"—a bloc which includes a significant portion of the American public, leading members of Congress, then-attorney general John Ashcroft, and President George W. Bush himself (Pew Forum 2004; Abernathy 2002). It is no wonder, then, why fears about an American-led crusade or holy war against the Muslim world are so pervasive and seemingly impossible to shake.

For the record, President Bush himself has not only made several "Islam is a religion of peace" comments, but he has also been reproached by prominent members of his own evangelical Christian base for publicly stating his conviction at a press conference that Christians and Muslims pray to the "same God."[19] Nevertheless, such diplomatic niceties and gestures of ecumenical solidarity can appear to be mere lip service or even grandstanding when considered alongside of the White House and the U.S. Agency for International Development (USAID)'s refusal to prohibit or at least regulate the work of American missionaries abroad if they are private charitable organizations that receive no funding from the government. And yet, the continued presence of these missionaries has led to both politically embarrassing and dangerous situations, as in the well-publicized cases of occupying forces scrambling to rescue foreign missionaries in Iraq who have been attacked or taken hostage by insurgents (Waldman 2003; Caldwell 2003a; Cha 2004). In short, even if their refusal to intervene does not itself suggest any concealed hopes on the part of the Bush administration for more Muslim conversions to Christianity, it at least lends credibility to the widely-held criticism that the U.S. International Religious Freedom Act (IRFA) of 1998 was passed by Congress upon heavy pressure from the New Christian Right and designed, in part, to promote American missionary activities abroad (Gunn 2000, 841–55; Caldwell 2003a).[20]

Perhaps these missionaries and proselytizing relief agencies would respond to accusations of neo-colonial ambition by claiming that they are not so much interested in furthering the geo-political objectives of the U.S. through force as they are simply taking advantage of missionary opportunities that American foreign policy makes possible. Even if this explanation were credible, however, one could still fault Samaritan's Purse, the Southern Baptist Convention, and other like-minded churches and "faith-based organizations" for insensitivity in rushing to win more souls for Christ so closely after the onset of hostilities. For many of these groups share a close relationship with the U.S. military and coordinate their activities accordingly: the Rev. Franklin Graham intimated as much when he stated that he would have stopped "Operation Desert Save" and, by implication, other forms of diplomatical-ly-compromising proselytism in the Gulf region, if only the chaplain from General Schwarzkopf's office had directly asked him to desist (Graham 1997, 239). To take another example, Dr. Richard Land, the President of the Ethics and Liberty Commission of the SBC, pledged his support for the war in Iraq in an open letter to the President (dated on October 3, 2002) that was co-signed by four prominent conservative Christian leaders. Further examples of this close interplay between American militarism and Christian proselytism can be found in the warnings by several evangelical Christian groups in De-cember 2003 to their readership that the historic "window of opportunity" for evangelism would soon close at the formal end of the American-led oc-cupation of Iraq in June 2004 (Rennie 2003; Caldwell 2003b; Cha 2004). For these and other reasons, it would be naïve at best and disingenuous at worst for these evangelists and missionaries to plead innocence with respect to their association with and even dependence upon the movements of coali-tion forces.

It would therefore be appropriate to regard American missionaries in Iraq as part of a new chapter in the history of Western missions who either pre-cede or follow in the wake of imperial powers, traders, or soldiers (Walls 2002, 38; Stahnke 2004, 634–35).[21] Missionaries from the West, particu-larly evangelical Protestants from the U.S., must accordingly acknowledge that their religion is and perhaps always has been "perceived as political, at home and abroad" (Walsh 2003; Sharkey 2005, 56–57).[22] Nevertheless, now that South Korea is the world's second largest source of Christian missionar-ies and Brazil is not far behind, the relationship between humanitarianism and military action has become even more complicated in contemporary times (Walls 2002, 45; Onishi 2004).[23] For as Gulf War II amply reveals, Korean missionaries can now preach a Christianity without their own bag-gage of Christendom, while still benefiting from the opportunities for pros-elytism that other states with legacies of imperialism and superior military power make possible. In addition, as half of the world's Christians now come from Africa, Latin America, Asia, and the Pacific and as Christianity contin-ues to expand in these regions, perhaps we might expect a further loosening of the common association between Christianity, proselytizing Christians, and the West.

Conclusion

Proselytism continues to create problems between religious groups and states, among religious traditions themselves, and even within particular religions as they wrestle with the appropriate posture to take toward the religiously *Other*. We have seen how the logic of anti-proselytization differs according to how proselytism itself is defined, and what it purportedly threatens: the well-being and self-determination of individuals or that of entire groups. We have also seen how these multiple types of anti-proselytism range in reasonableness and warrantability. To review, it can be argued that the first and fifth types of anti-proselytism, "appropriate targets and tactics" and "anti-imperialism," occasionally exaggerate their claims. Yet the facts that some proselytizers continue to employ morally questionable techniques, interact with vulnerable targeted audiences under the cover of humanitarian assistance or other false pretenses, and link their activities so closely with the movements of occupying military forces suggest that opponents of proselytism for these reasons have genuine cause to be concerned. Likewise, the second and third types of anti-proselytization, "substitution" and "non-recruitment," do much to discredit proselytism, though arguably in a self-serving or otherwise partial manner: the former by denouncing evangelistic outreach only when it is directed at other Christians and the latter by censuring attempts at conversion only in its religious, but not secular, forms. Finally, the fourth type of anti-proselytism issues a cautionary tale about the fragility and susceptibility of groups to either "outsiders" with superior power or resources, or dissident "insiders" who have subversive aims. We can accordingly appreciate the desire to preserve the unity of groups that consider themselves to be besieged by these entities, but must also acknowledge the false histories and other founding myths that often undergird such calls for "group protection."

Postscript

While our study has focused almost exclusively on the question whether anti-proselytization can be *justified*, a separate question remains whether these five types are, or at least have the potential to be, *successful* in preventing would-be proselytizers from engaging in proselytism—or at least its most problematic varieties. It is here, however, where we are likely to report more modest gains in our answer, since the reasons commonly marshaled against proselytism neither counteract, nor even directly address the reasons why many individuals and groups proselytize in the first place. To illustrate, non-intervention, territorial integrity, and respect for sovereignty sound more Westphalian in language than conventionally or traditionally religious, just as individual autonomy, self-determination, and the right to be "left alone" from proselytizers incline more toward the values of modern liberalism than anything else. The methods employed by many of the missionaries who flocked to tsunami-stricken areas in the aftermath of the 2004 Indian Ocean earthquake also reveal that concerns about "appropriate targets and tactics" failed to persuade or deter. The example of Minos Kokkinakis in the Greek anti-proselytism case further suggests that neither respect for the law, nor the likelihood of punishment for its violation, are sufficient to prevent the doggedly determined from proselytizing. As the experience of Gulf War II additionally reveals, even the real possibility of capture and death can fail to stem the tide of foreign missionaries who continue to enter into Iraq and neighboring states at their own peril. All of this is not to suggest, however, that these arguments for anti-proselytization would be inefficacious. Rather, the point is directed more at their inadequacy as a long-term strategy to eradicate proselytism altogether, so long as proselytizers continue to subscribe to worldviews that not only understand the religious conversion of others as entirely necessary for their own good, but also encourage insubordination to the law in some cases, and valorize martyrdom in others.

It is here where the example of Judaism becomes instructive once again for illustrating how effective anti-proselytization can be when argued from the "inside" of any given religious tradition. This is to say that the logic of anti-proselytization might be better served if it directly responded to and accordingly interrogated the logic of proselytization itself. For example, if Christian evangelism toward Jews is largely premised upon supercessionism and replacement theology (*i.e.,* the view that the Church has become the sole authentic continuation of Israel after Christ's sacrifice and now possesses what was once Israel's inheritance of blessings and covenantal promises), it is more than likely that only alternative theologies involving God's eternal election of Israel could successfully counter them. Of course, such counter-theologies will not convince all proselytizing Christians, but they will most likely have a greater chance of undercutting the reasons that drive evangelism toward Jews in the first place. This manner of engaging the logic of proselytism on its own terms has the additional benefit of showing respect for those who would proselytize, thereby drawing them into genuine dialogue with others who have been critical of their activities (An-Na'im 2005).

A number of practical implications might follow from this proposal. First, if counter-theologies have the best chance of rebutting theological arguments for proselytism, then anti-proselytizers as a whole would be wise to become conversant in that mode of discourse. Moreover, if it is true that co-religionists are generally the most competent speakers of this discourse, it may follow that it is they—and *not* the proselytizer's intended targets—who hold the greatest responsibility in advancing the cause of anti-proselytization (assuming first that they eschew proselytism). That is, it would be up to non-proselytizing Christians to rein in other proselytizing Christians (and non-proselytizing Muslims to deter other proselytizing Muslims and so forth) by using resources internal their own traditions to re-conceptulize how best to respond to and interact with the religiously *Other*.

It might be argued that the proposal to find reasons internal to each tradition for anti-proselytization shows disrespect to the proselytizing religions themselves, since it encourages them to stop doing the very things that have been central to, and perhaps even constitutive of, their collective identity (Coleman 2003, 17, 22–33). Put differently, one wonders if Mormonism without missions, or evangelical Christianity without the spreading of the Gospel, would even make sense, or if the abandonment of the proselytizing component in these (and other) religions would do irrevocable damage to their integrity. In response to these questions, we acknowledge first that it is for adherents of these traditions themselves to determine the direction in which they would like to be headed. We acknowledge second, however, that authentic and significant change *is* possible in ways that would most likely have been totally unforeseen and incomprehensible by earlier generations. To illustrate with respect to our earlier example, the very supercessionism that was embraced in some form by all three branches of Christianity and contributed to the forced conversions of Jews in the Middle Ages, severe persecutions during the Crusades and the Inquisition, pogroms in the nineteenth century, and the Holocaust of the twentieth century has now been largely abandoned and officially denounced by the Catholic Church and many mainline Protestant denominations. Is it not therefore reasonable to expect or even hope for future changes of this magnitude in either Christianity or other religions?

Notes

1. A version of this chapter was presented at the Symposium on Proselytization at the nineteenth World Congress of the International Association for the History of Religions (IAHR) in Tokyo, Japan (March 24–30, 2005). I would like to thank the symposium coordinator, Rosalind I.J. Hackett, for the invitation to participate as well as her detailed suggestions for improvement. I would also like to thank Johannes Harnischfeger, Patsy Rahn, Heather Sharkey, and all those who participated in the Faculty Interdisciplinary Forum at Virginia Tech on March 16, 2005, especially William FitzPatrick, for stimulating discussion, encouragement, and helpful feedback on earlier drafts.

2. In what follows, I will examine some of these pressing social and ethical problems in the first, fourth, and fifth types of anti-proselytization and will especially focus on theological considerations in the second and third types. Andrew F. Walls, emeritus director of the Centre for the Study of Christianity in the Non–Western World at the University of Edinburgh, discusses four major motives that spawned the nineteenth century Christian medical missionary movement: (1) imitative or obedientiary reasons—to follow Christ's injunction to "do good," (2) humanitarian or philanthropic reasons—to respond to unnecessary suffering, (3) utilitarian reasons—to forestall missionary mortality and improve efficiency, (4) strategic reasons—to minister to others medically when no other form of mission could gain a hearing (1996, 211–220).

3. Of course, passengers on public transport who take advantage of the confined space to preach to their fellow travelers can also be said to be proselytizing to a "captive audience," even in the absence of a power imbalance (Rosalind Hackett, pers. comm.). Moreover, while the Church of Jesus Christ of Latter-day Saints contends that the posthumously baptized are offered an opportunity—not an obligation—to join the religion in the afterlife, the dead nevertheless remain powerless to prevent, escape, or even consent to their baptism-by-proxy and in this sense remain "captive." It is worth noting that the LDS Church agreed on April 11, 2005 to end the practice of posthumously baptizing Jewish survivors of the Holocaust in light of an earlier 1995 agreement with the American Gathering of Jewish Holocaust Survivors to discontinue the practice of posthumously baptizing Holocaust survivors, celebrities, or persons unrelated to the Mormon participants (Thiessen 2005).

4. The IFC of Metropolitan Washington was founded in 1978 and today includes members from the Baha'i, Hindu, Jain, Mormon, Sikh, and Zoroastrian traditions, as well. More information about the Interfaith Conference can be found on their website at http://www.ifcmw.org/.

5. In lieu of offering the promise of material gain, some proselytizers have threatened punishment for non-compliance, be it food or sleep deprivation, psychological terror, force or violence, or even death (Anderson 2003, 125; Arzt 1999, 90; Rambo 1993, 16, 76).

6. The term "rice Christian" was coined by nineteenth century missionaries to China and India who were frustrated by the fact that many came to the missions, sat through their services, and even accepted baptism and claimed to be Christian because of the missionaries' daily distribution of food. Similar results obtained in other contexts throughout the world even when the missionaries did not deliberately entice their audiences with these or other fringe benefits.

7. The Islamic Defenders Front is perhaps best known to Westerners for destroying bars and discos in Jakarta, and the Laskar Mujahidin for sectarian conflict with Christians in Indonesia as well as alleged links to al-Qaeda.

8. Though WorldHelp had already raised $70,000 in donations and planned to raise $350,000 more, the group changed its fundraising appeal on its website and abandoned plans to move the children when Indonesian officials declined to grant them permission to do so (Cooperman 2005; Sampson 2005).

9. Similar concerns were raised in the aftermath of Hurricane Katrina, the costliest and one of the deadliest hurricanes in American history that made its second landfall as a Category 3 storm in Southeast Louisiana on August 29, 2005. Operation Save America (an anti-abortion group formerly known as Operation Rescue) dispensed food and clothing along with Bibles and tracts (Cooperman and Williamson 2005). Samaritan's Purse sent 4000 volunteers to repair and clean more than 6500 houses to "demonstrate God's love" at the same time that they "spread the Gospel" and "offer[ed] the hurricane survivors hope" (Graham 2006). Texan and Louisianan Southern Baptists "serv[ed] more than 1 million meals, distribut[ed] 11,000 evangelistic tracts and 1200 Bibles, and s[aw] at least 45 new professions of faith in Christ" (Curry 2005). As understood by civil libertarians, supporters of a firm "wall" separating church and state, and those who were already opposed to President Bush's Faith Based and Community Initiative, the situation went from

bad to worse when the Federal Emergency Management Agency (FEMA) declared on September 26, 2005 that it would use taxpayer money to reimburse eligible churches and other "faith-based organizations" that provided essential social services to survivors of hurricanes Katrina and Rita (Cooperman and Williamson 2005).

10. Anthropologist Don Seeman examines the complex situation of the Ethiopian *Felashmura* (descendants of members of Beta Israel who converted to Christianity) who are claiming the right to "return to Judaism" by mass migration to Israel. According to some of his informants, this desire to "return" has been connected to a variety of reasons, including a "desire to benefit from citizenship in a relatively prosperous welfare state" (2003, 40).

11. Farid Esack, a South African Muslim liberation theologian, detects the following analogous belief among many Muslims: while the world would be a better place if everyone was a member of the one true faith (Islam), it is still possible that some persons are already "anonymously Muslim" (1999, 123).

12. If Islam really were a totalized entity encompassing *all* aspects of a Muslim's way of life as conservative Islamist discourse suggests (*e.g.*, a people, a civilization, an entire history, a culture, and a way of being) then apostasy or conversion out of Islam would indeed entail a total metamorphosis and dissolution of all past ties (Ismail 1998, 204, 210).

13. I owe this example of this major difference between (religious) proselytism and secular advocacy to William FitzPatrick, who also supplied the example of global warming.

14. The Keston Institute is an Oxford, England-based organization that records and monitors the attitude of communist and former communist countries toward religions in general and Christianity in particular. Michael Bourdeaux founded the organization in 1969 and later won (in 1984) the Templeton Prize For Progress Toward Research or Discoveries about Spiritual Realities.

15. To those who would counter Mutua's bleak assessment by emphasizing their revulsion to imposed uniformity and appreciation of the human right to religious freedom, Mutua would remind them that the human rights corpus nevertheless forces all religions to compete for adherents on a playing field that is neither now, nor ever has been, level (1996, 418; 2004, 652).

16. With respect to the much-discussed veil controversy in France, some have argued that the very existence of French Muslims who do not conform to mainstream attitudes about the value or interpretation of *laïcité* "call[s] into question the long accepted tenet that life in a Western democracy will increasingly secularize adherents of all faiths" (Mathoz and Saunders 2005, 17).

17. Mark Elliott extends this line of reasoning in a way that thwarts the objectives of its proponents: if we were to take seriously the claim that any "majority Christian confession" should be granted "territorial prerogative," the past activities of Orthodox Christians would be rendered suspect, as well (*e.g.*, the argument would imply that Saints Cyril and Methodius should not have begun their work in Moravia, since missionaries from Rome had already been in evidence) (2000, 2).

18. The Southern Baptist Convention of which Jerry Vines once served as two-term president is the largest Protestant denomination in the U.S. and reportedly enjoys the highest

receptivity to their concerns under the George W. Bush White House since the Reagan years (Land 2004).

19. President Bush has publicly distinguished the actions of a few terrorists from the "true faith of Islam" at his visit to the Islamic Center of Washington, D.C. on September 17, 2001, as well as in his address to a joint session of Congress on September 20, 2001. His "we worship the same God" comments were made in response to a reporter's questions on November 20, 2003, when he and Prime Minister Tony Blair presented the case for war with Iraq at the Foreign and Commonwealth Offices in London.

20. President Bush's appointment of the SBC's Dr. Richard Land to multiple terms on the very governmental agency that IRFA created, the U.S. Commission on International Religious Freedom, serves as further confirmation for many critics of both of these suspicions.

21. Again, this interpretation is meant neither to impute belligerent motives on the part of these missionaries, nor to imply that the advancement of Western cultural or socio-political hegemony is their primary goal. For it remains possible that it is truly evangelism—not the tasks of "civilizing" indigenous or otherwise local populations or securing foreign domination—that is their chief or even exclusive aim, as it was for some missionaries even during the heyday of Western imperialism in the nineteenth and early twentieth centuries (Hutchison 1987; Merril 1993).

22. To be sure, the precise nature of the relationship between imperial powers and proselytizing missionaries was more complicated than what much of conventional wisdom (including my previous statement) suggests. There were, in fact, some cases in the modern period of either clear separation or even antagonism between these two parties, as when missionaries served as important advocates for indigenous peoples in light of foreign rule or slavery by the imperialists, or where colonial governments expressly prohibited missionaries from proselytizing for a variety of reasons (Rambo 1993, 69; Yengoyan 1993, 254; Walls 2002, 94–96).

23. See Paul Freston's chapter in this volume for more on this point.

References

Anderson, Robert T. 2003. Constraint and Freedom in Icelandic Conversions. In *The Anthropology of Religious Conversion,* eds. A. Buckser and S.D. Glazier, 123–31. Lanham, MD: Rowman and Littlefield.

An-Na'im, Abdullahi. 2005. The Interdependence of Religion, Secularism, and Human Rights: Prospects for Islamic Societies. *Common Knowledge* 11(1): 56–80.

Appiah, Kwame Anthony. 2006. *Cosmopolitanism: Ethics in a World of Strangers.* Issues of Our Time. New York: W.W. Norton.

Austin-Broos, Diane. 2003. The Anthropology of Conversion: An Introduction. In *The Anthropology of Religious Conversion,* eds. A. Buckser and S.D. Glazier, 1–12. Lanham, MD: Rowman and Littlefield.

Arzt, Donna. 1999. *Jihad* for Hearts and Minds. In *Sharing the Book: Religious Perspectives on the Rights and Wrongs of Proselytism,* ed. J. Witte, Jr. and R.C. Martin, 79–95. Maryknoll, New York: Orbis Books.

Barker, Eileen. 2004. Why the Cults? New Religious Movements and Freedom of Religion or Belief. In *Facilitating Freedom of Religion or Belief: A Deskbook,* ed. Tore Lindholm, W. Cole Durham, Jr., Bahia G. Tahzib-Lie, 571–93. Leiden, The Netherlands: Martinus Nijhoff Publishers.

Berman, Harold J. 1996. Religious Rights in Russia at a Time of Tumultuous Transition: A Historical Theory. In *Religious Human Rights in Global Perspective: Legal Perspectives,* ed. J.D. van der Vyver and J. Witte, Jr., 285–304. The Netherlands: Kluwer Law International.

Braiker, Brian. 2004. The Persuader: Billy Graham's Son and Heir Apparent Discusses Evangelism, Iraq, and Why He Feels Christians are "Under Attack." *Newsweek,* December 17, web exclusive. [http://www.lexis-nexis.com/].

Buckser, Andrew. 2003. Social Conversion and Group Definition in Jewish Copenhagen. In *The Anthropology of Religious Conversion,* ed. A. Buckser and S.D. Glazier, 69–84. Lanham, MD: Rowman and Littlefield.

Broyde, Michael. J. 1999. Proselytism and Jewish Law: Inreach, Outreach, and the Jewish Tradition. In *Sharing the Book: Religious Perspectives on the Rights and Wrongs of Proselytism,* ed. J. Witte, Jr. and R. C. Martin, 45–60. Maryknoll, NY: Orbis Books.

Caldwell, Deborah. 2003a. Should Christian Missionaries Heed the Call in Iraq? *New York Times,* April 6; late ed.-final. http://www.lexis-nexis.com/.

———. 2003b. Despite Controversy, Iraq Beckons as Evangelical Mission Field. *Religion News Service,* April 24. http://pewforum.org/news/display.php?NewsID=2186 [accessed June 10, 2005].

Carmody, Brendan. 1988. Conversion and School at *Chikun,* 1905–39. *Africa: Journal of the International African Institute* 58(2): 193–209.

Casey, Michael. 2005. Muslims, Christians Battle for Souls on Sumatra Island in Wake of Tsunami. *Associated Press,* January 13. [http://www.lexis-nexis.com/].

Cha, Ariana Eunjung. 2004. Missionaries, Too, Battle for Iraq; Christian Groups Share Religion, Humanitarian Aid. *Washington Post,* May 16; final ed. http://www.lexis-nexis.com/.

Cooperman, Alan and Carolyn Murphy. 2003. Two Christian Groups' Aid Effort Questioned. *Washington Post,* March 28; final ed. http://www.lexis-nexis.com/.

Cooperman, Alan. 2005. Group Says it Relocated 300 Orphans; Virginia Missionaries Talk of Raising Muslim Tsunami Victims in Christian Home. *Washington Post,* January 13; final ed. http://www.lexis-nexis.com/.

Cooperman, Alan and Elizabeth Williamson. 2005. FEMA Plans to Reimburse Faith Groups for Aid: As Civil Libertarians Object, Religious Organizations

Weigh Whether to Apply. *Washington Post*, September 27.

Curry, Erin. 2005. Louisiana Church Steps Up to Fill Void, Texas DR Volunteers Redeploy. *Baptist Press News*, Sept. 23. http://www.bpnews.net/bpnews. asp?ID=21706 [accessed April 1, 2006].

Coulter, Ann. 2001. This is War: We Should Invade their Countries. *The National Review*, September 13. http://www.lexis-nexis.com/.

Cottle, Michael. 2003. Bible Brigade: Franklin Graham *v.* Iraq. *The New Republic*, April 21. http://www.tnr.com/doc.mhtml?i=20030421&s=cottle042103 [accessed July 1, 2005].

De Brennan, S. 2005. Critique, Culture and Commitment: The Dangerous and Counterproductive Paths of International Legal Discourse. *Law, Social Justice and Global Development Journal (LGD)* 2. http://www.go.warwick. ac.uk/elj/lgd/debrennan [accessed April 1, 2006].

Dulles, Avery. 2002. Covenant and Mission. *America: The National Catholic Weekly* 187 (12). http://www.americamagazine.org/gettext.cfm?textID=2550&arti cleTypeID=1&issueID=408 [accessed March 15, 2005].

Elegant, Simon. 2003. Voices of Islam: Five leading Muslim Thinkers Speak Out About War in Iraq. *Time Asia* 161(11), March 24. http://www.time.com/ time/asia/covers/501030324/ muslim.html [accessed March 15, 2005].

Elliott, Mark. 2000. Evangelism and Proselytism in Russia: Synonyms or Antonyms? *East-West Church and Ministry Report* 8(4): 1–3.

Esack, Farid. 1999. Muslims Engaging the Other and the *Humanum*. In *Sharing the Book*: *Religious Perspectives on the Rights and Wrongs of Proselytism*, ed. J. Witte Jr. and R.C. Martin, 118–41. Maryknoll, NY: Orbis Books.

Fautré, Willy, Alain Garay, and Yves Nidegger. 2004. The Sect Issue in the European-Francophone Sphere. In *Facilitating Freedom of Religion or Belief: A Deskbook*, ed. Tore Lindholm, W. Cole Durham, Jr., Bahia G. Tahzib-Lie, 595–618. Leiden, The Netherlands: Martinus Nijhoff Publishers.

Joint International Commission for Catholic–Pentecostal Dialogue. 1998. Evangelization, Proselytism, and Common Witness: The Report From the Fourth Phase of the International Dialogue (1990–1997) Between the Roman Catholic Church and Some Classical Pentecostal Churches and Leaders. *Cyberjournal for Pentecostal-Charismatic Research* 4. http://www.pctii.org/ cyberj/cyberj4/rcpent97.html [accessed on March 17, 2005].

Fagan, Geraldine and Lawrence Uzzell. 2002. Malign Intervention. *The Moscow Times*, July 24. http://www.themoscowtimes.com/stories/2002/07/24/006. html [accessed March 17, 2005].

Fraser, Giles. 2003. The Evangelicals Who Like to Giftwrap Islamophobia: The World's Largest Children's Christmas Project has a Toxic Agenda. *The Guardian*, November 10; final ed. http://www.lexis-nexis.com/.

Ghanea, Nazila. 2004. Apostasy and Freedom to Change Religion or Belief. In *Fa-*

cilitating Freedom of Religion or Belief: A Deskbook, ed. Tore Lindholm, W. Cole Durham, Jr., Bahia G. Tahzib-Lie, 669–88. Leiden, The Netherlands: Martinus Nijhoff Publishers.

Glazier, Stephen D. 2003. "Limin' wid Jah": Spiritual Baptists who Become Rasta-farians and Then Become Spiritual Baptists Again. In *The Anthropology of Religious Conversion,* ed. A. Buckser and S.D. Glazier, 149–70. Lanham, MD: Rowman and Littlefield.

Goodman, Peter S. 2005. For Tsunami Survivors, A Touch of Scientology. *Washington Post,* January 28; final ed. http://www.lexis-nexis.com/.

Goodstein, Laurie. 2005. Air Force Academy Staff Found Promoting Religion. *New York Times,* June 23; late ed.-final. http://nytimes.com/.

Graham, Franklin. 1997. *Rebel with a Cause.* Nashville, TN: Nelson Books.

———. 2006. Update: Volunteers Restore Hope Along Gulf Coast. *Samaritan's Purse,* February 1. http://www.samaritanspurse.org/Country_Article_NLA.asp?ArticleID=104 [accessed on April 1, 2006].

Gunn, T. Jeremy. 1996. Adjudicating Rights of Conscience Under the European Convention on Human Rights. In *Religious Human Rights in Global Perspective: Legal Perspectives*, ed. J.D. van der Vyver and J. Witte, Jr., 305–30. The Hague: Martinus Nijhoff Publishers.

———. 2000. A Preliminary Response to Criticism of the International Religious Freedom Act of 1998. *Brigham Young University Law Review* 3: 841–65. http://www.law2.byu.edu/ lawreview/archives/2000_3.htm [accessed on May 25, 2005].

———. 2003. The Complexity of Religion and the Definition of "Religion" in International Law. *Harvard Human Rights Journal* 16: 189–215.

———. 2004. Religious Freedom and *Laïcité*: A Comparison of the United States and France. *Brigham Young University Law Review* 2 (International Law and Religion Symposium): 419–506. http://www.law2.byu.edu/lawreview/archives/2004_2.htm [accessed May 30, 2005].

Heard, Christine. 2003. Samaritan's Purse. *SBS News,* June 26. http://news.sbs.com.au/ insight/trans.php?transid=550 [accessed March 10, 2005].

Hefner, Robert W. 1993. Of Faith and Commitment: Christian Conversion in Muslim Java. In *Conversion to Christianity: Historical and Anthropological Perspectives on a Great Transformation,* ed. R. Hefner, 99–125. Berkeley: University of California Press.

Hubbard, L. Ron. 1981. *The Way to Happiness: A Common Sense Guide to Better Living.* Los Angeles: The Way to Happiness Foundation International. http://www.twth.org/The_Way_ to_Happiness_Free_ebook.htm [accessed May 25, 2005].

Hutchison, William R. 1987. *Errand to the World: American Protestant Thought and Foreign Missions.* Chicago, IL: University of Chicago Press.

Interfaith Conference of Metropolitan Washington (IFC). 1987. IFC Statement on Proselytism, March 16. http://www.ifcmw.org/archives/archives.htm [accessed on March 10, 2005].

Ismail, Salwa. 1998. Confronting the Other: Identity, Culture, Politics, and Conservative Islamism in Egypt. *International Journal of Middle East Studies* 30(2): 199–255. http://www.jstor.org/.

Judge, H. 2004. The Muslim Headscarf and French Schools. *American Journal of Education* 111: 1–24. http://www.jstor.org/.

Kipp, Rita Smith. 1995. Conversion by Affiliation: The History of the Karo Batak Protestant Church. *American Ethnologist* 22(4): 868–82.

Lincoln, Bruce. 2002. *Holy Terrors: Thinking About Religion after September 11*. Chicago, IL: University of Chicago Press.

Lynn, Barry, Marc D. Stern, Oliver S. Thomas. 1995. *The Right to Religious Liberty: The Basic ACLU Guide to Religious Rights*. An American Civil Liberties Union Handbook, 2nd ed. Carbondale: Southern Illinois University Press.

Marthoz, Jean-Paul and Joseph Saunders. 2005. Religion and the Human Rights Movement. New York: Human Rights Watch. http://hrw.org/wr2k5/religion/index.htm [accessed July 6, 2005].

Mutua, Makau wa. 1996. Limitations on Religious Rights: Problematizing Religious Freedom in the African Context. In *Religious Human Rights in Global Perspective: Legal Perspectives*, ed. J.D. van der Vyver and J. Witte, Jr., 417–40. The Netherlands: Kluwer Law International.

———. 2004. Proselytism and Cultural Integrity. In *Facilitating Freedom of Religion or Belief: A Deskbook*, ed. Tore Lindholm, W. Cole Durham, Jr., Bahia G. Tahzib-Lie, 651–68. Leiden, The Netherlands: Martinus Nijhoff Publishers.

Menon, Kalyani Devaki. 2003. Converted Innocents and their Trickster Heroes: The Politics of Proselytizing in India. In *The Anthropology of Religious Conversion,* ed. A. Buckser and S.D. Glazier, 43–53. Lanham, MD: Rowman and Littlefield.

Merrill, William L. 1993. Conversion and Colonialism in Northern Mexico: The Tarahumara Response to the Jesuit Mission Program, 1601–1767. In *Conversion to Christianity: Historical and Anthropological Perspectives on a Great Transformation,* ed. R. Hefner, 129–63. Berkeley: University of California Press.

Norris, Rebecca Sachs. 2003. Converting to What? Embodied Culture and the Adoption of New Beliefs. In *The Anthropology of Religious Conversion,* ed. A. Buckser and S.D. Glazier, 171–81. Lanham, MD: Rowman and Littlefield.

Novak, David. 1999. Proselytism in Judaism. In *Sharing the Book: Religious Perspectives on the Rights and Wrongs of Proselytism,* ed. J. Witte, Jr. and R.C. Martin, 17–44. Maryknoll, NY: Orbis Books.

Nussbaum, Martha. 2001. *Women and Human Development: The Capabilities Approach*, new ed. New York: Cambridge University Press.

Onishi, Norimitsu. 2004. Korean Missionaries Carrying Word to Hard-to-Sway Places. *New York Times*, November 1; late-ed.-final. http://www.lexis-nexis.com/.

Perlez, Jane. 2005. Islamic Militants Volunteer to Aid Muslims in Indonesia. *New York Times*, January 10; late edition-final. http://www.lexis-nexis.com/.

Rambo, Lewis R. 1993. *Understanding Religious Conversion*. New Haven, CT: Yale University Press.

Rennie, David. 2003. Bible Belt Missionaries Set Out on a "War for Souls" in Iraq: Evangelists Out to "Save" Muslims. *Daily Telegraph* (UK), December 27. http://www.lexis-nexis.com/.

Rohde, David. 2005. Mix of Quake Aid and Preaching Stirs Concern. *New York Times*, January 22; late ed.-final. http://www.lexis-nexis.com/.

Sampson, Zinie Chen. 2005. Virginia Group Quits Effort to Place Muslim Orphans in Christian Home. *Associated Press*, January 13. http://www.lexis-nexis.com/.

Seeman, Don. 2003. Agency, Bureaucracy, and Religious Conversion: Ethiopian "Felashmura" Immigrants in Israel. In *The Anthropology of Religious Conversion,* ed. A. Buckser and S.D. Glazier, 29–41. Lanham, MD: Rowman and Littlefield.

Sharkey, Heather J. 2003. A New Crusade or an Old One? *ISIM Newsletter* (Leiden: International Institute for the Study of Islam in the Modern World) 12: 48–49.

———. 2004. Arabic Antimissionary Treatises: Muslim Responses to Christian Evangelism in the Modern Middle East. *International Bulletin of Missionary Research* 28(3): 112–18.

———. 2005. Empire and Muslim Conversions: Historical Reflections on Christian Missions in Egypt. *Islam and Christian-Muslim Relations* 16(1): 43–60.

Sipress, Alan. 2005. Christian Group Never had Custody of Orphans; World Help Partner in Indonesia Says No Steps Were Taken to Obtain 300 Children. *Washington Post*, January 15; final ed. http://www.lexis-nexis.com/.

Stahnke, Ted. 2004. The Right to Engage in Religious Persuasion. *Facilitating Freedom of Religion or Belief: A Deskbook*, ed. Tore Lindholm, W. Cole Durham, Jr., Bahia G. Tahzib-Lie, 619–49. Leiden, The Netherlands: Martinus Nijhoff Publishers.

Stockman, Farah. 2005. In Indonesia, Some Groups Mix Relief, Religion. *The Boston Globe*, January 16, third ed. http://www.lexis-nexis.com/.

Teoctist, His Beatitude Patriarch. 2002. *Homily of His Beatitude Teoctist, Sunday 13 October 2002.* http://www.vatican.va/latest/documents/teoctist_hom_20021013_en.html [accessed May 29, 2005].

Thiessen, Mark. 2005. Jews, Mormons to Examine Proxy Baptisms. *Associated Press,*

April 11. http://www.lexis-nexis.com/.

Uzzell, Lawrence A. 2002. Russians and Catholics. *First Things* 126: 21–23.

———. 2004. Don't Call it Proselytization. *First Things* 146: 14–16.

———. 2005. Politics, Propriety, and Proselytism in Russia. *The Review of Faith and International Affairs* 3 (2). http://www.globalengagement.org/edu/cfia/tbr_archive/archive-vol3-no2.htm [accessed April 1, 2006].

Vatican II Council. 1964. *Lumen Gentium.* http://www.vatican.va/archive/hist_councils/ii_vatican_council/documents/vat-ii_const_19641121_lumen-gentium_en.html [accessed on March 15, 2005].

Waldman, Steven. 2003. Jesus in Baghdad: Why We Should Keep Franklin Graham Out of Iraq. *Slate.* April 11. http://slate.msn.com/id/2081432/ [accessed July 1, 2005].

Walls, Andrew F. 1996. *The Missionary Movement in Christian History: Studies in the Transmission of Faith.* Maryknoll, NY: Orbis Books.

———. 2002. *The Cross-Cultural Process in Christian History: Studies in the Transmission and Appropriation of Faith.* Maryknoll, NY: Orbis Books.

Walsh, Andrew. Summer 2003. The Trouble with Missionaries: Franklin Graham Follows the Flag into Iraq. *Religion in the News* 6(2). http://www.trincoll.edu/depts/csrpl/RINVol6No2/ contents_vol6no2.htm [accessed May 29, 2005].

Woodward, Ken. 2003. Graham's Crusade: Should Evangelicals Invade Iraq? *Commonweal* 130(11). July 6. http://www.commonwealmagazine.org/article.php?id_article=747 [accessed July 1, 2005].

World Council of Churches (WCC) Central Committee. 1997. Towards Common Witness: A Call to Adopt Responsible Relationships in Mission and to Renounce Proselytism. Document No. 2.3A. http://www.wcc-coe.org/wcc/what/mission/prosel-e.html [accessed March 12, 2005].

World Health Organization. 1991. Guiding Principles on Human Organ Transplantation. Geneva: WHO. http://www.who.int/ethics/topics/transplantation_guiding_principles/en/ [accessed on Jun 1, 2005].

———. 2004. Ethics, Access and Safety in Tissue and Organ Transportation: Issues of Global Concern, Madrid, Spain, 6–9 October 2003: report. Geneva: WHO. http://www.who.int/ethics/en/ [accessed June 1, 2005].

Yengoyan, Aram A. 1993. The Pitjantijatjara of Central Australia. In *Conversion to Christianity: Historical and Anthropological Perspectives on a Great Transformation,* ed. R. Hefner, 233–57. Berkeley: University of California Press.

CHAPTER 5

The Changing Face of Christian Proselytizing: New Actors from the Global South Transforming Old Debates

Paul Freston

Introduction

The chapter looks at the implications, for global debates on the rights and wrongs of religious proselytization, of Christian missions originating from what is now often called the "Global South" (Latin America, Africa, Asia and the Pacific), a growing phenomenon on which very little academic study has been done. This new reality will be briefly outlined and then related to the controversies surrounding, and real or attempted political restrictions on, religious proselytization. How do these controversies affect the phenomenon analyzed? And, conversely, how does the "changing face" of Christian proselytizing affect the debate on proselytization, its social acceptability and its political legitimacy? To what extent is the validity of various arguments for or against proselytization cast in a different light when the identity of the proselytizers changes radically, especially when the new actors have the legitimacy of being from the oppressed "Global South" and are not obliged to carry post-colonial stigma?

Proselytization and global civil society

The article on religion and global civil society by George Thomas (2001) will serve as an introduction to our topic. How, he asks, can we construct a global civil society in which people may be intensely religious and yet live together? What Thomas calls the "world cultural principles" structuring global civil society are inherently hostile to proselytizing. This is seen as illegitimate because, firstly, it depicts one religion as truer than all others, thus falling foul of the now commonplace principle that affirmations to be the one true religion are of the same essence as intolerance and civil exclusion. Missionaries are charged with being manipulative and coercive, of strategically preying on the vulnerable, and of having suspect motives. In the second place, Thomas affirms, proselytizing is stigmatized because it presumes the need for other-worldly salvation; it makes the scandalous affirmation that a fellow world citizen is evil and will be punished by God. It thus calls into question the sovereign collective project of progress and this-worldly post-millenialism.

Thomas illustrates with the case of Protestant evangelical Christianity (which together with Roman Catholicism represents the main proselytizing thrust of contemporary Christianity). Evangelical religion, he says, both articulates and disarticulates with "world culture:" it is acceptable in its non-territorialism, voluntarism and individualism, but is offensive in its exclusivist doctrines and in the fact that most evangelical proselytizers have historically been from the United States. "In an emerging world culture there are increasingly pervasive principles that all peoples everywhere are one and that using religious absolutes to judge other traditions is illegitimate" (2001, 531). We may note that this emerging world culture thus echoes Rousseau's famous dictum, when talking of civil religion, that

> those who distinguish civil from theological intolerance are, to my mind, mistaken. The two forms are inseparable. It is impossible to live at peace with those we regard as damned... Wherever theological intolerance is admitted, it must inevitably have some civil effect... Tolerance should be given to all religions that tolerate others, so long as their dogmas contain nothing contrary to the duties of citizenship. But whoever dares to say "outside the Church is no salvation," ought to be driven from the State.
>
> (Rousseau as quoted in Mullen 1998, 186)

Thomas concludes that the working out of these contradictions is likely to have profound effects on the direction of world cultural models of religious liberty.

Heather Sharkey's chapter in this volume refers to "two major debates" (she is talking of Egypt in the first half of the twentieth century, but they arguably also apply to the global debate today): the relationship of Christian missions to Western imperialism, and the Islamic response to apostasy. But, we may ask, what happens when one of these debates (the relationship between missions and imperialism) radically changes its terms of reference? Similarly, Beach (1999) refers to how "some ecumenists see evangelism as largely associated with US evangelical foreign missions that tend to promote

US power." In the immediate post-colonial era, an alliance of anthropologists and leaders of Christian ecumenical organizations such as the World Council of Churches joined in denouncing missions as instruments of cultural imperialism and even "ethnocide." As scholar of World Christianity Lamin Sanneh states, a rule for measuring tolerance became the degree to which one opposed Christian exclusivism and traditional missionizing. Mainline missions, well-integrated into the cultural elites of Western countries, beat a hasty retreat. But, as Sanneh continues, the decline of Christianity failed to follow from the end of colonialism (2003, 16–17). The result, as Thomas points out, is that missions are neither monolithic nor immutable, and that their legitimacy will probably increase as their composition becomes more and more non-white (2001, 530).

This final point dovetails with Stahnke's (1995) discussion of proselytism as resulting in inevitable conflict. The problem, he avers, is not proselytism per se, but rather the difficulty in finding a "proper balance" between free speech and other interests. This difficulty cannot be solved in the abstract, but only in the empirical details of each case. The line between "proper" and "improper" proselytism varies with four primary factors: the characteristics of the source (who is doing the proselytizing); the characteristics of the target (who is being proselytized); where the proselytizing takes place; and the nature of the exchange. Our discussion here regards changes in the characteristics of the sources of much Christian proselytizing today, which in turn affect the nature of the exchanges which occur.

The changing face of Christian proselytizing

As Rosalind Hackett points out in her introduction to this volume, new technologies (especially in the mass media) have facilitated the global expansion of conversionist religions. But, at the same time that we talk about new technologies, we need also to talk about new actors. In the twenty-first century, the Christian proselytizers will not necessarily be the same as those of the two previous centuries.

It is true, of course, that most Christian proselytizing around the world has always been done by local agents, often after an initial impetus given by missionaries from abroad. In fact, post-colonial prohibitions on foreign missionaries often had the unintended effect of stimulating more rather than less expansion of the churches. The huge increase in missionaries in India since independence is overwhelmingly due to the mobilization of Indian Christians; most missionaries targeted by the anti-conversionist activities of the radical Hindu organizations are not Westerners but south Indians of low caste origins. Already in the nineteenth century, the Christianization of the

Pacific was achieved largely by missionaries from the islands themselves who went out to other islands.

So Christian transcultural proselytizing, even during the colonial and immediate post-colonial eras, was never limited to white Westerners. But recent decades have seen considerable changes, both in terms of the numbers of non-Westerners involved and in terms of greater transnational reach (rather than just remaining within one's own country or region). The significance of this has also been highlighted by the simultaneous decline in the number of missionaries from the West (with the exception of the United States).

The backdrop of this change in missions personnel has been a shift in the composition of the global Christian community. In Sanneh's characterization (2003, 80), at the same time as the West has become more and more post-Christian, Christianity has become more and more post-Western. Indeed, Christianity is now probably the largest religion in the Global South, even though its geographical spread is uneven. A key sector of this global Christianity is that of evangelical Protestantism, but it is one that has registered comparatively little on scholars' radar screens. This "invisibility" has resulted partly from the fact that evangelicalism (unlike Catholicism) has no global centre to organize or register its multifarious activities, many of which result from non-Western initiatives; and unlike Islam, it has not been involved in the sort of political activities that attract the attention of the global media.

What are "evangelicals"? There is no globally accepted definition, but for the purposes of this article the term refers to a sub-set of Protestants, distinguished by doctrinal and practical characteristics but not by denominational affiliation or even necessarily by self-labelling. Many recent studies have borrowed a working definition from British historian David Bebbington (1989, 1). This consists of four emphases: conversionism (need for change of life), activism (evangelistic and missionary efforts), biblicism (a special importance to the Bible, though not necessarily the fundamentalist idea of "inerrancy") and crucicentrism (centrality of Christ's sacrifice on the cross). Evangelicals are therefore found in many Protestant denominations (including "mainline" ones such as the Anglican and Methodist churches or the various Reformed and Presbyterian churches, as well as Baptist, Pentecostal and independent churches).

Evangelical Protestantism can be cautiously estimated at around 5 or 6% of world population, its importance enhanced by high levels of practice (in churchgoing and proselytism) and by global distribution (the US, Brazil, South Africa, Nigeria, South Korea and the Philippines being among the major centres). In comparison with the Protestantism of the developed West, the Global Southern version tends to be considerably more evangelical (and indeed largely Pentecostal, that is, composed of highly supernaturalistic believers who emphasize the contemporary manifestations of "gifts of the Holy Spirit" such as speaking in strange tongues to worship God, as well as divine healing, prophecy and exorcism of evil spirits). It is overwhelmingly an indigenous movement rather than one funded and run from the West. In fact, international contacts of any sort may often be totally absent. It is also usually strongly practising, rapidly expanding, organizationally divided and decidedly non-traditional. Only in a few peripheral Asian areas such as the North-East Indian state of Nagaland (where large-scale conversion is already at least a couple of generations old) has it acquired something of a traditional status. Much less is it a state religion, and rarely does it enjoy an unofficial privileged relationship to governments. Usually, Global Southern evangelicalism does not have strong institutions; it is often composed disproportionately of the poor in poor countries (though South Korea is an exception to this on both counts), so its cultural and educational resources are limited.

David Martin discerns two main lines of global evangelical expansion: the attraction of voluntaristic popular Christianity which emphasizes the Spirit, "spreading in partial alignment with the English language and Anglo-American influence;" and ethnic-minority evangelicalism (especially in South and South-East Asia), which has "to do with the emergence of minority self-consciousness which leaps over the pressure exercised by the local majority and links itself to evangelicalism as an expression of transnational modernity" (2004, 277).

Thus, while Christianity as a whole (in terms of nominal members) neither declined (as often thought in the West) nor grew during the twentieth century, this masks a vital change in its composition. We need to throw out our "pre-Columbian" maps of the Christian world (as historian Andrew Walls puts it) and realize that Christianity is only 40% European and North American today, as opposed to 80% in 1900, as Barrett (2001) shows. For the first time since some point in the Middle Ages, the majority of Christians are not of European origin. Only in the second half of the twentieth century was the impulse of the first centuries effectively resumed, i.e. a multidirectional spreading with a high degree of distance from the flows of world political and economic power. Post-colonialism has been far more favourable to Christian expansion than colonialism, and it is no longer correct to treat Christianity as *par excellence* the religion of the developed West (as many comparative religion courses still do). Not to mention the fact that the latter's Christianity is more and more concentrated among Third World immigrants. It is said that half of all churchgoers in London (UK) on an average Sunday are black. Within a couple of decades, half the world's Christians will be in Africa and Latin America. By 2050, on current trends, there will be as many Pentecostals in the world as there are Hindus, and twice as many Pentecostals as Buddhists.

This shift in the "centre of gravity" of world Christianity underlies current changes in the direction of its global flows, referring not only to migrations (which are important in the global spread of evangelicalism as they are with many other religions), but also to a missionary effort which transcends migrant communities. The old unilateral missionary flows are more and more replaced by the polycentricity of a globalized world. A range of new Protestant missionary "sending countries" has emerged, including South Korea, Brazil, the Philippines, India, South Africa, Ghana, Nigeria, and Guatemala.

Despite the general decline in Protestant missionary effort from the traditional sending countries of the First World, the United States is still by far the major missionary power. However, the second force is now South Korea, and other "emerging" centres of evangelical propagation are also apparently *en route* to overtake the declining numbers coming out of traditional centres such as Canada, Britain, Germany and Scandinavia.

Christian missionaries from the Third World now go all over the world. The complex global flows of contemporary evangelical Christianity can be illustrated by the large number of Korean missionaries in Russia, or by the recent case of the Naga missionary (from Nagaland in North-East India) sent to the Central African country of Burundi, or by the case of the Pakistani converted in a Brazilian church in Russia who then went back to Pakistan to start a branch of that Brazilian denomination there! From Brazil to Russia to Pakistan... the developed West is totally omitted from this trajectory. When *Time* magazine asked on its front cover whether Christians should try to convert Muslims (30 June 2003), the presupposition was that the Christians were white Westerners, but that is less and less the case.

Brazilian missionaries around the world

The case of Brazilian missions, which the author knows best (Freston 2001a, 2003, 2004a, 2005), is indicative. There are now around 2,500 Brazilian evangelical missionaries abroad, nearly 90% of whom are sent by missionary societies resulting from Brazilian initiative (the remainder being sent by the Brazilian branches of foreign missionary societies). The receiving countries (over 80) cover all the continents. Latin America receives 41%, Africa 19% and Europe also 19% (a significant inversion of historic flows). There are probably nearly 100 Brazilian missionaries in the United Kingdom today. Asia receives 12% and North America 9%. The countries with the largest contingents are Paraguay, Bolivia and the United States, followed by Portugal, Spain, Mozambique, Guinea-Bissau, Uruguay and Argentina.

Brazilian missionaries go overwhelmingly (nearly 80%) to countries with cultural or linguistic similarities to Brazil (Latin America, the Iberian Peninsula, the Portuguese-speaking countries in Africa), but increasingly to countries which are more distant in cultural terms (English- and French-speaking Africa, Europe, Asia, the Middle East). Choice of destination is influenced by criteria which go beyond utilitarian calculation and evoke a sense of gratuitous devotion, gratitude and adventure. As the *Sunday Times* (1 July 2001) reported, Brazilian missionaries spreading the word in "heathen" Britain say "we always thought of Britain as the land of the good until a Baptist minister visited us and told us about the decay... The British gave us our inheritance when they went to Brazil as missionaries. Now we are like the grandchildren coming home to help the grandparents." But Brazilian missionaries also work in Mongolia, Afghanistan and Albania, evoking the mystique of the "ends of the earth" which Christ's disciples were instructed to evangelize. However, most of Europe is not only expensive, but also too demanding and sceptical. As one missions leader says, "few churches want to invest in a missionary going to Europe. They think 'what's he going to do in the First World, tourism?' It is easier to sensitize churches for inhospitable countries with war and famine than for Europe."

Brazilian evangelical missionaries come from a range of churches (some Pentecostal, others not), but one controversial church that has attracted a lot of attention at home and abroad is the Universal Church of the Kingdom of God (UCKG). It is possible that no Christian denomination founded in the Third World has ever been exported so successfully and rapidly; only twenty-eight years after its establishment in a poor suburb of Rio de Janeiro in 1977, it has over a thousand churches in some eighty countries around the world, outside its native Brazil. It sends about one hundred Brazilian pastors abroad per year, besides sending a considerable number of Portuguese missionaries into other parts of Europe and many black South Africans into other countries of Africa and the Caribbean. In Israel, besides its Brazilian missionaries, this Brazilian church has also made use of a Ghanaian and an Angolan.

New actors and their implications

This surge of transnational proselytizing from the Third World has many implications. For one thing, autonomous transmission of an originally imported message, and especially transmission outside one's ethnic or national frontiers, point to a high degree of internalization of one's new identity. While missions reflect the self-confidence generated by numerical growth in the homeland, they also reflect an independent spirit, the capacity to see oneself not as the end of the process, or in Biblical language as "the ends of the earth," but rather as a new centre of Christianity from which the ends of the earth must be reached. For churches resulting from North American or

European missions, this often requires a costly change in mentality; but it is much easier for churches initiated in the Third World without any foreign connections.

Organizational dependence on the West is minimal; we have seen that only about 11% of all Brazilian missionaries go abroad with international missions. And academic concentration on "ideological dependence" is impoverishing in a globalized world in which the cult of the local is globally sustained and questions of "authenticity" have become immensely complex. Many studies of Third World churches with foreign links show the subtle ways in which such links are actually expressions of local initiative and jostling for position, rather than of foreign ideological domination. A more fruitful image for understanding these missions is to think of them as a "globalization from below," impelled by the spread in the Third World of the pietist concept of missionary "calling" (independent of institutional confirmation, autonomous from the state and little concerned about educational or social qualifications), creating genuinely popular social movements.

Brazilians and others have developed a sizeable missions presence around the globe, despite coming from a national context which can (at times) include rampant inflation, the limitations of a "soft" currency and brutal fluctuations in the exchange rate, as well as a geopolitical status involving a "soft" passport and lack of economic or intellectual prestige, but also often the "privilege" (in terms of legitimacy) of being from the poor and oppressed underbelly of the world. Often, this is the formerly colonized proselytizing the former colonizers; the poorer proselytizing the richer. This is a very long way from John Mott's perspective in 1900 (quoted in Sharkey's chapter in this volume), that "over one-third of the inhabitants of the unevangelized world are under the direct sway of Christian rulers. Moreover, the Protestant powers are in a position to... make possible the free preaching of the gospel to the remaining two-thirds." The flows of Christianity today (through missions and migrants) are more and more distinct from the flows of worldly power and wealth. This is closer to the situation of early Christianity (the centre of the empire is proselytized by the periphery) than to the era of the classical missions movement of the nineteenth century.

The new actors' religious identity: Christian

What do these new actors represent for the future of Christian proselytizing and how will their growing activities influence debates on the issue? There is no simple answer, since the phenomenon is varied and ambiguous. We can begin by examining the implications of these new actors' religious identity in terms of being Christian, Protestant evangelical and (largely) Pentecostal.

Stahnke (1995) stresses how religions may hold a wide variety of views on the propriety of proselytism, ranging from obligation to prohibition (or even incomprehension of the notion). Views may also vary depending on the identity of source and target. Global Southern evangelical missionaries fall very much into the classic characterization of the Christian position regarding tolerance and intolerance by one of the "founding fathers" of sociology, Georg Simmel. Simmel (1997, 203–06) contrasts the anti-proselytizing "God of the group" posture of ancient and ethnic religions, with the "God of humanity and of the individual" introduced by Christianity. For Simmel, any religious tradition is "tolerant" in one way and "intolerant" in another at the same time, and indeed tolerance/intolerance are two sides of the same coin. Christianity, Simmel says, introduced a new "intolerance" (the all-embracing inclusiveness that denies the existence of other gods) and a new "tolerance" (as compared to the anti-conversionist intolerance of particularistic religions; and in relation to the breadth of activities and inner states pleasing to God). Thus, for Simmel, Christianity is non-exclusive in the sense that God is not possessed by the group (although Christian history has provided many examples of attempts at ethno-nationalist appropriation of the Christian God, as in Afrikaner volk theology). This non-exclusiveness and its implications are sometimes forgotten in discussions of tolerance. Simmel cites the Anabaptists and the later Calvinists as exemplifying the principle that, rejecting all outward symptoms, the community must claim for its inner states the absolute tolerance of other authorities (e.g. the state) and must practice the same tolerance toward other communities.

In a discussion of western culture and pluralism, Mullen stresses that the general acceptance of pluralism does not have a lengthy history; "tolerance is a new virtue." Yet it is a virtue that developed in a distinctively religious milieu marked by voluntaristic non-territorial Christianity and using thoroughly religious arguments. Mullen concludes that "the assumption that religious pluralism can stand only on a platform of an almost complete mistrust for one's own creed will prove to be a very poor one. Rather, each society and tradition must find the basis for religious liberty near its own heart" (1998, 2). In a similar vein, Alexis de Tocqueville affirmed in the mid-nineteenth century that "proselytism does not arise simply from sincerity of belief, but from the idea of the *equality* of men and especially the *unity* of the human race"; moral beliefs with universal scope and the proselytizing urge in Christianity are thus two sides of the same coin (Alexis de Tocqueville quoted in Siedentop 1994, 108).

The new actors' religious identity: Protestant evangelical

Of all the major religions, Protestant Christianity has the longest historical links with processes leading towards religious freedom and democratization. John Witte (1993) speaks of three waves of Christian democratizing impulses which accompanied, or even anticipated, Samuel Huntington's (1991) "three waves" of democratization. The first of Witte's waves was Protestant, in the Northern Europe and North America of the seventeenth and eighteenth centuries. Of course, this first wave was largely an unintended result of the fracturing of the religious field and the experience of wars of religion, rather than the intended result of most Protestant leaders' convictions regarding democracy. Even so, "most of democracy's original exponents were deeply rooted in verities derived from Christian faith and ethics" (De Gruchy 1995, 49). In addition, "principled pluralism" was one of the early Protestant postures towards the state. This position, which first achieved political importance in the 1640s with the Levellers in England and the Baptist Roger Williams in Rhode Island, supplied the theological basis which allowed Protestant sectarian theology (intended for exclusive voluntary communities) to overflow into democratic politics by rejecting any division of the political world between the godly and the ungodly. The situation of Old Testament Israel was seen as entirely exceptional; today, the state should be non-confessional.

Whether through theological principle or the wisdom of experience, Protestantism became the first major religious current to give a positive answer to the fundamental question of its "compatibility" with political democracy. In consequence, today's Protestants, wherever they may be, are not usually required to allay fears regarding their religion's ultimate ability to co-exist with democracy. This is not just a question of having links with the West (which do not, in fact, always exist); it is a matter of theological resources and historical examples.

That, of course, far from settles things. In reality there have always been *Protestantisms* in the plural. Not only was early Protestantism far from immediately or uniformly favourable to democracy (besides the "principled pluralist" position of religious freedom in a non-confessional state, there was also the "Christian nation" idea of the state helping to promote true religion and morals, and the apolitical "rejection" of the state), but also some non-democratic regimes in modern times have enjoyed Protestant support or at least acquiescence. This plurality of postures was likely to be reinforced, and even amplified, if Protestantism managed to achieve a significant presence beyond its historic homeland in northern Europe and in areas of northern European immigration. By the late twentieth century this had in fact happened. As Protestantism was transformed into a global religion, it became involved in politics in very diverse settings. As a result, we see evangelical Protestantism being put to a variety of political uses across the globe.

That is not surprising; evangelical religion means different things to different people, and holds different positions in the social and religious fields of each country, besides varying from one denomination to another. This is accentuated by "local subversion," in which local contextual factors in church practice overwhelm the universal heritage of the church; a danger all the greater in churches with local autonomy. Being a decentralized faith, the globalization of evangelicalism may produce a splintering of political perspectives unable to dialogue with each other. Since it has no Rome or Mecca, evangelicalism has difficulty finding a broader view, and its politics tends to be caught up in ethnic, national or local ecclesiastical questions.

However, one of the most influential books on global Christianity, Philip Jenkins' *The Next Christendom*, has put forward a definite and controversial hypothesis regarding Third World Christian politics. In the first place, he says, "if there is one thing we can reliably predict about the twenty-first century, it is that an increasing share of the world's people is going to identify with one of two religions, either Christianity or Islam, and the two have a long and disastrous record of conflict." Muslim-Christian conflict, both within and between states, will intensify. He even foresees a "coming crusade" of Christians against Muslims, in desperate competition for converts (the more so as people of third religions become scarcer). "Issues of theocracy and religious law, toleration and minority rights, conversion and apostasy, should be among the most divisive in domestic and international politics for decades to come" (2002, 190). In the second place, Jenkins foresees a "new Christendom," a new wave of Christian states which may eventually form an African and Latin American axis of common belief in which faith is the guiding political ideology, a reversion to medievalism. And third, he regards Christians from the Global South as likely allies on social questions for First World religious conservatives, such as the Christian Right in the United States.

In favour of Jenkins, one must say that Muslim-Christian conflict is on the increase in certain areas (particularly West Africa and South-East Asia) and, while it is probably true to say that most of the violence has been perpetrated by Muslims, the Christians have been far from blameless. However, Jenkins tends to read Global Southern Christianity throught the lens of "northern" polemics. It is unlikely that Christians in the Global South will line up automatically with the Christian Right of the developed West on most issues. While abortion and homosexuality may be common ground (though not necessarily with as much salience as in the United States), gender issues are less uniformly so, and socio-economic and geopolitical issues still less. And if international politics in coming decades does indeed revolve around interfaith conflict (especially between Christianity and Islam), as Jenkins predicts, that will be more because of the actions of northern governments than because of southern Christianity.

As to Jenkins' prediction regarding a new Christendom, Sanneh replies caustically that there is

> little evidence that Christian Africa will repeat the disasters of Christian Europe… there have been no ecclesiastical courts condemning unbelievers, heretics and witches to death; no bloody battles of doctrine and polity; no territorial aggrandizement by churches; no jihads against infidels… no amputations. (2003, 39)

As Sanneh's slide from medieval Christian to modern Muslim deeds indicates, it is not only European Christendom which is the supposed model for future southern Christian deviations, but also radical Islamism. Yet southern Christianity lacks the ecclesiastical unity and political muscle necessary for a reconstituted Christendom, while also lacking the Islamist nostalgia for a glorious past and a vanished caliphate. And above all, almost no southern Christians have political projects similar to those of militant Islamists, even in Zambia. There (Freston 2004b, 83–91), the influence of charismatic evangelicalism led to the nation being declared "Christian" in 1991 by newly-elected president Frederick Chiluba. After his electoral victory (which had not been on a specifically religious platform), he had State House "cleansed" of evil spirits, organized an "anointing" service modelled on the biblical anointing of King David, and then declared Zambia to be a "Christian nation" in a covenant relationship with God.

While some Christians criticized Chiluba for this act, others approved it but felt it had not gone far enough. Among the latter was Nevers Mumba, a leading televangelist who ran for president in 2001 for his own political party, promising a "revolution of morality and prosperity." It was not good enough, he said, merely to have a president and vice-president who were Christians; all political positions should be occupied by God-fearing people. His intention was to "uphold the declaration of Zambia as a Christian nation, with a view to making it more practical." This did not mean religious discrimination, he explained; rather, it meant leaders with a different character. "Abuse of office, high levels of selfishness and overall lack of character in politicians have impeded economic growth… Good governance cannot be achieved by bad people." Even, it seems, by bad people who have declared the nation to be Christian. Zambia is not a Christian nation, insisted Mumba, because its leaders do not live by Christian norms (since President Chiluba was by then accused of wholesale corruption). "Manifestos alone do not change nations, but good people do" (Freston 2004b).

Mumba was, in any case, heavily defeated at the polls (although he became vice-president in 2003 at the behest of the winning candidate). But we should notice what is *not* going on in Zambia. It is the *nation* that is declared to be Christian and not the *state*. There is no established church, no legal discrimination of non-Christians in public life and no limitation on religious freedom, much less any Christian equivalent of *Shari'a* law. Even Mumba and others who lament the inadequate implementation of the "Christian nation" concept do not advocate such measures.

Their proposals are all perfectly compatible with democratic life. Mumba's programme says little about specific laws to make the country more "Christian", but it does talk a lot about public morality and qualities of leadership. While it makes questionable assumptions about the relationship between personal faith, good governance and national prosperity, there is no idea that a Christian nation should have a "*Shari'a*." Although it may produce hypocrites, it is not producing Christian equivalents of radical Islamists, nor is it producing American-style Christian "reconstructionists" who wish to apply the Old Testament laws (and punishments) today and insist that Christians must impose those laws on non-Christians. With all the limitations of Zambian Christian politics, this is an encouraging sign for the political future of the Christian Global South, however much the shrill rhetoric and political panic of some West African Christian leaders may be contributing to worsening inter-religious tensions there. There is little basis for the belief expressed by Davie, Heelas and Woodhead that certain forms of sub-Saharan Christianity, "hard and exclusivistic," have a serious terrorist potential. The only example they give is the Ugandan Lord's Resistance Army. "Sub-Saharan [Christian] movements as yet lack the knowledge, skills and technology to be dangerous on an international scale. Throw in what was available to the Taliban/al-Qaeda, however, and the prediction is that they will become correspondingly more dangerous." And the epicentre of danger is likely to be the world's most impoverished region, sub-Saharan Africa (2003: 13). However, Davie, Heelas and Woodhead's conclusion seems strained. The Lord's Resistance Army is totally marginal to sub-Saharan Christianity (the founder is of Catholic origin, has created an eclectic belief system including the Ten Commandments and elements of Islam and traditional Acholi religion, and is funded from Muslim sources) and enjoys no sympathy among African Christians in general. On the other hand, while Islam is clearly extremely diverse, al-Qaeda does enjoy considerable sympathy in the Muslim world.

I have dwelt on the Zambian case because, in extreme form, it highlights something about the evangelical Christianity from the Global South which is now heavily involved in transnational proselytizing. I disagree with the portrayals of religion under globalization which suggest that a globalized world must lead either to religious relativism or to clashing fundamentalisms. These seem to be religious equivalents of the contrast between Fukuyama's global triumph of liberal capitalist ideology and Huntington's clash of civilizations. For Malcolm Waters (1995), the options appear to boil down to ecumenical or fundamentalist alternatives. Similarly, Peter Beyer (1994) sees two options for religion if it desires to have any public influence: the "liberal" option, ecumenical and tolerant and making few really religious demands; and the "conservative" option which reasserts the religious tradition "in spite of modernity" and champions the cultural distinctiveness of a particular region of the globe, such as the New Christian Right and Islamist movements.

In fact, however, a revival of peaceful conversionism is a third possibility. The dynamic of conversion places evangelicalism in a very different relationship to global cultural processes from either pan-religious ecumenism (tending to global homogeneity) or fundamentalism (tending to irreducible pockets of anti-pluralism). As generally a non-traditional religion (in the Global South) spreading by conversion, its interests are usually the opposite of those of a reactive fundamentalism. For evangelicalism, pluralism and cultural diffuseness would seem to be advantageous, whereas fundamentalisms (and religious nationalisms) constitute one of its most serious barriers. It may be that evangelicalism flourishes best in a world that is *tranquilly religious*, rather than one that is either *secularized* or *defensively religious*.

The new actors' religious identity: Pentecostal

But that is not the whole story. Most evangelicals in the Global South are, broadly speaking, *Pentecostal*. Protestant Pentecostals comprise a large and growing global community, cautiously estimated by David Martin (2002: 1) at a quarter of a billion, or 4% of world population. Although Pentecostals are a minority of evangelicals in the developed world, they are a huge majority in most of the Third World. This has important effects.

A few years ago at an international consultation, a leading European scholar made an astonishing remark in response to my presentation on global pentecostalism. He said: "wherever there are Pentecostals, there is trouble." The comment did not seem to shock many people present, and I was too taken aback to do more than murmur my amazement. Later, I reflected on what would have been people's reaction if, instead of Pentecostals, he had referred to Muslims or Jews. I am sure there would have been an outcry, because it is definitely not politically correct any more to speak that way about Muslims or Jews. But it is still acceptable to do so about Pentecostals.

This is partly a question of social class. In most of the Third World, pentecostal churches have a genuinely popular nature in which both leaders and led are from humble origins. As in early modern Europe (Mullett 1980: 52f), grassroots Christian churches overturn accepted intellectual hierarchies, based on a recognition of the intellectual rights of the common person. Largely lower-class Pentecostals are, therefore, distant from the centres of political, cultural and academic power, and they often do not conform to the standards of "polite" discourse. In addition, their theology is uncompromising and often seen as intrinsically "aggressive." The Universal Church of the Kingdom of God (UCKG) illustrates well this side of Pentecostalism (while itself being roundly condemned by some other Pentecostals), in its theology and its methods. In the most famous controversy, in 1995, a UCKG bishop, in a live Brazilian television programme, kicked an image of Our Lady of Aparecida, patron saint of Brazil, to show it could not answer prayers. The church also routinely portrays other religions (especially the Afro-Brazilian ones) as demonic.

Stahnke (1995) stresses that, in an increasingly plural society, it is necessary not only to respect other religions but also to protect them from ridicule and contempt. Yet he also insists that the substance of a message must generally be tolerated by the state; it is the manner, not the content, which may justify some restriction on freedom of religion. The UCKG has not ceased portraying the Afro-Brazilian religions as demonic, but it did apologize publicly for the manner in which its bishop treated Our Lady of Aparecida on television. Having become a large institution with considerable media and political interests, it realized that it had overstepped the mark and has since evolved somewhat in the direction of a more "civilized" proselytizing style.

Yet it is in some other Pentecostal circles that we see a tendency which is, in the long run, more problematic. Like those pseudo-democrats who want "one man, one vote, one time," some Pentecostal proselytizers appear to want freedom to "win" and then close down religious freedom. We time and again see questions of religious freedom (for others) and acceptance of a non-confessional state as still problematic. This may be because the locally dominant religion itself does not accept these things. But sometimes evangelical leaders themselves do not accept them, or at least cannot understand and live with the self-restraining implications, especially as their power increases and they face the other side of the dilemma.

This is compounded by the curious return of a concept of territoriality in new versions of macro-level "spiritual warfare" frequently associated with theocratic currents. The idea of a "Christian nation" is a return to the territoriality of Christendom, under the aegis of the new charismatic theology of territorial spirits. The sacralization of power in such "spiritual warfare" concepts (the other side of the coin of its demonization when in the hands of non-believers), makes criticism impossible. Introducing the dynamic of territoriality into a pluralistic and democratic situation could bring considerable dangers for democracy and religious freedom. If Tertullian ridiculed the pagans who cried "Away with the Christians to the Lions!" whenever the Tiber rose as high as the city walls or the Nile did not flood properly, today it is "spiritual warfare" Pentecostals who blame such calamities on the particular religious rival or socially "degenerate" group of their choice.

Evangelicals and violence

What is the potential of all this for violence and even terrorism? If terrorism is one of the weapons of the weak, we need to know what the *religions* of the weak are, and what their roles might be in legitimizing or delegitimizing that or alternative options. It may be that more of the world's poor and geopolitically disadvantaged are now Christian than Muslim; how does this other portion of the world's "weak" regard the use of political violence?

Evangelicals in the Global South have indeed used violence. Nigerian bishops have approved the taking up of arms by Christians during inter-religious rioting in that country. Evangelicals in Kano have killed Muslims who (they would say in justification) were attacking them. In another incident, Christians killed those who could not say the Lord's Prayer. In May 2004 a Christian militia massacred over a hundred Muslims. Peru also exemplifies an evangelical option for the use of violence, albeit in an extreme situation and in self-defence. During the brutal Maoist guerrilla emergency in the Andes in the 1980s, evangelicals filled the Peasant Patrols which were formed (sometimes on evangelical initiative) to defend the local communities from the guerrillas in the absence of other support. In their armed action, these Pentecostals saw themselves as fighting against the anti-Christ.

In several contexts, ethnic separatism is an important element in evangelical politics in the Global South. Many national boundaries are, after all, the artificial fruit of colonialism, and there is no *a priori* reason why Christian political activists should accept them. And when they choose to challenge those boundaries, for whatever mix of religious, ethnic and regional motivations, they sometimes feel they have the right to appeal to force of arms. An example of this is the Indian state of Nagaland, almost totally Christian and largely Baptist. The main guerrilla group, the National Socialist Council of Nagaland, is so influenced by evangelical Christianity that it has an evangelistic music group which preaches to Naga villagers on the less Christianized Burmese side of the border. We thus find a group of Asian socialist guerrillas spreading the evangelical message! But their founding manifesto also says "we rule out the illusion of saving Nagaland through peaceful means. It is arms and arms alone that will save our nation."

A missionary report on Rwanda has analyzed the "close involvement of Christians" in the ethnic violence of 1994 when about 800,000 people were killed. For many evangelicals abroad, Rwanda had always been associated with the beginnings of the East African Revival, and it was hard for them to understand how such a setting could witness such slaughter. But the Revival's combination of pietism and dispensationalism could lead either to withdrawal or to uncritical support of whoever was in power, and both reactions were discernible in Rwanda in the run-up to the genocide. Rwanda is thus a vivid example of the impotence and collusion of anti-political evangelicalism, and of the price that can be paid for the lack of a theology of the public sphere (Freston 2001b, 134–38).

A recent book on *Terror in the Name of God* (Stern 2003), in its survey of religious terrorists, mentions three candidates for inclusion in a category of "evangelical terrorists." Two are found in the United States. The first group are the "Identity Christians" who see Anglo-Saxons as the "true Israel" and America as a sacred land. As the dominant religion of the racist right in the U.S., it is not very exportable to the Global South. The second group are the extreme anti-abortionists who have bombed abortion clinics and murdered staff who carry out abortions. This is potentially a more exportable position, and we should only find out how exportable if most parts of the Global South were to adopt abortion policies similar to those of the United States. The third group Stern mentions are the Indonesian Christian militias who have reacted to the activity of Muslim militias (seemingly encouraged by the Indonesian army) in some of the eastern islands. As the transmigration of Javanese Muslims to the eastern islands upset the local religious and ethnic balance, people like Benny Doro emerged. The leader of a Christian militia, he claims to have caught a bullet in his hand with the help of Jesus Christ. "He can no longer count the number of Muslims he has killed." The Christian militia groups are nominally led by prominent religious figures but their field commanders tend to be local thugs (Stern 2003, 73).

Of course, for some analysts, cases such as Indonesia and Nigeria simply show how religious labels do duty for ethnic, class and other divisions. Religion in general is thus exculpated. The opposite extreme is the view that mixing religion and politics always leads to intolerance and sometimes even to violence. The argument that religion fosters irrational violence has been restated not only in relation to the former Yugoslavia but also by Nobel Prize winner José Saramago who attributes terrorism to the "God factor." David Martin (1997) has replied to the "argument from Bosnia," saying that the more religious identity acquires institutional autonomy, the more it works against violence. Indian sociologist T.K. Oommen (2001) advances basically the same argument: when religion is seen as independent of states, nations and ethnies, it is rarely a distinct source of violence. But whereas Oommen speaks of religions in general, Martin is more cautious, saying modernity has advanced a central feature of primitive Christianity (the separation of religious identity from other markers of social belonging) which is precisely *not* shared by every religious tradition. But we must always remember that no religion is frozen in time, and the idea of separation can both be lost where it was original (as happened with Christianity) and acquired by religions where it was not. Sanneh (1996) feels there are resources in most religious traditions for this, and he exemplifies with Islam and Christianity in West Africa.

Thus, as Hefner (1993) says, attitudes towards state power vary among the world religions and even within the same religion, but he detects a relative "political modesty" in Christian history due to its origins on the margins of empire. As Hamilton (1998, 4) points out, origins are particularly important in the world religions since they acquire enormous normative significance. But doctrinal constraints do not prevent a certain latitude of contextual flexibility. Evangelical groups in the Global South can in fact oscillate rapidly between apoliticism and some form of "Christian nation" ideal. Some authors find an actual or potential connection between global pentecostal growth and violence, especially in Central America, often giving as example of the dangers involved the bloody anti-insurgency strategy of General Efraín Ríos Montt, president of Guatemala in 1982–83. But this is to underestimate the capacity of Pentecostals to comprehend their own militant metaphors of "spiritual warfare" and "crusade," and drives a wedge between Ríos Montt and other equally repressive (but non-pentecostal) Central American military presidents. What is certain is that Ríos' conversion did not *prevent* him acting in that way.

Nevertheless, does it make any difference that the strong association of Christianity with territoriality ("Christendom") was a phase (albeit lengthy) in the *middle* of its history, whereas in Islam the connection with territoriality seems to be more original and central? Barring an unlikely return to a sort of medievalism, does the weaker sense of territoriality in Christianity mean that, however much the religion may come to be associated with the poor and oppressed, it will find it hard to generate a broad sense of the "Christian umma" as under threat, a generalizable sentiment of belonging to a distinct religiously-defined community with a common fate? If so, there would be no diffused feeling of alienation to underpin a cultural cauldron in which Christian terrorist organizations could emerge and find sufficient recruits and broad enough sympathy (for their causes, if not for their methods).

Missionaries from the Global South: light and shade

Besides being (largely Pentecostal) evangelical Christians, these new actors in global proselytism are also *inexperienced missionaries* who come from *mostly poor and formerly colonized countries*. Stepping straight into a post-colonial world (in Africa and Asia) and a post-Christian one (in Europe), they are often unaware of the minefields into which they wander. The horror stories abound. Of Korean missionaries pressured to show results back home, who resort to holding raffles of bicycles, motorbikes or gas refrigerators for families who have attended all the services during the year (they especially want a full church when their supervisor comes). Of Brazilian missionaries among Muslims who feel the existence of mosques in Brazil ought to be conditional on reciprocity for churches in the Middle East. Of the Filipinos in the late 1990s who smuggled twenty-thousand Bibles into Saudi Arabia and claimed that country "for Christ" by the year 2000. "They were running out of time and still had all these Bibles. So they started to walk down the streets of Riyadh, throwing Bibles over the walls, literally hitting unsuspecting Muslims on the head" (cited in Seiple 2005).

The large Brazilian church we have talked about, the Universal Church of the Kingdom of God, habitually makes verbal attacks on the other religions of the countries where it works, both from the pulpit and in its media. Apart from Catholicism and Umbanda in Brazil, examples include traditional African religions in Africa (*Folha Universal* 9/8/98), Anglicanism in England (*The Sower*, May 1996, 19), the Orthodox Church in Russia (*Folha Universal* 18/8/02), "Japanese superstitions" (Furucho 2001) and the "thousands of Indian gods" (*Folha Universal* 13/6/99). In South Africa, the Zion Christian Church and the Catholic Church "preach demonic doctrines." All the sangomas of African religions are held to be demon-possessed and responsible for the recent spate of Muti murders (Freston 2005, 52).

The implications of this for physical violence in Africa are hotly debated. While Maxwell (2000) talks of the cyclical societal cleansing movements of parts of Africa, characterized by the demonizing of a range of religious entities, and concludes that such movements have now been Christianized, Hackett (2003) feels that discourses of demonism and satanism are increasingly prevalent in Africa (especially among Pentecostals) and have a deleterious effect for civil society, religious pluralism and freedom of religion. Democratization has created uncertainties which allow rumours of witchcraft to flourish. With an eye on the tensions in Nigeria, Hackett says that "it seems only a matter of time before others latch onto the terrorist trope and anti-Christ depictions of bin Laden and Saddam Hussein" (Hackett 2003, 67). But it must be stressed that the UCKG does not seem to be involved in anything like this. Demonization is not necessarily anti-democratic; such discourses only become a danger to democracy if they seek forcibly to curtail the activities of other religions or to inflame to violence. But in fact it is the UCKG itself whose activities have twice been curtailed by the Zambian government (with the support of many evangelical leaders) because it itself has been accused of Satanism! The biter bit, perhaps; but the fact is that while the Universal has never (yet) attempted to forcibly curtail its opponents' activities, it has been the victim of such attempts by other religious actors, the media and the state (in Zambia and elsewhere).

Another controversial aspect is the UCKG's portrayal of Africa. Their description of the continent in the church's Brazilian media is overwhelmingly negative, and the massive Christianization of sub-Saharan Africa in the past fifty years is written out of the record. We read, for example, that (in response to the work of the Universal Church) "Africans abandon their gods and surrender to Jesus" (*Folha Universal* 11/10/98). "The continent needs evangelizing… Besides the superstition of the blacks, it has been invaded by the Hindu and Muslim religions, which have nothing to do with African traditions and customs" (TV Record 11/10/97). "The continent is the victim of deceiving spirits [who] disguise themselves as ancestors… Even some traditional evangelical churches accept the worship of ancestors… The mission of the UCKG in the continent is to awaken the people to the truth and free them from the oppressing spirits" (*Folha Universal* 11/10/98).

Many Brazilians (not only UCKG missionaries) still regard Africa as "a privileged place for the work of invisible forces" (Oro, Corten and Dozon 2003, 101). The UCKG media talk of Africans as "a people who have for centuries suffered in the iron grasp of malignant forces," referring to spiritual entities rather than to geopolitical exploitation. Indeed, with the help of the Universal Church, "the land of witchcraft and idolatry… is freeing itself from the evils which centuries ago transformed its people into slave labour." This is not to deny other historical and contemporary causes:

> African leaders, in general, just as the colonizers before them, have not
> cared about the fate of the people. [But] this does not exclude the spiritual
> side of the problem… Africans live under the dominion of spiritual forces,
> worshipping demonic beings… Their pagan teachings lead to conformism,
> indifference and what we might call a "culture of submission"… Hunger is a
> consequence of poverty and the domination which divides people into rich
> and poor… But who says that those who are politically dominated always
> have to be poor? (*Folha Universal* 9/8/98)

With regard to South Africa, "theoretically apartheid is over, but in practice it still exists inside each person, since the African people (especially the blacks) do not fight and do not take hold of what should be theirs" (*Folha Universal* 17/10/99). This does not seem to be a recipe for expropriation of white property, but rather for a spiritual struggle and change of mentality. As Bishop Macedo said on a trip to Africa, "people here think the black man was born to die like a dog. That is their mentality. We are changing this. The African cannot have this way of thinking. He must believe that he was born to grow" (*Folha Universal* 17/10/99).

Bishop Crivella, leader of the work in Africa for many years and now a member of the Brazilian senate, says that "God is family, and if Africa suffers [from Aids] it is because it does not have this notion" (*Folha Universal* 20/6/99). Indeed,

> the African people do not have the same concept of marriage, home and faithfulness as Brazilians do. Constituting a family is not taken seriously in Africa... Each woman is worth twelve cows. This reflects the current stage of development of the African continent. (*Folha Universal*, 12/9/99; 9/8/98)

But lest this be thought to be pure racial prejudice, the same paper quotes its pastor in Luxemburg: "the Luxemburgers are cold, racist and very closed" (*Folha Universal*, 20/6/99). Perhaps, in the last analysis (and in view of its considerable success in Africa and the multi-racial composition of its pastorate), the UCKG vision of the world owes more to ethnocentrism and lack of empathy with the host populations, whoever they may be.

But generalizations about Brazilian missionaries are risky: while one missionary in Senegal says of the fast of Ramadan that it "exposes [Muslims] to the devil," another in Ivory Coast uses the occasion to "greet our Muslim friends and as far as possible avoid talking about the gospel" (Freston 2004a, 139). Meanwhile, a Brazilian missionary in the United Kingdom talks implicitly of missions as an antidote to intolerance. Commenting on the fact that Protestant missions took at least two centuries to emerge, he says that "the Reformers went on for 200 years doing theology without missions and burning witches and anyone who thought differently" (Freston 2004a, 139). When they got past that stage, they started doing missions. In other words, in this view, missions are connected with peaceability, tolerance and freedom. This is a far cry from the idea that missions are related to coercion and the colonization of consciousness. Perhaps a less dogmatic approach is to admit that both scenarios are possible, as in Max Stackhouse's entry on missions in the *Encyclopedia of Religion* (1987). Since it is difficult, he says, for the great missionary faiths to accept relativization, the possibilities of (potentially violent) confrontation are troubling in a globalizing world. But there is another possibility:

> dialogic exchange and/or openness to mutual conversion by allowing free

and open debate. Since direct confrontation is perilous in a nuclear age, we can only pray for a social openness to religious freedom and religious missions in all lands. (Stackhouse 1987, 577)

If the twenty-first century brings us a world increasingly divided between Christians and Muslims (as Jenkins [2002, 167] affirms), neither of whom can accept that "all roads lead to God," is the world condemned to chronic religious violence? Should one see the rising tide of Christian missionaries from the Global South as an appalling prospect, as the last piece in an apocalyptic jigsaw of religious fanaticism that will lead the world over the brink? Probably not. While there is undoubtedly light and shade, we are on the whole talking about peaceable activities based on the very supposition of religious freedom and openness to dialogue.

Generally, religious violence is not the work of those who are dedicated to peaceful proselytizing. And the Brazilian leader of a mission which places professional people in Muslim countries told me soon after September 11th 2001:

> American policies are not helping, and the participation of American evangelicals is very pro-Israel... We [Brazilian missionaries, on the other hand] have no difficulty taking a position which is not in favour of Israel. We repudiate the terrorist attacks, but we have to recognize they did not happen in a historical vacuum. The West must reflect on its international policies and abandon the double standard it applies when it knows there are no political or economic advantages at stake. The great majority of Muslims are peaceful and hospitable, lovers of tradition and good customs; they do not breathe hatred for the West and they have other more immediate problems. We need to show the world we are moved by a different spirit from the one in which prejudices are stronger than respect and dignity.
>
> (Freston 2004a, 140–41)

Even more idealistically, another Brazilian missions leader affirms that:

> the Christian community had an opportunity to evangelize the world on September 11th... If the representative of the greatest Protestant Christian nation had gone on that podium to speak of forgiveness and not of revenge, the world would really have known the message of the gospel. If he had said, 'we forgive what you have done, and we want to ask forgiveness for what we have done to you over the years.' (Freston 2004a, 140–41)

In the research that I have been carrying out amongst Brazilian evangelical missionaries abroad (and amongst the leaders of Brazilian missionary-sending agencies), I have been struck by how uniformly opposed to the Bush administration policies my interlocutors have been.

"Acceptable" religion in globalizing times

Clearly, global evangelicalism cannot adequately be studied in a manner which is hostile in principle to conversionist religion. But it is also clear that the question of the limits of "acceptable" religiosity for globalizing times has become pressing. We need to be aware of the new historical phase that inter-religious relations are entering. Even excellent works on the global expansion of Christianity (such as the volumes edited by Hefner [1993] and by van der Veer [1994]) are mostly concerned with conversion from a "traditional" to a "world" religion, but have little on the interaction *between* world religions. But the phase of fairly mutually isolated processes of conversion from a "traditional" to probably the only world religion on offer locally, while not complete, is now passing. There is now increased interaction (including conversion and attempts to convert) among world religions themselves. This is not to imply that the world religions have never encountered each other before (militarily or peacefully), but the encounters were more limited, affected fewer people and took place often with little mutual knowledge. Today, through the media, diasporas and missions, they affect more people, even in the heartlands of the respective traditions, and increasingly through peaceful propagation. As potential converts from outside the world religions become scarcer, the conversionist world religions will increasingly target each other's traditional populations (the recent evangelical missions slogan about the "10/40 window" of countries especially resistant to Christianity, all of them basically dominated by the other world religions, already reflects this). Debate over the rights and wrongs of proselytism will become more and more salient not only for that reason, and because of concerns over terrorism, but also because a globalized world reduces the space for any "other side" and means that any exclusion has graver consequences. In addition, the end form of a globalized world is still "up for grabs" and distinct visions of it will come into greater conflict as the stakes get higher. At the same time, the greater the need for consensual norms, the greater the tendency to use the proselytism debate itself as a weapon in religious or political competition.

Tooth-and-nail religious competition is not necessarily incompatible with democracy. Rousseau's dictum that civil and theological intolerance are inseparable is questionable. It is not impossible for people to disagree strongly about things they regard as of supreme importance (such as the need to convert others, and even the advisability of exorcising them of demons), and still be good democrats. In fact, they may regard democracy as an aid to genuine conversion, since it avoids the tendency to hypocrisy created by alliances between religion and political power. Luiz Eduardo Soares (1993, 48) suggests this when analysing the "holy war" of some Brazilian Pentecostals against the

Afro-Brazilian religions. "In our holy war there is a dialogue, however abrasive, with the beliefs which are criticized," which is more than can be said for the "complacent and superior tolerance" of the older churches which "do not feel their own superiority to be threatened... Warring pentecostalism is carrying out our modernizing revolution, based on egalitarian principles."

An illustration of this can be seen in the defence made by a UCKG politician when the church's media was sued by Afro-Brazilian religious groups. He distinguished between "offensive" religious speech and repressive legal actions. "The Catholic Church adores images. This offends us. The sacrifices [of animals in Afro-Brazilian religions] offend us. But we do not take legal action against these religions. We respect the person's right to profess their faith, but we do not need to respect their gods" (*Folha de S. Paulo*, 14/12/03).

New proselytizers and old debates

What about the effect of the specifically "Global Southern" identity of these new proselytizers? They themselves are quick to point out that they are both necessary and effective. Necessary because European missions are in decline and American missions are, as it were, geopolitically compromised. And effective, because their national identity brings advantages. As one Brazilian missionary told me, during the Gulf War and again after 2001,

> the great majority of non-Latin missionaries were leaving the Arab countries, but for us it was as if nothing was happening. [The Arabs] know we are a poor country and were once conquered, and that ends up creating affinities. (Freston 2004a, 139)

Brazilian missionaries worldwide seem to find their Brazilian identity to be an advantage in their relations with the local people. In Portuguese-speaking countries, Brazilians are part of the known universe, if only through music and TV soap operas. One blonde Brazilian missionary in Angola in the 1980s found she was often taken to be Russian; upon discovering she was Brazilian, Angolans would exclaim: "then you are our sister!" Even outside the Lusophone sphere, Brazilian identity (as "a peaceful country which wins the World Cup") is generally an advantage, usually supplemented by the impression of exuding greater "human warmth" than other foreign missionaries.

Global Christianity relativizes post-colonial guilt. Lamin Sanneh says "the West should get over its Christendom guilt complex about Christianity as colonialism by accepting that Christianity has survived" in the Third World (2003, 74). Its very lack of geopolitical privilege may be an advantage in certain circumstances. Even before the terrorist attacks of 2001, a Brazilian couple working among Muslims found that their work only started to progress when they dissociated themselves from an American missionary living in the same town. The mentality of the Brazilian missionaries in Britain who talk of themselves as the (spiritual) "grandchildren coming home to help the grandparents," while still implying a critique of the spiritual condition of Britain, is a far cry from nineteenth century ideas of "the white man's burden." Indeed, Bonk (2006, 86) talks of how "the material and social culture of Western missionaries served as a miraculous sign… There was little need for spectacular displays of tongues, healings, resurrections and the like." But this Western missionary model, associated with conspicuous material power, is not widely imitable by today's Third World missionaries, who have to rely not on "the marvels of sophisticated machines… and incomprehensible wealth", but on "healing the sick" and "exorcising demons." All this is in line with Montgomery's (1996) analysis of the historical diffusion of the world religions, stressing the importance of intergroup relations (diffusion from "below," by proselytizers who are not associated with the source of any geopolitical threat, has generally been far more effective).

Thus, at one level Brazilian missionaries find their identity a great advantage. They are seen as being from a country which is poor, peaceful and geopolitically uncompromised; they do not suffer from post-colonial guilt and they are not associated with conspicuous material power. In short, they are perceived as coming "from below."

But all is certainly not plain sailing for Brazilian missionaries. Besides (sometimes) manifesting intolerant and prejudiced attitudes, they have also (on occasion) been the victims of intolerant attitudes and actions, whether by the populace or by the state. An example of intolerance from civil society comes from the case of the UCKG in Portugal, perhaps one of the few places in the world where Brazilians can plausibly be regarded as in any sense a "threat" (cultural and linguistic, in this case). In 1995 some of the Portuguese media encouraged state intervention against the UCKG and mobs attacked some of its churches chanting anti-Brazilian slogans. In parts of Africa it has been popularly accused of Satanism. In Zambia, evangelical leaders appealed to the government to ban it, which did in fact happen (temporarily) in 1998. The UCKG has also been banned in some other African and Latin American countries, in one case on the absurd accusation that it had "burnt Bibles." In India, it complains of persecution from Muslim and Hindu fundamentalists. In some cases, its identity as a Brazilian church may be a liability: when its missionaries are mistreated by the local population, governments may be less concerned to offer succour than they would be in the case of missionaries from powerful Western countries.

If a fundamental presupposition of missionary activity is that people ought to be free to choose even "foreign" truth (especially if it comes from a geopolitically non-threatening source), and if in a truly globalized world no truth will be foreign any longer, then one might suppose that anti-proselytism's days are numbered. However, since anti-proselytism can have varied motivations, only in some cases will a missionary's "Global Southern" identity be of any help. For example, in India the anti-proselytism of the Sangh Parivar (the "family" of Hindu nationalist organizations such as the RSS and the VHP) is based on arguments of a religious nature. Clearly, in this case, the national identity of the proselytizers is irrelevant. In other cases, missionaries from the Global South may be initially more acceptable, as Brazilians seem to be in North Africa, but that does not mean that, with time, their identity as Christian missionaries will not become known and be problematic from the point of view of Muslim attitudes to apostasy. Thus, in cases where anti-proselytism is motivated merely by political opportunism or by relativistic or "world cultural" or even "Christian ecumenical" concerns, a "Global Southern" identity can be of at least partial help. But in religious nationalist or Islamic contexts, the change in the proselytizers' identity is likely to be irrelevant once the intention to proselytize becomes known.

In short, the "downward trend in recognition of the right to proselytize and to change one's religion in United Nations instruments" (1948, 1966, 1981) which Lerner (1998) detects is *in part* associated with decolonization and the rise of nationalisms, firstly secular and then religious. Inasmuch as that is so, the "changing face" of Christian proselytizers may have some effect in strengthening the legitimacy of their activities. Although Samuel Huntington says that "soft" power follows hard power (Huntington 1998: 109), most proselytising today (transcultural or not) is done by the relatively powerless of the world. With the shift in the centre of Christianity (in numerical predominance and in worldwide expansionist impulse), conversion is now flowing again, as it did in the primitive church, from the periphery of world power to the centre rather than vice versa.

Thomas, with whom we began our discussion, stresses that evangelical missions are in flux and that their increasingly "Global Southern" composition will increase their legitimacy and assist them in making coalitions with religious or non-religious allies who will help them in opening up territories to proselytizing activities. They will also use discursive strategies based on natural law and human rights, which in turn will have substantial effects on their own identity (2001: 530). It must be said, however, that missions from the Global South still have a steep learning curve to go through if they are to maximize those potentialities.

References

Barrett, David, George Kurian and Todd Johnson (eds.). 2001. *World Christian Encyclopedia* (2nd edition). New York: Oxford University Press.

Beach, B.B. 1999. "Evangelism and Proselytism—Religious Liberty and Ecumenical Challenges." www.irla.org/documents/articles/bbbeach-proselytism.html.

Bebbington, David. 1989. *Evangelicalism in Modern Britain.* London: Unwin Hyman.

Beyer, Peter. 1994. *Religion and Globalization.* London: Sage.

Bonk, Jonathan. 2006. "*And they marveled* ... Mammon as Miracle in Twentieth Century Missionary Encounter." In *Evangelical, Ecumenical, and Anabaptist Missiologies in Conversation. Essays in Honor of Wilbert R. Shenk,* ed. J. Krabill, W. Sawatsky and C. van Engen, 78–87. Maryknoll, NY: Orbis.

Davie, Grace, Paul Heelas and Linda Woodhead (eds.). 2003. *Predicting Religion.* Aldershot: Ashgate.

De Gruchy, John. 1995. *Christianity and Democracy.* New York: Cambridge University Press.

Freston, Paul. 2001a. "The Transnationalisation of Brazilian Pentecostalism: the Universal Church of the Kingdom of God." In *Between Babel and Pentecost: Transnational Pentecostalism in Africa and Latin America,* ed. André Corten and Ruth Fratani, 196–215. London: Hurst / Bloomington: Indiana University Press.

———. 2001b. *Evangelicals and Politics in Asia, Africa and Latin America.* New York: Cambridge University Press.

———. 2003. "A Igreja Universal na Ásia." In *Igreja Universal do Reino de Deus,* ed. Ari Pedro Oro, André Corten and Jean-Pierre Dozon, 197–229. São Paulo: Paulinas.

———. 2004a. "Les Dynamiques Missionnaires Internationales du Pentecôtisme Brésilien." In *Le Protestantisme Évangélique: un Christianisme de Conversion,* ed, Sebastien Fath, 123–43. Paris: Brepols.

———. 2004b. *Protestant Political Parties: a Global Survey.* Aldershot, UK: Ashgate.

———. 2005. "The Universal Church of the Kingdom of God: a Brazilian Church Finds Success in Southern Africa." *Journal of Religion in Africa* 35(1): 33–65.

Hackett, Rosalind I.J. 2003. "Discourses of Demonisation in Africa." *Diogenes* 50(3): 61–75.

———. 2008. "Revisiting Proselytization in the Twenty-first Century." In *Proselytization Revisited: Rights Talk, Free Markets and Culture Wars,* ed. Rosalind I.J. Hackett, 1–34. London: Equinox.

Hamilton, Malcolm. 1998. *Sociology and the World's Religions.* New York: St. Martin's Press.

Hefner, Robert (ed.). 1993. *Conversion to Christianity*. Berkeley: University of California.

Huntington, Samuel. 1991. *The Third Wave*. Norman: University of Oklahoma Press.

———. 1998. *The Clash of Civilizations and the Remaking of World Order*. London: Touchstone Books.

Jenkins, Philip. 2002. *The Next Christendom*, New York: Oxford University Press.

Lerner, Natan. 1998. "Proselytism, Change of Religion, and International Human Rights", www.law.emory.edu/EILR/volumes/win98/lerner.html.

Martin, David. 1997. *Does Christianity Cause War?* Oxford: Clarendon Press.

———. 2002. *Pentecostalism: the World their Parish*. Oxford: Blackwell.

———. 2004. "Evangelical Expansion in Global Society." In *Christianity Reborn*, ed. Donald Lewis, 273–94. Grand Rapids/Cambridge: Eerdmans.

Maxwell, David. 2000. "Christianity without Frontiers: Shona Missionaries and Transnational Pentecostalism in Africa," paper presented at the congress of the African Studies Association of the United Kingdom, Cambridge, September.

Montgomery, Robert. 1996. *The Diffusion of Religions*. Lanham, MD: University Press of America.

Mullen, David (ed.). 1998. *Religious Pluralism in the West*. Oxford: Blackwell.

Mullett, Michael. 1980. *Radical Religious Movements in Early Modern Europe*. London: George Allen and Unwin.

Oommen, T.K. 2001. "Religion as Source of Violence", *Ecumenical Review* 53(2): 168–75.

Oro, Ari Pedro, André Corten and Jean-Pierre Dozon (eds.). 2003. *Igreja Universal do Reino de Deus*. São Paulo: Paulinas.

Sanneh, Lamin. 1996. *Piety and Power*. Maryknoll, NY: Orbis.

———. 2003. *Whose Religion is Christianity?* Grand Rapids/Cambridge: Eerdmans.

Seiple, Robert. 2005. "From Bible Bombardment to Incarnational Evangelism", paper presented at the conference on Proselytism and Persecution, Seattle Pacific University, April.

Sharkey, Heather 2008. Muslim Apostasy, Christian Conversion, and Religious Freedom in Egypt. In *Proselytization Revisited: Rights Talk, Free Markets and Culture Wars*, ed. Rosalind I.J. Hackett, 139–166. London: Equinox.

Siedentop, Larry. 1994. *Tocqueville*. New York: Oxford University Press.

Simmel, Georg. 1997. *Essays on Religion*. New Haven, CT: Yale University Press.

Soares, Luiz Eduardo. 1993. "A Guerra dos Pentecostais contra os Afro-Brasileiros: Dimensões Democráticas do Conflito Religioso no Brasil." *Comunicações do ISER* 44: 43–50.

Stackhouse, Max. 1987. "Missions." In *Encyclopedia of Religion*, vol 8., ed. Mircea Eliade, 563–78. New York: Macmillan.

Stahnke, Ted. 1995. "Proselytism and the Freedom to Change Religion in International Human Rights Law," www.irla.org/documents/articles/stahnke-proselytism.html.

Stern, Jessica. 2003. *Terror in the Name of God*. New York: HarperCollins.

Thomas, George. 2001. "Religions in Global Civil Society." *Sociology of Religion* 62(4): 515–33.

Van der Veer, Peter (ed.). 1994. *Conversion to Modernities*. London: Routledge.

Waters, Malcolm. 1995. *Globalization*. London: Routledge.

Witte Jr., John (ed.). 1993. *Christianity and Democracy in Global Context*. Boulder, CO: Westview Press.

Chapter 6

Muslim Apostasy, Christian Conversion, and Religious Freedom in Egypt: A Study of American Missionaries, Western Imperialism, and Human Rights Agendas[1]

Heather J. Sharkey

Introduction

In early twentieth century Egypt, American Protestant missionaries evangelized actively among Muslims while working under the protective influence of British imperialism. However, missionaries encountered local resistance to their work in the form of what they called the Islamic apostasy principle (Zwemer 1924), the doctrine that conversion into Islam was acceptable but that conversion out was forbidden. They also encountered resistance in the form of Islamist and nationalist opposition, which intensified in the interwar period. Occasionally Muslims did convert to Christianity under missionary sponsorship, though converts came under heavy communal pressures to recant, and faced stiff social sanctions, including disinheritance, ostracism, assault, forced marriage, and sometimes death threats from their kin (Watson 1906; Watson 1907, 174–77, 179, 240; Gairdner 1909, 187–88). These barriers of Islamic doctrine and custom, combined with a mounting array of legal and organizational obstacles, help to explain why Protestant missionaries in Egypt could only point to two hundred converts from Islam by 1953. The vast majority of Egyptian converts to Protestantism came instead from Coptic Orthodox Christian backgrounds (Philips 1953, 7).

This article looks at the history of American missionary activity in Egypt in order to consider the development of conflicting ideologies of religious liberty, conversion, and individual rights.[2] It studies how and why American missionaries emerged as such strong and vocal supporters of universal religious liberty, even while they sought to articulate a platform for what one might call the "appropriate means" or ethical standards of proselytization (Kao, this volume). The article also studies why the Egyptian government in the twentieth century never gave legal support to unfettered individual religious choice, and why it never abandoned legal sanctions against apostasy, even after Egypt ratified the U.N. Universal Declaration of Human Rights (UDHR) of 1948. Article 18 of the UDHR, which many American Christian groups strongly endorsed then and later, and which many Muslim groups and governments have since questioned or partly rejected, states that "everyone has the right to freedom of thought, conscience and religion; this right includes freedom to change his religion or belief, and freedom, either alone or in community with others and in public or private, to manifest his religion or belief in teaching, practice, worship and observance."

This essay is divided into five parts. Part I traces the history of the American mission in Egypt from 1854 to the interwar period of the twentieth century, and discusses the mission's relationship to British colonialism in the region. Part II considers the rise of anti-missionary agitation in the late 1920s and early 1930s—a decisive period for the missionary enterprise in Egypt and for the Egyptian nationalist and Islamist movements at large. This section also considers the statement on religious freedom that American and British missionaries drafted in Egypt in 1932—a statement that presaged the religious liberty clause of the U.N. Universal Declaration of Human Rights (1948) in terms of its endorsement of unlimited religious choice. Part III examines the impact that local nationalist and Islamist activism had on government policies towards missions, and surveys the ways in which the government increasingly sought to regulate missionary activities, particularly in the decolonization period that followed the Free Officers revolution of 1952. Part IV considers the experiences of the American mission and of Egyptian Christian society in the postcolonial period. Finally, Part V addresses continuing debates over universal human rights and Islamic restrictions on religious freedom in Egypt and the wider Muslim world.

This article ultimately concludes that Egyptian government policies towards Christian evangelism in the twentieth century cannot be dismissed either as a mere invocation of traditional Islamic doctrines of apostasy in its various forms, or as a rejection of the ideal of universal individual liberties. Rather, Egyptian government policies must also be understood, to some degree, as a defensive reaction to Western imperialism, arising from an impulse to protect the country's Muslim majoritarian culture from Christian missionaries who benefited from and contributed to the panoply of Western power. This defensive reaction to Western imperialism continues to shape Egyptian government policies and public debates on the role and interpretation of Islam as the religion of state.

I. American evangelization and British imperialism in Egypt

American Presbyterian missionaries began work in Egypt in 1854, just two years before the Ottoman Empire issued the *Hatt-i Humayun*, one of its landmark nineteenth century reforms. The *Hatt-i Humayun* took the radical and unprecedented step of affirming the equality of Muslims, Christians, and Jews within the empire and, in theory, eliminated the institutionalized subordination of non-Muslims as *dhimmi*s (protected peoples living at the sufferance of a Muslim state). In reality, the decree may have represented an imperial maneuver to curry favor both with Europeans, at a time of growing Western imperial influence, and with Ottoman Christians, at a time when ethnic nationalist (and potentially separatist) sentiments were mounting in the Balkans. Contrary to its aims, the *Hatt-i Humayun* may have strained rather than eased Muslim-Christian relations in the empire by bolstering Muslim perceptions of Christian minorities as beneficiaries of Western imperial patronage (Masters 2001, 137–39).

For Christian missionaries in Egypt (which was then a quasi-autonomous part of the Ottoman Empire) the *Hatt-i Humayun* appears to have made little practical difference to their options for evangelization. Missionaries knew that they could try to evangelize among indigenous Christians but that the Muslim authorities of Egypt would not tolerate comparable efforts among Muslims. This rejection of proselytization among Muslims derived from traditional understandings of the Koran, the Prophet Muhammad's example, and early Islamic historical precedents. It reflected the belief that Islam was the culmination and perfection of monotheistic faith, and that individuals were free to join but not leave Islam. That is, an individual, once Muslim through birth or conversion, could not abandon the community and faith either by converting out or by lapsing into disbelief. The traditional sanction prescribed for abandoning Islam was death (Friedmann 2003).[3]

Writing in 1897, a Presbyterian missionary reflected that his predecessors in mid-nineteenth-century Egypt had "found Islam utterly opposed to the idea of religious liberty" (Watson 1904, 50). Although the missionaries wanted to convert Egyptian Muslims to Christianity *en masse*, the Muslim population's (and government's) deep antipathy to Muslim out-conversion led missionaries to concentrate their efforts on the Copts, Egypt's indigenous Christian minority, among whom they hoped to produce a kind of Protestant Reformation. In time, Coptic Orthodox Christians, converted to Protestantism, formed the core of what the missionaries called the "Evangelical" (or in Arabic, "*Injiliyya*") church—named in the hope that its members would spread the gospel to all the peoples in their midst.

After 1882, when Britain invaded and occupied Egypt, both American and British missionaries began to pursue a more ambitious program of work among Muslims (Sharkey 2005). They believed at this juncture that the presence of a Christian colonial power would enable them to do what had once been unthinkable in Islamic state domains: to attempt openly to convert Muslims to Christianity and to receive guaranteed protections for such converts. Britain's presence did lower barriers to Muslim evangelization by offering stronger protection for Protestant missionaries. Yet, the willingness of British authorities to protect foreign missionaries did not extend to local converts from Islam, who remained highly vulnerable. Missionary sources give the impression that, during the era of British colonial influence, the Egyptian courts did not pursue charges of apostasy. Nevertheless, the courts did apply inheritance laws that disinherited converts, because of the traditional stipulation that a non-Muslim could not inherit from a Muslim. Moreover, those who left Islam faced informal reprisals for their apostasy, meted out by relatives and neighbors who tried to persuade or coerce them to come back into the fold (Zwemer 1924; A. Watson 1906; C. Watson 1907).

This British policy of non-interference vis-à-vis Muslim conversions— undoubtedly a policy calculated not to arouse Muslim popular sentiment against British colonialism—led to an ideological rift between missionaries and British officialdom, not only in Egypt, but also in India, Northern Nigeria, and other Muslim regions of the British empire (Porter 2004, 296, 298–99). But this rift was not visible to many Muslims in Egypt, who instead saw missions and empire as allies, and who interpreted the expansion of Christian missions as a stark reminder of the political and military impotence of the Islamic world in the face of Western imperialism. Muslims knew, in short, that Christian proselytizing would have been unsustainable in an earlier age of Islamic imperialism, and that Christian evangelization was a symptom of weakness in a period of rapidly waning Ottoman power.[4] As the nineteenth century drew to a close, the assertive evangelization of the American missionaries in Egypt reflected the confident spirit of the global Protestant missionary movement. In 1900, John Mott, a leading American figure in this movement, published a book noting that worldwide Christian evangelization was possible as never before. He wrote,

> [o]ver one-third of the inhabitants of the unevangelized world are under
> the direct sway of Christian rulers. Moreover, the Protestant powers are in a
> position to exert an influence that will make possible the free preaching of

the Gospel to the remaining two-thirds of the people of the earth who have
not heard of Christ. (Mott 1900, 115)

In spite of the fact that British colonial authorities did not support the
freedom of Christian conversion in the ways that missionaries had hoped,
the half-century following the British occupation of Egypt (1882–1932) was
a reasonably good one for American missionaries. Foreign missions enjoyed
tremendous support in churches throughout the United States and funds
were abundant (Hutchison 1987). In Egypt, American Presbyterians were
able to draw upon these resources to deploy larger missionary staffs, buy
properties, erect buildings, and open institutions ranging from primary
schools and colleges to hospitals. By the standards of the late twentieth century (the postcolonial period), missionaries in the late nineteenth and early
twentieth centuries were able to evangelize with remarkable openness. In
cities, towns, and villages throughout Egypt, they held outdoor meetings,
tent shows, and public assemblies to which Muslims and Christians were
invited; they ran Sunday Schools and Vacation Bible Schools for Muslim
and Christian children; and they traveled by steamboat, railway, automo-
bile, and donkey—widely "itinerating," to use their term—while distributing
Arabic Bible excerpts and Christian tracts along the way (Elder 1958). In
their schools, which by 1936 enrolled over 12,000 students, a large proportion of them Muslim, they taught children about Christianity (Parker 1938,
177–78).[5] Relatively few students ever converted from Islam to Christianity,
but missionaries reported that many students had absorbed Christian ideas
and values nonetheless, and that some went on to live as "secret believers"—
Muslims in their public personae, but Christians in heart and mind (Philips
1953, 8; Rice 1910).

II. Anti-missionary agitation and the 1932 mission statement of religious freedom

By 1930, American missionaries were facing growing constraints on their
work as a result of three developments: the sharp contraction of funds from
American sources (largely the result of the economic Depression); the growth
of anti-colonial Egyptian nationalism against the factionalized context of parliamentary politics; and the emergence of new Islamist organizations which
called upon the Egyptian government to curtail Christian missionary activities and to promote Islam instead. The most important Islamist organizations
in this regard were the Muslim Brotherhood (founded in 1928), the Young
Men's Muslim Association or YMMA (modeled on the Young Men's Christian Association, or YMCA, which had a strong presence in Cairo), and the
Society for Defense of Islam, led by Muslim scholars associated with al-Azhar

university mosque (Carter 1984, Sharkey 2005).

It complicated matters that the Egyptian Arabic press, in the years from 1927 to 1932, presented a series of stories that accused American, British, and other foreign missionaries, both Protestants and Catholics, of abusing Muslim orphans; of abducting, brainwashing, and converting Muslim youths; and of publicly defaming Islam (Carter 1984).[6] A few of these incidents resulted in court cases, and one case in particular was especially important to the Americans since it involved one of their Egyptian lay evangelists, a former Muslim named Kamil Mansur. In 1930, this protégé of the American missionaries was accused of vilifying Islam at a public meeting in a Christian assembly hall; the Arabic press picked up the story and urged the government to put him on trial, which it did. "What could one expect from a missionary who gets a salary from evangelizing," asked the newspaper *al-Siyasa*, "except calumny on the Islamic religion by calling it superstition and by calling the Koran stories and tales that are incompatible with the modern age?"[7] According to the story presented in missionary records, Kamil Mansur only narrowly escaped a jail sentence, even though missionaries alerted the British colonial authorities and U.S. State Department officials to the case. Missionaries later ascribed Kamil Mansur's acquittal to the misstep of a high-ranking Egyptian official who damaged the prosecution by announcing that the accused was guilty even before the trial began.[8]

The Arabic news coverage of the early 1930s suggested that missionary behavior was part of a broad pattern of cultural denigration and assault on Egyptian Islamic society. It suggested that missionaries were undermining parental authority and family cohesion by preying upon vulnerable schoolchildren, and emphasized that the conversion of individuals threatened the social collective. The Arabic newspapers also linked missionary activities in Egypt to missionary activities in other parts of the Middle East where colonial powers were in place—for example, in Palestine under the British mandate—and pointed to wider patterns of Muslim cultural suppression, for example, in Algeria, where French colonial rulers were seeking to shut down village Koran schools.[9] All of this coverage appeared at a time when Egyptian nationalists were pressing Britain to cede the country a fuller and truer independence and to end the legal and fiscal privileges for foreigners known as the Capitulations. Newspapers of the early 1930s thereby connected the scandals of Christian missionary conversions to larger questions of cultural integrity and national sovereignty in the face of European colonialism. One article even asserted outright that Christian "evangelization is one of the forces of imperialism."[10]

In 1930, as the evangelist Kamil Mansur awaited trial on the charge of defamation (*ta'n*) of Islam, the secretary of the American Presbyterian mission warned his colleagues about deeper concerns. "From the standpoint of all the Missions in Egypt," he wrote, "the question of religious liberty and the future of mission and church work is much more important than the release of Kamil Effendi from prison....".[11] Like members of the other organizations that belonged to the Inter-Mission Council of Egypt, an ecumenical forum for Protestant missions that also included the Cairo YMCA and the American University in Cairo, the American missionaries believed that religious liberty entailed individual, universal freedom to choose and change one's sect or religion. They also believed that it entailed the right to think freely within each faith. Christians, they maintained, should be free to embrace Islam; Muslims should be free to embrace Christianity; and converts should be free to revert to their prior religion or even to change religions again.[12] Responding to the Kamil Mansur case, however, Egyptian politicians and legal thinkers asserted a different notion of religious liberty which harmonized with traditional Islamic laws regarding the rights of *dhimmis*.[13] Living in a Muslim state, Christians (like Jews) had the right to practice their religion freely and in an atmosphere of public security; Christians (like Jews) had the right to convert into Islam; but Muslims had no need of out-conversion since they already belonged to the superior faith. By extension, converts into Islam could not revert to their former religion.

In Egypt in the early 1930s, Egyptian Muslim politicians asserted that Muslims, if anything, had the right to freedom *from* Christian evangelism. In a confidential discussion with mission representatives in 1932, Ismail Sidqi Pasha, the Prime Minister, reportedly said that "while evangelistic work might be [acceptable] in primitive countries like Tanganyika, it was not suitable in a Moslem country like Egypt, especially as Egypt is firmly attached to a religion of its own, and is civilized." Christian proselytization among Muslims, he told the missionaries, constituted an "attack" on Islamic integrity.[14] A.W. Keown-Boyd, a British official in the Ministry of the Interior who was responsible for foreign and expatriate communities in Egypt, attempted to clarify such sentiments for the missionaries. He explained that Egyptians in the government interpreted the country's 1923 constitutional affirmation of religious freedom and belief to mean rights of worship in officially designated places, though these rights did not extend to any proselytizing that "involves criticism, or unfavorable comparison of the Moslem religion with other religions...."[15] Perhaps it was this conviction that had prompted a judge assigned to Kamil Mansur's case in 1930 to reject the defense lawyer's claim that the law affirmed blanket freedoms of religious expression. "A person who is employed for the purpose of [Christian] evangelization (*tabshir*)," the judge reportedly declared, "especially in a country whose inhabitants are not heathen, has no liberty and no opinions."[16]

As the Arabic press called for crackdowns on Christian evangelistic work and as Egyptian political and Muslim religious figures spoke out in turn against missionary proselytism, missionaries braced themselves for future government restrictions on their work.[17] In an attempt to forestall the worst and to demonstrate goodwill, mission groups began in 1932 to prepare a collective statement that went through multiple drafts before being submitted to the Egyptian government the next year. Entitled "The Policy of the Foreign Missionary Societies of the Egypt Inter-Mission Council, and certain other missionary bodies with regard to their work in Egypt, as formulated by them on October 18, 1932", this statement asserted belief in universal and unfettered rights of religious choice, thought, and expression; "repudiate[d] any symptoms of religious imperialism that would desire to impose beliefs and practices on others in order to manage their souls in their supposed interests"; and affirmed a policy of non-coercion and non-deception in evangelization. Privileging the value of the individual over the collective, the statement added that it is "a fundamental conviction of our religion that individuality, as part of the Divine order in creation and providence, should be held in reverence." The statement also equated religious liberty with social progress and with the features "of a humane and liberal culture." More specifically, the statement urged the Egyptian government to recognize the legal status of Muslim converts to Christianity (since such converts otherwise occupied a legal limbo), and to establish a procedure like the one already in place for legally recognizing Christian conversions to Islam.[18] In an attempt to safeguard rights of evangelizing on mission grounds, the statement declared that Christian mission schools reserved the right to teach Christianity—a right that they wished non-Christians to respect as a term of enrollment.[19]

The Egypt Inter-Mission Council statement on missionary policy also hailed the freedoms that it claimed were enshrined in Egypt's 1923 constitution. It quoted relevant excerpts from this document, notably, its clauses stating that "there shall be absolute freedom of conscience," that "the State shall, in conformity with established custom in Egypt protect the free exercise of all religion or belief, on condition that there shall be no violation of public order or morals," and that "freedom of thought shall be guaranteed. Within the limits of the law all persons shall have the right to express fully their views by word, writing, pictures or otherwise."[20] The statement suggested that the Egyptian government had the power to interpret its constitution as upholding unlimited religious freedom. An alternate reading of the constitution, however, and one more in line with Egyptian practice and indeed with practice throughout many parts of the twentieth-century Muslim world, was that its reference to the "limits of the law" implied not the limits of Egyptian law, but rather of the *Shari'a*—that is, of Islamic codes that set boundaries on permissible behavior within religious and social affairs.[21]

Missionary concerns over religious freedom in Egypt gained a wider forum in the International Missionary Council (IMC), an organization founded in 1921 that drew together Protestant missionaries from the English-speaking world and from Europe. In the early 1930s, concerns over the barriers to Muslim conversion in Egypt found a hearing in the New York and London offices of the IMC (where concerns over religious liberty in other countries, such as Mexico and China, were also aired). IMC leaders went on, in turn, to notify U.S. State Department and British Foreign Office authorities of their concerns about Egypt in an effort to gain safeguards for missionaries and converts.[22] Approximately fifteen years later, as the United Nations considered plans for drafting a universal human rights credo, American missionaries in the Middle East recognized Dr. O. Frederick Nolde, an American Lutheran theologian, as their emissary to the U.N. Nolde was director of the Commission of the Churches on International Affairs (CCIA), set up jointly by the World Council of Churches and the International Missionary Council (IMC) in 1946, and he represented Protestant organizations in urging members of the UDHR drafting committee to include protections of religious liberty.[23] Thus the IMC, in which the United Presbyterian Church (the sponsor of the American mission in Egypt) participated, took an active interest in framing the statement of universal religious freedom as enshrined in the UDHR.

III. Egyptian pressures on missions: nationalism, Islamism, and decolonization

Although they attempted to appeal to universal values, Christian missionaries in Egypt had ideas about evangelization, religious choice, and conversion that clashed with prevailing Muslim beliefs in Egypt. In the early 1930s, therefore, when missionaries in Cairo, London, New York, and elsewhere were engaged in debates over religious freedom, Egypt's Islamist and nationalist leaders were writing to newspapers, organizing demonstrations, and sponsoring lectures or conferences to urge the government to impose restraints on missionary work or to discuss ways of combating it. Some Islamist leaders even encouraged the courts to impose censorship on missionary lectures and publications.[24] Meanwhile, the Egyptian government began to implement laws and policies that signaled the growing regulatory powers and bureaucratization of the state as well as the state's ambition to break free from the constraints of British colonialism. In the early 1930s Egyptian authorities ordered mission institutions to comply with new building codes and asserted rights of inspection. Responding more pointedly to popular pressure, they increased the amount of Islamic education in government schools (which many Coptic children also attended) so that over one-third of classroom hours were dedicated to Islamic study; soon, too, they established a mandatory Koran examination for all first-and second-year secondary school students, Muslims and Christians alike (Carter 1986, 225–28; Mitchell 1993, 284–86).

Egyptian politicians gained more room to act against missionaries after the signing of the Anglo-Egyptian treaty in 1936 and the Montreux Convention in 1937, which led to the undoing of the Capitulatory rights that had given various privileges to foreigners. Over the next twenty years, and continuing beyond the 1952 revolution that brought Gamal Abdel Nasser to power, the Egyptian government applied an ever-tightening range of restrictions on missionaries. It made missionary entry and work visas much harder to secure, applied new taxes to mission institutions, and required mission schools and hospitals to "Egyptianize" their staffs increasingly. It also required American mission doctors to pass Egyptian medical tests before practicing—an unobjectionable requirement in theory but which, in practice, convinced mission doctors that Egyptian examiners were bent on rejecting them.[25]

Meanwhile, the government slowly elaborated rules about Christian instruction in mission schools. In the late 1940s it issued directives prohibiting mission schools from teaching Christianity to Muslim students and ordering them to provide instruction to Muslims on Islamic subjects. For several years the government allowed mission schools to satisfy the latter provision by arranging off-site Islamic instruction or by getting parents to accept responsibility for teaching their children after school hours.[26] Restrictions on missions tightened further under Nasser's Arab socialist regime. In 1956, and under threat of seizing mission buildings and assets, the government ordered mission schools to provide Islamic instruction on site to Muslim students, without exceptions.[27] At the same time the government denied mission schools the option of restricting enrollment to Christian students as a way of preserving their Christian focus. Since the national demand for education was pressing, the government decreed that mission schools could not discriminate in admission on the grounds of religion: they had to accept Muslim students *and* hire Muslim instructors to teach them Islam on the spot (Sharkey 2005, 51).[28]

The Egyptian government did not regard its measures as an assault on Christianity or on religious freedom. Rather, it viewed these measures as an assertion and affirmation of national sovereignty vis-à-vis foreign cultural agents. In any case, from the policies it pursued, one may infer that by the time the dust settled from the Suez Crisis of 1956 (an event that sealed the process of decolonization in Egypt) the Egyptian government had asserted a definition of religious freedom that was effectively this: Egyptian Christians had the freedom to practice Christianity or to join Islam, while Egyptian Muslims had the freedom to practice Islam free from Christian evangelization.

IV. The American mission and Christian society in postcolonial Egypt

Unlike its British counterparts, the American Presbyterian mission in Egypt survived decolonization.[29] Yet circumstances had dramatically changed relative to the early twentieth century. Missionaries could no longer openly, or easily, evangelize among Muslims, and they could no longer teach Christianity to Muslim children in schools. Instead they focused their efforts on the advancement of Egyptian Christians, and on the provision of social services (above all, literacy and rural development campaigns) that consciously took an interfaith-relations rather than evangelistic approach. In the 1960s and 70s, missionaries were more likely to work to provide potable water facilities or lending libraries for mixed Christian-Muslim (or Protestant-Coptic Orthodox) communities than to seek to evangelize and to convert. In this early postcolonial period, the mission theories of Kenneth Cragg, a British Anglican church leader, were extremely influential among American Presbyterian missionaries in Egypt and the wider Middle East.[30] Cragg became associated with the idea of "respectful witness" to Muslims. He asserted that giving witness to the faith, through words and deeds, was an obligation of Christian faith, but at the same time emphasized the importance of Muslim-Christian comity, mutual respect, and interfaith dialogue. In other words, Cragg advocated a form of mission that entailed friendly encounter, not polemical conflict (Lamb 1997).[31] His ideas were well-suited to the realities of Christian missions in postcolonial Muslim societies.

Despite the fact that Nasser's regime has often been portrayed as a secular regime (in part because of its violent suppression of the Muslim Brotherhood after 1954), religious politics remained important during the Nasser era, as well as during the Sadat and Mubarak eras that followed. In 1963, an American journalist named Edward Wakin described the Copts (by which he meant all indigenous Egyptian Christians, including the Coptic Orthodox as well as the much smaller Protestant and Catholic communities) as a "lonely minority." In the aftermath of the Jewish exodus of the 1950s and 1960s,[32] Copts were lonely as the sole native non-Muslim community. Copts also felt beleaguered as a minority in a country where, in their view, Muslim government ministers increasingly favored Muslims in the allocation of university places, foreign scholarships, and government jobs (Wakin 1963).[33] Writing forty years later in 2003, S.S. Hasan, an Egyptian Muslim social scientist, reached similar conclusions. "[T]here can be no doubt," she wrote, "that the condition of the Copts steadily deteriorated during the second half of the twentieth century, as Egypt was ineluctably drawn into the Islamic orbit." As a result, she observed, Copts increasingly turned for solace and assistance to church organizations and social service programs. These helped "to compensate for a discriminatory state which, as the pie shrank in relation to an exponential growth in population, denied the Christian minority its fair share" (Hasan 2003, 3, 150). Hasan was referring to the Egyptian government's inability to provide sufficient education, health care, and other social services to meet the public demands that Nasser's socialist revolution—a "revolution of expectations"—had stimulated (Hasan 2003, 153; Wickham 2002).

In 1996, Saad Eddin Ibrahim, an Egyptian-American sociologist and a professor at the American University in Cairo, chaired a report on the Copts for the London-based human rights organization, Minority Rights Group International. The report suggested that the Egyptian state discriminated against Copts in many ways—for example, by implementing a series of 1934 laws that placed tight restrictions on the building or renovations of churches and that, in practice, made it difficult for Christians to get government permission even for trivial church plumbing repairs. What the report did not explain is that these laws evoked restrictions on Christian and Jewish communities that harkened back to the early Muslim empire of the first Islamic century (i.e., the seventh century C.E.), and to a set of strictures called the Pact of Umar.[34] No comparable restrictions have affected mosques, which have proliferated in postcolonial Egypt, often wholly unregulated by the government.[35] On this point, the report urged the Egyptian government to pursue a policy of "giving equality to all citizens in matters of building both churches and mosques in relation to the population statistics." The report also called upon the government to give Copts fair representation in government jobs, including high-ranking positions as diplomats, mayors, university presidents, and the like. More radically still, after noting that an estimated 50,000 Coptic university graduates had converted to Islam "for economic reasons" in the 1980s and 90s, the report suggested that "there should be protection for those who want to convert to Christianity" (Ibrahim 1996, 11, 27).

This controversial report about the Copts was cited as one of several factors that prompted the Egyptian government in 2001 to put Saad Eddin Ibrahim on trial for "tarnishing Egypt's image abroad"—a trial that led an Egyptian court to sentence him to a seven-year jail term. Yet some Egyptians—including some Copts—were reportedly skeptical of Ibrahim's motives in addressing the "Coptic question." They felt that his report played into "American interests in the region," and that his focus on the Copts may have reflected not so much "genuine scholarly concern" for their situation but rather more "for what plays well in the West," particularly among human rights groups.[36]

This critique of Saad Eddin Ibrahim feeds into a larger debate that shows no signs of abating—namely, a debate over the Western moorings of universal human rights discussions and issues of national sovereignty and integrity.

V. Religious agency in an age of Western power: the big debates

Are universal human rights, including rights of unfettered religious choice, ultimately rooted in Western agendas? The question has had particular relevance in the case of American Christian missionaries. For, in the twentieth century, when U.S. power was mounting in economic, political, and cultural spheres, missionaries stood to gain by securing religious "free markets" that would open doors to evangelization in Muslim societies and further afield. Bluntly put, freedoms of proselytization and conversion served local missionary interests.

Among Middle East historians, debates over the motives of missionaries— and over their altruism, self-interest, and connection to Western powers— have been growing more intense (Tejirian and Simon 2002). They have also been building on some earlier discussions (Tibawi 1966, Finnie 1967, Grabill 1971). Increasingly attuned to the local dynamics and consequences of Western imperialism, historians of the Middle East are identifying American missionaries as influential proponents of Western modernity, as transformers of gender relations in the Western mode, and as forerunners of U.S. imperialism—that is, as cultural and sometimes political imperialists who stimulated significant social changes (Makdisi 1997; Doumato 2000; McAlister 2001; Doumato *et. al.* 2002; Sharkey 2005; Baron 2005). These discussions reflect the burgeoning growth of interest in missionaries as important participants in British colonial encounters around the world (Stanley 1990; Comaroff and Comaroff 1991, 1997; Robert 1997; Peel 2000; Cox 2002; Hall 2002; Porter 2004).

Missiologists (that is, scholars of missions who tend to come from Christian institutions or theology programs) have also been reassessing long-standing debates over missionary complicity in Western imperialism (Beaver 1964, Neill 1966). Some have examined the ways in which American and European missionaries interacted with or represented local cultures (Robert 1997; Stanley 2005). Others have cast a critical eye on missionaries for trying to introduce Christianity in their own ethnocentric mold, not only in "foreign" locales, but also in "home" missions, for example, among Native Americans (Banker 2003). In a related vein, some have asked whether U.S. missionaries were sometimes transmitters of an American culture that was distinct from a Christian one (Walls 1990, 8, 11–14; Pierard 1990, 165). These debates over American- and Euro-centrism continue to gain momentum as the demographics of global Christianity increasingly tilt towards the populations of Africa, Asia, and Latin America, and away from the U.S. and Europe (Jenkins 2002; Walls 2003; Sanneh and Carpenter 2005).

The question of the American nature of Christian culture and power remains relevant today given that the U.S. is still an important base for the global deployment of evangelical missionaries and a strong advocate of universal religious liberty. Indeed, the U.S. government signaled a special interest in religious freedom in 1998, a year that coincided with the UDHR's fiftieth anniversary, when the U.S. Congress passed a new bill after sustained Christian lobbying. The "International Religious Freedom Act" of 1998 authorizes the U.S. State Department (in particular, its Bureau of Democracy, Human Rights, and Labor) to compile annual country reports on religious freedoms and to advise the U.S. government to apply political and economic sanctions on countries that egregiously violate its norms. In 2005, these egregious violators of religious freedom, designated CPC's (Countries of Particular Concern), included Burma, China, North Korea, Iran, Sudan, Eritrea, Saudi Arabia, Vietnam, Pakistan, Turkmenistan, and Uzbekistan.[37]

In her study of *Islam and Human Rights*, Ann Elizabeth Mayer suggested that the Freedom from Religious Persecution Act (as an earlier version of the International Religious Freedom Act was known) was an "ill-judged" U.S. initiative. Upon its inception the bill provoked suspicion rather than goodwill in the Middle East, largely because of the strong support that it drew from Christian evangelical groups and the American religious right-wing. "Although some countries like China are included in the list of putative offenders," Mayer wrote in 1999, "there has been sufficient initial targeting of Middle Eastern countries to provoke anger and wariness in the region." She added that the bill's focus on religious rights threatened to detract from larger sets of human rights, and that it might only make Middle Eastern Christians more vulnerable, by confirming for Muslim-majority communities an impression of the triadic links between foreign Christian missionaries, Middle Eastern Christian minorities, and the forces of Western imperialism (Mayer 1999, 132–33). Certainly, in 2005, the U.S. government's selective invocation of religious human rights risked the appearance of hypocrisy, given recent prisoner abuse scandals involving American troops at Abu Ghraib prison in Iraq, along with continuing questions about the international legality and ethics of the U.S. government's incarceration and treatment of prisoners (suspected Muslim militants) at Guantánamo Bay in Cuba. After all, the treatment of prisoners in Abu Ghraib and Guantánamo Bay contradicted clauses of the U.N. Universal Declaration of Human Rights—the same document used as the benchmark for religious freedoms.

For some critics, Muslim and non-Muslim alike, the inconsistent and selective invocation of human rights has sometimes added to perceptions of the UDHR and other U.N.-sponsored human rights agreements as Western constructs that serve Western political power—that is, as documents that are more "culture-bound" and less universal than they appear (Mayer 1994, 309). It has also stimulated efforts among some Muslim thinkers to formulate "Islamic" human rights declarations or to assert differences between "Islamic" versus "Western" human rights philosophies.[38] Ann Elizabeth Mayer has pointed out, however, that

> Muslims who oppose international human rights and demand their replacement by Islamic law have not to date conceived of Islam affording more extensive protections for human rights than are provided by international law. ...[D]istinctive Islamic criteria have consistently been used to cut back on the rights and freedoms guaranteed by international law, as if the latter were deemed excessive. (Mayer 1999, 2)

The restrictions placed by the Islamic human rights schemes of the late twentieth century tended to apply to minority and women's rights, and included the traditional rejection of apostasy in its various forms (e.g., out-conversion, heterodoxy, and atheism). Strikingly, one of these Islamic human rights schemes—the Cairo Declaration on Human Rights in Islam, issued in 1990—specifically condemned and prohibited colonialism as "one of the most evil forms of enslavement."[39]

In spite of the efforts of some Muslim thinkers to assert Islamic human rights specificities, many other Muslims have accepted or welcomed the notion of universal human rights that transcend religious distinctions. To this end, for example, human rights organizations in Tunisia and Egypt celebrated and commemorated the fiftieth anniversary of the UDHR in public forums (Idris 1998; Okasha 1999).

Moreover, the UDHR has a long history of support within the Muslim world. In 1948 as the Universal Declaration of Human Rights took shape within the U.N. General Assembly, Muslim delegates registered support for most or all of the ideals that this manifesto sought to articulate. When the document came up for the final vote in the U.N. General Assembly, the only Muslim-majority country to abstain was Saudi Arabia, which objected to various clauses that it deemed at variance with Islamic restrictions—particularly the clauses pertaining to equality among religious groups and unrestricted religious choice. The Saudi representative insisted that Islam provides for choice and religious freedom, but within bounds and with certain restraints (Morsink 1999, 24–25). Otherwise, eight of the forty-eight affirmative votes for the UDHR came from independent Muslim-majority states: Pakistan, Afghanistan, Iran, Iraq, Lebanon, Syria, the People's Democratic

Republic of Yemen, and Egypt (Arzt 1990, 216). In 1966, following a wave of decolonizations, several other Muslim countries—Albania, Algeria, Jordan, Libya, Mali, Morocco, Niger, Somalia, Sudan, and Tunisia—ratified the U.N. International Covenant on Civil and Political Rights (ICCPR) which also endorses the individual's "freedom to have or to adopt a religion or belief of his choice" (Saeed and Saeed 2004, 14). It is worth noting, however, that four Muslim countries, Pakistan, Saudi Arabia, Turkey, and the United Arab Emirates, refused to ratify the ICCPR (Mayer 1999, 18–19).

Although Egypt was one of the countries that passed both the UDHR and the ICCPR, its court system, to this day, does not recognize conversion out of Islam. By contrast, it has longstanding procedures in place to register conversions *into* Islam, notably from the ranks of Egypt's Coptic Christian minority. Registering conversion is not an abstraction of spiritual identity; rather, in states that apply Muslim personal status laws, a change of religion into Islam can have important legal consequences for marriage and divorce, child custody, and inheritance.

Modern Egyptian courts have not attempted to apply the death penalty for apostasy, as Islamic law traditionally prescribed, and as some Muslim countries, such as Sudan and Saudi Arabia, prescribe today (see, for example, Human Rights Watch 1998). Yet as the case of Nasr Hamid Abu Zayd showed in 1994–96, a court verdict of apostasy against a Muslim man can lead in Egypt, if not to execution, then to "civil death." Nasr Hamid Abu Zayd was an Egyptian Muslim professor whom a third party charged with apostasy on the grounds of errant belief. The court reviewed the professor's writings, which advocated a revision of laws away from traditional Koranic interpretations, and unilaterally divorced him from his wife, on the grounds that Islamic law forbids the marriage of a Muslim woman to a non-Muslim man (Mayer 1999, 154–55; Ayalon 1999, 1, 4). In other words, the court convicted him of apostasy not on the grounds of conversion but of heterodoxy.[40] (Note that, following the Egyptian court judgment, Abu Zayd and his wife sought asylum in the Netherlands in order to preserve their marriage.) Egyptian courts have continued to pursue charges of deviant belief as recently as December 2004 when thirteen Muslims were charged with "insulting heavenly religions." Concern over this trial and other episodes prompted the U.S. Commission on International Religious Freedom to keep Egypt on its "watch list" in 2005 (U.S. Commission on International Religious Freedom 2005, 28, 105–10).[41]

In Egypt during the 1930s and 40s, Muslim officials sometimes justified restrictions on evangelization and conversion—notwithstanding the 1922 Egyptian constitution's guarantee of religious freedom—on the grounds of maintaining public order, arguing that the preservation of communal cohesion trumped individual liberties.[42] In the late twentieth century, interpretations of the U.N. International Covenant on Civil and Political Rights or ICCPR (1966)—a covenant that Egypt ratified—provided Egypt with the same potential escape clause. For indeed, the third clause of Article 18 of the ICCPR—an article that otherwise provides for religious freedom—suggests that laws may restrict "freedom to manifest one's religion or beliefs" for the sake of protecting public order.

No mass movement for religious free choice appears to be looming on the Muslim world horizon. Nevertheless, a small number of Muslim thinkers are now engaged in vigorous debates over the future of Islam and its relevance for, and relationship to, a culturally pluralist world. Among the leading revisionist thinkers is the Sudanese scholar Abdullahi An-Na'im who has called for an Islamic "Reformation" (An-Naim 1990, Emory University School of Law 2005). Two other scholars, the Malaysian brothers Abdullah Saeed and Hassan Saeed, have explicitly proposed revisions of Islamic laws on out-conversion and apostasy. Drawing upon the Koran and other sources of Islamic jurisprudence, Saeed and Saeed argue that Islamic teachings are in line with the free choice implied in the Universal Declaration of Human Rights, and that Muslim governments in today's world should abandon apostasy laws. They argue that Islam will be most robust and successful when it is purely voluntary and non-coercive. They contend, too, that many Muslims "are moving away from the notion of an enforced religion to one of the profession of a religion as a covenant between an individual and God" (Saeed and Saeed 2004, 172).

Saeed and Saeed nevertheless acknowledge that the histories of Western imperialism and Christian evangelization complicate efforts towards revising Islamic world policies towards conversion. "For many Muslims," they observe, "a close relationship exists between colonialism, Christian missionary activities among Muslims, conversion and apostasy." They add, "The fear was, and still is, that increasingly aggressive Christian missionaries, supported by a once-colonizing West, want nothing less than Christianization of large parts of the Muslim world. Where direct Christianization failed, Westernization and secularization (linked again indirectly to Christianity and the West) are believed to be intent on achieving it" (Saeed and Saeed 2004, 116). In other words, they point out that, for many Muslims, apostasy is associated with fears of Western cultural invasion.

Conclusion

This article has attempted to explore the history of an idea, religious free choice, against the context of the history of Christian missions to Muslims in Egypt during the nineteenth and twentieth centuries. The article has explained how an American Presbyterian mission was able to operate and flourish in Egypt under the protective influence of British imperialism until decolonization in the 1950s, and how its missionaries encountered a strong barrier to Muslim conversion in the form of traditional Islamic attitudes towards apostasy. The article also considered how Christian missionaries became a focal point, and counterpoint, for Egyptian nationalist and Islamist activities that led to mounting restrictions on Christian missionary work.

Egypt's twentieth century restrictions on evangelization and conversion cannot be attributed to Islamic values alone, though Islamic legal and customary attitudes towards apostasy certainly figured in their implementation. Nationalist sentiment, reflecting a range of secular and religious (Islamist) expressions, also played a role in rallying opposition to Christian missionary activities, just as it did in within the Hindu-majority culture of India, where proponents of *Hindutva* (Hindu nationalism) took strong anti-missionary positions (Menon 2003; Mayer this volume). The anti-missionary activism of Buddhist nationalists in Sri Lanka has followed a similar pattern as well (Berkwitz this volume). The common denominator in the Egyptian-Islamic, Indian-Hindu, and Sri Lankan-Buddhist equations was colonialism, that is, the local histories of Western imperialism that triggered defensive reactions.

The case of Egypt shows that local Muslim leaders often regarded the evangelization of Christian missionaries as a cultural assault connected to larger political and economic manifestations of Western power. The Egyptian case leads, in turn, to two broad conclusions that have cross-cultural relevance. First, religious conversion and proselytization of any kind may be regarded as a form of conquest by peoples who find themselves on the receiving end of imperialism. Second, as long as Christian missionaries are associated with Western imperialism, and with its stores of wealth and power, resistance to Christian evangelization will take nationalist, anti-colonial, and religious communitarian forms. These collective movements will occasionally clash with the claims of individuals to supra-national, supra-religious rights and choices.

Notes

1. The author would like to thank the American Philosophical Society (Franklin Research Grant) and the University of Pennsylvania's University Research Foundation for supporting this research, and the American University in Cairo for according visiting faculty status in summer 2005. She would also like to thank the staff of the Presbyterian Historical Society in Philadelphia, Dar al-Kutub in Cairo, and the special collections library of the American University in Cairo.

2. Reflecting Christian missionary usage of the early twentieth century, this article uses the

terms "religious freedom" and "religious liberty" interchangeably.

3. Friedmann notes that most medieval Muslim jurists agreed on a death penalty for apostates but differed over whether apostates could avoid this penalty by recanting and if so, how much time they should have to recant (Friedmann 2003, 127).

4. Friedmann makes this point powerfully when he writes that, throughout most of the pre-modern era in the Middle East,

> ...Muslims faced the other religions from the position of a ruling power, and enjoyed in relation to them a position of unmistakable superiority. They were therefore able to determine the nature of their relationship with the others in conformity with their world-view and in accordance with their beliefs. Barring the earliest years of nascent Islam in Mecca, the first two or three years in Medina, the period of the Crusades in certain regions and a few other minor exceptions, this characterization holds true for the pre-modern period of Islamic history in its entirety. (Friedmann 2003, 1)

5. This tally was based on enrollments at 160 schools. Note that these figures did not include the 174 additional schools (mostly village primary schools), enrolling 17,051 students, for which the Evangelical Church assumed responsibility in the same year.

6. The missionaries against whom such charges were leveled included not only Americans, but also Britons, Swedes, Germans and others.

7. "al-Tabshir al-musallah fi dar al-Amrikan" (Armed Evangelism in the House of the Americans), *al-Siyasa* (Cairo), April 14, 1930, 3 (my translation). *Al-Siyasa* published other articles calling on the government to crack down on missionary evangelization, such as "al-I'tida' al-munazzam 'ala al-islam wa-wajib al-hukuma fi al-mubadara ila qam'ihi" (Organized Assault on the Islamic Religion and the Duty of the Government to Suppress It," *al-Siyasa* (Cairo), April 14, 1930, 1 (front page lead article).

8. Presbyterian Historical Society, Philadelphia, United Presbyterian Church of North America (henceforth abbreviated PHS), RG 209-1-08: J.W. Acheson Papers, Translation of an article, "An Explicit Statement by the Shaykh of al-Azhar," that appeared in *Kawkab al-Sharq*, Cairo, April 19, 1930, with annotation added by J.W. Acheson. Apparently the official (variously identified by Acheson as the Minister of Justice and the Minister of the Interior) had made his assertion about Kamil Mansur's guilt to Shaykh Muhammad Ahmad al-Zawahiri, who reported the conversation to journalists, who published these comments in turn. It may have helped their defense, too, that the first judge assigned to the case had spoken freely of Kamil Mansur's presumed guilt during pre-trial meetings, and had reminded him (according to a missionary source) that "the Gospel had described him, as an evangelist, as a 'wolf in sheep's clothing'." PHS RG 209-1-08: J.W. Acheson Papers, [Unsigned] letter to Paton, April 16, 1930.

9. "Al-Qur'an fi al-Jaza'ir" (The Koran in Algeria), *al-Balagh* (Cairo), June 1, 1933, 2; "Khatr al-haraka al-tabshiriyya, wa-wajib al-umam al-islamiyya fi al-ta'awun li-dar'ihi" (The Danger of the Evangelical Movement and the Duty of Islamic Nations to Cooperate in Repelling It), *al-Siyasa, Mulhaq* (Cairo), Literary Supplement to No. 2733, 24 Shawal 1350/ 26 February 1932, 15.

10. "Al-Tabshir Khatr Mushtarak" (Evangelization is a Shared Danger [between Egyptian Muslims and Christians]), *al-Balagh* (Cairo), July 1, 1933, 8.

11. PHS RG 209-1-08: J.W. Acheson Papers, Acheson to Anderson, Cairo, April 18, 1930.

12. A case that arose in 1862 suggested that the American missionaries were prepared to support the liberties of an agnostic or atheist as well, although it would have been unwise for them to announce this to the Egyptian authorities in their statement, since atheism was a form of apostasy more heinous than out-conversion. Andrew Watson wrote of this case in his retrospective history of the American mission: he noted that the missionaries interceded to save the life of a Muslim man, educated in France and resident in Cairo, who had written a series of articles criticizing the Prophet Muhammad. He claims that the man was about to be exiled and drowned [*sic*] in the Nile when the missionaries contacted their consuls to intercede on his behalf. Watson noted, "I am sorry to add, however, that the man does not seem to have any religion, though he is a man of good moral character, and occasionally pays a visit to our Cairo bookshop" (Watson 1904, 151–52).

13. By definition, *dhimmi*s in Islamic states lived under social contracts by which "the Muslim community accords hospitality and protection to members of other revealed religions, on the condition that they acknowledge the domination of Islam" (van Donzel 1994, 84).

14. PHS RG 209-1-10: J.W. Acheson Papers, Resumé of an interview between R.S. McClenahan and S.A. Morrison of the Inter-Mission Council and H.E. Ismail Sidky Pasha, Prime Minister of the Egyptian Government, February 20, 1932.

15. PHS RG 209-1-10: J.W. Acheson Papers, Keown-Boyd to Morrison, Cairo, April 26, 1932.

16. PHS RG 209-1-08: J.W. Acheson Papers, Translated excerpt from *al-Siyasa*, April 16, 1930, p. 5.

17. A thorough study of the anti-missionary Arabic press coverage of the late 1920s and early 1930s is provided in Carter 1984. Note that some of the newspapers that Carter consulted were missing from Dar al-Kutub (the Egyptian national library in Cairo) when I visited there in summer 2005.

18. Women converts remained especially vulnerable given the lack of a legal procedure for recognizing conversion from Islam to Christianity throughout the court system and given the tendency of Islamic courts to order their return to Muslim male guardians. For commentary on the case of a young woman named Nazli Ghunaym, see PHS RG 209-1-11: J.W. Acheson Papers, Adams to Anderson, Sidi Bishr, July 25, 1933. Adult male converts, at least, enjoyed independence of movement—they could move to another town or country and reinvent themselves more easily.

19. In drafting the statement, the member organizations of the Egypt Inter-Mission Council had debated certain provisions reflecting different attitudes and policies within and between the missions, notably regarding the teaching of Christianity in mission schools—whether it should be compulsory for all or open to exemption on the grounds of conscience—and regarding the conversion of minors. The final printed version appears in PHS RG 209-1-13: J.W. Acheson Papers, Statement, "The Policy of the Foreign Missionary Societies of the Egypt Inter-Mission Council, and certain other missionary bodies with regard to their work in Egypt, as formulated by them on October 18, 1932." See also PHS RG 209-1-11: J.W. Acheson Papers, for the penultimate draft.

20. Quoted in PHS RG 209-1-11: J.W. Acheson Papers, Statement, "The Policy of the Foreign Missionary Societies of the Egypt Inter-Mission Council, and certain other missionary bodies with regard to their work in Egypt, as formulated by them on October 18, 1932."

21. Mayer makes this point throughout her book on *Islam and Human Rights* and notes, "The result [in legal practice] is a mélange—and often a very awkward one—of international law principles and concepts that are taken from the Islamic legal heritage or that are presented as having Islamic pedigrees" (Mayer 1999, 24). Certainly the 1990 Cairo Declaration on Human Rights in Islam asserts the *Shari'a* as a limiting framework for all rights and freedoms (see Articles 24 and 25).

22. PHS UPCUSA Commission on Ecumenical Mission and Relations (COEMAR) RG 81-26-20: International Missionary Council Papers, Religious Liberty, 1930–1935.

23. PHS UPCUSA Syria Mission RG 115-13-7: Near East Christian Council, Foreign Missions Conference of North America, Committee on Work among Moslems, Digests of Reports presented to the Committee for the Restudy of Christian-Moslem Relations. "Suggestions for the work of the Study Committee from the meeting of the enlarged Executive Committee of the International Missionary Council at Whitby, 1947," presented by Dr. Fred Field Goodsell, Exec.Vice-Pres. Of the American Board of Commissioners for Foreign Missions, report no. 13, 1948.

24. PHS RG 209-1-08: J.W. Acheson Papers, Muhammad Madi Abu al-Azayim, Chairman of the Socieyt of the Islamic Caliphate in the Nile Valley, "An Open Letter to the President of the Chamber of Deputies, Wissa Wassef Effendi," *al-Siyasa*, Cairo, April 22, 1930, translated typescript; Morrison to Paton, Cairo, April 22, 1930 (including a summary of the letter from the YMMA published in *al-Ittihad* on April 19th). Missionaries noted that another call for censorship came from a writer in the April 22, 1930 edition of *al-Dunya al-Musawwara*; this particular writer added that since missionaries attacked Islam in order to earn their daily bread, their "mouths should be stopped by stuffing them with food". PHS RG 209-1-08: J.W. Acheson Papers, Morrison to Paton, Cairo, Mary 2, 1930. In organizing the Muslim Brotherhood, its founder, Hasan al-Banna, sought to devise a system of Islamic social services (e.g., schools, adult training programs, sports clubs for young men) to rival and supplant missionary services (Mitchell 1993, 2, 13, 231, 274–75).

25. PHS RG 209-3-40: Charles A. Laughead Papers, Laughead to Anderson, Cairo, October 25, 1936; Laughead to Taylor, Tanta, June 18, 1936; and Taylor to Laughead, [Philadelphia] February 27, 1936. PHS RG 209-2-09: E.M. Bailey Papers, Bailey to Black, July 6, 1955.

26. PHS RG 209-2-05: E.M. Bailey Papers, Bailey to Reed, Assiut, January 20, 1947. As late as June 1956 the mission sent a letter to Muslim parents (in response to a stricter law issued in 1955), stating that "acceptance of your child in the next school year is dependent upon the willingness of the government to interpret the law so that the parents may accept the responsibility for the teaching of any religion other than Christianity." PHS RG 209-2-10: E.M. Bailey Papers, American Mission in Egypt, "Notice Now Being Sent to Muslim Parents," Translation of Arabic typescript, [June] 1956. See also Bailey to the Egyptian Minister of Education, Cairo, May 14, 1956.

27. On the new laws requiring on-site Islamic instruction and on the threat of government seizure, see PHS RG 209-2-10: E.M. Bailey Papers, "Government to Exercise Control over All Private Schools," typescript copy of article from *Egyptian Gazette*, May 21, 1956; Bailey to Black, Cairo, May 18, 1956; Bailey to Black, January 24, 1956; Confidential, "The Report on the Field Deputation by Dr. Reed and Dr. Black Concerning Teaching of Islam in Schools in Egypt, June 23-July 8, 1956." The government did in fact seize the assets of the Egypt General Mission before deporting its British workers; however, anti-British sentiment in the context of the Suez Crisis figured into its action. PHS RG 209-2-11: E.M. Bailey Papers, Bailey to Black, Cairo, February 18, 1957.

28. Missionaries hailed it as a minor consolation that the new rulings did not require them to provide Muslim prayer space, and that they could still teach Christianity to enrolled Christians.

29. The British Church Missionary Society (CMS), Egypt General Mission (EGM), and Nile Mission Press (NMP) were forced either to dismantle their operations in Egypt or to transfer authority to Egyptian nationals. The CMS succeeded in transferring its operations, the EGM stopped functioning, and the NMP moved to Lebanon.

30. Interview with John Lorimer, retired missionary to Egypt, Pasadena, California, August 27, 2004; UPCUSA PHS RG 115-13-9: Near East Christian Council, Report on Islamics Conference in Amman [1954]. The latter report summarized the key points that Cragg made in a lecture and called these the most significant conclusion of the conference. One of these points was that missionaries

    are responsible for developing within Islam a complete concept of freedom [*sic*]. Historically the Moslem has been free to remain what he is born; but this is only the freedom of a prison. If Islam seriously regards itself as rational, then it must not only encourage the Moslem to examine his religion objectively and rationally, but it must also allow him the freedom to follow his persuasion, even if this should lead him outside Islam.

31. Kenneth Cragg has been a prolific writer, but his classic work is *The Call of the Minaret*, which was first published in 1956 and was re-issued in 1985.

32. The Jewish dispersion reflected local manifestations of the Arab-Israeli conflict, when the Egyptian government deported some Jews, and harassed or seized the assets of others (Beinin 1998).

33. Wakin suggested that Copts accounted for 15% of the Egyptian population (Wakin 1963, 4), but many sources suggest a lower figure—commonly around 7%. The most recent edition of the CIA World Factbook suggests 6% (CIA 2005).

34. The standard if somewhat dated study of the Pact of Umar is Tritton (1930/1970).

35. On mosque construction in Egypt, see Wickham (2002, 98); on the restrictions regarding church-construction in Egypt, see The Middle East Research Institute (1999).

36. Ibrahim spent more than a year in jail before a higher court exonerated and released him. For background on the case, see El-Ghobashy (2002).

37. For general information on this law, see U.S. State Department, "International Religious Freedom Act", http://www.state.gov/g/drl/irf/ (Accessed March 7, 2005). Country reports are available at http://www.state.gov/g/drl/irf/rpt/ The 2005 listing for CPC's is

available at: U.S. Commission on International Religious Freedom, *Annual Report*: 2005, 27–28, http://www.uscirf.gov/ (accessed July 28, 2005).

38. For an Arabic academic study exploring the distinct historical trajectories of Islamic and Western rights philosophies, see, for example, Kamal al-Din (2000).

39. This condemnation of colonialism appears in Article 11(b) of the Cairo Declaration on Human Rights in Islam (Islamic Conference of Foreign Ministers, 1990).

40. For a discussion of the different types of apostasy from Islam as traditionally understood, followed by a series of autobiographical accounts by a diverse group of these "apostates", see Ibn Warraq (2003).

41. Besides Egypt, the countries on the watch list included Bangladesh, Belarus, Cuba, Indonesia, and Nigeria.

42. Officials invoked public order arguments to restrict the teaching of Christianity in mission schools, for example. American University in Cairo Archives (henceforth abbreviated AUC), Charles R. Watson Papers, Missions and Government File, Strictly Confidential, Minutes of the Joint Meeting of the Committees of the Egypt Inter-Mission Council on "Education" and "Missions and Government" held at AUC on March 19, 1941, prepared by S.A. Morrison. In 1937 the Egyptian Prime Minister affirmed that Christian mission institutions, acting "within the limits of the customs recognized in Egypt regarding religions other than the State religion," could enjoy rights of worship "on condition that there is no offense against public order or morals." AUC Watson Papers, His Excellency Moustapha Nahas Pasha to Euan Wallace, Head of the Delegation for the United Kingdom, dated Capitulations Conference, Montreux, May 8, 1937 (copy in the papers of the Egypt Inter-Mission Council). One missionary, in 1928, resisted a "public order" argument while trying to justify medical evangelization. AUC Watson Papers, George Swan [of the Egypt General Mission] to A.W. Keown-Boyd, Public Security Dept, European Section, Minister of Interior, dated May 18, 1928.

References

Archival Sources and Rare Materials

American University in Cairo, Cairo, Egypt (AUC), Rare Books and Special Collections Library: Charles R. Watson Papers.

Dar al-Kutub, Cairo, Egypt (the Egyptian national library): Arabic periodicals including *al-Siyasa* (Cairo) and *al-Balagh* (Cairo).

Presbyterian Historical Society, Philadelphia (PHS): Egypt mission papers of the United Presbyterian Church of North America (UPCNA) and the United Presbyterian Church in the U.S.A. (UPCUSA).

University of Pennsylvania, Van Pelt Library Rare Books & Manuscripts Collection, al-*Siyasa, Mulhaq* (Cairo), literary supplements 1932–1934.

Other References

An-Na'im, Abdullahi Ahmed. 1990. *Toward an Islamic Reformation: Civil Liberties, Human Rights, and International Law*. Syracuse: Syracuse University Press.

Arzt, Donna E. 1990. The Application of International Human Rights Law in Islamic States. *Human Rights Quarterly* 12(2): 202–30.

Ayalon, Ami. 1999. *Egypt's Quest for Cultural Orientation*. Tel Aviv: The Moshe Dayan Center for Middle Eastern and African Studies.

Banker, Mark. 2003. Of Missionaries, Multiculturalism, and Mainstream Malaise: Reflections on the "Presbyterian Predicament". *Journal of Presbyterian History* 81(2): 77–102.

Baron, Beth. 2005. Women's Voluntary Social Welfare Organizations in Egypt. In *Gender, Religion, and Change in the Middle East: Two Hundred Years of History*, ed. Inger Marie Okkenhaug and Ingvild Flaskerud, 85–102. Oxford: Berg.

Beaver, R. Pierce. 1964. *From Missions to Mission*. New York: Association Press.

Beinin, Joel. 1998. *The Dispersion of Egyptian Jewry*. Berkeley: University of California Press.

Berkwitz, Stephen C. Buddhism and the Politics of Conversion in Sri Lanka. In *Proselytization Revisited: Rights Talk, Free Markets, and Culture Wars*, ed. Rosalind I.J. Hackett, 199–30. London: Equinox.

Carter, B.L. 1984. On Spreading the Gospel to Egyptians Sitting in Darkness: The political problem of missionaries in Egypt in the 1930s. *Middle Eastern Studies* 20: 18–36.

———. 1986. *The Copts in Egyptian Politics*. London: Croom Helm.

Central Intelligence Agency (CIA). 2005. Egypt: People. In *The World Factbook*. https://www.cia.gov/library/publications/the-world-factbook/geos/eg.html#People [accessed July 29, 2005].

Comaroff, John L. and Comaroff, Jean. 1991. *Of Revelation and Revolution, Vol. 1: Christianity, Colonialism, and Consciousness in South Africa*. Chicago: The University of Chicago Press.

Comaroff, John L. and Comaroff, Jean. 1997. *Of Revelation and Revolution, Vol. 2: The Dialectics of Modernity on a South African Frontier*. Chicago: The University of Chicago Press.

Cox, Jeffrey. 2002. *Imperial Fault Lines: Christianity and Colonial Power in India, 1818–1940*. Stanford: Stanford University Press.

Cragg, Kenneth. 1985. *The Call of the Minaret*, 2nd revised edition. Maryknoll, NY: Orbis Books.

Doumato, Eleanor Abdella. 2000. *Getting God's Ear: Women, Islam, and Healing in Saudi Arabia and the Gulf*. New York: Columbia University Press.

Doumato, Eleanor Abdella (ed.) 2002. *Islam and Christian-Muslim Relations*, special issue on "Missionary Transformations: Gender, Culture and Identity in the

Middle East." *Islam and Christian-Muslim Relations* 13(4).

Elder, Earl E. 1958. *Vindicating a Vision: The Story of the American Mission in Egypt, 1854–1954*. Philadelphia: The United Presbyterian Board of Foreign Missions.

El-Ghobashy, Mona. 2002. Antinomies of the Saad Eddin Ibrahim Case. *Middle East Report Online*, August 15. http://www.merip.org/mero/mero081502.html [accessed March 7, 2005].

Emory University, School of Law. "Islam and Human Rights." http://www.law.emory.edu/IHR/ [accessed October 5, 2005].

Finnie, David H. 1967. *Pioneers East: The Early American Experience in the Middle East*. Cambridge, MA: Harvard University Press.

Friedmann, Yohanan. 2003. *Tolerance and Coercion in Islam: Interfaith Relations in the Muslim Tradition*. Cambridge: Cambridge University Press.

Gairdner, W.H.T. 1909. *The Reproach of Islam*. London: Student Volunteer Missionary Union.

Grabill, Joseph L. 1971. *Protestant Diplomacy and the Near East: Missionary Influence on American Policy, 1810–1927*. Minneapolis: University of Minnesota Press.

Hall, Catherine. 2002. *Civilising Subjects: Metropole and Colony in the English Imagination, 1830–1867*. Chicago, IL: The University of Chicago Press.

Hasan, S.S. 2003. *Christians versus Muslims in Modern Egypt: The Century-Long Struggle for Coptic Equality*. Oxford: Oxford University Press.

Human Rights Watch. 1998. Human Rights Causes of the Famine in Sudan. http://www.hrw.org/campaigns/sudan98/context.htm [accessed March 9, 2005].

Hutchison, William R. 1987. *Errand to the World: American Protestant Thought and Foreign Missions*. Chicago, IL: The University of Chicago Press.

Ibn Warraq. 2003. *Leaving Islam: Apostates Speak Out*. Amherst, NY: Prometheus Books.

Ibrahim, Saad Eddin. 1996. *The Copts of Egypt*. London: Minority Rights Group.

Idris, al-Rashid. 1998. *Tunis wa huquq al-insan: fi dhikra al-khamsin lil-i'lan al-'alami li-sanat 1948* ("Tunisia and Human Rights: In Commemoration of the Fiftieth Anniversary of the Universal Declaration of 1948"). Tunis: Markaz al-Nashr al-Jami'i.

Islamic Conference of Foreign Ministers. 1990. Cairo Declaration on Human Rights in Islam. http://www.humanrights.harvard.edu/index.php?option=com_content&view=article&id=74&Itemid=39 [accessed July 29, 2005].

Jenkins, Philip. 2002. *The Next Christendom: the Coming of Global Christianity*. Oxford: Oxford University Press.

Kamal al-Din, Muhammad Hasan. 2000. *Huquq al-insan bayna hilf al-fudul wamithaq al-umam al-muttahida* ("Human Rights between the Alliance of the Virtuous and the United Nations Charter"). Beirut: Dar al-Mahajja al-Bayda'.

Kao, Grace Y. The Logic of Anti-Proselytization, Revisited. In *Proselytization Revisited: Rights Talk, Free Markets, and Culture Wars*, ed. Rosalind I.J. Hackett, 77–108. London: Equinox.

Lamb, Christopher. 1997. *The Call to Retrieval: Kenneth Cragg's Christian Vocation to Islam*. London: Grey Seal.

Makdisi, Ussama. 1997. Reclaiming the Land of the Bible: Missionaries, Secularism, and Evangelical Modernity. *American Historical Review* 102(3): 680–713.

Masters, Bruce. 2001. *Christians and Jews in the Ottoman Arab World: The Roots of Sectarianism*. Cambridge: Cambridge University Press.

Mayer, Ann Elizabeth. 1994. Universal versus Islamic Human Rights: A Clash of Cultures or a Clash with a Construct? *Michigan Journal of International Law* 15: 307–404.

———. 1999. *Islam and Human Rights: Tradition and Politics*. 3rd ed. Boulder: Westview Press.

Mayer, Jean-François. Conflicts of Proselytism: An Overview and Comparative Assessment. In *Proselytization Revisited: Rights Talk, Free Markets, and Culture Wars*, ed. Rosalind I.J. Hackett, 35–52. London: Equinox.

McAlister, Melani. 2001. *Epic Encounters: Culture, Media, and U.S. Interests in the Middle East, 1945–2000*. Berkeley: University of California Press.

Menon, Kalyani Devaki. 2003. Converted Innocents and Their Trickster Heroes: The Politics of Proselytizing in India. In *The Anthropology of Religious Conversion*, ed. Andrew Buckser and Stephen D. Glazier, 43–53. Lanham, MD: Rowman and Littlefield.

Middle East Research Institute, The. 1999. Anti-Christian Legislation in Egypt, December 21. http://memri.org/bin/articles.cgi?Page=countries&Area=egypt&ID=SP6599 [accessed March 9, 2005].

Mitchell, Richard P. 1993. *The Society of the Muslim Brothers*. Oxford: Oxford University Press.

Morsink, Johannes. 1999. *The Universal Declaration of Human Rights: Origin, Drafting, and Intent*. Philadelphia: University of Pennsylvania Press.

Mott, John R. 1900. *The Evangelization of the World in This Generation*. New York: Student Volunteer Movement for Foreign Missions.

Neill, Stephen. 1966. *Colonialism and Christian Missions*. New York: McGraw-Hill Book Company.

Okasha, 'Amr. 1999. *al-Karakatir wa'l-shir'a al-dawliyya li-huquq al-insan* ("The International Human Rights Conventions in Caricature"). Cairo: Jama'at tanmiyat al-dimuqratiyya, Barnamaj asdiqa' al-dimuqratiyya [Group for Democracy Development, Friends of Democracy Program].

Parker, Joseph I. 1938. *Interpretative Statistical Survey of the World Mission of the Christian Church*. New York: International Missionary Council.

Peel, J.D.Y. 2000. *Religious Encounter and the Making of the Yoruba*. Bloomington:

Indiana University Press.

Philips, H.E. 1953. *Blessed Be Egypt My People*. Philadelphia: The Judson Press.

Pierard, Richard V. 1990. Pax Americana and the Evangelical Missionary Advance. In *Earthen Vessels: American Evangelicals and Foreign Missions, 1880–1980*, eds. Joel A. Carpenter and Wilbert R. Shenk, 155–79. Grand Rapids, MI: William B. Eerdmans Publishing Company.

Porter, Andrew. 2004. *Religion versus Empire? British Protestant Missionaries and Overseas Expansion, 1700–1914*. New York: Manchester University Press.

Rice, W.A. 1910. *Crusaders of the Twentieth Century, or the Christian Missionary and the Muslim: An Introduction to Work among Muhammadans*. London: Church Missionary Society.

Robert, Dana L. 1997. From Missions to Beyond Missions: The Historiography of American Protestant Foreign Missions since World War II. In *New Directions in American Religious History*, ed. Harry S. Stout and D.G. Hart, 362–93. New York: Oxford University Press.

Saeed, Abdullah and Saeed, Hassan. 2004. *Freedom of Religion, Apostasy and Islam*. London: Ashgate.

Sanneh, Lamin and Carpenter, Joel A. (eds). 2005. *The Changing Face of Christianity: Africa, the West, and the World*. Oxford: Oxford University Press.

Sharkey, Heather J. 2005. Empire and Muslim Conversion: Historical Reflections on Christian Missions in Egypt. *Islam and Christian-Muslim Relations* 16(1): 43–60.

Stanley, Brian. 1990. *The Bible and the Flag: Protestant Missions and British Imperialism in the Nineteenth and Twentieth Centuries*. Leicester: Apollos.

———. 2005. Do Africans Have Religion? Answers from Edinburgh 1910 and since. Paper presented at the Conference of the Yale-Edinburgh Group on the History of the Missionary Movement and Non-Western Christianity, New Haven, CT, July 9.

Tejirian, Eleanor H. and Simon, Reeva Spector (eds). 2002. *Altruism and Imperialism : Western Cultural and Religious Missions in the Middle East*. New York: Middle East Institute, Columbia University.

Tibawi, A.L. 1966. *American Interests in Syria 1800–1901: A Study of Educational, Literary and Religious Work*. Oxford: Clarendon Press.

Tritton, A.S. 1930. *The Caliphs and Their Non-Muslim Subjects: A Critical Study of the Covenant of 'Umar*. London: Oxford University Press. Reprinted London: Cass, 1970.

United Nations. 1948. Universal Declaration of Human Rights (adopted December 10, 1948). http://www.un.org/Overview/rights.html [accessed March 7, 2005].

United Nations, Office of the High Commissioner for Human Rights. 1966. International Covenant on Civil and Political Rights [ICCPR] (adopted December 16, 1966. http://www.unhchr.ch/html/menu3/b/a_ccpr.htm [accessed March 9, 2005].

U.S. Commission on International Religious Freedom. 2005. *Annual Report.* http://www.uscirf.gov/ [accessed July 28, 2005].

U.S. State Department. 1998. International Religious Freedom Act. http://www.state.gov/g/drl/irf/ [accessed March 7, 2005].

Van Donzel, E. 1994. *Islamic Desk Reference.* Leiden: E.J. Brill.

Wakin, Edward. 1963. *A Lonely Minority: The Modern Story of Egypt's Copts.* New York: William Morrow and Company.

Walls, Andrew F. 1990. The American Dimension in the History of the Missionary Movement. In *Earthen Vessels: American Evangelicals and Foreign Missions, 1880–1980,* ed. Joel A. Carpenter and Wilbert R. Shenk, 1–25. Grand Rapids, MI: William B. Eerdmans Publishing Company.

———. 2003. Cross-cultural Encounters and the Shift to World Christianity. *Journal of Presbyterian History* 81(2): 112–16.

Watson, Andrew. 1904. *The American Mission in Egypt, 1854 to 1896.* 2nd ed. Pittsburgh: United Presbyterian Board of Publication.

———. 1906. Islam in Egypt. In *The Mohammedan World of To-Day,* ed. S.M. Zwemer, E.M. Wherry and James L. Barton, 23–29. New York: F.H. Revell.

Watson, Charles R. 1907. *Egypt and the Christian Crusade.* New York: Young People's Missionary Movement.

Wickham, Carrie Rosefsy. 2002. *Mobilizing Islam: Religion, Activism, and Political Change in Egypt.* New York: Columbia University Press.

Zwemer, Samuel M. 1924. *The Law of Apostasy in Islam: Answering the question why there are so few Moslem converts, and giving examples of their moral courage and martyrdom.* London: Marshall Brothers.

CHAPTER 7

Seeing is More than Believing: Posters and Proselytization in Nigeria[1]

Asonzeh F-K. Ukah

Religion, religious practices, and institutions play important roles in the private and public lives of Nigerians. The Nigerian Constitution provides the legal framework for freedom of religion and belief in the country. According to the Constitution,

> Every person shall be entitled to freedom of thought, conscience and
> religion, including freedom to change his religion or belief, and freedom
> (either alone or in community with others, and in public or in private) to
> manifest and propagate his religion or belief in worship, teaching, practice
> and observance.[2]

This legal provision is what Simeon Ilesanmi (2001, 540) calls the "the free exercise norm" by which individuals are in principle free to worship a divine being of their choice, change their religion and form religious associations with people of like minds. To a large extent, therefore, religion is unregulated by government, meaning that officially, the government does not support or adopt any religion as "state religion." This provision is regarded as the "non-establishment norm." These two norms may be taken to constitute a legal framework or basis for unrestricted religious enterprise as well as proselytism in Nigeria. In practice, however, this is not the case as government funds are used to subsidize pilgrimages to Mecca (for Muslims) and Jerusalem or Rome (for Christians). In addition, although Nigeria is a "non-secular" but religiously plural (some prefer the term "multi-religious") country with three major religious traditions, (African traditional religions [ATR], Islam and

Christianity), Islam and Christianity have gained ascendancy in the competition for power and status in the country, with these two receiving recognition in the armed forces and police, for example.

Notwithstanding some of these irregularities, Nigeria is resolutely laissez-faire in religious matters, (except of course, in the twelve Northern States[3] where the *Shari'a* law has been expanded since 1999).[4] There is a highly competitive marketplace of religious ideas, practices and groups where public and free exercise of religion holds sway. The contradiction that exists between the constitutional provisions for free exercise of religion and the expansion and reintroduction of *Shari'a* in some parts of the country is very obvious: *Shari'a* law discriminates against non-Muslims on religious grounds. It also protects Muslims from being proselytized, while encouraging non-Muslims to be actively proselytized. Under the new *Shari'a* dispensation, issues of proselytism have come to the fore once more because Islam does not accept the right (legal, human, social or even personal) of Muslims "to abandon and adopt another religion or the right to remain without a religion."[5] In this sense, the right to maintain Islam's religious orthodoxy appears to clash with the right to individual self-determination, as well as the constitutional right to change one's religious affiliation. In these ways, the full exercise of freedom of religion is effectively curtailed or hampered. For Christian groups in the country, however, the constitutional provision is the basis for deploying a variety of strategies aimed at bringing people into their religious organizations, thereby expanding their religious influence and activities. Such expansion has come primarily through effective proselytization. This chapter examines one such strategy which newly formed Christian groups have popularized in recent times: the poster.

All the different strands of religious traditions in Nigeria employ the media in varying degrees to disseminate their beliefs and practices. Of all the groups, Pentecostal organizations use the mass media the most extensively. Many Pentecostal churches meticulously employ professional media and marketing professionals to design, display and market their activities. The Redeemed Christian Church of God (RCCG), for example, extensively uses the electronic and print media in its activities. The church, founded in 1952 as a breakaway group from the Cherubim and Seraphim (C & S) movement, was rebranded in the 1980s by the founder's successor through incorporation of new faith movement teachings (such as the emphasis on "health and wealth," positive confession, giving in order to receive, see: Adeboye 1989; 2003; Hunt 2000; Price 2005). The church also introduced new ritual ceremonies, and intensive and extensive production of the media materials such as audio cassettes, videos, advertisements (posters, billboards), identity media (writing materials branded with church logo, bumper stickers, branded tennis caps, key-holders and T-shirts), radio and television programs, use of a broad range of Internet resources and web-casting, satellite broadcasting and the production of video-films (Ukah 2003c, 155–59). The church owns Dove Media, a complex of cable television, radio and movie company. Furthermore, the church owns an Outside Broadcasting Van (OBV), purchased at more than 200,000 British pounds sterling in 2002, with which it relays its ritual activities to satellite stations across the world. In addition to these, the RCCG operates Transerve Disc Technologies Limited, a company that controls more than 40 percent of the importation and marketing of blank compact discs in Nigeria. In the early 1990s, the leader of the church, Pastor Enoch Adeboye (b. 02 March 1942) recruited Nigeria's foremost corporate marketer, Felix Omoikhoje Aizobeoje Ohiwerei (b. 18 January 1937), the Chairman/Managing Director, and later the Chairman/Chief Executive Officer, of Nigerian Breweries Plc, to market the church's services to corporate Nigeria.[6] As the Chairman of the Nigerian Investment Promotion Commission (since December 2003) and an elder of the RCCG, Felix Ohiwerei coordinates and liaises with corporate organizations to sponsor the church's activities through the donation of cash and equipment or technical expertise. For example, the church's production of a home video about its early history, *The Covenant Church: The Genesis* (Dove Media 2006),[7] was sponsored by Intercontinental Bank Plc.

Many other churches literally imitate what they perceive as trendsetting practices of the RCCG in order to reproduce the church's spectacular material and media successes. Aside from deliberate attempts at cloning RCCG business strategies, many Pentecostal church leaders incorporate business strategies described in books written by American economists, business and marketing scholars, and professionals. Pentecostal bookstores, which are now ubiquitous, are inundated with books on the latest techniques of advertising, marketing and business management such as *Marketing Moves* (Kotler, Jain and Maesincee 2002); *Marketing as Strategy* (Kumar 2004); *Ice to the Eskimos: How to Market a Product Nobody Wants* (Spoelstra 1997). One of the most popular is Kotler's *How to Create, Win and Dominate Markets* (1999).[8] Despite its relatively high cost, this book is a popular item in many Pentecostal bookstores in southern Nigeria. It is fast becoming an important *textbook* of choice on Pentecostal media and marketing strategy for the "New Religious Class" (NRC) (Ukah 2005a, 271). Books on marketing and advertising are assuming a quasi-religious character among Pentecostal leaders in the country. Pastors and their collaborators frequently cull ideas from these books and from professional marketers and advertisers in designing and staging their church advertising campaigns. The Pentecostal advertising industry is a sophisticated arena where complex professional skill, personnel and resources are usually employed in the production and display of competitive religious strategies.

Regulating deregulation

Unlike in the United Kingdom, where religious and other charity organizations are monitored and regulated by the Charity Commission, there is no government body that oversees what religious organizations do to their members or with the immense resources available to them. As a result, their associations are not investigated and the truthfulness or otherwise of the contents of their advertising campaigns are not scrutinized. This means that campaign strategies are determined by each individual church leader-owner. So far the only attempt at regulating an aspect of religious communication in the media is the one made by the National Broadcasting Commission (NBC), the government agency responsible for regulating electronic broadcasting of radio and television. There are more than 181 government-owned television and radio stations in Nigeria. In addition to these, there are over 95 privately owned and operated television, radio, cable, satellite and direct-to-home television stations. On 30 March 2004, the NBC directed all electronic media broadcast stations in the country thus: "broadcast stations which indulge in transmitting [...] programmes that profess indiscriminate miracles as events of daily fingertip occurrence [should] put a stop to this by the 30th of April 2004."[9] The NBC effectively accused the churches of "false advertising" and "false claims" which, according to the agency, endanger the good of the society by exploiting the gullible.

Obviously the body was visibly worried that liberalizing the broadcast industry need not entail a mentality of "anything goes,"[10] which was actually the reality in the electronic broadcast industry at that time. Commenting on the action of the NBC, Magbadelo (2005, 44) writes that its aim "was to protect innocent Nigerians against extortion by some notorious evangelists whose deception may have become public knowledge", for there have been "instances when exposés were published ... on some fake Pentecostal pastors who use magical powers and cultic medium to manipulate and cajole their unscrupulous adherents." A national news magazine claimed the NBC action was because of "miracle lies" disseminated through the broadcast media by Pentecostal entrepreneurs.[11] The then President of the Pentecostal Fellowship of Nigeria (PFN),[12] Bishop Mike Okonkwo, founder-owner and presiding bishop of The Redeemed Evangelical Mission (TREM), Lagos, was unequivocal about the reason for the NBC order: there are Pentecostal pastors "who have modernized occultism by injecting the name of Jesus Christ into their largely unbiblical practices" and use the broadcast media to deceive the simple and gullible public.[13]

Following on the heels of the NBC order was another important development, this time from the Advertising Practitioners Council of Nigeria (APCON) insisting that from 1 January 2005 all religious adverts must go through its vetting body, the Advertising Standards Panel (ASP), and comply with the provisions of the Code of Advertising Practice (CAP) before they are aired.[14] The APCON reiterated that religious advertisements must "not mislead members of the public or coerce, cajole or compel anyone to subscribe to any particular religion or participate in any religious function or programme." All religious promotions containing messages of "services, claims and offerings" are to be scrutinized for "exaggeration or spurious testimonials likely to mislead the audience" before they are allowed to be broadcast or displayed in the public domain.[15] The anxiety of the NBC and the APCON borders on the "media panic" resulting from the "media war" among certain prominent pastors because of the competition over membership and property. In 2001, three church-owners were for several months engaged in accusations and counter-accusations, using the public mass media to denounce one another. The reason for the altercation was about the nature and sources of the power of two of the pastors, Chris Oyakhilome and Temitope Joshua to work miracles.[16] These two were accused by another high-profile pastor, Kris Okotie, of resorting to occultic means in their claims to heal and cure all manners of diseases.[17] The protracted publicity which the quarrel generated impinged on the role of the media in proselytization particularly in the context of religious and media deregulation.[18] It is one thing however, to make the regulations and another to enforce them. Like many other aspects of the Nigerian society, the rules are observed mainly in their glaring breach. For example, the CAP explicitly prohibits the use of promise of financial prosperity, negative references to other religious groups and the exploitation of the weaknesses, shortcomings or state of desperation of people in religious promotion, yet these elements are the central ingredients of all forms of Pentecostal promotional displays.

The anxiety expressed by the above bodies is all the more significant because umbrella associations of religious groups, such as the Christian Association of Nigeria (CAN), the Pentecostal Fellowship of Nigeria (PFN) or the Supreme Council for Islamic Affairs (SCIA) lack any powers of legal enforcement to monitor proselytization strategies or sanction and discipline "erring" member groups.[19] Hence various religious actors engage in public exhibition of their religious beliefs, the founding of new religious groups and a diverse range of overt and covert proselytic strategies. Often, these different groups compete between each other for public and government attention and support, each group aiming to secure greater resources than its competitor. Such competition between Muslim and Christian groups for patronage aims at increasing membership, but also attracting high-profile individuals. This practice exacerbates religious tension generally, but especially in tertiary educational institutions where there is suspicion of Christian proselytism directed at Muslims.[20] In other words, the legal foregrounding of religious liberty (freedom of belief, practice and association) also underpins the practice of religious proselytization (freedom to disseminate one's religion or switch affiliation). Put together, these freedoms have accelerated religious transformation in the country, particularly in the last three decades of the twentieth century. Especially in the Christian south of the country, the proliferation of Pentecostal and neo-Pentecostal groups has led to the emergence of diverse forms of proselytism.

Proselytism and its cognates have had a long history of usage originally from the positive meaning of "approaching" or converting to Judaism,[21] to the neutral meaning of spreading a faith or belief (religious, ideological or political) among people who were not members of a group and bringing them to conversion, to the positively pejorative meaning of inducing conversion through unfair means such as the provision of medical services, education, access of political and economic resources, etc.[22] As used in this chapter, proselytization is taken to mean the diverse attempts by a religious group to propagate and publicly affirm its beliefs and recruit members from other religious groups or the general public (see Martin and Winter 1999, 30). The end product of the process is to bring about a movement from one religious group to another. Particularly relevant to our discussion (which relates proselytization to proselytism in some sense), is the targeting of those who are already Christians by Christian groups, eliciting the charge of "sheep-stealing" and unfair methods of bringing about religious reaffiliation and a changed worldview. In line with Stark and Finke (2000, 114; cf. Stark and Bainbridge 1996, 197; Stark 2001, 50, 112), I make a distinction between *reaffiliation* as "shifts within religious traditions" (as when a Catholic joins a Pentecostal group) and *conversion* as "shifts across religious traditions" (as in when a Christian becomes a Muslim or a Buddhist, cf. Rambo 1993; 1999). The relevance of this distinction is seen in how it features in frequent charges, mainly against Pentecostal pastors, of using the media in making/spreading false claims in order to lure people who are already members of other Christian groups into their churches. Pastors are often accused of misrepresenting themselves and their ministries, of selling miracles and promising too much in the media than is the case in reality.[23] According to Magbadelo (2005, 44), "there have been several reports [in the media] regarding the doubtful intentions and machinations of some Pentecostal pastors who engaged in magical acts to delude and mollify their unsuspecting devotees." Tunde Bakare, the founder-owner of Latter Rain Assembly, Lagos, recently accused many of his fellow pastors and church founder-owners of not being "called by God but by their bellies."[24] According to him, "[t]he [Pentecostal] ministry has become a secure place for many people who are jobless." Continuing, he called the pastors "traders" who market church membership and ecclesiastical positions to the rich and powerful in the society and in government.[25] Top-ranking officials of the PFN voice similar sentiments. According to the national secretary of the PFN, the biggest challenge to Pentecostal Christianity in Nigeria is the ever-growing presence of men and women who were not called by God but by their stomach and who have "hijacked the altar."[26]

Particularly cogent in these recriminations is the charge that the use of media advertising has come to aid religious entrepreneurs in deceiving, manipulating and exploiting the public for mercantile motives, in the guise of exercising religious freedom to recruit new members.[27] Effectively, this is a charge that alleges that new Pentecostal entrepreneurs actively engage in proselytism, the unfair deployment of deceitful, deceptive means and promises to lure and entice those who are already Christians to switch religious affiliation or allegiance. For example, John Moyibi Amoda, a Nigerian Pentecostal pastor, charges that "the merchandising of the Gospel of the Lord Jesus Christ" is "the primary source of all the problems enervating the spiritual life of the church" (Amoda 1997, vii). He laments that leaders and founders of Pentecostal churches and ministries "rule over their congregation as captains of industries oversee business empires" (Amoda 1997, xi) and pastors administer their congregations "as fiefdoms and principalities" (Amoda 1997, x). It has been alleged that the media have played important roles in transforming these new churches into "thriving businesses" (Maier 2000, 263; also Marshall-Fratani 1998, 282), and that "[t]he turnover of some churches is far in excess of some multinationals," prompting some moves by the Nigerian legislature to again consider imposing some form of taxes on "church businesses."[28]

Explicit in the NBC ban on the broadcast of miracles on national television stations is the acceptance of the power and role of the media in furthering the self-interest of pastors who engage the medium of television for religious purposes. The deregulation of the broadcast media industry through the promulgation of Decree No. 32 of 1992 by General Ibrahim Babangida's military regime witnessed the establishment of many privately owned television and radio broadcast stations. As a result of the protracted economic difficulties of the country, starting from the early 1980s, government media houses were grossly underfunded. With the boom in Pentecostal activities, notably competition for membership, the media soon became the arena for the display of a variety of proselytizing strategies. Pentecostal pastors with the wherewithal bought (and some still buy) airtime on the electronic media to showcase their prowess in preaching and working miracles of healing and financial breakthrough. While the pastors soon became famous media personalities, the media houses raked in large revenues from hosting religious events which often made up more than a half of the total broadcasting slate of some sta-tions. Soon, religious advertising became a multi-million naira industry, "the second biggest spender on prime time television" (next only to alcohol and tobacco advertising combined).[29] Before the NBC ban, the media houses nei-ther vetted nor "regulated" the contents of what the pastors brought to them for broadcast because "the piper dictates the tune" (Jibo and Okoosi-Simbine 2003, 182). Consequently, television stations were inundated with a bar-rage of unverified—and unverifiable—miracle claims. Central to the NBC's ban on miracle programmes is not the miracle claims in themselves but the financial gains that accrue from such claims. In the fraught situation in which most Nigerians find themselves, many transformed into "miracle seekers," moving from church to church in search of "a powerful man of God" who could radically transform their circumstances. Furthermore, it was common knowledge that pastors solicited for funds during their programmes in ad-dition to marketing their products, such as anointed handkerchiefs, audio-visual materials, books and magazines. While the general public hailed the ban as appropriate even though belated, it raised the paradox of how to regu-late a deregulated religious media sphere.

Furthermore, the accusations of manipulation, exploitation and profiteer-ing coming from pastors, non-pastors, as well as non-Christians against some Pentecostal pastors, highlight a paradox of proselytism: that these attempts at bringing new people into a particular church or the Christian community more generally, in practical terms represents the splintering of the Christian community into "irreconcilable" small groups.

Furthermore, it is argued that while conversion brings in new people into a religious tradition, proselytism seeks to bring in people into particular sectar-ian groups. For example, Pentecostal proselytization does not simply seek to get people to become Christians, but to reaffiliate them to particular Pente-costal churches and ministries. This charge is obvious from an examination of the use of posters, for example, in Pentecostal advertising (Ukah 2004b; 2003a), as well as other church-marketing strategies (see Barna 1992) now common among Pentecostal churches in Nigeria.[30]

While it is easy to regulate the electronic media of radio and television, and to a lesser extent, audiovisual productions, it is practically impossible to control what pastors put out on billboards, stickers, church signposts, "identity media," church bulletins, magazines and posters (Kotler 1999). In other words, small media elude official state control. These diverse, slippery ways of projecting image and identity have become pervasive in Nigeria. All Pentecostal churches are aggressively engaged in the intensive production and distribution of these media forms which have significant implications for charges of unfair proselytization methods and conflict. We shall critically examine the Pentecostal poster, which is arguably the most widely used of the advertising strategies of Nigeria's "New Pentecostalism," a potent instrument of client acquisition for the new "church–firms."[31]

The Nigerian Pentecostal poster

The poster is a visual form for communication as well as a consumer medium of advertising, publicity, and propaganda (Schmidt 2005). The development of mass production techniques and consumer society heightened the development of all forms of advertising for consumer goods, including the poster (Morgan 1999, 15f). A strong element in the emergence of the poster in advertising is that it is an outdoor form designed to be seen, to be put on display, to be aestheticized. Hence, Baricoat (1972, 12) calls it "the art gallery of the street." This is where its communicative potential resides. Aside from this obvious advantage of accessibility, it is readily adaptable to the needs of individuals and can be cheaply produced in large quantities. Its popularity among Nigerian religious entrepreneurs lies in its perceived power in selling a product or an ideology, mobilizing, and propagating an idea, person or product (Miescher 2001, 137). In the face of its ubiquity in urban Nigeria, both scholars of religion and visual communication have neglected the religious poster as a form of visual communication.[32] In a recent history of visual communication in southern Nigeria, there was no single mention of the religious poster (Fourchard 2003).

While it is hard to define the "typical" Nigerian Pentecostal poster, we can still describe the basic features which characterize the many varieties found posted on utility poles, parked vehicles, pedestrian bridges, classroom walls, etc. As exemplified by Figure 1, the narrative structure of a poster comprises a plot (the general outlay of image and text on paper); an actor/performer (the charismatic figure who functions as a channel of grace and bounty); a mood (sentiments the poster evokes in the minds of its viewers/readers, such as optimism and cheerfulness); and a resolution (which is always suspended until the viewer/reader attends the advertised programme). These features constitute the communicative ingredients of the poster; they work together to bring about "a sale" of the message/image of the pastor. Pentecostal posters carry a catchy (or seductive) caption, usually stylistically designed with bold, colourful letterings. Examples of such captions are: "Twenty-Four Hour Miracle;" "Miracle Bonanza;" "Miracle Explosion;" "Signs and Wonders

Figure 1.   A Pentecostal Poster. Photo: Asonzeh Ukah, Lagos, October 2002

Extravaganza;" "Eradication of Witchcraft;" "Instant Prosperity Breakthrough;" "Breaking your Fallow Ground," "Divine Connection to the New
Millennium;" "It's War!;" "Anointing for Distinction." These headings not
only attract attention, they make promises, organize desire and create expec-

tations in the minds of those who read them (Ukah 1999, 37; 2004b). Below the caption is the text that articulates the perceived socio-material or spiritual lack to which the programme that is being advertised is constructed as a solution. Poster messages are often addressed to those who are presumed to have specific problems by a pastor who promises them instant solution in the context of the advertised event (Ukah 1999, 41). Thus, central to the content of the poster is the assumption of a lack, a need in viewers to which there is a ready remedy which the pastor promises to provide; it offers a "redemption" from a perceived problem (Parsons 2000, 52). The poster carries a colour image of the principal actor(s) as well as an anchoring text: "an anointed man of God;" "the phenomenon of our time."[33] Also on the poster is the information regarding time, venue and date(s) of the events advertised. Lastly, the poster offers a promise, invitation or affirmation: "Your life will never be the same;" "Come and receive your breakthrough;" "Come expecting and you'll surely be blessed;"[34] "Unction will be released into your life;" "Jesus is Lord;" "Jesus Saves." Not all religious posters advertise religious events; some are strictly commercial posters advertising specific products of a pastor/church-firm (books, magazines, audio-visual materials), such as in the example in Figure 2 below. In this type of poster, the image of the self-defined "man of God" is significant in the valorization of the product on sale. The consump-

Figure 2.   Commercial Poster of Christ Embassy Church, Lagos, Nigeria. Photo: Asonzeh Ukah, Benin City, February 2005.

tion of such material products is the outward sign of divine prosperity and extravagant blessing.

In the above example, the image on the poster is that of the church owner-founder, Chris Oyakhilome,[35] who is not only the most prominent Nigerian televangelist with his programme "Atmosphere for Miracles" aired on more than 60 local and international television stations and monthly devotional, *Rhapsody of Realities*,[36] but also a media mogul producing a wide range of media products. He owns "Love World Christian Network," a satellite television channel transmitting from South Africa. Signals from this network cover all of Africa, Europe, the Middle East, Australia and New Zealand. In addition, his programmes are transmitted daily on three other satellite channels in Europe and North America. He has used the media to penetrate tertiary educational institutions in the country, as well as other African cities. He claims to have more than one million members in Nigeria alone, this feat largely accomplished through effective media use.[37] His image gives added value to the products advertised, the consumption of which both creates difference and defines membership identity and expectations (Coşgel and Minkler 2004). In this advert, there is perhaps little difference between religious advertising and commercial advertising.[38] The statement on the poster saying "the more you buy the more your chances of winning" depicts the church as a lottery/gambling company that encourages people to "try their luck" in investing in the hope of making a fortune.[39] Also, the phrase "keep buying, keep winning" is popular in Nigeria in the sales promotion of both soft and alcoholic drinks. Consuming his products is also buying into his image rhetoric: consumers may come to believe in sharing in his charismata.

Increasingly, there are posters that carry the photograph of a pastor and his spouse, as shown in Figure 3. The frequent occurrence of this type of advertising material, particularly on billboards, provides a local metaphor pointing to a stable and united domestic front; it emphasizes marriage as the "divine" institution of monogamy, an important element in Pentecostal beliefs (Ojo 1998; 2005). Many Nigerians have problems managing their family life in the face of serious economic stress. So the image of "pastor and spouse," connoting marital stability and family values, appears more appealing than ever before. Furthermore, the image helps to manufacture and market the woman's charismata to audiences who are predisposed to accepting the leader's divine authority (Ukah 2004b). Aside from lending social and media visibility to certain classes of women (spouses of pastors), the practice points to growing female empowerment and the mobilization of the public gaze on the female face and body as surfaces for the inscription of power and control, not in the marketing of secular goods and services as is frequently the case in popular advertising, but in the marketing of divine goods: grace and charismata.[40] The power of the female image to sell consumer products is transposed into marketing divine products, into a realm that abrogates the distinction between male and female.

The poster is the hub around which all advertising campaigns of Pentecostal churches, for big or small events, revolve (Reid 1987, 91–101). Although poster usage in Nigeria has evolved slowly over many years from plain words without images printed on white cardboard, contemporary posters are a product of high technology; they are complex, multi-dimensional and

Figure 3.   A Pentecostal Poster of "Pastor and Spouse," Owerri, October 2006. Photo: Asonzeh Ukah.

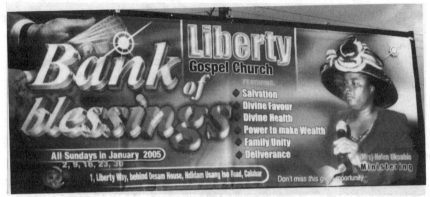

Figure 4.   A Pentecostal poster that was also resized as billboard and handbill, Calabar, February 2005. Photo: Asonzeh Ukah.

highly aestheticized. It is rare now to find a black and white religious poster in Nigeria. Also a rarity is locating image-less posters; almost all Pentecostal posters carry colour photograph(s), a fact that points to the increasing under-standing of the power of the image as "tangible attributes" that support the claims and promises of pastors (Scott 1994, 253). The ubiquity of colourful, image-saturated Pentecostal posters has influenced the emergence in Nigeria of Muslim posters with pictures, a completely new phenomenon.[41]

What defines the contemporary Pentecostal poster is its ability to attract, compel and seize attention. A singular element that helps it achieve this objective is the coercive, or rather, seductive, power of the image. In Figure 4 above, the pastor is an icon of modernity, a bringer of financial blessings depicted by United States of America dollar bills. On this particular poster and similar ones like it frequently produced and distributed widely, the pas-tor is framed as a superhero, a spectacle to be consumed voyeuristically by admirers and followers. Generally, the poster aesthetically stages the power of the pastor to mediate miraculous changes in health and wealth. The photos on posters explicitly portray religious leaders as icons of modernity and grace; they also connote special persons imbued with the unusual presence of divin-ity.[42]

In Figure 5, the full face of the female pastor demonstrates her power and resolve to conquer the evil of witchcraft; she is depicted like the female superhero, Xena the Warrior Princess, who goes about defeating evil in or-der to make up for her own evil past (Kennedy 2007). The sacred is not far away, but saturated in the image on the poster. Hence, there are many instances when believers are exhorted to hold on to the poster as "a point of contact" with the divine for their miracle. Because God is spectacularly powerful, his ministers are instruments of spectacle (Kramer 2005, 104). For the "New Pentecostalism," there is no distinction between the two meanings (of modernity and grace): the presence of divinity carries with it an overflow of modernity and well-being.[43] While there is a great internal variety in the posters, many of them are iconic texts with high symbolic value, all of them competing for symbolic supremacy (Watts 2004) in a Pentecostal media marketplace. The overplus of meanings in the poster creates the possibility for multiple interpretations by viewers: each consumer negotiating out of the visual text his/her desired meaning or sense. The posters also carry the ambiguity of belief in a transcendent God and the immersion of the believer in a world of plenty: a rich God seeks and merits publicity. For both poster designers and sponsors, this ambiguity serves a deliberate intention to captivate an audience: Is the sacred a "wholly Other," or residing in the person whose photo is splashed on the paper or in the material object itself? This is not easy to resolve one way or the other. Considering the level of aestheticization, financial commitment and devotion shown in the production, distribution and circulation of posters, all the elements are carefully coordinated in such a way as to create a complex field of interrelatedness in generation of meaning and appropriation.

Nigeria's new Pentecostalism emphasizes the doctrine of "the God of the rich," who deliberately befriends the rich.[44] Such a religion evaluates this present world as a place to be enjoyed to the fullest. This doctrinal orientation partly predisposes pastors to be fixated with the power of the image as well as market strategies of selling goods and services. R. Laurence Moore (1994) amply demonstrates a similar "religious logic" that coincides with a "commercial logic" from the history of "American religion in the marketplace of

Figure 5.   A Pentecostal Poster. Lagos, 2004. Photo: Asonzeh Ukah.

culture," as the sub-title of his book goes. The wealth of God requires his ministers to "invest heavily in advertising and in the techniques of efficient business management" (Moore 1994, 206). Because God is so rich, he demands a great deal of investment such that even commercial firms are required to bring in their own investment into the church with the expectation of making a profit. According to the leader of the Redeemed Christian Church of God (RCCG), Pastor Enoch Adeboye (1989, 29), "those who trade with God never lose." Godliness is a profitable, gainful enterprise (Okwori 1995). For big firms as well as for mega-churches such as the RCCG, image is reality; the image of a rich God is the present reality within which church-firms must settle and operate. In the socioeconomic context in which these new churches operate, the mercantile motive of a great deal of religious activities does not debase religion but rather elevates it because of the explicit exchange relationship which religious participation entails.

The aesthetics of the poster, therefore, reflects the underlying doctrines of Pentecostalism with its thematic emphasis on an expansive God whose wealth is located in the marketplace of commercial practice. Its commercial culture is partly governed by the local practice of exhibiting one's best as a way of seeking notice, of symbolically communicating one's worth to a public that recognizes and desires wealth and grandiosity. Part of the proselytizing potential of the poster thus is located in its design to appeal to an audience that understands the logic of its image, a public that wants to share in the wealth of God as manifested in the life of the pastor, whose image proudly gazes out from the poster. The power of the gaze to focus, channel and organize attention is generally recognized therein (Downing, Dodds and Bray 2004; Rashotte 2003); the function of the religious image to articulate religious sentiments is also amply stated in the work of Morgan (1998; 1999; 2005), for example. These images demonstrate particular ways of envisioning spiritual agency and potency. For both producers and consumers, posters with images are regarded as capable of mediating miracles and divine presence, eliciting a sort of sacred gaze (Morgan 2005) that structures belief, ritual exchange, religious allegiance and moral sentiments. The use of the image is rooted in the local obsession that "to be seen" is "to be acknowledged," to be valued. According to Morgan (1998, 3), "the act of looking itself contributes to religious formation and, indeed, constitutes a powerful practice of belief." It has been argued elsewhere, for example, that New Pentecostalism entrenched its hold on the Nigerian popular imagination when its principal ideas were matched with images, particularly home video images which emerged in the early 1990s (Ukah 2003b; 2005b). The (poster) image is a central element that focuses and organizes gaze and attention by concretizing abstract ideas in tangible, recognizable forms. It is an economical way of saying many things in a few colour images anchored by cryptic texts. Such texts include: "Your life will never be the same;" "Jesus is Lord;" "God is waiting for you;" "Jesus Saves;" "Come expecting and you will surely be blessed." These standardized texts give the impression of pious slogans.

With the presence of many churches in southern Nigeria, the poster fulfils an important function of providing information for their activities. These activities function as contexts of proselytization. It is ordinarily assumed that adequate publicity makes church activities successful. One of the reasons adduced for the failure of Benny Hinn's "Four Million Dollars" crusade in Lagos in April 2005 was the lack of sufficient publicity.[45] When churches behave as "religious firms" that must compete for limited resources, they tend to fill each day of the week with a specific event requiring intense advertising campaign in order to draw in people. The poster has become a medium of choice in carrying out this enterprise. The poster initiates the public performance of these events as media items even before their actual commencement. With poster publicity, public attention and curiosity is aroused and mobilized. The function of posters as inviting attention and presence relates it to a proselytizing medium which may be different from its use as a publicity strategy.[46] The poster does not provide neutral information; it provides information coloured by self-interest of the producing church and its leadership. The promises of grandiosity and subliminal satisfaction are meant to attract people and these can be as seductive as they are misleading. Intense competition can breed the danger of competitors providing fraudulent information (Darby and Karni 1973). In Nigeria, many advertisements are fraudulent as Limbs and Fort (2000) have discovered; Pentecostal advertisements are not exceptions. Hence the anxieties of both the NBC and the APCON.

Nigerians are judged the "largest church-goers in the world;"[47] the ubiquitous display of religion, of which the use of posters is one, gives visual evidence to this.[48] Since religion is a commodifiable practice, it is designed to be consumed and to be reproduced in some form. The display of religion is a process in the commodification and reproduction of religion. Thus, the use of posters assumes a definite economic and commercial relationship between producers and consumers (see Percy 2000). The production of posters is an economic enterprise demanding the channelling of scarce resources. It costs labour, often expensive professional skill, energy and money to display religion. While church members are the primary distributors of posters, there are a number of commercial firms whose services include the distribution of posters nationwide; their services are hired frequently by churches to ensure wide publicity. The cost for the production and distribution of posters is part of the responsibility of the members of a church who make financial contributions to this end. This fact supports the observation of Downes and

Miller (1998, 87) that the "marketing costs [of goods] are included in the purchase price of the goods in the shop." Even in this sense, consumers of religious posters who may finally buy into what is displayed become active producers of aspects of what they in turn consume.

There are indeed few studies of audiences of religious media in Nigeria. The worries of the NBC pertaining to "miracle broadcasts" did not emanate from any empirical research "finding" about the negative "effects" or influences of religious television. A basic assumption of the ban, however, is that religious broadcasting predisposes viewers to switch affiliation, to search for and patronise miracle-worker-pastors who literally sell miracles and other fantastical interventions to consumers in search of material gain. A significant factor in understanding the function of the poster as a proselytizing strategy, therefore, is to consider who views the displays and to what end. This particular issue relates to the audiences/consumers of public religion.

Consumers of the Pentecostal poster

In a study carried out in Ibadan metropolis between 1998 and 1999 and reported in detail in Ukah (1999), it was found out that posters enjoyed a varied readership among Pentecostal Christians drawn from seven different churches. Poster readership comes second only to the audience of Christian music. Not unexpectedly, more women read posters than men (women far outnumber men in almost all Pentecostal churches). Aesthetically enhanced posters in terms of outlay, design, colour and familiarity with the image displayed receive the greatest attention. The flashy and shocking captions ("It's War!," "Total Recovery," "Slaying your Giant," and others) often arouse curiosity and attract people to read the posters. The majority of our subjects (82.7%) agreed that poster publicity should be encouraged even when 60 (25.5%) respondents affirmed that "posters advertise pastors rather than Jesus Christ." There appears to be some inconsistency in the finding that the majority of our respondents said the primary message of poster is "salvation" but none said he/she was converted through reading posters. All our respondents, except five who were converted from Islam, reaffiliated from other Christian denominations, the majority (52.2%) from other Pentecostal churches (26.6% from the mainline churches and 13.3% from the African Independent Churches).

Nigerian poster audiences are fundamentally diverse and plural. Like other forms of visual advertisements in the public gaze, the poster is usually observed by numerous publics and never by any specific, normative or representative audience. Because posters are ubiquitous, there are multiple publics who view them; these viewers are made up of individuals from almost all social and economic strata of the society. The careful choice of sites of display, even within government offices and corporate buildings, makes the presence of posters almost inescapable to passers-by and motorists but also to workers engaged in their daily work. I have witnessed a bank worker distributing posters to colleagues, dropping copies on working desks of friends, during official working hours. It is a particular strength of the poster that it is displayed where it *must* be seen, which I refer to as "targeted display" (unless it is destroyed by long-term exposure to the elements or deliberately by supporters of an opposing pastor or church which sometimes happens!). The political power of the poster is an issue that relates to where it is exhibited, what Promey (2000) calls the "micropolitics" of the religious image or its geographical referent of display. A pastor whose posters are displayed widely in a city asserts a measure of social power. Because posters can be moved around easily, placed in strategic places where a target audience is known to frequent, they have an advantage over other media as billboards, church signs and other print adverts that are difficult to move around.

Consumers of posters actively reconstruct the material, its place and meaning in their private and public life from many different perspectives (Promey 2001, 32). They are active agents who bring their biographies to bear on the meaning they derive from what they consume (Ukah 2003b). This fact is also true of the consumption of other religious media products like Christian videos, as a recent survey demonstrates (Ukah 2005b). Viewers' expectations and life circumstances are important elements in the complex process of constructing meaning out of posters. The poster may not have an independent life and meaning of its own but is brought to life by the interpenetration of diverse factors interacting in the social and religious construction of meaning. It is this capacity to generate fresh meaning in its audiences that predisposes some pastors to use it as a proselytizing instrument, frequently directed at members of other churches rather than at non-Christians.

However, the significance of the poster is not to be found in a single aspect of its complex life but in the combination of all the factors such that meaning is made possible and it attracts people to events and also helps in creating a public face and brand name for a pastor and his church. Pentecostal advertising materials function to manufacture consumers of Pentecostalism. These consumers are recruited primarily from Christian background rather than from other non-Christian confessions. This finding from our small survey mitigates its role in proselytization understood as conversion (a shift from one religious tradition to another), but not in proselytism understood as reaffiliation and church-switching. Many Pentecostal church-founder/owners are aware of "sheep-stealing" within the Pentecostal community. Frequently, a pastor tells his congregation "to bring along their friends as they come to church next Sunday." These friends, who often belong to other Pentecostal churches, are subjects of proselytism. As a result of the fear of losing members to big-time, popular preachers, some church-founder/owners have refused to affiliate with a body like the Pentecostal Fellowship of Nigeria for fear of having to share the pulpit with a prominent pastor who might have the capability to lure away their members. Such fear intensifies their own use of poster advertising as a way of promoting their own self-image and marketing their charismata to a wide audience or public, consolidating their hold on their members and encapsulating them from external influences, as well as targeting members of other congregations, particularly those in the moneyed professions of banking and the financial sector. For the new prosperity Pentecostalism in Nigeria, demography is both salvation and destiny. Proselytizing members of professional groups ensures a steady supply of money, as well as quality members whose influence and networks extend to other facets of the society. The poster becomes an instrument of targeted, focused and reinforced proselytism. Even when such activity fails to win over its targets, it nonetheless weakens resistance, softens opposition and creates the environment for future success in proselytizing events. It is in this sense that the presence of the poster becomes a proselytizing influence on a public that has been frequently exposed to its subtle propaganda effects.

Conclusion

Religious advertisement in Nigeria constitutes a rich source of information on the existential circumstances of ordinary citizens. It is a significant source of social and daily commentary on what people find attractive and appealing, the nature of their problems, as well as the state of the various institutions within which they seek meaning. Adverts that emphasize healing, for example, provide commentary on the failed state of health facilities in the country. Those claiming to make congregants wealthy contrast with the deep state of poverty, deprivation and squalor that remain the practical experience of the majority of Nigerians. In this context, religious adverts provide information on a people's self-understanding as a community as well as their expectations and desires. They desire change and would willingly invest time and resources in its pursuit. In the advertisements we also observe a narrative of pride where pastors and church-owners bask in colour, splendour and contentment; pride of being called on a mission with a purpose and promise of glory and wealth. Posters frame pastors as spectacles of power and icons of modernity. In addition, there is evidence of a narrative of suspicion of pastors who decry the activity of fellow pastors who are intent on "sheep-stealing." Apart from the promise of wealth and prosperity advertised on posters, there is some degree of unease and incomprehension that is attached to the vitriol levelled at witches and the devil as the sources of people's problems.

There is a paradox in poster narratives. Although the advertisements comment on the state of affairs in the society, they do this by utterly neglecting that reality. The adverts are replete with sublimal promises of radical changes and self-transformation. For example, a common slogan of these posters is "Come and you will not be the same again." But these and similar promises are rarely fulfilled. As an aspect of religious promotional culture, poster adverts only present positive images of the sponsoring churches and their leaders. The primary element of the success story contained in the adverts is that of the church-owner and the spouse or other testifiers. The principal appeal of these materials derives from their messages about success, material status, and well-being (Smith 2001a, 2001b; Meyer 2004).

Thus, the symbolic inscriptions of Pentecostal advertising inspire as well as mislead. They inspire people *seeking* change but mislead those who *actually* expect to be changed by its promises. They embody the ideals of the scarcity-driven "New Pentecostalism" with its undercurrent of social, economic and political strains caused by decades of downward slide into near-anarchy. They also point to the strong character of a "New Religious Class" (NRC) that operates as business entrepreneurs mining an exuberant "fee for service" religion (Weller 2000, 477) that unabashedly deploys a diverse range of marketing mix aimed at "finding, keeping and growing profitable customers" within the religious market (Kotler 1999, 121). In the emergent marketing culture, the image has emerged as the singular most important device in nurturing profitable clients, cultivating market segments and niches, in competing and strategically repositioning both religious producers and products, and in invigorating and expanding the Pentecostal economy. It is a veritable strategy of dominating the new Pentecostal market.

As we saw from the analysis of the survey, the poster does not convert non-Christians; it is rather a formidable instrument of proselytism, inducing church-switching mainly within the ranks of miracle-seekers and God-shoppers who are attracted towards the miraculous, the spectacular, the unusual and the powerful. Because of this function, critical and anti-Pentecostal opinions have arisen from within the movement as well as from outside. Many individuals now denounce the "selling of miracles" and "sheep-stealing" through the provision of false and exaggerated claims and promises by pastors. Hence the import of NBC's ban and the insistence of APCON on monitoring and regulating religious advertising. The "unofficial" nature of the poster makes such regulation of deregulation impossible to carry out beyond the usual government rhetoric. Because of these different factors, the poster is an effective instrument of advertisement by pastors hungry for church growth.

Thus, understanding the social, economic and religious impact of Pentecostal poster advertising requires insights from the economics of religion, a field that construes churches as firms, pastors as religious producers or entrepreneurs and adherents as consumers willing to pay for the services they receive (Iannaccone 1994; 1998; Iannaccone, Olson and Stark 1995). Under this model, Pentecostal expansion is less a function of evangelism, conversion or proselytization and more a question of inter-firm rivalry, competition and splits from within as well as proselytism (sometimes referred to as church-switching and sheep-stealing). Pentecostal advertisement turns prominent pastors into media celebrities imbued with social and economic power (Bartholomew 2006, 11; see also 2004, 2005; Pringle and Binet 2005).[49] Nowhere is this "rivalry of iconic texts" (Watts 2004) more dramatically demonstrated in Nigeria as in Pentecostal poster advertisement.

Notes

1. I thank the President of International Association for the History of Religions (IAHR), Professor Rosalind I.J. Hackett for inviting me to the IAHR meeting in Tokyo, Japan, in early 2005, where she read on my behalf a first draft of this paper. Her encouragement and comments helped me in refining this paper to its present state. I am grateful to Bill Dewey for his assistance and comments in respect of this paper. I also benefited from the expert opinions of Professor David Morgan who read and commented on an earlier draft of the paper. The usual caveat holds.

2. *Constitution of the Federal Republic of Nigeria*, 1999, art. 38.1.

3. The *Shari'a*, which is the ethical and legal code of Islam, and derived from both the Qur'an and the Sunnah, has always been a source of legal and political controversies in the postcolonial legal and constitutional history of Nigeria. The twelve Northern States which, as at January 2007, have expanded or reintroduced *Shari'a* law, are as follows: Zamfara, Sokoto, Jigawa, Kano, Kaduna, Katsina, Yobe, Gombe, Niger, Bauchi, Bronu, Kebbi (see John Paden "Islam and Democratic Federalism in Nigeria," *Africa Notes*, published by the Center for Strategic and International Studies [CSIS], Number 2, March 2002). On some of the social and legal consequences of the revitalization of the *Shari'a* legal code in Nigeria, see Ado-Kurawa (2000); Kalu (2003, 389–408); Ostien, Nasir and Kogelmann (2005); Danfulani (2005); cf. Kenny (1996).

4. Governor Yerima of Zamfara State was the first to initiate this expansion of *Shari'a* on 27 October 1999, barely five months after a civilian regime was put in place following a 15-year military dictatorship, (see Ruud Peters, "The Reintroduction of Islamic Criminal Law in Northern Nigeria," A Study conducted on behalf of the European Union, September 2001, http://ec.europa.eu/comm/europeaid/projects/eidhr/pdf/islamic-criminal-law-nigeria_en.pdf, [accessed 22.07.06].

5. Natan Lerner "Proselytism, Change or Religion, and International Human Rights," (http://www.law.emory.edu/EILR/volumes/win98/lerner.html [accessed 03.12.04, no longer available].

6. Ayo Arowolo, "Ohiwerei at 70: A Tribute", http://www.guardiannewsngr.com/editorial_ opinion/article04//indexn3_html?pdate=170107&ptitle=Ohiwerei%20At%2070:%20 A%20Tribute&cpdate=170107 [accessed 17.01.07, now archived].

7. Produced and directed by Charles Novia; Executive producer, Ope Banwo.

8. All the titles are among the best selling books found in Pentecostal bookstores in Lagos in late 2004 and 2005.

9. See "NBC's Order on Miracles", *The Punch* (Lagos), Tuesday 18 May 2004, 17; Geoffrey Ekenna, "Miracles or Magic?", *Newswatch* (Lagos), 19 April 2004, 12–14.

10. Ex-president Olusegun Obasanjo (1998, 55–58) had previously described Nigeria as a "country of anything goes".

11. *Newswatch* (Lagos), cover page, 19 April 2004.

12. The Pentecostal Fellowship of Nigeria was established in 1985 as an umbrella body of Pentecostal groups in the country, although not all Pentecostal churches have embraced or agreed to join the organization. Dr. Badejo of the Four Square Gospel Church was elected as its first president and Bishop Mike Okonkwo of The Redeemed Evangelical Mission (TREM) who later became the association's president, was its first secretary. See *The Guardian* (Lagos), Sunday 6 February 2005.

13. Interview cited in *Newswatch* (Lagos), 19 April 2004, 14.

14. The APCON was set up by Decree 55 of 1988. Item 12 of the Code of Advertising Practice of APCON, which is the only item explicitly dealing with religious advertising, states: "Advertisements must not disparage the religious beliefs of the people, nor deceive people into believing that miracles are common place events. The propagation of religious faith deserves utmost care" (Ozoh 1998, 230).

15. "APCON seeks Media Cooperation against Unwholesome Ads" *This Day* (Lagos), 4 April 2005, 40.

16. See Reuben Abati, "The Clash of Pastor Generals, *The Guardian on Sunday* (Lagos), 11 November 2001, 10.

17. Kris Okotie, "My Grouse with Oyakhilome", *The Guardian on Sunday* (Lagos), 11 November 2001, 30; also *ThisDay on Sunday*, (Lagos), 28 October 2001, 43.

18. See the two part interview granted by one of the protagonists of the "media war", Chris Oyakhilome, on the role of media in shaping public perceptions of the crisis, *National Standard* (Abuja), vol. 1, no. 6, December 2004, 23–30; *National Standard* (Abuja), vol. 1, no. 7, January 2005, 18–24.

19. For peculiar reasons, law enforcement groups in Nigeria are very reluctant to investigate the activities of religious leaders or bodies even when there are public complaints regarding some of their activities partly for fear of being accused of religious victimization, and partly because of the belief in the arcane capabilities of religious leaders to cast a hex on people who disagree with them. The municipal authorities also decline to oversee the religious organizations that exist within their jurisdiction, because often those who are expected to carry out these functions are sometimes members or sympathizers of these

organizations and are unwilling to do so.

20. See David A.A. Obasa, *SCM UI: 50 Years in Retrospect*, Ibadan: Students' Christian Movement, UI, (n.d.).

21. See Acts of the Apostles 2:10b, where "proselytes" is used to describe "converts to Judaism." In this vein, "proselytizing" means bringing willing Gentiles into the covenant community through a three-fold process of i) circumcision (if male), ii) baptism, and iii) offering a sacrifice at the temple.

22. Carlos A. Valle, "Communication and Proselytism, " (http://www.religion-online.org/showarticle.asp?title=136) (accessed 03.12.2004). Valle cites David Bosch as suggesting that the word was first used by the Jesuits as a description of the "spreading of the Christian faith among people (including Protestants) who were not members of the Catholic Church."

23. See, for example, the charges levelled against pastors by the Founder-owner-General Overseer of Latter Rain Assembly, Pastor Tunde Bakare, "Pastors are Turning to Traders", *Sunday Sun* (Lagos), 25 September 2005, 2, 47.

24. Tunde Bakare, "Pastors are Turning to Traders", *Sunday Sun* (Lagos), 25 September 2005, 2.

25. Tunde Bakare, "Pastors are Turning to Traders", *Sunday Sun* (Lagos), 25 September 2005, 47.

26. "Touts have Hijacked the Pulpit, says PFN scribe", *Daily Sun* (Lagos), Tuesday, November 14, 2006, http://www.sunnewsonline.com/webpages/features/manpulpit/2006/nov/14/manpulpit-14-11-2006-001.htm [accessed 14.11.06].

27. See the two-page advertorial "Jesus Christ Satisfies Hunger for Righteousness not for Money" sponsored by one "Evangelist Dr. Adegboluga Olusegun Adenuga", *Encomium* (Lagos), Tuesday 10 August 2004, 32, 33.

28. *The Week* (Lagos), 5 July 2004, 10.

29. "Miracle Pastor: Sources of Power, Controversial Healings, the Big Bucks on TV", *The Week* (Lagos), 2 September 2002, vol. 16, no. 22, 14–19.

30. George Barna's *A Step-by-Step Guide to Church Marketing: Breaking Ground for the Harvest* (1992) is one of the most popular and widely available church-marketing textbooks among Pentecostal pastors..

31. The analysis of the religious organization as a commercial firm is found in Adam Smith's *Wealth of Nations*. Anderson (1988) and Iannaccone (1991) provide brilliant expositions of Smith's analysis and its contemporary applications within the theoretical framework of the religious markets. Ekelund *et al.* (1989) and Hull and Bold (1989) treat the medieval church as an economic firm. The theory of the religious market or the religious economy is anchored on treating the religious group as a "firm," the religious believer as a consumer and the pastor/prophet as a supplier of religion which is conceived of a "marketable good" (Stark and Bainbridge 1985; 1996 [1987]; Stark and Finke 2000; Iannaccone 1990). Several scholars have applied insights from this theory to different areas of religious practice and participation. O'Connor and Falola (1999, 117) have

examined Orisha worship in Nigeria and the United States of America as "a client religion in which services are purchased, not unlike a consultant or tax accountant." Rey (2004) examines Bourdieu's analysis of prophets/pastors as "independent entrepreneurs of salvation." In a similar way, Redden (2005) examines the New Age movement using the market/firm model while Lu (2005) attributes the evolution and success of Falun Gong to the movement's entrepreneurial logic and "firm" character. Passas and Castillo (1992, 103) argue convincingly that the "clear" business character of the Church of Scientology "helps explain its survival and success." Stolz (2006) provides an insightful analysis of the theoretical fruitfulness of the religious market model in discussions of religious organizations and participation in contemporary times.

32. For exceptions, see Ojo (1994); Ukah (1999).

33. This text is unique to the posters and banners of Pastor Femi Emmanuel of Living Spring Chapel, Ibadan and Lagos.

34. This closing text is unique to Glory Tabernacle Ministry, Ibadan.

35. From Edo State, Nigeria, Chris Oyakhilome studied architecture at Ambrose Ali University, Ekpoma, Edo State and worked briefly in the banking sector in Benin City before moving to Lagos and starting his church, Believers' Love World Inc. (alias "Christ Embassy"), in 1989.

36. In order to ensure wider circulation, this devotional is translated into 25 languages including Hausa, Igbo, Yoruba, French, Russian, Dutch, German and Spanish.

37. Chris Oyakhilome, published interview, *National Standard* (Lagos) vol.1, no. 6, December 2004, 24.

38. Because the new churches are increasingly being recognized as business or economic empires, there is an ongoing debate in Nigeria regarding the need to review their tax-exempt, charity status. See Dayo Thomas "A Due to Ceasar [*sic*]", *The Week* (Lagos), 5 July 2004, 9–16; *Daily Sun* (Lagos), 8 March 2005, 36.

39. Gambling shares some significant features with religious practice and behaviour. Religious advertising also shares some features with gambling advertising, hence in some societies, religious advertising is considered "offensive". On gambling, see Sauer (2001); on gambling advertising, see Youn, Faber and Shah (2000); on religion as a controversial product whose advertising is seen as offensive, see Waller (1999), Waller and Fam (2000), Fam, Waller and Erdogan (2004).

40. The rhetoric of power and control is a dominant one among Pentecostals. The exercise of power and control is a demonstration of being in charge of one's circumstances and one's destiny, material and spiritual. For more on this see, Wilson and Clow (1981); Enoch Adeboye, "Jesus, Our Symbol of Dominion", *Redemption Light*, vol. 9, no. 11, December 2005, 8, 11–12, 37.

41. Muslims, because of their religious beliefs, are generally reluctant and careful in using images in advertisements (Rice and al-Mossawi 2002).

42. Much as in African traditional religion where ritual specialists are revered and held in high honour as people set apart from the rest of the community, Pentecostal pastors are

so revered and in some cases held as "the God we see now" (see Ukah 2003c, 116). Some Nigerian Pentecostal Christians hold their pastors as "Jesus Christ in the flesh," sometimes with disastrous consequences, see "Rev. King's Day in Court," Editorial Article, *The Guardian* (Lagos), online edition 23 January 2007.

43. A leading pastor maintains that one cannot be a believer and be either poor or ill (see Ukah 2003c, 197). According to Enoch Adeboye of the Redeemed Christian Church of God, "God does not make people poor. People are poor because of their own attitude to certain principles. The principles are there: You sow, you reap; you don't sow, you don't reap," *Congress News & People* (Lagos), vol. 1, no. 2 (Dec. 2005), 7.

44. See Adeboye (1989) for the doctrine of "a God of the rich," cf. Ukah (2004a, 2005a).

45. See "Holy Anger", *Daily Sun* (Lagos), 9 May 2006, 1, 4 and 5; Also, "Top Pastors Plotted Failure of Benny Hinn Crusade"—Bishop Joseph Olanrewaju Obembe, *Daily Sun* (Lagos), 9 May 2006, 4 and 5; "Benny Hinn $4m Saga, Pastor Adeboye Opens Up," *Motivation* Magazine(Lagos), vol 3, no. 7, December 2005, 5.

46. The poster can be used by an organization to create awareness, for example, for the use of condom. It can also be used to publicize a product such as a religious service and at the same time proselytize, that is, to recruit membership. It is these distinct functions that I underscore here. In Pentecostal usage of the poster, the functions of publicity and recruitment are merged and reinforce each other.

47. *Daily Sun* (Lagos), 8 March 2005, 36.

48. "The Changing Face of the Church", http://www.thehumbleway.org/resources/newsweek. pdf (accessed 21.07.06, no longer avaialbe). Also see "Nigeria Leads in Religious Belief," http://news.bbc.co.uk/1/hi/programmes/wtwtgod/3490490.stm [accessed 21.07.06].

49. On how the media help in creating a "star" or a "celebrity" and the different ramifications of power and appeal, see Marshall (1997).

References

Adeboye, Enoch Adejare. 1989. *Turning your Austerity to Prosperity*. Lagos: CRM Press.

———. 2003. *Sixty-Five Steps to Prosperity and Wealth*. Lagos: CRM Press.

Ado-Kurawa, Ibrahim. 2000. Shari'a *and the Press in Nigeria: Islam versus Western Christian Civilization*. Kano: Kurawa Holdings Limited.

Amoda, John Moyibi. 1997. *Pentecostalism in Chains: The Merchandising of the Gospel of the Lord Jesus Christ*. New York: Civiletis International.

Anderson, Gary M. 1988. Mr. Smith and the Preachers: The Economics of Religion in the Wealth of Nations. *Journal of Political Economy* 96(5): 1066–88.

Baricoat, John. 1972. *Posters: A Concise History*. London: Thames and Hudson.

Barna, George. 1992. *A Step-by-Step Guide to Church Marketing: Breaking Ground for the Harvest*. Ventura, CA: Regal Books.

Bartholomew, Richard. 2004. "Community and Consumerism: The Case of Christian Publishing," PhD. Dissertation, School of Oriental and African Studies, University of London.

————. 2005. Religious Mission and Business Reality: Trends in the Contemporary British Christian Book Industry. *Journal of Contemporary Religion* 20(1): 41–54.

————. 2006. Publishing, Celebrity, and the Globalisation of Conservative Protestantism. *Journal of Contemporary Religion* 21(1): 1–13.

Coşgel, Metin M. and Lanse Minkler. 2004. Religious Identity and Consumption. *Review of Social Economy* 62(3): 339–50.

Danfulani, Umar H. 2005. *The* Shariʻa *Issue and Christian-Muslim Relations in Contemporary Nigeria.* Stockholm: Almqvist and Wiksell International.

Darby, Michael R. and Edi Karni. 1973. Free Competition and the Optimal Amount of Fraud. *Journal of Law and Economics* 16(1): 67–88.

Downes, Brenda and Steve Miller. 1998. *Teach Yourself Media Studies,* London: Hodder Headline.

Downing Paul E., Chris M. Dodds and David Bray. 2004. Why Does the Gaze of Others Direct Visual Attention? *Visual Cognition* 11(1): 71–79.

Ekelund, Robert B. Jr., Robert F. Hébert and Robert D. Tollison. 1989. An Economic Model of the Medieval Church: Usury as a Form of Rent Seeking. *Journal of Law, Economics, and Organization* 5(2): 307–31.

Fam, Kim Shy, David S. Waller and B. Zafer Erdogan. 2004. The Influence of Religion on Attitudes towards the Advertising of Controversial Products. *European Journal of Marketing* 38(5/6): 537–55.

Fourchard, Laurent. (ed.) 2003. *Modern History of Visual Art in Southern Nigeria.* Ibadan: IFRA.

Hull, Brooks B. and Frederick Bold. 1988. Towards an Economic Theory of the Church. *International Journal of Social Economics* 16: 5–15.

Hunt, Stephen, 2000. "Winning Ways:" Globalisation and the Impact of Health and Wealth Gospel. *Journal of Contemporary Religion* 16(2): 85–105.

Iannaccone, Laurence R. 1990. Religious Practice: A Human Capital Approach, *Journal for the Scientific Study of Religion* 29(3): 297–314.

————. 1991. The Consequences of Religious Market Structure: Adam Smith and the Economics of Religion. *Rationality and Society* 3(2): 156–77.

————. 1994. Progress in the Economics of Religion. *Journal of Institutional and Theoretical Economics* 150(4): 737–44.

————. 1998. Introduction to the Economics of Religion. *Journal of Economic Literature* 36: 1465–96.

Iannaccone, Laurence R., Daniel V.A. Olson and Rodney Stark. 1995. Religious Resources and Church Growth. *Social Force* 74(2): 705–31.

Ilesanmi, Simon. 2001. Constitutional Treatment of Religion and the Politics of Human Rights in Nigeria. *African Affairs* 100: 529–54.

Jibo, Mvendaga and Antonia T. Okoosi-Simbine. 2003. The Nigerian Media: An Assessment of its Role in Achieving Transparent and Accountable Government in the Fourth Republic. *Nordic Journal of African Studies* 12(2): 180–95.

Kalu, Ogbu. 2003. Safiyya and Adamah: Punishing Adultery with *Shari'a* Stones in Twenty-First Century Nigeria. *African Affairs* 102: 389–408.

Kenny, Joseph. 1996. *Shari'a* and Christianity in Nigeria: Islam and a "Secular" State. *Journal of Religion in Africa* 26(4): 338–64.

Kotler, Philip. 1999. *Kotler on Marketing: How to Create, Win, and Dominate Markets*. New York: The Free Press.

Kotler, Philip, Dipak C. Jain and Suvit Maesincee. 2002. *Marketing Moves: A New Approach to Profits, Growth, and Renewal*. Boston, MA: Harvard Business School Press.

Kramer, Eric. W. 2005. Spectacle and the Staging of Power in Brazilian Neo-Pentecostalism. *Latin American Perspectives* 140 (32/1): 95–120.

Kumar, Nirmalya, 2004. *Marketing as Strategy: Understanding the CEO's Agenda for Driving Growth and Innovation*. Boston, MA: Harvard Business School Press.

Lerner, Natan. 1998. "Proselytism, Change of Religion, and International Human Rights." (http://www.law.emory.edu/EILR/volumes/win98/lerner.html) [accessed 03.12.04].

Limbs, Eric C. and Timothy L. Fort. 2000. Nigerian Business Practices and their Interface with Virtue Ethics. *Journal of Business Ethics* 26: 169–79.

Lu, Yunfeng. 2005. Entrepreneurial Logics and the Evolution of Falun Gong. *Journal for the Scientific Study of Religion* 44(2):173–85.

Magbadelo, J.O. 2005. Pentecostalism in Nigeria: Exploring or Edifying the Masses? CODESRIA Bulletin 1/2: 44–50

Maier, Karl. 2000. *This House is Fallen: Nigeria in Crisis*, London: Penguin Books.

Marshall, David P. 1997. *Celebrity and Power: Fame in Contemporary Culture*, Minneapolis, MN: University of Minneapolis Press.

Marshall-Fratani, Ruth. 1998. Mediating the Global and Local in Nigerian Pentecostalism. *Journal of Religion in Africa* 28(3): 278–315.

Martin, Paul J. and Harry Winter. 1999. Religious Proselytization: Historical and Theological Perspectives at the End of the Twentieth Century. In *Proselytization and Communal Self-Determination*, ed. Abdullahi Ahmed An-Na'im, 29–50. Maryknoll, NY: Orbis Books.

Meyer, Birgit. 2004. "Praise the Lord:" Popular Cinema and Pentecostalite Style in Ghana's New Public Sphere. *American Ethnologist* 31(1): 92–110.

Miescher, Giorgio. 2001. Posters as Source. Collecting and Researching Posters at the Basler Afrika Bibliographien. In *Documenting and Researching Southern Africa: Aspects and Perspectives*, ed. Dag Henrichsen and Giorgio Miescher,

137–59. Basler: Basler Afrika Bibliographien Publication.

Moore, Laurence R. 1994. *Selling God: American Religion in the Marketplace of Culture*. Oxford: Oxford University Press.

Morgan, David. 1998. *Visual Piety: A History and Theory of Popular Religious Images*. Berkeley: University of California Press.

———. 1999. *Protestants and Pictures: Religion, Visual Culture and the Age of American Mass Production*. Oxford: Oxford University Press.

———. 2005. *The Sacred Gaze: Religious Visual Culture in Theory and Practice*. Berkeley: University of California Press.

Obasanjo, Olusegun. 1998. The Country of Anything Goes. *New York Review of Books*, September 24, 56–58.

O'Connor, Kathleen and Toyin Falola. 1999. Religious Entrepreneurship and the Informal Economic Sector: *Orisa* Worship as "Service Provider" in Nigeria and the United States. *Paideuma* 45: 115–35.

Obasa, David A.A. ND. *SCM UI: 50 Years in Retrospect*. Ibadan: University of Ibadan Students' Christian Movement.

Ojo, Matthews A. 1994. Material Inscriptions of the Spiritual World among Nigerian Charismatic Movements. Paper presented at the Institute for the Advanced Study and Research in African Humanities, April, Northwestern University.

———. 1998. Sexuality, Marriage and Piety among Nigerian Charismatic Movements. In *Rites of Passage in Contemporary Africa*, ed. James Cox, 180–97. Cardiff: Cardiff Academic Press.

———. 2005. Religion and Sexuality: Individuality, Choice and Sexual Rights in Nigerian Christianity. Understanding Human Sexuality Seminar series 4. Africa Regional Sexuality Resource Centre (ARSRC), Lagos, June 9.

Okwori, E. M. 1995. *Godliness for Gain: An Evaluation of the Nigerian Version of the Prosperity Gospel*. Jos, Nigeria: CAPRO Media Services.

Ostien, Philip, Jamila M. Nasir and Franz Kogelmann. 2005. *Comparative Perspective on* Shari'a *in Nigeria*. Ibadan: Spectrum Books Limited.

Ozoh, Hilary Chidi. 1998. *Principles and Practice of Advertising*. Lagos: APCON.

Paden, John. 2002. Islam and Democratic Federalism in Nigeria. *Africa Notes, Center for Strategic and International Studies (CSIS)*, no, 2, March.

Parsons, Susan F. 2000. Redeeming Media: The Promises and Pretext of Advertising. *Studies in Christian Ethics* 13(1): 49–65.

Passas, Nikos and Manuel Escamilla Castillo. 1992. Scientology and its 'Clear' Business. *Behavioral Sciences and the Law* 10: 103–16.

Percy, Martin. 2000. The Church in the Market Place: Advertising and religion in a Secular Age. *Journal of Contemporary Religion* 15(1): 97–119.

Peters, Ruud. 2001. The Reintroduction of Islamic Criminal Law in Northern Nigeria. http://ec.europa.eu/comm/europeaid/projects/eidhr/pdf/islamic-criminal-law-nigeria_en.pdf, [accessed 22.07.06].

Price, Frederick C. 2005. *Name it and Claim it: the Power of Positive Confession.* Benin City: Marvellous Christina Publications.

Pringle, Hamish and Les Binet. 2005. How Marketers can use Celebrities to Sell more Effectively. *Journal of Consumer Behaviour* 4(3): 201–14.

Promey, Sally M. 2000. The Visual Culture of American Religions: An Historiographical Essay. In Exhibiting the Visual Culture of American Religions, eds. David Morgan and Sally M. Promey, 1–8. Valparaiso, IN: Valparaiso University Press.

Rambo, Lewis R. 1993. *Understanding Religious Conversion.* New Haven, CT: Yale University Press.

———. 1999. Theories of Conversion: Understanding and Interpreting Religious Change. *Social Compass* 46(3): 259–71.

Rashotte, Lisa Slattery. 2003. Written versus Visual Stimuli in the Study of Impression Formation. *Social Science Review* 32: 278–93.

Redden, Guy, 2005. The New Age: Towards a Market Model. *Journal of Contemporary Religion* 20(2): 231–46.

Reid, Gavin. 1987. *To Reach a Nation: The Challenge of Evangelism in a Mass-Media Age.* London: Hodder and Stoughton.

Rey, Terry. 2004. Marketing the Goods of Salvation: Bourdieu on Religion. *Religion* 34: 331–43.

Rice, Gallian and Mohammed al-Mossawi. 2002. The Implications of Islam for Advertising Messages: The Middle Eastern Context. *Journal of Euro-Marketing* 11(3): 71–96.

Sauer, Raymond D. 2001. The Political Economy of Gambling Regulation. *Managerial and Decision Economics* 22: 5–15.

Schmidt, Wendelin. 2005. Mass Media and Visual Communication: Popular Posters in West Africa. *Third Text* 9(3): 307–16.

Scott, Linda M. 1994. Images in Advertising: The Need for a Theory of Visual Rhetoric. *Journal of Consumer Research* 21: 252–73.

Smith, Jordan Daniel. 2001a. Ritual Killing, 419, and Fast Wealth: Inequality and the Popular Imagination in Southeastern Nigeria. *American Ethnologist* 28(4): 807–26.

———. 2001b. "The Arrow of God:" Pentecostalism, Inequality, and the Supernatural in South-Eastern Nigeria. *Africa* 71(4): 587–613.

Spoelstra, Jon, 1997. *Ice to the Eskimos: How to Market a Product Nobody Wants.* New York: Harp Business Books.

Stark, Rodney. 2001. *One True God: Historical Consequences of Monotheism,* Princeton, NJ: Princeton University Press.

Stark, Rodney and Roger Finke. 2000. *Acts of Faith: Explaining the Human Side of Religion.* Berkeley: University of California Press.

Stark, Rodney and William Sims Bainbridge. 1985. *The Future of Religion: Seculariza-tion, Revival, and Cult Formation.* Berkeley: University of California Press.

——. 1996. *A Theory of Religion*, New Jersey: Rutgers University Press. [1987].

Stolz, Jörg. 2006. Salvation Goods and Religious Markets: Integrating Rational Choice and Weberian Perspectives. *Social Compass* 53(1): 13–32.

Ukah, Asonzeh F.-K. 1999. Poster Publicity and Religious Proselytization: A Study of Pentecostalism in Ibadan, MSc. project, Department of Sociology, University of Ibadan, Ibadan, Nigeria.

——. 2003a. Reklame für Gott: Religiös Werbung in Nigeria. In *Afrikanische Reklamekunst*, ed. Tobias Wendl, 148–53. Wuppertal: Peter Hammer Verlag.

——. 2003b. Advertising God: Nigerian Christian Video-Films and the Power of Consumer Culture. *Journal of Religion in Africa* 30(2): 203–31.

——. 2003c. *The Redeemed Christian Church of God (RCCG), Nigeria. Local Identities and Global Processes in African Pentecostalism*, PhD. Dissertation, University of Bayreuth. http://opus.ub.uni-bayreuth.de/volltexte/2004/73/pdf/Ukah.pdf.

——. 2004a. Pentecostalism, Religious Expansion and the City: Lesson from the Nigerian Bible Belt. In *Resistance and Expansion: Explorations of Local Vitality in Africa*, ed. Peter Probst and Gerd Spittler, 415–41. Münster: LIT Verlag.

——. 2004b. Religiös Propaganda in Afrika. In *Plakate in Afrika*, ed. Dieter Kramer and Wendelin Schmidt, 83–88. Frankfurt: Museum der Weltkulturen.

——. 2005a. "Those who Trade with God Never Lose:" The Economics of Pentecostal Activism in Nigeria. In *Christianity and Social Change in Africa: Essays in Honor of John Peel*, ed. Toyin Falola, 251–74. Carolina: Carolina Academic Press.

——. 2005b. The Local and the Global in the Media and Material Culture of Nigerian Pentecostalism. In *Entreprises religieuses transnationales en Afrique de l'Ouest*, ed. Laurent Fourchard, André Mary and René Otayek, 285–313. Paris: Karthala and Ibadan: IFRA.

Valle, Carlos A. nd. "Communication and Proselytism", (http://www.religion-online.org/showarticle.asp?title=136) [accessed 03.12.2004].

Waller, David S. 1999. Attitudes towards Offensive Advertising: An Australian Study. *Journal of Consumer Marketing* 16(3): 288–94.

Waller, David S. and Kim Shyan Fam. 2000. Cultural Values and Advertising in Malaysia: Views from the Industry. *Asia Pacific Journal of Marketing and Logistics* 12(1): 3–16.

Watts, James W. 2004. Ten Commandments Monuments and the Rivalry of Iconic Texts. *Journal of Religion and Society* 6: 1–12; http://moses.creighton.edu/JRS/pdf/2004-13.pdf [accessed 18.07.06].

Weller, Robert P. 2000. Living at the Edge: Religion, Capitalism, and the End of the

Nation-State in Taiwan. *Public Culture* 12(2): 477–98.

Wilson, John and Harvey K. Clow. 1981. Themes of Power and Control in a Pentecostal Assembly. *Journal for the Scientific Study of Religion* 20(3): 241–50.

Youn, Seounmi, Ronald J. Faber and Dhavan V. Shah. 2000. Restricting Gambling Advertising and the Third-Person Effect. *Psychology and Marketing* 17(7): 633–49.

CHAPTER 8

Religious Conflict and the Politics of Conversion in Sri Lanka[1]

Stephen C. Berkwitz

Religious conversion, commonly viewed in the West in terms of personal experience and individual rights, has emerged as a source of major public debate and political struggle in Sri Lanka at the turn of the twenty-first century. Given the other challenges facing the Sri Lankan state at present—including a protracted civil war, post-tsunami reconstruction and rehabilitation, and serious disruptions to the national economy from rising oil prices and renegotiated textile trade agreements—it may seem somewhat surprising that the issue of religious conversion would become a pressing political issue. However, whereas those other problems are linked to concerns over the territorial sovereignty and economic wellbeing of the state, the current conflict over conversion in Sri Lanka is closely tied to disputes over the *identity* of the state. Debates over religious and national identities, human rights, cultural sovereignty, and the "foremost place" granted to Buddhism in the country's constitution frame the politics of conversion in Sri Lanka. One result of these debates is the sustained effort on the part of some actors to draft and pass legislation to make "unethical conversions" illegal in Sri Lanka. The Sri Lankan case makes clear that religious conversion is not simply a matter of individual faith and conscience, but it is, to quote Gauri Viswanathan, "among the most destabilizing activities in modern society, altering not only demographic patterns but also the characterization of belief as communally sanctioned assent to religious ideology" (Viswanathan 1998, xvi). In Sri Lanka, religious communities and ideologies frequently become the grounds upon which conflicting visions of national identity and culture are fought, making conversion a matter of central importance in public debates.

The conflict over conversion in Sri Lanka principally involves, on one side, Buddhist nationalists who wish to protect the religious freedom of the Sri Lankan Buddhist community from what they perceive to be coercive conversions, and on the other side, evangelical Christians and human rights organizations who wish to protect the religious freedom of local and international Christian organizations from limitations on proselytism imposed by, in their view, a coercive, Buddhist-dominated government. Other groups, such as the island's Catholic, Muslim, and small mainline Protestant communities have either expressed ambiguous sentiments over the issue or have chosen to remain silent. But the "anti-conversion" controversy has high stakes for everyone, as it is connected with efforts to define religious identity, legislate the parameters for acceptable religious conduct, and protect religious liberty at the national and international levels.

An island in the Indian Ocean, Sri Lanka is a multi-ethnic and multi-religious nation state comprising around twenty million people. Geographically close to India, Sri Lanka is nevertheless distinguished from its much larger neighbor by the fact that a majority of its citizens are Buddhists. Demographic statistics, which play a large role in fomenting the anti-conversion debate and other political conflicts, typically reveal that Sinhalas make up the largest ethnic group, followed by Tamils, Muslims (formerly "Moors" and "Malays"), and Burghers (the descendents of the Dutch and other European colonialists). Approximately 70% of the population is described as Buddhist, 15% Hindu, 8% Christian, and 7% Muslim.[2] Although these numbers are not uncontested and the control of large sections of the north and east of the island by the Tamil rebel group the Liberation Tigers of Tamil Eelam (LTTE) make accurate census-taking difficult in some regions, it is still the case that around two-thirds of Sri Lankans are Sinhala Buddhists. These numbers are freighted with heavy implications for contemporary debates over conversion and the degree to which national identity is subsumed under religious identity in the Sri Lankan context.

A convergence of recent events has sparked the contemporary debate over conversion in Sri Lanka. In December 2003, a popular Buddhist monk named Ven. Gangodawila Soma, who denounced, among other things, Christian organizations distributing aid in Sri Lanka, died suddenly of heart failure while traveling to Russia to accept an honorary degree from a little-known theological institute. These circumstances fueled speculation among Buddhist nationalists that Soma's death was not an accident. A rash of arsons and other acts of vandalism against Christian churches followed Soma's funeral. A few months later, a newly formed political party comprised of Buddhist monks called the Jathika Hela Urumaya (National Sinhala Heritage party) put forth a block of over two hundred candidates for parliamentary elections and won nine seats. The JHU ran chiefly on a platform to safeguard the sovereignty of the nation, the territorial integrity of the country, and the position of Buddhism as the official religion of the state (Deegalle 2004, 88).

Upon entering the parliament as MPs, the JHU mobilized efforts to draft and pass a bill called the "Prohibition of Forcible Conversion of Religion" to prohibit "unethical conversions" in the summer of 2004. The government then drafted a stronger bill called the "Protection of Religious Freedom Act," which like the JHU bill criminalizes any attempt to convert a person to another religion "forcibly or by use of force or inducement, or by fraud, or by unethical means or in any other manner as well as to provide for matters connected there unto." The Supreme Court ruled that the JHU bill was legislating against forcible conversion in order to protect freedom of thought against aggressive evangelism, and was therefore legitimate under the country's constitution (Deshapriya and Welikala 2004, 194). But the Court also found numerous clauses such as the definition of fraudulent means, the requirement for a convert to give official notice of his/her conversion, and the bill's specification for punishment to be overly broad and unconstitutional, necessitating revisions to the bill.

The original and revised anti-conversion bills have triggered considerable public debate, with large numbers of monks, Buddhist nationalists, and several politicians advocating its passage, and a coalition of local and international Christian and human rights organizations opposing it. The dispute has occasionally been pushed aside in favor of other issues, most notably when the Indian Ocean tsunami hit coastal Sri Lanka on December 26, 2004, causing approximately forty-five thousand deaths and widespread destruction around the island. However, in the tsunami's aftermath, the controversy over Christian conversion was revived, particularly by local and international reports of some Christian groups mixing relief work with proselytism (Rohde 2005, Lampman 2005). It seems clear that the controversy over conversion in Sri Lanka will remain intense, as it draws upon a long history of hostility towards Christian missions, and involves a seemingly irreconcilable dispute over how religion itself is to be conceived: a personal acceptance of certain beliefs and morals in one's private conscience or an essential element of a group's cultural heritage and national identity.

I. Historical antecedents of Christian missions in Sri Lanka

Two of the major legacies of European colonialism in Sri Lanka are the categorization of Sri Lanka's population into distinct religious and ethnic groupings and an enduring distrust of Christian missionary work. This colonial history, which began in the early sixteenth century with the initial Portuguese presence and culminated in the intensive colonization of the island by the British in the nineteenth century, colors the contemporary debates over religious identity. The Portuguese are remembered for introducing Catholicism to this island and for their looting and destruction of Buddhist and Hindu temples. The first missionaries who arrived in 1543, led by the Franciscan friar João de Vila de Conde, initially sought to convert the Buddhist king of the Kotte kingdom. The king's reluctance, and the hostility the Franciscans encountered outside of the coastal areas populated by lower castes, led early Portuguese observers to conclude that the refusal of many Sinhalese to convert to Catholicism was because they were blinded by the Devil and heathen priests, while their leaders feared the political repercussions of abandoning the religion of the Buddha (Queyroz 1992, 258–61). However, Portuguese missionaries were persistent in their goal to save souls, and they generally received the support of the Portuguese military commanders, as well as of Sri Lankan rulers allied with them. While destroying Buddhist temples and monastic colleges, as well as Hindu temples, the Portuguese also appropriated lands granted to native houses of worship and redirected their incomes toward the maintenance of Catholic orders and churches (Paranavitana 2004, 6). During this period, numerous letters sent back to Portuguese authorities in Lisbon and Goa mention the number of churches built, and people baptized and converted, making conversion appear as an index to Portuguese power and influence in the island.

The Dutch, who replaced the Portuguese in the seventeenth century, were less openly hostile to Buddhist and Hindu religious traditions, but they still required church membership for natives seeking high offices and church attendance for students in schools (K.M. De Silva 1995, 556–57). Seeking to avoid alienating the local populace, the Dutch usually refrained from violent forms of religious persecution. Still, the new colonial rulers took steps to prohibit the free exercise of Roman Catholicism, Buddhism and other non-Calvinist traditions in the territories they controlled (Paranvitana 2004, 8). During this period, the first forms of Protestant Christianity were introduced into the island, although the numbers of converts remained comparatively small.

The British arrived in the late eighteenth century and assumed direct control over the entire island in 1815. The colonial administration left religious affairs largely to British missionaries, but implemented a number of policies that fostered a modern ethnic consciousness and the rise of identity politics among the island's residents. As they did in India, the British mapped and counted their colonial subjects in Sri Lanka, strengthening notions of Sinhalas, Tamils, and other ethnic groups as substantively distinct from one another. In response to what was seen as a heterogeneous population, the British recognized and codified differences in language, religion, custom, and even clothes to mark the racial variation of the island's inhabitants (Nissan and Stirrat 1990, 27). Later, some of these differences would become even more salient when it came to establishing the basis for communal representation in politics (Wickramasinghe 1995, 27–33). Colonial authorities sought to select members from each community to represent their people's interests at the national level. As indicated above, one of the many results of the censuses and administrative policies was to sharpen the awareness of ethnic and religious difference in the island.

Also in the nineteenth century, British missionaries traveled to Sri Lanka primarily to convert the Buddhists and Hindus to the Christian faith. Missionaries preached and wrote tracts in pursuit of their aim—winning converts to Christianity. Their publications, produced on the island's first printing presses, were aimed as much at Buddhists as local Christians, and frequently were polemical in tone, containing attacks on the "idolatrous superstition" and "stronghold of Satan," which Buddhism was sometimes called (Malalgoda 1976, 204–05). When, to the missionaries' chagrin, Buddhist monks and laypersons initially refused to be drawn into polemical disputations over religious "truth," the attacks on Buddhism became more pointed. In response, Buddhists first decided to petition the government urging its intervention to uphold religious tolerance by ordering the withdrawal of offensive Christian publications and proclaiming that publications likely to offend and harm the feelings of other religious groups should not be circulated (Malalgoda 1976, 213–14). A tepid government response had little practical effect on the activities of the missionaries. Then in 1849, a Wesleyan missionary named Daniel J. Gogerly published a treatise in Sinhala called *Kristiyani Prajñapti* (The Evidences and Doctrines of the Christian Religion), which compared Christian and Buddhist doctrines in an effort to prove the superiority of the former. Gogerly's work challenged Buddhists to disprove its theses, and it was reissued twice before the author added a long section entitled "Proofs that Buddhism is Not a True Religion" in 1861.

In the 1860s, in response to repeated denunciations and challenges of the missionaries, Buddhist monks launched a more energetic and organized response. Acquiring their own printing presses, monks began publishing tracts defending the Buddhist religion from the missionaries' attacks and attacking them in turn. Meanwhile, missionaries who believed that Gogerly's work had decisively demonstrated the truth and superiority of Christianity attempted to bait Buddhist monks into public debates over religion. When a group of monks finally accepted a debate, the missionaries and local seminarians were surprised by the large turnout of monks and lay Buddhist supporters. A series of debates were held in sites around the southern and central parts of the island between 1865 and 1873. While local Christian converts argued the case for Christianity, a number of monks representing different monastic ordination lineages held forth on behalf of Buddhism. Ven. Mohottivatte Gunananda was among the leading spokesmen who contested the missionaries' claims, and he argued in a lively and energetic style reminiscent of the missionaries themselves. Gunananda and the other monks, supported by a mainly Buddhist audience in the thousands, met the missionaries' rhetoric head on, raising counter-objections and challenging them to prove their own scriptural claims (Malalgoda 1976, 228–30).

Despite what by most accounts was a triumphant effort by the monks, Christian missionaries continued to augment their influence through the establishment of missionary schools. The English education offered at those schools held the key for social advancement in colonial society, and many Sinhala Buddhists felt obliged to attend them (Ruberu 1967, 90–93). Moves to establish Buddhist schools to counter the missionary institutes were slow and halting for several decades. Only in the latter part of the nineteenth century, with the assistance of Colonel Henry Steel Olcott and the Ceylon branch of the Theosophical Society that he founded, did efforts to establish Buddhist schools meet with success.

The colonial periods of Sri Lanka's history link religious conversion with the imposition of foreign rule, a fact that looms large in twenty-first century religious and political discourse. But even earlier, Sinhala Buddhists expressed skepticism and resentment against the efforts of Christian proselytization. The early eighteenth century Sinhala work entitled *Rajavaliya* (The Lineage of Kings) evinces this fact when it asserts that the leading persons in the city of Kotte converted to Christianity out of a desire for the wealth of the Portuguese (Suraweera 1997, 230). Likewise, the *Culavamsa* records that the Portuguese "used gifts of money and the like to get their creed adopted by others" (Paranavitana 2004, 4). Over time, the efforts of Christian missionaries to convince Buddhists of the supposed falsehoods and inferiority of their religion sparked a broader Buddhist revival that was characterized by a more aggressive defense of the tradition and the gradual conflation of Buddhism and Sinhala identity in nationalist thought. Missionaries became implicated in colonial British efforts to "disestablish" Buddhism as the primary religion in the island, taking over the social and welfare activities previously managed by the monks and teaching Sinhala children to look down upon and despise their Buddhist culture as low and base (Rahula 1974, 90).

Nationalist sentiments were mobilized by Sinhala leaders like the Buddhist layperson Anagarika Dharmapala (1864–1933) who, humiliated by the denigration of Buddhism by the religious teachers at Christian schools, began to argue later for the reform of Buddhism in the name of creating a progressive and prosperous modern society (Seneviratne 1999, 28–31). Although Dharmapala praised the ancient heritage of Sinhala Buddhists, as evidenced in their long literary and archaeological history, the type of Buddhism he promoted was distinctly modern and reactionary. He emphasized puritan values of discipline, hard work, and punctuality, while charging monks with the duty to revive Buddhism at home and abroad through active social service and preaching (Seneviratne 1999, 34–35). Dharmapala popularized the image of Christian missionaries as working hand-in-hand with the British administrators to turn the country's Buddhists into subservient drunkards who adopt Christian names and customs at the expense of their country's great traditions (Guruge 1991, 512, 524–25). He also spread the idea that the British had betrayed Buddhism by failing to live up to their obligations from the Kandyan Convention of 1815, wherein they pledged to maintain the Buddhist religion and preserve the ancient laws and customs of the land.

Owing to the anti-Christian and anti-colonial rhetoric of Gunananda, Dharmapala, and others, modern Buddhist nationalism in Sri Lanka has been articulated largely in opposition to Western and Christian forces. And after Independence was granted in 1948, many Sinhala Buddhists began to advocate for a nation governed by and supportive of their own community and religious heritage. The resulting split between the Sinhala and Tamil populations as a result of the ethnic politics that shaped legislation has been well-documented elsewhere (e.g., Manor 1989, Tambiah 1992, Daniel 1996). Since the 1950s, a sizable contingent of Buddhist monks has actively lobbied in the political sphere to uplift the conditions of Buddhism in the country. Blaming British policies that allegedly favored the promotion of Christianity in mission schools, these new Buddhist activists called upon the Sinhala-dominated government to recognize and promote Buddhism as a policy of the state.

These efforts culminated in 1972 with the inclusion of an article in the Constitution affirming that Buddhism would be given the "foremost place" as the religion of the majority of Sri Lankans. Currently, Article 9 of the Constitution certified in 1978 states: "The Republic of Sri Lanka shall give to Buddhism the foremost place and accordingly it shall be the duty of the State to protect and foster the Buddha Sasana [i.e., the historical dispensation of the Buddha's religion], while assuring to all religions the rights [granted to all persons to freely adopt and manifest the religion of their choice]." This legal act has the effect of officially stating what many Sri Lankan Buddhists accept as a matter of fact: that Sri Lanka is a "Buddhist state" and the homeland of the authentic Buddhist tradition as laid out by the Buddha himself some 2500 years ago. A statement attributed to the Buddha from the sixth century

Buddhist chronicle *Mahavamsa*, similarly asserts, "In Lanka, O' Lord of the Gods, will my Dispensation be established" (Buddhadatta 1959, 42; cf. Geiger 1912, 55). This pronouncement, together with the historically conservative ethos of the Theravada school of Buddhism in Sri Lanka, helps to explain why there are many in Sri Lanka who proudly claim that their country acts to preserve the "True Buddhism" founded and taught by the Buddha long ago.

II. Coming to the defense of Buddhism

From the perspective of political history, modern Buddhist nationalism would seem to have succeeded in accomplishing its aims. The state has awarded Buddhism the foremost place among all religions and is active in promoting the religion and preserving many of its institutions and historical monuments. The majority of the population remains Buddhist, and Buddhist educational institutions are no longer disadvantaged compared to Christian ones. However, in recent years, Buddhist nationalists have consistently decried the impoverished state of the religion and the many external threats it faces. For several decades, Tamil separatist aspirations and particularly the LTTE, which has occasionally targeted Buddhist sites and monks for terrorist attacks in their campaign for a separate Tamil state, have been cast as the chief threat to Sinhala Buddhists. Anti-colonial and postcolonial Sinhala nationalism has discursively linked the state with Buddhism, so that any threat to one is seen as a threat to the other. The calls of Buddhist nationalists and "political monks" to oppose Tamil separatism and the devolution of state powers to regional authorities, even by military force if necessary, must be understood in that light (Bartholomeusz 2002).

Since the late 1990s, however, Christian proselytism, in the forms of newer evangelical movements and, allegedly, certain non-governmental organizations (NGOs), has emerged in Buddhist nationalist discourse as a comparable threat to the existence of the Buddhist religion and the Sinhala nation. Citing the presence of evangelical denominations and organizations, and anecdotal reports of their activities in Sri Lanka, a growing chorus of Buddhist nationalist voices has arisen to condemn Christian methods for converting Buddhists and Hindus to Christianity. One of the more influential voices in this regard was that of Ven. Gangodawila Soma (1948–2003), a Buddhist monk who was openly critical of Christian missionaries, Sri Lankan politicians, and the immoral activities of large segments in the Sinhala Buddhist laity (Berkwitz 2003, 67; 2008, 82–6). Ordained in a monastic lineage well-known in Sri Lanka for its austerity and social service, Soma became a popular and controversial monk in the late 1990s after he returned from founding two Buddhist temples in Australia to work on behalf of the Buddha Sasana in Sri Lanka.

He employed an engaging preaching style to address issues of relevance and importance to the laity, often infusing his sermons with sarcastic humor and biting critiques of those forces seen to compromise or threaten the Buddha's authentic Teaching (i.e., Dharma).

Ven. Soma typically denounced immoral politicians for seeking to earn personal wealth at the expense of the welfare of the people and the unity of the state. Specifically, he accused the island's leading politicians of working in partnership with other external forces to exploit people's desires for alcohol, cigarettes, money, and so forth, effectively undermining their commitment to Buddhist morality. He described this type of activity as "missionary politics," linking contemporary efforts among politicians to profit from liquor and cigarette sales to efforts undertaken by the British colonialists earlier to spread immoral conduct for economic gain and to turn the Sinhalas toward Christianity (Soma 2004, 5; 2002, 22). Ven. Soma's critiques were thus wide in scope and conspiratorial in tone. Often dismissed as an "extremist" and "anti-Christian" by his detractors, many of whom lack much familiarity with the content of his sermons and writings (cf. Severino 2005), Ven. Soma's public comments actually incorporated a broad range of themes and critiques not limited to Christian conversion, such as the internationalization of Sri Lanka's peace negotiations and economic policy-making (Berkwitz 2006; 2008, 90–5).

Nevertheless, Ven. Soma frequently denounced the activities of Christian NGOs with foreign ties. He accused foreign NGOs of going to poor villages and bribing the inhabitants, saying they will extend the help that is needed if the people come over to their religion (Soma 2001, 75). In a country where foreign aid is necessary and commonplace, the charge that unscrupulous NGOs are operating covertly to convert poor Buddhists to Christianity, and turn them against their cultural traditions, is indeed grave. Ven. Soma argued further that converting Buddhists from a religion that clearly espouses the truth and that facilitates good fortune in the present and next life was no easy matter. Consequently, the British colonialists and, more recently, Christian NGOs were forced to resort to bribing Sinhala Buddhists with material inducements and to promoting alcohol to weaken their moral resolve (Soma 2004, 5). These activities, according to Ven. Soma, are economically profitable for the politicians who license and sometimes own liquor stores, and they are consistent with religious goals of converting Buddhists to Christianity.

If local politicians promoted immoral conduct for selfish gain, Ven. Soma attributed even more devious intentions to foreign NGOs. According to him, those organizations use aid distribution from foreign sources as a cover for their proselytizing activities. Ven. Soma charged that NGOs were partnering with Christian missionary organizations to offer money and jobs to people who would convert to Christianity, with the clear goal of establishing a Christian government in Sri Lanka (Munasinghe 2004, 28). By promoting immoral conduct such as drinking and gambling, the foreigners could make Sri Lankans poorer and more dependent on the aid offered by missionaries in return for their conversions (Munasinghe 2004, 29). As such, Ven. Soma's religious critique of Christian proselytism was inextricably linked to political and economic critiques of the country's misguided leaders and the relatively low standard of living of many of its citizens. In response, he called upon Buddhist monks and laypeople to initiate a re-awakening of Buddhist culture in the island and to demand that the government fulfill its constitutional obligation to protect Buddhism.

Ven. Soma's sudden death at age fifty-five accelerated the momentum behind the campaign to prevent the "unethical" conversions of Buddhists to Christianity. First, as mentioned above, the unusual circumstances surrounding his death fanned the flames of conspiracy theorists, who suggested that the reverend monk was assassinated by his opponents. Subsequently, two of the three members of a special commission appointed by then President Chandrika Kumaratunga to investigate his death did find that "Christian Fundamentalists" first conspired to embarrass the monk by awarding him an honorary doctorate from a Christian institution, and then, when he fell ill, conspired to delay the necessary medical attention and heart by-pass that could have saved his life (Weerapperuma 2005). The large public funeral for Ven. Soma in December 2004 attracted crowds in the tens and even hundreds of thousands along the route of his funeral cortege, as well as the many people who watched the event live on one of several television channels. It also coincided with a sharp spike in attacks on Christian churches in the island (U. S. Department of State 2004). Some of the monks who spoke at his funeral went on to form the JHU party and contest the parliamentary elections four months later. The surprising success of the JHU, winning nine seats and becoming an influential swing bloc, inspired its leaders to move energetically towards drafting and presenting legislation to outlaw "unethical conversions," a perceived problem that Soma was instrumental in publicizing.

The JHU is the first political party in Sri Lanka comprised primarily of monastic legislators. Whereas sections of the Sri Lankan monkhood have long been involved in political causes and campaigns, the extraordinary steps of monks forming a new party and serving as a legislative bloc in the country's parliament were unprecedented. The JHU ran on a platform of twelve points to establish a righteous state (*dharmarajyayak*) in line with Buddhist principles. The first item in its manifesto asserts "all unethical conversions are illegal," clearly indicating that the JHU would make legislative action on this issue a priority once they entered parliament (Deegalle 2004, 95). Item five dictates that the government should control and monitor all the activities and monetary transactions of the NGOs that operate in the country, again indicating that the party leaders view the activities of registered NGOs as primarily concerned with Christian evangelism (Deegalle 2004, 95). The newly elected JHU MPs attempted to follow through on these issues by presenting the "Prohibition of Forcible Conversion of Religion" bill to the parliament. The submission of a similar, even stronger, bill by the governing party sidetracked the JHU effort, as did the judgment of the country's Supreme Court that parts of the bill were unconstitutional. The JHU submitted a revised draft of the bill that deleted all the unconstitutional clauses and problematic sections according to the Supreme Court, and a Standing Committee of Parliament is at the time of this writing examining the bill.[3]

Public statements given by the JHU monks are consistent with Soma's critiques of Sri Lankan politicians and evangelical Christian missionaries. Ven Ellawala Medhananda, one of the JHU parliamentarians, has warned that the forces that destroyed Soma also threaten to destroy other monks who work to preserve the country's Buddhist heritage (Munasinghe 2004, 76). JHU leaders express common Buddhist nationalist concerns, warning that the future of Buddhism and the Sinhala people are at risk from Tamil terrorism and fundamentalist Christian sects. They continually maintain that their efforts are focused on overcoming all of society's evils through adherence to Buddhist teachings, and that there will be no effort to restrict the freedom of other ethnic groups or believers in other faiths to practice; only unethical conversions would be stopped (Wijethunge 2004). However, the JHU focus on restricting the actions of "fundamentalist" Christians, namely the newer evangelical movements that proselytize more aggressively than the established Christian denominations in the island, makes many Christian groups nervous about the potential abuse of an anti-conversion law in restricting or penalizing their everyday church activities.

Although the JHU monks are empowered to present the anti-conversion bill to Parliament and remain the movement's most visible leaders, there are many other individuals and groups working to combat unethical conversions. The activism among Sinhala Buddhist nationalists is exemplified by several recent publications. For example, one such work offers a sustained critique of Christian arguments for the existence of God and inerrancy of the Bible, offering Buddhists specific responses to the pointed questions asked of them by evangelical Christians (A.L. De Silva 2003). Another pamphlet accuses evangelicals of a concerted effort to tarnish the reputation of Buddhism by, among other things, dashing Buddha statues on the ground and urinating on them, as well as paying men to impersonate monks and misbehave in public (Ranawaka-Das 2002, 13–14). An English language newspaper called *Buddhist Times* has been particularly vocal in denouncing and publicizing instances where Christian evangelicals and NGOs have engaged in unethical conversions. In the inaugural issue from May 2002, the editorial "Why a *Buddhist Times?*" explains the rationale behind the paper. It claims that Buddhism in Sri Lanka is under threat from numerous sources, including the LTTE, political corruption, and especially evangelical sects who "come here in the guise of tax-exempt foreign investors or as plain and simple proselytizers loaded with dollars to distribute amongst the poor" (Anon. 2002a, 4).

The *Buddhist Times* appears designed in part to raise awareness of Christian proselytism in Sri Lanka and to mobilize public opposition to it. The first issue lists thirty names of Christian "Evangelist organizations registered with the Registrar of Companies" and contains articles explaining why Sri Lanka is vulnerable to Christian sponsored NGOs and the abuse of religious freedom by evangelists. A subsequent issue contains an article warning Buddhists about the conversion techniques employed by Christian organizations from the US, South Korea, the UK, and The Netherlands. It bemoans the plan of foreign evangelical organizations "to slowly and systematically destroy all moral values that are sacred to Theravada Buddhists and change the cultural as well as religious practises [*sic*] like respect for elders, parents, teachers and the Buddhist clergy" (Anon. 2002b, 7). The article lists conversion methods such as setting up a "Community Centre" for prayer meetings, conducting free tuition classes to lure young people to convert, opening preschools where children are taught Christian hymns, conducting faith healing programs, and employing young men to impersonate monks and get them to misbehave in public (Anon. 2002b, 7). Readers of the article are further encouraged to take action by being alert to signs of conversion activities and to notify the head monk of the local temple should conversion activities arise.

A similar article about the activities of the Christian aid organization called World Vision appears in a 2004 issue of *Buddhist Times*. World Vision is a large NGO working to alleviate poverty through child sponsorship programs and other aid distribution internationally. It has had a fairly visible presence in Sri Lanka for several years, although it has become a focus of controversy for its allegedly aggressive methods of proselytizing. The article alleges that World Vision engages in covert conversion activities under the guise of poverty alleviation in various parts of Sri Lanka (Amarasekera 2004, 8). Citing the NGO's efforts to take over preschools in economically depressed Buddhist villages and construct drinking wells in others, the writer argues that readers should be aware of these efforts to conceal its proselytizing efforts with projects aimed at school children. The means by and degree to which World Vision engages in proselytism in Sri Lanka are in dispute, and it may be singled out more because of its greater visibility among Christian aid organizations than its actual activities.[4] Some opponents of the anti-conversion legislation assert that there are no unethical conversions taking place anywhere in the island. But World Vision has become a prominent target of Buddhist nationalist anger, sparking public condemnations and, occasionally, threats and violent attacks on its offices and staff (U.S. Department of State 2004).

Generally speaking, Sinhala Buddhist nationalists view evangelical Christian proselytism as a threat to longstanding cultural traditions that is frequently concealed within relief and development work performed by foreign NGOs. Resentful of the historical legacies of European colonialism and the Christian proselytism that accompanied it, Buddhist nationalists are alarmed by the appearance of evangelical churches that convert poor Buddhists, hold unorthodox religious services, and encourage people to sever ties with their local customs and relationships. The anti-conversion debate thus appears as part of a broader Buddhist reaction against perceived intrusions by evangelical Christian groups in Sri Lankan society. While it is probably fair to say that most Buddhist nationalists are not opposed to Christianity as a religion, they do resent efforts by well-funded groups to change the religious demographics of a predominantly Buddhist country (Fernando 1995, 208).

The movement to counter Christian proselytism has given rise to some innovative ideas among Sinhala Buddhist nationalists. One recent initiative, in the wake of the devastating tsunami of 2004, involved a meeting of Buddhist monks and laypersons, funded largely by the Buddha Light International Association based in Taiwan, to work towards founding a Buddhist relief and care movement parallel to the International Societies of the Red Cross and Red Crescent (Edirisinghe 2005, 2). The impetus behind this Colombo-based effort to form what has been tentatively called a "Red Lotus Society" appears, at least in part, to be concerned with establishing a humanitarian agency that can distribute relief aid without depending on the efforts of Christian-sponsored groups that may combine aid with proselytism. Further, in the summer of 2006, the All Ceylon Buddhist Congress appointed a commission of inquiry to investigate the issue of the conversion of Buddhists to other religions. The nine-member commission has been charged to document and report any evidence for the conversion of Buddhists by "fraudulent and unethical means" and to ascertain the effects of conversion on families and society as a whole.[5] Whether or not these efforts ultimately succeed, they illustrate some of the ways that contemporary Buddhists are seeking to curb the influence of Christian proselytism in Sri Lanka.

III. Protecting the religious freedoms of Christians

The politics of conversion in contemporary Sri Lanka also involves groups who wish to preserve their ability to proselytize and others who object to the possible infringement on individual rights from the anti-conversion legislation. The opposition comprises local and international actors, with the most vocal being representatives of the evangelical Christian community. Evangelical Christianity has historically maintained that a person's salvation is achieved by an acceptance of Jesus Christ as the Savior and Son of God. As a consequence, numerous charismatic and evangelical sects of Christianity emphasize the moment of acceptance as a monumental act of being saved or sometimes "born again." In these same sects, faithful Christians are expected to display or "witness" their faith to others, seeking to help others to convert to their church owing to a scriptural commission to spread the Word of God or a feeling of being directed by the Holy Spirit to do so (Anderson 2004, 206–07). Although many traditional and mainline Christian churches have come to deemphasize the call to convert and instead focus on ministering to the already faithful, fast-growing evangelical bodies embrace this call through sponsoring or participating in mission activities at home and abroad.

From a theological perspective, conversion to Christianity is typically seen as an intensely personal and transformative event in the life of an individual. Imagined largely in terms of the biblical story of the apostle Paul, conversion is thought to combine notions of a sudden revelation, a radical reversal of previous beliefs and allegiances, and an underlying assumption that converts are passive respondents to outside forces (Rambo 2003, 213). The convert is theoretically overcome by the experience of being saved or filled by the Spirit in what is characterized as a life-changing moment. From that point on, the convert is expected to be faithful and committed to his or her new religious orientation, leaving past habits and practices that contravene the new faith behind. Although anthropological research has cast doubts on the ideal picture of conversion as a complete and total transformation in a person's identity, the idealized image of a sudden and complete change still carries rhetorical force in determining the self-understanding and self-worth of Christian evangelists (cf. Comaroff and Comaroff 1991, 248–51; Coleman 2003, 17–18).

Theological justifications and motivations aside, the emphasis given to conversion among Christian evangelical groups carries with it certain institutional efforts and political implications. Many of the Christian aid organizations working in Sri Lanka have some connection to evangelical groups, and other bodies have moved to establish "indigenous churches" to spread the faith. Though exact figures are hard to come by in Sri Lanka, most analyses point to increased numbers of evangelical Christians in recent years, although these groups are still far outnumbered by Catholic bodies (U.S. Department of State 2004). Evangelical Christian Sri Lankans, who include members from the Sinhala and Tamil ethnic groups, are usually affiliated to an indigenous church led by local pastors. These churches are often relative newcomers to the religious landscape of Sri Lanka, and many are independent. Thus, since their churches came into existence only after the end of colonialism in the island, evangelicals typically excempt themselves from the history of earlier Christian missions in Sri Lanka. Still, advocacy groups such as the National Christian Fellowship of Sri Lanka (NCFSL) and the National Christian Evangelical Alliance of Sri Lanka (NCEASL) have emerged and are organizing much of the opposition to the anti-conversion legislation.

One of the main arguments presented by the evangelicals is that the proposed anti-conversion legislation discriminates against Christians and violates their freedom of religious worship. Broadly speaking, the campaign to defeat the legislation, which is being waged both locally and internationally, complains that the anti-conversion legislation, together with an increase in violent attacks against churches and Christians in Sri Lanka, are evidence of systematic religious persecution. The Christian opposition has frequently employed the language of human rights to express its views against the bills. Citing Articles 10 and 14(e) in Sri Lanka's Constitution, evangelicals have been joined by many traditional Christian leaders in affirming their right to the freedom to have or to adopt a religion or belief of one's choice and to manifest one's religion or belief in public or in private. From an evangelical perspective, conversion to the Word or Spirit of God is an inherent good that can only be effected by divine power. In this view, there is nothing unethical about encouraging non-believers to accept Jesus Christ, as this is thought to facilitate the individual's salvation.

The reliance of Christian evangelicals on a discourse of rights to contest the anti-conversion legislation is largely a consequence of being a religious minority that is empowered by the values of multiculturalism and certain legal protections. In the wake of ethnic violence, particularly the riots of 1983 that witnessed the deaths of up to 2000 Tamils and extensive destruction of property around Colombo, Sri Lankan governments have stressed the virtues of tolerance and the peaceful coexistence between ethnic and religious groups. At the same time, minority groups have become more vocal about the rights guaranteed to them by Sri Lanka's Constitution, criticizing the government when it fails to ensure them. The language of rights has also been popularized by and borrowed from international groups who have been monitoring the controversy and have been petitioned by local actors to intervene.[6]

Evangelical associations, human rights organizations, and western governments are among the international bodies that have entered into the fray of Sri Lanka's anti-conversion debate. In each case, western governments and NGOs have sided with the Christian cause in the name of promoting religious liberty. Although protecting freedom of religion has long been a priority among human rights groups, the defense of religious liberty has become an even greater priority of the United States government since passing the "International Religious Freedom Act" (IRFA) of 1998, which mandated the establishment within the Department of State of an Office on International Religious Freedom and required the government to sanction states deemed to violate religious freedom. The move to make religious freedom a central aim of U.S. foreign policy was made in part due to concerns of evangelical Christians about persecution (Hackett, Silk, and Hoover 2000). Indeed the act itself specifically notes congressional resolutions denouncing the persecution of Christians worldwide (with the Baha'is in Iran being the only other group mentioned).

The 2005 Annual Report of the United States Commission on International Religious Freedom, the preparation of which is required by IRFA, is a large document that lists "Countries of Particular Concern" (CPC), documents examples of religious freedom violations, and makes formal recommendations to the President, Secretary of State, and the leaders of Congress. Sri Lanka is not listed as a CPC, as this designation is currently reserved for "countries whose governments have engaged in or tolerated systematic and egregious violations of religious freedom," such as Burma, China, Iran, North Korea, Saudi Arabia, and Uzbekistan, among others (U.S. Commission on International Religious Freedom 2005, 27–28). Nor has Sri Lanka been added to the commission's "Watch List." However, the annual publication of reports on religious freedom, and the responses these reports mandate. does raise the stakes for Sri Lanka, as it can ill-afford to be reprimanded and sanctioned by the U.S. government under IRFA, which could result in the delay or cancellation of official and state visits to the U.S., the reduction or termination of certain assistance funds, and the imposition of targeted or broad trade sanctions.

The 2006 Annual Report has again left Sri Lanka off its CPC list, yet it does express the need for the U.S. Commission on International Religious Freedom, which issues the Annual Report, to continue monitoring the situation in the island. The 2006 report notes a decrease in the number of attacks against churches, but it faults the government and the state's judicial system for failing to investigate and prosecute all perpetrators of religious violence (U.S. Commission on International Religious Freedom 2006, 217). As it stands, IRFA has given added impetus for U.S. diplomatic personnel, particularly Embassy officials, to discuss U.S. concerns over the anti-conversion issue in meetings with Sri Lankan government officials at the highest levels, including President Chandrika Kumaratunga (U.S. Department of State 2004). In addition, some members of the Commission made a fact-finding trip to Sri Lanka in February 2006 to investigate allegations of Christian persecution and the proposed legislation, and the Commission notes that it issued formal statements of concern in July 2005 about ongoing violence against religious minorities and the proposed anti-conversion bill, and in September 2005 about a proposed constitutional amendment prohibiting conversion of Buddhists and forcing Buddhist parents to raise their children as Buddhists (U.S. Commission on International Religious Freedom 2006, 216, 218–19).

While the U.S. government continues to monitor religious freedom issues in Sri Lanka and to express its concern over attacks on churches and the anti-conversion bill, western NGOs are registering their concerns and opposition as well. For instance, the Virginia-based Jubilee Campaign USA, an NGO advocating for religious liberty and the "persecuted church" around the world, prepared an official report based on the fact-finding mission it made to Sri Lanka on the invitation of the evangelical National Christian Fellowship of Sri Lanka. Having interviewed political leaders, a U.S. diplomat, pastors and laypeople from NCF-affiliated churches, Catholic and mainline Protestant representatives, and *one* Buddhist monk over a two-and-a-half day period in October 2004, the Jubilee Campaign concludes that there is "a continuing campaign of harassment, intimidation, vandalism and violence against the minority Christian community" by Sinhalese Buddhists that could amount to "religious cleansing" (Jubilee Campaign 2005, 4–5). The Jubilee Campaign report singles out the proposed anti-conversion legislation and the attacks on evangelical churches as evidence that religious liberty in Sri Lanka is under threat. It also asserts that it found no evidence of unethical conversions by evangelical Christians, leading the group to conclude that it subsists only in "hearsay, rumor, and anecdotal allegations" (Jubilee Campaign 2005, 27–28).

The Jubilee Campaign has evidently taken steps to assist the evangelical Christian community in Sri Lanka beyond simply raising awareness of the attacks on churches and the anti-conversion legislation. Its report notes that it arranged a meeting between NCF officials and the Human Rights Officer from the U.S. Embassy in Colombo to allow the indigenous Christian leaders to make contact with American diplomats and to share their stories of persecution (Jubilee Campaign 2005, 23). While it acknowledges that Christians could do a better job of reaching out to members of other religions and ought to enforce a code of ethical conduct for evangelism, it does suggest that militant Buddhists and monks in particular are to blame for the tensions. Significantly, it also calls upon the U.S. government to make the protection of religious liberty in Sri Lanka "a central part of all negotiations" between the two countries, especially with reference to the Millennium Challenge Account development assistance program (Jubilee Campaign 2005, 5).

Another organization, the Washington D.C.-based Becket Fund for Religious Liberty, has also investigated the state of religious freedom in Sri Lanka and has begun lobbying the U.S. government to take action. An attorney with the Becket Fund named Roger Severino was sent on a fact-finding trip to Sri Lanka, and his findings have formed the basis for the group's advocacy program. The Becket Fund has focused its efforts on arguing that the proposed anti-conversion legislation violates accepted international human rights codes, including those protecting the freedom of religion in the International Convention on Civil and Political Rights (ICCPR). In a legal analysis it sent to Sri Lanka's President and Prime Minister in 2004, the Becket Fund argued that the proposed Cabinet and JHU anti-conversion bills "egregiously violate" the rights protected by ICCPR Article 18 by infringing upon the freedom of an individual to choose a belief by obstructing his or her access to religious ideas and by extinguishing the freedom of a believer to manifest his or her beliefs regardless of the intent to convert or not (Becket Fund 2004, 3). The memorandum goes on to argue that the proposed legislation would unfairly discriminate against religious minorities who may influence someone else to convert unintentionally by their actions or who are called to manifest their belief through seeking conversions or offering religious charity. It asserts that religious expression and religious conversion are inseparable, and the anti-conversion law would effectively shut off the opportunities for religious seekers to find out information in their search for religious truth (Becket Fund 2004, 4).

The Becket Fund's legal analysis of the proposed anti-conversion laws is thorough and highly critical based on its interpretation of the legality of the acts in terms of human rights conventions. More interesting, perhaps, is the political action it is taking in conjunction with its studies. In addition to sending its appeal and critique to the leaders of Sri Lanka's government, the Becket Fund has drafted a letter to Secretary of State Condoleezza Rice and Paul V. Applegarth, the head of the Millennium Challenge Corporation, informing them of the situation in Sri Lanka and advocating the withholding of U.S. development assistance given through the Millennium Challenge Account. This letter asserts that the Government of Sri Lanka has tolerated the religious persecution fomented by "radical Buddhists" and should be held accountable for its obligation to protect the freedom of religious expression.[7] Roger Severino also prepared remarks on the "persecution" of Christians by "militant Buddhists" for a congressional briefing in Washington, D.C. on January 28, 2005. In these remarks, Severino provides a shorthand historical overview of the controversy and a report of the alleged religious discrimination handed down to Christians in Sri Lanka by two recent Supreme Court decisions and the anti-conversion bills.[8] Severino's remarks warn that the anti-conversion bill is nearing passage due to the efforts of Theravada Buddhists in Sri Lanka (who, according to him, are unlike the supposedly peaceful Tibetan and Zen Buddhists), and he urges his audience to organize a U.S. congressional delegation to visit Sri Lanka to follow-up on this issue and to request that the State Department and USAID make monthly reports on religious liberty in Sri Lanka and offer support to the religiously affiliated NGOs in tsunami relief (Severino 2005).

The significance of the statements made by western governments and NGOs on the conversion controversy in Sri Lanka is threefold. First, they establish a direct link between the anti-conversion legislation and violent attacks on the Christian minority. Although the State Department and Commission reports are generally more restrained in their conclusions, the Jubilee Campaign and the Becket Fund explicitly argue that the JHU legislators and their supporters are part of a larger Buddhist "extremist" movement that is virulently opposed to the practice and spread of Christianity in the island. Rhetorically speaking, in their view, the legislation is merely one aspect of a systematic campaign of persecution. Secondly, it illustrates the powerful intervention of western actors into the debate, raising the stakes of Sri Lanka's proposed laws prohibiting unethical conversions by explicitly alluding to possible economic and diplomatic sanctions if a law is eventually passed. And, thirdly, it is suggestive of the extent to which religious liberty is imagined in the west to comprise the freedom to proselytize and distribute Bibles (see IRFA).

IV. An analysis of the controversy

One of the most remarkable features of Sri Lanka's anti-conversion debate is the extent to which the two sides, bitterly resentful of each other, actually share a similar politics and are engaged in parallel pursuits. To be sure, there is vast disagreement between Sinhala Buddhist nationalists and evangelical Christians along with their international supporters. Both sides operated from distinctly different understandings of what conversion entails. Buddhist proponents of the acts view conversion in the active sense of encouraging (or coercing) someone to abandon their religion for a new one. Thus they advance moral arguments in support of anti-conversion legislation, claiming that it is "unethical" to use threats of infernal damnation and financial inducements to persuade people to relinquish their religion, which they view as a core part of the Sinhala cultural heritage. Evangelical Christians, in contrast, understand conversion to be a passive experience wherein one is led by a higher spiritual power to embrace a new religious identity. Accordingly, evangelicals and the religious freedom lobby emphasize the universal rights people have to adopt and manifest a religion of their choice.

Nevertheless, the politics of conversion in Sri Lanka tends to push the claims of all parties in similar directions. The basic views of the anti-conversion proponents and opponents converge in the rhetoric they employ. Buddhist nationalists and evangelical Christians both evince a common theme of victimization. Buddhist activists assert that the country's Buddhist majority is being victimized by wealthy, foreign-based missionary groups intent upon making Buddhism extinct in Sri Lanka. They warn that their tradition is in danger of disappearing due largely to the efforts of Christian missionaries to convert Sinhalas away from their native religion (Munasinghe 2004, 40). At the same time, Christian evangelicals claim that their churches and communities are being persecuted by forces aligned with an extremist Buddhist majority community seeking to criminalize their activities and expel them from Sri Lanka. Thus, because both sides depict themselves as victims in a religious conflict, they both make appeals to law to safeguard their interests. Buddhist activists seek anti-conversion legislation to protect their co-religionists against unethical conversion techniques. Meanwhile, Christians are appealing to national and international statutes to protect the freedom to manifest their faith.

Further, both sides engage in methods to essentialize and demonize their opponents. Buddhist nationalists condemn all attempts of Christians to convert Buddhists and Hindus to their religion, portraying missionaries and aid-workers as singularly bent on making them turn away from the religion of their parents for a foreign tradition. Relatively unconcerned about the activities of local, longstanding Catholic and mainline Protestant churches, Buddhist nationalists are highly suspicious of the evangelical and charismatic Christians, whom they believe are funded by wealthy foreign donors. NGO workers distributing relief aid or development assistance are also believed to be working covertly to convert needy people to Christianity by any means necessary. On the other hand, the views of Buddhist monks among evangelical Christians and their supporters are scarcely more positive. Many comments speak negatively of the entire Buddhist monkhood and portray it as uniformly hostile to Christianity. Sri Lankan Buddhists are characterized as "radical," "militant," and "extremist," drawing on much of the same loaded language frequently used by Sri Lankan Tamil nationalists to justify their calls for a separate state. In both cases, the depiction of Sinhala Buddhists as uniformly militant and chauvinistic works to make foreign intervention and mediation seem necessary, as the Buddhist majority is held to be incapable of and unwilling to recognize the rights of minorities. As such, both sides of the debate accuse their opponents of being religiously intolerant, either by actively working to convert people away from their religion or by using both legal and violent means to persecute them for their religious beliefs and traditions.

The Buddhist nationalists and Christian evangelicals reveal another similarity in their politics in how they respond to the views of their opponents. Both groups have shown themselves to be incapable of accepting the legitimacy of the arguments made against them. Buddhist nationalists are unable to acknowledge that any Buddhist might choose to convert to Christianity out of his or her free will (cf. Menon 2003, 44–45). Instead, they argue that Christian organizations, funded by large foreign bank accounts, are using subtle and devious methods such as giving bribes, brainwashing people, and targeting impressionable children (Anon. 2002b, 7; Dhammananda 2002, 6). Such rhetoric resembles earlier claims of conversion through bribery in the pre-modern Buddhist texts mentioned above. From this perspective, the evident superiority of Buddhism makes any conversion away from it to a religion of "blind faith" (as Christianity is often pejoratively described) suspect. Nor do Buddhist nationalists see their own attempts to spread the Buddha's teaching abroad and to the indigenous Vedda community in Sri Lanka as equivalent to Christian missions, arguing instead that such *dharmaduta* ("Dharma-messenger") activity consists of explaining the Dharma and letting people make up their own minds or, in the case of the Veddas, helping to revive Sinhala culture in the island (Soma 2001, 76; Dharmadasa 1990, 161–62).

Evangelical Christians also fail to acknowledge aspects of the opposing Buddhist argument. For them, conversion is a miraculous event from a divine source and has no connection with the imposition of colonialism and western power whatsoever. It is much easier for them to affirm that the opposition to Christian evangelism is part of a broader, systematic persecution of Christianity rather than for reasons that are local and historical in nature. They believe that modern Christians share no culpability in or association with the unethical tactics employed by earlier missionaries. Nor do they seem ready to acknowledge that they operate out of a position of political and economic power, drawing upon the socio-economic hegemony of North America and Western Europe for the support of their proselytizing activities in developing countries (Perera 1998, 108–09). Moreover, Christian evangelicals cannot admit that any rational person could object to their methods and motives of conversion on moral grounds. Hence, their Buddhist opponents are typically cast as "extremists" who are seemingly gripped by an anti-conversion hysteria.[9]

Furthermore, the rhetoric and logic of both sides reveals their dependence on a notion of religious identity as something discrete and more or less fixed. One is either a Buddhist or a Christian (or a Hindu or a Muslim). The attempts to legislate against unethical conversions and to manifest one's religion in an effort to bring about a conversion in others are both premised on the idea that one can clearly discern and establish an individual's religious identity. But it remains unclear just how one could establish one's identity as a Buddhist at a police station when filing a complaint of unethical conversion, or whether a Catholic could lodge a similar complaint against an evangelical Christian.[10] How would the courts rule on a case involving someone who was baptised a Christian but affirms a belief in karma and occasionally participates in Buddhist rituals of alms-givings to monks? Could a nominal Buddhist born into the religion but not actively practising it file a complaint if approached by an evangelical? Should a Buddhist who occasionally goes to a Hindu temple to worship Vishnu or Kali be considered a Hindu instead of or in addition to being a Buddhist? Whether making an accusation of unethical conversion or attempting to convert someone else, both actions tend to ignore the fact that religious identities can be fluid and difficult to pinpoint in practice.

Moreover, the positions of both sides display important shortcomings that tend to undermine some of their respective arguments. The Buddhist position that all, or at least most conversions to Christianity are facilitated by unethical means ignores the fact that some converts express rather different reasons for becoming Christians. Field interviews conducted by Dr. Sasanka Perera of Colombo University have revealed that many Buddhists and Catholics who joined evangelical Christian groups complained that their motivation for abandoning their former traditions was because of the disinterest their religious establishments had shown towards their existential and emotional needs (Perera 1998, 64–65). In these cases, the sympathy and assistance offered by evangelicals to people experiencing problems in life appears to be a major factor in conversions. At the same time, the arguments from the other side that there is no evidence of unethical conversions taking place in the island appear disingenuous. While such incidents are difficult to track and prove, there are examples of aggressive evangelizing that seem either out of ignorance or deliberate provocation to be culturally insensitive and liable to provoke violence (Perera 1998, 115–17). Perera also notes that when people experiencing general poverty or lack of access to adequate education, food, sanitation and health needs were approached with offers of help from evangelical groups, they regularly express the belief that continued support or better support would be offered to them only if they joined the group formally (Perera 1998, 67–69). In instances such as these, the line between charitable acts and unethical economic inducements can become easily blurred.

It is also clear that the politics of conversion in Sri Lanka is not wholly local. There are powerful international interests represented by NGOs and foreign governments who are invested and involved in the anti-conversion debate. And it is this fact that demonstrates how Sri Lanka's debate over conversion is implicated more broadly in the crisis of the declining authority of the nation-state in the current era. Arjun Appadurai has persuasively argued that the deeply disjunctive relationships between mass migration of peoples, technological flow, and financial transfers, among other new cultural processes, have transformed national landscapes into more fluid, less bounded spaces of cultural and economic transactions. Whereas nation-states previously enjoyed near-monopolies over the control and regulation of what their residents saw, heard, and aspired to, the transnational flow of people and electronic media has curtailed the power of nation-states to direct their respective paths of modernization (Appadurai 1996, 10). In practice, this means that the authority of a state like Sri Lanka to set the terms of its political, economic, and cultural realities is tempered by the competing interests and agendas of transnational agencies and discourses. This may involve global economic entities such as the World Bank and the International Monetary Fund, but it may also involve groups that adjudicate cultural issues. For example, the claims for human rights and multiculturalism, often championed by NGOs, may conflict with a nation-state's policies for managing its different religious and ethnic communities and defining the public sphere (Appadurai 1996, 22).

These modern realities that function to limit sharply that ability of a small nation-state like Sri Lanka to determine its own economic and cultural policies are clearly at stake in the anti-conversion debate. One aspect of the modern crisis of the nation-state involves the failure of multiculturalist values and policies to do more than just reproduce the status quo or go beyond an identity politics based on simplistic notions of sameness and difference (Radhakrishnan 2003, 40–42). In Sri Lanka, this results in endless appeals for ethnic and religious representation and consideration in government policy and patronage. Beyond the calls for protecting vulnerable citizens from unscrupulous evangelists, the critics of Christian conversions denounce the failure of Sri Lankan's politicians to protect Buddhism out of fear of being unfair to other minorities and not conforming to the wishes of western powers (Soma 2004, 5; Wijethunge 2004). The proponents of the anti-conversion bills are thus not simply "anti-Christian," although their opponents characterize them this way, but it is more accurate to describe them as seeking to marshal powerful local allegiances to resist the intrusion of global threats to their cultural sovereignty.[11] Buddhist nationalists are more "anti-conversion," since the practice itself works to subvert the religious boundaries of the state that are accepted as normative and that regularize the relations between groups of people (Viswanathan 1998, 16).

To the degree that Sri Lankan Buddhists depend on foreign assistance from western governments and NGOs, they are pressured to accept the prescriptions and mandates attached to such aid. The effect of this unequal relationship is that Sri Lanka, as an aid-receiving country, finds itself obliged to adopt the models of "civil society" that its donors wish to see. Today's donors tend to privilege and reward "good" civil society organizations such as professional groups, the Church, and human rights lobbies that support global connections and the economic status quo, while neglecting the "bad" civil society made up of ethnically inspired, more nationalistic groups (Wickramasinghe 2005, 480). An important result of these donor priorities is a move away from issues of social inequity and critiques of global forces towards a focus on issues of rights and advocacy that preclude significant social and economic changes (Wickramasinghe 2005, 482). As a result, the conditions and mechanisms for receiving aid are widely seen by Buddhist nationalists to be transforming Sri Lankan society into one modeled after western capitalist and Christian-dominated ones.

At root, this religious controversy involves a contest to define the state. Buddhist nationalists who support anti-conversion legislation are becoming frustrated with the constraints they face to protect and preserve the integrity of Buddhism and Sinhala culture in the face of what seems to them hostile and imperial forces. They seek legal recognition of the state as essentially Buddhist in nature and safeguards to preserve its preeminent status. Christian evangelicals, in Sri Lanka and across the globe, wish to require states to give unfettered access to their groups in order to be considered democratic and free, and thus entitled to development aid and other forms of economic support from the West. Human rights advocates, meanwhile, seek to insure that the state respects and guarantees internationally recognized rights to citizens of all religious communities. In this sense, Sri Lanka's conversion debate involves various, conflicting attempts to imagine and refashion the state in accordance with the values of one's community.

The politics of conversion in Sri Lanka are intricately woven within these larger debates over rights, national autonomy, and cultural sovereignty. Sinhala Buddhist nationalists reject arguments that limiting conversions would infringe on the religious freedom for evangelical Christians. And they are becoming more aware that international governments and agencies are influencing the outcome, with overt warnings of adverse consequences on aid and trade concessions should the law pass.[12] Although several international human rights instruments are generally silent on the issue of proselytism per se, there is clear momentum internationally behind ensuring the freedom to attempt to convert others to one's religion (Stahnke 2004, 648). To this end, it seems probable that the Government of Sri Lanka will try to find a compromise solution to assuage the demands of Buddhist nationalists without going so far as to provoke condemnation and sanctions from foreign governments and international bodies.

As it stands, human rights discourse on religion tends more often than not to include broad provisions to "manifest" one's religion, and thus the legal case to restrict or prohibit proselytism by Christians or anyone else is questionable. The problem with the discourse of rights, however, is that it obscures the contingencies of its arguments with a universalist appeal to human freedoms. The diverse array of opponents of Sri Lanka's anti-conversion legislation have been effective in employing the language of rights to denounce the legislation and quite possibly prevent it from being enacted. Yet such discourse does not address the open dispute over whether proselytism constitutes a "right" that exists beyond state regulation (cf. Hunter and Price 2001), nor does it acknowledge the coercive means with which some definitions of religious liberty are promoted in ways that benefit some religious groups (i.e., those that actively proselytize) while harming others.

The Sri Lankan case demonstrates that the issue of conversion is intensely political and far from a strictly personal affair. Conversion alters the boundaries and the make-up of religious communities, causing the transfer of one's allegiance to a different group. In Sri Lanka, it also comprises attempts to influence public policy either to protect local cultural norms and traditions from external forces deemed hostile or to protect the rights of religious minorities to practice their faiths without interference from states that seek to limit their activities. This conflict, moreover, illustrates that converts have become the ground for articulating competing claims of what the nation is and what rights to religion entail (Viswanathan 1998, 76). Sinhala Buddhists generally view Sri Lanka as essentially a Sinhala Buddhist state, whereas Christians in Sri Lanka and abroad generally view proselytism and religious charity as integral acts that witness to their faith. Attempts to convert and to prohibit conversion in Sri Lanka comprise agonistic practices to contest the perceived infringements upon one's human rights or the integrity of one's cultural heritage.

The ongoing legal efforts seem unlikely to succeed in resolving the conflict or addressing the constellation of larger issues and disputes pertaining to national autonomy, quality of life issues, and cultural integration that revolve around Sri Lanka's anti-conversion debate. Indeed, the legislation and threats of sanctions from donor countries are not even designed to settle the underlying arguments over preserving cultural autonomy and promoting religious freedom, which in Sri Lanka is understood differently by different groups.

Rather, it is doubtful that any legal decision could fully satisfy any party, as the law is unable to prevent individuals from converting to another religion or to condone the unfettered right to proselytize even if it is judged to offend accustomed community rights or to disrupt social harmony. As long as the conflict resorts to legal means to determine religious identity, adjudicate "ethical" behavior, and preserve the right to "manifest" one's religion, serious differences over the role of conversion in determining religious affiliation and the identity of the state will doubtless persist.

Notes

1. I would like to thank Ananda Abeysekara, Jack Llewellyn, John Schmalzbauer, and Heather Sharkey for their perceptive suggestions for improvements on an earlier draft of this essay. I also wish to thank Rohan Edrisinha, Jean-François Mayer, and Sasanka Perera for providing me with additional information related to the anti-conversion controversy in Sri Lanka. Needless to say, the views herein are mine, and any and all shortcomings in this work are my responsibility alone. I presented a version of this piece at the International Centre for Ethnic Studies in Colombo, Sri Lanka on June 30, 2006 and benefited from the questions and comments of those who were present.

2. While this contextual listing of the percentages for Sri Lanka's ethnic communities is useful for the purposes of an introduction, I am aware of the problems associated with such data. Recent critiques of contemporary scholarship on Sri Lanka point out the tendency to portray the island nation-state in essentialist terms as the home to violence and an intractable struggle between the majority Sinhalas and minority Tamils (Abeyesekara 2004, 978–79). Accordingly, some voices have responded by calling upon scholars to "dehistoricize" history and the view that ethnic communities have a constancy and causality with respect to current political events (Scott 1999, 105). The works of Abeyesekara and Scott, among others, are useful for reminding scholars of the serious problems that come with hypostasizing ethnicity and religion in Sri Lankan studies.

3. Rohan Edrisinha related this information to me in a personal communication (July 24, 2006). He also informed me of a behind-the-scenes initiative to work out a compromise by the lawyers for the JHU and the lawyers for the evangelical opponents of the bill. Another ongoing effort to resolve the controversy involves forming an inter-religious council made up of religious leaders from the country's different faiths to investigate claims of unethical religious conduct and to issue official statements and recommendations to the government. Such a council, however, would not have the force of law. Edrisinha has told me that this effort has been slowed due to disagreements over determining the representative make-up of the council.

4. It should be noted that World Vision does not openly advocate mixing aid with evangelism, noting on its website that sponsors of children who live in "sensitive countries" where Christians are a minority should not write letters using evangelistic language or make references to Jesus or the Bible in their correspondence with the children they sponsor.

5. The public notice for the appointment of the Commission of Inquiry into and Report

on the Conversion of Sri Lankan Buddhists into other religious traditions, which has been appointed by the All Ceylon Buddhist Congress, contains sixteen charges for the commission to carry out, including ascertaining the operations and sources of funding behind organizations engaged in converting Buddhists, ascertaining whether promotions or other inducements are being withheld from Buddhists because of their religion, and investigating whether certain media institutions are purposely distracting the country's youth from observing the traditional cultural norms and preparing them for conversion. Additional details about this commission may be found online at http://www.acbc.lk/ commission.htm.

6. One example of this can be found on the website of the Evangelical Fellowship of Canada (http://www.evangelicalfellowship.ca), which alerted evangelicals to the "deteriorating" situation for Christians in Sri Lanka, instructed them to pray for those Christians and that the anti-conversion law would not pass. It also contained an appeal from the NCEASL asking its Canadian brethren to write letters to the Sri Lankan High Commissioner in Canada and the Canadian Department of Foreign Affairs to protect the country's Christians and prevent the enactment of the anti-conversion law.

7. This letter may be downloaded from the Becket Fund's website at http://www.becket-fund.org/index.php/case/91.html.

8. These decisions revolved around the Supreme Court of Sri Lanka ruling in 2003 to refuse to allow two separate Christian organizations to register as corporations, claiming that a religious group could not incorporate if it was involved in proselytizing and providing material benefit.

9. The Becket Fund for Religious Liberty's website consistently characterizes Sri Lankan Buddhists in disparaging terms. Emilie Kao, the Becket Fund's Director of International Advocacy, gave a speech to the 60th Session of the United Nation's Commission on Human Rights on April 8, 2004, wherein she depicted the controversy over conversion in Sri Lanka as a "battle between those who treasure religious freedom and those who would destroy it" (htyp://www.becketfund.org/index.php/case/91.html).

10. I wish to acknowledge Ainslie Joseph of the Christian Alliance for Social Action in Athurugiriya, Sri Lanka for pointing out these potential problems with the proposed anti-conversion legislation to me.

11. It is interesting to note in this regard that in the summer of 2006 the JHU came out in support of Catholic calls to ban the showing of the film "The Da Vinci Code" in Sri Lanka, citing the need for the state to protect the "religious sensitivities" of its citizens. Such a move allowed the party to demonstrate their sympathies with the country's Catholic leaders. See Dhananjani Silva, "JHU backs Da Vinci Code ban," *Sunday Times*, May 28, 2006.

12. Confirmation of the potential international repercussions of the anti-conversion legislation appeared in a front page article entitled "US warns Lanka on Religious Bill" in the *Sunday Times* newspaper on July 31, 2005. The piece went on to explain that the US Assistant Secretary of State Christine Rocca had told Sri Lanka's ambassador to the United States that the State Department was receiving numerous messages from Senators and

Congressmen about the proposed legislation, and that the pressure was building up in the United States against the move. This report confirms the existence of a substantial lobbying effort to oppose the anti-conversion bills. The recognition of this political reality appears in an editorial by Dayan Jayatilleka published in the *Sunday Observer* newspaper on April 30, 2006. Therein, he specifically notes that if the JHU succeeds bringing the religious bill before the House and it gets approved, Sri Lanka may lose the support from the United States that it currently enjoys in trying to isolate the LTTE worldwide as a terrorist organization.

References

Abeysekara, Ananda. 2004. Identity for and against Itself: Religion, Criticism, and Pluralization. *Journal of the American Academy of Religion* 72(4): 973–1001.

Amarasekera, Lt. Col. A.S. 2004. World Vision Changes Its Strategy. *Buddhist Times* 3(2), June edition.

Anderson, Allan. 2004. *An Introduction to Pentecostalism: Global Charismatic Christianity.* Cambridge: Cambridge University Press.

Anonymous. 2002a. Why a *Buddhist Times*? *Buddhist Times* 1(1), May edition.

_____. 2002b. The Current Religious Environment in Sri Lanka: The Dangers Faced by Buddhists, What Signals to Watch and How to Respond. *Buddhist Times* 1(3), July edition.

Appadurai, Arjun. 1996. *Modernity at Large: Cultural Dimensions of Globalization.* Minneapolis, MN: University of Minnesota Press.

Bartholomeusz, Tessa J. 2002. *In Defense of Dharma: Just-War Ideology In Buddhist Sri Lanka.* London: Routledge Curzon.

Becket Fund for Religious Liberty. 2004. "Legal Memorandum." http://www.becket-fund.org/index.php/case/91.html [accessed July 26, 2005].

Berkwitz, Stephen C. 2003. Recent Trends in Sri Lankan Buddhism. *Religion* 33(1): 57–71.

_____. 2006. Buddhism in Sri Lanka: Practice, Protest, and Preservation. In *Buddhism in World Cultures: Comparative Perspectives,* ed. S.C. Berkwitz, 45–72. Santa Barbara: ABC-CLIO.

———. 2008. Resisting the Global in Buddhist Nationalism: Venerable Soma's Discourse of Decline and Reform. *Journal of Asian Studies* 67(1): 73–106.

Buddhadatta, A.P. 1959. *The Mahavansa: Pali Text together with Some Later Additions.* Colombo: M.D. Gunasena.

Coleman, Simon. 2003. Continuous Conversion?: The Rhetoric, Practice, and Rhetorical Practice of Charismatic Protestant Conversion. In *The Anthropology of Religious Conversion,* ed. A. Buckser and S.D. Glazier, 15–27. Lanham, MD: Rowman and Littlefield Publishers.

Comaroff, John L. and Jean Comaroff. 1991. *Of Revelation and Revolution: Chris-*

tianity, Colonialism, and Consciousness in South Africa, vol. 1. Chicago, IL: University of Chicago Press.

Daniel, E. Valentine. 1996. *Charred Lullabies: Chapters in an Anthropography of Violence*. Princeton, NJ: Princeton University Press.

Deegalle, Mahinda. 2004. Politics of the Jathika Hela Urumaya Monks: Buddhism and Ethnicity in Contemporary Sri Lanka. *Contemporary Buddhism* 5(2): 83–103.

Deshapriya, Sunanda and Asanga Welikala. 2004. Paradise Lost: Sri Lanka's Monks Threaten to Destroy over 2,000 Years of Buddhist Tradition and Take Down the Island's Democracy with It. *Index on Censorship* 33(4): 190–94.

De Silva, A.L. 2003. *Beyond Belief: A Buddhist Critique of Fundamentalist Christianity*. Dehiwala, Sri Lanka: Global Graphics and Printing.

De Silva, K.M. 1995. Conclusion. In *University of Peradeniya History of Sri Lanka, Volume II (c1500 to c1800)*, ed. K.M. de Silva, 553–66. Peradeniya, Sri Lanka: University of Peradeniya.

Dhammananda, Ven. Medagama. 2002. Buddhism in Confrontation with Christian Evangelism. *Buddhist Times* 1(2), June edition.

Dharmadasa, K.N.O. 1990. The Veddas' Struggle for Survival: Problems, Policies and Responses. In *The Vanishing Aborigines: Sri Lanka's Veddas in Transition*, ed. K.N.O. Dharmadasa and S.W.R. de A. Samarasinghe, 141–70. New Delhi: Vikas Publishing House.

Edirisinghe, Padma. 2005. A Universal Buddhist Movement. *Buddhist Times* 4(1), May edition.

Fernando, Antony. 1995. Understanding the "Sinhala-Buddhist" Movement in Sri Lanka: Are Buddhists anti-Christian, Are Sinhalese anti-Tamil. *Journal of Dharma* 20(2): 207–23.

Geiger, Wilhelm, trans. 1912. *The Great Chronicle of Ceylon*. London: Pali Text Society.

Guruge, Ananda, ed. 1991. *Return to Righteousness: A Collection of Speeches, Essays and Letters of the Anagarika Dharmapala*. 2nd ed. Colombo: Department of Cultural Affairs.

Hackett, Rosalind I.J., Mark Silk, and Dennis Hoover. 2000. *Religious Persecution as a U.S. Policy Issue: Proceedings of a Consultation held at Trinity College, Hartford, September 26–27, 1999*. Hartford, CT: Center for the Study of Religion in Public Life, Trinity College.

Hunter, Howard O. and Polly J. Price. 2001. Regulation of Religious Proselytism in the United States. *Brigham Young University Law Review* 2001(2): 537–74.

Jayatilleka, Dayan. 2005. What Now? *Sunday Observer*. April 30. News: 11.

Jubilee Campaign. 2005. *Fact-Finding Mission to Sri Lanka: A Report by the Jubilee Campaign USA*. Fairfax, VA: Jubilee Campaign.

Lampman, Jane. 2005. Disaster Aid Furthers Fears of Proselytizing. *Christian*

Science Monitor January 31 online edition.

Malalgoda, Kitsiri. 1976. *Buddhism in Sinhalese Society, 1750–1900: A Study of Religious Revival and Change.* Berkeley: University of California Press.

Manor, James. 1989. *The Expedient Utopian: Bandaranaike and Ceylon.* Cambridge: Cambridge University Press.

Menon, Kalyani Devaki. 2003. Converted Innocents and Their Trickster Heroes: The Politics of Proselytizing in India. In *The Anthropology of Religious Conversion*, ed. A. Buckser and S.D. Glazier, 43–53. Lanham, MD: Rowman and Littlefield Publishers.

Munasinghe, Chamika, ed. 2004. *Ape Dharma Kathikavatha.* Colombo: Dayawansa Jayakody and Company.

Nissan, Elizabeth and R.L. Stirrat. 1990. The Generation of Communal Identities. In *Sri Lanka: History and the Roots of Conflict*, ed. Jonathan Spencer, 19–44. London: Routledge.

Paranavitana, K.D. 2004. Suppression of Buddhism and Aspects of Indigenous Culture under the Portuguese and the Dutch. *Journal of the Royal Asiatic Society of Sri Lanka.* New Series, 49: 1–14.

Perera, Sasanka. 1998. *New Evangelical Movements and Conflict in South Asia: Sri Lanka and Nepal in Perspective.* Colombo: Regional Centre for Strategic Studies.

Queyroz, Fernão de. [1930] 1992. *The Temporal and Spiritual Conquest of Ceylon*, vol. 1. Trans. S.G. Perera. New Delhi: Asian Education Services.

Radhakrishnan, R. 2003. *Theory in an Uneven World.* Malden, MA: Blackwell Publishing.

Rahula, Walpola. 1974. *The Heritage of the Bhikkhu: A Short History of the Bhikkhu in Educational, Cultural, Social, and Political Life.* Trans. K.P.G. Wijayasurendra. New York: Grove Press.

Rambo, Lewis R. 2003. Anthropology and the Study of Conversion. In *The Anthropology of Religious Conversion*, ed. A. Buckser and S.D. Glazier, 211–22. Lanham, MD: Rowman and Littlefield Publishers.

Ranawaka-Das, Prema. 2002. *Why Go From Light into Darkness?: Against Conversion.* Dehiwala, Sri Lanka: Global Graphics and Printing.

Rohde, David. 2005. Mix of Quake Aid and Preaching Stirs Concern. *New York Times* January 22 edition.

Ruberu, Ranjit. 1967. Missionary Education in Ceylon. In *Educational Policy and the Mission Schools: Case Studies from the British Empire*, ed. B. Holmes, 77–118. London: Routledge and Kegan Paul.

Scott, David. 1999. *Refashioning Futures: Criticism After Postcoloniality.* Princeton, NJ: Princeton University Press.

Seneviratne, H.L. 1999. *The Work of Kings: The New Buddhism in Sri Lanka.* Chicago, IL: University of Chicago.

Severino, Roger. 2005. Relief and Religion in Post-Tsunami Sri Lanka: Prepared Remarks-Congressional Briefing (1-28-05). http://www.lankaliberty.com/index.html [accessed July 25, 2005].

Silva, Dhananjani. 2006. JHU backs Da Vinci Code ban. *Sunday Times*, May 28th issue.

Soma, Gangodawila. 2001. *Misaditu Bindina Handa*, ed. Indu Perera. Colombo: Dayawansa Jayakody and Company.

_____. 2002. *Deshaya Surakina Ran Asipatha*. Colombo: Dayawansa Jayakody and Company.

_____. 2004. Sudda langa Konda naemu Upasaka Candalayo. *Janavijaya* June 2 edition.

Stahnke, Tad. 2004. The Right to Engage in Religious Persuasion. In *Facilitating Freedom of Religion or Belief: A Deskbook*, ed. T. Lindholm, W.C. Durham, Jr., B.G. Tahzib-Lie, 619–49. Leiden: Martinus Nijhoff Publishers.

Suraweera, A. V. [1976] 1997. *Rajavaliya:Vicaratmaka Sanjñapanaya saha Sastriya Samskaranaya*. Sri Lanka: Educational Publications Department.

Tambiah, Stanley Jeyaraja. 1992. *Buddhism Betrayed?: Religion, Politics, and Violence in Sri Lanka*. Chicago, IL: University of Chicago Press.

U.S. Commission on International Religious Freedom. 2005. *Annual Report of the United States Commission on International Religious Freedom*. http://www.uscirf.gov [accessed July 20, 2005].

_____. 2006. *Annual Report of the United States Commission on International Religious Freedom*. http://www.uscirf.gov [accessed July 19, 2006].

U.S. Department of State. 2004. "Sri Lanka: International Religious Freedom Report 2004." http://www.state.gov/g/drl/rls/irf/2004/35520.htm [accessed July 20, 2005].

Viswanathan, Gauri. 1998. *Outside the Fold: Conversion, Modernity, and Belief*. Princeton, NJ: Princeton University Press.

Weerapperuma, E. 2005. Politics not for Bhikkhus – Ven. Dhammaloka Thera. *Daily News*, October 24th issue.

Wickramasinghe, Nira. 1995. *Ethnic Politics in Colonial Ceylon, 1927–1947*. New Delhi: Vikas Publishing House.

_____. 2005. The Idea of Civil Society in the South: Imaginings, Transplants, Designs. *Science and Society* 69(3): 458–86.

Wijethunge, Shan. 2004. Sangha Power!: Discussion led by Shan Wijethunge with the Venerables who registered for the Sri Lankan polls on Feb 24, 2004. http://www.jathikahelaurumaya.lk/index.php?prm=news [accessed May 14, 2005, now defunct, printed copy in library of S. Berkwitz].

CHAPTER 9

Promoting World Peace through Inner Peace: The Discourses and Technologies of Dhammakāya Proselytization

Rachelle M. Scott

In December 1998, at the intersection of Phetburi and Ratchadamri roads in the heart of the busy Pratunam shopping district of Bangkok, passers-by were confronted by a massive electronic billboard displaying flashing photographs of the Dhammakāya Temple (*Wat Phra Thammakai*), one of Thailand's largest modern temples. This grand, public slide-show moved through a sequence of images which included photographs of Dhammakāya practitioners meditating and offering gifts to monks, photographs of the Temple's new reliquary monument, the *Mahādhammakāya Chedi*, which was the site of the much-publicized "miracle in the sky," and photographs of weeping Dhammakāya practitioners looking with amazement at the sky. For tourists shopping in this area of Bangkok, which encompasses the World Trade Center (one of Bangkok's largest shopping malls) and Pantip Plaza (a paradise of technological gadgetry), the sight of such overt religious advertising must have seemed curious, especially for those who envision Buddhism as a quiet, contemplative tradition with an ethos of simplicity and renunciation. Had one reacted in this way to the in-your-face, larger-than-life automated billboard, she would not have been alone, for in 1998 and 1999 the Dhammakāya Temple was embroiled in a nation-wide controversy over its so-called aggressive marketing techniques and its dissemination of alleged heretical ideas about *nirvāṇa*.

In this essay, I explore the discourses and technologies of Dhammakāya proselytization within a context typified by the competing forces of globalization and localization. I will demonstrate how the Temple adapts its message to suit the differing needs and sensibilities of divergent local and global audiences. At the same time, I will argue that these re-envisionings of Dhammakāya Buddhism are not mutually exclusive, for the Thai form of Dhammakāya Buddhism is becoming increasingly global as "Thai-ness" itself is being contested. Following the thesis advanced in *Conversions to Modernities* (van der Veer 1996), which emphasized the integral relationship between conversions to particular ways of being religious and particular ways of being modern, my examination of Dhammakāya proselytization links conversions to Dhammakāya Buddhism (a particular way of being Buddhist) to conversions to global modernity—a process that entails a careful negotiation between being local (i.e. attractive to local Thai audiences) and global (i.e. attractive to non-Thai, non-Buddhist, and even "secular" audiences). Lastly, I will examine the controversy in Thailand over the content and methods of Dhammakāya proselytization, a controversy that involved two of Grace Kao's forms of anti-proselytization (see Chapter 4 in this volume): the anti-proselytization of appropriate means and the anti-proselytization of group protection.

Proselytization and the politics of conversion

The use of the term "proselytization" to refer to the activities of the Dhammakāya Temple may, at first glance, appear problematic. Proselytization literally entails the making of proselytes who have "come from one opinion, belief, creed, or party to another."[1] Proselytization aims at the conversion or dramatic alteration of one's religious orientation and affiliation. For some scholars, it is the strong conversion element within proselytism that distinguishes it from evangelism since the latter implies the dissemination of a particular religious view without the requisite of conversion (Beach 1999). The Thai translation and usage of the term proselytization captures this distinction. In Thai, proselytization is usually translated as *plian satsana* (literally, to change religion), and it tends to refer to the missionary activities of non-Buddhists (especially Christians and Muslims). When Thais refer to the activities of monks who disseminate the *dhamma* (the teachings of the Buddha) to Buddhists and non-Buddhists, however, they typically use the Thai verb *phoei phrae* (to spread, publicize, broadcast) to describe their efforts. Dhammakāya monks, for instance, describe their efforts to spread *wicha thammakai* (knowledge of the *dhammakāya* path) to Buddhists and non-Buddhists as an act of *phoei phrae*, not *plian satsana*. In Thailand, therefore, the usage of the English term proselytization is intimately linked to the act of radical conversion; as a result, it typically is not associated with the activities of monks who seek to spread the *dhamma* to others. The Thai usage, therefore, supports the thesis put forward by De Roover and Claerhout in this volume that the "problem of conversion" exists only within and among the traditions of Christianity, Judaism, and Islam (De Roover and Claerhout 2008).

My usage of the term proselytization to refer to Dhammakāya activities is also made problematic by the pejorative connotations of the term. Many of the standard definitions of proselytism emphasize the use of dubious motives and means as key characteristics of proselytizing activities:

> Proselytism is false or corrupt witness, using wrong methods. Proselytism is sheep-stealing with a view to enlarging one's own church and empire-building, using false motivation. Proselytism is evangelizing the wrong people, using false targets. Proselytism is interfering with the belief and religious life of other people, false tactic. Proselytism is keeping people ignorant about real faith and religion, in essence, keeping them captive in the church of the accidental birth, false confession/formalism. Proselytism is a conscious effort with the intention to win members of another church. (Beach 1999)

Beach suggests that these pejorative connotations are abundant due to "a tendency to give proselytism a sectarian connotation, by using it to refer to witness and evangelism by other religious confessions." At the same time, Beach notes that there is also a tendency to label the evangelizing efforts of one church among members of another church as "false proselytism." As we will see, critics of the Dhammakāya Temple frequently level such charges against the Temple.

Given these negative connotations and its problematic usage in reference to Buddhist teaching in Thailand, why do I choose to use the term proselytization to refer to the activities of the Dhammakāya Temple? My usage of the term is not an attempt to pass judgment on the motives and methods of the Dhammakāya Temple, for I do not attribute any intrinsic negative qualities to the term proselytization. For me, the term proselytization connotes a pro-active missionary campaign whose primary aim is to invoke a significant change in the religious thought, practice, and identity of others.[2] I prefer the term, despite its recent pejorative history, because it adequately captures the conversion element of the Dhammakāya mission to spread *wicha thammakai* throughout Thailand and around the world.[3] Dhammakāya conversion, particularly in the Thai context, is defined by the adoption and subsequent use of one method, *dhammakāya* meditation, for religious development. Dhammakāya practitioners tend to ignore other well-established meditation methods (or, in some cases, they insist that *dhammakāya* meditation incorporates all other methods). Moreover, Dhammakāya practitioners tend to be exclusively affiliated with the Dhammakāya Temple. In the past, such exclusive affiliation was due to local patronage (people would frequent temples in close proximity to their homes). In the Dhammakāya case, however, practitioners travel from all regions of Thailand (and around the world) to the main temple in Pathum Thani in order to practice a specific type of Buddhist meditation with Dhammakāya adepts. When they do, they don Dhammakāya clothing (uniforms and t-shirts) that mark them as Dhammakāya practitioners. It is because of this tendency toward exclusive practice and affiliation that I find term proselytization apposite when describing Dhammakāya missionary activities.

As we shall see, however, the methods of Dhammakāya proselytization, and the nature of Dhammakāya conversion, depend heavily on cultural and historical context. As many of the contributors in this volume attest, the terms proselytization and conversion are multivalent. While some may conclude that there is a need to delimit their meanings in reference to specific religious traditions, others prefer to use the terms while simultaneously acknowledging that their meanings and fields of reference will vary according to context. In this essay, I will explore how the discourses and technologies of Dhammakāya proselytization vary according to audience (local versus global), and how this ultimately affects the nature of Dhammakāya conversion (i.e. the nature of one's religiosity). The Dhammakāya case demonstrates how the discourses and technologies employed for the dissemination of the *dhamma* are context-sensitive; as such, they reflect the forces at play within specific cultural and historical contexts.

The missionizing forces of modern Theravāda Buddhism

The Buddhist tradition, along with Christianity and Islam, is often classified as a "missionary religion" due to its universalism (it transcends particular places, cultures, and ethnicities) and its phenomenal spread throughout the world. A contemporary map of Buddhist influence shows a small sprinkling of Buddhists in the tradition's homeland of India, but many more concentrations of Buddhists in other parts of South Asia, Southeast Asia, and East Asia, as well as a growing sphere of influence in Europe and North America. This map reflects how the dual forces of migration and proselytization have dramatically changed the Buddhist landscape over the course of the past two millennia.

Recently, however, scholars have questioned the "missionary" character of the Buddhist tradition. At the forefront of this discussion is the thesis, advanced by Jonathon Walters, that pre-modern Theravada Buddhism was not a missionary religion (Walters 1992). Walters contends that modern

Buddhist historians have mis-read the Buddha's directive that monks should wander (*carikam*, Pāli) "for the good of many people, for the happiness of many people, out of compassion for the world, for the good and the happiness of gods and men, don't two of you go by one [road]" (Walters 1992, 218).[4] According to Walters, *carikam* should not be interpreted as wandering as a "mission" to spread the dharma to others, but rather as a form of Buddhist practice or simply as another word for teaching (presumably to those already within the Buddhist fold). Walters contends that our classification of Buddhism as a "missionary religion," therefore, fundamentally misrepresents the ethos of pre-modern Theravada. Moreover, he argues that our viewing of Buddhism as a missionary religion also leads us to ignore the novelty of modern expressions of Buddhist proselytization. The missionary efforts of Dharmapala in Sri Lanka, for instance, not only conveyed a new Buddhist orthodoxy, but also redefined Buddhist practice to include proselytization as one of the primary activities of a faithful Buddhist. In other words, Walters contends that the missionary zeal of Buddhist modernists such as Dharmapala is a modern phenomenon, and that it represents a radical change in orientation within the tradition.

In a recent collection of essays on modern Buddhist missionaries, Learman and Kemper acknowledge the utility of Walters' critical examination of the categories of "mission" and "missionary," but question his restriction of the definition of a "missionary religion" to one that views proselytization as a defining and essential characteristic (Learman 2005; Kemper 2005). For them, this definition is far too limited. Clearly Buddhist monks served as "missionaries," as purveyors of the dharma, to communities with little to no previous knowledge of the Buddha's teachings. Proselytization may not have been the defining characteristic of the *sangha* in pre-modern societies, but it nevertheless existed. Having said that, Learman and Kemper recognize how the processes of modernity, colonialism, and Christian missionization have dramatically influenced the field in which Buddhist monks and laypersons advance their religious convictions and identities.

Two examples that highlight the effects of modernity on the content, style, and purpose of Buddhist proselytism are the missionary efforts of Anagarika Dharmapala (1864–1933) in Sri Lanka and the modern "development" monks of Thailand. In the first example, Dharmapala's promotion of a reformed version of Theravāda Buddhism in Sri Lanka emerged within the contexts of British colonial rule and active Christian proselytization. His campaign of religious reform sought not only to purify the tradition but also to fortify the tradition against considerable external threats. Sri Lanka had endured four hundred years of colonial rule (the Portuguese and Dutch preceded the British), which "made Sri Lanka one of the most thoroughly missionized societies in the world, as each wave of Europeans established schools, converted people, and attended to small communities of the faithful" (Kemper 2005, 22). Given this context, it is not surprising that Dharmapala's reformist Buddhism mirrored the Protestantism of his Christian contemporaries, with its emphasis on canonical Pāli texts (over and against vernacular texts and rituals), its critique of contemporary monastic practice, and its rejection of "magical Buddhism" and the worship of the devas.[5] Like Christian Protestantism, it promoted a this-worldly asceticism whose aim it was to produce "respectable," "rational" and "moral" Sinhalese Buddhists. Unlike Protestantism, however, Dharmapala maintained that this reformation would be accomplished through the efforts of the *sangha* (Seneviratne 1999, 36). Of course, Dharmapala argued that the *sangha* needed to undergo a process of purification first in order to purge the *sangha* of its "traditional" trappings and to instruct monks in "proper" Buddhism, but once that was accomplished, these revitalized Sinhalese monks could then disseminate the *true* dharma to the laity. With this rejuvenated system of moral and mental training, Sinhalese Buddhists could then regain their cultural pride, which had been devastated by centuries of colonialism. Sinhalese monks and laypersons could become patriots "for the preservation of our nation, our literature, our land, and our most glorious religion, at whose source our fore-fathers drank deep for nearly seventy generations..." (Dharmapala 1965, 501).

Dharmapala became a new kind of *dharmaduta* (messenger of the dharma), one whose proselytization was aimed at teaching Sinhalese Buddhists not only the "true" form of dharma, but also practical knowledge about modern life. As Kemper points out, Dharmapala's promotion of Buddhist reform entailed a new mode of proselytization: "Dharmapala redefined the nature of a Buddhist sermon (Pali: bana), sloughing off the incantatory parts and reducing the night-long act merit making to something resembling a Christian sermon (dhammadeśena)" (Kemper 2005, 29). This reformation of teaching styles also affected the content:

> To Sinhala audiences, he offered moral instruction and practical advice
> about handling money, table manners, and personal hygiene. For Western
> audiences, preaching in a way that resembled a Christian sermon made it an
> easily recognized social practice. Clarity allowed the brilliance of the Bud-
> dha's teaching to be easily communicated, and nothing was lost, he thought,
> by sloughing off the repetitive and time-consuming quality of the traditional
> form. (Kemper 2005, 29)

Dharmapala's proselytization both at home and abroad clearly reflected his modernist agenda of elevating the consciousness of Sinhalese Buddhists and countering the prevailing negative stereotypes of Buddhism put forward by

Western colonialists and missionaries.

Another example of modern Buddhist proselytization is the government-sponsored missionary work of Thai monks in the north, northeast, and southern provinces—those areas on the periphery of Bangkok's authority. The first wave of this proselytization in the late nineteenth and early twentieth centuries involved the sending of modern reformist monks from the *Thammayutnikai* throughout Thailand in an effort to homogenize Buddhist practice within the kingdom, and to secure central authority over local abbots.[6] Although Thailand was not subjected to direct European colonization, it nevertheless was influenced by the forces of colonization and Western imperialism, which necessitated the centralization of power in Bangkok. One expression of this was the dissemination of a new Buddhist orthodoxy through the missionizing efforts of *Thammayutnikai* monks.

The second wave of this government-sponsored proselytization began in the 1960s with the creation of the *thammathut* (*dharmaduta*, Pāli) and *thammacarik* (*dhammacarika*, Pāli) programs in Thailand. These programs sent Bangkok monks to the periphery in order to aid the government in its program of national development. Among other things, they were to aid in the shaping of a national identity among peripheral groups and thereby strengthen ties to the centralized political establishment. The government saw the Buddhist *sangha* as a safeguard against alien ideologies, especially in the north and northeast where Thais were most susceptible to "subversive elements." The *thammathut* (ambassador of dharma) program was established by the Department of Religious Affairs in 1965. The purpose of the program, according to a catalogue from Mahāchulalongkorn University, was to aid "community development." In addition to teaching Buddhism, the Thammathut monks were to demonstrate how the developmental goals of the nation applied to their daily lives. Charles Keyes argues that "the main impact of the program has been to provide villagers in these areas with clear evidence that the Sangha approves and supports the economic development efforts of the government" (Keyes 1971, 561). The *thammacarik* (wandering dharma) program started in 1964, and its aim was to convert tribal peoples to Buddhism, namely the Meo, Yao, Lisu, Lahu, Akha, Karen, and T'in peoples. These conversions were to aid the central government in asserting its influence over these northern tribes in matters relating to social and economic policy, as well as engendering a sense of national loyalty (Keyes 1971, 564). These *thammathut* and *thammacarik* monks were not merely messengers of the dharma, they were messengers of Thai nationalism; they constituted a force against communism and ethnic separatism.

Both Dharmapala and the modern missionary monks of Thailand demonstrate how the forces of modernity influenced both the content and technologies of Buddhist proselytization in the nineteenth and twentieth centuries. Today, new forces are influencing Buddhist proselytization in the twenty-first century. They are the forces of globalization, particularly global communication and the global economy. While these forces are broadly influencing the lives of Buddhists around the world, a select number of temples and new Buddhist movements are promoting a global Buddhism that expressly embraces aspects of this global transformation. Soka Gakkai, Foguang Shan, and the Dhammakāya Temple are all examples and products of this transformation.[7] All three movements actively promote their distinctive messages to audiences throughout the world, while simultaneously seeking to create and maintain their place within the religious landscape of their local communities. While all Buddhists must balance the competing forces of globalization and localization in their constructions of religious identity and authority, those who proselytize on a global scale face the added challenge of negotiating multiple identities to varied audiences.

Dhammakāya proselytization

The Dhammakāya Temple is one of the largest temples in Thailand; in fact, one might classify it as a mega-temple, for it resembles the explicitly modern and larger-than-life qualities of mega-churches in the United States. It began in 1970 as a small meditation group (a *samnak*) devoted to the technique of the late Luang Pho Sot of Wat Paknam. From this humble origin, it has grown into a large complex that services hundreds of thousands of practitioners in Thailand and around the world. When one arrives at the Temple, in Pathum Thani, a suburb of Bangkok, one is greeted by a fifty-foot tall billboard depicting the Dhammakāya insignia. After passing through the entrance, one is immediately struck by the sheer size of the Temple compound with its large parking lots, its assembly hall (which can house up to 300,000 people), and condominium-style monastic residences. On Buddhist holidays, the Temple grounds overflow with families, buses, and monks from around the country. Greeters are strategically placed in the parking lot to welcome "seasoned" practitioners and newcomers alike. Loudspeakers and television sets cover the expanse of the assembly hall in order for everyone to hear and view monks preaching at the front. At lunchtime, laypersons join long queues to receive food and water from volunteers. On special occasions, tens of thousands of monks and laypersons pose before official Temple photographers in order to be immortalized in one of the Temple's popular publicity photographs. The sheer size of the Temple and its congregation speak to the enormous success of the Temple in marketing its distinctive practice to local and national audiences, and more recently, to global audiences throughout the world.

Two reasons for the Dhammakāya Temple's success has been its ability to package traditional practices, such as meditation and merit-making, in modern garb, and the Temple's promotion of these practices through modern mass media (books, videos, audiocassettes, the Internet, billboards, mass-mailings, radio and television). One Dhammakāya pamphlet reads:

> The Buddhist temple traditionally has a significant role in the Thai community. The temple is a centre to teach and exemplify ethical practice that is an implicit part of everyday life… This temple perpetuates the temple's traditional role but is characterized by adherence to the Dhammakaya tradition of meditation and adaptation of traditional values to modern society.[8]

The adaptation of traditional values to modern society includes an embracing of modern technology and modern standards of living. Dhammakāya monks often don expensive foreign-made robes, acquire business degrees, and appear on radio and television programs, while prominent laypersons drive expensive cars and exchange business cards.

Another principle index of the modern character of the Temple is its promotion of Dhammakāya meditation (*wicha thammakai*, Thai; *vijjā dhammakāya*, Pāli) for all practitioners. Unlike traditional Thai temples, which reserved meditation practice for monks and exceptionally pious laypersons, the Dhammakāya Temple recommends meditation for everyone— monks and laypersons, men and women, children and the elderly. As with modern Theravāda lay meditation movements in Sri Lanka and Myanmar, the Dhammakāya Temple offers a streamlined form of meditation that does not require the rigors of traditional monastic practice and study.[9] Dhammakāya meditation enables practitioners to access "the body of insight that exists in every sentient being,"[10] which can improve one's relationships, occupational skills and health, and thereby lead to happiness and prosperity. Temple publications provide detailed descriptions of the technique, and commonly display photographs of practitioners during meditation. One such photograph is of a family—a mother, father and two daughters, donning crisp, white Dhammakāya uniforms, meditating outside near a tranquil stream, with serene expressions on their faces.[11] This photograph speaks to the Temple's emphasis on meditation as the principal religious practice for all people (regardless of age, occupation and religion), as well as the Temple's marketing of Dhammakāya Buddhism as a modern alternative to traditional Thai temple Buddhism, which is often tacitly portrayed as out-dated and out-of-touch with the concerns of modern life.

The modern character of the Temple is also exemplified in its active proselytization of Dhammakāya Buddhism throughout the country and around the world. The active agent of this proselytization is the Dhammakāya Foundation, which is comprised of high-ranking Dhammakāya monks and laypersons who work in concert to promote the Temple and its practices. At the head of the Foundation are Phra Dhammachayo (the abbot of Wat Phra Dhammakāya and President of the Foundation) and Phra Tatthacheevo (the assistant abbot of the Dhammakāya Temple and Vice President of the Foundation). Over the past three decades the Dhammakāya Foundation has created an impressive bureaucratic machine devoted to the maintenance and promotion of the Temple. It has five divisions: an administrative center that handles accounts and personnel; a support center which oversees such things as construction, public maintenance, ritual management, registration, receptions, bus services, flower decoration, and cleaning; a fund mobilization division; an education division which deals with foreign affairs, the student *dhamma* training program, and educational materials; and the propagation division that serves to promote the dissemination of Dhammakāya practice (Apinya 1993, 162–63). It is through the Dhammakāya Foundation that the Temple has been able to spread its message of *wicha thammakai*. According to the Foundation's web-site, it has seven primary objectives:

1. To propagate the Dhammakaya meditation technique to the general public regardless of race, nationality, and religion in order to bring peace to the world,

2. To promote and support Buddhist studies,

3. To promote and support Dhamma education among monks, novices, laymen, laywomen, and the general public,

4. To provide general support for monks, novices, laymen, and laywomen of Wat Phra Dhammakaya as appropriate,

5. To build and maintain World Dhammakaya Centre,

6. To build and maintain Wat Phra Dhammakaya,

7. To build and maintain an academic institute that offers all levels of education: pre-school, elementary school, middle school, high school, vocational school, and university to provide intensive Dhamma education and training in addition to normal curriculum (in the near future).[12]

These stated objectives mix support of Dhammakāya institutions and practitioners, which is a common function for temple bureaucracies, with an active campaign to foster "world peace" around the globe through the spread of its distinctive meditation method. The importance of Dhammakāya proselytization within the broader sphere of Temple activities is made evident by its placement at the beginning of the list of objectives. Most recently, the aim of Dhammakāya proselytization has led to the creation of a new satellite television station, DMC (Dhammakāya Meditation Channel), which broadcasts meditation instruction, Dhammakāya news, sermons, and children's programming to temples and homes in Thailand and across the globe.

The creation of the World Dhammakāya Center

The global aspirations of the Dhammakāya Temple are also reflected in its creation of the World Dhammakāya Center, which serves as an international center for Buddhist study and practice. About ten years ago, Phra Thatthacheevo, the assistant abbot of the Temple, announced that, "The Catholics have their Vatican, the Moslems their Mecca, we Buddhists therefore await our World Thammakaay Center" (Apinya, 154). As of 2007, the Temple has made great strides towards the completion of its World Dhammakāya Center as it has now finished the construction of three new buildings: an assembly hall that covers over forty acres, and which is lauded as the "largest public building in the world;" the *Mahādhammakāya Chedi*, which contains relics of the Buddha and which serves as a focus for communal ritual; and the Phramongkolthepmuni Memorial Hall, which is dedicated to the life and teachings of Luang Pho Sot, the monk who "re-discovered" the Dhammakāya meditation technique.

The creation of the World Dhammakāya Center marks a transformation in the Dhammakāya community from a distinctively Thai Buddhist movement to a global movement that crosses national and religious boundaries. This shift in identity, however, is not entirely new, for the Temple has always maintained a broader conceptualization of its religious field than the average Thai temple. Most Thai temples service local communities, but the Dhammakāya Temple has purposively sought to draw its membership from all over Thailand by inviting monks and laypersons from other temples to participate in its services. In recent years, the Temple has established centers in provinces throughout Thailand while maintaining the locus of its authority in Pathum Thani. Donald Swearer suggests that the Dhammakāya Temple "proposes in effect to recreate the old galactic polity" with the Pathum Thani temple at the center of power (Swearer 1991, 657). In the past, therefore, the Dhammakāya Temple sought to broaden its field from a relatively small area in Pathum Thani to the entire country. With the creation of the World Dhammakāya Center, however, the Temple is now reaching beyond Thailand to emigrant Thais and foreigners in countries throughout the world. Once again, in the words of Phra Thattacheevo, the World Dhammakāya Center will be like Mecca and the Vatican; it will become, in the eyes of its practitioners, the locus of Buddhist practice in the world.

Dhammakāya proselytization within Thailand

With this re-conceptualization of the Temple as a global center for Buddhist practice, however, the Temple did not entirely abandon its identity as a Thai Buddhist temple. Despite its global-laden rhetoric, most Dhammakāya practitioners are Thais living within Thailand. As a result, the Temple's marketing discourses are replete with narratives entrenched within Thai Buddhist culture. The automated Pratunam billboard at the corner of Phetburi and Ratchadamri roads, for instance, advertised an attractive package of Dhammakāya meditation mixed with traditional merit-making practices and popular stories of miracles and amulets.

The Temple's promotion of its *Mahādhammakāya Chedi*, the second project in the temple's construction of the World Dhammakāya Center, provides one example of the use of these narratives. First, the *chedi* was to become one of the main focal points for Dhammakāya meditation. Temple publications describe it as a *sunruamplangsattha* (a center for the power of "faith"),[13] which would draw people from around the world to promote, in the words of one popular slogan, "world peace through inner peace."[14] This slogan emphasized the importance of Dhammakāya meditation for the realization of the Temple's goals of personal and social transformation and the role of the *Mahādhammakāya Chedi* as a catalyst for this transformation. The linkage of the *chedi* with meditation and transformation was made explicit in one of the Temple's t-shirts which depicted an image of the *chedi*, surrounded by practitioners in deep meditation, with the slogan "world peace through inner peace" written underneath.

The *Mahādhammakāya Chedi* was promoted as a preeminent field of merit (*puñña khetta*) for all potential donors. The Temple utilized modern technology to spread its message and solicit donations, but its advertisements employed the traditional Theravāda narratives of merit-making that correlate acts of *dāna* (generous giving) with beneficial results. Donations for the building of a temple were considered by many to be the pinnacle act of *dāna*, and as such, they were seen as a great source of merit (*bun*, Thai; *puñña*, Pāli). In Southeast Asia, the karmic theory of action centers on merit-making (*tam bun* in Thai). Traditionally, the making of merit has meant offering gifts to the *sangha* (the order of monks), gifts that can range from the daily offering of food, to new robes during the rainy season, or the commissioning of a Buddha image or monument.

In the campaign for the construction of the *chedi*, the Temple emphasized how individual donations would benefit both Buddhism and the individual donor. The front page of one Dhammakāya pamphlet reads, "How YOU can become one part of the Dhammakāya [Chedi]...and the Dhammakāya [Chedi] can become a part of you." The inside of the pamphlet reads: "Ever since ancient times, Buddhists have always come together to build holy sanctuaries." The pamphlet explains that Buddhists construct *chedis* in order to pass down knowledge of the triple gem (the Buddha, *dharma*, and *sangha*) to future generations, and thereby ensure the continuation of the tradition. We are told that the design of the *Mahādhammakāya Chedi* follows the style of the oldest surviving Indian Buddhist *chedi* at Sañchi. On the right side of the pamphlet is another image of Phra Dhammakāya, with the words, "Claim your own inner refuge for eternity." Here the pamphlet refers to the commissioning of individual Buddha images that bear the names of their donors. These images are now permanently affixed to the exterior of the *chedi* and housed within its interior. Since these images were made by a special process that combined silicon bronze with titanium gold ion plating, they should, according to the Temple, last at least 1,000 years.

This pamphlet presents two main themes: first, the act of donating money for the building of a *chedi* is an act of great piety that has been done "ever since ancient times," and second, that such donations will engender benefits for the donors. The idea of "being a part of tradition" links contemporary donors to the narratives of exemplary donors of the past, such as Anānthapindika and Visākhā.[15] There is, however, one notable distinction and the Temple refers to this explicitly. In the past, only wealthy patrons could afford to build a *chedi* or commission a Buddha image. However, at the Dhammakāya Temple, an individual alone does not need to sponsor the entire project, only a portion of it. For instance, whereas there is a main Buddha image enclosed within the *chedi*, the Temple arranged for the creation of one million small Buddha images that were commissioned by individual patrons. For 30,000 baht (which in 1998 would have been about $750), one's personal Buddha image was placed on the top of the dome; for 10,000 baht (about $250), one's image was housed in the interior of the *chedi*. Moreover, if the patron did not have sufficient funds to pay up front, she could opt for the Temple's installment plan. Since each image has the name of the donor inscribed on the base, the *chedi* represents not only the *triratanā* (the triple gem of the Buddha, the *dhamma*, and the *sangha*), but also the collective generosity of the donors.

The second theme relayed in this pamphlet is that of "receiving benefits" for donations. This idea draws upon the rich narrative tradition of exemplary donors and the rewards that they received for their generosity—rewards such as good health, increased wealth, or a heavenly rebirth. These rewards derive from the cultivation of merit in this life or in past lives. Generosity (*dāna*) is one of the main bases of merit, along with *sīla* (ethical conduct) and *bhāvanā* (meditation). While the fruits of one's merit are typically unknown, Dhammakāya Temple publications make them explicit. On the back page of one pamphlet is a list of benefits that one might gain by commissioning a personal Dhammakāya image, including wealth and prosperity, personal beauty, career success, purity and radiance of mind, and endowment with worldly riches, heavenly riches, and the riches of *nirvāṇa*.

The Dhammakāya Temple's promotion of the *Mahādhammakāya Chedi* as a preeminent field of merit was not the only theme that played well to Thai audiences. The Temple tapped into the popular "cult of amulets" in Thailand by marketing its own distinctive amulet, the *Phra Mahāsiriratdhatu amulets.*[16] Like other amulets in Thailand, these amulets are thought to possess special powers. Temple publications suggest that these amulets will help donors to overcome problems and to obtain wealth and possessions. In fact, in April of 1998, the Temple started to publish magazines entitled, "*Anuphap Phra Mahāsiriratdhatu*" (the Power of the *Mahāsiriratdhatu* amulet). These publications, which were distributed on a monthly basis, contain stories of miraculous events in the lives of people who possessed these amulets— there were miraculous healings (people with cancer or disabilities are cured), miraculous rescue stories (people who escape severe accidents without injury), and stories of wealth and prosperity (businesses that go bankrupt, but then remarkably recover).

The Dhammakāya Temple's distribution of magical amulets played into popular narratives of religious power and miraculous events. This theme continued in the Temple's promotion of miraculous events at the Temple, most notably the "miracle in the sky" which purportedly occurred on September 6, 1998 on the grounds of the *Mahādhammakāya Chedi*. On this day, the sun was reported to have disappeared from the sky, and then was replaced by an image of Luang Pho Sot, the "re-discoverer" of the dhammakāya meditation technique. The Temple was not shy about advertising this event in the press. In a full-page advertisement in the *Bangkok Post*, the Temple described the miracle, while simultaneously advertising the amulet. On the top of the page was a picture of the *chedi* with thousands of supporters around it, and in the sky is a super-imposed picture of a golden Luang Pho Sot. Underneath this picture were photos of Dhammakāya practitioners crying as they looked into the sky. Two long testimonials describing the miracle were on the bottom half of the page, while at the right-hand side there was an image of the *Mahāsiriratādhatu* amulet and a description of its powers.

This advertisement aptly displays the Temple's strategic packaging of Dhammakāya meditation alongside popular forms of Thai religiosity, namely merit-making, the collection of amulets and tales of miraculous events, for the wider Thai populace in its proselytizing activities. During the campaign for the construction of the *chedi*, the Dhammakāya Temple wanted to broaden its field of proselytization to include Thais who had little to no previous experience with Dhammakāya meditation. Thais, who otherwise might not be interested in Dhammakāya practice, responded to narratives of merit-making, amulets, and miracles. While these technologies of proselytization proved effective for a period of time, we will see later how they became the subject of heated debate within Thai public discourse.

Global Dhammakāya

The narratives of Dhammakāya meditation, merit-making, amulets and miracles were not confined to Thais living within Thailand. The Temple promoted these ideas to emigrant and migrant Thais in centers throughout the world, through the distribution of Temple publications, such as the popular *Anuphap Phra Mahāsiriratdhatu* magazines, through resident and guest Dhammakāya monks, and through the use of the Internet. The Dhammakāya Foundation's Thai language website provides detailed information on home Temple activities, and it provides downloads of weekly teachings by renowned Dhammakāya monks. Moreover, the Foundation provides a live broadcast over the Internet of Dhammakāya activities in Thailand, which can be viewed at one's local Dhammakāya center. Needless to say, the audience is predominantly Thai.

At the same time, however, these international centers service non-Thais who are attracted to Dhammakāya meditation, but who have little to no interest in stories of powerful amulets and miracles in the sky. The first goal of the Dhammakāya Foundation is "to propagate the Dhammakaya meditation technique to the general public regardless of race, nationality, and religion in order to bring peace to the world." To this end, the Foundation has established centers throughout Thailand and abroad. The first international center was established in 1992 in Azusa, California; since then, centers have been founded in twenty other countries in Europe, the Middle East, Southeast Asia, and East Asia. According to the Foundation's website, "each center is staffed by qualified teachers of meditation from the Dhammakāya Foundation headquarters in Thailand, and offers a range of activities for training in the quality of mind for people of all ages."[17] Therefore, the principal practice for non-Buddhist locals from these countries is Dhammakāya meditation.

At the Dhammakāya center in Chicago, where I attended a six-week course in Dhammakāya meditation in the spring of 2001, non-Thai practitioners were introduced to the techniques of Dhammakāya meditation outside of the context of Thai religious philosophy and practice. In this cultural context, Dhammakāya meditation was couched in the language of healthy living and self-improvement, and we were informed that one need not "convert" to Buddhism in order to reap the health benefits of Dhammakāya meditation. Each session began with a series of yoga poses, followed by meditation practice, and a discourse by the instructor on the benefits of meditation. On one occasion we received excerpts from one of Andrew Weil's popular books on healthy living in which he writes about the benefits of simple breathing meditation. [18] The self-improvement discourses linked our own personal development to the world community, emphasizing how the power of our collective meditation could influence the efforts for peace around the globe. While photographs of the Dhammakāya Temple in Thailand were present at the center, there were no references to the Temple at our sessions. Rather, the focus was on the microcosm of each individual and the macrocosm of the world. The distinctive Thai qualities of the Dhammakāya Temple, therefore, were not apparent to non-Thais interested in Dhammakāya meditation.

In its platform of universal proselytization, the Dhammakāya Foundation de-emphasizes the Thai Buddhist aspects of Dhammakāya practice, namely the importance of monasticism, merit-making, miracles, and amulets. Even the Temple's slogan, "World Peace through Inner Peace," is sufficiently vague as to allow for non-Buddhist interpretations. For Thai audiences, "inner peace" easily translates to Buddhist meditation practice, but for non-Thais, this phrase can be situated within secular discourses on healthy living and self-improvement. On the Azusa, California website, for instance, the benefits of meditation that are listed are "reducing stress, enhancing memory, creating mental clarity, experiencing calm, joy, and inner pace, gaining self improvement, and harmonizing body and mind." [19] Dhammakāya meditation, for these individuals, therefore need not be understood within a religious framework at all. In fact, the Asuza website distinguishes between information for Buddhists (which includes a calendar of important Buddhist holidays and merit-making opportunities) and information for non-Buddhists (which details meditation courses and retreats that are explicitly labeled as "non-religious"). Similarly, "world peace" is promoted as a universal human goal, which transcends national and religious differences. One instance of this global message is found in a Dhammakāya music video, which displays images of the world, with children holding hands and doves flying in the air, while strands of the following lyrics fill the background:

> Peace on earth it's a dream we all share; only now it's close to reality; would you listen carefully and spare a little bit of your time? Meditation—haven't you heard that it is the key word for everyone?; it is the next human evolution, and you would be the one to share it with the world? Now we join together and make it happen. Let's make the world at peace through meditation." [20]

In this vein, the Dhammakāya Temple taps into universal discourses of world peace promoted by other Buddhist leaders, such as the Dalai Lama, Thich Nhat Hahn, and Soka Gakkai, who insist that the goal of world peace transcends religious, ethnic, and cultural divides.

While the Dhammakāya Temple's discourses often obfuscate the religious aspects of Dhammakāya practice for its world audience, the Temple remains steadfastly committed to promoting its practice of Dhammakāya meditation. In this respect, the Temple's message of world peace differs from that of the Dalai Lama and Thich Nhat Hahn. David Chappell argues that Buddhists like the Dalai Lama and Thich Nhat Hahn tend to "nurture a sense of global community" rather than demand a particular religious orthodoxy or orthopraxy (Chappell 1999). For Chappell, this reflects a primary difference between Buddhist and Christian forms of proselytization. The Dhammakāya Temple, however, does put forth a single practice, dhammakāya meditation, as the most effective means for bringing about personal, social, and world transformation. One may interpret meditation from either a religious or secular perspective, but one must still follow the Dhammakāya technique. Once again, it is the Temple's exclusive promotion of *wichā thammakai* that has led me to describe its activities as acts of proselytization. And in this respect, Dhammakāya proselytization resembles that of Soka Gakkai International with its focus on the exclusive practice of *daimoku* for individual and global transformation (Seager 2006).

Conclusion: The Dhammakāya controversy and its implications

The discourses and technologies of Dhammakāya proselytization have been shaped by the competing forces of local Thai culture and globalization. Within the Thai context, the Temple has drawn from popular narratives of merit-making, miracles, and amulets to extend its field of proselytization. In the global context, however, the Temple has abandoned these features in order to cast as large of a net as possible—to reach individuals interested in "world peace" and "inner peace," but who are not necessarily Buddhist "converts." In both local and global contexts, the Temple has utilized sophisticated media as a means by which to disseminate its message.

The Dhammakāya methods of proselytization, however, are not without detractors. In fact, in 1998 and 1999 they were one source of criticism in a series of allegations leveled against the Temple. In this volume, Grace Kao identifies five distinct types of anti-proselytization; of these, the anti-proselytization of appropriate targets and tactics and anti-proselytization of group protection best describe the rationale behind many of the criticisms aimed at the Dhammakāya Temple's discourses and technologies of proselytization. According to Kao, the anti-proselytization of appropriate tactics finds fault with the methods of a particular group, especially the "targeting of the particu-larly vulnerable populations for religious conversion or the offering of material inducements to bring about the same" (Kao 2008: 78). In the Dhammakāya case, critics condemned the scale of the Temple's proselytization—its use of billboards, mass-mailings, television, and "direct-sale" marketing in order to extend its reach to Buddhists throughout the nation. These activities, accord-ing to some critics, were clear examples of the commercialization of Buddhism (*phuttha phanit*). During the peak of the controversy in 1999, many people with whom I spoke at temples around Thailand described the Temple's activities as *thurakit* (business), not *satsana* (religion). They cited stories printed in the var-ious newspapers or discussed on television that "proved" that the Temple was interested only in money, not religion. Stories in popular newspapers involv-ing the "purchase" of honorary sashes, installment plans for large donations, the permanent millionaire club, and the infamous "asset sucking amulets" were popular subjects of discussion. It is not irrelevant that these questions regarding Dhammakāya proselytization arose during the Asian economic cri-sis. As the Temple was expanding its scope of proselytization, the newspapers were reporting on the decline of donations at other Buddhist temples. While other temples were struggling to receive enough food or to pay their monthly bills, the Dhammakāya Temple advertised its *Mahādhammakāya chedi* on their enormous automated billboard in the heart of Bangkok.

While the charges of "selling merit" occupied a prominent space within the daily newspapers due to their sensational character, another criticism was leveled against the Temple that focused more on the integrity of Thai Bud-dhism. Some critics, especially those who were monks or Buddhist scholars, classified the Dhammakāya Temple's interpretation of *nirvāṇa* as a place of perpetual bliss as heretical and akin to Mahāyāna conceptions of *nirvāṇa*. As such, they argued that the dissemination and popularization of this idea could lead to the downfall of the Thai *sangha*.[21] These critics were concerned with the impact of these alleged "heretical" ideas on both monastic and lay Thai Buddhists. Kao's category of anti-proselytization for group protection clearly fits these charges against the Dhammakāya Temple. Kao describes the premise behind this type of anti-proselytization as the perceived need to safeguard one's self and one's community from the corrosive influences of others—"be they proselytizers from afar or even dissidents from within " (Kao 2008: 87). Kao argues that this type of anti-proselytization contains "a logic that combines ethnic essentialism with entitlements that ances-tral precedence purportedly provides." In the Dhammakāya case, the logic behind the anti-proselytization for group protection combines a nationalis-tic essentialism with a specific conception of authentic Theravāda Buddhist practice and doctrine.

These criticisms of Dhammakāya proselytization highlight an important point in our analyses of the phenomenon of proselytization. As the concepts of "mission," "missionary," "proselytization," and "conversion," are fluid in relation to historical and cultural contexts, so too is the role and place of proselytization within traditions at specific moments in history. What is and is not an appropriate method of proselytization, and what is and is not a legitimate motive for proselytization, are matters of contestation within religious communities. The Buddha's message of going forth "for the good of many, for the happiness of the many, out of compassion for the world" (*bahujanahitāya bahujanasukhaāya lokānukampāya*) therefore, not only raises questions concerning the missionary ethos of Theravāda Buddhism, it also highlights how disparate Buddhist communities might assess the actions which purportedly lead to the good and happiness of the many.

Notes

1. This definition was taken from the Oxford English Dictionary, s.v. "proselyte."

2. Ted Stahnke similarly tries to avoid the negative connotation of proselytyism as an act of coercision by defining it as an "expressive conduct undertaken with the purpose of trying to change the religious beliefs, affiliation, or identity of another" (Stahnke 2004, 256).

3. The neutral use of the term proselytization, therefore, resembles that of the term "fundamentalism" in the multi-volume series of the Fundamentalism Project (University of Chicago). Marty and Appleby, the editors of the series, use the term fundamentalism to refer to the activities of various religious groups that share common characteristics, despite its negative connotations and its historical linkage to Christianity. See Marty and Appleby (1991).

4. The entire passage from the Vinaya (IV, 20) reads: Go forth for the good of the many, for the happiness of the many, out of compassion for the world, for the welfare, the good and the happiness of gods and men. Let no two of you go in the same direction. Teach the Dharma which is beautiful in the beginning, beautiful in the middle and beautiful at the end. Proclaim both the letter and the spirit of the holy life completely fulfilled and perfectly pure. This translation was taken from Venerable S. Dhammika in *The Buddha and his Disciples*, which is available electronically at http://www.buddhanet.net/e-learning/buddhism/disciples06.htm [accessed on September 13, 2005].

5. Dharmapala's reformist Buddhism was also influenced by Colonel Olcott, one the founders of the Buddhist Theosophical Society in Sri Lanka. Olcott viewed contemporary Sinhalese Buddhism as a degenerate form of the tradition. He sought to reform the content of Sinhalese Buddhism and to mobilize Sinhalese Buddhists, both monastic and lay, to become active participants in the revival of their tradition. Kemper argues that Olcott followed the lead of Christian missionaries by stimulating the revival through institutional reforms such as fund-raising at church bazaars, the creation of Buddhist Sunday schools,

and making the Buddha's birthday a public holiday (Kemper 2005, 26). Olcott's platform of revival led him to take Dharmapala under his wing, fostering new conceptions of Buddhist doctrine, practice, and identity.

6. For an extensive study of the use of the Thammayutnikai for the purpose of religious centralization, see Taylor (1993).

7. For excellent descriptions of the proselytization activities of Soka Gakkai, see Hammond and Machacek (1999) and for Foguang Shan, see Chandler (2004, 2005).

8. From a *Dhammakāya* pamphlet distributed at the main temple in Pathum Thani, Thailand in January 1999.

9. For more information on new lay meditation movements in Sri Lanka, see Bond (1988, 2003) and Gombrich and Obeyeskere (1988).

10. This is unlike traditional Theravāda interpretations of *dhammakāya* as the body of dhamma, as the teachings of the Buddha or the sum of his perfections as a *Samyaksambuddha* (a perfectly awakened one).

11. This image is in an advertisement for a telecommunications company (UCOM group), which is commonly found on the back cover of the Dhammakāya Foundation's magazine, *Kalyanamit*.

12. www.dhammakaya.th.org [accessed on January 11, 2005].

13. Dhammakāya English-language materials translate the word *srattha* (*saddhā*, Pali) as faith, whereas many Buddhist scholars prefer to translate *saddhā* as confidence since the concept of faith is so thoroughly wedded to Protestant Christianity. Theravāda Buddhists typically argue that *saddhā* marks the beginning of the path rather than its culmination (as in Protestant Christianity), and they, therefore, place little emphasis upon it. The conscious decision of Dhammakāya representatives to use the word faith, therefore, may reflect an attempt to globalize Dhammakāya practice by using religious terminology well known to Christian audiences, or perhaps, it is simply an attempt at a straightforward translation of the word *saddhā*.

14. One such publication is *Mahathammakai chedi: Mahachedi phua santi phap lok*, which was published in 2000 by the Dhammakāya Foundation.

15. For a substantive analysis of donor narratives, see Falk (1990).

16. Tambiah (1984) provides an extensive overview of the origins and expression of the modern "cult of amulets" in Thailand.

17. www.dhammakaya.or.th [accessed on January 11, 2005].

18. On the excerpt that was distributed in class, the title of Weil's book is listed as *Breathing: The Master Key to Self-Healing*, but since this is available only in audio format it is unknown which of his books was copied for the class.

19. www.dimc.net/Azusa.2004B.htm [accessed on February 20, 2005].

20. This song is entitled, *World Peace through Meditation*. It is available on-line at www.dmc.tv, the homepage of DMC (Dhammakāya Meditation Channel), the Foundation's twen-

ty-four hour satellite channel.

21. Since there is no central religious figure within the Therāvada tradition, the *sangha*, as a whole, has the duty to preserve the *dhamma*. As a result, Theravāda societies place an emphasis on maintaining the purity of the *sangha*, which is principally done through the strict adherence to the monastic discipline of the *Vinaya*.

References

Apinya, Fuengfusakul. 1993. Empire of Crystal and Utopian Commune: Two Types of Contemporary Theravada Reform in Thailand. *Sojourn* 8(1):153–83.

Beach, B.B. 1999. Evangelism and Proselytism—Religious Liberty and Ecumenical Challenges. International Religious Liberty Association. http://www.irla.org/documents/articles/bbbeach-proselytism.html.

Bond, George. 1988. *The Buddhist Revival in Sri Lanka: Religious Tradition, Reinterpretation and Response*. Studies in Comparative Religion. Columbia: University of South Carolina Press.

———. 2003. The Contemporary Lay Meditation Movement and Lay Gurus in Sri Lanka. *Religion* 33(1): 23–55.

Chappell, David. 1999. Buddhist Interreligious Dialogue: To Build a Global Community. In *The Sound of Liberating Truth: Buddhist-Christian Dialogues in Honor of Frederick J. Streng*, ed. Sallie King and Paul Ingram, 3–35. Richmond, UK: Curzon.

Chandler, Stuart. 2004. *Establishing a Pure Land on Earth: The Foguang Buddhist Perspective on Modernization and Globalization*. Topics in Contemporary Buddhism. Honolulu: University of Hawaii Press.

———. 2005. Spreading Buddha's Light: The Internationalization of Foguang Shan. In *Buddhist Missionaries in the Era of Globalization*, ed. Linda Learman, 162–84. Honolulu: University of Hawaii Press.

De Roover, Jakob and Sarah Claerhout. 2008. Conversion of the World on the Universal Declaration of Theological Trouble. In *Proselytization Revisited: Rights Talk, Free Markets and Culture Wars*, ed. Rosalind I.J. Hackett, 53–76. London: Equinox.

Dharmapala, Angarika. 1965. *Return to Righteousness: A Collection of Speeches, Essays and Letters of the Anagarika Dharmapala*. Ed. Ananda Guruge. Sri Lanka: The Anagarika Dharmapala Birth Centenary Committee, Ministry of Education and Cultural Affairs.

Falk, Nancy Auer. 1990. Exemplary Donors of the Pāli Tradition. In *Ethics, Wealth, and Salvation: A Study in Buddhist Social Ethics*, ed. Russell F. Sizemore and Donald K. Swearer, xx–xx. Columbia: University of South Carolina Press.

Hammond, Phillip and David Machacek. 1999. *Soka Gakkai in America: Accommodation and Conversion*. Oxford: Oxford University Press.

Gombrich, Richard and Gananath Obeyesekere. 1988. *Buddhism Transformed: Religious Change in Sri Lanka.* Princeton, NJ: Princeton University Press.

Kemper, Steven. 2005. Dharmapala's Dharmaduta and the Buddhist Ethnoscape. In *Buddhist Missionaries in the Era of Globalization,* ed. Linda Learman, 22–50. Honolulu: University of Hawaii Press.

Kao, Grace. 2008. The Logic of Anti-Proselytization, Revisted. In *Proselytization Revisited: Rights Talk, Free Markets and Culture Wars,* ed. Rosalind I.J. Hackett, 77–108. London: Equinox.

Keyes, Charles. 1971. Buddhism and National Integration in Thailand. *Journal of Asian Studies* 30(3): 551–67.

Learman, Linda. 2005. Introduction. In *Buddhist Missionaries in the Era of Globalization,* ed. Linda Learman, 1–21. Honolulu: University of Hawaii Press.

Marty, Martin and Scott Appleby, eds. 1991. *Fundamentalisms Observed.* Chicago: University of Chicago Press.

Seager, Richard. 2006. *Encountering the Dharma: Daisaku Ikeda, Soka Gakkai, and the Globalization of Buddhist Humanism.* Berkeley: University of California Press.

Seneviratne, H.L. 1999. *The Work of Kings: The New Buddhism in Sri Lanka.* Chicago: University of Chicago Press.

Swearer, Donald. 1991. Fundamentalistic Movements in Theravada Buddhism. In *Fundamentalisms Observed,* ed. Martin Mary and Scott Appleby, 628–90. Chicago: University of Chicago Press.

Tambiah, Stanley J. 1984. *The Buddhist Saints of the Forest and the Cult of Amulets: A Study in Charisma, Hagiography, Sectarianism, and Millennial Buddhism.* Cambridge Studies in Social Anthropology. Cambridge: Cambridge University Press.

Taylor, J.L. 1993. *Forest Monks and the Nation-State: An Anthropological and Historical Study in Northeastern Thailand.* Singapore: Institute of Southeast Asian Studies.

van der Veer, Peter, ed. 1996. *Conversions to Modernities: The Globalization of Christianity,* New York: Routledge.

Walters, Jonathan S. 1992. Rethinking Buddhist Missions. 2 vols. Ph.D. diss., University of Chicago.

CHAPTER 10

Asia's Antioch: Prayer and Proselytism in Singapore[1]

Jean DeBernardi

Evangelical Christian leaders often remind Singaporeans that they must seek to fulfill the Great Commission to preach the gospel to all nations, observing that God has given them a special "role and responsibility in His Kingdom agenda—an Antioch for Asia" (*Prayerlink* 1998, 4). Antioch was a multiethnic city in what is today Turkey, and in the first century AD was the cradle of Christianity; many see Singapore as the cradle of Christianity for twenty-first century Asia. In support of their goal, Singaporean Christians provide extraordinary levels of financial support to local charitable outreach, church-planting in Singapore's so-called heartland, and global missions. Christians often observe, however, that the power to convert rests not with their own powers of persuasion but rather with the Holy Spirit and with God. Because they attribute their success to divine will, prayer seeking divine assistance is one important dimension to the practice of proselytism. Some contemporary forms of intercessory prayer also serve as an adjunct to fundraising and the support of missionary outreach, since these forms of prayer are designed to both inform and raise interest in less developed world areas.[2]

Based on ethnographic research and interviews conducted in Singapore between 1995 and 2005, I examine the rhetoric and practice of prayers and rituals that seek stable conversion—of the non-Christian other, but also the self—as an outcome. These include spiritual warfare prayers and spiritual mapping, but also the ministry of deliverance, bridge-burning rituals of conversion, praying for nations, and praying through the 10/40 window, a term that Christians use to refer to an area stretching from West Africa to East Asia that falls from 10 degrees north to 40 degrees north of the equator whose populations encompass the majority of the world's Muslims, Hindus, and Buddhists. Although prayer and bridge-burning rituals of conversion entail a much smaller financial and personal commitment than Christian educational work or social services, nonetheless we may regard these as a useful focus for analysis.

Anticipation of the millennial year energized the popularity of these forms of prayer and ritual practice, since many prophesied that the year 2000 would be a date by which Christians worldwide, including Singaporeans, would achieve extraordinary levels of success in proselytism. Consequently, in the 1990s, many Singaporeans—charismatic and non-charismatic alike—found innovative forms of prayer, including C. Peter Wagner's proposals for spiritual warfare, compelling. When the year 2000 arrived, many of these programs lost momentum for a time, their participants disappointed at having failed to achieve their goals. Meanwhile, in the wake of the attack on the World Trade Center on September 11th, 2001, the government has emphatically reinforced its policies on religious harmony, which include stern anti-proselytism measures.

I begin by examining the political and social context for proselytism in multi-religious, multi-ethnic Singapore, including government efforts to safeguard religious harmony by means of legislation and grass-roots campaigns. I then examine Singaporean Christians' use of prayer and ritual practice in the 1990s, including spiritual warfare, the ritual of deliverance, praying for nations, and the global campaign of coordinated prayer known as the AD2000 United Prayer Track.

The Global and the Local in Asia's Antioch

Singapore is a multicultural, multireligious city-state with a large Chinese majority and smaller Malay and Indian minority populations. From its establishment in the early nineteenth century by Sir Stamford Raffles as an entrepôt for the East India Company's China trade, British and other missionaries took the conversion of Malay Muslims in Singapore and its hinterland as a goal. But these evangelists met with local resistance both from the Muslim Imams and the Sultans of the nearby Malay states, who often imposed restrictions on the scope of their activities. Consequently, most converts were drawn from Chinese or Indian immigrant populations, together with the long-settled Straits Chinese population and other residents in this polyglot, heterogeneous city.

The 2000 Singapore Census of Population sketches out the main dimensions of Singapore's social and religious diversity. Chinese form 76.8%, Malays 13.9%, and Indians 7.9% of a total population of 3.26 million citizens and permanent residents. If the population figures are broken down by religious affiliation, Muslims comprise 14.9% of the total population, a number that includes 99.6% of Malays, but also 25% of the Indian population. In Singapore Islam is internally diverse, but the most prevalent form is the Shafi'i school of Sunni Islam, which also is the orthodox form of Islam in Malaysia. Many Chinese identify themselves as Buddhist (42.5%) or Taoist (8.5%), and 16.5% of ethnic Chinese are Christians. Hindus comprise 4% of the total population, and 55.4% of Indians identify themselves as Hindu. 12.1% of Indians profess Christianity, and that number showed a slight decrease between 1980 and 2000 (Singapore Census of Population 2000).

Although 14.8% of Singaporeans identify themselves to census takers as having no religion, many still identify with religious traditions that are ethnically linked: Buddhism and Taoism for Chinese, Hinduism, Islam, and Sikhism for Indians, and Islam for Malays. The small Christian minority tends to be English-educated and affluent and from Chinese and Indian ethnic backgrounds. Christianity has shown steady growth since 1980, drawing most of its new converts from among better-educated Chinese. The 2000 census figures show that 33.5% of Christians have graduated from university, as compared with 3.5% of Muslims and 2.7% of Taoists (Singapore Census of Population 2000).

In his or her everyday life, a Singaporean Christian often negotiates religious diversity. A first generation Christian's social environment almost certainly will include family members who maintain private shrines in their homes for devotion to their favorite Hindu or Daoist deities, Buddhas or Bodhisattvas. The state also mandates ethnic and religious diversity in its management of the Housing Development Board (HDB) high-rise flats in which the overwhelming majority of Singaporeans live. As a consequence of the application of an ethnic ratio system designed to prevent the formation of ethnically exclusive enclaves, a Christian's neighbors will typically include Buddhists, Muslims, Hindus, and Taoists. Indeed, Chinese spirit mediums commonly locate unregistered private altars in their flats, and often celebrate festivals on the HDB basketball court, where self-mortifying spirit mediums may fall into trance and lead their devotees on processions, accompanied by lion dancers and musicians.

As residents in a global city-state that is a major transportation hub, and also a regional center for Asian missions—Asia's Antioch—Singaporeans Christians move through international Christian networks with ease. Globetrotting evangelists frequently visit Singapore to participate in or lead events at Singapore's Indoor Stadium, and ideas and practices also flow through the books, videotapes and video-CDs that are available for sale at these mass events. At the same time, Singapore's prominent Christian leaders travel extensively to participate in global conferences and workshops, and in the 1990s the model for the urban cell church developed at Singapore's Faith Community Baptist Church was marketed successfully to American churches.

Churches, Christian bookstores, and websites also offer the Singaporean Christian consumer a wide range of products. These include self-help books like Joel Osteen's *Your Best Life Now* (2004) and Rick Warren's *The Purpose Driven Life* (2002), Christian fiction like Tim LaHaye and Jerry B. Jenkins' influential *Left Behind* series, Christian music, recorded teachings, multilingual CD-ROMs like the "Jesus" film (a 1979 movie created as an aid to evangelism that has since been translated into hundreds of languages) and probably most Singaporean Christians have been to see Mel Gibson's *The Passion of the Christ* (2004). Singapore's Christian leaders are keenly aware that they may utilize innovative practices and teachings to mobilize interest and participation, and many make selective use of elements drawn from the competing theologies now in circulation, including the spiritual warfare movement and the Health and Wealth Gospel.

At the same time, Singapore's churches exist within a local nexus of relationships that includes a range of different denominations, from the conservative Bible Presbyterians and Brethren to the Methodists, Anglicans, and Presbyterians, and independent churches like the Church of Singapore, Faith Community Baptist Church, and City Harvest. Although connected with groups elsewhere, each denomination and independent church has its own local history and lineage, as Bobby Sng (2003 [1980]) has documented in detail, and often transmit unique heritages defined by their relationship to their local founding ancestors. Local leaders undoubtedly combine new practices with Christian practices inherited from their training and from previous waves of revival.

Although these diverse churches may vary in terms of their networks or the degree to which they have adopted charismatic practices, they share a focus on evangelism. Like evangelical Christians worldwide, Singaporean Christians are committed to furthering the Great Commission to preach the gospel in the entire world "for a witness to all peoples" before Jesus' return. For these Christians, activism—the "expression of the gospel in effort"—remains an important foundation for their programs of proselytism and outreach (Bebbington 1989, 3).

In North America and Europe, denominations that scholars typically categorize as Mainline Protestant like Anglicans, Methodists, Lutherans, and Presbyterians, are internally diverse, with evangelical and non-evangelical wings. Indeed, many liberal Protestants in North America and Europe now question whether or not proselytism is appropriate in a pluralistic, post-colonial world, rejecting the absolutist view that only Christians will receive salvation.

But since most of Singapore's Christian leaders reject the liberal Protestant perspective, the non-evangelical wing of mainline Protestantism is virtually non-existent there. Meanwhile, in the post-colonial period, the Anglican Church in Singapore has incorporated charismatic forms of Christian practice and engages in evangelical outreach. Some speculate that the turn towards charismatic and evangelical practices has been a strategy by which Anglican leaders in Singapore and Malaysia seek to shake off negative associations with colonialism—the Anglican Church remains, after all, England's national church.

With few exceptions, Singapore's Christian leaders strongly emphasize evangelical forms of practice, including social outreach (education, medical care, and social programs) and foreign missions. As Asia's Antioch, Singapore hosts local, regional, and international mission organizations and initiatives, and churches frequently support independent missionaries and send members on Vision trips to less developed areas of the region, including China, where they may volunteer educational, medical, or dental services. Singapore's churches also engage in diverse forms of proselytism at home, albeit in an increasingly restricted field of action.

The maintenance of religious harmony

As a group, Singapore's Christians enjoy considerable social influence. Nonetheless, since Singapore's independence in 1965 they have experienced increasing controls on their public practices. These restrictions have only intensified since the 1990 enactment of the Religious Harmony Act, an important instrument by which the government seeks to maintain not only religious but also ethnic harmony in this cosmopolitan city.

In contemporary Singapore, freedom of religion is constitutionally guaranteed. Article 15 of Singapore's Constitution (1963) is entitled "Freedom of Religion," and provides that:

(1) Every person has the right to profess and practice his religion and to propagate it.
(2) No person shall be compelled to pay any tax the proceeds of which are specially allocated in whole or in part for the purposes of a religion other than his own.
(3) Every religious group has the right (a) to manage its own religious affairs; (b) to establish and maintain institutions for religious or charitable purposes; and (c) to acquire and own property and hold and administer it in accordance with law.
(4) This article does not authorize any act contrary to any general law relating to public order, public health or morality.

But Singapore's Societies Act requires that all religious groups must be registered, and the government has deregistered some groups, including the Singapore Congregation of Jehovah's Witnesses and the Unification Church.

Singapore's Constitution further provides for the special position of the Malays in Part XIII (Special Provisions), including protection of their religious, cultural, and linguistic heritage, and the regulation of Muslim religious affairs:

> Article 152 Minorities and Special Position of Malays (1) It shall be the responsibility of the Government constantly to care for the interests of the racial and religious minorities in Singapore. (2) The Government shall exercise its functions in such manner as to recognize the special position of the Malays, who are the indigenous people of Singapore, and accordingly it shall be the responsibility of the Government to protect, safeguard, support, foster and promote their political, educational, religious, economic, social and cultural interests and the Malay language.
> Article 153 Muslim Religion The Legislature shall by law make provision for regulating Muslim religious affairs and for constituting a Council to advise the President in matters relating to the Muslim religion (Singapore - Constitution 1963).

With respect to the Muslim community, the government has followed a strategy of bureaucratic centralization and control (see Kadir 2004).[3]

All Singaporeans (including Muslims) are free to change their religion. But since Islam is closely interwoven with Malay ethnic identity, the issue of conversion is highly sensitive, especially since Singapore is a small city-state with two powerful Muslim-majority neighbors—Malaysia and Indonesia. In Singapore, a child's ethnicity is determined by that of the father, and is the basis on which the so-called mother tongue of Singapore's bilingual education system is determined: a Malay child studies Malay and English; a Chinese child Mandarin and English. Although apostasy is **not** considered to be an offense in Singapore, nonetheless on conversion Singaporean Malay Christians reportedly experience social stigma and ostracism. As the census data would suggest, the number of Singaporean Malay Christian converts is very small, perhaps no more than a few thousand individuals.[4]

Singapore's government has set strict limitations to proselytism. Since 1970, the government has prohibited public proselytizing, including the open-air evangelism so central to local evangelical programs of outreach during the colonial period. Christians must use discretion in the distribution of tracts, especially if they may be seen as seeking to address Muslims with their message. Indeed, they now label some potentially sensitive publications distributed in their churches "For Christians only" to avoid the charge that they are proselytizing non-Christian populations. Restrictions also have been imposed on the organization of religious events in schools, which has hampered the recruitment of youth, a serious limitation that some Christian leaders describe as responsible for the stagnation of growth.

In 1990 Parliament further enacted the Maintenance of Religious Harmony Act in order to create a means to respond to perceived threats to religious harmony, including insensitive proselytism and the entry of religious groups into the political arena. The latter issue came to the fore in the 1980s when a number of Catholic priests and social workers, inspired by Liberation Theology, decided that it was their responsibility to become involved in raising awareness of social issues. On 21 May 1987, sixteen people were arrested under Singapore's Internal Security Act. In subsequent media coverage, the Home Affairs Ministry portrayed participants as being pro-communist and leftist, and as having used the Catholic Church and other religious organizations to further their goals (see Hill n.d., 10–12; Kuah-Pearce 2003, 147–54).

With the Maintenance of Religious Harmony Act, the government sought to establish working rules by which to ensure peaceful coexistence among Singapore's diverse religious groups, many of which are identified with ethnic or subethnic groups (see Sinha 2005). The Act created a Presidential Council for Religious Harmony with representatives of the major religions to monitor religious matters and further empowered the Minister to issue restraining orders against anyone whose actions were deemed a threat.[5] The response to infringement of the Religious Harmony legislation is often cautionary, but may be more severe, including prosecution, fine or imprisonment, and restrictions on the individual's exercise of leadership in a religious group.[6]

As Kuah-Pearce Khun Eng concludes, the Religious Harmony Act sets definite limits to Constitutional guarantees of freedom of worship:

> Individuals can chose whatever they want to worship. They can also encourage family members, friends and colleagues to participate, but cannot coerce or force them to join. The line dividing the act of persuasion and coercion is very thin. If there are no complaints, then it is an act of persuasion; but if there is dissatisfaction and complaints, it becomes coercion. Also, when a group engages all its members to go out and persuade others whom they do not know, particularly in public places, it is coercion. Within the law, they can be stopped from such acts of proselytism (2003, 164).

As a consequence, Christians must exercise considerable discretion in their outreach efforts. In particular, Singaporeans express awareness of their vulnerable geopolitical situation as a Chinese majority city-state whose two closest neighbors are Muslim-majority states, Malaysia and Indonesia, sometimes comparing their situation to that of Israel in the Middle East. Since openly seeking converts among Muslims could potentially lead to the charge of causing antagonism between ethnic groups and possibly even prosecution for violation of the Religious Harmony Act, few Christians would actively seek to convert Singaporean Muslims.

The September 11th attack on the World Trade Center raised fears that Singapore might become a target for terrorist attacks, but also increased tensions between Muslims and non-Muslims. To give but one anecdotal example, after 9-11 some Chinese passengers reportedly berated Malay Muslim taxi drivers and criticized their religion, blaming the attacks on Islam. Concerned about the potential for violence, the government swiftly mobilized the city-state to revisit the issue of religious harmony. After consultation with national bodies representing a wide range of religious groups, in October 2002 the government adopted a Declaration on Religious Harmony, and formed the consultative committee into an Inter-Religious Harmony Circle (IRHC). The government further organized a number of grass-roots Inter-Racial Confidence Circles and Harmony Circles to promote "mutual understanding, respect and support between the races" (Ministry of Community Development, Youth and Sports 2003).

As its creators describe it, the Declaration is not a legal document but rather an "ethos" and a "code for conduct" that "affirms the values that have helped to maintain religious harmony in Singapore; and serves as a reminder of the need for continued efforts to develop stronger bonds across religions in Singapore" (*Channel News Asia* 2002). The text is as follows:

Declaration on Religious Harmony

We, the people in Singapore, declare that religious harmony is vital for peace, progress and prosperity in our multi-racial and multi-religious Nation.

We resolve to strengthen religious harmony through mutual tolerance, confidence, respect, and understanding.

We shall always
> Recognise the secular nature of our State,
> Promote cohesion within our society,

> Respect each other's freedom of religion,
> Grow our common space while respecting our diversity,
> Foster inter-religious communications,

and thereby ensure that religion will not be abused to create conflict and disharmony in Singapore.

The text, which is scripted for public recitation, is available on wallet-sized cards in all official languages (English, Mandarin, Malay, and Tamil), and is very much like a credo (Ministry of Community Development, Youth and Sports, 2003).

As it has done with other social engineering projects, the government uses campaign-strategies to promote religious harmony. The government portrays religious and racial harmony as intimately linked, and actively encourages Singapore's religious organizations to celebrate Racial Harmony Week, which is held annually during the week in which Racial Harmony Day falls. Racial Harmony Day (July 21) commemorates an outbreak of rioting and violent conflict between Chinese and Malays in 1964 in which 23 died and many were injured, an event that occurred during a mass religious procession on Prophet Mohammed's birthday. This racial riot, together with communal riots that occurred in 1950, 1964, and 1969, figure prominently in government arguments for strict state controls over religion.

During Racial Harmony Week in 2005, the government formally promoted religious harmony through education, posters, attractive gifts, and an obligatory social practice: collective recitation of the Declaration on Religious Harmony. The Ministry of Community Development, Youth and Sports (2005) further announced that the Inter-Religious Harmony Circle (IRHC) was making a gift of a story book entitled *Colours of Harmony* to all primary school children, and also distributed Declaration on Religious Harmony notepads and posters to "all schools, the Inter Racial Confidence Circles (IRCCs) and the various Harmony Circles."

Evangelism at home: public outreach and prayer

Although Singaporean evangelical Christians may reject liberal theology, they must conform to government restrictions on proselytism. Most recently, Christian leaders must conform to the requirement that they affirm the goals of religious harmony, and are called on to participate in inter-religious dialogues. Although some Christian leaders have welcomed the opportunity for greater dialogue with non-Christians (in particular Muslim leaders), others participate grudgingly or delegate the responsibility to others.[7]

Although the government may seek to set limits to proselytism, and although many Christians are not interested in engaging in outreach to non-Christians, at least some Singapore Christians actively seek to convert non-Christians. Many focus their efforts on family members, friends, or co-workers, but some even use chance encounters with strangers as an occasion to promote Christianity. Because the government regards proselytism as potentially sensitive and limits the distribution of tracts, open-air proselytizing, and outreach in schools, evangelical Christians must find other strategies to enact the requirement that they seek to influence the non-Christian other to accept the Christian message.

A common form of outreach involves the organization of church-based evangelical events to which members invite non-members, including traditionally staged revival meetings at which locally popular or visiting evangelists exhort their audience. More innovative are dramatic skits scripted and performed by younger members. For example, in 1999 the Frankel Estate Brethren Assembly staged an elaborate allegorical musical drama entitled *Phil* to a standing-room only audience. The local authors based the musical style and some plot elements of their Christian musical on the American film "Grease," and the event closed with a young evangelist offering a biblical interpretation and exhortation.

Evangelism at home also includes support for services in languages like Filipino, Indonesian, and Burmese, aimed at guest workers in Singapore, including the maids of Christian employers. But Christian leaders also often instruct their members to take advantage of every opportunity to proselytize, even providing them with workbooks where they may keep a log of persons whom they sought to convert, from parents and grandparents to friends and fellow-workers. Indeed, this may be the most controversial aspect of their practice, since the conversion of one or more family members may result in conflict, and outreach to strangers risks offending practitioners of other religions (see DeBernardi 2005, 2007).

Proselytism involves persuasion, but as I discuss above, Christians assert that the actual power of conversion rests not with their rhetorical skills but with God. Consequently the conversion of the world requires not only human effort but also prayer. Meanwhile, with increasing restrictions on public evangelism, prayer may be the most common form of proselytizing activity that many Christians engage in (aside, of course, from the donation of funds in support of missions efforts and charitable outreach).

Marcel Mauss broadly defined prayer as "a religious rite which is oral and bears directly on the sacred" (2003 [1909], 57). He observed:

> Prayer is precisely one of these phenomena where ritual is united in belief.
> It is full of meaning like a myth: it is often as rich in ideas and images as a
> religious narrative. It is full of power and efficacy like a ritual and it is often
> as powerfully creative as a ceremony based on sympathetic magic.
>
> (Mauss 2003 [1909], 22)

He further observed that in Protestantism prayer had become "practically the whole of religious life," and has engulfed other religious expressions: "prayer has been the remarkable tree which, having grown up in the shade of other trees, has ended by smothering them under its vast branches" (Mauss 2003 [1909], 23).

Protestant Christians engage in prayer in formats that vary from set liturgies and the scripted stanzas of hymns to spontaneous improvisations and speaking in tongues. Among the most common are prayers of thanksgiving for blessings won, but also common are intercessory prayers by means of which individuals or groups pray to God for divine assistance. The potential beneficiaries are many: the person or group praying may seek to intercede with God on behalf of any individual or group. Some Singaporean Christians have adapted to an Asian context new forms of intercessory prayer like "praying for nations" and "taking cities for God," using collective forms of prayer and ritual practice to symbolically challenge competing non-religious social forces, including politics, materialism, secularism, and intellectualism.

Spiritual Warfare

In the discussion that follows, I consider diverse forms of prayer and ritual practice that Singaporean Christians (and especially charismatic Christians) adopted and promoted in the 1990s. I begin with spiritual warfare, a form of prayer evangelism that captured the imagination of many Christians. Drawing together certain Bible passages with contemporary revelations and experiences, those who support spiritual warfare theology argue that unconverted regions of the world are under the control of territorial spirits (which one author identifies as "cultural ethnic demons") who are rooted in specific "geographical areas and population centres" (Wagner 1991, 3). They further propose that Christians adopt a constellation of practices, including spiritual mapping to identify the so-called spiritual strongholds controlled by these territorial spirits, and three forms of focused prayer: (1) prayer walking, in which they walk inconspicuously in small groups to pray, targeting areas that they have identified as spiritual strongholds (like a red light district, a bar-filled street, or a Masonic lodge); (2) prayer marches, in which they gather en masse to process through city streets to a site where they hold a well-publicized rally; and (3) prayer journeys, where they travel in groups to visit powerful "spiritual strongholds" that transcend local communities, like Ephesus and Mount Everest, where they prayed against the Queen of Heaven (Wagner 1998; see also DeBernardi 1999; Lowe 1998).

One important non-Biblical source for the spiritual warfare movement is Christian fiction that invokes demonic possession to explain dark events. In particular, the Christian novel is a popular genre through which the theology of spiritual warfare finds an important outlet. Take, for example, Frank Peretti's 1986 best-selling Christian novel, *This Present Darkness*. This influential publication precedes most of the published Christian books on spiritual warfare, and has sold an estimated six million copies worldwide. Peretti's vivid account of demonic possession and expulsion is, as the book's cover announces, a novel. But for those who believe in demonic possession, these fictional events compel belief, transcending the allegorical dimension of this story.

These programs stirred considerable interest especially among charismatic Christian leaders, many of whom found the spiritual warfare framework of interpretation convincing and relevant for Singapore. In 1998, for example, Wagner published a book entitled *Confronting the Queen of Heaven* in which he proposed that the Queen of Heaven was in fact a "manifestation of the principality of darkness," a "demonic principality who is most responsible under Satan for keeping unbelievers in spiritual darkness" (Wagner 1998, 16–17). He further proposed that the Queen of Heaven had taken different forms, including the moon goddess, Diana of Ephesus, the "counterfeit Mary" venerated by Catholics, and even Mount Everest, whose Nepali name *Sagarmatha* means "Mother of the Universe" (Wagner 1998, 36–37). Some Singaporean Christians localized Wagner's ideas readily, proposing in their teachings or in interviews with me that in Singapore the Queen of Heaven took the form of the popular bodhisattva known as the Goddess of Mercy (*Guanyin*).

That the concept of territorial spirits was so readily accepted by Singaporean Chinese is not surprising, since we may discern a striking congruency between the metaphor of territorial spirits and the practices of Chinese popular religious culture. One of the most common forms of traditional Chinese temple organization is the territorial temple, whose ritual practices include periodical festivals, collective offerings of food and incense to protective spirits, and processions that demarcate community boundaries (see Feuchtwang 2001; Watson 1985). This form of territorial temple is now rare in Singapore, where development has marginalized popular temples and state planning has broken down ethnic enclaves. Nonetheless, spirit mediums commonly locate private altars in apartment units in Housing and Development Board (HDB) flats, and periodically plant flags on the side of major roads to announce that they will be using the collective space of the high-rise flat to celebrate a festival. Although limited in their activities, they nonetheless draw massive crowds to their ritual performances, processions (which must travel from place to place by car and truck), and open-air opera performances, sometimes to the displeasure of other residents.

In a recent book promoting a program of "community penetration" in Singapore's heartland, including lower-cost HDB flats, a charismatic Christian leader identifies these popular religious practices as a form of territorial possessing (*sic*), comparing them to Christian prayer walking:

> The enemy believes in territorial possessing as well. His devotees do prayer
> walk as well. They offer prayers and sacrifices to exert control over the

community where they are situated. They plant flags and they go for prayer processions. Judges 11:24 illustrates territorial claims and the argument that Chemosh the national god of the Moabites and Ammonites had given them certain territory.

The enemy takes territorial ownership and possession seriously. We too must take community commitment seriously. We have observed that there are blocks that are very difficult to penetrate because of the meddling with idols and demons by the residents in the block. Therefore, where there are house temples situated at any particular block, that block becomes more difficult to reach. (Chua 2004, 55–56)

He proposes a four-part program of outreach that includes deeds of kindness, intercession (i.e. prayer), preaching, and strengthening. The process of strengthening, he notes, includes deliverance, since

Most of them were Taoists before their conversion and would have been to temples, taken enchanted waters, and consulted temple mediums. Many of them would have dedicated their children to various temple deities they need to be ministered to in deliverance. (Chua 2004, 68–69)

But he also adds that since they may have suffered deep emotional pain, they also required inner healing, and that since many may not be well-educated, they also require life-skills training (Chua 2004, 68–69).

In 2000, the Lausanne Committee for World Evangelism, an international network of evangelical Christians, convened a meeting in Nairobi to discuss the practice of spiritual warfare. They concluded that there was some danger that these practices were in fact a reversion to a pagan worldview and emphasized power more than truth, and cautioned that the practice was potentially divisive. Nonetheless, most of the authors who contributed to an edited volume based on that conference heartily endorsed this theology, and indeed many of the contributing authors identified non-Christian religions as occult (Moreau *et. al.* 2003 [2002]). Malaysian Methodist Bishop Rev. Dr. Hwa Yung, for example, contributed an essay entitled "A Systematic Theology that Recognizes the Demonic" in which he concluded that while "most religions contain some things that are high and noble, in practice they are often linked in different ways to occult practices," adding that "priests in Buddhist and Hindu temples and Muslim Sufis leaders are often involved in such practices" (Hwa 2003, 16).

Simon Coleman has observed of charismatic Christians in Europe that proselytism often is not so much about converting others as it is about reinforcing one's commitments by pronouncing them to others under the guise of proselytism. Consequently, he concludes that "[m]issionization is not merely a matter of attempting to transform the potential convert, but also—perhaps even primarily—a means of recreating or reconverting the charismatic self" (Coleman 2003, 17). But as contextualized in Singapore, practitioners of prayer evangelism and spiritual warfare vividly imagine the deities of non-Christian religious practice as demonic opponents, whom they seek to over-come in a war waged against dark principalities. Consequently, these forms of prayer further serve not only to reinforce the charismatic self, but also to reinforce the boundary between the supplicant's own beliefs and practices and those of Asian religions that dominate the total field of religious practice.

In the post-September 11th era in Singapore, the government's efforts to promote awareness of issues regarding religious harmony have led many Christian leaders to become sensitive to the potential problems that spiritual warfare theology and prayer could cause. And indeed, the local application of spirit warfare theology in multi-religious Singapore has the potential to deeply offend non-Christians. Spiritual warfare is no longer as popular or influential as it was in the 1990s, but the rhetoric of the spiritual strongholds and territorial spirits continues to circulate and have influence in Singapore and elsewhere (see DeBernardi 2005).

The ministry of deliverance and the smashing of idols

Another globally popular form of ritual practice that finds enthusiastic local acceptance in Singapore is the ministry of deliverance. Whereas the spiritual warfare proponents used prayer to wage war with territorial spirits, those who perform the ministry of deliverance use verbal and ritual formulae to expel them and dispel their influence. As with spiritual warfare, in the process of localizing the practices of the ministry of deliverance some Singaporean lead-ers teach their followers to imagine the deities of popular religious culture as demonic opponents or intruders.

The concept of deliverance is complex, often engaging simultaneously with psychological issues (in particular guilt over moral lapses) and external sources of disturbance that are identified as demonic or occult with varying degrees of specificity. For example, at a three-day rally at Singapore's Indoor Stadium on the occasion of a 1999 visit to Singapore by Brazilian prayer evangelist Ed Silvoso, a Singaporean charismatic pastor proposed that spiritual warfare included both "radical holiness" and dealing with "areas of darkness" in people's lives. He discussed sin at length, and publicly confessed to having been a secret smoker who had lied about his smoking, and also to having masturbated as a teenager.

Although he emphasized sin, the speaker also proposed that idolatry was a serious problem in Singapore. Since many Singaporean Christians were first generation believers, he concluded, many had been "given to demons at birth," i.e. been given in adoption to deities as a means of seeking their protection—a traditional ritual response to childhood afflictions. He noted that he himself had been dedicated to the Monkey God (joking, "people say that I am so agile!"), and called on participants: "Reject the Goddess of Mercy, the Monkey God, the God of the Earth, the God of Prosperity. Do it together!" He further warned against having any kind of demonic images in the home, including images from Bali, pictures of Lucifer, or so-called demonic computer games, since proximity to these images was like "waving a flag of invitation to the devil."

Based on interviews that I conducted in 1999, I conclude that many took these recommendations seriously, not only destroying deity images, but also throwing away batik shirts with ambiguous designs and destroying objects decorated with dragon images. Many still deplore the actions of a charismatic Anglican minister who, the story goes, destroyed a valuable antique altar that had legs designed to look like Chinese dragons. Meanwhile, conversion from traditional Chinese religion in many churches typically entails the requirement that a new convert must destroy their idols in a bridge burning ritual of conversion. Although in 2004 a charismatic minister reported that this was voluntarily done, in the 1990s it appeared that many churches strictly enforced the requirement. In 1995, for example one Christian leader noted that when a wealthy Chinese man had joined their church, they had gone to his house and smashed his very costly porcelain idols, which he estimated to be worth six or seven thousand Singapore dollars.

Although the ministry of deliverance tends to follow a stereotyped form in which a person's difficulties are attributed to affliction by a local spirit, often as the consequence of an unresolved bond created when they were "adopted" by that deity as a child, the ritual process sometimes takes on the tone of a psychodrama. In 2002, for example, a Christian lay leader performed the ministry of deliverance on a high-ranking minister in a British-based denomination. Although he initially exorcized the minister of idols, he later asked him to break soul ties with the colonials of the East India Company and to renounce the influence of Freemasonry. British missionaries brought Singapore's oldest churches to Singapore and Freemasonry was popular with elite members of those churches. This deliverance ritual suggests that a powerful obstacle to winning converts in contemporary Singapore is the perception that Christianity is a European rather than an Asian religion.

Christian conversion opens up the possibility for an individual to transform his or her life through an act of personal choice, a choice that often involves disengagement from tradition forms of social obligation. But the act of conversion takes place within social networks and cannot fail to have repercussions in the total field of practice that includes family and community. Sometimes the parents of Christian converts themselves are baptized on their deathbeds because they are concerned that their children will not respect their memory with the rituals of ancestor worship, and consider that this will give them a chance for reunion with their children in a Christian heaven. But when the parents and other family members refuse to convert, deep divisions and conflicts may arise.

Praying for nations and unreached people groups

In the 1990s, intercessory prayer on behalf of nations and unreached people groups was enormously popular with Singaporean Christians. Two works enjoyed especial influence: Patrick Johnstone's *Operation World* (1993 [1974]) and George Otis Jr.'s *Strongholds of the 10/40 Window: Intercessors Guide to the World's Least Evangelized Nations* (1995). Their influence persists. Singaporean Christians still regularly produce prayer guides inspired by these works as strategies for promoting their own vision of evangelism, and generating support for locally based evangelical programs.

Operation World is a detailed compendium of information on all the world's nations designed as a prayer diary, with prayer tasks assigned for every day of the year. In the book's preface, Johnstone explains that prayer is fundamental to Christian practice and intercession essential in order for God's purposes to be realized:

> As intercessors what power we wield! We reign in life with the Lord Jesus. He has raised us up to share his throne and his authority. . . . We have authority over Satan to thwart his plans, pull down his strongholds, release his captives. Our prayers change the world, open closed doors, make resistant people receptive, put down and raise up leaders and extend the kingdom of our Lord Jesus. (Johnstone 1993 [1974], 11)

He further identifies two purposes in writing the book: first, to inform for prayer, and second, to mobilize individuals for witness as part of a growing mission movement around the world (Johnstone 1993 [1974], 13).

Singapore, for example, is scheduled as the country of the day on October 9th. The entry for Singapore includes a map and background information on its geographical location, population, economy, and politics. The entry further offers detailed statistical information on religious diversity, including a detailed breakdown by Protestant denomination, and identifies the less reached sectors of the population, including Malay Muslims and non-English speaking Chinese. The author praises Singapore for its "missions vision" and observes that "Singapore might well claim to be the Antioch of Asia," observing that some of Singapore's Christian leaders were committed to "pray and work for" Singapore to become 30% Christian by the census in 2000 (Johnstone 1993 [1974], 488). Despite considerable activism, this goal was not achieved.

George Otis Jr., the author of the second influential book, *Strongholds of the 10/40 Window: Intercessors Guide to the World's Least Evangelized Nations*, is the founder and president of the Sentinel Group, a Christian research and information agency in Lynnwood, Washington. Together with C. Peter Wagner, he coordinated the "A.D. 2000 and Beyond Movement's United Prayer Track," which until its closure in 2001 used the Internet to coordinate global events of simultaneous prayer and fasting.

Otis has articulated a vision of evangelism that focuses on what he identifies as the "Strongholds of the 10/40 Window." As I briefly discuss above, this term refers to the countries that lie within the area from 10 degrees to 40 degrees north of the equator, including Northern Africa, the Middle East, India, China, and Mainland Southeast Asia. This area, he notes, "is littered with an astonishing diversity of natural and man-made sacred sites" which are "important points of contact with the spirit world," but also "targetable elements in the Enemy's deceptive web" (Otis 1995, ii). As the book's cover blurb also notes, "the 10/40 Window contains the birthplace of every major non-Christian religion on earth: Islam, Hinduism, Buddhism, Shintoism, Taoism, Confucianism, Bahai, Sikhism, Judaism, and Jainism."

Otis's definition of spiritual strongholds suggests that they are simultaneously occult and social:

> . . . spiritual strongholds are the invisible structures of thought and authority that are erected through the combined agency of demonic influence and human will. In this sense they are not demons, but the place from which demons operate (Otis 1995, ii).

Specific entries for nations provide detailed information on local spiritual strongholds so that intercessors can target them in their prayers.

There is no entry for Singapore, but the entry for Malaysia proposes that intercessors pray over specific "Spiritual Power Points"—the Shah Alam Mosque, near Kuala Lumpur, and Penang's Snake Temple and Mahayana Buddhist temple, Kek Lok Si—and also during spiritual events like the Hindu festival Thaipusam and the Islamic Ramadan (Otis 1995, 156). Prayer points like the Penang Snake Temple are designed as a basis for intercessory prayer, with God as the primary audience. Undoubtedly the speaker's explicit purpose (and the prayer's illocutionary force) is to request that God act on behalf of a population of unreached people.

But these prayers also act on those who pray. For example, in 2004, a Singaporean NGO called the X-PACT Society published an attractively produced pamphlet entitled *Harvesting Souls through Prayer: a 30-day prayer guide for Cambodia* (Lau and Goh 2004). The editor identified four potential uses for the pamphlet: for prayer during personal devotions, for sharing and prayer during prayer meetings, worship service, Sunday School, cell groups, etc; for special prayer meetings focused on Cambodia; and for preparing a mission team "through a season of prayer."

Like *Operation World* and *Strongholds of the 10/40 Window*, *Harvesting Souls through Prayer* offers general information about Cambodia, including recent history, population statistics, details about major ethnic minorities, and a map. The prayer guide further offers a thirty-day prayer diary, identifying a theme and prayer point for each day of the month, and offering background discussion and a prayer point on these selected themes. Many of these are pressing social problems for which the participant is asked to pray for solutions. At the same time, the pamphlet is designed to educate the Singaporean Christian, including individuals planning to go to Cambodia on a Vision trip, for whom a special entry "How to Keep Your Sanity in Cambodia" has been appended. In affirming their commitments through prayer and possibly activism, Christians confirm the evangelical self as one that is socially responsible and caring.

Although the authors of this prayer pamphlet vividly describe the plight of disabled Cambodian children, the disastrous impact of landmines, and the inadequate public health system, they do not openly request funds. This suggests that they are following the practice called living by faith, which involves praying to God about financial needs rather than directly approaching potential donors or relying for support on missionary agencies. In the nineteenth century Plymouth Brethren George Müller (1805–1898) and J. Hudson Taylor (1832–1905), who founded the China Inland Mission, widely popularized living by faith among evangelical Christians. Contemporary evangelical Christians continue to circulate the details of their extraordinary successes in pamphlets and on internet websites, and in particular take Müller's reliance on prayer and his faith in God's providence as an exemplary model for evangelical practice.

During his philanthropic career, Müller raised over 1.6 million pounds to support the education of British orphans, Bible publication and distribution, and the work of independent missionaries. He publicized his work through the annual reports of the Scriptural Knowledge Institution that he founded and also through six autobiographical accounts of his work published between 1837 and 1886. His fundraising was global in its reach: in 1852, for example, he reported receiving donations from Europe, North and South

America, Africa, and Australia. When he needed funds he prayed, and he attributed the success of his evangelical work to prayer and to God rather than to his ability as a fundraiser (see Müller 1861; DeBernardi n.d.).

Contemporary proponents of prayer evangelism now promote new forms of prayer like spiritual warfare and praying for nations, but when they employ prayer as one foundation for their evangelical work they follow the example set by Müller. Although their prayers are addressed to God, prayer also has what British J.L. Austin has termed a perlocutionary effect, meaning an intendend or unintended effect on the person who reads or hears the utterance (see Austin 1975). Undoubtedly Christians are aware that their prayers may inspire the person who prays (or those who hear their prayers) to do or realize something about their Christian commitments, mobilizing interest and support for evangelical work.

AD 2000 and Beyond

In the 1990s, a variety of programs and movements for world evangelism coalesced around a remarkable global movement entitled "AD 2000 and Beyond," which participants describe as a "movement of movement, and a network of networks." The AD 2000 and Beyond movement was launched in Singapore in 1989 at a meeting of the Global Consultation on World Evangelism, and took as its goal "a church for every people and the gospel for every person by the year AD 2000." They took as their focus the 10/40 Window, and sought to mobilize evangelical Christians worldwide in the decade leading up to the year 2000.

As one aspect of the AD2000 and Beyond Movement's evangelical strategy, participants formed a global partnership of "international prayer networks and ministries" that they called the AD 2000 United Prayer Resource Network or, more commonly, the AD 2000 United Prayer Track. This network served as the "prayer mobilization arm" of the AD2000 and Beyond movement, and participating groups included the Spiritual Warfare Network (C. Peter Wagner), Generals of Intercession (Cindy Jacobs), Reconciliation Coalition (John Dawson), Prayer Evangelism (Ed Silvoso), and the Sentinel Group (George Otis Jr.).

Through websites, publications, videos, and evangelistic tours, this network of evangelists developed and promoted a range of innovative prayer practices, all of which found fertile ground among Singapore's well-organized and well-funded Christian leaders. In a retrospective report, Wagner identified "The 10 Major Prayer Innovations of the 1990s" (2000), each of which he associated with the Christian leader or leaders who had promoted that particular form of prayer. As he describes them these included:

1. Strategic-level spiritual warfare. The idea of taking authority over high-ranking principalities and powers assigned by Satan to keep social networks of various kinds in spiritual darkness was the focus of the Spiritual Warfare Network starting in 1990. Key authors included Cindy Jacobs, Dick Eastman, and C. Peter Wagner.

2. Identificational repentance. The body of Christ began to learn that it is possible to heal the wounds of the past through identificational repentance and thus to weaken strongholds that Satan has built. The key author was John Dawson.

3. Prayer evangelism. Prayer has ordinarily been an add-on to evangelism, but now we know that prayer itself, when intelligently strategized and focused, can be a direct force for winning people to Christ. The key author was Ed Silvoso.

4. Personal intercession for leaders. For pastors and other Christian leaders, identifying and relating positively to personal intercessors can mean the difference between success and failure in ministry. Key authors included John Maxwell, Terry Teykl, and C. Peter Wagner.

5. Two-way prayer. Prayer is not just speaking to God, but also hearing directly from Him. Derivatives of this include prophecy, the office of prophet, and prophetic intercession. Key authors included Cindy Jacobs and Chuck Pierce.

6. On-site praying. Prayer began to move out of the church and into the community through praise marches, prayer expeditions, prayer journeys, and prayer-walking. Key authors included Graham Kendrick, Steve Hawthorne and C. Peter Wagner.

7. City transformation. Through prayer, the kingdom of God can move out of the church and penetrate all levels of society, thereby transforming cities and other territories. Key authors included George Otis, Jr., Ed Silvoso, John Dawson, and C. Peter Wagner.

8. The AD2000 United Prayer Track. A vehicle for mobilizing prayer for the lost at a level never before seen in church history. Key authors included Luis Bush, Beverly Pegues, and Dick Eastman.

9. Commitment to the land. Spiritual authority of pastors and other leaders increases proportionately to their commitment to the territory in which God has placed them. The key author was Bob Beckett.

10. Spiritual mapping. Spirit-guided research can help target our prayers and produced informed, and thus more effective, intercession. The key author was George Otis, Jr.

In the 1990s, Singapore's charismatic Christian leaders made full use of all of these prayer innovations in activities associated first with the AD 2000 United

Prayer Track, and later with a still active network called LoveSingapore.

A pivotal event in the development of the AD 2000 United Prayer Track in Singapore was the 1994 "Day to Change the World," which coincided with a global March for Jesus: "Some 10 million people took to the streets in 1,500 cities of 171 nations....It was a day of unprecedented unity and unbroken intercession across time zones." Due to government restrictions Singaporean Christians could not have a street march, but they held a version of the event at the Hougang Stadium. Following the *Day to Change the World*, the AD2000 United Prayer Track leaders decided to organize Singapore's own national day of prayer as an annual event, which they scheduled on the Saturday before National Day (*Prayerlink* 1998, 4–5).[8]

The local organizers described the *Day to Change OUR World* and its associated activities, which commenced in 1995, as a "full-scale mobilization encompassing a diversity of prayer strategies" (*Prayerlink* 1998, 6). And indeed, events organized by the AD2000 United Prayer Track that I observed in 1997 included all ten of the forms of innovative prayer listed by Wagner, including notably strategic-level spiritual warfare, prayer evangelism, identificational repentance, and prayerwalking.

The event commenced in July with a 40-day prayer fast whose participants met every noon at Singapore's Anglican Cathedral to "pray for nations" and concluded on August 9th—Singapore's National Day—with a mass prayer rally in Singapore's Indoor Stadium. A postcard advertising the event announced the theme for 1997—"Let my People Go!"—on one side above a map of the 10/40 Window, and "Thy Kingdom come!" on the other above a map of Singapore against a background showing an enormous wave, an allusion to the event's title, "Prayerwave Asia."

On the first day of the fast, the organizers presented participants with the Prayerwave Asia declaration, which began, "LORD JESUS, WE ENTHRONE YOU Sovereign Lord over Asia," and prayed "Your Kingdom come, Your will be done in Asia as it is in Heaven." The declaration prayed "for the revelation of Your Love and Your Light among the hundreds of unreached people groups across Asia," and requested that God "[i]ntervene in every arena of influence, every seat of power in the nations of Asia." A prayer in a sidebar added a note of spiritual warfare: "Ask God to expose, restrain, contain and overthrow the pharaoh-spirits that are conspiring against His Church and His agenda in Asia." Below this, the tract defined Pharoah-spirits as "anti-God systems and structures" manifested in political, cultural, religious, secular, intellectual, and materialistic mindsets.

At prayer sessions that I attended, participants held up signs with the names of diverse countries, and individuals divided into small groups to pray for the country of their choice, taking turns in offering spontaneous prayer. As an aid to prayer, organizers also distributed flyers with the wave image, the names of individual countries, and a Bible verse from the *Book of Exodus*. The theme "let my people go!" suggests that Asia's peoples were living in bondage and required divine deliverance, by analogy to the parting of the Red Sea as the Jews returned from exodus.[9] One of the countries so prayed for was Malaysia, where the government prohibits the proselytization of Muslims. Although proselytism may be prohibited, Christians still may pray for societal transformation and conversion.

At the conclusion of the 40-day Prayer Fast in 1997, seventy-two churches and Christian organizations (the majority of which were charismatic in their practices) cooperated to organize the National Day Festival of Praise.[10] In keeping with the event's theme, "Jesus Christ, Hope of the Nation," participants sought to ritually heal some of the wounds of Singapore's national past, including both British colonialism and the Japanese occupation of World War II. According to a later report, to which I have added some details in square brackets, the ritual drama of identificational repentance addressed:

> …the deep-seated fears and insecurities; resentment and bitterness linked with British colonialism and Japanese atrocities of World War II. British Prayer Track leader, Roger Mitchell stood in identification with England [repenting British racial superiority and exclusivity]; while Paul Ariga, the "Billy Graham of Japan," repented on behalf of Japan. Many tears were shed as Paul Ariga sobbed before Elizabeth Choi, an elderly lady who had been tortured for 200 days at the hands of Japanese soldiers; and before Anglican Canon James Wong, whose father was murdered by the Japanese. As the aggrieved parties extended heartfelt forgiveness ["We forgive you and your people. We release every debt that has stood between us because Jesus has cancelled these debts"], walls of hatred and bitterness tumbled down. "Love covers a multitude of sins." Putting the past behind her, the Singapore Church arose to release blessings upon Britain and Japan!
>
> (*Prayerlink* 1998, 7)

During the ritual performance, the British and Japanese ministers lay prone on the floor in an "attitude of repentance." The Singaporean ministers responded with forgiveness, and also with grateful acknowledgment of Britain's and Japan's contributions in transferring technology and investments to Singapore.

August 9th also was the date of a coordinated Citywalk. The organizers gave participants a set of six maps marked with walking tours of downtown Singapore together with a lengthy scripted declaration, an excerpt of which I provide here:

Figure 1. Singapore's National Day Festival of Praise, 1997 (Photograph: Jean DeBernardi).

Today, as priests of the Most High God standing at this historical site of our nation, we acknowledge as one people that this land of Singapore is the Lord's, and all that it contains, our economy and all who dwell therein. For the Lord our God is the God of our past, God of our present, and God of our future.

Since the occasion was designed to celebrate and strengthen the Singaporean nation, and (I infer) also to "enthrone" God over Singapore, the maps identified as key prayer points specific locations like government ministries, the Prime Minister's office, Parliament House, banks and financial houses, shopping malls and entertainment centres, as well as Sir Stamford Raffles' landing site and statue, and Singapore's national symbol, the merlion (an imaginary creature with the head of a lion and the body of a fish) in Merlion Park.

Finally, the event ended with "Citylight," a program of coordinated prayer whose beginning was timed to coincide with the strike of the national anthem during Singapore's National Day Parade. The common prayer focus for the Citylight event was threefold: "Open Heavens" (the revival of Christians in Singapore), "Open Hearts" (citywide harvest, i.e. conversion), and "Open Homes" (establishing a cell group in every HDB flat).

Conclusion

I began my study of Christianity in Singapore in 1995 with questions about the syncretism of traditional Chinese culture and Christianity expressed in an emergent Asian Theology that Taiwanese theologian Choan Seng Song and others have recently promoted (Song 1990 [1979]). I discovered instead an anti-syncretic stance that concealed a syncretic fusion of Asian and Western notions of the occult: the deities of popular religious culture take on new energy when they are identified not as powerless beings, but rather as territorial spirits, and made the target of strategic-level spiritual warfare. But I also found in the activities and organizational strategies of the AD 2000 and Beyond Movement in Singapore a drive to adapt evangelical Christianity to the symbolism and practices of the modern nation and of urban life.

Singaporeans are known for their efficiency, competitiveness, and bureaucratic rationality and Singaporean Christians deploy formidable skills in the planning and execution of these programs. Indeed, Singapore's Christian leaders are swift to recognize and adopt new trends in Christian evangelical practice, and have the education, financial resources, and organizational backing to fully realize the potential of an evangelical prayer movement like the AD 2000 United Prayer Track. But their activities also demonstrated remarkable parallels with the social structures and social programs of the modern state.

The government promotes national unity on its National Day; Singapore's AD 2000 United Prayer Track promoted Christian unity with a concurrently scheduled event entitled "The Day to Change OUR World." The government uses education and marketing to promote its social programs; Christians similarly publicize their events and propagate their values through attractively designed posters, handouts, brochures, magazines, and on-line resources. Both the government and the Christian leaders have created carefully scripted declarations designed for public recitation. The Christian declaration is of course a prayer whose audience is God, whereas the State declaration is seeking to create a shared secular ethos or code for conduct for its citizens. The government now promotes religious harmony by organizing Inter-Racial Confidence Circles and Harmony Circles, whereas the AD 2000 United Prayer Track took as one of its goals planting cell groups in every HDB highrise in Singapore's largely non-Christian heartland. Here, we may guess that the state is imitating, or perhaps competing with, the church and other religious organizations in its drive for grassroots influence.

Although both seek to shape people's core values and behavior, there are key differences. Singapore's government has a well-funded army, navy, and air force equipped with some of the most technologically advanced military hardware in the region, which the government puts on public display during its National Day Parade. The nation-state also has the power to levy taxes, and to manage many aspects of individuals' lives, from the content of the educational curriculum to mandating that religious leaders attend harmony circles and engage in inter-religious dialogue.

Singaporean Christian leaders may imagine themselves as prayer warriors, but when they use prayer as a weapon, they are in fact seeking to conquer their own followers, whose adherence is purely voluntary, and from whom they regularly seek donations and volunteer labor. Charismatic ministers are far more likely to wear business suits than clerical robes (or military uniforms), and those who lead Singapore's megachurches are members of its managerial elite. Unlike the government, they do not have the power to tax, regulate, or conscript their followers.

As I have discussed above, the novelty of innovative programs of prayer evangelism like spiritual warfare prayer and praying for nations conceals deeper continuities with the practice of living by faith and praying for God's providential help. Where evangelical movements like the AD 2000 United Prayer Track succeed most visibly is not in proselytism or making new converts but rather in mobilizing interest and support among Singaporean Christians for their programs. This support is most evident in voluntary donations made in support of Christian social programs and charitable outreach in traditional areas of evangelical concern, including providing medical care, education, and social assistance to the disadvantaged both within and outside Singapore. Since the nineteenth century, when the first Protestant faith missionaries rejected a salary and prayed instead for voluntary donations, prayer has had this function: Christians address their prayers to God, but when they pray, often many are listening.

Notes

1. This paper is based on research conducted in 1995, 1997, and 1999 with support from the University of Alberta Humanities, Fine Arts, and Social Science Research committee, the Social Science and Humanities Research Council of Canada, and the Wenner-Gren Foundation for Anthropological Research. I wish to thank the Institute of Southeast Asian Studies and the Center for Advanced Studies at the National University of Singapore for providing me with research affiliation in Singapore, and especially thank Diana Wong, Lai Ah Eng, C. J. W. L. Lee, and Brenda Yeoh for their support. For assistance with this research and/or comments on earlier drafts of this paper, I owe special thanks to Carol Berger, Simon Chan, Timothy Jenkins, Stephen A. Kent, Rosalind Hackett, Lai Ah Eng, and Heather Sharkey.

In this paper, I also draw on research conducted on behalf of the Singapore Institute of Policy Studies (IPS) in 2004–2005 as part of a collaborative research project on "Religious Diversity and Harmony in Singapore." I would like to thank IPS and especially project director Dr. Lai Ah Eng for their support for this research and for permission to tap into these research findings for this article (see also DeBernardi 2005, 2008).

2. As Rosalind Hackett notes in the Introduction to this volume, the term proselytism often carries with it a heavy freight of negative connotations. Indeed, some Singaporeans even regard the term "evangelism" as sensitive. I conclude that however it is labeled, the practice of seeking religious converts has the potential to be controversial. Because it is well-entrenched in the scholarly literature I have chosen to use the term proselytism in this article. I have sought to use the term neutrally to refer to the practice of seeking to cause or convince someone to enter into a new religious group.

3. The 1965 Administration of Muslim Law Act synchronized the management of Muslim affairs and created a statutory advisory board, the Islamic Religious Council of Singapore (the Majlis Ugama Islam Singapore, or MUIS). As its website announces, MUIS's strategic priority is "To set the Islamic agenda, shape religious life and forge the Singaporean Muslim." (see *MUIS: Vision and Mission*). Global Islamic revivalism and trends originating in multiple centers of religious authority have influenced the practice of Islam in Singapore, which like Christianity is internally diverse (see Kadir 2004). Since the 2001 attack on the World Trade Center, and in cooperation with the Singapore Islamic Scholars and Religious Teachers Association (Persatuan Ulama & Guru Guru Agama Islam, or PERGAS) MUIS has promoted a moderate Islamic agenda, screening local religious leaders, vetting visiting religious speakers, and monitoring students attending madrassahs overseas (Rahil Ismail and Shaw 2006, 42).

4. By way of comparison, Article 160 of the Malaysian constitution defines a Malay as someone who professes Islam, habitually speaks the Malay language, and conforms to Malay custom (*Constitution of Malaysia* 1958). Consequently Malays may not leave Islam at will, and Malaysia's *Shari'a* courts have the authority to punish Malays who abandon Islam by fines, detention, and imprisonment. At present there is no civil procedure by which a Muslim may change their religion: in October 2006, a Malaysian civil court ruled that a Malay convert to Christianity must appeal to a *Shari'a* court to officially renounce Islam, and unless that appeal is granted, she cannot legally marry her Christian fiancé (Alford 2006). For an insightful discussion of religious pluralism and inter-faith relationships in Malaysia, see Yeoh (2005).

5. Grounds for the charge of promoting religious disharmony include: a. Causing feelings of enmity, hatred, ill-will or hostility or prejudicing the maintenance of harmony between different religious groups; b. carrying out activities to promote a political cause, or a cause of any political society while, under the guise of, propagating or practicing any religious belief; c. carrying out subversive activities under the guise of propagating or practicing any religious belief; or d. exciting disaffection against the President or the Government (Kuah-Pearce 2003, 162).

6. The individual might also be prohibited from publicly addressing a congregation, printing and distributing any publication, or holding an office on an editorial board or committee of any publication produced by the group in question.

7. I base this observation both on interviews with Christian leaders that I conducted in 2004, and also informal conversations that I had with participants in an Intercultural Dialogue that I led at the Singapore Institute of Policy Studies in November 2004 and at a conference in 2005.

8. At an International Spiritual Warfare Network Consultation in Seoul, Korea in 1993, C. Peter Wagner officially appointed Pastor Lawrence Khong of Faith Community Baptist Church as Singapore Coordinator for the Spiritual Warfare Network. On his return, Rev. Khong began to convene small AD2000 monthly prayer meetings for pastors. Before the next Global Consultation on World Evangelism in 1995—an event attended by nearly 4,000 Christian leaders representing 186 countries, the Singaporean delegation chose Anglican Archbishop Moses Tay as the AD2000 National Coordinator for Singapore (*Prayerlink* 1998, 4–5).

9. The text on this prayer sheet was: LET MY PEOPLE GO! Then Moses stretched out his hand over the sea, and all that night the Lord drove the sea back with a strong east wind and turned it into dry land. The waters were divided, and the Israelites went through the sea on dry ground. Exodus 14:21–22.

10. These included a number of independent Charismatic churches (including City Harvest Church, the Church of Singapore, Faith Community Baptist Church, and New Creation Church), but also some denominational churches (Anglican, Assembly of God, and Methodist) and organizations like the Bible Society of Singapore, the Full Gospel Business Men's Fellowship International, and Women's Aglow Fellowship of Singapore.

References

Alford, Deann. 2006. Malay Melee. *Christianity Today.* November 2006. http://www.christianitytoday.com/ct/2006/november/3.21.html [accessed 26 December 2006].

Austin, J. L. 1975. *How to Do Things with Words.* 2nd ed. Cambridge, MA: Harvard University Press. Original date?

Bebbington, David. 1989. *Evangelicalism in Modern Britain: A History from the 1730s to the 1980s.* Grand Rapids, MI: Baker Book House.

Channel News Asia. 2002. Need to Tackle Proselytism when Drafting Religious Code: Minister. 24 October 2002. http://www.wwrn.org/article.php?idd=7466&sec=36&con=28 [accessed 10 June 2006].

Chua, Lawrence. 2004. *CP101 Reaching the Under-Reached. A Handbook for Community Penetration.* Singapore: Living Sanctuary Brethren Church.

Coleman, Simon. 2003. Continuous Conversion? The Rhetoric, Practice, and Rhetorical Practice of Charismatic Protestant Conversion. In *The Anthropology of Religious Conversion,* ed. Andrew Buckser and Stephen D. Glazier, 15–27. Lanham, MD: Rowman and Littlefield Publishers.

Constitution of Malaysia. 1957. http://www.pogar.org/publications/other/constitutions/malaysia-e.pdf [accessed 26 December 2006].

DeBernardi, Jean. 1999. Spiritual Warfare and Territorial Spirits: The Globalization and Localization of a "Practical Theology." *Religious Studies and Theology* 18(2): 66–96.

———. 2005. Christianity and Chinese Religious Culture in Singapore: Anthropological Perspectives. In *Facing Faiths, Crossing Cultures: Key Trends and Issues* in a Multicultural World. Dialogues with Chandra Muzaffar, Ibrahim Abu-Rabi', and Jean DeBernardi, ed. Lai Ah Eng, 178–225. Singapore: Institute of Policy Studies and SNP Reference.

———. 2008. Evangelical Christianity in Singapore: Global Christian Culture in the Antioch of Asia. In *Religious Diversity and Harmony in Singapore*, ed. Lai Ah Eng, 116–41. Singapore: Institute of Policy Studies.

———. n.d. If the Lord be not Come: Evangelical Christianity and the Brethren Movement in Singapore and Penang, Malaysia. Unpublished manuscript.

Feuchtwang, Stephan. 2001. *Popular Religion in China: The Imperial Metaphor*. Richmond, UK: Curzon.

Hill, Michael. n.d. Conversion and Subversion: Religion and the Management of Moral Panics in Singapore. Working Paper, Asian Studies Institute, Victoria University of Wellington. http://www.victoria.ac.nz/asianstudies/publications/working/08ConversionandSubversion.pdf [accessed 2 June 2006].

Hwa Yung. 2003 [2002]. A Systematic Theology that Recognizes the Demonic. In *Deliver Us From Evil: An Uneasy Frontier in Christian Mission*, ed. A. Scott Moreau, Tokunboh Adeyemo, David G. Burnett, Bryant L. Myers and Hwa Yung, 3–17. Petaling Jaya: Glad Sounds, Asian edition published with permission from Marc Books, World Vision International.

Johnstone, Patrick. 1993 [1974]. *Operation World*. 5th ed. Carlisle: OM Publishing.

Kadir, Suzaina. 2004. Islam, State and Society in Singapore. In *Inter-Asia Cultural Studies* 5(3): 357–71.

Kuah-Pearce, Khun Eng. 2003. *State, Society and Religious Engineering: Towards a Reformist Buddhism in Singapore*. Singapore: Eastern Universities Press.

LaHaye, Tim and Jerry B. Jenkins. 1995. *Left Behind: A Novel of the Earth's Last Days*. Wheaton, IL: Tynedale House Publishers.

Lau Pak Soon and Goh Kailin. 2004. *Harvesting Souls Through Prayer: A 30-day prayer guide for Cambodia*. Singapore.

Lowe, Chuck. 1998. *Territorial Spirits and World Evangelism?: A Biblical, Historical and Missiological Critique of Strategic-Level Spiritual Warfare*. Ross-shire, UK: Mentor/OMF.

Mauss, Marcel. 2003 [1909]. *On Prayer*. Ed. and introd. W.S.F. Pickering. Trans. Susan Leslie. New York: Durkheim Press/Berghahn Books.

Ministry of Community Development, Youth and Sports, Declaration on Religious Harmony. 2003. Press release, 9 June 2003. Http://www.mcys.gov.sg/MCDSFiles/Press/Articles/press-release-9Jun-final.html [accessed 6 June 2006].

———. 2005. Press Release: Children to See the "Colours of Harmony" (A Story Book on Religious Harmony for Chinese). Media Release No.: 24/2005. http://209.85.173.104/search?q=cache:1sPWctO70bAJ:www.mcys.gov.sg/MCDSFiles/Press/Articles/ReligiousHarmonyForChildren.pdf+%22childr en+to+see+the+%22colours+of+harmony%22&hl=en&ct=clnk&cd=1&client=safari [accessed 6 June 2006].

Moreau, A. Scott, Tokunboh Adeyemo, David G. Burnett, Bryant L. Myers and Hwa Yung. 2003 [2002]. *Deliver Us From Evil: An Uneasy Frontier in Christian Mission*. Petaling Jaya: Glad Sounds, Asian edition published with permission from Marc Books, World Vision International.

MUIS: Vision and Mission. 2006. http://www.muis.gov.sg/cms/aboutus/mission.aspx?id=181 [accessed 23 December 2006].

Müller, George. 1861. *The Life of Trust being a Narrative of the Lord's Dealings with George Müller*. Ed. H. Lincoln Wayland. Boston, MA: Gould and Lincoln.

Osteen, Joel. 2004. *Your* Best Life *Now: 7 Steps to Living at your Full Potential*. New York: Warner Faith.

Otis, George Jr. 1995. *Strongholds of the 10/40 Window: Intercessors Guide to the World's Least Evangelized Nations*. Seattle, WA: YWAM.

Peretti, Frank E. 1986. *This Present Darkness*. Wheaton, IL: Crossway Books.

Prayerlink. 1998. Singapore.

Rahil Ismail and Brian J. Shaw. 2006. Singapore's Malay-Muslim Minority: Social Identification in a Post-"9-11" World. *Asian Ethnicity* 7(1): 37–51.

Singapore – Constitution. 1963. Adopted 16 September 1963. http://www.oefre.un-ibe.ch/law/icl/sn00000_.html. [accessed 2 June 2006].

Singapore Census of Population. 2000. Religion. Advance Data Release No. 2, 2000. http://www.singstat.gov.sg/pubn/popn/c2000adr/chap5.pdf [accessed 23 December 2006].

Sinha, Vineeta. 2005. Theorising "Talk" about "Religious Pluralism" and "Religious Harmony" in Singapore. *Journal of Contemporary Religion* 20(1): 25–40.

Sng, Bobby E. K. 2003 [1980]. *In His Good Time: The Story of the Church in Singapore, 1819–2002*. 3rd ed. Singapore: Bible Society of Singapore and Graduates' Christian Fellowship.

Song, Choan-Seng. 1990 [1979]. *Third Eye Theology*. Revised edition. Maryknoll, NY: Orbis Books.

Wagner, C. Peter. 1991. Territorial Spirits. In *Territorial Spirits: Insights on Strategic-Level Spiritual Warfare from Nineteen Christian Leaders*, ed. C. Peter Wagner, 43–50. Chichester: Sovereign World.

———. 1998. *Confronting the Queen of Heaven*. Colorado Springs, CO: Wagner Institute for Practical Theology.

———. 2000. Summary Report: AD2000 United Prayer Track. http://www.ad2000.org/re00623.htm, 2000. [accessed 6 June 2006].

Warren, Rick. 2002. *The Purpose Driven Life*. Grand Rapids, MI: Zondervan.

Watson, James L. 1985. Standardizing the Gods: The Promotion of T'ien Hou ("Empress of Heaven") Along the South China Coast, 960-1960. In *Popular Culture in Late Imperial China*, ed David Johnson, Andrew J. Nathan, and

Evelyn S. Rawski, 292–324. Berkeley: University of California Press.

Yeoh Seng Guan. 2005. Managing sensitivities: religious pluralism, civil society and inter-faith relations in Malaysia. The Round Table: the Commonwealth Journal of International Affairs 94(38): 629–40.

CHAPTER 11

False Consciousness and the Jargon of Authenticity: Proselytization in the Christianized Lowland Philippines

Paul-François Tremlett

In this essay, I focus on a single site or place called Mount Banahaw in the Philippines. Mount Banahaw is an extinct volcano widely believed, by Filipinos, to be a centre and repository of spiritual power and potency. Since about 1840 it has been a centre of pilgrimage, healing and home to nationalist religious movements, and has also been associated with banditry, anticolonial armed groups, as well as communist/Maoist insurgents, encounters with UFOs and so-called new age religion. This essay references field work conducted in and around Mount Banahaw among Tagálog-speaking peoples of central-southern Luzón in the Philippines (1999–2000 and 2003) and attends to the contested representation and production—both discursively and in material practice—of Mount Banahaw by the state, Protestant missionaries working in the area, and elements within the Catholic Church. Critically, these different discursive and material representations and productions of Mount Banahaw are mediated by understandings of Filipino identity and the implication of Mount Banahaw—as a site of anti-colonial resistance and by the fact that the religious movements that have settled on its slopes worship or venerate the national hero of the country, José Rizal—in Filipino official and popular nationalisms.

In this essay, I will conceive of the representation and production of Mount Banahaw as integral to the proselytizing strategies of state and religious agents and agencies. As such, the essay will consist of three parts. In the first, I will examine Rizal as an ambivalent site for the imagining of the nation. One significant element of the literature about Rizal and so-called Rizalist religious movements is the attempt to de-legitimize the popular worship or veneration of Rizal and to establish strict interpretive parameters for reading Rizal's life and death. Nationalism emerges here as an ideology to be inculcated and proselytization thus ceases to be purely a matter pertaining to religion, as indeed sociological analyses of education, nationalism, and marginality attest (Durkheim 1956; Althusser 1971; Gellner 1983). In the second, I will examine Protestant missionary discourse and practice, whereby Mount Banahaw is produced as a site of error and superstition—indeed of false consciousness—that requires urgent attention from a missionary intellectual. One important consequence of this is the de-legitimation of the worship or veneration of Rizal by local religious movements and the implicit construction of boundaries to determine the precise separation of the political from the religious. Here, ironically, mission appears to be an agent of secularization. In the third, I will focus on writings about Banahaw by two Filipino Jesuit scholars, and I will pay particular attention to a theological jargon of authenticity (Adorno 2003) and the romanticization of the mountain. Here, Banahaw emerges not as a site that requires instruction, but is itself constituted as a site from which others may learn to experience God—and daily life—in a more spiritually authentic manner.

Rizal, religion, nation

The largest of the religious groups in Mount Banahaw is known as Ciudad Mistica de Dios—the Mystical City of God—and was established on the mountain's lower slopes in the late 1950s (Quibuyen 1991; Claussen 2001; Lahiri 2002). Like almost all of the other churches and religious groups on the mountain, José Rizal—a European-educated Tagálog novelist and doctor—figures prominently in Mistica's theology, and he is considered by some Mistica members to be the Tagálog Christ. For the state, Rizal's life and body (Tremlett 2006, 11–13) have been critical sites for mediating modernity and for imagining the nation. For Mistica, however, Rizal is not merely an object of memory or cognitive recall but a source of potency and power that functions to reinforce values of reciprocity, pity and empathy. For Ileto (1999a), the veneration and remembering of Rizal by groups such as Ciudad Mistica de Dios subverts state or official commemorations of the national hero. For Lahiri (2002), however, the veneration and remembering of Rizal by religious groups and movements signifies the colonization of Mount Banahaw—a former border area—and its transformation into an ideological prop for official nationalism. I will argue that official discourses about Rizal are directed towards the de-legitimation of religious nationalism. I will read a selection of nationalist accounts of the life and death of José Rizal through Foucault's

(1983) notion of pastoral power. Foucault's work is concerned with the shift to modernity and, like Weber (2002), the processes of rationalization that accompany it. He argues that the break from feudalism constitutes an abrupt transformation in the organization and production of power and knowledge in Western Europe. For Foucault, pastoral power describes certain social relations particular to modernity such as those between teacher and pupil and doctor and patient that constitute the individual as a subject that has a mind to be trained and a body that must be constantly monitored for signs of sickness. However, pastoral power describes not simply procedures, techniques and strategies of what Foucault calls "individualization" (1983, 215), but also the modes of (knowledge) production peculiar to modernity.

Pastoral power also denotes a form of power that has a specifically Christian origin, and the emergence of nation-states and capitalism in the nineteenth century as new modes of social, political and economic organization sees pastoral power modified towards secular objectives. According to Foucault, from the nineteenth century onwards the pastoral function is no longer one of "salvation," but rather one of "health, well-being (that is, sufficient wealth, standard of living), security, [and] protection against accidents" (1983, 215). If the idea of the shepherd and the flock once characterized the relationship of the pastor as an agent of salvation towards Others defined in terms of a particular lack (sin), then government-as-administration—indeed, as medicine—discloses the continuous development of pastoral power and its new modalities and domains of operation notably in the fields of education, health and law.

Pastoral power is, then, an uplifting and correcting power that can be taken to denote, in this context, the necessity of a civilizing agent for the preservation and extension of the state and nationalism. After the Spanish-American War in 1898 the Philippines came under U.S. control, and the new colonizers made José Rizal—whose acerbic novels incurred the ire of the previous Spanish colonial régime so much so that they executed him—the national hero to orient Tagálogs and Filipinos towards an advocate of constitutional nationalism, scientific and moral education and peace (Constantino 1970; Ileto 1999b). In other words, the strategic deployment of Rizal by the Americans, and his elevation to the status of national hero was part of the U.S. strategy to pacify the archipelago. The textualization of Rizal's life and death that followed was part of a deliberate strategy to construct Rizal as a civilizer and as an educator—in fact, as a paragon of pastoral power.

One arena in which Rizal was deployed was that of education. High-school text books by both Filipino and American writers advanced the notion that Rizal, and not Andres Bonifacio, the founder of the Katipunan that had initiated the 1896 revolution against the Spanish régime, was the proper symbol for the new nation. After independence, Rizal's novels *Noli Me Tangere* (translated as *The Social Cancer* 1996) and *El Filibusterismo* (translated as *The Reign of Greed* 1997) were made compulsory reading for Filipino school children and university students (Republic Act 1425, approved June 12, 1956). Although this move was resisted by the Catholic Church—Rizal's novels contain certain pointed criticisms of the Church and particularly the missionary Orders—the compulsory study and structured remembering of Rizal's life and works was conceived of as a means to help build and sustain—through reference to a death framed as a sacrifice to freedom and independence—a national consciousness of service to the nation. That this remembering of Rizal should simultaneously involve the forgetting of Bonifacio is not without significance.

Zaide's *Jose Rizal: Life, Works and Writings* (1992), and Gagelonia's *Rizal: Our Noble Heritage* (1968) were both written to supplement Republic Act 1425. Gagelonia was a Knight Commander of the Order of the Knights of Rizal, a Protestant group in part responsible for the Rizal Law passed in 1956. These texts are notable for their hyperbole. Rizal is variously described as a "peerless genius," "the greatest man the Malay race has ever produced," and as "a benefactor of all Asia and perhaps of all mankind," while his execution at the hands of the Spanish régime is described as a "sublime martyrdom" and "Christ-like." The relentless list of facts presented in both books discloses the vast effort undertaken to construct a very specific hermeneutic for reading Rizal. Yet, despite these and other official investments in and deployments of Rizal by indigenous administrations and the American régime that preceded Philippine independence, Rizal continuously exceeds the interpretative limits they try to establish. As Ileto has remarked, Rizal was, from the beginning, (and, of course, the beginning was, concomitantly, Rizal's material end), "implicated in the very world which…[the American and indigenous élites]… sought to efface" (Ileto 1999a, 31).

In a collection of annual Rizal day lectures delivered under the auspices of the (Philippine) National Historical Institute between 1977 and 1985 (see Aquino 1987; Bernardino 1987; Enriquez and Torres 1987), a period that, it ought to be remembered, constituted the latter half of Ferdinand E. Marcos's presidency, a consistent theme emerges. This theme or hermeneutic refers essentially to Rizal's interests in education and science as tools with which to uplift "the *common tao*" or peasantry (Bernardino 1987, 31). Critically, many of the lectures reference the four years Rizal spent exiled to Dapitan in Mindanao (see Orendain 1966). While there, he opened—among other things—a school and a clinic. He also set up a co-operative for local farmers, helped to improve local fishing methods, and even introduced street lighting.

On the one hand, this might be read as an attempt to inscribe the correct form that social relations between members of the élite and the peasantry should take. In these constructions of Rizal, such relations are presented fundamentally in terms of care. As such, his activities—carried out on behalf of, or for others—serve as a model of social, political, economic, developmental and pastoral action. These lectures, then, could be construed as a mode of critique against the Marcos régime for which bribery, corruption, murder and general wholesale economic plunder seem to have been routine.

On the other hand, one might pause to reflect on the constitution of the so-called common *tao* as an object in need of the civilizing and uplifting attention of an élite missionary agent. Interestingly, as a missionary object, the *tao* remain essentially the same savage, superstitious, duplicitous and indeed common subject of Spanish and American colonialisms. One function of this Rizalian hermeneutic, then, is to reproduce political and economic relations of domination predicated upon the presupposed qualifications of an élite-civilizing Self and the lack that is held to constitute the peasant Other. Yet, there remains a paradox, for the successful uplifting of the peasantry would constitute the disappearance of the peasant Other, which in turn would disclose the completion—or the end—not simply of the mission-to-uplift, but, critically, of the hegemony of the Filipino élite. As such, the American colonial régime and subsequent indigenous administrations might be said to have depended upon Rizal as a nexus of truth, where the proper subordination of the so-called common *tao* could be inscribed and maintained.

This notion of Rizal-as-missionary is also articulated in *In Excelcis: The Mission of Jose P. Rizal, Humanist and Philippine National Hero* (Maria Sta 1996), a text produced to coincide with the centennial commemoration of his execution by firing squad at the hands of the Spanish colonial régime. This text—complete with a Foreword from the then president of the Philippines Fidel V. Ramos—encourages the reader not only to interpret Rizal as a messenger (the chapter titles are, respectively, The Prophecy, The Call, The Crusade, The Calm and The Glory), but worse, that modernity and the nation-state were that message. It is clear that this text was intended not only to locate Rizal as a role-model of service to the nation, but further to situate him in world history as part of an unfolding towards liberal-democracy, the nation-state and capitalism as inevitable and desirable social forms.

Jose Rizal and the Asian Renaissance (Rajaretnam 1996) is a collection of essays that emerged from a conference on Rizal held on the October 2–3, 1995 in Kuala Lumpur, Malaysia, and includes papers given by Fidel V. Ramos and the then Deputy Prime Minister of Malaysia, Anwar Ibrahim. Intended to complement the activities of the Philippine Centennial Commission and the Rizal Martyrdom Centennial Commission, Rizal is presented as a "*homo universalis*" (Ibrahim 1996, 38) and as a figure whose "importance and reputation...have transcended his time and place" (Rajaretnam 1996, vi).

As a pan East Asian intellectual described as being on a par with Mahatma Gandhi, Rabindranath Tagore, Muhammad Iqbal and Sun Yat-Sen, Rizal is interpreted as having been part of a particular East–West dialogue through which a synthesis of aspects of the cultures and thought of Europe, America and Asia became possible. Although this dialogue is understood as having been instrumental in Asia's struggle against colonialism, it more importantly reveals the dominance of Western political and economic values in marking out the boundaries and limits of thought *vis-à-vis* ideas of culture, nationhood and identity in the Philippines and elsewhere in Asia. Rizal, then, is speaking to the present, but the present of this speaking is defined in terms of capitalism, trade agreements, nation-states and co-operation and security spheres. This is, however, a Rizal somewhat at odds with the Rizal venerated and worshipped by the peasants of central and southern Luzon in the Philippines, who, in places such as Mount Banahaw have remembered his death and have conducted their own ceremonies to do so. They have also ascribed him extraordinary abilities and powers, such as the ability to become invisible, and the ability to remain invulnerable to harm from blades and bullets (Santos 1973). Interestingly, the same kinds of abilities have also been commonly ascribed to rebel and bandit leaders in the Philippines.

For example, on March 29, 1897—some three months after Rizal's execution—the Spanish governor-general received the following report from one of his agents:

> The natives...in this capital believe in the rumours circulating that Jose Rizal, executed last 29 December [sic] in Bagumbayan is not dead as stated in the papers, but, on the contrary, is alive and well because of a miracle. After the execution of Rizal, the body was wrapped and loaded into a carriage which was enveloped by a rose-coloured cloud, which followed the carriage all the way to the cemetery where, upon reaching the gates, the soldiers discovered that Rizal's body had disappeared and in its place was a beautiful white cock which then flew in the direction of Cavite to join the soul of Fr. Burgos executed in 1872 who was alive and hiding in that province... The natives also believe that the corpse of Rizal transfers itself miraculously from place to place within the [Paco] cemetery! (Ocampo 1990, 16)

It seems that Rizal's death—and it is clear that he met his death with considerable dignity—generated meanings well beyond those approved by the American colonial régime and later indigenous administrations. In particular, comparisons of the deaths of Rizal and Christ produced stories that suggested that Rizal was not dead after all, but was merely waiting for the appropriate time to return. The commemoration of Rizal's death by the ruling political and economic élite could not limit these other readings of Rizal.

In a survey of various Rizalist groups, movements and churches by Foronda (1961), Rizalism is explained away in terms of indigenous, pre-Hispanic religious beliefs and practices of so-called ancestor worship (1961, 37). Indeed, Foronda's explanation unfolds in terms reminiscent of a Frazerian anthropology. Rizalism, for Foronda, is an empty signifier to a distant pre-Hispanic past defined in terms of ignorance, ancestor worship and paganism. "The poor unlettered folk...living in mountain areas and far-flung barrios" remain an object of pastoral intervention, and they must be shown the error of their false beliefs. By approaching the worship/veneration of Rizal in terms of Frazerian utilitarianism religion is relegated to the realm of (false) consciousness. Belief, as purely a matter of faulty reasoning, can thus be set up for correction by a missionary or vanguard intellectual of one kind or another.

Nowhere is all this more apparent than in a short document containing three short lectures on Rizal, published in 1969 by the (Philippine) National Historical Commission, which was presided over at that time by Ferdinand E. Marcos. The most interesting of these was delivered by Leon Ma. Guerrero at Fort Santiago, on December 30 1968. The lecture begins with Guerrero trying to imagine Rizal in the present as a presidential candidate running for election. Guerrero argues that Rizal was a man relevant to a particular historical moment and further, that the concerns of that moment are no longer shared by the present:

> He [Rizal] was mainly employed, to begin with, in securing reforms in the colonial government of his day, by which he meant the recognition of and respect for the "liberties" of the people or what we would call their fundamental rights. These are now proclaimed in our own Constitution, and, however imperfectly, enforced by our own judiciary. They were threatened in the not so distant past, they must be preserved with eternal vigilance, but in principle they are no longer a valid issue. Rizal was also deeply concerned with the emergence of a united Filipino nation, and nationalism is still one of the most significant and powerful influences in our political life. But the ultimate goal of Rizal's nationalism, masked by the dissimulation that prudence required under an intolerant colonial regime, was independence, and independence has already been acquired. (Guerrero 1969, 6–7)

Guerrero's text is haunted by Black Sunday and the bloody events of May 1967, when members of a Rizalist religious group known as Lapiang Malaya led by Valentin de los Santos were massacred on the streets of Manila by government soldiers. They had been attempting to stage a demonstration (see Sturtevant 1969). Guerrero refers to Black Sunday as a "gaudy and unforgivably sanguinary farce" and declares that "there is, after-all, a limit to the relevance of the past to the present, and the transgression of that limit leads to tragedy and folly" (1969, 9). Guerrero wants to negate de los Santos' invocation of Rizal. According to Guerrero, then, the dead cannot, indeed must not come back: the coffins and the tombs must be secured, and the work of mourning and of remembering must be placed within strict parameters to ensure proper closure.

Interestingly, Ileto's *Pasyon and Revolution* begins with an account of Black Sunday. Ileto uses this to argue that the events of Holy Week and the *pasyón* did not only structure the so-called traditional mind in the nineteenth century:

> The Lapiang Malaya affair is not an isolated event in Philippine history. It is not an aberration in an otherwise comprehensible past. We should be able to find meaning in it, not resorting to convenient explanations like "fanaticism," "nativism" and "millenarianism," which only alienate us further from the kapatid [lit: "brother" or "sister"] who lived through it. But what we modern Filipinos need first of all is a set of conceptual tools, a grammar, that would help us understand the world of the kapatid, which is part of our world. Twentieth-century economic and technological developments have produced the modern Filipino culture to which we belong, but as Marx himself often pointed out, cultural transformation proceeds in an uneven, sporadic manner so that in a given historical situation we find cultural modes that reflect previous stages of development. In the interest of social reform we can either further accelerate the demise of "backward" ways of thinking (reflected in the Lapiang Malaya) in order to pave way for the new, or we can graft modern ideas onto traditional modes of thought. Whatever our strategy may be, it is necessary that we first understand how the traditional mind operates, particularly in relation to questions of change.
>
> (Ileto 1979, 2).

Ileto's use of the word "*kapatíd*" is critical to a spatializing of Self/Other relations that defines this piece of text. His use of "we" and the later identification of that "we" with a modernity that might be opposed to and thus distanced from "the traditional mind" is transformed through the use of a kinship term (*kapatíd*) to reference not only élite-urban Filipinos, but all Filipinos as a single family. However, if, at the beginning of this passage Ileto seeks to "understand the world of the *kapatid*, which is part of our world," by the end these two worlds have been re-inscribed in a hierarchical relationship. Ileto's apparent advocacy of corrective surgery—note the use of the word "graft" in the quotation above—is an attempt to operate on that which is still, ultimately, understood as a problem or as an error requiring correction. The "world of the *kapatíd*" is a world that belongs to the past, and "the traditional mind" is a mind that needs to be modernized. The problem with these pronouncements is that Ileto re-inscribes the masses as a subject requiring cognitive instruction from some kind of vanguard intellectual. In other words, the question of religion is a question being answered in terms of consciousness, reason and cognition, with religious beliefs and practices being assessed, measured, judged and evaluated in terms of their use-value and also in nationalist terms.

Each year, on December 30—the day of Rizal's execution by the Spanish colonial régime—state-sanctioned mourning and remembrance occurs at the Rizal monuments and shrines that are to be found in the central plazas of towns and cities across the Philippines. However, he is also remembered by members of Ciudad Mistica de Dios, with the singing of nationalistic hymns and the *Pagtaás ng Watawat* or Flag-raising Ceremony. The differences and similarities in these mournings are worth remarking on.

The Rizal Day celebrations in San Pablo City on December 30, 1999 included political speeches and Tagálog songs and dances from the nineteenth century, together with a flag-raising ceremony. They ended with a re-enactment of Rizal's execution by firing squad at Bagumbayan field in Manila. In other words, Rizal was killed again, and, no doubt, he is re-killed year in year out all over the Philippines. This requirement of re-killing is a means of preserving state sanctioned or official readings of Rizal that emphasize that the things that Rizal died for (i.e., for constitutional government and independence), have already been acquired. Moreover, if the constant repetition of Rizal's death threatens to lead that death into meaninglessness, it also functions as a grim reminder of state-power and state-violence.

For Mistica, the remembering of Rizal is an element in a series of mournings for the "*labindalawáng ilaw ng Pilipinás*"—the twelve lights of the Philippines[1]—all of whom were involved in the struggle against Spanish rule. Rizal and the twelve disciples of Philippine nationalism—as they are depicted in paint on the inside of Mistica's church—are clearly rendered in parallel to Jesus Christ and his disciples. This veneration of Rizal as Christ, and/or the remembering of Rizal and other Filipino revolutionary heroes in terms of Christ and his disciples, might suggest a form of national memory radically at odds with those approved by official nationalism. Yet, the apparent substitution of—or perhaps better—blurring of a religious ritual with a civic ceremony, Mount Banahaw's emergence as a national shrine to anti-colonial resistance and the dealings of Banahaw's religious leaders with wealthy patrons and politicians might equally suggest an effort by one waning source of power to negotiate with another apparently more fecund source, i.e., the state, and perhaps the colonization of the former by the latter. Moreover, the endless and serial reproduction of Rizal by both the state and religious groups in stone, paint, hymn, song and text ensures Rizal's disappearance out of time and place and his transference to a mythical realm. Finally, with both official and subaltern memories focused on Rizal, a number of important figures and events in Philippine history can be conveniently glossed or forgotten.

On June 12 2000, I was in Manila for the celebrations at the Luneta, for the yearly commemoration of Emilio Aguinaldo's declaration of independence in 1898, and the establishment of the Malolos Republic, the first independent Republic to be established in Asia. Central to the celebrations was a procession of floats and various characters from Philippine history, including not only Lapu-lapu, José Rizal, Emilio Aguinaldo and Andres Bonifacio, but also Macario Sakay and Papa Isio. The presence of religious rebels such as Macario Sakay (Ileto 1979) and Papa Isio (Cullamar 1986) in the procession led me to pause, because the activities of the likes of Isio and Sakay have generally been constituted as aberrations of an essentially rational history and at best, as proto-nationalists (Zaide 1957; Agoncillo and Alfonso 1968; Corpuz 1970; Constantino 1975). However, it soon became clear that this procession constituted a kind of hermeneutic of obedience. As each figure or float reached President Estrada, he, she or they would fall to one knee in an act of fealty and obeisance. It seemed as if Estrada was attempting to summon all of Philippine history's disparate elements in an attempt to forge a coherence and unity among them through a single act of obedience to the present. If the entirety of the past could be summoned such that it was at once both transparent and coherent, then perhaps the dead could be both acknowledged and silenced simultaneously through a combined act of necromancy and exorcism. It was a statement to the effect that the past is the servant of the present, and that the dead shall obey the will of the living. Furthermore, it exposed the fragility of nationalism as a ritual practice (Hobsbawm and Ranger 1983) and as a kind of proselytization that in the Philippines has been forced to contend with commemorations and ceremonies that sit ambivalently beside state-sanctioned proceedings.

False consciousness

San Pablo City is home to a number of small Protestant congregations and missionary schools, including the Christian Reformed Church which is actively working in the villages on the lower slopes of Mount Banahaw. In this section I want to explore briefly firstly how this group of missionaries conceive of the beliefs and practices of those Tagálogs living on the mountain, secondly the work of conversion itself, and thirdly the consequences of conversion for Rizal and the theologies of groups such as Mistica.

The first people I established any kind of relationships with in San Pablo

City were connected to a group known as the Banahaw for Jesus Movement (BJM). According to their analysis, Mount Banahaw and the religious activities that go on there are examples of idolatry, superstition and error. As such, they took me around the various shrines (*puwesto*) on the lower slopes of the mountain to "prove" to me that the Filipinos in Mount Banahaw are worshipping "idols." They also introduced me to locals who regaled me with stories of Banahaw's alleged miracles. This evidence showed that Banahaw's residents are superstitious and that, given the fantastical nature of these stories, the people of Mount Banahaw are in desperate and urgent need of cognitive instruction to save them from the Devil. Indeed, I was advised by the leader of the BJM group not to conduct research with Ciudad Mistica de Dios as their members were "witches" and "Satanists."

The religious beliefs and practices of the villagers of Mount Banahaw are understood by BJM members as elements of a discrete system, some of which are recognisably Christian, others of which are pagan or even Satanic deviations. The first move, then, for a BJM missionary is to separate or de-contextualize local religious beliefs and practices both from the economic, political and cultural history of rural central-southern Luzón and the Philippines more generally, and to measure and evaluate them in terms of their accordance or lack of accordance with the Bible. Missionary work involves, then, identifying what are considered to be false or erroneous beliefs and practices—the worship or veneration of Rizal being a conspicuous example—and targeting them for correction. Their principal weapon in this task is the Biblical text itself, and Bible-reading classes in which they practice a hermeneutic known as "scripture interprets scripture." As missionary or vanguard intellectuals, they endeavour to demonstrate the lack of fit between local beliefs and practices and what is permitted and prohibited in the Bible. Their mission, then, is to cognitively instruct Mount Banahaw's residents in how to read the Bible correctly and to apply that reading to their own daily conduct. They begin the process of re-education by distributing free medicines to villagers. Slowly they gain the trust of local people, suggesting that they should read the Bible together. They target village leaders for these Bible-reading sessions and were proud to inform me that they had the ear of the leadership of another religious group on the mountain called Tatlong Persona Solo Dios (Three Persons in One God or TPSD). The effect of their interventions in and around Mount Banahaw remains to be seen. However, a significant consequence of their missionary work and their effort to expose the lack of scriptural authority for the worship or veneration of Rizal, is the inscription of normative boundaries to demarcate the political from the religious. This secularizing effect can be seen in the Mistica compound. Although BJM have failed to convert any Mistica members, Mistica completed construction of a new church in their compound in 2000. Significantly, while in the old church can be found the paintings of Rizal and Christ discussed earlier, in the new church the walls are blank. When I asked about the reason behind this I was told that Mistica was concerned that representations of the group as Rizal worshippers had constituted the group as theologically naive.

The jargon of authenticity

In this section I am going to engage in an analysis of two texts produced by Jesuit scholars about Mount Banahaw. The first is Marasigan's book about TPSD, a group established by Agapito Illustrisimo—a former pulahan or so-called Red One—in the village of Kinabuhayan in 1936. As with Ciudad Mistica de Dios, its priests are women, and José Rizal figures prominently in its theology. Mount Banahaw is likewise considered by this group to be a place of great power, and the site for the future emergence of the New Jerusalem (see Elesterio 1989; Claussen 2001). The second is a more general work about the various religious communities living in Mount Banahaw and the kinds of religious beliefs and practices that can be found there. Critically, both works reflect a re-positioning that took place within the Catholic Church inspired by the Second Vatican Council (1962–1965). Both these works, then, constitute attempts to apply ideas derived from Vatican II to the study of so-called folk religion.

Marasigan's work with TPSD in the village of Kinabuhayan is framed by his reading of *Evangeli Nuntiandi*. This document, prepared for the tenth anniversary of the Second Vatican Council, reaffirms the role of the Church in the struggle against oppressive political and economic structures, arguing that the message of liberation "is not foreign to evangelization" (41). On so-called "popular religiosity" (59), it declares that "it manifests a thirst for God which only the simple and poor can know" (60) and further that "pastoral charity...must be sensitive to it, know how to perceive its interior dimensions and undeniable values, be ready to help it overcome its risks of deviation" (60). Further, Marasigan's long years of engagement with the religious groups and movements of Mount Banahaw attest to his belief that although the religiosity of the poor needs monitoring to prevent deviation, it nevertheless authentically and genuinely expresses the presupposed essential human search for God. Marasigan writes:

> The study [of Tatlong Persona Solo Dios] arose out of a seminar-workshop
> at the Loyola School of Theology, Ateneo de Manila University, during
> the first semester of 1979. The participants were trying to apply Loner-
> gan's "Method in Theology" to specific problems of inculturation in the
> Philippines. The problems were tentatively contextualized as a polarization

between two cultures—the more Westernized and the less Westernized Filipino cultures, between the urbanized minority and the rural majority of the Christian population, between official religion and popular religiosity. This cultural polarization was seen as a significant aspect of the country's four centuries of colonial history. The participants agreed that studies of popular piety before Vatican II, although well-documented, lacked the insights into the cultural pluralism of Vatican II; these uncritically assumed that the culture of medieval Western Europe or the modern technocratic culture of industrialized nations was the "norm" for all other cultures, and that cultural progress consisted in making these other cultures conform to the "norm." Historically, as a result of this assumption, some expressions of the people's search for God and the faith are despised and pejoratively labelled as "popular religiosity" or "folk Christianity." Pope Paul VI has since exhorted Catholics, in *Evangelii Nuntiandi* to rediscover the positive elements in popular piety and to purify it of its negative elements. (Marasigan 1985, 1)

Marasigan sets out an opposition that he claims is characteristic of documents on so-called "popular piety" prepared before Vatican II. These documents distinguish between urban and rural populations, and between an urban minority in the Philippines that is the bearer of "official religion" and is "more Westernized" and a rural majority which remains, somehow, inadequately Christianized. In other words, a position is advanced whereby the rural Philippines continues to be a missionary space, a space that, for a whole host of complex reasons, has somehow remained beyond the pastoral project of both the Church and the state. In this analysis, "folk Christianity" is, as it were, a poor copy or imitation of an official master religion.

The pre-Vatican II period approaches the folk of folk religion as in need of cognitive instruction. The inadequacy of this position, according to Marasigan, demands that new studies be undertaken that emphasize "participant observation" and what Marasigan terms "immersion experiences" (1985, 2). Marasigan claims that living among the TPSD in the village of Kinabuhayan led him to question and reflect on his own assumptions about rural religiosity, and then to adopt a position of sympathy towards the TPSD. However, it is Marasigan's sympathetic approach to the TPSD, and their theology and the documents that they made available to him, that ultimately leads Marasigan into romanticism as he claims that "they [the TPSD members] are very close to nature and extremely sensitive to its beauties and changing moods, and they commune with nature in a very intimate way, almost intersubjectively" (1985, 3).

This is by no means an isolated example. Later on, the faith of TPSD members is described as "serene" and in terms of "ineffable peace" (1985, 10), while a complex of cave shrines beside Kinabuahyan's river are described as "awesome and fascinating" (1985, 4). These caves are full of icons, burning candles and incense, and are visited by pilgrims daily. According to Marasigan, the dusky half-light of the cave shrines produces an experience that might bring "a poet or musician to peeks of artistic inspiration and a contemplative to the verge of ecstasy" (1985, 4).

While Marasigan's is very much a scholarly work, Gorospe's text is much more a book for the coffee table with its large print, question and answer format and numerous colour photographs. The reader is informed, in a Foreword, of Gorospe's background, and the circumstances that formed the context for his journeys to the "Power Mountain" (1992, 6), which have involved, among other things, taking his students from the Ateneo de Manila to visit Mount Banahaw's religious communities and shrines.

Gorospe's approach to Mount Banahaw, its history, his discussion of the pilgrimage route and the various shrines and the religious beliefs and practices of those who live there is framed explicitly in terms of the opposition of rural life versus city or urban living. This opposition closely resembles the way a number of people, including healers, Mistica members and middle-class Manileños, represented Mount Banahaw to me. It is assumed that those who live close to nature (sic) somehow have unmediated access to the divine and more authentic spiritual experiences than city dwellers, because "it is the city that is artificial and Banahaw that is natural. We were not meant to live like a thousand chickens cooped in cement cages and choked by smog and deafened by urban noise" (1992, 73). Moreover:

> Even without belief in the local folklore, complying with the rituals develops
> the virtue of respect and understanding—virtues that are in themselves very
> spiritual. For as long as moments of silence are observed, private prayers are
> said, nature is observed and enjoyed, a different kind of high is provoked,
> a lightness of feeling induced, an inner peace made possible. All these
> promote spirituality. Our oneness with nature, represented by water, trees,
> rocks, open skies, clean air, is our first hint of what it is to be united with
> the Creator of all these—the same Creator of us all. If it is difficult to know
> God directly, then, we can make it a little easier for ourselves by knowing
> him through what he has directly created—that means through human
> beings and nature. From the ritualism of prayer before a rock, prayer while
> bathing in the stream, prayer inside the cave, prayer among the trees and the
> stars, we can transcend to a higher and deeper journey—a journey to our
> spirituality. (1992, 70)

The legacy of Vatican II in the Philippines, then, beyond the Church's discursive interventions on the political stage (for example, Cardinal Jaime Sin's very public condemnation of Estrada's alleged gambling and womanizing were critical to the mobilization of Manileños for EDSA II which led to Estrada's downfall) has been to provide a framework for the romanticization of the countryside generally and rural religion in Mount Banahaw in particular. The most important function of the Catholic construction of Mount Banahaw would appear to be the inscription of the memory of God in what is held to be authentic examples of pre-Hispanic religio-spiritual beliefs and practices. Although the beliefs and practices of Mount Banahaw's religious groups implicitly deny the authority of the Catholic Church to interpret scripture and clearly reflect and negotiate with local and national experiences of colonialism and nationalism, the same beliefs and practices are nevertheless recuperated as a source that can revitalize not only modern, urban existence, but Philippine Catholicism and indeed the nation as a whole.

Conclusions

In this essay I have attempted to demonstrate the complex discursive and material production of Mount Banahaw as a site of nationalist inculcation—a form of state proselytizing or pastoral power—to de-legitimize the veneration and worship of the Philippine national hero José Rizal by local religious movements, as a site of superstition and paganism by Protestant missionaries whose activities have important consequences for Banahaw's religio-nationalist movements and their theologies and, finally, as a space of authentic religiosity that can revitalize Philippine Catholicism and the nation. In each instance, proselytization was understood as a form of cognitive instruction. However, I would also suggest, given the inflection of proselytizing discourses and practices with wider discourses in the Philippines about national identity and culture, that proselytization articulates new relations between nation and locality, as well as certain institutions and groups.

A weakness of this essay has been the tendency to constitute Banahaw's residents and religious groups as passive objects of state, missionary and church interventions, rather than as agents and authors of their own history. In 2003, in my final conversation with Mistica's Secretary-General before returning to London, he concluded with the words, "we are hog farmers. That's all we know." These words captured a sense of betrayal and of Banahaw's dissipating power and potency, that indeed Mistica's members—largely poor, tenant farmers and migrant workers—have become objects of capitalist exploitation, state manipulation (particularly during elections), unwanted missionary attention and scholarly enquiry. Moreover, the lure of Banahaw's power is lost on the children of Mistica members who are attracted rather by the seductions of the city and global media images of wealth, glamour and power, allegedly available there. If it is proper to talk about the conversion of Mount Banahaw then it is as a touristic and new age curio for middle class Manileños who, in increasing numbers, are spending their weekends and building second homes on the mountain's lower slopes in search of an authentic experience of the sacred.

Acknowledgment

I would like to thank Rosalind Hackett for her extended comments on an earlier version of this essay. Of course, all errors in fact and in interpretation remain my own.

Note

1. The *"labindalawáng ilaw ng Pilipinás"* are, in alphabetical order, Melchora Aquino 1812–1919 (better known as Tandang Sora, she nursed and fed wounded *Katipuñeros* and was captured and exiled by the Spanish régime, but was able to return in 1898 when America occupied the archipelago), Andres Bonifacio 1863–1897 (founder and leader of the Katipunan that instigated the revolution against Spain, he was murdered by Aguinaldo in a power struggle for leadership of the revolution), Fr. José Apolonio Burgos 1837–1872 (he was a Filipino priest who opposed the turning over of the parishes to the friars, and was executed after being implicated in the Cavite Mutiny), Emilio Jacinto 1875–1899 (he was a political essayist who wrote in Tagálog rather than Spanish), G. Lopez Jaena 1865–1896 (he was a member of the self-styled Propaganda Movement based in Spain), Gen. Antonio Luna 1868–1899 (considered to be the best general in the revolutionary army, he was assassinated by Aguinaldo's agents), Juan Luna 1857–1899 (a painter who won considerable accolade in Spain, he was imprisoned on the outbreak of hostilities between revolutionary and Spanish forces), Apolinario Mabini 1864–1903 (he was political adviser to Emilio Aguinaldo), Gen. Miguel Malvar 1865–1911 (he was a general in the revolutionary army), Pedro Paterno 1857–1911 (he was the writer of the first Filipino novel in Spanish), Gen. Gregorio Del Pilar 1875–1899 (he was a general in the revolutionary army famous for his defence of Tirad Pass where he and his entire force were killed by American troops), and Marcelo del Pilar 1850–1896 (he was also a member of the Propaganda Movement in Spain).

References

Adorno, T. 2003. *The Jargon of Authenticity.* Trans. K. Tarnowski and F. Will. London and New York: Routledge.

Agoncillo, T.A. and O.M. Alfonso, 1968. *History of the Filipino People.* Quezon City: Malaya Books.

Althusser, L. 1971. Ideology and Ideological State Apparatuses (Notes towards an Investigation). *Lenin and Philosophy, and Other Essays,* 127–86. Trans. B. Brewster. London: NLB.

Aquino, C. P. 1987. Rizal's Social Humanism: A Design for Our Times. In *Jose Rizal Annual Lectures 1977–1985*, 1–9. Manila: National Historical Institute.

Bernardino, V. 1987. Jose Rizal, The Total Man/Hero. In *Jose Rizal Annual Lectures 1977–1985*, 29–34. Manila: National Historical Institute.

Claussen, H.L. 2001. *Unconventional Sisterhood: Feminist Catholic Nuns in the Philippines*. Ann Arbor: University of Michigan Press.

Constantino, R. 1970. Veneration Without Understanding. In *Dissent and Counter-Consciousness*, 125–146. Quezon City: Malaya Books.

———. 1975. *The Philippines: A Past Revisited*. Quezon City: Tala Publishing Services.

Corpuz, O.D. 1970. *The Philippines*. Englewood Cliffs, NJ: Prentice-Hall and Manila: National Bookstore.

Cullamar, E.T. 1986. *Babaylanism in Negros 1896–1907*. Quezon City: New Day Publishers.

Durkheim, E. 1956. *Education and Sociology*. Trans. Sherwood D. Fox. New York: The Free Press.

Elesterio, F.G. 1989. Ultra-Nationalist Filipino Religions. In *Three Essays on Philippine Religious Culture*, 40–56. Manila: De la Salle University Press.

Enriquez, J. T. 1987. Rizal: Balikatan Sa Barangay. In *Jose Rizal Annual Lectures 1977–1985*, 11–19. Manila: National Historical Institute.

Foronda Jr. M. A. 1961. *Cults Honouring Rizal*. Manila: De la Salle College.

Foucault, M. 1983. Afterword, The Subject and Power. In *Michel Foucault: Beyond Structuralism and Hermeneutics*. Ed. H. Dreyfus and P. Rabinow, 208–26. Brighton: The Harvester Press.

Gagelonia, P.A. 1968. *Rizal: Our Noble Heritage*. Manila: Cruz and Sons Bookstore.

Gellner, E. 1983. *Nations and Nationalism*. Oxford: Blackwell.

Gorospe, V.R. 1992. *Banahaw: Conversations with a Pilgrim to the Power Mountain*. Makati, Manila: Bookmark.

Guerrero, L.M. 1969. Rizal and the Faustian Generation. In *The Second Annual Jose P. Rizal Lectures*, 1–15. Manila: National Historical Commission.

Hobsbawm, E. and Ranger, T. 1983. *The Invention of Tradition*. Cambridge: Cambridge University Press.

The Holy See. n.d. Apostolic Exhortation *Evangeli Nuntiandi* of His Holiness Pope Paul VI. London: Catholic Truth Society.

Ibrahim, A. 1996. Jose Rizal: The Discourse on the Asian Renaissance. In *Jose Rizal and the Asian Renaissance*, (ed). M. Rajaretnam, 38–42. Kuala Lumpur: Institut Kajian Dasar and Manila: Solidaridad Publishing House.

Ileto, R.C. 1979. *Pasyon and Revolution: Popular Movements in The Philippines 1840–1910*. Quezon City: Ateneo de Manila University Press.

———. 1999a. Rizal and the Underside of Philippine History. In *Filipinos and Their Revolution: Event, Discourse, and Historiography*, ed. R.C. Ileto, 29–78. Quezon City: Ateneo de Manila University Press.

———. 1999b. The Philippine Revolution of 1896 and U.S. Colonial Education. In *Knowing America's Colony: A Hundred Years from The Philippine War*, ed. R.C. Ileto, 1–17. Philippine Studies Occasional Papers Series 13. University of Hawaii at Manoa: Centre for Philippine Studies.

Lahiri, S. 2002. Materializing the Spiritual: Christianity, Community, and History in a Philippine Landscape. PhD Thesis: Cornell University.

Marasigan V. 1985. *A Banahaw Guru: Symbolic Deeds of Agapito Illustrisimo*. Quezon City: Ateneo de Manila University Press.

Maria Sta. F.P. 1996. *In Excelcis: The Mission of Jose P. Rizal, Humanist and Philippine National Hero*. Makati City: Studio Five Designs.

Ocampo, A.R. 1990. *Rizal Without the Overcoat*. Manila: Anvil Publishing.

Orendain, J.C. 1966. *Rizal: Model Citizen of Dapitan*. Quezon City: International Graphic Service.

Quibuyen, F. 1991. *"And Woman Shall Prevail Over Man:" Symbolic Sexual Inversion and Counter-Hegemonic Discourse in Mt. Banahaw: The Case of the Ciudad Mistica de Dios*. Philippine Studies Occasional Papers Series 10. University of Hawaii at Manoa: Centre for Philippine Studies.

Rajaretnam, M. 1996. Preface to *Jose Rizal and the Asian Renaissance*. (ed). M. Rajaretnam, v-ix. Kuala Lumpur: Institut Kajian Dasar and Manila: Solidaridad Publishing House.

Rizal, J. 1996. *The Social Cancer*. Trans. C.E. Derbyshire. Quezon City: Giraffe Books.

———. 1997. *The Reign of Greed*. Trans. C.E. Derbyshire. Quezon City: Giraffe Books.

Santos, A.P. (ed). 1973. *Rizal Miracle Tales*. Manila: National Book Store.

Sturtevant, D.R. 1969. *Agrarian Unrest in the Philippines*. Ohio: Centre for International Studies, Papers in International Studies Southeast Asia Series 8. Place: Publisher.

Torres, J. P. 1987. Rizal's Continuing Dialogue. In *Jose Rizal Annual Lectures 1977–1985*, 21–27. Manila: National Historical Institute.

Tremlett, P-F. 2006. *Power, Invulnerability, Beauty: Producing and Transforming Male Bodies in the Lowland Christianised Philippines*. Gender and Religion Centre Occasional Paper. London: School of Oriental and African Studies, University of London.

Weber, M. 2002. *The Protestant Ethic and the Spirit of Capitalism*. Trans. T. Parsons. London and New York: Routledge.

Zaide, G.F. 1957. *Philippine Political and Cultural History*, vol 1 and 2. Manila: Philippine Education Company.

———. 1992. *Jose Rizal: Life, Works and Writings*. Manila: National Book Store.

CHAPTER 12

Proselytization as Secular Protest: Rearticulating the Falun Gong Message

Patsy Rahn

In July 1999, a cultivation practice known as Falun Gong (FLG) was banned in the People's Republic of China (PRC). In response, FLG became a protest movement using non-violent means to advocate their cause and seek redress. Their goal was to counteract the Chinese government's negative portrayal of the movement, and end the ban and alleged mistreatment of its members within China. The founder of the group, Li Hongzhi, developed teachings to explain the crisis to his followers, and, over time, changed the tasks of his disciples, moving them from a primary goal of personal cultivation into a culture of protest and salvation. This chapter explores, therefore, how religious dogma and goals, here in the case of FLG, become transformed in response to events, and how a sacred, soteriological message becomes embodied in a secular message. It illustrates how salvation is articulated, not just in terms of acceptance of a strict religious perspective, but also by adherence to a secular view. Finally, this case study reveals how the interface of media with goals of religious ultimate concern and political protest creates a rich environment for proselytization. In the case of FLG, this proselytization is of both a secular and religious nature.[1]

I will begin with a brief description of FLG's background in the PRC and its shift from a legitimate group to a banned group in crisis. I will then explore the attitude of FLG practitioners towards proselytization and salvation, and how these beliefs developed progressively within a culture of protest and salvation. The third section will discuss the attitude of FLG practitioners toward the media, and how their teachings influence their use of informational and communicational technologies for proselytizing activities.

Background: from legitimacy to crisis

In 1992 Li Hongzhi founded a movement in China called Falun Gong. The group defines itself as a "cultivation practice" that teaches people to be good, kind and moral. A disciple achieves this by practicing certain exercises, and believing in Li's teachings, a process called "cultivation." One of its most publicized creeds is that the ultimate principles of the universe are "Truthfulness, Compassion and Forbearance." For many Chinese, its initial attraction is a promise of good health and healing.[2] Before the ban, FLG was legally registered with China's national *qigong* organization, the Chinese Qigong Scientific Research Organization.[3] Li taught for several years throughout China under its auspices. In 1995, his teachings came under criticism for promoting "superstition," and, in 1996, his publications began to be banned.[4] In 1996, Li informed the *qigong* organization that FLG would no longer provide training seminars in China, and he withdrew the group from the Qigong Association (Tong 2002b, 640). This act lost the group its registration and effectively made it illegal. Li then left China to travel and teach in North America and Europe. In 1998 he emigrated to the United States.

The group's size, meanwhile, grew to between two million (government low-end estimate) to eighty million (FLG estimate), making it one of the largest non-governmental organizations in China (Tong 2002b, 636). In order to provide a legitimate organizational base, at Li's request, several Falun Gong members in China tried to re-register the group as a social organization. When this failed, FLG re-defined itself as having a loose organizational structure in the hope that this would allow it to legally exist without being registered as an organization.[5] During the years of growing criticism before it was banned, the group organized approximately three hundred demonstrations to protest media reports critical of them (Tong 2002a, 795). This process culminated in the 25 April, 1999 day-long gathering of between 10,000 to 18,000 practitioners outside the government headquarters in Beijing. It was this demonstration that caused the Chinese government, under President Jiang Zemin, to investigate and eventually ban the group on 22 July, 1999.[6]

Particularly in the initial years following the ban, using propaganda directed at the public, as well as re-education and intimidation of FLG followers, the government waged an intense campaign to discredit and suppress the group. The government burned books, jailed leaders, detained thousands, and sent thousands more to reform-labor camps. Since the ban, Falun Gong claims that many practitioners have been tortured and thousands of practitioners have died in jail, or shortly thereafter. The government denies these claims, and counters that over a thousand people have died due to believing in FLG teachings. Outside China, Falun Gong continues to advocate both its cause and its plight to the Western public, politicians, human rights groups, the United Nations, and the U.S. courts, in an attempt to gain redress and remedy. The Chinese government, for its part, tries to convince the same constituencies that Falun Gong is a dangerous cult that causes harm to its practitioners and to society, and therefore deserves to be banned.

Falun Gong was pro-active in China before the ban, willing to protest and demand redress for critical commentary and censorship. Once banned, and with its center moved to the United States, the group evolved into a protest movement operating on an international scale. The suppression in China, and the FLG campaign to reverse this, constitute the environment in which Li Hongzhi continued to develop his teachings using feedback and response from his disciples, the Chinese government, and actors in the international community.[7] It was out of these needs and in this environment that a culture of protest and salvation was developed, with the media, particularly the Internet, playing a significant role in mediating their goals.

The combining of religious and secular goals

I will begin by discussing the group's attitude towards proselytization, and then examine how the response to the ban has generated teachings that comprise both religious and secular goals. I suggest that the group's goals led to a need for proselytization, and influenced its methods. Briefly, Falun Gong practitioners believe that a person has a predestined relationship with Falun Dafa (another name for the group). Ultimately, Master Li will save practitioners and anyone else deserving of salvation. Prior to the ban, however, proselytizing to save others was rarely talked about as a task for disciples. As stated above, this changed after the group was banned. Some background is necessary to explain how the religious task of disciples shifted from cultivating oneself to saving others.

On 20 July, 1999, two days before the official ban, Li Hongzhi went into hiding, and had no contact with his followers or the media for nine months. It was during this time that FLG followers in China suffered the initial, and most severe, period of repression. Li later explained his absence by saying he was busy battling and eliminating the evil forces in other dimensions that were causing the tribulations for his disciples.[8] On 20 May, 2000, Li ended his seclusion by once again starting to post new articles, or teachings, to the FLG Minghui website also known as Clearwisdom. His new postings became a major source of motivation, inspiration, and direction for the movement. Postings included transcripts of his talks given at FLG experience-sharing conferences, and subsequent question and answer sessions, as well as new writings.[9] Before this time, the main goal and responsibility of practitioners was to cultivate themselves so as to reach "Consummation," i.e., to ascend to one's Falun Dafa paradise where they would become a god and reign as a king.[10] Once Li reappeared in May 2000, his teachings changed to require disciples to take an activist stance, and protest the events in China. This meant they had to "step forward" to "clarify the truth" and "validate the Fa" (*Fa* literally means law and in FLG terminology means the teachings of Falun Dafa). If they did not "step forward" they ran the risk of losing their chance to "Consummate."

For FLG practitioners in China, "stepping forward to clarify the truth" could be very dangerous to the point of losing one's life. It could mean a loss of job, family problems, isolation from neighbors, detention, arrest, questioning, incarceration in labor camps, prisons or mental hospitals, and possibly even torture or death. Actions of "stepping forward" could include going to Tiananmen Square to protest, and hence being detained, going on a hunger strike once in detention, passing out flyers to the public, as well as printing and distributing FLG website articles and Li's teachings. It also included contacting Western reporters, reporting information on abuses, detentions, etc., to the FLG website, as well as sending in testimonials. To "clarify the truth" meant convincing others that the Chinese Communist Party's (CCP) view of FLG was wrong and reveal CCP injustices towards FLG. "Stepping forward to clarify the truth" and being pro-active for the movement was, and still is, necessary proof that one is a true disciple. Not to be pro-active was at best to lose one's status as a good practitioner and, at worst, to lose one's chance of Consummating.

Thus, after Li's reappearance in 2000, the action of being able to "clarify the truth" was connected to saving sentient beings and both these tasks were connected to a disciple's chance of Consummation. During a conference in 2003, Li stated:

> Looking at it from an ordinary person's perspective, we indeed want to tell
> the world's people the real truth about us. And from the Fa's perspective,
> we're indeed saving them from being eliminated because of that.
>
> (Li 2003a)

"Elimination" is what will happen to non-believers and evil-doers at the moment of Fa-rectification.[11] A simple explanation of Fa-rectification is that it is both a process and an end-point. It is the process through which the inhabitants of a multi-dimensional cosmos will return to their appropriate places in the cosmos, based on their level of moral achievement and relationship to the Fa. During this process, the good will be separated from the bad.

At the end-point, those who do not accept Falun Dafa, and those who were evil in that they opposed Falun Dafa, will be punished and eliminated. Once this moment is completed, there will be overall acceptance of Falun Dafa as the universal truth, thereby returning the Dafa to its appropriate place in the cosmos.

This concept of Fa-rectification appears to have been introduced by Li as a means to explain the ongoing repression. The repression was explained as a period of "tribulations," a test for the disciples of FLG, one that would "weed out" those not worthy of Consummation. The tribulations and trials provided opportunities to increase one's virtue (*de*) and raise the level of cultivation through suffering.[12] The greater one's level of virtue, the more one was likely to Consummate at the end-moment of Fa-rectification. A disciple could earn virtue by actively stepping forward to end the ban, and now this task included saving others. If a disciple did not do enough to clarify the facts in order to save others, their cultivation level would be insufficient and they would not be able to leave at the moment of Consummation. Since the period before Fa-rectification was short, it was imperative for a disciple to be pro-active in saving others. In this way, participation in the secular goal of ending the ban in China was given religious motivation and legitimation.

Salvation

How could a person be saved? A person who became a true practitioner would, of course, be saved. Furthermore, even if someone simply believed that FLG was good, and especially if they disbelieved what the Chinese government said about the group, they too would be saved. However, the FLG believe "ordinary people" (in contrast to FLG disciples who are not ordinary people but gods) are in imminent danger of being eliminated in the Fa-rectification if they are under the evil and destructive influence of the Chinese government's propaganda. Thus, as part of their proselytizing, FLG wish to turn others away from wrongful ideas about FLG, particularly those propagated by the CCP. The goal of FLG proselytization was not necessarily for conversion to a spiritual belief, although that is the primary aim. The goal was also to convert a person from a negative view of FLG to a positive one; in particular, to a view that believes the Chinese government's propaganda to be evil or wrong, thereby motivating the target to support FLG in its protest movement. If a person became a disciple, all well and good, but if not, the goal was to have the person think correctly about the group so they can be saved in the final judgment.[13]

The religious goal to save others

Starting in 2004, Li's announcements indicated a new priority and urgency for disciples to clarify the facts in order to save sentient beings. At a conference in Chicago he stated: "As Dafa disciples have clarified the facts you have saved many beings who were supposed to be saved, but that is not enough… [you] should allow more sentient beings to be saved." He also stated that, "clarifying the facts…far transcends your personal cultivation" and "is something you *must* do, and you must do it to the end" (Li 2004a). Since time is short before the moment of judgment arrives, it is an urgent task. This doctrine has the effect of motivating followers to increase their public relations work in support of the protest and redress goal. Dogmatic motivation is provided by the following: the urgency of having little time left before the Fa-rectification arrives, the fact that this is a disciple's only and last chance to earn enough virtue so they can Consummate, and linking the saving of others to their own salvation.[14] In this manner, Li links the public goal to the spiritual goal, the cosmic to the personal. The priority of "clarifying the facts" is directly linked to a disciple's chances of being saved and of saving others. At the same time, this translates into a need to increase media coverage of both the group's crisis in order to end the ban, and, simultaneously, save as many of the world's people as possible. The sense that time is running out, and that the moment of Fa-rectification is imminent, intensifies disciples' work and also may increase their anxiety and expectation. In an article posted to the FLG website in 2005, a practitioner states:

> every Dafa disciple can feel the rapid pace of the Fa-rectification progressing to the human world… We feel very much encouraged and realize that we should make special efforts… and hurry up to save the world's people during this last period of time… but at the same time, a considerable number of practitioners have also developed a new wave of anxiety and attachment to time, thinking that all will soon come to an end…If we cannot let go of this strong attachment, then it is very likely that it will result in various kinds of obstacles and lead to unexpected tribulations at this last state, causing Dafa disciples to be unable to smoothly reach Consummation as one body. (Dafa Practitioner 2005)[15]

Mass-mediating the message

Initially, the task of clarifying the truth via press releases and media coverage was defensive and used to repudiate the propaganda disseminated by the Chinese government. In September 2000, however, tactics became more offensive, and the task shifted to defying and criticizing the government, particularly China's leader at the time, President Jiang Zemin. In 2005, the critique shifted again, this time to the CCP, including predictions of the elimination of the CCP in the near future.

Initially, the FLG was effective in terms of its press relations. The group and its situation was, for the most part, given sympathetic coverage by the media.[16] Over time, however, a certain skepticism toward the press developed within the movement. During the question and answer period of the February 2003 experience-sharing conference "Explaining the Fa During the 2003 Lantern Festival at the U.S. West Fa Conference," in response to a disciple's question regarding the "façade of China's economy" (its promise of huge rewards) being an obstacle to clarifying the truth, Li replied:

> And why is it that in the international community so many media outlets
> and governments are all so quiet on this, and why are they able to look the
> other way in the face of this catastrophe? They have a lot of vested interests
> and a lot to gain wrapped up in this. (Li 2003a)

Thus, on a prosaic level, Falun Gong viewed any lack of media or Western government support as resulting from their privileging of financial gain over human rights. For FLG, investing in China was also funding the Communist government's campaign against FLG, and therefore committing a sin. Other doctrinal explanations, such as the interference of old gods and evil forces, are also posited to explain the lack of support.

The group found it difficult to engage others in its cause through discussions over their ultimate religious concern. Sharing the "high-level" teachings about the Fa-rectification of the cosmos, and the ability to save oneself from elimination through one's acceptance of Falun Gong, did not attract the support desired. An approach was therefore developed to address the interests of "ordinary people." Li expressed this as follows, at the aforementioned 2003 conference:

> When clarifying the truth, have you discovered a problem? They can
> accept everything when you talk about people being persecuted. Talk about
> freedom of belief getting trampled, the violation of human rights and so on,
> and they can accept it all, but as soon as you talk about the truths of the Fa
> they're blocked.
>
> When you're clarifying the facts, if you go above the human principles by
> just one little bit, people won't be able to accept it. So when you're clarifying
> facts, you must not talk about high-level things. What you know are things
> that Gods should know. Those things are what I taught to you, not worldly
> people. So you shouldn't tell those things to ordinary people. You can only

talk about our being persecuted, about our real situation, about our being good people and being wrongly persecuted, about our freedom of belief being violated, about our human rights being violated. They can accept all these things and then will immediately support and express to you their sympathy. . . . Of course, what's going on is, your intention is to turn him into a Dafa disciple…[however] Our number one task at this time is to help them learn the truth. (Li 2003a)

I contend that the group's frustration at what they saw as lack of concern and involvement in their cause by others, plus the need to rearticulate their identity, and the Chinese government's treatment of them, as well as the urgency of their ultimate concern of Fa-Rectification, led the group to develop its own media outlets. For Falun Gong, no event on earth can equal the importance of Fa-rectification of the cosmos: not the attacks of 9/11, nor the war with Iraq, nor problems in the Middle East. Terrorism is seen by Li as a distraction created by the "old forces" so that the United States is unable to turn its attention to the ban and persecution of FLG in China.[17] Since their ultimate concern was not receiving the world-wide attention they felt it deserved, gaining direct control over some media was a logical solution. Talking to his disciples about running websites and media outlets at a 2004 conference in New York, Li said:

[i]t's all for the singular purpose of clarifying the facts. At this point the Chinese communist government and that arch fiend's evil, villainous faction have used financial leverage so that they now have society's media in the palm of their hand. Nobody is reporting on the persecution we're being subjected to, so with no other recourse, Dafa disciples have worked together to do these things. (Li 2005a)

In 2004, controversy arose over whether certain New York-based media organizations, such as the newspaper group *The Epoch Times* and New Tang Dynasty Television (NTDTV), were FLG organizations. The Chinese government claimed they were propaganda tools for the FLG to damage the reputation of the Chinese government. The FLG claimed they were independent news organizations.

At the very least, a close association exists between these media groups and the FLG practitioners who operate them. In discussing media issues with his followers, Li referred to *The Epoch Times* as "a newspaper run by Dafa disciples." Of NTDTV he stated: "The Chinese New Year Gala sponsored by New Tang Dynasty TV aims to reach out to and engage more Chinese people so as to clarify the facts to them and save them" (Li 2005a). In early 2004, Li gave his one and only interview, since the group was banned, to NTDTV.

According to a report in the *Far Eastern Economic Review*, prominent FLG spokespeople serve as directors for NTDTV and on the board of *The Epoch Times*; both organizations give the FLG prominent coverage. In addition, both organizations are staffed by volunteers, often FLG followers, whose main jobs are unrelated to journalism (Lawrence 2004).

One reason why the group might deny its association with these news organizations, notable for their focus critical of the CCP, is that Li Hongzhi teaches his followers that they must not be political. Falun Gong is very sensitive to having the term "political" applied to them or their actions. This is partly due to Li's early teaching that FLG practitioners must never be "political." This functioned as good survival advice when the group was doing well in China. They also refuse the term because the Chinese government accuses Li of political motivations to overthrow the Communist government, insinuating that Li wants to obtain political power for himself. The FLG adamantly deny any desire for political power. However, their actions have undoubtedly become increasingly political over time. This is certainly true of recent developments such as FLG predictions of the imminent demise of the CCP. An editorial posted to the FLG website on 22 February 2005, entitled "People in Mainland China For Whom it Would be Dangerous to Publicize Their Names Can Publicly Announce Their Withdrawal from the CCP using an Alias," stated:

> The evil spirit of the Chinese Communist Part (CCP) chooses to go against Dafa, and is doomed to be thoroughly eliminated by all of the cosmos's gods before the Fa reaches the human world. All the world's people who have joined the CCP or various Party organizations for various reasons bear the mark of the evil, the mark of the beast, as a result. If they can promptly withdraw from the Party, the Youth League and Young Vanguard League, and erase the evil markings, when earthshaking changes occur in near future in the human world, and when the doomsday of the evil party arrives, they can escape from the calamity brought by the CCP.
>
> (Clearwisdom Editors 2005)

Thus, proselytization has been extended to those in China's ruling party with the goal being a mass exodus of people from the Party. Concurrently, FLG disciples must add "eliminating the Communist evil specter" to their ritual tasks. This has added the more specific, and political, task of removing a ruling party from power to the religious task of eliminating evil from the cosmos.

The Epoch Times has since written and widely distributed a treatise entitled "Nine Commentaries on the Communist Party," giving a highly critical presentation of Chinese history and the role of the Communist Party. At an

April conference in 2005, Li stated that "there are divine factors behind the *Nine Commentaries* and they will have a positive impact on people, Asians and Westerners alike" (Li 2005d). The primary target audience for the Nine Commentaries are people living in China. At another conference in April, Li claimed: "[t]he primary goal of publishing the *Nine Commentaries* was to expose the Chinese Communist Party's (CCP) nature so that people who had been deceived by the CCP could see it for what it is and recognize the CCP's evilness, and thus be saved" (Li 2005e). The *Epoch Times Special Report* of April 13, 2005 declared: "Global withdrawals from the Chinese Communist Party (CCP) membership, including its youth league, is [*sic*] approaching one million." It then goes on to give credit to the treatise: "the impact of The Epoch Times special publication: *Nine Commentaries on the Communist Party* has been linked to the mass departure from the CCP inside and outside China." It also claimed that "825,000 CCP members have publicly withdrawn their membership from the Party via the Epoch Times website."[18] These figures are refuted by the Chinese government, and since Li approved the practice of people using aliases to make public withdrawals, and of FLG practitioners removing deceased relatives from the CCP, the figure for actual withdrawals from the CCP remains to be verified (Li 2005d).[19]

In her study of Chinese millenarian movements, Jan Nattier (1988, 42) suggests that such movements may create apocalyptic myths predicting the downfall of an oppressive ruler, and try to actualize such beliefs through revolutionary activity when several factors are in place. One factor is infusing the political system with religious significance so that it becomes a "key element in the cosmic structure." Under this condition, Nattier states, the political system is seen as an affront to the cosmic order, calling for a religious response: "When concrete action (i.e., the removal of the usurper or other offender) is impossible, one response is the creation of apocalyptic mythology." Nattier concludes that when followers believe that "their enterprise is divinely sanctioned," and that the political system is a key evil element in the cosmic structure, then millennial revolt may be undertaken under sacred justification (Nattier 1988, 42). The above conditions are present in FLG belief. Catherine Wessinger (2006), employing her categories for millennial movements involved in violence, states that FLG, although pacifist in orientation, has acquired characteristics of a revolutionary millennial movement as it works toward the elimination of the CCP. As such, the conflict between the Chinese government and FLG continues to be polarized, with FLG developing dogma of an increasingly political and revolutionary nature. However, FLG disciples are told by Li not to place hope or trust in any human agency to end the ban in China. Only Fa-rectification will right the cosmic environment and resolve the situation. This teaching is likely to prevent violent

revolutionary action on the part of the group since it is up to cosmic powers, not human agency, to bring about the revolutionary change.[20] Yet it is
still the task of FLG disciples to publicize the truth to save sentient beings,
including those in the CCP who must leave their political affiliation in order
to be saved.

Thus, to recap the main points of this section, in reaction to crisis, FLG
developed a protest culture, within which a salvational phase developed, and
out of which a political phase emerged. From the beginning of this new orientation, FLG used media technologies to proselytize, invoking both a spiritual message and a secular one. The secular message focused on human rights
issues, and aimed at both political influence and individual "conversion" to
support its cause of ending the ban on FLG in China. The secular message
has become increasingly political and now includes efforts to bring down
the Chinese Communist Party. However, the spiritual message, embedded
within the secular message, is the ultimate concern of the group. The religious
and secular goals are mutually inclusive, and the group's proselytizing efforts
automatically involve both types of messages. What has become noteworthy,
however, is the covertness of the spiritual message, and the increasing prominence of the secular within their proselytization strategies.

Also of interest is the soteriological potential of the secular message.
Although the goal of FLG proselytization is ultimately salvation through
conversion to a spiritual belief, a person may also be saved if they accept a
change of viewpoint. The secular salvific goal is thus to convert a person from
a negative view of FLG to a positive one. In particular, they seek a conversion
to the view that the Chinese government's propaganda against the group is
evil or at least wrong, thereby motivating the target to support FLG in its
protest movement. In other words, not only converting a person to become
a disciple, but also converting a person to think correctly about the group,
is held to be successful proselytization. In this way, I suggest that FLG proselytization does not elicit the same negative responses or conflict as evidenced
elsewhere in this book where the proselytic message is primarily religious.
In the case of FLG, the human rights issue raised in their secular message is
less threatening to targets than a form of proselytization that calls into question or challenges the target's religious belief (or non-belief). Therefore, while
some methods of FLG secular proselytization, such as the distribution and
exhibition of persecution literature, may face problems in terms of civil challenges over permits to assemble, for example, the secular message is accepted
and protected under the right of free speech. In brief, the FLG religious message is tied to the secular one, and salvation is obtainable from the lighter
investment of adopting the specific secular view. Salvation from conversion
to discipleship is the fuller destiny, but reserved for those "destined" to come

to it of their own accord. "Clarifying the truth" about the group's secular concerns is the way to attract those predestined to join and to change the view of others, thus offering salvation to all. In this way, the secular message houses the ultimate (religious) concern.

The future of FLG proselytizing efforts

FLG teachings and activities continue to develop in response to both external and internal factors. External factors include actions of the Chinese government, interaction with the international media, and the success or failure of FLG proselytization in regards to both their secular and religious goals. Internal factors include the response of FLG disciples to the teachings and tasks, and the success or failure of tactics tried by disciples in their proselytizing efforts. This case study shows how both the goal(s) and strategies of FLG proselytization changed in response to circumstances. It was, and continues to be, a fluid and dynamic situation in which FLG practitioners are likely to continue to innovate in their methods of dissemination.

Regardless of how one views the controversy over the control of various media organizations, it is clear that FLG and its members are producing news and information for public consumption.[21] The message has changed over the years as the group's goals have shifted. At first, the information centered on explaining the ban to the world, publicizing their protest actions, and asking for help. During the next stage they shifted to a more offensive approach, attacking President Jiang Zemin and defining those opposing FLG as evil demons. Li's teachings then emphasized the need to save sentient beings as part of the truth clarification. This increased the need for disciples to proselytize and encouraged the development of FLG news organizations. The most recent phase adds the task of bringing about the demise of the Communist Party through proselytization to Party members. Since religious proselytization is covertly embedded in secular proselytization, I contend that this is one reason why FLG proselytization has avoided the negative response and conflict in the West that is at times associated with new religious movements. An exception to this could be the FLG hijacking of satellite and cable TV broadcasting signals in China. Here again, the combination of secular and religious goals complicates the event. Although this is an innovative and non-violent method of protest, it is also illegal (as many non-violent forms of protest are), and a form of proselytization thrust upon a non-consenting constituency. It has also raised some controversy amongst FLG practitioners as to the appropriateness of the method. In response, Li posted a message to the FLG website on March 8, 2002, three days after the first cable-TV hijacking. In the article entitled, "Look at Things with Righteous Thought," he tried to calm these doubts by justifying the action as legitimate due to its ability to help save others. He stated:

> Right now, the Dafa disciples of Mainland China using television to let people know the truth is exposing the evil's persecution, is saving the sentient beings whose minds have been poisoned by the evil's deceit, and is a magnificent act of mercy. The group of evil political scoundrels has never followed the law in dealing with Dafa disciples, so don't disapprove of the actions Dafa disciples are taking as they clarify the truth, due to your attachment of fear. No matter how the evil persecutes, what awaits Dafa disciples is still Consummation, and what awaits the evil beings in nothing but eternally paying in Hell for all they have done to interfere with and persecute the Fa-rectification and Dafa disciples.

Practitioners continue to post articles periodically, demonstrating support and justification for the TV-signal hijacking campaign, perhaps reflecting an ongoing uneasiness by some practitioners with the illegality of the actions, although the actions have not created any bad publicity for the group in the West.[22]

While understanding the group's need for publicizing its human rights problems and seeking redress, it is also true that, without the conflict and the high profile secular message, the religious proselytization of FLG would need to find new forms of justification and outreach. The mutual imbrications of conflict and proselytization in relation to the more secular goal have become the primary identity marker of the group, and a large part of its motivation and cohesion. This is not to say the group would lose its identity should the secular goals be reached, but a new doctrinal emphasis would need to be developed.

This is further complicated by the teachings of Li Hongzhi, where much about the future is left undefined. The Fa-rectification is said to be imminent, but Li has recently developed new teachings to project FLG into the future. There is now a two stage Fa-rectification. The first Fa-rectification is of the cosmos and the second Fa-rectification is of the human world. However, those disciples who have been faithful during this time of trial and tribulation will Consummate and ascend to their Falun Dafa paradise at the end of the first Fa-rectification. After that, there is no chance for them to return to earth. Apparently, the second stage of Fa-rectification of the human world will be accomplished by those new followers successfully proselytized in the latter part of the first stage. It is in this second stage that Falun Dafa will spread to all parts of the world and become accepted as universal truth. How and when the ban in China and its attendant repression will end is left undisclosed. A disciple is not to think about when the Fa-rectification will take place, or when the proscriptions will end; this would constitute an attachment of the disciple's and harm his or her chance of Consummation.

Concluding remarks

It is the conflict in China that is at the core of the FLG's public identity and secular proselytic activity. It is the concept of Fa-rectification, a concept developed to explain the conflict, that lies now at the core of the group's rationale and orientation. Through a process of response to circumstances, the group's religious goal became embedded in its secular goal. It is the use of media for advancing their secular goal that gives the group a public dynamic and opportunity for religious outreach. Thus, it was out of both the group's secular and religious goals that the need for proselytization arose, and its methods of proselytization developed.

Notes

1. Catherine Wessinger states that "A *religion* is a comprehensive world view that makes sense of the universe and of human existence. Religion explains where we came from and where we are going. Religion teaches what is right, and what is wrong. Religion is an expression of an *ultimate concern*, which is the most important thing in the world for an individual or group," *How the Millennium Comes Violently: From Jonestown to Heaven's Gate* (2000, 5). According to Wessinger, "an ultimate concern is the religious goal or religious commitment…as expressed within a belief system" *Millennialism, Persecution, and Violence: Historical Cases* (2000, 8). See these two works by Wessinger for the important role "ultimate concern" can play in new religious movements.

2. Good health and healing benefits of practicing FLG have recently become re-emphasized on the FLG website. See for instance, the link to "My Master" webpage and testimonials. Interestingly, the testimonials refer to the time when Li taught in China and tell of personal contact with him, his benevolence and miraculous healings, etc. Stories of Li's personal charisma and powers may balance out the "on-line" presence of Li experienced by followers since 1999 http://www.clearwisdom.net/emh/141/ [accessed 21 February 2004].

3. *Qigong* is a general term designating a system for improving and maintaining good health based on ideas found in traditional Chinese medicine and culture. It involves a wide range of physical, mental and breathing exercises. Falun Gong does not use breathing exercises and does not consider itself a *qigong* practice, even though the movement arose within the context of the *qigong* boom in China during the 1970s and 1980s.

4. In "A Letter Clarifying Rumors About Falun Gong" by Falun Dafa practitioners in Hong Kong, 21 May 1999, referring to the 1996 decision, states: "Only after the News and Publication Department banned the books on Falun Gong did the Qigong Association change its attitude" and let Li Hongzhi "voluntarily withdraw" from the Qigong Association in November, 1996. http://falundafa.org/fldfbb/to_rumor_eng.doc_ [now defunct]. This letter is reprinted in Shi-min Fang and Zixian Deng "The Two Tales of Falun Gong" presented at the annual conference of the American Family Foundation, 28 April 2000.

Also see: "China Bans Publications on Falun Gong," *China Daily* Beijing, 23 July 1999. Report on a circular from the Press and Publications Administration. www.chinadaily. com.cn/falun/7236.htm [accessed 1 Sept. 1999, now defunct]. It states that on 5 June 1998 another FLG book was banned, and on 10 May 1999 various cassette tapes and videos of a "sermon" given by Li Hongzhi were banned, and on 1 June in Qinghai Province, four books "mostly collections of Li Hongzhi's sermons delivered abroad, were banned."

Note: Many of Li Hongzhi's articles are only available via the Falun Gong website Minghui (Clearwisdom). Because the website addresses for these articles change over time, if you cannot locate the article at the webpage cited, go to the Falun Gong homepage, http://www.clearwisdom.net, where many of Li's articles can be searched by title and date under "Daily Archive." As of April 2008, the earliest archived postings start in June 1999. For Li's books, search by title under "Falun Dafa Books."

5. James Tong (2002b) traces this change to a loose organizational structure at the end of 1997. However, in "Further Giving Up Attachments" written 1 January, 1996, and included in Li's *Falun Buddha Law: Essentials for Further Advances* (English version, Translation Group of Falun Xiulian Dafa, Beijing 1998), Li states: "I want to have a loose administration simply because you cling to ordinary people and thus will loose your mental balance in your work." So the idea of shifting to a loose structure may have begun as early as 1996.

6. For an analysis of the government's response to the *Zhongnanhai* demonstration and the ensuing ban, see Tong (2002a).

7. Susan J. Palmer states:

    The emergence of Falun Gong's protest movement can be analyzed as the result of a give-and-take relationship between the charismatic Master and his disciples. While Master Li supplies the ideas, his disciples choose how to put them into action. Master Li then responds to their actions in his next article, alternately commending, encouraging, cautioning or castigating. He provides occult interpretations of the ongoing struggle in China, and fresh spiritual motivation for continuing dissent. (2003, 355–56)

8. Li explained:

    From the outset I tried my best to eliminate them. But they were extremely huge. No matter how fast you eliminate them, a certain amount of time is needed. It took me nine months to eliminate them… You can't just eliminate it, so you have to bear it. But I knew that if the students were to bear it, it would be hard for them to make it through. So I could only let the students bear the evilness played out by humans, whereas I bore the real things. (Li 2000, 6)

    Three years later he described his absence again:

    So to lessen the pressure and the persecution of Dafa disciples, I separated Dafa disciples and these things. I had those evil things come to me, and eliminated them quickly and on a large scale at the same time, so back then there was a lot of harm done to my surface material body. Later on I'd almost cleaned out all of those things, it took a year to do it, and if I didn't do that my Dafa disciples really couldn't bear it. I blocked them all off. In fact, what the Dafa disciples endured wasn't proportionate to their enormous number and how wicked they were. (2003a, 10)

9. Li's writings are considered scripture. The main sacred book, written prior to the ban, is Li Hongzhi's *Zhuan Falun* (*The Turning of the Dharma Wheel*).

10. At the moment of Consummation a disciple will ascend bodily in broad daylight to a paradise where they will be a god and reign as a King. Li states: "When the day of Consummation really comes, let me tell you, Dafa disciples really will Ascend in Broad Daylight, and the whole world will be able to see it" (Li 2003b). Regarding becoming a god, in answer to a question Li states that at the moment of Consummation "one instantly goes from being a human to being a god. And at that instant you will know everything, and at that instant you will become an omnipotent, magnificent god" (Li 2004b). Regarding reigning as a King, Li states that one must establish mighty virtue (*de*) so that one may "truly reach Consummation and become a King who presides over his own domain (2003c)."

11. Li does not give much detail about how this will happen except to say it will be over in an instant. At one conference he makes reference to "dead people strewn everywhere in the streets" (Li 2003c).

12. Regarding the necessity of suffering for spiritual advancement, see Gareth Fisher (2003).

13. See for instance, Li's February 15, 2005 statement in "Turning the Wheel Towards the Human World." He states:

I look only at a sentient being's attitude toward Dafa during the Fa-rectification. In other words, no matter which beings they are or how huge the mistakes and sins they committed in history, as long as they do not play a negative role with regard to the Fa-rectification, I can give them benevolent solutions and eliminate their sins and karma. That is the greatest mercy and true salvation. (Li 2005b, 1)

14. Another important motivation is the pragmatic one of saving FLG in China from arrest and abuse. This involves issues of human rights and is the main topic in FLG media releases and reports. Publicly, the FLG identity is based in their culture of protest, while the in-group identity is based on the salvational message.

15. Personal names are usually not given when posting to the FLG website. Articles are often signed "a Dafa Practitioner."

16. Mark R. Bell and Taylor C. Boas state that: "Western press coverage has been overwhelmingly supportive of Falun Gong and critical of PRC authorities, and negative assessments of the movement outside of the PRC are few and far between" (2003, 287). For an alternative view that more reflects the view of the Falun Gong, see Danny Schechter, *Falun Gong's Challenge to China: Spiritual Practice or "Evil cult"?* (2000). For a discussion of early media coverage, see Patsy Rahn *The Falun Gong: Beyond the Headlines* (2000). Regarding the use of the Internet and media in the conflict, see John Powers and Meg Y.M. Lee, Dueling Media: Symbolic Conflict in China's Falun Gong Suppression Campaign (2002); Also see: Falun Dafa and the Internet: a Marriage Made in Web Heaven, July 30, 1999. From the website http://www.virtualchina.com, category InfoTech, subcategory Perspectives, page 1 of 4. [accessed 2 January 2000, now defunct].

17. For instance, Li states:

> I'd say that it is because the old forces have been stirring up trouble in the Middle East, which has kept the U.S. tied up and prevented it from having the energy to focus on China and do something about the persecution of Dafa disciples. If it weren't tied up with the issue of terrorists right now, I believe the U.S. government definitely wouldn't tolerate evil like this being so rampant in today's world. (Li 2005c)

18. *The Epoch Times: Epoch Times International.* Australia Epoch Pty Ltd. Exclusive Report. "Nine Commentaries on the Communist Party". Received 17 July 2005 as a handout in Sydney Australia.

19. A disciple asked Li:

> Some students want to help withdraw their deceased relatives or family members from the Party. Is that necessary?" Li replied: "That's fine. There is no problem with that, for they have passed away and it's not as if they can come over and ask the *Epoch Times* to publish their statement in print or online, right? So yes, you can do that. And does it make any difference? Yes, it does! (2005d)

20. For further discussion of why the FLG is unlikely to develop violent means of protest, see Patsy Rahn (2002).

21. As of March 2005, media and information groups organized and/or run, or seemingly affiliated with Falun Gong include: the main FLG website Minghui also known as Clearwisdom; *The Epoch Times*; *Washington China Review*; New Tang Dynasty Television (NTDTV); Association for Asian Research (AFAR); World Falun Dafa Radio; World Organization to Investigate Persecution of FLG (WOIPFG); Global Coalition to Bring Jiang to Justice (GCBJJ); Falun Gong Human Rights Working Group (FLGHRWG); China Mental Health Watch (CMHW).

22. For FLG justification of the TV-signal hijacking campaign, see Ouyang Fei posting to Clearwisdom November 28, 2004. The posting concludes: "…tapping into the TV system to broadcast truth clarification videos is one of the most effective ways to combat the Jiang faction's terrorist acts and an admirable act of justice under the present conditions". Regarding satellite interference, see Tao Zhongren (2002) "My Thoughts on the Authenticity of the Report about Tapping into Satellite Programs" and also a practitioner's posting, "Thoughts After Reading Practitioners Broadcast TV Documentaries that Clarify the Truth of the Persecution of Falun Dafa in Xingtai and Shahe Cities, Hebai Province." It states: "Tapping into the TV networks is a good way to save sentient beings." Beginning in 2002, FLG cut into Chinese television cable or satellite signals, and replaced programming with FLG videos promoting their views. According to Chinese reports, this included interruption of the 2002 satellite broadcast of the World Cup soccer game and celebrations commemorating Hong Kong's return to China. Regarding the first cable-cutting incident see, Phillip P. Pan (2002), "Falun Gong Seized City's State-Run TV to Broadcast Message," and "Falung Gong uses guerilla tactics to fight," *Reuters* Sunday, July 21, 2002, and "China: Falun Gong Stage TV Hijacking" by Ted Anthony. The Associated Press, September 24, 2002.

References

Anthony, Ted. 2002. China: Falun Gong Stage TV Hijacking. The Associated Press, September 24.

Baird, Robert D. 1971. *Category Formation and the History of Religions.* The Hague: Mouton.

Bell, Mark R. and Taylor C. Boas. 2003. Falun Gong and the Internet: Evangelism, Community and Struggle for Survival. *Nova Religio* 6(2): 277–93.

Clearwisdom Editors. 2005. www.clearwisdom.net/emh/articles/2005/2/22/57791p. html [accessed 1 Mar 2005].

Dafa Practioner. 2004. Thoughts After Reading Practitioners Broadcast TV Documentaries that Clarify the Truth of the Persecution of Falun Dafa in Xingtai and Shahe Cities, Hebai Province. February 19, 2004. http://minghui.org/mh/articles/2004/2/1/66261.html [accessed 8 July 2004].

——. 2005. One Cannot Reach Consummation without Letting Go of the Huge Attachment to Time. www.clearwisdom.net/emharticles/2005/2/23/57813. html [accessed 10 May 2005].

Fei, Ouyang. 2004. Tapping into the TV System to Broadcast Truth Clarification Videos is a Form of Resistance against State-Run Terrorism. http://www.clearwisdom.net/emh/articles/2004/11/28/55033p.html [accessed 30 Nov 2005].

Fischer, Gareth. 2003. Resistance and Salvation in Falun Gong: The Promise and Peril of Forbearance. *Nova Religio* 6(2): 2294–311.

Lawrence, Susan V. 2004. Falun Gong Uses Free Speech as a Sword. *Far Eastern Economic Review* 167(15): 26–29. (Hong Kong edition).

Li, Hongzhi. 2000. Master Li Hongzhi's Lecture at the Great Lakes Conference in North America, 9 December. www.clearwisdom.net/eng/2000/Dec/23/JingWen122300.html [Accessed 28 December 2000].

——. 2003a. Explaining the Fa During the 2003 Lantern Festival at the U.S. West Fa Conference, 15 February. www.clearwisdom.net/emh/articles/2003/3/21/2003lajiefa.html [Accessed 30 March 2003].

——. 2003b. Teaching and Explaining the Fa at the Metropolitan New York Fa Conference, April 20, 2003. www.clearwisdom.net/emh/articles/2003/5/6/2003nyjiefa.html [accessed 3 Aug 2003].

——. 2003c. Teaching the Fa at the 2003 Atlanta Fa Conference, Nov. 29. 2003: 22. http://www.clearwisdom.net/emh/articles/2004/1/26/2003_Atlanta_Lecture.html [accessed 28 June 2004].

——. 2004a. Teaching the Fa at the 2004 Chicago Conference." 23 May. www.clearwisdom.net/emh/articles/2004/6/10/49079.html [Accessed 15 June 2004].

——. 2004b. Teaching the Fa at the Meeting with Asia-Pacific Students. www.

clearwisdom.net/emh/articles/2004/5/28/2004_Asia-Pacific_Lecture.html [accessed 28 June 2004].

———. 2005a. Teaching the Fa at the 2004 International Fa Conference in New York: Questions and Answers Section, Part II. 1 January. www.clearwisdom. net/emh/articles/2005/1/10/56449.html [Accessed 17 February 2005].

———. 2005b. Turning the Wheel Towards the Human World. February 15, 2005. www.clearwisdom.net/emh/articles/2005/2/18/57688.html [Accessed 20 February 2005].

———. 2005c. Teaching the Fa at the 2004 International Fa Conference In New York: Questions and Answers Section, Part III, 21 November 2004 www. clearwisdom.net/emh/articles/2005/1/27/56991.html [Accessed 4 August 2005].

———. 2005d. Teaching the Fa at the Western U.S. International Fa Conference: Question & Answer Section, Part I 2005." http://www.clearwisdom. net/emh/articles/2005/4/19/2005_SF_Lecture.html [Accessed 3 August 2005].

———. 2005e. Teaching the Fa at the 2005 Manhattan International Fa Conference" April 24, 2005. www.clearwisdom.net/emh/articles/2005/5/14/60765.html [accessed 22 May 2005].

Nattier, Jan. 1988. The Meanings of the Maitreya Myth: A Typological Analysis. In *Maitreya, the Future Buddha*, eds. Alan Sponberg and Helen Harcare, 23–47. Cambridge: Cambridge University Press.

Palmer, Susan. 2003. From Healing to Protest: Conversion Patterns Among the Practitioners of Falun Gong. *Nova Religio* 6(2): 348–64.

Pan, Philip. P. 2002. Falun Gong Seized City's State-Run TV to Broadcast Message. *Washington Post Foreign Service*. Friday, March 8, A20.

Powers, John and Meg Y.M. Lee. 2002. Dueling Media: Symbolic Conflict in China's Falun Gong Suppression Campaign. In *Chinese Conflict Management and Resolution*, ed. G.M. Chen and R. Ma, 259–74. Westport, CT: Ablex.

Rahn, Patsy. 2000. The Falun Gong: Beyond the Headlines. *Cultic Studies Journal: Psychological Manipulation and Society* 17: 168–86.

———. 2002. The Chemistry of a Conflict: The Chinese Government and the Falun Gong. *Terrorism and Political Violence* 14(4): 41–65.

Reuters. 2002. Falung Gong uses guerilla tactics to fight. Sunday, July 21.

Schechter, Danny. 2000. *Falun Gong's Challenge to China: Spiritual Practice or "Evil cult?"* New York: Akashic Books.

Tong, James. 2002a. Anatomy of Regime Repression in China: Timing, Enforcement Institutions, and Target Selection in Banning the Falun Gong, July, 1999. *Asian Survey* (November–December): 795–820.

———. 2002b An Organizational Analysis of the Falun Gong: Structure, Communications, Financing. *China Quarterly* 171: 641–65.

Virtual China: Perspectives 1999. Falun Dafa and the Internet: A Marriage Made in Web Heaven. 30 July. www.virtualchina.com/infotech...perspective-073099. htm [accessed 2 January 2000, now defunct].

Wessinger, Catherine. 2000. *How the Millennium Comes Violently: From Jonestown to Heaven's Gate.* New York: Seven Bridges.

———. 2000. *Millennialism, Persecution, and Violence: Historical Cases.* New York: Syracuse University Press.

———. 2006. New Religious Movements and Violence. In *Introduction to New and Alternative Religions in America*, vol.1 History and Controversies, eds. Eugene V. Gallagher and W. Michael Ashcraft, 165–205.Westport, CT: Greenwood Press.

Zhongren, Tao. 2002. My Thoughts on the Authenticity of the Report about Tapping into Satellite Programs, comments posted to Clearwisdom July 30, 2002 http://clearwisdom.net/emh/articles/2002/7/30/24672.html [accessed 25 June 2004].

CHAPTER 13

The Social and Legal Context of Proselytization in Contemporary Japan

Mark R. Mullins

A century ago proselytization in Japan was most commonly associated with the intrusive presence and evangelistic activities of Christian missionaries from Europe and North America. For the past several decades in Japan, however, it has usually been connected with the recruitment activities of controversial new religious movements. Soka Gakkai, Jehovah's Witnesses, the Unification Church, Aum Shinrikyo, and Honohana—often referred to as "cults" by representatives of established religions and Japanese lawyers' association—are just some of the religious organizations that have attracted regular media attention. The followers of these and other groups have actively engaged in membership recruitment in a variety of public places, including train stations, parks, and busy commercial streets. It has not been unusual for individuals to be stopped at the crowded entrance of a train station by dedicated followers and offered purification rituals (*okiyome*) on the spot, in addition to literature, invitations to attend a meeting or seminar, or asked to make a financial donation to some worthy cause promoted by the group. Some religious movements (Seicho no Ie and the Jehovah's Witnesses, for example), are widely known for their outreach strategy of making regular home visits in neighborhoods throughout Japan.[1]

Media coverage of such new religious movements in recent years has been so extensive that it is easy to lose sight of the fact that the history of Japanese religion has been intertwined with various forms of proselytization for centuries. Folk religion and Shinto are the only traditions usually recognized as native or indigenous to Japan (though scholars will be quick to point out that these so-called "native" traditions were deeply shaped by transplanted foreign influences from China as early as the sixth century). Very few Japanese today, however, identify themselves exclusively as followers of Shinto. Survey research over the past several decades has consistently found that only about thirty percent of the Japanese population claims a personal religious commitment of any kind; more remarkable is that only three percent of that number identify Shinto—Japan's indigenous tradition—as their personal religion.[2] This means that the majority of individuals with a clearly defined religious identity belong to a missionary religion of one kind or another.

In order to appreciate the complexity of the contemporary situation, it is necessary to have some understanding of the development of the dominant forms of religious association and the evolution of state policies and laws regulating religion that shape current attitudes and responses toward proselytizing religions. Following a brief overview of these major developments, this chapter will consider the current social climate and the predicament of religious groups. The free practice of religion has been guaranteed by the post-war Constitution (1947), but most Japanese today hold negative attitudes toward the activities of religious organizations and an increasing number even regard membership recruitment in public places as an activity that should be regulated more strictly by the law. Our analysis will consider some of the factors that have contributed to the growing "gap" between this social reality and the ideals and positive legal status accorded religious organizations.

Historical background: religion as social obligation

The genealogy of contemporary patterns of religious affiliation can be traced to the diffusion of foreign-born missionary religions in relation to native Shinto traditions in the pre-modern period. Buddhism was transplanted to Japan via China and Korea in the sixth century and initially adopted by politically powerful clans and, eventually, by the imperial court. By the eighth century, Buddhism had become a quasi-state religion and temples were being built in each province. Multiple Buddhist schools and traditions were transplanted, indigenized, and widely diffused for almost a millennium before Christianity was added to the mix in the sixteenth century. The Roman Catholic mission to Japan began with the arrival of the first Jesuit missionaries in 1549. Their relative success in a rather short period of time has led some scholars to designate this period as the "Christian century."

Although these diverse religious beliefs, practices, and traditions have existed for centuries, one should not mistakenly assume that the religious economy of Japan has been a "free market" that offered a wide range of individual choice. In fact, there has been a general tendency for Japanese to be embedded in a system of "layered obligations that has little to do with personal beliefs or convictions" (Davis 1992, 31). These "obligations" have been rooted in the fact that the practice of religion in everyday life has often been controlled by those holding the reigns of political power throughout much of Japanese history. During the Tokugawa period (1600–1867), for example, Buddhism received state patronage in exchange for services to the shogunate. By administering the *danka seido*, a system in which all the residents of a given area were required to register their household with a local temple and record births, marriages, and deaths, Buddhist priests were used by the Tokugawa regime to monitor and control the entire population. Priests also issued certificates (*tera-uke*) to individuals each year attesting that the person in question was not a member of the proscribed religion (Christianity), which had met with considerable success during the late sixteenth century.[3] While the "top-down" forced affiliation with Buddhist temples is clearly a key factor that connected many Japanese to the Buddhist tradition, it should also be noted that there were also a number of active Buddhist priests who spread their religious teachings "from below;" that is, proselytizing without added pressure and support of political authorities.[4] The Tokugawa policies, nevertheless, need to be recognized as an important source of the widespread Japanese participation in religious ritual because of social "obligation" rather than personal "choice," which characterizes attitudes of many toward religion, even today.[5]

Over the course of Japan's modernization a layer of civil religious obligations was added to this traditional religious division of labor. From the Meiji Restoration (1868) until the end of World War II, the government pursued a policy of uniting the people of Japan under the canopy of a state-sponsored and emperor-centered civil religion. The national religion created by the government bureaucrats was largely an "invention of tradition"[6]—projected back on Japanese history—and differed considerably from the previous forms of Shinto belief and practice. It was used, nevertheless, to unify and integrate the heterogeneous population and mobilize the people for nation-building, modernization, and military expansion for over half a century.

"National Evangelists" (recruited from among Shinto and Buddhist priests) propagated this new layer of religious "obligation" on behalf of the state as a part of the Great Promulgation Campaign, which lasted some fourteen years (1870–1884). By 1876 there were already over ten thousand evangelists mobilized for this work and under the direction and control of the Ise Shrines (Hardacre 1989, 45). As most Japanese were embedded in particularistic communal Shinto traditions, the local responses to this missionary campaign were generally less than enthusiastic. The government was eventually forced to turn to the public school system and military training to effectively propagate this new civil religious obligation over the course of several decades. In 1890 the Imperial Rescript on Education (*Kyoiku chokugo*) was issued and provided the normative framework that would define the limits of religious freedom for half a century. The Rescript was distributed to all schools and quickly became a sacred text for religious socialization. Shrine visits (*jinja sampai*) became regular school-sponsored events, and most schools maintained a *kamidana* (god shelf) and enshrined the imperial photo, various kami, and sometimes a talisman from Ise Shrine.

By the late 1930s the government became increasingly totalitarian, and members of every religious group were required to participate in civil religious rituals and conform to the state-defined orthodoxy. The authorities defined Shinto as a "non-religious" institution of the state, and participation in its rituals came to be viewed as the "patriotic" duty of all Japanese, regardless of personal religious convictions. While new religious movements and Christian churches attracted some new members during this period, the various pre-existing religious duties and obligations created a difficult environment for the propagation of religious alternatives.

The changing legal context

In order to appreciate the situation of missionary religions in contemporary Japan, we must also give some consideration to the government policies and constitutional provisions for religion that have evolved over the past century. This is a complicated story with significant shifts in government policy and strategy. The restoration of imperial rule in 1868 initiated a series of changes that radically transformed the role and status of religion in Japanese society. As noted above, the most fundamental religious change resulting from the restoration was the development of an emperor-centered national religion. Buddhism lost the state patronage it had enjoyed during the Tokugawa period, and Shinto was revived to provide the foundation for the new political order. Largely due to foreign pressure, the government removed the notices proscribing Christianity in 1873 and included an article on religious freedom in the Meiji Constitution (1889). Article 28 guaranteed citizens religious freedom "within limits not prejudicial to peace and order, and not antagonistic to their duties as subjects." Under State Shinto, however, it became obvious that "duties as subjects" would be in conflict with and override individual freedoms during the wartime period.

All of this changed abruptly with Japan's defeat on 15 August 1945 and the arrival of the Occupation Forces. Before the end of the year, the Supreme Commander for the Allied Powers (SCAP) issued the Directive for the Disestablishment of State Shinto (15 December 1945) and set in motion policies that effectively reduced Shinto to the status of a voluntary organization without special legal authority or financial support from the state. In accord with the Directive, the wartime laws regulating religion were subsequently abolished and all religious groups, including Shinto shrines, were placed on equal footing as "voluntary" organizations. Articles 20 and 89 of the post-war Constitution of Japan (1947) clearly articulated the principle of religious freedom and separation of religion and state, and thus fulfilled the consti-tutional reform objectives of the Occupation authorities. This "freedom of religion" guaranteed by the postwar Constitution, as one Japanese scholar (Tanaka 1959, 80) emphasized years ago, "includes the freedom to keep silent about one's faith or to propagate one's faith."[7]

Under the 1951 religious corporation law (*shukyo hojin ho*) religious groups were able to register with the government as "religious juridical persons" (*shukyo hojin*), which were understood to be a part of a larger legal category defined as "public benefit organizations" (*koeiki hojin*). This gave registered religious groups the legal basis to own properties and buildings for worship and religious activities, as well as to operate various business enterprises to support the religious aims of the organization. A basic assumption behind this legislation was that registered religious bodies contribute to the "public good" (*koeki*) and for this reason should be permitted to engage in economic activities to support their religious work and public welfare activities. While the postwar constitution and religious corporation law are based on the posi-tive view that religious institutions represent a social good and make signifi-cant contributions to civil society, this understanding is not widely shared by the general public today.[8]

Proselytization and social conflict in modern Japan

These constitutional and legal changes marked the beginning of a new period of religious vitality and proselytizing activities. The postwar con-stitution clearly established religious freedom and liberated Japanese from civil or national religious obligations connected with State Shinto and the emperor system. Equally important was the demographic shift of the popula-tion from rural to urban areas that accompanied the postwar rebuilding and development of the Japanese economy, which weakened territorial religious affiliations and obligations and encouraged "the growth of the more transient religious style of individuals" (Davis 1977). While the older ritual obliga-tions connected to family and community have by no means disappeared, they have certainly lost some of their power, and religious involvements have increasingly become a matter of personal choice.

This rapidly changing social environment created a new opening for recruitment activities by many religious entrepreneurs and groups. Literally hundreds of new religions blossomed in the new environment to create what McFarland (1967) referred to as the "rush hour of the gods." Some new religions that had been suppressed during the war re-emerged, and scores of others were organized in the early postwar period. The groups that experienced the most phenomenal growth during this time were Soka Gakkai, Rissho Koseikai, Reiyukai, Seicho-no-Ie, and PL Kyodan. Soka Gakkai, for example, grew from 35,000 households to a membership of over one million households in just over a decade. It was not just the home-grown new religions, however, that were competing in the new free-market religious economy. In response to General MacArthur's call for Christian missionary reinforcements to join in building a new Japan, over fifteen hundred missionaries arrived from North America and Europe between 1949 and 1953. While the Christian missionary enterprise in Japan has largely been a Western one, the number of missionaries from Europe and North America has declined significantly over the past three decades. Since the 1970s, however, Christian missionaries from South Korea have been investing considerable efforts in Japan.[9]

According to recent government statistics (2004), there are 182,223 religious bodies legally registered with the government.[10] Most of these organizations are Shinto (46.7 percent) and Buddhist (42.5 percent); other religions (i.e., new religious movements, with 8.4 percent)[11] and Christian churches (2.4 percent) are clearly Japan's religious minorities, albeit with a significant social presence. The government also reports statistics for *fukyosho*, which basically refers to centers of religious outreach or propagation centers. Out of a total of 26,497 such centers, some 21,574 are related to the last category of "other religions," which includes a variety of new religious movements. Established religions—including older Christian denominations in Japan— clearly invest fewer resources in such outreach activities today and rarely have training programs to mobilize members for recruitment. Given the disproportionate investment of resources in such centers, it is not surprising that the public perception of proselytizing religions today is associated more with new religions.

The new religions and Christian mission groups that have met with relative success in the postwar period share a good deal in common. They tend to emphasize religious experience, are "member-oriented" groups (rather than clergy-centered institutions), and aim for the effective employment of lay leaders in recruitment work. These movements usually encourage individuals to cultivate their own spirituality, rather than simply depend on the ritual performance of a priestly order. Personal salvation or self-cultivation (*kokoronaoshi*) is only the first step in the religious life. Most new religions teach that individuals are also expected to draw others into the path of salvation and make a contribution to world transformation (*yonaoshi*). Many of the larger movements in Japan have made a significant impact in such areas as politics, education, social welfare, and volunteer activities.[12]

Whereas established religions and churches tend to monopolize spiritual power in the hands of an elite clergy, these groups provide opportunities for rapid upward spiritual mobility.[13] With only a few days of training, any member can achieve spiritual power and be mobilized for outreach through household meetings, testimonials, and healing activities. Serious commitment to the religious organization, in fact, is often measured in terms of the time spent on behalf of the movement and the number of new members recruited. In sum, it has been the mobilization of the laity that made the postwar growth of Japanese new religions possible. Women, in particular, have been empowered in new ways to take charge of their own spiritual cultivation—rather than depend upon male clerics—and allowed to assume leadership roles within these new movements. Often denied opportunities in the larger society, many new religions rewarded women who were successful in recruitment activities with significant leadership positions.[14]

Several studies of Japanese new religions shed some light on the role of laity in recruitment activities and the spread of new movements through established family networks and relationships. Most available research indicates that the *michibikikata* ("recruiting-person" or "introducing person") is usually not a religious professional or stranger, but a follower who simply invites a personal acquaintance or family member to attend a meeting or service to find a solution to their problems or healing of an illness.[15] Winston Davis' (1980) survey of converts to Mahikari discovered that 39 percent were introduced by a relative, 23 percent attracted by newspapers and advertisements, and 22 percent by a friend; only 6 percent became involved through introduction by a stranger. Similarly, Earhart's (1989, 98–101) study of Gedatsu-kai found that individuals were usually guided into the new religion by a family member or relative (53.2 percent) or an acquaintance (40.5 percent), a category that included friend, neighbor, or co-worker. Religious professionals or branch leaders accounted for only 5.4 percent of the introductions to this movement. It would appear, therefore, that proselytization by strangers and clergy—anonymous individuals outside of these relationships and bonds of trust—is generally not very effective.

There are apparently some exceptions to this generalization. In contrast to conversion and recruitment in these home-grown Japanese religions—in which networks of family, relatives, and friends play such a prominent role—Sugiyama's (2004, 166) study of Mormons in Japan discovered that 48.5 percent were recruited by missionaries through home visitation, contact on the street, or in English classes taught by the missionaries. Foreign-born missionary religions, it appears, depend more upon the professional proselytizer than other Japanese religions, though this study also found that 39.7 percent indicated that a family member or friend was the key contact and connection with the group. The roles and relative contributions of the laity and professional missionary in recruitment activities is clearly an area in need of more systematic and comparative research.

Both Christian mission groups and new religions have constituted a fundamental challenge to conventional or established religions and Japanese religiosity over the past century. By encouraging individuals to consider alternative interpretations of reality, lifestyles, and spiritual disciplines, these new traditions can cause conflict and division in many situations and be disruptive of the *wa*—or social harmony—of traditional Japanese society. Although some new religions encourage members to fulfill traditional religious obligations, as well as adopt new disciplines and practices, most Christian groups and new religions introduce an element of tension by stressing the distinction between the "world as it is" and the "world as it should be."

The social conflict generated by proselytism can be clearly seen in the history of Christian missionary activity in Japan. As a proscribed religion for over two centuries (until 1873), Christianity was popularly understood and referred to as a heretical religion and evil teaching (*jakyo*). The exclusivism emphasized by early Protestant missionaries in the late nineteenth century, and their criticism of indigenous religious practices, did little to alleviate this widespread perception. The history of Christian mission abounds with stories of individuals being cut off from their families or isolated in their communities because of the demands of their new faith and refusal to participate in household ancestor rites or community festivals. It has not been uncommon for zealous new Christians, following the instructions of their missionary teachers, to burn the family Buddhist altar and ancestral tablets, as well as the Shinto godshelf, understandably creating innumerable family conflicts.

There have been other "single practice" religious traditions demanding exclusive commitment from their followers that have also generated their share of social conflict and critical reactions from the larger public. Soka Gakkai, a modern expression of Nichiren Buddhism, for example, was often the target of criticism for its aggressive recruitment tactics (*shakubuku*) during the early postwar period. Similarly, Aum Shinrikyo generated considerable conflict with the larger society in the early 1990s—several years before the subway sarin gas attack—because of its push to rapidly increase the number of its world-renouncing members, who cut off familial relationships and obligations. Since most Japanese have been integrated into the system of household (Buddhist) and communal (Shinto) religious obligations, and usually participate in the annual rituals and festivals related to both traditions, any religious group that requires exclusive commitment or makes high demands on members tends to clash with Japanese religious sensibilities and generates conflict.

The role of the mass media

While high-demand and exclusivistic religions may have done their share to generate negative feelings toward missionary religions, these attitudes have undoubtedly been cultivated by the media coverage of deviant behavior, financial scandals, high-profile court cases, and incidents of violence related to religious groups. Several examples from the past two decades are worth brief consideration here.

The Jehovah's Witnesses is one foreign-born missionary movement that has a significant public presence in Japan. First of all, it has a membership of just over 200,000, many of whom have been effectively mobilized as "publishers," dedicated followers who regularly distribute materials and engage in witnessing activities at train stations and through home visits. These activities have not led to particularly impressive results in Japan's difficult religious environment. According to their own reports, "in Japan it takes about 18,000 hours of preaching to gain one baptism," whereas in countries like Zambia and Nepal it requires 2000 hours or less to gain one baptism.[16] In addition to the relatively high-profile recruitment activities of the Jehovah's Witnesses, their public presence is also heightened by the newspaper coverage of incidents related to the movement that reveal a serious tension between its values and that of society at large. In 1985, for example, a ten-year-old child injured in a traffic accident died, shortly after her parents—dedicated followers of the Jehovah's Witnesses—refused to allow a blood transfusion. This incident attracted considerable negative attention, but other convictions of Jehovah's Witnesses regarding other areas of social life also clash with Japanese values and religious sensibilities. Parents with children enrolled in Japanese public schools, for example, often refuse to participate in PTA activities and do not allow their children to sing the national anthem at official school events or participate in martial arts classes.[17]

Another group that comes under public scrutiny even more frequently is the Unification Church. "Problems" that are regularly covered by the news media, and shape public opinion, include the mass weddings held in Seoul, high-pressure recruitment methods, and fundraising activities through "spiritual sales" of sacred objects that are said to guarantee the salvation of one's ancestors. According to many claims in court cases, members have been pressured by leaders to take out loans to support the activities of the church, and often find themselves in difficult circumstances and unable to repay the loans. The National Network of Lawyers Against Spiritual Sales, which includes some 300 lawyers concerned with Unification Church activities in Japan, reports that it received some 18,000 complaints over a ten-year period (1987–1997). The Unification Church has been taken to court numerous times and found to be "legally liable for the unlawful procurement of monetary donations" in numerous judgments determined by courts in Japan over the past few years.[18]

Financial scandals and problems are hardly confined to the Unification Church. Over the past two decades, suspicions of widespread abuse of the existing laws led the tax authorities to increase their investigation of public benefit organizations (*koeki hojin*). Some 73 percent of these 250,000 registered corporations are religious organizations. According to a 1995 National Tax Agency report, for example, 321 of 381 religious corporations investigated by the agency (that is, 84.3 percent) had failed to report the required information, and 44 had actual "hidden" income. In addition to these cases of tax evasion, there have been numerous complaints regarding the deceptive and high-pressure membership recruitment tactics and fund-raising methods used by a number of religious organizations. According to one report, between 1987 and 1994 the Tokyo Lawyers Association and Consumer Centers across Japan received a total of 16,575 complaints of exploitation by various religious organizations (Kito 1995: 24–44).[19] In light of these findings, it is not surprising that there are many outspoken critics of the 1951 Religious Corporations Law, which they maintain has allowed for too much abuse by religious groups and lack of accountability and government oversight.

All of the above examples pale in comparison to the negative impact on Japanese attitudes that resulted from the sarin gas attack on the Tokyo subway system by Aum Shinrikyo members just over a decade ago. On the morning of March 20, 1995, during rush hour, close disciples of the Aum's charismatic founder, Shoko Asahara, released the deadly sarin nerve gas on Chiyoda, Hibiya, and Marunouchi subway lines. Within minutes, thousands of commuters and scores of subway employees began stumbling out of some 16 stations in central Tokyo. After the gas attack and allegations of Aum's involvement, the daily newspapers, weekly magazines, and television programming gave almost constant coverage to the developments regarding Aum for several months. The peak of media coverage was on May 16, the day Asahara was arrested at the Kamikuishiki facilities and transported to the Metropolitan Police Department in Tokyo. Hundreds of employees from each TV broadcasting company were deployed to cover the story and all regular programming was bumped by Aum coverage and special reports. Across the country some 50 newspapers also issued special editions to provide full coverage of the Aum investigation.[20]

In the end, Asahara and 104 of his followers were indicted on various charges, including murder in relation to the Tokyo subway sarin gas attack on March 20, 1995, which killed 12 people and injured another 5,500; another sarin gas attack in Matsumoto, Nagano Prefecture, which killed seven and injured 600 in June 1994; the kidnapping and murder of Tsutsumi Sakamoto, a lawyer representing concerned parents of Aum members, along with his wife and son; and the kidnapping and death of Kiyoshi Kariya, a Tokyo notary public, in February 1995.

In view of the many tragic deaths, thousands of injuries, and widespread sense of insecurity that followed the gas attack, it is understandable that many Japanese became more concerned that the government protect the public from dangerous and abusive religious groups, rather than be overly concerned about the protection of religious freedoms. Frightening images connected with religion were seared into the Japanese consciousness through months of daily and extensive coverage. Furthermore, the general public was shocked to learn that such a small religious movement could turn so violent and cause such damage and suffering. Naturally, serious concerns were raised regarding the adequacy of the postwar laws regulating religion by the fact that a group like Aum could be legally registered with the government and receive tax-breaks that supported its various business and activities (including the production of drugs and sarin gas).[21]

In response to these concerns, on December 8, 1995—that is, less than one year after the subway incident—the Diet passed a bill to amend the Religious Corporations Law. The new law now requires more transparency in reporting of financial transactions and allows individuals with legitimate interests (both members and government officials) to request additional information from religious bodies. To my knowledge, no proposals to limit propagation activities were considered during the debate regarding the revision of the law.

In light of the media coverage of controversial religious groups over the past two decades, it is not surprising to find a general social climate of suspicion and mistrust toward religious groups in Japan. Survey research has shown that the majority of Japanese today regard religious institutions as untrustworthy, gloomy, closed, and since the Aum crisis, increasingly as dangerous (*abunai*). A national survey conducted in 1995 discovered that the most commonly held images of new religions in particular were that they were primarily out for money, were characterized by annoying and intrusive recruitment activities, and were scary.[22] These negative attitudes tend to be especially strong among young people, particularly individuals in their twenties. This is relevant to our concerns here because young people and students are often regarded as a prime target of proselytizing religions. In fact, many religious groups have an organized presence on university campuses across Japan. Over the years, these groups have been the source of considerable difficulties for university administrators. Parents hold universities responsible if their son or daughter joins a problematic religious group while enrolled in the institution. Hence, on most campuses the office of student affairs provides information about religious groups as a part of their orientation program and bulletin boards carry notices that warn students about surreptitious groups working on campus with misleading advertisements about seminars and retreats, which do not reveal their ties to religious organizations.

In this context, it is interesting to consider the findings of surveys of Japanese college students conducted in 1995, 1996, 1998, and 1999, which questioned students regarding their attitudes toward street proselytization.[23] Each time approximately 60 percent of the students agreed with the statement that "*Proselytization on streets is an annoyance and should be restricted by law*" (emphasis mine). The religious groups most recognized and identified by students in this survey were the Jehovah's Witnesses, various other Christian sects, Soka Gakkai, Honohana Sanpogyo, and Kofuku no Kagaku (Science of Happiness). Over 50 percent of the students surveyed had experienced some form of solicitation from a religious organization, which most frequently occurred around a train station (on the street) or at home (Inoue 2003, 34–35).

Whatever the good intentions of proselytizing religions may be, it seems apparent that at least one of the unintended consequences of current methods of public engagement is the strengthening of rather negative stereotypes among most Japanese. If such perceptions of religious organizations and their activities continue to intensify, the free practice of religion—including proselytization activities—may face some regulation in the future. While at the moment it is hard to imagine that any serious legislation to limit this activity will be forthcoming, another "crisis" of some kind could mobilize politicians and generate public support for some kind of restrictions.

Conclusion

In this brief review, we have only considered some aspects of the social and legal context of proselytization in contemporary Japan. It is important that we recognize, however, that this is not an exclusively domestic concern. For almost a century, representatives of many Japanese religions have been involved in carrying their traditions beyond the shores of Japan. The Japanese have not, in other words, simply passively accepted the advances of outside religions; rather, they have creatively responded with their own religious initiatives, and exported new and old Japanese religious traditions, through both emigration and missionary activity. As Peter Clarke (2000, 2) has reminded us, globalization is not a unidirectional process of Westernization as sometimes portrayed in the literature; rather, the development of "global society" has its share of "reverse influences" from non-Western societies. Japanese have clearly become significant actors in global proselytism and the expansion of their religions overseas is rapidly becoming a significant new field of research.[24]

While it might be possible to speak of the relative success of some Japanese religions abroad—Zen and Soka Gakkai in the United States and Sekai Kyusei Kyo in Brazil, for example—in most locations the gains have been rather modest.[25] Nevertheless, both established and new Japanese religions now have a global presence. The most active movement internationally is undoubtedly Soka Gakkai, which already has an organizational presence in some 82 countries and territories. The "old unilateral missionary flows," as Paul Freston points out elsewhere in this volume, truly are a thing of the past. The evangelists of various Western missionary organizations are likely to encounter equally dedicated representatives of Japanese religions in most regions of the world. While many Japanese religions are welcomed in some overseas contexts—Brazil, for example—their activities are sometimes viewed with a great deal of suspicion and concern. In the years ahead, we should anticipate significant conflict and public debate as Japanese religions continue to expand in areas that for centuries were regarded as part of Christendom or, more recently, a "secular" society with little use for religion of any kind.[26]

Notes

1. The Japanese terminology used for "proselytization" varies from group to group, but includes such terms as *fukyo* (to spread teachings), *dendo* (to transmit the way), *michibiku* (to guide, introduce), and *shakubuku* (a term emphasized by the Soka Gakkai movement several decades ago, which literally means "to break and suppress"). What these terms share is the common concern to disseminate beliefs and recruit new members to some organized form of religion, which is hardly a feature restricted to the controversial groups mentioned above. A number of scholars studying Japanese religions have adopted several terms closely connected to the Christian tradition, such as evangelism and evangelist, and used them in discussions of proselytization and membership recruitment by Japanese religions. Since this chapter draws on the work of many different scholars, the terminology used varies accordingly.

2. See Ishii (1997) for a helpful overview of survey research on Japanese religious belief and practice in the postwar period.

3. The Tokugawa authorities had determined that Christianity—with its close connection with European nations with expanding colonial empires—represented a serious threat to Japan. Christianity was designated as an "evil religion" (*jakyo*),and a policy of national seclusion was instituted in order to eliminate this disruptive and

politically subversive movement. Government decrees ordered the expulsion of European missionaries and mandated the systematic persecution of Japanese converts. In spite of the widespread persecution, arrest, and execution of Christians, as well as effective methods of social control instituted by the authorities, Christianity continued "unofficially" for the next two centuries as the "hidden Christians" (*Kakure Kirishitan*) sought to survive in the hostile environment and secretly carry on the faith they had received.

4. Goodwin (1989, 137–49) provides a helpful study of Buddhist missionary activity, fundraising, and social engagement (i.e., proselytization "from below") in the Heian and Kamakura periods; that is, centuries before the Tokugawa authorities forced affiliation with Buddhist temples.

5. It is worth noting here that the pattern of "proselytization from above" was also rather typical of the first Christian mission in Japan. While Jesuit missionaries and their Japanese assistants traveled from village to village in various feudal domains, it was the conversion of the feudal lord or village heads that led to the phenomenon of mass conversions, as those below in the hierarchical order followed the decision of those above. The spread of religious voluntarism and individualism in religious matters only becomes a taken-for-granted reality in the twentieth century.

6. This interpretation and the following brief discussion of State Shinto draws on the work of Hardacre (1989).

7. Tanaka goes on to elaborate this point as follows:

    as a result of these freedoms being guaranteed, the state is not only forbidden to compel an individual to believe in a certain specific religious faith, to make a confession of faith, to perform acts running counter to his faith, or to restrict or prohibit him to propagate his faith. (1959, 80)

8. It should be noted that many religious groups are involved in the support of many public welfare activities, including medical work, social welfare, and education. These activities, however, do not receive the media attention that more sensational scandals always attract.

9. The largest church in the world today, in fact, is the Yoido Full Gospel Church in Seoul, which claims over 700,000 members and a Sunday attendance of over 200,000. The growth of the Korean church has also been accompanied by the development of numerous mission agencies and overseas missionary work. In the last decade of the twentieth century, the number of Korean missionaries serving overseas grew from 1,645 serving in 87 different countries in 1990 to 10,745 serving in some 162 different countries in 2002. While many different Korean Christian groups are active in Japan—Presbyterian, independent evangelists, and the controversial Unification Church—it has been Paul Yonggi Cho's Full Gospel Church that has made the most concerted evangelistic efforts over the past two decades. The mission to Japan began in 1976 with the organization of a church in Osaka. Two years later another church was established in Tokyo, and numerous branch churches and home cell groups have been organized since that time. Cho also began television evangelism in Japan in 1978, broadcasting his programs on seven different stations across Japan. See Mullins (1994) for a

preliminary study of this Korean missionary enterprise in Japan.

10. These statistics are taken from the *Shukyo nenkan: Heisei 15 Nen* [Religion Yearbook, 2003] (2004, 30–33). In addition to these legally registered religious groups, it should also be noted that there are other unregistered groups—without legal status and tax benefits—that are still engaged in recruitment activities (Aum Shinrikyo, for example).

11. Actually, the percentage of new religions is actually higher since the statistics of some Buddhist and Shinto-related new religions are listed along with established Buddhist and Shinto institutions rather than in the "other" category.

12. Regarding the larger social impact of new religions, see Robert Kisala (1992), which provides a helpful analysis of the social ethics and activities of such new religions as Tenrikyo and Rissho Koseikai (including peace activities and social welfare work in their care for refugees, the disabled and the elderly). The political involvements of new religions in Japan, particularly Soka Gakkai, is covered by Shupe (1993) and Kisala (1999), especially chapter 3.

13. Shimazono (1992, 120–21) refers to this pattern of laicization with Japanese phrases such as *taishu shugi* (roughly, salvation for the masses) and *zaike shugi* (principle of lay religion), which approximates the traditional Protestant slogan of the "priesthood of all believers." According to the teachings of many groups based on the Lotus Sutra (Soka Gakkai and Reiyukai, for example), lay people are fully capable of taking control of their religious destiny without dependence on a professional priesthood, and can become religious leaders in their own right as they lead others to the daily practice of Buddhism through household gatherings and *hoza*.

14. A helpful overview and analysis of the different understandings, approaches, and methods of proselytization in representative Japanese new religions may be found in the article, "Fukyo to Kyoka" [Propagation and Education], in the massive *Shinshukyo Jiten* [Encyclopedia of New Religions] Nobutaka Inoue *et al*, eds., (1990, 307–24).

15. In the case of Reiyukai, a Buddhist new religion, Hardacre explains that the organizational structure of the group itself is based on

> the personal connection established by proselytization. These links are conceived of in familistic terms; the person who proselytizes is the 'parent' (*michibiki no oya*), and the convert is the 'child' (*michibiki no ko*). This relationship is the individual's most basic tie to the group as a whole. He will attend the meetings (*hoza*) held by the 'parent,' and he cannot ordinarily change his membership to another *hoza*. (1984, 54–55)

16. See the "Statistics of Jehovah's Witnesses: Graphic Presentation of Jehovah's Witnesses Activities in the World, 1988–2004," http://www.jwic.com/stat.htm [Accessed 16 January 2007].

17. For a more detailed discussion of problematic aspects of the Jehovah's Witnesses in the Japanese social context, see Shimazono (2001, 223–28).

18. For a brief synopsis of these court cases and the activities of this lawyers' association, see http://www1k.mesh.ne.jp/reikan/english/index-e.htm [Accessed 16 January 2007]. Another source in English on problems connected with the Unification Church in Japan is Sakurai Yoshihide (2004), "Illegal Missionary Work Lawsuits and Exit Counseling for Unification Church Members."

19. One of the most recent cases to attract considerable attention is that of Hogen Fukunaga, founder of Honohana Sampogyo, who was indicted in 2000 for illegal financial activities and fraud related to charging outrageous fees for counseling and predictions based on a technique of "reading the soles" of an individual's feet.

20. See Gardner (2001, 133–62) for a critical analysis of the media converage of the Aum affair.

21. See Kisala and Mullins (2001) for a more detailed treatment of the post-Aum religious situation in Japan.

22. The results of this survey are reported by Ishii (1997, 152).

23. See Inoue (2003, 2–16) for details on the methods and samples of these surveys.

24. For some useful materials in English related to this developing area of study, see Shimazono (1991), Mullins and Young (1991), Clarke and Somers (1994), Clarke (2000), and Learman (2005).

25. Sekai Kyusei Kyo (also known as the Church of World Messianity) in Brazil, is one of the few success stories of Japanese new religions abroad. Initially established in 1965 in Sao Paulo, today it has 186 churches or mission centers across Brazil, 300,000 members, and approximately three million participants nationwide. Although membership in the religion was initially Japanese, today less than three percent of the membership is confined to the ethnic community. As Clarke (2000, 161) points out, the Church of World Messianity's success in Brazil is closely related to its "policy of inculturation." This is in sharp contrast to other established Japanese religions in Brazil—Zen, Pure Land, Shingon, and Tendai—which have largely maintained transplanted traditions and serve as "ethnic religions" for Japanese or Brazilians of Japanese descent.

26. There is already evidence that this is a likely scenario. A 1995 report to the French government identified the following Japanese religious movements active in France as problematic "cults:" Kofuku no kagaku, Shinji Shumeikai, Reiyukai, Seimeikyo, Sukyo Mahikari, and Soka Gakkai. This Report on the "Inquiry into Cults" was unanimously adopted by the French Government Commission on December 20, 1995 (the full report is available at http://cftf.com/french/Les_Sectes_en_France/cults.html [Accessed 16 January 2007].

References

Clarke, Peter B., ed. 2000. *Japanese New Religions in Global Perspective*. Richmond, UK: Curzon Press.

Clarke, Peter B. and Jeffrey Somers, eds. 1994. *Japanese New Religions in the West*. Sandgate, Folkestone, UK: Japan Library/Curzon Press.

Davis, Winston. 1977. *Toward Modernity: A Developmental Typology of Popular Religious Affiliations in Japan*. Cornell University East Asia papers 12. China-Japan Program, Cornell University; Rev. edition.

———. 1980. *Dojo: Magic and Exorcism in Modern Japan*. Stanford, CA: Stanford University Press.

————. 1992. *Japanese Religion and Society: Paradigms of Structure and Change.* Albany: State University of New York Press.

Earhart, H. Byron. 1989. *Gedatsu-Kai and Religion in Contemporary Japan: Returning to the Center.* Bloomington: Indiana University Press.

Gardner, Richard A. 2001. Aum and the Media. In *Religion and Social Crisis in Japan: Understanding Japanese Society Through the Aum Affair,* ed. Robert Kisala and Mark R. Mullins, 133–162. Basingstoke and NY: Palgrave and St. Martin's Press.

Goodwin, Janet R. 1989. Building Bridges and Saving Souls: The Fruits of Evangelism in Medieval Japan. *Monumenta Nipponica* 44(2): 137–49.

Hardacre, Helen. 1984. *Lay Buddhism in Contemporary Japan: Reiyukai Kyodan.* Princeton, NJ: Princeton University Press.

————. *Shinto and the State: 1868–1988.* 1989. Princeton, NJ: Princeton University Press.

Inoue, Nobutaka. 2003. *Japanese College Students' Attitudes Towards Religion: An Analysis of Questionnaire Surveys from 1992 to 2001.* Tokyo: Kokugakuin University.

Inoue, Nobutaka, Komoto Mitsugu, Tsushima Michihito, Nakamaki Hirochika and Mishiyama Shigeru, eds. 1990. *Shinshukyo Jiten* [Encyclopedia of New Religions] Tokyo: Kobundo.

Ishii, Kenji. 1997. *Da-ta bukku: Gendai Nihonjin no Shukyo* [Data Book: The Religion of Modern Japan]. Tokyo: Shinyosha.

Kisala, Robert. 1992. *Gendai Shukyo to Shakai Rinri* [Contemporary Religion and Social Ethics]. Tokyo: Seikyusha.

————. 1999. *Prophets of Peace: Pacifism and Cultural Identity in Japan's New Religions.* Honolulu: University of Hawaii Press.

Kisala, Robert and Mark R. Mullins, eds. 2001. *Religion and Social Crisis in Japan: Understanding Japanese Society Through the Aum Affair.* Basingstoke/NY: Palgrave and St. Martin's Press.

Kito, Masaki. 1995. *21Seiki no Shukyo Hojinho* [A Religious Corporations Law for the 21ˢᵗ Century]. Tokyo: Asahi Shinbun Sha.

Learman, Linda. Ed. 2005. *Buddhist Missionaries in the Era of Globalization.* Honolulu: University of Hawaii Press.

McFarland, H. Neill. 1967. *The Rush Hour of the Gods.* New York: Macmillan.

Mullins, Mark R. 1992. Japan's New Age and Neo-New Religions: Sociological Interpretations. In *Perspectives on the New Age,* ed. James R. Lewis and J. Gordon Melton, 232–46. Albany: State University of New York Press.

————. 1994. The Empire Strikes Back: Korean Pentecostal Mission to Japan. In *Charismatic Christianity as a Global Culture,* ed. Karla Poewe, 87–102. Columbia: University of South Carolina Press.

————. 1997. Aum Shinrikyo as an Apocalyptic Movement. In *Millennium, Mes-*

siahs and Mayhem: Contemporary Apocalyptic Movements, ed. Thomas Robbins and Susan E. Palmer,313–24. London: Routledge.

———. 1998. *Christianity Made in Japan: A Study of Indigenous Movements.* Honolulu: University of Hawaii Press.

Mullins, Mark R., Shimazono Susumu and Paul Swanson, eds. 1993. *Religion and Society in Modern Japan.* Berkeley, CA: Asian Humanities Press.

Mullins, Mark R. and Richard Fox Young. Eds. 1991. Introduction to Special Double Issue on "Japanese New Religions Abroad." *Japanese Journal of Religious Studies* 18(2–3): 95–103.

Shimazono, Susumu. 1991. The Expansion of Japan's New Religions into Foreign Cultures. *Japanese Journal of Religious Studies* 18(2–3): 105–32.

———. 1992. *Gendai Kyusai Shukyoron* [Salvation Religions in Contemporary Society]. Tokyo: Seikyusha.

———. 2001. *Posutomodan no Shinshukyo* [Post-Modern New Religions]. Tokyo: Tokyodo Shuppan.

Shukyo nenkan: Heisei 15 Nen. 2004. [Religion Yearbook 2003]. Tokyo: Gyosei.

Shupe, Anson. 1993. Soka Gakkai and the Slippery Slope from Militancy to Accommodation. In *Religion and Society in Modern Japan*, ed. Mark R. Mullins, Shimazono Susumu and Paul Swanson, 231–38. Berkeley, CA: Asian Humanities Press.

Sugiyama, Sachiko. 2004. *Shinshukyo to Aidenteitei—Kaishin to Iyashi no Shukyoshakaishinrigaku* [New Religions and Identity—A Social-Psychology of Conversion and Healing]. Tokyo: Shinyosha.

Tanaka, Jiro. 1959. The Meiji and Present Constitutions Compared. In *Religion and State in Japan.* Occasional Bulletin 7. Tokyo: International Institute for the Study of Religions.

Yoshihide, Sakurai. 2004. Illegal Missionary Work Lawsuits and Exit Counseling for Unification Church Members. *Cultic Studies Review* 3(3) http://culticstudiesreview.org/

CHAPTER 14

Negotiating Proselytism in Twenty-first Century Russia

Olga Kazmina

Debating the issue of proselytism is quite new in Russia. Moreover, the term was virtually unknown prior to the 1990s. Since that time, significant changes in public discourse have taken place. In order to comprehend the significance of contemporary debates on the subject it is necessary to situate the problem of proselytization in historical perspective, as well as to distinguish its theological, cultural, social, and political aspects. Furthermore, Russia's traditional non-Christian denominations, which are found predominantly within certain ethnic groups, have not yet felt the full impact of proselytism. For this reason, this chapter will focus primarily on the Christian segment of Russia's religious landscape. There will be some examination of the key terms in this debate, as well as the various understandings of the nature and the tasks of missionary activity by the various parties involved.

The influx of multiple new denominations into Russia in the 1990s, and the attendant rise in proselytizing activity, attracted the attention of religious figures, academics, policy makers and the mass media in Russia. It also provoked scholarly interest abroad. For example, Emory Law School's, Law and Religion Program, Proselytism Project published a volume entitled, "Proselytism and Orthodoxy in Russia: The New War for Souls" (Witte and Bourdeaux 1999). I will refer to the contents of this book in my analysis, especially when covering the divergent views that each denomination holds concerning evangelism, missionary work, and proselytism. Since the publication of this book, many of the positions of the core denominations within Russian society have changed, new church documents have appeared, and some elements of the inter-denominational debates have shifted. All of this points to the need for further exploration of the proselytism problem and its current reinterpretation in the contemporary Russian context.

To understand why proselytizing claims and activities have become so contentious in contemporary Russia I will pose the following key questions: How do denominational views of proselytism differ? Who have been the core participants in the debate? How has the negotiating of proselytism been shaped by political and social changes? How has the issue been shaped by identity questions? What has been the impact of legislation? What role have the mass media played in the process? How do state and society create and foster a context for the re-imagination of religion, in general, and public discourse over proselytism, in particular?

Historical perspective

The Orthodox Church has historically been involved in the politics, power claims and "land gathering" of the Old Russian state. Traditionally, church and state were closely interrelated, and religion was incorporated into the state's ideology. Despite this doctrine of "symphony" between church and state, they often competed with each other for social dominance. This competition ended only under Peter the Great in the early eighteenth century, when the Patriarchate was abolished and the Czar was proclaimed to be the head of the Orthodox Church. In general, Peter's reforms attempted to integrate religious life with the centralized imperial administration (Meyendorff 1978, 170). The Church's functioning was thus subject to state control. At the same time, the Russian Orthodox Church remained the largest and most influential denomination in the country. With nearly 100 million members at the beginning of the twentieth century, 50,000 priests, and some 95,000 monks and nuns in more than 950 monasteries, it was also the world's largest national church (Tsypin 2000, 132). More importantly, as the established church, it enjoyed many privileges that other denominations did not. Its membership was protected by the state: conversion from the Russian Orthodox Church to other denominations (even Christian ones) was forbidden by law. Hence, there were few places for proselytization, and the issue of proselytism was not even on the Church's agenda.

The advent of religious freedom in Russia is usually connected with "The Act of Toleration" adopted in 1905. It guaranteed a better position for non-Orthodox denominations and permitted cross-over from the Russian Orthodox Church to other Christian communities. The Russian Orthodox Church benefited from it as well, though it remained still greatly dependent on the state. This led to an atmosphere of renewal, which stimulated the movement for the restoration of the Moscow Patriarchate (abolished in 1721), independence from the state, and church reform. However, religious freedom and the possibilities for proselytization were short lived: the Bolshevik revolution of October 1917 ended all hopes of its continuance. Instead, cruel repression hit the Russian Orthodox Church, and, sometime later, other religious organizations. Under Soviet authority, "freedom of conscience," while formally proclaimed, in reality resulted in persecution of believers and the elimination of many religious organizations. After the death of Patriarch Tikhon, the authorities did not permit the Church to elect his successor. During World War II, the Nazis (while hostile to Christianity in their own country) allowed the profession of Christian religion on the occupied territories primarily for tactical reasons. The Soviet government reacted to these measures in 1943 by improving conditions for religious organizations, especially the Russian Orthodox Church and Muslims. In particular, some churches, monasteries and convents were reopened, certain priests and bishops were released from prisons, and the Russian Orthodox Church was permitted to elect the Patriarch. During the postwar period, atheism was not a major policy objective. However, in the late 1950s and early 1960s, Nikita Khrushchev initiated a powerful anti-religious campaign which included the mass closure of churches, increased atheistic propaganda, and the discrediting of clergy and official interference in church affairs (Tsekhanskaia 2002, 19). During the Brezhnev era, the religious situation continued to deteriorate; even though there were no large-scale church closings, the losses of the Khrushchev attack were not reversed and new ones were added (Davis 1995, 46).

Church-state relations began to change for the better only in the late 1980s, during Mikhail Gorbachev's *perestroika* campaign. In 1988, the Millennium of Christianity in Russia was celebrated as a national festival. In practice, this was the end of the Soviet policy on religion.

The Soviet experience and its effect on religious development can be generalized by emphasizing that religion during that period of time was encompassed in "state-church ideology." The state wanted, and to a certain extent succeeded in subjugating religion. Persecution and strict state regulations bred passiveness among religious organizations in social and political terms. The existing religious organizations needed to survive as institutions which meant that the question of proselytism was not a major concern. Another goal of the Soviet State, as Catherine Wanner (2004, 73) notes, was to eradicate religious practice, and by doing so, erase religious identities, especially those aligned with national identities. As the years that followed showed, these efforts failed. However, Soviet anti-religious policy had the effect of reshaping religion. By the end of the Soviet period, most people had experienced anti-religious socialization and had received no religious education. Religiosity was often latent or hidden, and not grounded in solid knowledge of church doctrine and practice. This would later affect the rise of proselytism as a problematic issue. Latent religiosity stimulated a religious revival in the late 1980s and the early 1990s. Simultaneously, the lack of religious knowledge made religious structure very flexible when new converts often passed from one denomination to another, and this structure did not stabilize until the mid-1990s.

Against this broader background, it will also be helpful to compare the history of Catholics and Protestants in Russia, the main challengers to the Russian Orthodox Church. Small groups of Catholics, descendants of settlers from Western Europe, appeared in Russia in the eleventh and twelfth centuries. Early on, no real antagonism existed between Western and Eastern forms of Christianity in Russia. Relations between the two branches of Christianity began to deteriorate with the fall of Constantinople to the crusaders in 1204, and subsequent German, Swedish and Danish invasions of the Russian lands further worsened relations between the two churches (Mchedlov 2003, 334–35). Only under Peter the Great did Russia's relations with the Roman Catholic Church improve. Simultaneously, the number of Catholics living in the Russian Empire increased, and Peter introduced the principle of tolerance toward Catholics on the part of the authorities, conditional upon their loyalty to the Russian state. This principle actually held until the Soviet period (Trofimchuk 2002, 282).

Catherine the Great, who reigned from 1762–1796, invited large numbers of Germans, including many Catholics, to migrate to Russia. During Catherine's reign the Russian Empire also acquired Polish lands, which were inhabited by adherents of the Roman Catholic Church. Gradually, Catholicism came to be seen as the religion of certain ethnic groups who lived in Russia. As such, the very notion of ethnic Russian conversions to Catholicism was inconceivable, and Catholic missionary work among non-Catholic ethnic groups was prohibited. Catholicism was also strongly associated with Western European culture, statehood, and policy, and the interest in Catholicism within Russia's population coincided with periods of reform and modernization. Eventually, the first ethnic Russian conversions to Catholicism occurred in the early nineteenth century during the reforms of Alexander I, who reigned from 1801–1825. Most of these new converts came from the upper classes of Russian society (Filatov and Vorontsova 1999, 96) and, following their conversions, they either left the country or had to keep their conversions a secret. A new phase of increased interest in Catholicism in Russia occurred at the beginning of the twentieth century, coinciding with a period of modernization. This time it resulted in the establishment of ethnic Russian Catholic parishes and even the creation of the Russian Catholic Church of the Eastern Rite in 1907. This church was, however, disbanded in the 1920s. Almost all Latin Rite Roman Catholic parishes were closed in the Russian Republic (RSFSR) by 1940. Only two churches remained open, and these only because they were officially registered as institutions of the French Embassy. The restoration of Catholic parishes began after Mikhail Gorbachev came to power in 1985, notably after his audience with Pope John Paul II in 1989.

Protestants also appeared quite early in Russia, with the first Lutheran community formed in Moscow in the mid-sixteenth century. Not long after, Lutheranism spread in Ingria, a territory around the current location of St. Petersburg. Under Peter the Great, the number of Lutherans in Russia also increased. These were mostly German specialists whom Peter invited to come to Russia. Throughout this period, the status of the Lutheran Church in Russia was quite stable. Because it was an ethnic church, there was little concern that Orthodox believers would convert to Lutheranism (Shlygina and Kazmina 1999, 185). During the Soviet period, however, the Lutheran Church, like other denominations, went through very hard times and actually ceased to exist officially in Russia, though it continued some of its activities underground. Active restoration of the Lutheran Church did not take place until the late 1980s.

In the second part of the eighteenth century the Mennonites appeared in the country at the invitation of Catherine the Great, who granted them some privileges, including exemption from military service. This was crucial for them because of their pacifist beliefs. After the 1917 Bolshevik Revolution, a significant portion of the Mennonite population left Russia. Those who stayed were subjected to repression in the 1930s and 1940s.

Baptists first arrived in Russia in the mid-nineteenth century. Initially, the only Baptists in Russia were Germans, but soon the denomination began to encompass other ethnic groups. In 1870, Evangelical Christians, who hold doctrinal views similar to the Baptists, also came to Russia. During the first decade of Soviet rule, when the state concentrated mostly on its struggle against the Russian Orthodox Church, evangelicals remained relatively free to operate and gained many converts. By the late 1920s, however, Soviet anti-religious repression affected them as well (Bolshakoff, 1950, 119–20).

Another Protestant denomination, the Pentecostals, appeared on the scene not long before World War I, with the first Pentecostal congregation being established in St. Petersburg in 1913. The first Pentecostal preachers were former Evangelical Christians who were converted to Pentecostalism by American missionaries. At first, Pentecostals pursued their missionary work among Baptists and Evangelical Christians, but then extended their efforts to the followers of other denominations as well. In the early 1920s their numbers grew dramatically, during a time when the Soviet authorities were preoccupied with their struggle against the Russian Orthodox Church and so did not hinder the Pentecostals and their work. Indeed, such was the success of Pentecostals, that when they applied to Lenin for permission to open a church in Petrograd (formerly St. Petersburg), their wish was granted. However, beginning in 1929, with the enactment of new anti-religious legislation, the Pentecostals, too, became targets of repression.

The rise of the proselytism problem in the early 1990s

The early 1990s were characterized by the appearance of many new denominations in Russia, and active missionary work by Western Christian denominations. The Russian Orthodox Church was becoming anxious at the rapidly growing competition and provoked sharp discussions over proselytizing activities. With this increase in popular interest in religion, politicians started to address the religious sentiments of the population and use religious elements in their activities. The issue of missionary activity now permeated political discourse. The problem of proselytism had been negotiated, not only in religious literature and scholarly works, but also in the secular press and mass media. Interestingly, the (Russian) term "prozelitizm" was first used in public discourse in condemning the activity of Protestant evangelical denominations and new religious movements.

The celebration of the Millennium of Christianity opened a new period in church-state relations. Religion was finally recognized by the state. Another turning point in religious politics, as attested by researchers, was Mikhail Gorbachev's meeting with the Pope in 1989. It meant that the state, while having recognized religion in general, did not grant any special support or favor to the Russian Orthodox Church, but initiated a policy of neutrality with regard to all denominations (Davis 1995, 73). This facilitated the arrival of religious organizations from abroad. Another fact that favored the appearance of new missions was that many people identified themselves not as adherents of some particular denomination, but simply as Christians (Byzov and Filatov 1993, 37).

Furthermore, for the first time in seventy years, people were given the freedom to profess their beliefs openly. The first liberal Law on Freedom of Conscience and Religious Organizations was adopted in the USSR on October 1, 1990, and later that month the Russian Republic's Law on Freedom of Beliefs came into force. The laws lifted all restrictions on the activity of religious organizations, guaranteed equal rights for all denominations, and permitted foreigners to be leaders of religious organizations. The overwhelming majority of new denominations began their activities exactly in the first half of the 1990s (Filatov 2002, 471)—the new period of religious freedom.

The early 1990s were also a period when both Russian mass media and public opinion were increasingly sensitive to the international discourse on religious freedom. Agadjanian argues that the 1990 law was too liberal for Russian society, which was not ready for such a degree of religious freedom (Agadjanian 2000, 121). In any case, the newfound religious freedom put the issue of proselytism squarely on the national agenda, and the term itself became known to the broader population at that time. Russia has traditionally been a country where the majority of the population professed Orthodox Christianity, but during the communist period many people became religiously inactive and inert, or even devoid of belief. Therefore, one of the major challenges of the early 1990s was the re-Christianization of the population. As described above, the Russian Orthodox Church was no longer the only key player in this field, and many Western evangelical denominations came to Russia from abroad. The Roman Catholic Church became active as well, and succeeded in attracting those who did not belong to traditionally Catholic ethnic groups. However, the most active missionary actors to emerge during this time, and hence main objects in the discourse over proselytism, were Protestant denominations.

At the beginning of the 1990s, there was a particular interest in Roman Catholicism on the part of the Russian citizens—especially young people—who did not have a traditional Catholic background, and some converted to Catholicism. It is unclear why Catholicism rather than Protestantism was more successful in Russia during this period, given Protestantism's very active missionary campaign. One factor may have been that traditionally in Russia, Roman Catholicism was the body associated with Western values and these values were very popular in the early 1990s. A further possibility may have been that people had difficulty in choosing among various Protestant denominations which they did not associate with Protestantism in general, while the Roman Catholic Church was well known. The fact that toward the end of the late Soviet period the main anti-religious sentiment was aimed at Protestant denominations might also have created negative stereotypes and prejudices.

Russia's Latin Rite Roman Catholics, for the most part, are associated with Poles, although other ethnic groups, too, can be found among Russia's Catholics (Lithuanians, some Belorussians, and others). In 1990–1991, the Vatican reorganized the structure of the Catholic Church in Russia to establish an Apostolic Administrator for Latin Rite Catholics of European Russia, based in Moscow, and an Apostolic Administrator for Latin Rite Catholics in the Asian part of Russia, based in Novosibirsk.

In the early 1990s with the tide of rising popular interest in religion, religious organizations found themselves more in competition with each other.

The Russian Orthodox Church felt threatened and insecure. The years of the communist regime had done their job: the Church had, in effect, become "locked" in its church buildings. It had lost its expertise in missionary work and had forgotten how to conduct community activities outside the church. By contrast, Protestant evangelicals and Catholics that came from abroad were very skilled in these types of activities.

The resultant tensions were aggravated by differences in viewpoints between the Russian Orthodox Church and Western Christian denominations on evangelism, missionary work, and proselytism. According to Protestant evangelicals, anyone who is just a "nominal" Christian, regardless of whether the person was baptized before, is a legitimate object of evangelism in any region of the world regardless of whether another Christian Church exists there. Thus a region like this would be viewed as a legitimate "missionary field" (Witte and Bourdeaux 1999, 21). The Russian Orthodox Church, while agreeing that every person must come into a personal relationship with Christ, believes that this relationship is strengthened through the sacraments and service. According to Russian Orthodoxy, most of the people of Russia (which is considered as a canonical territory of the Russian Orthodox Church) are under its spiritual protection, because they, or at least their parents, were baptized in the Russian Orthodox Church. Therefore, Russia is not an open field for missionary work. As Patriarch Aleksii II declared to the Bishops' Council in Moscow in 1997 that the Russian Orthodox Church considers missionary activity destructive when it is aimed at persons who were baptized into Orthodoxy or are linked with Orthodoxy historically. The Orthodox Church cites the words of the Apostle Paul: "It has always been my ambition to preach the gospel where Christ was not known, so that I would not be building on someone else's foundation" (Romans 15:20). The Moscow Patriarchate's message to Western Christians was the following:

> Do you recognize us, Orthodox, as Christians or not? If you do, then
> instead of trying to outwit and outmaneuver us..., you ought to help the
> Russian Orthodox Church in this dire moment of economic collapse, short-
> age of clergy and theological schools.... You ought to help the Orthodox
> Church to successfully carry out its mission on its native soil.
>
> (Pospielovsky 1995, 56)

The position of the Russian Orthodox Church, and the general context in which proselytism was being negotiated, were also shaped by identity issues. Traditionally, in Russia there has been a correlation between religion and ethnicity and the cultural dimension of religion has been very meaningful for ethnic identity (Kazmina 2000, 229–45). Frequently, religious affiliation was ascribed as a result of birth into a particular ethnic group (Barker 2000, 44).

This, in turn, created a situation in which religion is widely considered not just a private affair, but rather as a force of cultural tradition. Hence, proselytism was viewed as an attack on national identity. Also, the long period of existence under state domination weakened the institutional functionality of the Church. All this put the Russian Orthodox Church in a defensive position in the face of new challenges from proselytizing groups. Elizabeth H. Prodromou's analysis of Orthodoxy's ambivalence towards pluralism is apposite here. She notes three conditions:

> first, a historical long *durée* in which Orthodox churches, peoples or countries existed in contexts marked by the absence of democracy; second, institutional patterns of dysfunctional ecclesiastical behavior related to the formal and informal interpenetration of institutions of church and state; and third, conceptions of national (and collective) identity that have been permeated and shaped over centuries by Orthodoxy. (2004, 30–31)

The public debate over proselytism in the mid-1990s: the politicization of religion

Discussions concerning proselytism became more strained by the mid 1990s when religion became considerably politicized. Religion tended to be treated as a political force or a factor of political mobilization by various political agents and state bodies. While the latter displayed little trust and respect for the population, they still wanted to acquire prestige by demonstrating loyalty to the Russian Orthodox Church. During the nation-wide election campaigns of 1995 and 1996, almost all of major political blocs tried to play upon the prestige of the Church to gain votes (Verkhovskii *et al.* 1998, 176). Significantly, various political leaders also tried to appeal to public sentiments by using any opportunity to denounce proselytism, foreign missions, totalitarian sects, and destructive cults.

In the mid-1990s, the euphoria surrounding Western values gave way to more nationalistic tendencies (Filatov 2002, 471–72). These developments affected the religious sphere as well, where they engendered greater interest in Orthodox Christianity and other traditional religions. The very term "traditional religions" became widespread during this time. There was a rather widespread opinion that religious freedoms "had gone too far, that they threatened the true traditions of Russia, and that something must be done to curb them" (Bourdeaux 1995, 118). Also, there was the disappointment that foreign missions had little understanding of peoples, their cultures and histories (Guroian 1993, 242). This was the context for the public debates over the promulgation of the new law on religion. The reasons articulated were the lack of control on the observance of the law "On Freedom of Beliefs,"[1] concerns about so-called "totalitarian sects," and the concerns of the Russian Orthodox Church about the activity of some foreign religious organizations in Russia, and the Church's desire to have legal protection against proselytism.

It is noteworthy that the mass media were very involved in the debates over the drafting of the new law, as well as on the necessity of the adoption of the new law. There were two main positions represented in the media: traditionalist and liberal, according to Alexandr Agadjanian (2000, 122–28) and they were both centered on the proselytism problem. Traditionalists insisted that proselytization by Western Christian denominations and new religious movements threatened the predominance of the Russian Orthodox Church, and was dangerous for Russian culture and society. The theme of the danger of "totalitarian sects" and "destructive cults," and the obligation to protect the population against them, was extremely popular. The argument that a "traditionally Orthodox country must not give ground to foreign denominations" can be considered the quintessence of the traditionalist approach represented in the media.[2] Liberals, on the other hand, built their arguments on criticism of the Russian Orthodox Church, the defense of pluralism, the rights of minorities, and human rights rhetoric in general. A salient feature of the mid-1990s was that the liberal voices in the press were stronger than in society in general, which tended to lean toward a more traditionalist or conservative position (Agadjanian 2000, 127). Moreover, unlike the early 1990s, international opinion became less influential for the majority of the population.

The new law "On Freedom of Conscience and on Religious Associations" was finally adopted on October 1, 1997. According to the law, religious organizations that had operated since 1982 or earlier were put in a more favorable position in comparison with those which were created later. Only the former could obtain status as a legal entity. Those created later could only obtain the status of a religious group with lesser rights. In particular, their right to engage in missionary work was limited. It should be noted, however, that the acts that mitigated the most discriminatory provisions of the law (including the provision of the fifteen-year qualification, which met most critique) were adopted some years later.

The law also created a problem with the registration of certain denominations that included non-territorial formations, because it assigned each religious organization to a specific area. Whereas there were no problems with the new registration of the Catholic parishes, the new registration of Catholic orders such as Jesuits (Independent Russian Region of Christ Society) was problematic, because they were not included directly in the territorial bodies. The Constitutional Court settled this case in 2000. Having analyzed the provisions of the Constitution and of 1997 law, the Constitutional Court substituted a literal application of the latter. In fact, it changed the sense of the 1997 law. The Court determined three types of religious organizations that could be registered: local religious organizations, centralized religious organizations that included no less than three local organizations, and religious associations established by other religious bodies. As a result, the Independent Russian Region of Christ Society was given the opportunity to be registered as an organization of the third type.

In sum, the 1997 Law did not seriously change the situation in Russia with respect to religious freedom, but it did alter the general atmosphere and public opinion. Whereas proselytism was widely negotiated in political and public spheres in the 1990s, legislation did not react to it until later. As to the role of international law, there are references to international acts in the Russian Constitution in 1993, and there were also references to international acts, in the 1990 law on religion. In 1997, such references are absent. At the same time, despite substantial differences between the 1990 and 1997 laws, they both uphold the right to choose, the right to have and to change religious convictions, and the right to freely distribute religious views and convictions unless such activity violates the Law and infringes upon the rights of others (see for example Pchelintsev 1999, 5, 7–26; Schipkov 1998, 264–76).

New developments in negotiating proselytism since the late 1990s: The significance of Orthodox-Catholic relations

In the late 1990s, missionary events such as Protestant church services held in major stadiums receded into the past. The percentage of Protestants in Russia's population reached only one percent (including traditionally Protestant ethnic groups). Protestant evangelical missionary work brought the most success in Siberia and the Far East, where the Russian Orthodox Church's infrastructure is much weaker than in European Russia.

Historically, the Orthodox churches have created a particularly close relationship with the cultural identity of the people; this relationship was reconstructed and grew stronger in the second half of the 1990s. The competition between non-traditional denominations and the Russian Orthodox Church in the public sphere therefore turned to political and cultural arguments, while theological debates became the subject of interdenominational dialogue. One of the major arguments addressed was that the populations containing foreign denominations would divide Russian society and destroy Russian culture (Filatov 2002, 481). Unlike the early 1990s, in the mid- and late-1990s these arguments were received favorably by the general population. Thus, the theoretical discussion on proselytism became less interesting for the populace, and shifted away from popular newspapers and political discourse toward more specialized publications, both religious and secular. Later, these exchanges moved to the sphere of official inter-denominational relations.

In the social discourse reflecting inter-denominational relations, since the late 1990s the term "proselytism" has been the most widespread in the debates between the Russian Orthodox Church and the Roman Catholic Church over the activities of Catholics in Russia. The Roman Catholics became the core challenger to the Russian Orthodox Church, not the newer sects, as we might be led to believe. It happened that the denominations that were more remote in theological terms, became more isolated in their spheres of activities, while those more proximate (like Orthodoxy and Catholicism) competed in the same field. A nominal Orthodox person can convert to Catholicism more easily than to a denomination whose views are more theologically distinct. Furthermore, for Russia's general population with its minimal religious education and religious knowledge, there is no substantial perceived difference between the various Western Christian denominations and the new religious movements. They are all considered "others" or "sects," the only exclusion to this is Roman Catholicism (Agadjanian 2000, 123).

In Russia, inter-faith relations in general, and Orthodox-Catholic relations in particular, contain theological, historical, cultural and ethnic aspects, which implicate the key question of identity. Moreover, as argued above, the issues of theology and identity are interconnected, as the affiliation with Orthodoxy is closely bound to ethnicity. As Dimitry Pospelovsky (1995, 55) notes,

> the Orthodox Church may be tolerant and friendly toward other religions, but it will never subscribe to the Anglican branch theory. For the Orthodox there can be only one church, the Orthodox, with its direct succession from the ecumenical councils and denial of the right of any individual bishops, be they popes or Luthers, to establish new dogmas or doctrines. The more ecumenically minded Orthodox see Roman Catholicism as a part of that one church, although an erring part.

Since Orthodox and Catholic teachings are not that different in the eyes of people with minimal religious training, the conversion from nominal Orthodoxy to Catholicism can be considered by such people as merely a change of organization, and secular, rather than spiritual, interests can motivate such a change in affiliation. This observation can explain the very existence of the sense of competition, and the deep-seated concerns of the Russian Orthodox Church, even though demographic distribution is very unequal, namely sixty percent are Orthodox and less than one percent are Catholics. On the other hand, these figures demonstrate that despite all fears and concerns, Russian conversions from Orthodoxy are very infrequent, and the connection between religious and ethnic identities generally deters such conversions.

In general, the Russian Orthodox Church is disturbed by any Catholic activity in Russia which does not correlate with the numbers of traditional Catholics in the country. Whether that activity be the establishing of a Catholic diocese—or a Roman Catholic theological college in Moscow. In inter-church dialogue, the basic contention of the Russian Orthodox Church would be the unfairness of the Catholic doctrine concerning *filioque* and additional elements, and hence the possibility of full salvation only in Orthodoxy, together with the perception of the canonical territory of the Russian Orthodox Church. In that connection, the accusation of Catholic missionary work among real or potential adherents of the Orthodox Church is justifiable.[3]

This belief concerning canonical territory has proved to be the base argument of the Russian Orthodox Church in negotiating proselytism with all of its contenders during the post-Soviet period. It derives from Orthodox theology and points to the close connection between religious affiliation and national and ethnic identity. As the response of Metropolitan Kirill (of Smolensk and Kaliningrad, Chairman of the Department for External Church Relations) in 2005 clearly indicates:

> [t]he canonical tradition of the early undivided Church formulated the very important principle: one city, one bishop, that is, in one city, or speaking more broadly, in one place there is one Church. … We do not believe that the tragic division of the Church that followed … can, on the ontological level, eliminate this principle tracing back to the early Christian time. That is why Russia, where the word of God was preached by the Orthodox Church and where she existed from the very beginning as a local Church, that is the Church of this place, is considered to be the canonical territory of the Moscow Patriarchate. … Since the Baptism of Russia, Russian Orthodox missionaries became enlightening pioneers who played a key role in the Christianization of the country and the development of the national identity of the people to whom they brought the word of God. … The peoples of Russia whose cultural heritage is Orthodox expect to hear the word of the Gospel precisely from the Russian Orthodox Church and see precisely in her their spiritual guide. (Metropolitan Kirill 2005)

The basic points of the Catholic Church are its universalism and the special status of the Apostle Peter who is considered to be God's deputy on Earth and a founder of Catholic Church. This perception justifies missionary work all over the world as well as the appeal to the Orthodox Church for Eucharistic communion.

Igor Kovalevskii, General Secretary of the Conference of Catholic bishops in Russia, divides the problem of Catholic proselytism into two parts. On the one hand, he stresses that from the secular-legal perspective, the Russian Constitution guarantees religious freedom and hence everyone has the right to change their religious convictions. On the other hand, from a religious perspective, he argues for the special role of the Apostle Peter and insists that the Catholic Church has to build its relations with the Russian Orthodox Church in the framework of inter-Christian dialogue (Kovalevskii 2003). He also assigns two meanings to the term "proselytism." He argues that one meaning of proselytism is derived from inter-denominational relations and grounded in an understanding of the enticement of believers from one denomination to another using improper means. The Catholic Church is against such proselytism, according to Kovalevskii. At the same time, he stresses a theological and biblical understanding of proselytism, which is immediately connected with the missionary nature of the Christian Church and the command of Jesus Christ to make disciples. With this understanding in mind, every Christian must be a missionary, according to Kovalevskii. An Orthodox believer should bring/be an Orthodox witness, whereas a Catholic believer should bring/be a Catholic witness (Kovalevskii 2003).

Drawing the borders of such missionary work, the "Pro Russia" Commission of the Roman Catholic Church adopted the document entitled the "General Principles and Practical Norms of the Coordination of Evangelical Activity and Ecumenical Duties of the Catholic Church in Russia and Other CIS Countries" in 1992 (see Roman Catholic Church 2005, 501–10). While explaining the Catholic Church's mission of preaching to all people, this document does not approve of proselytism, which is understood as any pressure on conscience (Roman Catholic Church 2005, 503). In this document there is also a reference to the Vatican II Council with its statement that the Church strictly prohibits the proselytization of someone by tricks or enticing him or her to the Church (Roman Catholic Church 2005, 503). This document also states that the apostolic activity of the Catholic Church on the territory of CIS must be of ecumenical character. In the end, proselytism would not be the best way to reach this goal, but rather a fraternal dialogue between the followers of Christ aimed at the restoration of the full unity of Byzantine and Roman Churches, such as existed in the first millennium (Roman Catholic Church 2005, 504).

In response to this document, the Russian Orthodox Church published the "Basic Principles of the Russian Orthodox Church's Attitude to the Non-Orthodox," which was adopted by the Bishops Council in 2000 (Russian Orthodox Church 2000a). This document stresses that the essential goal of the Orthodox Church in relations with other Christian confessions is the restoration of that unity among Christians which is required of us by God (John 17–21; Russian Orthodox Church 2000c). The relationship of the Russian Orthodox Church with the non-Orthodox Christian communities in the former Soviet republics, the document says, should be carried out in the spirit of fraternal cooperation in order to coordinate social work, promote social harmony, and to put an end to proselytism on the canonical territory of the Russian Orthodox Church. The Russian Orthodox Church maintains that the mission of the traditional confessions is possible only if it is pursued without proselytism, and not at the expense of "stealing" the faithful, especially with the use of material benefits (Russian Orthodox Church 2000d). As to the relations with the Roman Catholic Church, in the appendix to "Basic Principles…" (Russian Orthodox Church 2000a), it is emphasized that unia and proselytism are the two most important issues to be settled in the dialogue with the Roman Catholic Church (Russian Orthodox Church 2000b).

Hence, in comparing these two documents, one can see similar points aspiring toward unity, fraternal dialogue, and the condemnation of proselytism. At the same time, proselytism remains among the major concerns that the Russian Orthodox Church has with the Roman Catholic Church. It is connected with various understanding of the scope of missionary work and the meaning of proselytism. The Russian Orthodox Church would like to see the activities of the Catholic Church in Russia contained to church services among so called ethnic Catholics.

In 2002, the previous structure of the Catholic Church in Russia was replaced by four Catholic dioceses, which formed a separate church province. Although the names of these new dioceses do not contain territorial affiliations, this reorganization angered the Russian Orthodox Church, which interpreted it as a form of proselytism. They interpreted it as an attempt by the Roman Catholic Church to expand its base in Russia by pursuing missionary activity on the canonical territory of the Russian Orthodox Church. This caused the conflict to escalate and became a new impulse for the debates over proselytism. Reacting to the establishing of Catholic dioceses in Russia, the Russian Orthodox Church identified this development as one of the most serious obstacles for improving relations between the two Churches, and labeled it as proselytism—as defined in the Declaration of Aleksii II, Patriarch of Moscow. In particular, the Patriarch found it unamicable to establish a Catholic Church province embracing the territory of Russia without any consultation with the Russian Orthodox Church. He also noted that, historically in Russia, the Catholic Church was viewed as a denomination of a few, rather small ethnic groups, and hence there had never even been Catholic dioceses in Russia in the past, much less a church province. The establishment of such a province made the Russian Orthodox Church suspicious of the missionizing aimed not only at ethnic Catholics, but also at the larger population (Aleksii II 2003, 123–26). The Ministry of Foreign Affairs of the Russian Federation also issued an Official Declaration where regret was expressed that the Catholic dioceses and province in Russia were established without any dialogue with the Russian Orthodox Church (Ministry of Foreign Affairs 2003, 126).

Since that time the problem of proselytism continues to be the main obstacle for improving relations between the Russian Orthodox and the Roman Catholic Churches. In his interview with *Corriere della Sera*, on August 27, 2004, Patriarch Aleksii II stressed that the division of the Christian world was profoundly tragic and that this division remained a serious obstacle for the ongoing witness of Christ. At the same time, Aleksii II noted that due to the current conditions of increasing secularization in Russia, uniting the efforts of all traditional churches in their witness for Christ was an urgent necessity. However, the response of Christians to the challenges of the contemporary world would be successful and convincing only in the case of cooperation based on mutual love and respect. According to him, this must be the basic principle of inter-religious relations and, in particular, Orthodox-Catholic dialogue. For this, the Patriarch is convinced: the Catholic Church should renounce proselytism as an unworthy pursuit which provides immediate benefits rather than a lasting contribution to the true witness of Christ. He further said that the Orthodox Church was awaiting a change of attitude within Catholic clergy and monks towards the Orthodox population on Russian territory (Aleksii II 2004).

Later, the Patriarch talked again about the complications in relations between the Russian Orthodox Church and the Roman Catholic Church. He said he regretted that his meeting with Pope John Paul II in 1997 in the Austrian city of Graz did not take place due to the declared refusal of the Catholic side to keep the condemnation of proselytism in the final document. He stressed that proselytism among the Orthodox population was one of the most acute and painful problems of Orthodox-Catholic relations in Russia. The Patriarch pointed out that he was for stronger coordination with the Roman Catholic Church in many spheres. However, for maximum effectiveness of such coordination, it was essential to overcome the differences and misunderstandings that complicate the dialogue (Aleksii II 2005).

However, though the problem of proselytism has not been resolved, the relations between the Russian Orthodox Church and the Roman Catholic Church have improved in 2006 and 2007, as noticed by representatives of both Churches as well as secular observers (See, for example, Anon. 2007a; Anon. 2007b; Anon. 2007c). Another characteristic feature of the current relations between the two Churches is the emphasis on similar positions over social problems and the solidarity in defending traditional Christian values. Thus, bishop Illarion, representative of Moscow Patriarchate in European international organizations said in one interview:

> ... [A]lthough the most significant problems, such as unia and proselytism, still remain unsolved, [...] nobody can prevent us from intensifying cooperation in defending traditional Christian values in Europe and all over the world before we reach the results in a theological dialogue.
>
> (Anon. 2007d)

One can also find similar motif in the words of archbishop Antonio Mennini, representative of the Holy See in Russia:

> We will try to multiply the signs of sympathy and respect towards the Russian Orthodox Church and set distrust and prejudice aside: we act only for the sake of Christ. (Mennini 2007)

The early 1990s saw the Russian Orthodox Church defending its position in regards to the proselytism problem. At a later date, the Church started to rethink its own position about how to carry out its own missionary work and, by the same token, to oppose what it viewed as proselytism by others. The perception of the Russian Orthodox Church on the issue culminated in the "Concept of Missionary Activity of the Russian Orthodox Church for 2005–2010," issued by the Missionary Department of the Moscow Patriarchate in April 2005 (Russian Orthodox Church 2005). In this document the Church formulated the forms and methods of missionary activity. Among these informational, apologetic, educational, and "external" missions are listed. The informational mission consists of Orthodox witness to large segments of the population through mass media, parish libraries and special publications. The apologetic mission aims to provide a comparison of Orthodoxy with the doctrines of non-Orthodox denominations, which are deemed inauthentic in the eyes of the Russian Orthodox Church. This comparison is intended to confront the proselytism of non-Orthodox organizations. The educational mission consists in providing a basic knowledge of Orthodoxy to those who are preparing to be baptized and those who are nominally Orthodox (i.e. were baptized but are not familiar with Orthodox teachings and practice), so that they become real churched persons. In particular, it explains why the Church attributes major importance to the introduction of a secondary school course "Bases of Orthodox Culture" for those willing to learn. Finally, the external mission encompasses the Orthodox witness to non-Christian peoples, and in particular immigrants. It also stipulates the protection of the local traditionally Orthodox population of Siberia and the Far East (with youth as a priority) from the intensive missionary activity of charismatic Protestant organizations from South Korea. In general, a strong emphasis is made in this "Concept" on the work with younger people, including those ethnic Orthodox who have converted to other Christian denominations but have preserved Orthodoxy and are open to the dialogue (Russian Orthodox Church 2005). Hence, while at the first encounter with proselytism, the Russian Orthodox Church had just reacted defensively, now the Church tends to act offensively, and has become the major player in its canonical territory in confronting the proselytism problem.

Revisiting the terms of proselytism

At this point, we can look back at the way the various strategic terms and concepts in this debate have been deployed. The discourse surrounding proselytism in Russia has been complicated by the absence of a single common definition. Moreover, the definitions of proselytism, which are used in the mass media, are often emotionally driven, which is evident in expressions such as "unfair missionary work." The problem is that the border between fair and unfair missionary work is not clarified within such definitions. International resources in terms of legislation and human rights documents, to which Russian discourse often referred in the early 1990s, does not clarify all these issues either. Natan Lerner (2000, 117), in trying to determine the limits of proselytism and having analyzed international law, suggests that "proselytism involving material enticement—money, gifts, or privileges—should be considered a form of coercion, and thus, may be limited by law." In Russia, the most active missionary activity took place during the hardest economic years, when material benefits were involved directly or indirectly, through free English-language classes, for example.

When talking about definitions it is also important to note that the concept of religious territory was commonly invoked in negotiating proselytism in Russia, but its understanding varied according to denomination. From the perspective of the Russian Orthodox Church, it would be the notion of the canonical territory, for Catholics it would be the perception of universalism, and for Protestants it would be the idea of the free missionary field, or missionary territory. Another issue which leads to misunderstandings in negotiating proselytism in Russia has been the ignorance on the part of foreign religious organizations concerning the close ties between religion and ethnic and national identities. Metropolitan Kirill (2002) notes that:

> In a significant degree Russia had formed as a state under the influence of religious factors, because exactly religious components mostly determined the national self-consciousness. To be Russian meant to be Orthodox, while

professing another faith was connected with belonging to another ethic group, another culture.

A majority of the population in contemporary Russia would share this sentiment. The cultural dimension of religiosity is the strongest and most meaningful for Russia's general population. That is why it is quite common in contemporary Russia for even non-believers to associate themselves with Orthodoxy (Mchedlov 2002, 45). From this perspective, the missionary activity of non-Orthodox preachers among such non-believers would raise "the anti-proselytization of substitution" as it is called by Grace Kao in her chapter elsewhere in this volume. Also, because of this close conjunction between religion and ethnicity, the non-Orthodox denominations did not attract larger percentages of Russia's population.

One final question remains. Do religious organizations use the same language of rights and freedom of religion as the state does? The answer will be both "yes" and "no." Yes, because they all advocate religious freedom, especially in church-state relations, and condemn proselytism. No, because the understanding of proselytism is not the same, as demonstrated above. In addition, whereas in church-state relations religious organizations operate within the provisions of the law and use common legal terms, in the debates between themselves they appeal to their own teachings, which can be different.

The academic community in Russia is not homogeneous when it comes to the question of proselytism. One part of the academy stresses the great predominance of the Orthodox Church in the religious structure of Russia's population, and its central role in Russian history and culture. Their argument is that the special status of the Russian Orthodox Church is quite natural (though it is not an established church), and they support the position of the Russian Orthodox Church as to the activity of other denominations on its canonical territory. At the same time, there is another branch of the academy which emphasizes that Russia is a multi-confessional country, and all denominations should be treated equally regardless of their numbers and their weight in the society.

Conclusion

In analyzing religious developments in post-communist Russia, with a spotlight on proselytism, it is important to identify two different periods: the early to mid 1990s, and the late 1990s to the present. When we talk about the revisiting of proselytism in these periods we should underline the shifts in the position of the Russian Orthodox Church, the change in core challengers to the Russian Orthodox Church, and the alteration in their polemics. In the early 1990s, Russia was viewed as a newly opened religious free market and numerous missionaries from a range of denominations arrived in the country. Missionary actions were not yet coordinated and new players competed not only with the local religious organizations, but also with each other. Their activities were considered by the Russian Orthodox Church as a threat to the status quo. The Russian Orthodox Church wanted legal protection from the state, whereas the state tended to remain neutral. Political actors, who tried to use religion as a factor to gain political power, did not appeal to religious organizations, but rather to the larger population. Many of the active players of the early 1990s had to learn to be content with their limited spheres, the numbers of their members and their restricted missionary activity. The position of the state was to change during this time—from demonstrative neutrality in early 1990s, to demonstrative solidarity with the Russian Orthodox Church in the late 1990s, to general neutrality and support for the Russian Orthodox Church at critical moments from 2000 onwards.

Another difference between the two periods was the attitude of the mass media. In the first period, the mass media were very involved with the religious debates of the time. In the second period, the secular press generally lost interest in the problem of inter-denominational relations. When this interest was reactivated by certain events, the press showed its solidarity with the Russian Orthodox Church. Currently, the secular press is not sensitive to the activities of Catholic parishes or orders in Russia. Its interest in Catholicism is limited by general politics of Vatican, while the interest in Catholic activities in Russia has considerably decreased. Since the early 1990s there have been significant shifts in the religious economy. As Eileen Barker notes:

> with the collapse of communism, there arose the opportunity for an individual's religion to be achieved through his or her personal choice. Instead of religion being imposed or denied from above, each person was invited to shop in the new religious supermarkets that were opening throughout Central and Eastern Europe and the F[ormer] S[oviet] U[nion]. Continuing the economic metaphor, new producers and new consumers were, in theory at least, ready to produce and to consume. (2000, 45)

In the early 1990s, this free market was open for all denominations in Russia. Using the economic metaphor again (having in mind, of course, its limitations), this market made its way from the initial accumulation and the competition of many non-numerous agents in the early 1990s to the positioning of "trans-national corporations" in the late 1990s. In the Russian religious context, the main actors in the debate over proselytism were the largest traditional state-supported church in the country and the world's largest Christian denomination.

Another difference between the two periods when proselytism was being negotiated and contested was that, in the early 1990s the competition between Protestants and the Russian Orthodox Church, addressed human rights issues and principles of religious freedom. In the late 1990s and early 2000s, when the main battle line in the debates over proselytism lay between the Russian Orthodox Church and the Roman Catholic Church, Catholic polemic focused on theological issues, namely, universalism and unity.

In sum, the resurgent problem of proselytism is closely tied to major religious changes in the contemporary Russian landscape, and was revisited with each new stage of Russia's post-communist development because of competing interests. The Russian Orthodox Church has a long history of both growth and survival under strong state control, and almost underground conditions. It made the Church anxious at the onset of competition in the new "free religious market." The principal opponents of the Russian Orthodox Church decided that Russia should be an open missionary field and shaped their activities accordingly in the first period. As to the Catholic Church, their perspective is that their community will eventually find its place as a minority group in Russia, seeing its universalist character in the very fact of the presence on the territory of Russia. Evangelicals, on the other hand, were satisfied with the success they enjoyed in Siberia and the Far East. The Russian Orthodox Church can now anticipate a new round of contested proselytism in this region. In general, the problem of proselytism is far from being settled. Future negotiations will encompass theological, cultural, social and political aspects, as well as reflect the different values of the competing groups. This will result in contradictions based on the inherent differences that lie at the heart of the controversy. Productive discussion on the proselytism issue can only be possible with the adoption of a more pluralistic attitude by all parties concerned.

Notes

1. According to the 1990 Law "On Freedom of Beliefs" the control of the observance of this law was placed mainly in the hands of the Soviets of People's Deputies (local authorities). Hence, after the Soviets ceased to exist in 1993, there was actually no more monitoring of the law.

2. *Nezavisimaia Gazeta* [newspaper], 28 March 1996.

3. I will not cover here the problem of Uniatism in Ukraine, which is among the areas of contention in relations between the Russian Orthodox Church and the Roman Catholic Church.

References

Agadjanian, Alexandr. 2000. Religioznyi diskurs v rossiiskikh mass-media: Entropiia, simfoniia, ideokratiia [Religious discourse in Russian mass-media: Entropy, symphony, ideocracy]. In *Starye tserkvi, novye veruiushchiie: Religiia v massovom soznanii postsovetskoi Rossii* [Old churches, new believers: Religion in mass consciousness of post-soviet Russia], ed. Kimmo Kaariainen and Dmitrii Furman, 116–47. St. Petersburg, Moscow: Letnii Sad.

Aleksii II. 1997. Interconfessional and Interfaith relations: Participation in the Activity of International Christian Organizations. Section 11 of *The Report to the Bishops Council in Moscow, 18–23 Feb. 1997* http://www.sedmitza.ru/index.html?sid=50&did=40 [Accessed 5 June 2005].

———. 2003. Zaiavleniie Patriarkha Moskovskogo i vseia Rusi Aleksiia II i Sviashchennogo Sinoda Russkoi Pravoslavnoi Tserkvi [Declaration of Alexii II, Patriarch of Moscow and All Russia and of Holy Synod of the Russian Orthodox Church]. In *Pirrova pobeda Vatikana* [*Pyrrhic victory of Vatican*], ed. S. Grigoriev and A. Stepanov, 123–26. Zhitomir: Ni-ka.

———. 2004. *Sviateishii Patriarkh Moskovskii i vseia Rusi Aleksii II otvetil na voprosy korrespondenta italianskoi gazety "Corriere della Sera" Armando Torno, 27 avgusta 2004 goda* [His Holiness Patriarch of Moscow and all Russia Aleksii II answered the questions of the correspondent of the Italian newspaper "Corriere della Sera" Armando Torno, August 27, 2004]. http://www.mospat.ru/text/ publications/id/7536.html [Accessed 10 June 2005, now defunct].

———. 2005. *His Holiness Alexy: "I sincerely hope that the next Primate of the Roman Catholic Church will enable relations with the Russian Orthodox Church to develop in a positive directions."* http://www.mospat.ru/text/e_interview/id/9050.html [Accessed 10 July 2005, no longer available].

Anon. 2007a. *Putin vpervye vstretitsia s Benediktom XVI* [Putin will have a meeting with Pope Benedict XVI for the first time]. http://religion.rin.ru/cgi-bin/religion/about.pl?idn=73773&id= [Accessed 22 March 2007].

———. 2007b. *Rossiiskiie katoliki otmechaut znachitelnoie uluchsheniie otnoshenii s pravoslavnymi* [Russian Catholics mark significant improvement in the relations with Orthodox]. http://religion.rin.ru/ cgi-bin/religion/about.pl?idn=73530&id= [Accessed 22 March 2007, now defunct].

———. 2007c. *Vizit Papy Rimskogo "ne stoit na povestke dnia"* [*Visit of the Pope of Rome "is not on the agenda"*]. http://religion.rin.ru/cgi-bin/religion/about.pl?idn=73835&id= [Accessed 22 March 2007].

———. 2007d. *Vstrecha Putina i Benedikta XVI pomozhet sovmestnoi zashchite Rossiiei I Vatikanom traditsionnykh tsennostei* [*The Meeting of Putin and Benedict XVI will help to joint defense of traditional values*]. http://religion.rin.ru/cgi-bin/religion/about.pl?idn=73801&id= [Accessed 22 March 2007].

Barker, Eileen. 2000. The Opium Wars of the New Millennium: Religion in Eastern Europe and the Former Soviet Union. In *Religion on the International News Agenda*, ed. Mark Silk, 39–59. Hartford, CT: The Leonard E. Greenberg Center for the Study of Religion in Public Life.

Bolshakoff, Serge. 1950. *Russian Nonconformity: The Story of "Unofficial" Religion in Russia*. Philadelphia: Westminster.

Bourdeaux, Michael. 1995. Glasnost and the Gospel. The Emergence of Religious Pluralism. In *The Politics of Religion in Russia and the New States of Eurasia*, vol. 3. ed. Michael Bourdeaux, 113–27. Armonk, NY, London: M.E. Sharpe.

Byzov, Leonid, and Sergei Filatov. 1993. Religiia i politika v obshchestvennom soznanii sovetskogo naroda [Religion and politics in mass conscience of the Soviet people]. In *Religiia i demokratiia. Na puti k svobode sovesti (Religion and democracy. On the way to freedom of conscience)*, ed Sergei Filatov and Dmitrii Furman, 9–42. Moscow: Progress.

Davis, Nathaniel. 1995. *A Long Walk to Church. A Contemporary History of Russian Orthodoxy*. Boulder, CO: Westview Press.

Filatov, Sergei. 2002. Poslesloviie. Religiia v postsovetskoi Rossii [Afterwords. Religion in post-soviet Russia]. In *Religiia i obshchestvo. Ocherki religioznoi zhizni sovremennoi Rossii* [Religion and society. Essays on the religious life of Ccontemporary Russia], ed. Sergei Filatov, 470–84. Moscow, Saint-Petersburg: Letnii Sad.

Filatov, Sergei, and Lyudmila Vorontsova. 1999. Russian Catholicism: Relic or reality? In *Proselytism and Orthodoxy in Russia: The New war for Souls*, ed. John Witte Jr. and Michael E. Bourdeaux, 93–107. Maryknoll, NY: Orbis Books.

Guroian, Vigen. 1993. Evangelism and Mission in the Orthodox Tradition. In *Sharing the Book. Religious Perspectives on the Rights and Wrongs of Proselytism*, ed. John Witte, Jr. and Richard C. Martin, 231–44. Maryknoll, NY: Orbis Books.

Kazmina, Olga. 2000. Integriruiushchaia i dezintegriruiushchaya rol religii i etnicheskie protsessy v sovremennoi Rossii [The integrative and disintegrative role of religion and ethnic processes in contemporary Russia]. *Ab Imperio* 2: 229–45.

Kovalevskii, Igor. 2003. *Katolichestvo v Rossii. Subkultura ili kontrkultura?* [Catholicism in Russia. Subculture or counterculture?]. http://religare.ru/analytics7799.htm [Accessed 15 November 2004].

Lerner, Natan. 2000. *Religion, Beliefs, and International Human Rights*. Maryknoll, NY: Orbis Books.

Mchedlov, Mikhail, ed. 2002. *Mnogonatsionalnaia Rossia: Dialog religii i kultur. Rol religioznykh ob'edinenii v mirotvorcheskoi deyatelnosti, ukreplenii mezhreli-*

gioznogo soglasiia i druzhby narodov [Multiethnic Russia: Dialogue of religions and cultures. The role of religious associations in peacemaking activity, strengthening of inter-religious accord and friendship of peoples]. Moscow: Bibloteka Assamblei Narodov Rossii.

Mchedlov, Mikhail, ed. 2003. *Rossiiskaia tsivilizatsiia* [Russian civilization]. Moscow: Akademicheskii Proekt.

Mennini, Antonio 2007a. *Predstavitel Vatikana v RF prizyvaet katolikov uvazhat pravoslavnyie tserkovnyie traditsii* [Representative of the Vatikan in the Russian Federation calls upon Catholics to respect Orthodox church traditions]. http://religion.rin.ru/cgi-bin/religion/about.pl?idn=73654&id= [Accessed 22 March 2007].

Metropolitan Kirill. 2002. *Tserkov prizvana vesti dialog s mirom na urovne serdtsa* [The Church is urged to pursue the dialogue with the world on the heart level]. *Metropolitan Kirill of Smolensk and Kaliningrad, Chairman of the Department for External Church Relations, speech at Moscow State Institute of International Relations. 02.19.2002* http://www.russian-orthodox-church. org.ru/ne2002.htm_ [Accessed 10 December 2004, now defunct].

———. 2005. *Orthodoxy and non-Orthodoxy. Metropolitan Kirill of Smolensk and Kaliningrad, Chairman of the Department for External Church Relations, answers questions from participants in the internet-conference held by the Lutheranism in Russia* www.mospat.ru/text/e_publications/id/7651.html [Accessed 1 August 2005, now defunct].

Meyendorff, John. 1978. Russian Bishops and Church Reform in 1905. In *Russian Orthodoxy under the Old Regime*, ed. Robert Nichols and Theofanis George Stavrou, 170–82. Minneapolis: University of Minnesota Press.

Ministry of Foreign Affairs. 2003. Zaiavleniie MID Rossii [Declaration of the Ministry of Foreign Affairs of Russia]. 2003. In *Pirrova pobeda Vatikana (Pyrrhic victory of the Vatican)*, ed. S. Grigoriev and A. Stepanov, 126. Zhitomir: Ni-ka.

Nezavisimaia Gazeta [newspaper], 28 March 1996. Cited in Agadjanian 2000, 124.

Pchelintsev, Anatolii. 1999. *Novoe zakonodatelstvo Rossii o svobode sovesti i o religioznykh ob'edineniiakh. Sbornik normativnykh aktov.* [New Russia's legislation on freedom of conscience and on religious associations. Collection of legal acts]. Moscow: Institute of Religion and Law.

Pospielovsky, Dimitry V. 1995. The Russian Orthodox Church in the Postcommunist CIS. In *The Politics of Religion in Russia and the New States of Eurasia*, ed. Michael Bourdeaux, vol. 3, 41–74. Armonk, NY; London, UK: M.E. Sharpe.

Prodromou, Elizabeth H. 2004. Orthodox Christianity and Pluralism. Moving beyond Ambivalence? In *The Orthodox Churches in a Pluralistic world. An Ecumenical* Conversation, ed. Emmanuel Clapsis. Geneva: WCC Publishers;

Brookline MA: Holy Cross Orthodox Press.

Roman Catholic Church 2005. Obshchie printsipy i prakticheskie normy koordinatsii evangelizatorskoi deiatelnosti i ekumenicheskie obiazatelstva katolicheskoi tserkvi v Rossii i drugikh stranakh SNG [General principles and practical norms of the coordination of evangelistic activity and ecumenical duties of the Catholic Church in Russia and other CIS countries]. In *Pravoslavie i katolichestvo: Ot konfrontatsii k dialogu. Khrestomatiia* [Orthodoxy and Catholicism: From confrontation to dialogue. A Reader], ed. Alexei Yudin, 501–10. Moscow: Bibleisko-Bogoslovski Institut sv. Apostola Andreia.

Russian Orthodox Church. 2000a. *Basic Principles of the Russian Orthodox Church's Attitude to the Non-Orthodox.*. http://www.mospat.ru/chapters/e_principles/ [Accessed 3 July 2005, now defunct].

———. 2000b. *Osnovnye printsipy otnoshenia Russkoi Pravoslavnoi Tserkvi k inoslaviiu* [Basic principles of the Russian Orthodox Church's attitude to the non-Orthodox)] www.wco.ru/biblio/books/inoslav1/ Main-Con.htm [Accessed 12 November 2004].

———. 2000c. The quest for the restoration of the unity. Part 2 of *Basic principles of the Russian Orthodox Church's attitude to the non-Orthodox* http://www.mospat.ru/text/e_principles/id/5546.html [Accessed 3 July 2005, now defunct].

———. 2000d. Relations of the Russian Orthodox Church with the non-Orthodox on her canonical territory, pt. 6 of *Basic principles of the Russian Orthodox Church's attitude to the non-Orthodox* http://www.mospat.ru/text/e_principles/id/5542.html [Accessed 3 July 2005, now defunct].

———. 2005. *Kontseptsiia missionerskoi deiatelnosti Russkoi Pravoslavnoi Tserkvi na 2005-2010 gody* [Concept of the missionary activity of the Russian Orthodox Church for 2005-2010]. 04.19.2005 http://www.religare.ru/print16807.thm [Accessed 6 June 2005, now defunct].

Shchipkov, Alexandr. 1998. *Vo chto verit Rossia: Religioznyie protsessy v postperestroechnoi Rossii* [In what does Russia believe: Religious processes in post-perestroika Russia]. St. Petersburg: Russian Christian Institute of Humanities Publishers.

Shlygina, Natalia, and Olga Kazmina.1999. Ingrian Finns of the Parish of Holy Trinity Church (Moscow). In *Ingrians and Neighbors: Focus on the Eastern Baltic Sea Region*, ed. Markku Teinonen and Timo J. Virtanen, 182–94. Helsinki: Finnish Literature Society.

Trofimchuk, Nikolai, ed. 2002. *Istoriia religii v Rossii* [A history of religions in Russia]. Moscow: RAGS.

Tsekhanskaia, Kira. 2001-2. Russia: Trends in Orthodox Religiosity in the Twentieth Century (Statistics and Reality). *Anthropology and Archeology of Eurasia* 40(3): 10-30.

Tsypin, Vladislav (Archpriest), and A. Nazarenko, eds. 2000. *Pravoslavnaia entsik-lopediia. Russkaia Pravoslavnaia Tserkov* [Orthodox encyclopnddia. Russian Orthodox Church]. Moscow: Pravoslavnaia Entsiklopediia.

Verkhovskii, Alexandr, Vladimir Pribylovskii, and Ekaterina Mikhailovskaia. 1998. *Natsionalizm i ksenofobiia v rossiiskom obshchestve* [Nationalism and xeno-phobia in the Russian society]. Moscow: Panorama.

Wanner, Catherine. 2004. Missionaries of Faith and Culture: Evangelical Encounters in Ukraine. *Slavic Review* 63(4): 732–55.

Witte, Jr, John. and Michael Bourdeaux, eds. 1999. *Proselytism and Orthodoxy in Russia. The New War for Souls*. Maryknoll, NY: Orbis Books.

CHAPTER 15

Education, Nationalism, and Hidden *Da'wa*: Turkish Missionary Movements in Central Asia and the Caucasus

Bayram Balcı

In the last decade, Fethullah Gülen's community, the so-called *fethullahci* community, has become one of the most powerful religious groups in Turkey. Established in the early 1970's in Izmir, where Gülen was in office as a preacher of the Republic or *vaiz*, the community appears to be the successful heir of the first *nurcu* movement founded by Said Nursi (1870–1960) in the second half of the nineteenth century. The *fethullahci* or neo-*nurcu* community benefited from the economic growth and liberal measures encouraged by Turgut Özal's government in the 1980's. Indeed, external conditions favoured the development of Gülen's community—often qualified as *cemaat* (although this is not a term they use publicly)—and it soon became an empire supported by a great educational network.[1] This chapter will demonstrate how the "nurcu" movement implemented private schools with the support of Turkish businesses, wherever Muslim Turks settled (mainly Central Asia and the Caucasus, or CAC) using an unorthodox method of proselytization. It will demonstrate that, in the case of Gülen's movement, their efforts to disseminate and revitalize Islamic belief and practice were influenced by Christian practice, in the sense that the *fethullahci* borrowed much from the Christian missionary movements of the beginning of the century in the Ottoman Empire. Lastly, this chapter will point out the contradiction between the movement's ideology and its pragmatic approach: while the *fethullahci's* identity in Turkey is essentially Islamic, their activities abroad contribute to the implementation of Turkish nationalism, rather than religious values.

Since the early 1990's, the former Soviet Union, and especially Central Asia and the Caucasus, have been focal points in Gülen's development strategy of a transnational network. In this study, we shall analyse the neo-*nurcu*'s international ambitions and their ultimate goals for the Turkic areas including Uzbekistan, Kazakhstan, Kyrgyzstan, Turkmenistan, Azerbaijan, and Russian Tatarstan and Bashkortostan. Furthermore, it may prove important to analyze the role of the CAC community in more detail, in order to understand its ramifications. The *fethullahci* are actively involved in all aspects of life: business, industrial production and trade, media, and education. High schools—[*liseler*]— are the most significant components of the community's presence outside of Turkey. Because of their long experience in the CAC area, they participate in the formulating of Ankara's policy toward the former Soviet Turkic Republics.

Gülen's disciples—or *shagird*—aim at re-introducing Islam at both the individual and social levels, eroded by seventy years of active atheism and systematic religious persecution under the communist regime. But, as I plan to demonstrate, the *cemaat* faces difficulties in spreading ideas in the CAC States, as the latter have proved to be suspicious about any foreign political or religious influence. Yet, Turkism has a better chance of spreading more widely than Islam, as local authorities fear and avoid radical Islam, whereas innocuous Turkism and pan-Turkism are believed to contribute to the building of a much-needed, new national identity.[2]

Implementation of the *fethullahci* international educational network

Central Asian and Caucasian children entered the first *fethullahci* schools in 1992/93 at a time when the relations between Turkey and these Republics were still favourable, and not yet eroded by disenchantment. At that time, all the "Turkic brothers" coming together again were expected to adopt the "Turkish model of development" (Bal 1997; Jalolov 1994). Gülen's school development benefited from the personal support they received from Turgut Özal, the well-known conservative and devout Turkish leader.

In fact, Gülen's pioneers did not wait for a favourable moment to launch their mission. Many *nurcu* from various Turkish cities prepared themselves to "conquer" Central Asia (Can 1997). Even prior to the collapse of the Soviet Union, many businessmen, students, teachers and journalists belonging to the movement, or close to it, had come to Central Asia to fulfil their mission, after Gülen and his advisors had urged them to do so (Erdoğan 1997). The method of implementation is typically the same: businessmen from one city in Turkey decide to concentrate their efforts on one city in the CAC area. Gülen's followers from Bursa for example, chose to work and invest exclusively in Tashkent. Besides business and trade, all kinds of cultural and human relations of the local community are to be nurtured. This strategy can be compared to town-twinning (*kardes sehir*) (Aras 1998).

In the *neo-nurcu* experience, missionaries are sent into the selected twin towns to-be to assess local needs in terms of economic development, education, and religion. Their first duty consists in identifying the real decision-makers in all sectors within the local community: major businessmen, administration officials, and politicians, and to develop contacts with those who may facilitate *nurcu* implementation locally. Then the latter are invited to come to Turkey and are welcomed there by local *vakıfs*—religious foundations—and other *nurcu* organizations to witness the movement's achievements at home in the private education sector. Once the visitors are convinced of their hosts' efficacy, the preliminary work for the establishment of *fethullahci* schools can start. They gather the necessary official authorizations to build or renovate one or more schools.[3] Yet, the new schools remain under the control of the state, which provides gas, water and electricity. All other expenses, such as furniture, computers, laboratories, text-books and other materials, are met by Turkish businesses supporting Gülen's mission.

The development strategy in CAC has been successful from the outset. In only two years, from 1991 to 1993, hundreds of companies and dozens of schools (see Table 1) were opened, and this does not include the local newspaper, *Zaman*, which is published in each capital city of the region.

Figure 1. The schools of Fetullah Gülen recall the life and works of Mustafa Kemal Ataturk.

A company can be qualified as *nurcu* when its managers and executives share the ideas of Said Nursi, and more precisely as neo-*nurcu* when they are close to Fethullah Gülen's ideas and actions in the field, especially in CAC. *Nurcu* or neo-*nurcu* businesses demonstrated this when in the first years of independence they imported and disseminated *nurcu* literature and journals.[4] In that respect, neo-*nurcu* bookshops belonging to the *cemaat*, like *Aydın* in Gogol street in Almaty and its branch in Tashkent on Alisher Navoï street or the *Nil* stationery and bookshop in Baku, played an important role in the distribution of *nurcu* literature (in Turkish, English, Russian, Uzbek, Kazakh, Kyrgyz and Turkmen).

In each country, most of the *nurcu* companies have linked up in business associations, favoring trade between the host country and Turkey, and networking with Uzbek, Kazakh, Kyrgyz, Turkmen, and Azeri companies in order to disseminate Nursi's and Gülen's ideas.[5] In Uzbekistan, for example, it is named UTID—*Özbekistan ve Türkiye Işadamları Derneği*—the Association of Uzbek and Turkish Businessmen; in Kyrgyzstan, KITIAD (*Kırgızistan ve Türkiye Işadamlari Derneği*); in Azerbaijan, TÜSIAB (*Türkiye Azerbaycan Sanayii ve Isadamlari Birliği*). Non-*nurcu* entities can join these organizations, but they are in the minority.

It is impossible to explain the *cemaat*'s success in the CAC area without mentioning the role of *Zaman*, the *nurcu* daily newspaper which is currently edited and distributed in three out of the four Central Asian Turkic capital cities: Bishkek, Ashgabat and Almaty, as well as in Baku for all of Azerbaijan.[6] After the collapse of the Soviet Union, *Zaman* rapidly established offices in CAC. Their initial implementation was relatively easy. An office was even

| Country | Number and type of institution | | | | Name of the support |
	Primary school	High school	University	International school	company and location of headquarters
Uzbekistan	1	18		1	Silm, Bursa
Kazakhstan	1	29	1		Feza et Şelale, Istanbul
Kyrgyzstan	1	11	1		Sebat, Adapazarı
Turkmenistan		15	1		Başkent, Ankara
Azerbaijan	1	12	1		Cağ *Eğitim Şirketi*, Istanbul
Russian Federation*	1	10			Ertugrul Gazi,Kayseri
Georgia	2	3	1		Caglar
TOTAL before 2000 (including Uzbekistan)	7	88	5	1	
TOTAL in 2005 (excluding Uzbekistan, schools closed in 2000	6	70	5		

Table 1.   The *fethullahci* school network in Central Asia and the Caucasus (* North Caucasus, Tatarstan and Bashkortostan).

Figure 2. Classes are mainly taught in English.

opened in Tashkent, and Uzbeks could read *Zaman* for two years, that is until the regime became hostile to Turkey and Turkish schools, and forbade the Uzbek edition.[7] Like other *nurcu* companies, the purpose of *Zaman* is to support schools in carrying out their mission. Some teachers work outside their classes for *Zaman* as journalists, and even pupils and students often take the opportunity to perfect their Turkish through training at a *Zaman* office.

By 2000, there were approximately one hundred *fethullahci* institutions in all of the CAC, belonging to the wider network of Gülen's schools and universities throughout Eurasia and the Balkans.

The neo-*nurcu* presence and distribution of institutions in each host country varies greatly. Uzbekistan, for example, is the most populated state of the region, but had no *nurcu* school operating in the country after 2000. There are a number of reasons for this. Tashkent has always endeavoured to keep Turkish influence at arms length, and even forbade schools to operate as of September 2000. Since Turkish authorities refused to extradite the Uzbek opposition leaders, Muhammad Solih and Abdurrahman Polatov, diplomatic relations with President Karimov deteriorated. Furthermore, Karimov was hostile to a strong Turkish foreign policy in Uzbekistan (in fact in the whole of Central Asia). As a matter of foreign policy, he prefers to deal with Russia and other strategically important countries like China, and not exclusively with Turkey.

Kazakhstan, where the *cemaat* presently runs twenty-eight high schools and the Süleyman Demirel University, has the greatest number of schools. Administratively less centralized, Kazakhstan favoured their spreading all across the country. In 1991/92, representatives of Gülen directly signed contracts with regional governors (*oblast*), who are empowered to conclude educational agreements with foreign companies. For the Kazakh government, this cooperation proved to be very successful as it contributed to the acceleration of society's "kazakhization," and to the limitation of Russia's extensive influence.

Figure 3. Classroom scene in Turkmenistan.

Turkish schools are quite numerous in Kyrgyzstan and Turkmenistan, despite the fact that they are not heavily populated. The *cemaat* has been very active and successful in the latter country and has had two of its members become close advisors to President Saparmurad "Turkmenbachi" Niyazov, one of whom was promoted to Minister of the Textile Industry and Minister of Education. In Ashgabat, one out of two universities belongs to the *cemaat*.[8]

Azerbaijan is a place where Fethullah Gülen and his followers were able to to establish a very strong presence for the movement in each major city of the country. Because of its geographic and linguistic proximity to Turkey, the movement had no particular difficulty implementing its activities there, even though Azerbaijan is sixty-percent Shia, compared to forty-percent Sunni. For the *fethullahci*, this aspect was never problematic. As with any other country, the movement adapted to local specifics and sought to establish a bridge between Shiism and Sunnism.

In the other regions of the Caucasus, primarily Georgia and Dagestan, the movement has excellent relations with the local governments, as well as with the central decision-makers in Moscow, who could help them develop more schools in the Caucasus, and even in Tatarstan and Bashkortostan should they wish to. However, after 2001, for very unclear reasons, the Russian government closed some of Gülen's schools, especially in the North Caucasus (Karatchaevo Tcherkessia).

Accounting for the success of *Fethullahci* schools

Fethullahci schools are under the control of a country-level management— *Genel Müdürlük*—located in the capital city of their host country and, at the same time, they are all affiliated with a *fethullahci* education company based in Turkey (see Table 1 for details). But these branches may loosen their dependence on the Turkish headquarters as they progress toward a greater autonomy in the host country, and become integrated in the national economic system.

The country general director—*Genel Müdür*—is the head of all the high schools in the country. Developing contacts with local and national officials, with the Ministry of Education, with universities, and with all other relevant organizations and institutions in the country, is part of his job. In the movement's internal hierarchy, the *Genel Müdür* is required to be in constant contact with Turkey's headquarters, as well as with the *fethullahci* businessmen or investors who finance and provide materials to schools. All school directors report directly to him. Once a month, he invites them all to his office to remind them of their mission, the development strategy, and inform them about the "foreign policy" and communication strategy of the group. Then in keeping with the strong hierarchy, each school director manages a team of teachers or *öğretmenler*. The latter are responsible for the tutors or *belletmen*, who work and reside with the pupils and students. Teachers are carefully selected in Turkey before they go on a mission. Most of the time, they are recruited from among the sympathizers of the *cemaat*. Every candidate must have known the *cemaat* for a long time. A digression is necessary here to detail the recruitment method used.

Becoming a member of the *fethullahci cemaat* differs greatly from any other type of club or party membership. First of all, there are no membership cards and no special initiation rites. Most of the *fethullahci* I met in Central Asia and Caucasus have become members through relatives, friends, or work acquaintances who are already members. Being a member implies a real involvement in the organization and activities, offering one's services or *hizmet*—to help disseminate the ideas of Nursi and Gülen (Yavuz and Esposito 2003), as well as accepting the mission set by the community. However, there is not one member profile within the community. Membership is quite blurred, which is why a simple sympathizer or an activist may also be considered members. The latter are trained in the private schools run by the community and the students campuses—the famous *ışık evleri*—which are flats belonging to the *cemaat*, rented out by *fethullahci* businessmen, where young and usually deprived students are allowed to stay during their studies. The headquarters of all the educational companies in Turkey: *Şelale, Başkent, Silm, Sebat,* or *Çağ*, are responsible for selecting teachers and *belletmen*. In that respect, all share the same willingness to serve the community, and are sufficiently qualified in mathematics, history or biology. Obviously, each recruited teacher is carefully prepared to insure the success of the mission, as the hidden proselytism of the *fethullahci* depends, in large part on the personnel involved.

The *Belletmen* or tutors are the second linchpin of the community in the field. Most of them are *fethullahci* students in Turkey, who decided to come to Central Asia for several reasons: some failed their exams at the university, while others were given the opportunity to discover new countries. Recruited by the educational company in Turkey, these student *belletmen* to-be are then assisted in their mission by the *cemaat* paying for their studies in local universities and allowing them to live on campus for free. They sleep in the dormitory beside the pupils they are responsible for.

Female membership within the *cemaat* is not forbidden, but it is rare for women to get involved, and even less common for them to go abroad alone to teach or study. Around ninety-percent of the *belletmen* (and teachers) are male, and the pupils call them *Abi* or "older brother." Indeed their mission is as simple as acting as an elder brother or as a parent to the young pupils, helping them with their homework, getting them ready for the lessons next day, insuring basic education on adequate nutrition, good hygiene, and community living, etc. In addition, they may resolve conflicts with the family or friends. While the pupils are in class, the *belletmen* go to university. For the *belletmen* the deal is attractive. Eventually, their most important mission is to pass on the idea of community to the children, preaching by example. In Uzbekistan, the first crisis between the *cemaat* and the government occurred when Uzbek authorities expelled *belletmen,* charging them with illegal proselytism.

Pupil selection in the *cemaat's* high schools is quite rigorous. In Turkey, the selection method is elitist, based on the *Altın Nesil* concept—the Gold generation—which aims to provide a perfect education for a perfect generation in order to obtain a perfect society. This concept also refers to a modern and disciplined young generation, but still shows great respect for religious and national values. To reach this objective and engender this Gold generation, the community offers the best schools and the best teachers. In Central Asia, the *cemaat* is pursuing the same objective, and that explains why they give particular attention to selecting only the best. Each year, all school managers organize highly selective entry competitions with the help of local teachers.

In the beginning, schooling was free in the CAC area. But nowadays parents have to pay a fee. So far, the cost depends very much on the level of sponsorship by Turkish businesses supporting the school in the host country.

Figure 4. Schoolboys from a Fetullah Gülen school in Turkmenistan.

Figure 5. Schoolboys from a Fetullah Gülen school in Kyrghizstan.

Therefore, the number or wealth of sponsors is inversely proportional to the fee parents have to pay, and some schools have not introduced fees, but all country managers agree that in the long run, schools will have to draw on financial contributions from the parents. In Kazakhstan, in 1998/99 parents were already paying a charge for school meals, as well as for textbooks (some of which, especially those in English), were very expensive as they were directly imported from Great Britain). The remaining expenses were covered by Turkish companies. In Turkmenistan, the schooling has now become so expensive that each pupil has to pay one-thousand U.S. dollars a year. In Uzbekistan, in 1999, the *Ulugbek International School* (including a high school and a university) charged five-thousand U.S. dollars for the year. The economic crisis in Russia in summer 1998 affected Central Asian economies and made the situation for parents and for Turkish schools more difficult. In the entire region, when Turkish businessmen and educators arrived in the early 1990s, they were convinced that local economies would quickly enable good working conditions, thanks to oil and gas or cotton income. In 2000, they were still waiting for that economic growth to happen.

After children pass their exams, a new life begins, in complete contrast to the one in the failed national educational system. As the boarding system came into general use, all pupils are required to stay in school full-time. Even if parents live close by, their children are expected to sleep in the dormitory. Pupils are only allowed to spend week-ends at home. Most of the time, however, the parents live too far away and children stay in school for a whole month, or even longer, without visiting their family. This boarding school system allows educators to exert a stricter control over their students. Outside classes in the private rooms and dormitories and far from parents' watchful eyes, teachers and *belletmen* may impart Nursi's and Gülen's teachings. In that respect, the *fethullahci* method is similar to the Jesuit educational model in the dissemination of Christianity around the world in past centuries. In both cases, children receive constant education in and outside the classroom, and in the dormitory. In these schools, pupils have to wear a specific school uniform to efface class differences, (as in Turkish schools or British private schools), while in the public schools pupils wear what they want.

The prestigious *Anadolu* and *Fen* high schools in Turkey are a model for Turkish schools in CAC. They share the same programs and materials, in the hope of providing the same quality preparation for university entrance exams. The *cemaat* has even developed its own publishing house, *Sürat Yayınları*. Pupils enter Turkish schools after the fifth or the sixth class (according to the former Soviet system), after taking highly demanding exams. During the first year, they learn English and Turkish, attending language classes for fifteen to twenty hours a week. This is a decisive moment, as from the second year on, all lessons are taught in English and Turkish. After the first (preparatory) class the schooling lasts four years, before pupils are entitled to take university entrance exams.

Priority is given to scientific subjects: mathematics, physics, biology, and computer science. Fethullah Gülen is as attached to this core *nurcu* principle as Said Nursi was (Yavuz 1999c). One of his main projects in the beginning was to teach sciences in koranic schools and religion in public schools (Söylemez 1997). Foreign languages and sciences are even more valued by pragmatic parents who consider these as strong assets for future professional careers, Student graduates from *fethullahci* schools usually get the opportunity to study further in famous universities, while foreign languages facilitate prestigious employment with international businesses or organizations. Even officials, including high officials belonging to national elites, show interest in these schools. They like to send their children there, contributing to the qualification and education of new elites.

In each school, the different subjects are shared between Turkish and local teachers. In general, the Turks control the sciences, while their colleagues teach local history and literature. In Uzbekistan, after a crisis in 1993, schools started to be managed by two directors: one Uzbek and one Turk. In the other Republics, the school management would remain in the hands of a Turk citizen. In the Russian Federation, especially in Tatarstan, the authorities have recently passed a law granting local educators full control over these institutions.

Nurcu schools and Fethullah Gülen's vision for Central Asia and the Caucasus

Fethullah Gülen has often been interviewed by Turkish media about his views and intentions for Central Asia and Caucasus. Before answering the questions, Gülen usually recalls that the schools do not belong to him personally, since all the *nurcu* companies in Turkey and CAC are independent. However, some businessmen and intellectuals accept his guidance as a spiritual leader and endeavor to fulfil his dreams for Central Asia and the Caucasus. What is this vision?

Nostalgic for the great Ottoman Empire, Gülen worships Central Asia. According to him, Anatolia is indebted to Asia for its high degree of civilization. Without Asia, Islam and Turkish culture would have never been present in Anatolia as we know it (Barkan 1954). Furthermore, in the ancient past, both arrived in Anatolia from Asia thanks to *dervishes* and mystics, known as *Alperen*. Fethullah Gülen often compares his followers to the *Alperen* (Köprülü 1993), but overestimates their influence. He mystifies them and seems to forget that before Islam and the Turks arrived there, great ancient civilizations had arisen in Anatolia. In his opinion, what the *fethullahci* are achieving in today's Central Asia is nothing but the repayment of *medyun* ("indebted" in Arabic), a moral debt that the Turks owe to Asia (Gülen 1997).

When we ask the followers of Fethullah Gülen about their motivations for coming to Central Asia, most of the time they give the same answers: "we are here to pay our moral debt—*vefa borcu*," paying respect to their ancestors who left Central Asia to civilize and spread Islam to Anatolia. There are no nationalist or pan-Turkist aspects in their approach. The representatives of *Türk Dünyası Araştırmaları Vakfı*, or Foundation for Turkic World Researches, are also present in some CAC schools, where its staff teach Turkish, economics, and other subjects. Like their leader, the *fethullahci* choose moderation and never express strong nationalistic or Islamic ideas. They insist that their mission in Central Asia consists in bridging the cultural gap between Turkey and the Turkic Republics of Central Asia (Sevindi, N. 1997).

In the Caucasus, the followers of Fethullah Gulen justified their presence differently. In Azerbaijan, where Turkism is strong (the majority of the population identify themselves with the Turks and display positive feelings towards Turkey), the *fethullahci* use the common Turkic legacy and ethnic discourse to implement their activities. In other areas like Georgia, or the Russian Federation where Islam or Turkish identity do not prevail, the *nurcu* justify their presence by their willingness to contribute to the dialogue between religions and civilizations. Dear to Fethullah Gülen, this dialogue is a recurring subject in his literature and philosophy and serves the missionary effort wherever Turkish ethnicity or Islam are not most prominent.

A closer examination of the activities and project of the *cemaat* shows that the *fethullahci* community, throughout the former Soviet Union, shares all the specific features of a missionary movement. In the case of the *fethullahci*, this mission consists in re-establishing Islam in the region after seventy years of domination by an atheist regime that persecuted Islam. But this is not the *da'wa* or *tabligh* of classical Islamic proselytism (Witte and Martin 1999). As we said before, although they do not profess the same religion, the *fethullahci*

Figure 6. School director between the Kazakh and Turkish flags at school in Kazakhstan.

borrowed much from European Christian experience, such as that of the Jesuits (Giacomelli, 1991) or the more recently established American Peace Corps (Schwarz, K. 1991), and several other American or European Protestant organizations who are active today in this region.

All these groups share a central focus on education. Those with a religious foundation focus on the establishment of schools to spread their religious ideology. The *fethullahci*, like the Jesuits, totally supervise the pupils day and night, in school or in boarding houses (Faguer 1991). All these missionary movements situated themselves very close to the target populations to convert them (or re-Islamize in the case of the *fethullahci*) by adapting to their culture, and then influencing them in return.

The *fethullahci* missionary method has its own distinctive characteristics. Schools, in spite of Turkish (kemalist) media allegations, are no direct instrument of proselytism (Balcı 2001). The *fethullahci* would definitely prefer to openly practice and spread their religion. However, upon their arrival in the Soviet Union, they soon realized that the inherited regimes were strongly attached to some of the Soviet legacy, and especially to secular legislation and institutions. Consequently, they judged open proselytism to be unrealistic, if not dangerous, preferring caution and a less conspicuous promotion of Islam by long-term involvement in the educational field.

Fethullah Gülen *Hocaefendi*—the "respected lord" as his disciples prefer to call him—justifies his method of hidden proselytism by distinguishing *tebliğ* from *temsil* (Balcı, 2001). Because societies are subject to extensive political, religious and philosophical propaganda, people are less easily influenced by ideologues in the long run. Gülen also asks his troops not to practice this form of open Islamic proselytism or *tebliğ*, because of the way it introduces an asymmetry between the proselytizer and the proselytized.

Instead of *tebliğ*, Gülen strongly encourages his disciples to put into practice *temsil*, meaning that teachers lead by example, never uttering the word "Islam" or any other word likely to upset the paranoid local authorities, and possibly jeopardize the activities of the *cemaat* in Central Asia. This representation—*temsil*—of the model Islamic life is expected from them at all times, and in all places.

In light of this, it seems inappropriate to use the term proselytism, when talking of societies which are primarily Muslim to begin with, even though present Central Asian and Caucasian forms of Islam differ very much from what there were when these regions were first Islamized. While the Soviets strove hard to break Islam in the region, at most they only weakened, and sometimes perverted, traditions of belief and practice, but failed to eradicate it completely (Gross 1998; Bennigsen and Wimbush 1986). The *fethullahci* movement aims currently at working with local people to revive Islam. Education is their choice, and schools are considered to be the optimal medium for their mission (Balcı 2001). In that respect, the *fethullahci* imitated the historical *jadid* movement, whose objectives at the beginning of the nineteenth century consisted in favouring the modernization of Turkish and Islamic communities in the Russian Empire (Dudoignon 1996).

The innermost nature of *nurcu* Islam, wherever it is in Central Asia or Turkey, claims to be modern and moderate, extremely elitist, but rejecting any confrontation with the authorities. The *fethullahci* have no difficulty in adapting to Central Asian or Caucasian Islam because they respect mysticism. Though the *cemaat* is not a brotherhood like the *Nakchibendiyya* or *Yeseviyya*, the most important movements in Central Asia, it respects their cultural significance and social role, and even shares some similar characteristics and values. For example, like all Muslims in Central Asia, Turkish missionaries often visit the graves of Bahauddin Nakchibendi in Boukhara (Uzbekistan) and Ahmed Yesevi in Turkestan (Kazakhstan). In Azerbaijan they also respect the legacy of local mysticism and the pilgrimages to the holy shrines of great men. Both *fethullahci* and CAC Muslims share similar practices in terms of prayers, while in contrast, the so-called "wahhabists," for example, brook no compromise in their religious practice, and completely reject the mystical elements of Central Asian and Caucasian Islam. Therefore, this serves to highlight the level of tolerance and openness within Gülen's movement.

Throughout Eurasia, the *fethullahci* carry out the *temsil* principle to the letter. For example, the administration of a *nurcu* high school will never impose Said Nursi or Fethullah Gülen's books on the children or local colleagues. So far, religious discussions or lectures of *Risale* only attract the Turkish population in the area. Teachers, businessmen or *fethullahci* students meet once a week for *çay sohbetleri*—tea discussions—where they try to perfect their Islamic and *nurcu* knowledge. While not officially present in schools, the *nurcu* and *fethullahci* literature is easily available in every local language (as well as in Russian) in almost every Central Asian or Caucasian city, in bookshops or around mosques.

Considered to be dangerous for the durability of the movement in Central Asia, *namaz* and *ramazan* (the prayers and the fast of Ramadan) are not even tolerated by the school managers, who officially forbade them in the schools after 1993 and the crisis with the Uzbek government. Yet, in that respect too, the movement has proved to be ambivalent. Officially, the school manager and teachers claim prayer and fasting are forbidden, even calling parents into school to remind them that these are not religious schools. But at the same time, the same managers encourage the *belletmen* to select a minority of pupils and secretly teach them prayers and elementary Islamic education. The *belletmen's* role consists in appearing as a confidant (*Abi*) to his pupils, and not as a teacher's representative, whose job is to keep an eye on them. Only small groups are selected for hidden religious education, but in the last year of schooling, *belletmen* intensify Islamic lessons to select pupils.

Naturally the model differs from one country to another. In Uzbekistan for example, President Karimov has never tolerated any form of Islamic proselytism. Because even the simplest act of devotion could merit arrest and imprisonment, the *fethullahci* could never engage in any form of open proselytic discourse or promotion of Islam. This situation is more or less equivalent in Turkmenistan, while in Kazakhstan or in Kyrgyzstan, it is easier for the *cemaat* to educate pupils in basic Islam.

In Azerbaijan, *fethullahci* associations, except for Turkish and other foreign groups, can easily implement their activities. The collapse of the Soviet Union facilitated Islamic revival and religious cooperation from Turkish public or private actors. Though much remains to be done, Azerbaijan is probably the most liberal and democratic country, compared to other Muslim republics that were born from the former Soviet Union. *Fethullahci* groups are not the only ones spreading the *nurcu* message in Azerbaijan. Other *nurcu* groups are present, especially in the north of the country where the population is more Sunnites than Shiite. So far, the *fethullahci* presence is accepted by the authorities, but this situation could change in the future if the *nurcu* successes increase and widen the gap between Sunnites and Shiites. Under Soviet rule, active atheism and religious persecution had ironed out differences between both these two branches of Islam, and the new regime is somewhat attached to this more unified perspective, and its potential for ensuring national integration.

Winning over Turkish diplomats and local authorities

As stated above, the *cemaat* prioritizes the reinforcement of Islam in Central Asia and the Caucasus. Whereas there were early successes after 1991, many members of Gülen's movement now realize that the task was more challenging than they originally imagined. In the early years of independence, new mosques were built and those turned into factories under Soviet rule were renovated and reopened for worship. The post-communist intelligentsia, striving to differentiate itself from the Soviet elites, supported Islamic revival as a means of generating a new nationalized identity. The leaders of the newly independent states, to mark the break with Russian and Soviet domination, approved some Islamic practices and distinguished national identities (Haghayeghi 1996). This situation gave the *cemaat* the illusion that it was possible to promote Islam and preach openly, but they soon realized that this official support for Islamic revivalism was only rhetorical, while state control over the freedom of conscience was more of a reality. In Uzbekistan, for example, when Islam became too powerful in the Ferghana Valley and threatened the new state, President Karimov decided to put an end to all Islamic activities, and strengthened control over every single beard or publication in Arabic (Babadjanov 1998). Some mosques in the Ferghana Valley and a couple of *fethullahci* schools were banned and immediately closed. Clearly identified by the Uzbek authorities as a potential Islamist threat, Gülen had to think of a subtler strategy to remain active in the area. Subsequently, Gülen's followers developed cooperation with local governments and Turkish embassies, contributing indirectly to the spreading of Turkism as a nationalist ideology in the Turkic Republics.

Far from its first missionary identity, the *cemaat's* image quickly turned into a type of private company with educational goals. The community developed contacts with many international, local, political, social, and civil actors among which embassies, ministries, governments, and universities were included. At first, the *cemaat* won the trust of parents and educators, thanks to their unrivalled success in preparing pupils for university entry examinations. A majority of pupils coming from Turkish schools entered prestigious universities in their country and abroad. In Tashkent, the renowned University of Diplomacy welcomed several students from Turkish schools every year. In Ashgabat, Almaty, Bishkek and Baku, *cemaat-* educated pupils today study in the best universities.

In the former Soviet Union, the *Olympiade* competitions were a very famous annual tradition, consisting of a special contest to identify the best pupils in schools at all levels (village, town, region, Republic). After their arrival in Central Asia, Turkish missionaries found out that this tradition could easily serve their interests and communication strategy. They organized *International Olympiades* throughout Central Asia. Students from Turkish schools generally do very well in these competitions for which they are carefully prepared. This success contributes to the good image of the schools, and they then become more popular in the eyes of parents and authorities.

Because, or thanks to, a very elitist method of recruitment and careful preparation for future careers, these pupils can be considered as future national elites (Balcı 2000). Many important businessmen and policy makers send their children to these schools because of the high percentage of guaranteed success. The *cemaat* uses these influential parents as a lobby, especially when the movement's activities and institutions need defending. In Uzbekistan, after the first 1993 crisis, the intervention of some powerful parents helped the *cemaat* to remain in the country. However, these parents did not prove to be strong enough to sacrifice their careers for the *cemaat*, as evidenced in Uzbekistan in September 2000.

The *cemaat*'s strategy involves targeting local governments also. In order to guarantee its presence in each country, the *cemaat* offers to strengthen the government's legitimacy. Fethullah Gülen's followers have become the unexpected supporters of new ideologies adopted by all post-Soviet regimes. In Gülen's schools, the children learn to worship the newly independent state, the president, the flag, the new institutions, as well as the new official national heroes and ideologies. In that connection, the *fethullahci* translated into Turkish some of the Uzbek president's books which they disseminate in Turkey. Eventually, the *fethullahci* became the ambassadors of the new Central Asian regimes in Turkey, where they promote culture, history and music and, inversely, the ambassadors of Turkish knowledge and culture in the formation of new elites.

Special attention must be paid to the relations between the *cemaat* and Turkish embassies in Central Asia and the Caucasus. These relationships, based on mutual suspicion over a long period and dominated by several conflicts, remained strained for some time. For example, in the early 1990's, the Turkish embassy in Tashkent was at odds with the *fethullahci* school administration. The crisis between the *cemaat* and the Uzbek government occurred when the Uzbeks became suspicious after a report was drawn up by the Turkish embassy and circulated to the local authorities, regarding the nature of the *fethullahci* movement. In this report, the Ambassador warned the Uzbek government about the allegedly fundamentalist danger in the *cemaat*'s activities.

But this incident proved to be an exception in Turkey's attitude towards the *cemaat*'s activities abroad. Usually, the Turkish government and especially Turgut Özal, more than his successors (Ciller, Demirel, Ecevit and Sezer) actively supported Gülen's projects in Central Asia. In Uzbekistan, and in other countries too, the creation of a school is made possible when the Turkish embassy, in the name of the government, gives its approval. In the Uzbek 255 Charter, which regulates the educational cooperation between Tashkent, Ankara and the *Silm* Company, all three parties must agree and sign before acting. The school authorities in each Central Asian country are in constant contact with the cultural and linguistic attaché (*Eğitim Müşaviri ve Kültür Ataşesi*) of the Turkish embassy, engendering real cooperation between them. For example, the embassy may help the *cemaat* with textbook supply, and sometimes the national Turkish holidays (23 April or 29 October) are prepared by both state and *nurcu* representatives.

The positive relationship between Turkish embassies and the *cemaat* results, in large part, from their respective missions and projects for Central Asia and the Caucasus. Ankara's dream of building a bridge between Turkey and the CAC area implies the development of strong cultural and economic relations. In this regard, the Turkish state opened two universities and a couple of state schools in the region, the Ahmed Yesevi University in Kazakhstan and Manas University in Kyrgyzstan (Balcı, 1999). But Turkish diplomats observe that their official efforts in Central Asia are nothing compared to the *cemaat*'s achievements so far. While state teachers from Turkey are paid six-hundred to one-thousand U.S. dollars a month, a *fethullahci* missionary teacher earns two-hundred to five-hundred U.S. dollars a month. The boarding system in the *cemaat*'s schools allows pupils to learn Turkish quicker and more easily. More prestigious than public schools, the *cemaat*'s high schools are very important for Turkish policy-makers in Central Asia, the Caucasus, and even in the Russian Federation, where they transmit Turkish culture. Besides, *Realpolitik* towards religious groups, and the presence of Turkish schools, favour the development of Turkism, whereas Turkish diplomacy experienced difficulties in exporting its own, large Turkish identity, comprising Turks of Turkey, Uzbeks, Kazakhs, Kyrgyzs, Turkmens, Azeris, etc. Unfortunately for the diplomats, from the start the fledgling states preferred to prioritize Uzbekism, Kazakhism, etc. While Ankara sought concord on points of common interest, the Turkic state authorities preferred to strengthen their own national identities. In every Uzbek, Kazakh, Kyrgyz or Turkmen state school, children are now taught the new grammar of state nationalism. In the *cemaat*'s schools, pupils learn about their two-layered identity: national and trans-national Turkic. During my participation in lessons, I was able to observe how these schools are simultaneously making use of the Uzbek and Turkic, or Kazakh and Turkic, or Kyrgyz and Turkic, or Turkmen and Turkic identities. Devoid of any irredentism or pan-Turkism, the *cemaat*'s schools are playing a significant role in fostering the formation of a common transnational Turkic identity within Central Asian societies.

Last but not least, these schools, with the support of *nurcu* companies and business associations (UTID, KITIAD, etc.), have proved strategic for the development of economic ties between Turkey and the republics. More than half of Turkish companies in Central Asia are *nurcu*-oriented, helping Turkey to develop important links with new Turkic republics.

Conclusion

For the *fethullahci*, the re-Islamization of Central Asian and Caucasian Turkic republics remains a primary goal. Interestingly, however, the *fethullahci* ideology, tinged with Turkish patriotism, has indirectly, and sometimes directly, ended up spreading the Turkish development model more efficiently than any religious message. Because of the deep-rooted distrust of Islam by the local powers, the *cemaat* can only act under the attractive cover of nationalism, and is obliged to disguise its genuine identity and *da'wa* mission. The movement was introduced there as a simple Turkish organization with the real, but apparently modest, intention of bringing all Turkic peoples closer together. Among the population, especially in provincial towns, the schools they establish are known as *turestkiy litsey* or, *turk maktabi*. They are never referred to as *nurcu* or *fethullahci* schools, as nobody is really aware of their basic religious orientation.

According to the *cemaat*, all students educated in the *fethullahci* school network will likely become the next generation of elites in their country, and will hopefully develop strong relations with Turkey. Meanwhile, there is no guarantee that they will adopt all *nurcu* ideas. The *cemaat* often organizes large meetings of its graduates in various capital and provincial cities, with the purpose of fostering their support for the *fethullahci* movement. Although many students remain in contact with their teachers, long after they graduate, they are also subject to many other influences.

It is too early to judge if the movement has been able to establish viable national and local *fethullahci* branches in Central Asia and the Caucasus. Our estimation is that the Turks still comprise close to ninety-five percent of the movement in the CAC area. Conversions to *fethullahci* ideas among nationals remain anecdotal, and most are kept clandestine, because of the ongoing surveillance of religious groups. The Azeri case is different, however, as there is already a national *fethullahci* branch in Azerbaijan. The close cultural relationship with Turks allowed the *fethullahci* community to establish deep roots in this part of the world. Gülen and his highly organized network of followers will likely continue their endeavors to develop such branches in Central Asia and the Russian Federation.

Notes

1. It is difficult to sort out the list of all *fethullahci* educative and media firms in Turkey. We can, however, point to that Fatih University, *Yamanlar Koleji* (Highschool), *Zaman* (Newspaper), *Samanyolu* (TV channel) *Burç FM* (radio), *Asya Finans* (Bank) and *Sürat Yayınları* (Publisher) as the main *fethullahci* establishments in Turkey. The leaders of all these organizations are close to Fethullah Gülen and share his ideas.

2. This study is based on field research carried out between November 1996 and May 2000 in Kazakhstan, Uzbekistan, Kyrgyzstan and Turkmenistan. The research work in Central Asia was completed with other field missions in the Caucasus, mainly in Azerbaijan. One short field research program was also conducted in Kazan (capital of Tatarstan), and in the North Caucasus, where the movement had several schools up to 2001.

3. The high schools are managed by a firm whose director is an influential member of the *cemaat*. Since their creation in Central Asia and the Caucasus, these schools have been managed by *Silm* (based in Bursa) for Uzbekistan, *Feza* and *Şelale* (based in Istanbul) for Kazakhstan, *Sebat* (based in Adapazarı) for Kyrgyzstan, *Başkent* (based in Ankara) for Turkmenistan and *Cağ* (based in Istanbul) for Azerbaijan.

4. Situated in Cağaloğlu-Istanbul, *Sözler Yayınevi* Publisher has translated into Turkic languages and Russian (and Serbo-Croatian) some chapters of Nursi's *Risale-i-Nur*. Usually the shortest and easiest parts of this extensive religious work have been translated. For example, it is possible to find in several Central Asian cities *Küçük Sözler* (Small Words), *Tabiat Risalesi* (Epistle of the Nature), *Yirmiüçüncü Söz* (23rd word).

5. The aim of *UTID* is to facilitate Turkish investments in Uzbekistan. Every Uzbek or Turkish company may become a member by accepting the legal conditions of the organization. In May 2000, the relation between the association and the Uzbek government deteriorated, because of the political crisis between Tashkent and Ankara. *UTID's* leader was declared *persona non grata* in Uzbekistan in April 2000.

6. See www.zaman.com.tr. This generic web site provides links to *Zaman* Kyrgyzstan, Kazakhstan, Turkmenistan and Azerbaijan.

7. Crises are chronic between Tashkent and Ankara. The first crisis occurred because of the presence of Uzbek opposition leaders in Turkey. Muhammad Salih, chairman of *Erk* and Abdurrahman Polat, chairman of *Birlik* chose Turkey as an exile when they were threatened by the Uzbek government. Karimov demanded that Turkish authorities expel them. The Uzbek president feared that these opponents might influence Uzbek students in Turkey. In 1994 all of the latter were called back to Uzbekistan.

8. The most important university is Mahdumkuli State University. Some teachers from the *cemaat* taught there, until the *cemaat* set up the *Uluslararasi Türk-Türkmen Üniversitesi* (International Turk-Turkmen University).

References

Aras, B. 1998. Turkish Islam's Moderate Face. *Middle East Quarterly*, 5(3): 23–29.

Babadjanov, B. 1998 Le renouveau des communautés soufies en Ouzbékistan. *Les Cahiers d'Asie centrale*. 5-6: 285–311.

Bal, I. 1997. Orta Asya ve Batının Dış Politika Olarak Türk Modeli [The Turkish model viewed by Central Asia and the West]. *Yeni Türkiye* 15: 936–45.

Balcı, B. 1999. Du mausolée à l'université: l'université turco-kazakhe Ahmet Yesevi au centre de la coopération universitaire entre la Turquie et le Kazakhstan. *Cahiers d'études du monde turco-iranien*. 27: 313–328.

———. 2001. *Missionnaires de l'Islam, Les écoles turques de Fethullah Gülen en Asie centrale*. Paris: Maisonneuve et Larose.

Balcı, A., Akkok, F. and Demir Engin, C. 2000. The Role of Turkish Schools in the Educational System and Social Transformation of Central Asian Countries: the Case of Turkmenistan and Kyrgyzstan. *Central Asian Survey* 19(1): 141–56.

Barkan, Ö. 1954. *Kolonizatör Türk Dervişleri* [Turkish Dervish Colonisers]. Istanbul: Diyanet Vakfı.

Bennigsen, A., Wimbush, E. Eds. 1986. *Muslims of the Soviet Union. A Guide*. Bloomington, IN: Indiana University Press.

Can, E. 1996. *Fethullah Gülen Hocaefendi ile ufuk turu* [A General Discussion with Fethullah Gülen]. Istanbul: A. D Yayıncılık.

Dudoignon, S. 1996. Djadidisme, mirasisme, islamisme. *Cahiers du monde russe* 37(1-2): 13–40.

Erdoğan, L. 1997. *Küçük Dünyam Fethullah Gülen Hocaefendi ile sohbet, 41. baskı* [An Interview with Fethullah Gülen]. Istanbul: AD Yayıncılık.

Faguer, J-P. 1991. Les effets d'une éducation totale, un collège jésuite en 1960. *Actes de la recherche en sciences social* 86/87: 25–43.

Giacomelli, R. 1991. *Vous avez dit Jésuites? Radioscopie d'une compagnie, dialogue avec Peter-Hans Kolvenbach, supérieur général de la compagnie de Jésus.* Montréal: Éditions Médiaspaul.

Gross, J-A. 1998. Islamic Central Asia: approaches to religiosity and community., *Religious Studies Review* 24(4): 351–58.

Gülen, F. 1997. Orta Asyada Eğitim Hizmetleri [Educative services in Central Asia]. *Yeni Türkiye* 15: 685–92.

Haghayeghi, M. 1995. *Islam and Politics in Central Asia.* New York: St Martin's Press.

Jalolov, J. 1994. *Bozor Iqtisodiyati: Turkiya Modelining Siri* [Market Economy: the Secrets of the Turkish Model]. Tashkent: Adolat.

Köprülü, F. 1993. *Türk Edebiyatında ilk Mutasavvıflar* [The First Mystics in Turkish Literature]. Ankara: Diyanet İşleri Başkanlığı. (Third ed.).

Schwarz, K. 1991. *What You Can do for Your Country: an Oral History of the Peace Corps.* New York: Morrow.

Sevindi, N. 1997. *Fethullah Gülen, New York Sohbeti* [Discussions in New York with Fethullah Gülen]. Istanbul: Sabah Yayınları.

Witte J., and R. Martin Eds. 1999. *Sharing the Book, Religious Perspectives on the Rights and Wrongs of Proselytism.* New York: Orbis.

Soylemez, M. 1997. *Problem ve çözümleriyle eğitimimiz* [Problems and Solutions for our Education System]. Izmir: Çağlayan yayınları.

———. 1999. Towards an Islamic Liberalism?: the Nurcu movement and Fethullah Gülen. *Middle East Journal* 53(4): 584–605.

Yavuz H. and J. Esposito. 2003. *Turkish Islam and the Secular State, The Gülen Movement.* Syracuse, NY: Syracuse University Press.

Main websites relating to Said Nursi, Fethullah Gülen, their movements and their schools

On Said Nursi and his movement:

- http://www.bediuzzamansaidnursi.net/
- http://www.risale-inur.org/
- http://www.nurpenceresi.com/
- http://www.nur.org [site in English]
- http://www.nursistudies.com [site in English, Russian, Arabic] http://www.saidnursi.de [German site]

For a general view of the Fethullah Gülen movement's philosophy:

- http://tr.fgulen.com
- http://www.fethullahgulen.info
- http://en.fgulen.com site en douze langues

On the movement's main newspaper, Zaman:

- http://www.zaman.com.tr

On the schools in Kyrgyzstan:

- http://sebat.edu.kg

On the schools in Georgia:

- www.caglar-k12.ge

On the Black Sea University in Tbilisi:

- http://www.ibsu.edu.ge

On the schools in Kazakhstan:

- http://www.katev.org

CHAPTER 16

The New Protestant 10/40 Window:
Korean Proselytism in the Asian Region of Russia

Julia S. Kovalchuk

This chapter seeks to illuminate the activities of Korean Protestant mission-aries in the Asian part of the Russian Federation, or, to be more specific —the autonomous republics of South-western Siberia, which are inhabited by a number of ethnic groups. I begin by exploring the contemporary reli-gious situation in that region, and give a brief description of the indigenous groups in the late 1990s. Then I introduce my fieldwork materials, collected in 2004–2005 in the Altai, Tuva, and Hakhasia regions, which focus on the interaction between Korean missionaries and representatives of the local cul-tures in Siberia. In conclusion, I discuss the main reasons why the Koreans succeeded in church-planting in some regions of Siberia, and not in others, in light of the general characteristics of Korean proselytizing strategies.

Overall, the phenomenon of Korean missionaries has generally been over-looked by religion scholars in Russia. From 2000 onwards, articles have begun to appear on Protestant expansion, but they tend to be localized stud-ies, offering no comparative perspective or analysis of broader trends.[1] There is some literature produced by anti-cult centers which decries the embracing of new Protestant sects over Orthodox tradition, and one region in the Far East of Russia (Primorski) is now making available online interviews with local officials regarding Protestant missionary activity. But, for the most part, my findings are taken from interviews with regional government officials, religious leaders, and pastors.

Following the liberalization of post-Soviet territories, Russia, as well as oth-er states, became the object of local and foreign missionary activities. To date,

4708 registered Protestant units constitute 23% of the total religious organizations which registered in the Russian Federation prior to 2004. Among the most active religious organizations in the Asian part of the Russian Federation, Protestants tend to dominate. The largest organizations are the Pentecostals, Baptists, Adventists, Jehovah's Witnesses and Lutherans. Foreign missionaries come mainly from the USA, South Korea, Germany and Scandinavia. There exists a wide range of denominations, from the conservative mainstream Protestant denominations to the more liberal Pentecostal churches.

After the collapse of "Soviet" identity, most of the people living in the Russian Federation had to reconfigure their social identities. Religion proved appealing in this period of social dislocation. In the autonomous republics of the Russian Federation, where the indigenous population practiced religions other than Russian Orthodox Christianity, the national elites revived traditional beliefs. They attempted to forge a new type of religious identity, based on local tradition, that would help spawn a new form of national consciousness.

The processes of ethnic consolidation and diaspora formation revealed a new need for defining ethnic identity on an ideological basis. In the process, religion became one of the most important factors in ethno-political identity formation. While searching for the appropriate religious resource, ethnic groups directed their attention towards similar cultural paradigms that included traditional religious beliefs and practices, common language and ancestors, and an historical homeland. Thus, the main group of Koreans living in the Russian Federation (especially in the Far East region, where over 60,000 Koreans live) took into consideration the potential benefits of relations with South Korea while searching for their new identity. In the 1990s, the relations between Russia and South Korea were characterized by cooperation in economic, trade, and cultural spheres, and included a religious component. For the Koreans living in the Far East of Russia, the success of their historical homeland became the key factor that influenced the choice of their new religious identity—Protestantism. As South Korea had its own economical and geopolitical interests in the Asian part of the Russian Federation, representatives from both sides became interested in the presence of Korean churches in the Far East region of Russia. By the beginning of the 2000s, 30% of all Protestant churches in Primorski region were Korean churches, constituting 17% of all registered religious organizations.

It soon became clear that the outstanding feature of Korean Protestantism was its proselytizing zeal. Their active missionary work in many countries of the world is legitimated by their self-perception as a special nation that is being "used by God" for building a new Christendom on earth. As South Korea itself is located in the so-called "10/40 window"[2] that fact makes

Korean pastors and missionaries interpret their mission as both historic and unique (Svichev 1999). In 1994, 29% of Korean missionaries worked in the "10/40 window," and by 1997, they constituted 47.7% of all Korean missionaries serving abroad. The main frontier of the "spiritual war" was concentrated by the close of the century along the 105 meridian (China, Vietnam, Laos, Cambodia, areas along Mekong River) and gradually moved west from there. Taking that fact into consideration, we can see how the Asian part of Russia, specifically the Far East and Siberia, also became territories for Korean proselytism.

The proselytizing initiatives of the Korean Church arguably reflect the exigencies of a modernizing and expanding South Korea, desirous of transcending its historically "shady" position and expanding Korean culture and geopolitical influence. Likewise, the theology and practice of Korean Protestantism constitutes a response to the social and psychological needs of a population that finds itself in a post-traditional phase and critical period of transition. Christianity served to valorize traditional Korean values on the one hand, while on the other, it facilitated the integration of Korean culture and nationalism into the process of global modernization.

Korean proselytism has enjoyed success in other Asian societies where the social and cultural structure is similar to Korean culture. Asian ethnic groups find it easier to convert to Christianity when the carriers have an "Asian face" and there is a sense of a common "Asian" identity. Besides, Korean missionaries can proselytize and be almost "invisible" in Asian countries such as China, where religious freedom is limited. By 2000, 46% of the total number of Korean missionaries worked in Asia, where, significantly, by 2001, 60.9% of the world's population lived.[3] The top ten host countries for Korean missionaries are China (781 missionaries), the Philippines (527), Japan (463), Russia (359), Germany (288), Thailand (233), Indonesia (216), USA (183), India (160), and Uzbekistan (138).[4]

In some regions, however, Korean missionary strategies proved inappropriate. Since Korean culture was closed to foreign influences for many centuries, the rapid modernization and globalization of the late twentieth century were somewhat overwhelming for a large sector of Korean society. Most Koreans are grounded in their traditional ways, and so their missionaries face numerous problems in understanding other cultures. This limited knowledge of cultural diversity has proved to be one of the primary problems for Korean missionaries abroad. Many of them do not speak foreign languages and are not familiar with the cultural and social practices of the regions where they are sent. As Pentecostal doctrine prevails in the majority of Korean churches, many missionaries rely on the "Holy Spirit" to "guide them" in missionary work, often at the expense of learning the local language and culture.

However, Korean churches nowadays have started to benefit from improved material support for missionaries going into the field. Now they are equipped with CD presentations, evangelization cartoons for children, and church Internet sites to assist them in their endeavors.

Korean proselytism in the Far East and Siberia

From here onwards, I will focus on Korean proselytism in the Asian part of Russia: namely, the Far East and Siberia. These regions are characterized by the presence of a variety of indigenous groups, all very different from the Russians in terms of language, ethnicity, history, culture and religious beliefs. The presence of the Russian Orthodox Church is limited here in comparison to the central part of Russia. This implies that the population is potentially more receptive to other religious organizations.

The first Korean church was planted in Sakhalin Island in 1991. When the first Korean missionaries arrived in the area, they encountered a group of Koreans already living there, who had formed an underground home church. This church was run by the Korean Protestants who had been exiled by the Japanese during the Pacific War to Sakhalin to work in the coal mines and the wood industry. In December 1991, Korean missionaries officially organized the first Protestant church—the Christian Sakhalin Church. During 1992, Korean missionaries visited eight cities and towns on Sakhalin and many new churches were planted, so by April 1995 there were twenty-seven Korean Protestant churches and a seminary for training forty local pastors. Sakhalin Koreans gradually substituted pastors from South Korea in the local churches. According to a Korean missionary who worked in Sakhalin in the 1990s, 20% of the Sakhalin population had converted to Protestantism by 1997.

The first Korean missionaries appeared in Vladivostok, the largest seaport of Far East Russia and its administrative center, by the end of 1991, and in Khabarovsk by 1992. In the 1990s, the Korean diaspora in this area was growing in numbers because of the migration of ethnic Koreans from Kazakhstan, Uzbekistan, and other regions. Korean business entrepreneurs were followed by a flow of missionaries. A large proportion of them came to the Far East without visas permitting religious activities. As Korean missionaries admit, the Far East was not considered a target region for evangelization by the late 1990s. However, even after the peak of missionary activity, more than 3000 Protestant missionaries from abroad came to the Far East on a legal basis from 1999 to 2004 (Kobyzov 2005).

These statistics can be partly explained by the fact that this region of Russia eventually became a strategic region for Korean proselytism in China, because the Russian-Chinese border turned out to be more transparent for missionaries than any other country's borders. As China was the first on the list of target regions for Korean proselytism, a presence in the Far East became a unique opportunity for Korean missionaries to proselytize: the largest Chinese diaspora lives in the Far East and on the territories along the Amur River. North China is also a region where sizeable populations of ethnic Koreans now live. Missionaries carry Christian literature (published in Chinese) into China, and organize radio and TV broadcasts for Chinese Christians from within Russian territory (Kobyzov 2003).

In 2002, the Chief of Public Relations and Information Support Department of the Far East region (Vladivostok), Mr. A. Smirnoff, had the following comments about missionary activity in the region:

> The religious life in the Primorski region has never been as active as it is now. Today, 266 religious organizations of 22 different denominations operate in the region. The number of religious organizations increased tenfold during the last 12 years. Besides these religious organizations, additionally 350 non-registered religious groups are engaged in religious activities in the region. A missionary boom was recorded this year. According to the data of our Department in the first eight months of 2002 our region received the same number of missionaries as recorded over the last 3 years: in 1999–2001, 418 people with religious objectives visited the region, in 2002, 406 missionaries came. Among these missionaries: those coming from the USA in 2001 numbered 67, in 2002, 114, and from South Korea in 2001 there were 65, in 2002, 265 people.[5]

This notable increase in the number of Korean missionaries generated both public debates and rumors. For example, one of the deputies of the Russian State Duma published a provocative online report about Korean intentions to consolidate all ethnic Koreans living in Russia for migration to the Far East, where later they would be able to form a separate state (Dudarenok 2005). The leading role in this potential secession was imputed to Korean missionaries.[6] Though the majority of people did not take the report seriously, it nevertheless served to generate tension around ethnic and religious issues in the region. For example, on February 10, 2004, during a conference entitled "The Questions of Spiritual Security in Sakhalin Region" organized by the Sakhalin Administration and Russian Orthodox Eparchy, the organizers referred to that report in order to underline the negative impact of Korean missionary activities in the regions of the Far East. As a result, the regional administration discussed the possibility of passing a regional law restricting missionary activities in Sakhalin.[7] Moreover, it was noted that Korean missionaries proselytizing in Sakhalin churches were attributing economic and social problems in Sakhalin to unskillful Russian management, and that

Koreans intended to create a separatist paradise in Sakhalin, distinct from the Russian Federation. It is important to emphasize that, prior to this, ethnic and religious relations in the region were very favorable. Yet it was not only ethnic Koreans and the Chinese who attracted Korean missionaries to the Far East and Siberia, but also the "unevangelized" regions, inhabited by indigenous ethnic groups. In the 1990s, these groups began to experience a disruption in their traditional mode of living and a worldview crisis. They became a target for proselytism. Yet, as time passed, Korean missionaries, one by one, started to lose interest in evangelizing Siberia, because of the severe winters, high cost of living, hard living conditions, and the difficulties in obtaining visas. But the main reason given by the missionaries as to why they left Siberia was, "too much effort and fruitless results."

Russians living for a century in a predominantly secular society were very skeptical of adopting religious ideas, especially if such ideas came from Koreans. Since the majority of the Russians subscribe to Russian Orthodoxy few were ready to change their identity to the alternative proposed by Korean missionaries. That notwithstanding, a certain number of Korean missionaries have continued their missionary activities in the years following 2000, and many continue to come from South Korea for short-term evangelization campaigns in the summer.

In the following sections I focus on the missionary practices of Korean missionaries in Siberia. The majority of the indigenous ethnic groups in Siberia belong to the Turkic group and, until recently, practiced a nomadic lifestyle. For historical reasons, these groups vary socially and culturally, and this has influenced their reception of Korean proselytization.

Altai Republic

According to the national census of 2002, the Altai ethnic population consists of 62,000 people who make up 30.6% of the total population of the Republic. In addition to the Russians and the Altaians, there are 12,000 Kazakh, 2,300 Telengit, 1,500 Tubalar, and numerous other small ethnic groups which inhabit the region.

The Altai people became acquainted with Russian Orthodox beliefs when the first Russians came to their territory in the seventeenth century. Coexistence with the Russians and their religious and cultural tradition influenced the lifestyles of Altai ethnic groups. As a result a section of the population started to adhere to Russian Orthodoxy. Nowadays, Russians make up 57% of the Altai Republic population, with 30% Altaians and 6% Kazakhs. Because of migration, several religions co-exist in Altai: Russian Orthodoxy, Islam (the Kazakhs), Buddhism, shamanism, and Burkhanism—a syncretic religion that appeared in the late nineteenth century. Recently there have been a number of public debates about religious choice within the Altai state. According to local press monitoring, the majority of the population is indifferent to religious debates, they simply contrast their own religion with that of others. They see "their" religion as a complex mix of beliefs and religious practices with quotidian relevance, and grounded in shamanism. The Altai elite, in contrast, are still attempting to create a religious ideology from this ethnic religion that could serve as a symbol of national renaissance. The government of the Altai Republic is keen to promote social stability, and so supports a dialogue between traditional religions, but limits the influence of new religious groups in the Republic. As shamanism beliefs are still strong in some areas of Altai, shamans are the requisite figures at traditional cultural festivals, such as "El'oyn," which takes place annually (Kovalchuk 2004).

Research conducted in the capital of the Altai Republic in 2004, Gorno-Altaisk, revealed that information sources on religious topics are limited: no books or magazines on subjects related to religion (except Russian Orthodox literature) are available in the bookstores, Internet access is limited, and the local press pays little attention to the contemporary religious situation. In 2005, the Ministry of Justice in the Altai Republic registered thirty-six religious organizations. The Russian Orthodox Church has twenty-three parishes and ten churches. Islam has four registered communities and three mosques. Buddhism has three registered communities of the Gelukpa tradition, and one from the Karma Kagyu tradition. The Roman Catholic Church has one registered community. Year after year Protestants gain strength in Altai and now have six registered religious organizations. From the beginning of this century Protestant leaders from Siberian regions, as well as from abroad, visited local churches and participated in evangelization campaigns in rural areas of the Republic. Nevertheless, from 2000 to 2005, according to the Republic Register there was no one coming into the republic with an entrance visa that permitted religious activities.

A popular topic for sermons in the burgeoning Protestant churches is for missionaries and pastors to focus on the topic of Altai revival, and overcoming nationalistic ideas and ethnic dissociation. The proposed new identity is based on: 1) the fact of "Holy Spirit baptism", and 2) the shared residential area, i.e. the Altai Republic, without ethnic priorities. A typical congregation includes both Russian and Altaian parishioners. As a result in some churches, sermons are conducted in two languages with hymns translated from Russian to the Altai language. Members of the churches with an evangelical/Pentecostal orientation visit each other's church in case if the outstanding religious figure visits one of the churches.

Prior to 2005, Protestant churches in Altai were seeking to avoid conflict with the local administration and battling strong social stereotypes that associated Protestant churches with "destructive sects." After 2005, field research demonstrates that as Protestantism became stronger in Russia more generally Protestant churches changed the way they identified themselves within the society. They started to stand up for their religious rights. Their welfare policy has also altered in some respects. Before they donated food, clothes, money to the hospitals, orphanages, and homeless people. Now churches prefer to open their own welfare organizations, such as rehabilitation centers for those addicted to drugs and alcohol. This form of ministry entails new opportunities for the evangelization of those whom they cater to.

So it was against this general background that Korean missionaries began to proselytize in the Altai Republic. A missionary from the Korean Presbyterian Church started evangelizing in the Altai capital near the end of 1990s through a non-governmental organization (NGO) called "Peace." But the local administration exposed the evangelization tactics of this NGO and restricted its activities. In 2001, Korean missionaries registered as the Gorno-Altaisk Christian Presbyterian Church. By 2004, the church had built a three-storey building, attracting mainly young people from poor families or those coming from rural areas to the capital. Later, the demographics of the church began to change with more representatives of the Altai middle class and even social elites starting to appear in the congregation. Sermons were delivered only in Russian. The leader of the church is a charismatic female Korean preacher. She is dedicated to the missionary work in Altai and had previous missionary experience in other countries. She belongs to the liberal wing of the Presbyterian Church of Korea; the doctrine is largely Pentecostal, and includes exorcism and healing. The strategy of team mission work in the rural areas of Altai is determined by her prophesies.

The first people to support a Korean preacher were the ethnic Koreans who migrated to Altai from Uzbekistan. As time passed, more young and middle-aged representatives from lower social strata became regular churchgoers. The church took root in other Altai towns: Ongudai and Shabolino. The cell group method of evangelization, where small groups of families gather in homes during the week for support and prayer, and which is popular in Korea, spread here as well. In time, more Altai intelligentsia started to attend the Presbyterian Church, and they began to publish a Christian newspaper called "Istochnik."

The church leader believes that "very soon Altai is going to be changed as it was in Korea, and more Altai missionaries will go to other regions to evangelize others." She claims that the "spiritual war" is really strong in Altai, as the society is predominantly secular. Protestantism encounters strong opposition and hostile public opinion. In her opinion, these conditions resulted in the departure of the majority of Korean missionaries from Siberia. She also notes that because of the long period of Russian influence on Altai, the intellectual component of Altai religion became more pronounced than the emotional component in the decision-making process.

Hakhasia Republic

According to the 2002 census, the population of the Hakhasia Republic was 65,000 people. By the end of nineteenth century, the majority of the Hakhas had been converted to Russian Orthodoxy. The national Hakhas elite places great weight on the historical memory of the Hakhas people. For them, their past is a heroic past. The reviving of the institution of family clans provides a foundation for the traditional values of Hakhas people. Similarly, the traditional shamanic beliefs and customs are seen as part of the cultural heritage

In Hakhasia, according to the data given by the Republic Committee in 2005, there were 64 religious organizations officially registered. During the Soviet period, many Baptists and Pentecostals were exiled to Hakhasia. Today, there are seven religious organizations belonging to the Pentecostals, six to the Jehovah's Witnesses, Evangelical Baptists have six, Evangelical Lutherans have five, the Seventh-Day Adventists have two, and the Evangelical Christians two, 50% of religious organizations in Hakhasia are therefore Protestant.

The Korean Presbyterian Church took steps toward planting churches in Hakhasia, and missionaries came for evangelization work, but no church creation resulted. The missionaries returned to South Korea, but declared their intention to return. They attributed their lack of success to the large proportion of Russians in the population, the strong position of Russian Orthodoxy, and disinterested attitude of the Hakhasia government regarding the presence of new non-traditional religious organizations.

Buryatia Republic

The religious policy of the government of the Buryatia Republic reflects the Buddhist roots of the region. Traditionally, there were strong ties between Buryatia, Mongolia, and Tibet. The Buryat people speak the language that belongs to the Mongolian language family, not Turkic, as in other republics of Siberia. According to Buryatia religious registration documents, 168 religious organizations, comprising ten religions, are present in the republic. Among those 168, forty belong to Protestant denominations (Manzanov, 2005). This is a significant number, considering that Buryatia is a Buddhist (Lamaist)-oriented Republic. In Buryatia, Korean missionaries began proselytizing in 1994. By 2005, they had succeeded in organizing about ten Presbyterian church-groups and about three Yoido Full Gospel church-groups. Local pastors have almost taken over from the Koreans, and according to one Korean pastor, a few hundred people attend Sunday services in Ulan-Ude, the capital of Buryatia. In the Buryatia Republic, many ethnic Koreans belong to the Republic elite: the first secretary of the Minister of Culture, and the first secretary of the Republic Prime Minister. The presence of Koreans in the local government may account in part for the growth of Korean Protestantism in the Republic.

Tuva Republic

In the Tuva Republic, our principal case study in this essay, changing religious priorities are influencing the geopolitical orientation of the region. The ethnic Tuva population is 235,000 which represents 77% of the total population of the Republic. The traditional beliefs of the indigenous Tuva people reflect both shamanic and Buddhist elements. At the end of the twentieth century, Tuva society still reflected traditional lifeways and social arrangements. Nowadays, the traditional nomadic mode of living does not provide sufficient livelihood for a family to survive, causing many more people to migrate to the city. Because of the close interrelationship of ethnic and religious ties, conversion to another religion means a loss of Tuva identity. Generally, the Tuva population maintains the idea that the basis for Tuva identity is their traditional religion; if some representatives of their ethnic group convert to Protestantism it is considered by many as a betrayal of the nation. Since the Tuva nation is small in size, many believe that a split on religious grounds will lead to its disappearance (Myshlyavtsev and Yusha 2002).

That notwithstanding, Korean missionary work in Tuva has attracted great interest from the locals. Until 2000, the religious situation in Tuva was characterized as a balance between the Russians belonging to the Russian Orthodox Church and the Tuva people practicing a blend of Buddhism and shamanism (Homushku 1998). By the middle of 2000, earlier negative attitudes towards Protestantism started to change. For Tuva people living in the city and towns the spiritual bond "people-nature" was now being displaced by the notion of "people-society," as agricultural occupations changed to other kinds of employment.

By 2005, there were about ten Pentecostal churches in the capital city of Kyzyl (population 105,000). The largest church in Kyzyl is Sunbokym, established by a Korean missionary from Yoido Full Gospel Church in Seoul in 1994. According to the words of the Tuva pastor from Sunbokym Church, about 10% of Kyzyl population has visited the Protestant church in Kyzyl at least once, a major proportion attends often, and some come from time to time. Sunbokym Church is seen as a part of Yoido Full Gospel Church that belongs to the Assemblies of God denomination in Korea. The head church for the Tuva Sunbokym Church is located in Chimkent, Kazakhstan. In Chimkent, Yoido Full Gospel has a training center for the local missionaries, who are able to study for three years free-of-charge at the Elim Seminary. Yoido Full Gospel does not proselytize among the Russians. Only two churches exist in Moscow and St. Petersburg. The presence of Yoido Full Gospel can be seen primarily in the areas inhabited by many indigenous ethnic groups: Tuva, Buraytia, Kazakhstan, and Uzbekistan. Korean missionaries say it is probably because of the personal reasons of David Yonggi Cho (the founding pastor of Yoido Full Gospel Church), that Yoido Full Gospel does not proselytize among Russians. According to information received from Korean missionaries, Koreans were asked to come to Tuva by some government officials in the 1990s. The latter hoped for material help from the Koreans on the one hand, and wanted to create moral and religious support for fashioning a new Tuva national religion on the other hand, as the shamanic/Buddhist past of Korea was similar to that of the Tuva Republic. It has not been possible verify this information. However, there is no disputing that Sunbokym Church is the only Protestant church in Tuva that has existed for more than ten years, with its own large building in the center of the capital Kyzyl.

The church began in Tuva with the arrival of Korean missionary families in 1994. By 1997, Sunbokym Church in Kyzyl had 600–700 people attending Sunday services in a rented cinema building. Before long, the church managed to buy a building in the center of Kyzyl. At that point, in 2003, the Korean pastor Lee considered his mission fulfilled and made a decision to return to South Korea. By that time, the local Tuva preachers had been trained in the Chimkent seminary, and returned to Tuva ready for service.

However, the departure of the Korean pastor resulted in a drop in the number of churchgoers at Kyzyl Sunbokym. They liked his sermons and they came to listen to a Korean pastor as a representative of Korean culture, considered to be a "higher culture" by the Tuva people. In addition, right after he left, a tragedy took place in the church that contributed to the decline in the parish. Tuva Preacher A. Maadygi was found hanged in the church attic, but during two months the services had been conducted under his dead body. This so shocked the parish that many left for other Pentecostal and Baptist churches in Kyzyl.

But new policy decisions by the incoming Tuva Pastor, to preach the sermon every Thursday in the Tuva language only, and to have simultaneous translation on Sundays, helped turn the church around. The Yoido Full Gospel hymns are also translated into both Russian and Tuva languages, plus the locals compose hymns in Tuva language to be sung in Tuva villages when church teams goes on evangelization campaigns. This is an example of a hymn written by a Tuva author who attends Sunbokym; it is often sung during evangelization services in the Tuva villages.

Our Father, Almighty God!
Please hear our prayers!
To our brothers, sisters, relatives
Give your Blessing!!!

Your blessed name
We praise!
The heart of our People
Awake!!!

God gave salvation
To Tuva people!
The hearts that suffer,
Our God, please heal!!!

I sing to You!
Almighty God!
For Tuva people
Give you Love!!!

I lived wandering,
I got tired.
But now I discovered You
And I found my happiness!!!

According to the senior pastor, these changes in language policy led to an increase in church attendance in Sunbokym. At the time of research in 2005, almost 100% of the churchgoers were ethnic Tuva, with 125 people attending Sunday services. In other Pentecostal churches in Kyzyl, where the pastors are Russian, the proportion of Russians attending is larger.

The language problem was not the only reason why the number of parishioners decreased in Sunbokym. This departure created a lacuna, since the Korean pastor's authority, and by the same token, his charisma, were more valued. Church members and supplicants believed that they could more easily benefit from healings and exorcisms in his church. His sermons, too, reflected a practical emphasis on problem-solving, miracles, and life-transformation, rather than on biblical exegesis. For the people, this represented not only greater accessibility but also greater resonance with their needs. During interviews conducted in Sunbokym Church almost all parishioners cited "blessings" as a reason for their coming to Sunbokym, such as: "was able to get to the university," "husband stopped drinking alcohol," "I was healed," etc. The best-selling books made available by the church are by David Yonggi Cho, the Korean founder of Yoido Full Gospel. His impressive portrait hangs on the wall in Kyzyl Sunbokym.

The perceived superiority of the Korean pastor also has consequences for church governance. The Tuva senior pastor claimed that the authority of the senior pastor of the church was stronger when a Korean pastor was the leader. Pastors and preachers in Tuva districts were not so predisposed to obey the Tuva senior pastor in the same way, in part because they prefer to act independently. In the view of the senior pastor, neglecting the system of church seniority prevents the church and its parishes from growing. The Tuva female preacher of Kyzyl Sunbokym Church cites the example of the behavior of the Korean student evangelization team that came to Kyzyl, as follows:

> The Koreans are the true Christians! They confessed Christianity for a hundred years; they understand the importance of seniority and obedience. But Tuva people do not understand. They are haughty and proud. But today, if you do not obey a senior pastor, tomorrow you do not obey Jesus Christ! Are you a real Christian then?

She does not take into consideration that Korean culture and society has always been hierarchical and influenced by Confucian values, and prefers to privilege the positive influence of Christianity over cultural traits.

Yet, at the same time, the senior pastor of Sunbokym Church himself and other preachers do not like to be dependent on a head church in Chimkent (Kazakhstan) in matters of funds distribution and other decision-making questions. Again the "culture-scale" approach puts Kazakh culture on the same level as Tuva culture: "Why should we obey Chimkent if they do not understand our needs?" argues the senior Tuva pastor of Sunbokym Church. Because of that reason, Kyzyl Church tries to solve all questions through the Korean pastor, appealing directly to Seoul, and undermining the role of the Chimkent head church.

In their interactions with Koreans, Tuva people also try to identify common cultural characteristics. For example, in a Tuva house during a dinner organized especially in honor of the arriving Korean evangelization team, one of the Tuva female preachers said: "We should meet each other more often! We have so much in common! You know, we, Tuva people, and the Koreans are offspring of Simeon!" This perceived common "Asian" identity also contributes to the success of the Koreans in Tuva.

Missionary teams from South Korea are evidently a major boost and support for the local Sunbokym Church. Church members report that evangelization team activities always lead to an increase in church membership. In August 2005, one of the Korean teams of eight students visited Kyzyl Sunbokym Church. The members of the team came from Yoido Full Gospel and the Presbyterian Church in Seoul. The mission plan involved activities in Kyzyl and some villages in the regions of Tuva. The team was dressed in

T-shirts especially designed for evangelization work in the region: there was a Tuva horseman in the background and a Tuva map in front, with the phrase "We pray for Siberia" on the back (Figure 1). The uniform was also given to all Tuva church members who participated in the evangelization campaigns.

Next, the Korean missionaries marked important objects such as a Central Shaman House, Buddhist temples, Tuva government buildings, etc. on the map of Kyzyl to pray for Jesus Christ to come and reclaim "dark" places. By the end of the evening's activities, the Korean missionaries spent several hours praying for the victory of Christendom in Tuva. Then, the outdoor evangelization work began. The preparations for street evangelism included the study of some Russian and Tuva language words, drawing pictures, and learning hymns translated into Russian. About twenty young people went into the streets with richly colored posters and loud singing, shouting, "God loves you" in the Russian language (Figure 2). This attracted a lot of attention. The team stopped near the central market square, where the missionaries continued to sing songs, and give away balloons and candy to children and young

Figure 1.   Korean missionary prays near the monument "Center of Asia" in Kyzyl.

Figure 2.   Street evangelism.

people (Figure 3). As the majority of the Russians would not be interested in Korean proselytizing on the streets of Kyzyl, the campaign was aimed mainly at Tuva people.   However, the interest of the latter waned when they were told about Jesus Christ, saying: "I am not interested in the Russian God." But the fact that the missionaries were Korean, and that they used their street campaigns the following day to declare: "We are from Korea. God loves you!" helped undermine the stereotype of "Jesus Christ—the Russian God."

In fact, the following Sunday, during the sermon, Pastor Choi, the Korean leader of the evangelization team, said, "Many people on the streets here in Kyzyl said that Jesus Christ was the Russian God and they did not want to hear about Him. It was very painful to hear that. Yes, this is true—Jesus Christ is the Russian God, but He is also the Korean God and the Tuva God!!! Jesus Christ is God of the world. He created this world!"

In the village setting, the proselytization strategy varied slightly. Korean missionaries together with Tuva Sunbokym church members split up into different groups. They stopped in each village where a small parish of Sunbokym existed. The Koreans wrote posters with the following signs: "We are from Korea", "We are Korean students," "We are interested in Tuva culture," "We do not have a night's lodging," "Please, give us a meal and place to sleep." The aim of each member of the missionary team was to spend a night in a local house and to bring the host family to church the next day. We should also notice here that nobody from the Korean team knew either the Russian or Tuva languages.

The Tuva senior pastor believes that the personal example of the Christian life is the best means for ordinary people to appreciate the merits of a newly propagated religion. He stated: "They know me for a long time. They see how my life has changed. The person I used to be and the person I am now. They see the difference. When they have respect for me they start to get interested in religion too."

It is important to underscore that Pentecostalism in Tuva took root in the 1990s because of proselytism efforts, but from 2004, the evangelization of the Tuva people became more of an internal, indigenous affair. By summer 2005, Tuva Sunbokym Church had parishes in eight Tuva regions. A Sunbokym pastor claimed that the main reason that the church was not growing as fast as it possibly could was due to a lack of preachers willing to live in Tuva villages. Many of the preachers who had received theological education decided to stay in the cities.

A number of reasons can account for the successful growth of these Pentecostal forms of Christianity in the region. First, the demographic shift from a nomadic to a settled lifestyle resulted in many people relocating to the city. Second, traditional beliefs, whether shamanic and Buddhist, ceased to be functional enough for those in these new social settings. In addition, Bud-

Figure 3.   Child evangelism.

dhist teachings are perceived as difficult and not well known by the majority of Tuva people. Third, the Pentecostal version of Protestantism with its emphasis on healing, exorcism, and blessings in both this and the next world, attracted a lot of people. They also liked the ease of access to the teachings, and the opportunity to hear sermons in their own language. Furthermore, the Korean style of worship, with active singing, movement, and speaking in tongues, shares a number of similarities with shamanic chanting. Fourth, psychologically, the conversion to Protestantism created a new identity for the adherents, making them feel as though they were "special" and "selected by God." This translated into a newfound confidence in their everyday lives, even sense of superiority, despite the economic difficulties of the area. Fifth, many Tuva believe that conversion to Protestantism is the only way for Tuva people to survive and rebuild the nation, which is beset with huge problems of alcoholism and drug addiction, in the midst of a deep social and economic crisis. So in the face of ethnic and religious divisions, the new urban Tuva population see the potential of conversion to Protestantism as not weakening, but strengthening, their national identity. Korean missionaries continue to send funding and missionary help to Tuva, helping Sunbokym Church in Kyzyl to survive and pay for the transportation costs of evangelization campaigns around the region.

The story of Korean proselytism in Tuva is really just "a bead in the necklace" of global Korean proselytism. It demonstrates well how the Koreans initially used members of the local Korean diaspora as missionary agents, eventually deploying more effective strategies for converting the local population.

Conclusion

The history of Christianity in Korea, where Christian groups had to endure under suppression and prohibition, taught Korean Christians how to survive and operate even in countries where governments or other institutions were not welcoming. In fact, some Korean missionaries often enter such countries illegally or as businessmen, and then combine business with evangelization work.

It is evident that Koreans prefer to work with indigenous ethnic groups. The latter perceive them as representatives of "an advanced culture," and an example of a people that built modern Korea "with the help of God." Moreover, the ideal target group for missionary agents is a society in a transitional period, looking for new sources of meaning. For such a nation or ethnic group, Christianity can legitimize traditional values, inscribe them in a new cultural and modern context, and provide a new high-status identity for the converts. Humanitarian work also helps bring in new converts and their families. It also helps that there is some form of cultural and psychological affinity between the proselytizers and the proselytized. It was not so long ago that Korean society made its own, fairly rapid transition to a more urbanized and modernized society. Many Korean missionaries are the representatives of the second and third generation of those who migrated to the cities.

In South Korea, Protestantism permeates all spheres of social life: education, medical and social care, popular culture, and the mass media, etc. Christianity began as a new religion and ended up becoming an integral part of the Korean cultural landscape. It passed through various stages of social, cultural, economic, and political adaptation along with Korean society more generally. This led to the creation of "ready to use" communications and instructional technology for effective proselytizing in transitional societies. Korean Protestant missionaries therefore have both the means and the goals to continue to succeed in the Asian societies discussed in this essay.

Notes

1. See the work of Schipkov (1998), Lunkin (2002) as well as Filatov ed. *Religion and Society: Contemporary Religious Life in Russia* (2002), on the adaptation of Protestantism to indigenous cultures in Russia.

2. The 10/40 window is a reference to latitude and longitude markings on the globe believed to consist of the least proselytized groups on the planet for the Christian church.

3. Operation World, 2001.

4. Steve S.C. Moon, The Acts of Koreans: A Research Report on Korean Missionary Movement. www.krim.org [Accessed 24 June 2005].

5. http://www.vladivostok.eparhia.ru/society [Accessed 17 November 2005].

6. http://stolica.narod.ru/docs_vl/duma/006.htm [Accessed 31 October 1997].

7. http://www.pravoslavie.ru/cgi-bin/news.cgi?item=2r040211133440 [Accessed 25 April 2005, now defunct].

References

Dudarenok S.M. 2005. Конфликт как одна из составляющих религиозной жизни российского Дальнего Востока конца XX—начала XXI вв. [Conflict as a part of religious life in Far East of Russia 19th–21st centuries.] Electronic Resource: Russian Association of scholars of religion. http://www.rusoir.ru/print/01/30/ [Accessed 4/03/2006].

Filatov S. (ed.) 2002. Религия и общество: Очерки современной религиозной жизни России [Religion and Society. Contemporary Religious Life in Russia]. Moscow: Letnii Sad.

Homushku O.M. 2000. Протестантские религиозные организации в Туве [Protestant organizations in Tuva: contemporary situation]. In современное состояние [Protestantism in Siberia], 165–69. Materials of International Scientific Conference, Omsk, 1998.

Kobyzov R. 2005. Ethnic and religious interaction of the Russians and Chinese. Unpublished PhD thesis, Amurski State University, Blagovechensk

Kobyzov R.À. 2003 Китайцы как объект миссионерской деятельности христианских конфессий [The Chinese population as the object of missionary activities of the Christians). In Россия и Китай: на дальневосточных рубежах. [Russia and China on the Far East Border] 3: 570–75. Blagovechensk: Amur State University Press.

Kovalchuk Yu. S. 2004. Современная конфессиональная ситуация в Республике Алтай по данным мониторинга 2004 г . [Contemporary religious situation in Altai Republic based on Monitoring done in 2004]. Проблемы археологии, этнографии, антропологии Сибири и сопредельных территорий [*Problems of archaeology, ethnography and anthropology of Siberia*] 10: 57–62.

Lunkin R.N. 2002. Нехристианские народы России перед лицом христианства // Религия и общество [Non-Christian peoples of Russia facing Christianity]. In Очерки современной религиозной жизни России [Religion and Society. Contemporary Religious Life in Russia], ed. S.B. Filatov, 361–82. Moscow: Letnii Sad

Manzanov G.E. 2005. Современное состояние религиозности в Республике Бурятия [Contemporary situation with religiosity in Buryatia Republic]. *Religiovedenie* 2: 79–87.

Myshlyavtsev B.A. and Zg. M. Yusha. 2002. Протестантизм и его влияние на этнические процессы в современной Туве [Protestantism and its influence on ethnic processes in contemporary Tuva]. In Проблемы межэтнического взаимодействия народов Сибири [Problems of ethnic contacts among peoples of Siberia], 96-105. Novosibirsk.

Svichev M.P. 1999. Миссионерская деятельность в контексте геополитики [Missionary activities in geopolitics context]. Moscow: Russian Academy of State Service Materials.

Schipkov A.V. 1998. Во что верит Россия: Курс лекций [What does Russia believe in]. St-Petersburg: St.Petersburg: Publishing house of Russian Christian Humanitarian Academy.

CHAPTER 17

Proselytization or Information? Wicca and Internet Use

Shawn Arthur

Common conceptions of "proselytization" include forcing one's beliefs upon another in the attempt to coerce that person into adopting one's own religious tradition and ideology, convincing a Christian to change his/her denominational affiliation, and attempting to bring about the conversion of a non-Christian to Christianity (See Kao this volume; Lindholm *et. al.* 2004, 668; Stalnaker 2002, 337, 347.[1] In these cases, "proselytism" is not merely the attempt to gain converts, but also includes the endeavor to persuade others to change their beliefs, practices, and/or community affiliations, as well as efforts to "extend ideological influence and political dominance" (Mayer, in this volume).

From this latter perspective, "proselytism" can be understood as quite commonplace in daily life. Although attempting to change the perspectives of others occurs in many aspects of routine conversations and discussions where two opposing opinions meet, the term "proselytism" is generally not used outside of the religious purview. Theologian Lawrence A. Uzzell, in critiquing this ambiguity of the term, recognizes that: "[p]hrases such as 'feminist proselytism' or 'environmental proselytism' are unknown; it is considered natural, even laudable, for adherents of those secular beliefs to seek converts all over the world" (2004, 14).

Arguably, the historical uses of proselytism by dominant religious traditions are more sophisticated than mere conversion techniques. The term often carries a pejorative connotation, especially for those who are the focus of such efforts, because the practice of proselytism "implies a moral judgment of error (in assent) and impropriety (in action)" on the part of those being proselytized (Griffiths 2002, 31). Furthermore, building on anti-proselytism sentiments in the constitutions of countries such as Zambia and Mauritius, proselytism also can be understood as having the more sinister implications of prejudicing the religious rights and freedoms of others through unsolicited intervention (see Lindholm *et al.* 2004, 664). Integrating these common elements, I define proselytism as "the persuasive attempt to change another person's pre-existing religious beliefs, practices, commitments, and/or affiliations."[2]

The subject matter of this chapter is case studies of religious websites, especially those of Wicca, a nature-oriented religious tradition that is based on the affirmation of life and spiritual growth through understanding the Divine as both immanent and transcendent, as manifest in the natural world, and as revealing itself in the natural rhythms and cycles of the cosmos. A subset of the larger contemporary Paganism movement of the past sixty years, Wiccans were among the first religious groups to utilize the Internet for group formation, communication, and maintenance, as well as for ritual performance and networking. The majority of Wiccan websites profess that they do not proselytize or seek converts, and this chapter examines those claims and other evidence for online proselytizing activities.

What functions do religious websites serve?

Over the past decade, there has been much academic research done on the informative and communicative aspects of the Internet, including ways that religious adherents interact and communicate online. This particular research project began by examining and analyzing religious uses of cyberspace and questioning the agendas of the founders of Wiccan websites and web-based communities (see Arthur 2002). Whereas scholars have indicated that online religious communities are regularly created and maintained for community members, my research indicates that religious websites often also contain explicit outreach elements intended to attract new members and to teach non-members about the religious tradition or group. This essay investigates the motivations of website creators and viewers, and discusses some of the important outreach activities that many religious groups are now attempting to accomplish via the increasingly competitive public sphere of the Internet. My examination culminates with a detailed analysis of the possibility of online proselytization, and the forms that proselytizing activities can assume in cyberspace.

There are many different types of religious websites in existence, including academic sites about religion, religious education sites, official sites run by religious groups and leaders, organized group and church sites, outreach and advocacy sites, information archives, online periodicals, sites for marketing and selling religious items, individual home pages with religious content, and many other types. With this variety, there is no doubt that online religion is continually growing in importance. In fact, the extensive survey conducted by Elena Larsen and the Pew Internet and American Life Project indicates the great significance that online religion has for Americans (www.pewinternet. org[3]; Larsen 2004). This survey claims that 25% of Internet users have utilized this medium to find information on religions or spirituality, and more than three million people per day use the Internet to find religious or spiritual materials individually or to interact with other religious people in support networks. Furthermore, this project found that at least 50% of people who look for information about religion on the Internet have actively sought information on religions other than their own (Larsen 2004, 17–18).

Larsen's research indicates that information dissemination is one of the most important aspects of religious websites. This comes in a variety of forms: basic information about religious beliefs and tenets; online directories and regional contact listings; time schedules and directions to meetings; scriptures and reference texts; and education resources. Information dissemination *is* an important facet of religious practice, especially for those religions—such as Wicca, Islam, Scientology, and Mormonism—that are fighting for legitimacy as minority religious traditions in the United States, and which are often perceived as eccentric and controversial (See Berger and Ezzy 2004, 179; Horsfall 2000, 154, 161, 173; Varisco 2000, 3). However, religious websites almost always have objectives beyond the mere sharing of relatively unbiased information about their own beliefs and organization.[4] In their zeal to provide information to wary audiences, the websites of religious groups and individuals are often filled with persuasive language, invitations for further face-to-face contact, and other outreach-oriented activities. It is my contention that when information dissemination becomes part of a public outreach or advertising program to attract newcomers, to persuade people to change their perceptions about the religion in question, or to critique the religious beliefs of others, then the website is no longer merely sharing information, it is part of a proselytization campaign.

Motivations for creating religious websites

Why create a religious website? There are three major categories of religious website creator: religious bodies, such as the Vatican and Scientology, which attempt to present "official views;" local religious groups, such as churches or Wiccan covens, which are generally information- and outreach-oriented; and individually-hosted websites that express personal opinions and/or religious beliefs—often by supporting the organization of which the author is a part, and/or by critiquing other religious groups.[5] Clearly, each category has particular motivations for hosting a website, some of which are specific, and others which are held in common.

Concurring with Clifford Geertz's argument that all communicative perform-ance is action, and driving each action is an implicit or explicit motive, I con-tend that creating a website implies a range of specific objectives. I also argue that is important to question the motivations behind the proliferation of per-sonal and group websites, and to explore the formats and functions—intended and/or realized—of these uses of Internet space (see Horsfall 2000, 173).

In many ways researchers can determine certain aspects of website "creator/ author"[6] motivation by closely examining the texts of the websites them-selves, as well as the perceived tone, words, choice of images, and structure of a website document (see Patte 1993; Beardslee 1993). However, while authors often think they are focused on one objective, such as providing information, their readers are capable of interpreting the documents from their own varying perspectives, thus missing the author's original intention (see McKnight 1993). For example, although Wiccans claim that they do not want to attract converts, repeated messages such as "Please contact us!" that might be intended for existing community members can easily be interpreted as implicitly proselytic invitations to practice Wicca and to become Wiccan. This tendency indicates that the differences between providing information and conversion tactics are often unclear, especially on the Internet.

The major website creation goals of which I have become aware through my research include both internally—and externally—directed motivations. Motivations of internal orientation include promoting and maintaining community adhesion, sharing information and resources between existing community members, facilitating communication between group members, and reproducing important aspects of the religion in cyberspace—such as scripture reading, prayers, and rituals—for (customized) consumption by group members.

Motivations of external orientation are more numerous, and can be grouped into four major public relations or outreach categories: informing non-members about the religion, its members, its beliefs, and its practices; advertising and promoting the group or individual and its message; perform-ing missionary activities in order to attract and invite new members; and extending the influence of the religion by persuading non-members to change their perceptions about the website's product (whether a physical commodity or a religious practice) and its legitimacy. A good example of external-orient-ed motivation is the most complex Wiccan-oriented website, The Witches' Voice (www.witchvox.com), which contains all four of these elements. It is meant to be informative, but it also hosts sizeable directories through which individuals and groups advertise themselves and network with others.

Although many religious websites are not explicitly focused on recruiting outsiders, websites commonly function as portals for inquiries, further contact, and possible conversion of interested parties.[7] Additionally, these websites also function as advertisements for the group or person who hosts them. Part of the Wiccan Internet presence, and its emergent public relations strategy more generally, is a means to further "develop awareness" of all things Wiccan. Although certain websites may be intended for newly self-identified Wiccans to learn about and to adopt the ideas and practices more commensurate with those of the website creator, most Wiccan websites seem to be oriented outwards—not for Wiccans to become aware of themselves, *per se*, but for non-members to learn about Wiccans and their religion. For example, Gavin and Yvonne Frost have advertised their "Church and School of Wicca" in the back sections of comic books since at least the early 1970s, and, as the Internet has gained prominence, they have bought advertising space for their website (www.wicca.org) on various search engines including Google.com.

An additional major public relations motivation is proselytization. It is widely recognized that many religious groups utilize the Internet as a medium to promote their particular message (Campbell 2004, 108; Horsfall 2000, 158, 160; Lord 2002, 202). In this regard, I argue that advertising oneself and one's group on a website clearly indicates that one is attempting to share one's beliefs, to locate like-minded others, and/or to potentially recruit new members.[8]

It is in the cyber-realm that a new trend is emerging: online apologetics—the practice of attempting to convince non-members to change their perceptions about the individual, group, or religion portrayed on the website. This is accomplished by persuading outsiders to interact with and eventually to join the group, and to see the group as legitimate. Thus, many minority religious groups can vie for acceptance and legitimization by the greater real-world society: for it is on the Internet that attractive and persuasive information can most easily be accessed and digested by those outside of the group (see Cowan 2004, 257; Horsfall 2000, 175).

Due to the proliferation of misinformation about Wicca, especially in cyberspace, proponents of the religion have developed Wiccan apologetic strategies on both information-disseminating websites and in physical groups. The earliest forms of Wicca in the United Kingdom and United States often valorized the individualist and socially marginal qualities that the religion offered. However, this practice is evolving as Wicca becomes more widespread and its public persona grows. More Wiccans want their religion to become accepted by the general populace—hence all of the Pagan Pride activities that are held across the United States. [9] These public gatherings occur complete with music, banners, parades, pamphlets, and many Pagans and Wiccans outwardly exercising their public voice to advocate Wicca's legitimacy and to counter negative stereotypes. I relate Pagan Pride Day activities to online Wiccan activities because they are often similar in orientation and practice. As Lorne L. Dawson and Douglas E. Cowan have argued, Internet activities most often have direct correlations to offline activities (2004, 6). In this case, Wiccan Internet sites and Pagan Pride celebrations are often used "to set the record straight [because there] are a lot of misconceptions about the pagan community out there" (quoted in O'Horan 2005, 1).

In the same ideological vein, the final major motivation for website creation is countering negative propaganda. Many religious groups that host websites are focused on negating opposing views about their beliefs and practices (see Cowan 2004, 267). For example, Islamic apologetics websites abound that include line-by-line rejoinders to conservative Christian anti-Muslim perspectives, and official Scientology websites actively promote their side of the story in an attempt to highlight the best characteristics of the tradition, and to explain away the worst (Varisco 2000, 4; Horsfall 2000, 162, 174, 179). Additionally, part of the overall Wiccan online presence includes reactions against other people's misperceptions. As Grove Harris argues,

> Pagans [and Wiccans] have historically been misunderstood as the quintessential other, the personification of evil (as in devil worshiping—a Christian construct) or of amorality. Years of outreach and educational efforts, along with active participation of Pagans in national and international interfaith efforts, have clarified that Pagans are earth-centered spiritualists who hold all of life as sacred and honor the interconnectedness of all of life.
>
> (2005, 67; see also Fernback 2002, 262)

The most visible aspect of this practice online, which can be found on nearly every Wiccan website, comes in the form of "Wicca 101" and "Frequently Asked Questions" web pages. These promote discussion of basic Wiccan practices and beliefs, and most often include a section attempting to correct Christian misinformation about the religion. Pagan author Taylor Ellwood argues that "the only way we can get past the ignorance and the attempts by Christians to change our ways of belief is to educate people about what we believe in" (2003).

In fact, a Google.com website search for "Wicca" on November 1, 2005 indicated that nineteen of the first twenty websites, owned and run by Wiccans, contain sections of apologetics concerned to explain Wicca in terms that explicitly contradict common Christian portrayals of the religion. [10] A prime example of this is on the "What Is Wicca?" page on "The Celtic Connection" (www.wicca.com). This page discusses the history of Wicca and contains a section entitled "What Wicca Is Not," explaining that Wiccans are not what Christians claim: they do not worship Satan, sacrifice animals or people, or hex people with spells.[11] Website claims such as these signify that a portion of each of these Wiccan websites is focused not on communicating with existing Wiccans but on an outreach agenda to persuade non-members to change their perceptions about Wicca—an increasingly common form of apologetics, or implicit proselytization, which is discussed in more detail below.

Marketing and advertising strategies employed on websites

If religious website creation is driven by the motives of attracting others and changing the opinions of non-believers, then questions of how those motives are articulated online need to be addressed. For motivations other than mere information dissemination, a variety of marketing and advertising strategies are regularly employed. Indeed, the Internet is more frequently being approached as a "religious supermarket" where one can encounter and interact with any religious tradition that hosts a website, and through which religions can easily advertise themselves and share information (See Cowan 2005, 257; Dawson and Hennebry 2004, 160; Fernback 2002, 270; Ko, *et al.* 2005, 57; Lature 1995; Mayer 2000, 273). In this light, I suggest approaching the Internet as a market phenomenon, with different religious groups and religious ideologies as the various products that are available for public consumption. With this approach, marketing and advertising research can help us to better understand some features and implications of the commodification of the Internet and its religious goods.

Because they recognize the effectiveness of advertising on the Internet, many marketing firms have developed "persuasion engineering" strategies to attract the attention of possible consumers, and to coerce them into becoming interested in their products (Freedman 2005, 73; see also Uzzell 2004, 14). Of the various advertising techniques used online, the most basic and important is the actual creation and placement of the website itself into the public sphere. Not only do websites advertise their own content, the website creator can attach a long list of keywords to the coded aspects of the site so that search engines are more likely to recognize it[12] and feature it prominently in the first few pages of any search that includes the relevant keywords (see Dawson and Hennebry 2004, 160). Other techniques include paying close attention to the aesthetic qualities of the website, posting testimonies and autobiographical materials, featuring welcoming sentiments and personalized invitations for further contact, providing interactive content to foster communication, and using persuasive language to increase the overall effectiveness of the website's agenda(s).

The creation of religious websites works in the same ways to market messages and to persuade outsiders of their importance in the sea of competing voices that is cyberspace. According to Helga Lénárt-Cheng, good advertisement strategy employs a methodology that conceals its strategy by making subtle rather than overt promotions, by making the content easy to understand, by making self-praise indirect, and by repeating the advertisement (2003, 122–7; see also Freedman 2005, 72). Therefore, I view personal and group website creation as a form of autobiography, a literary device which has been used throughout history as a means of manipulating public opinion and changing one's public image. Providing testimonies that indicate the author's affinity for particular religious practices or beliefs is a clever means by which readers will encounter praise of the website's subject matter without the website creator's interfering with the more "objective" presentation of information.

As Lénárt-Cheng further argues, "[w]hether the reason for manipulation is personal interest, public lobbying, or political maneuvering, the seductive power of autobiographical writing to manipulate public opinion has always attracted writers" (2003, 117). The effectiveness of the autobiographical technique lies in the fact that readers most often ignore the "seemingly innocent marketing strategies used by autobiographers," such as subtle self-aggrandizement, testimonials from others about the subject's importance and worth, and persuasive language, but these nonetheless greatly influence readers' perceptions and assessments of the writer (2003, 118). Twelve of twenty Wiccan websites that I researched contained autobiographical and testimonial content about people's conversion stories, and accounts of their positive experiences with Wiccan practices.

The website creator's proclivity for, and ability to produce, aesthetically pleasing websites, and to compose convincing prose, can also increase the website's appeal, the group's public profile, and the relative authority of its creators. Thus, an attractive website can increase the likelihood that visitors will contact the person(s) associated with the website, and this can augment the host's capacity for outreach activities (see Horsfall 2000, 163).[13] Each time a website is accessed another invitation is performed (Howard 2005: 173–4). Therefore, seemingly personal invitations to "Contact us for more information!" and "Come join us at open rituals!"[14] can operate on at least two levels: inviting self-proclaimed Wiccans to join the community represented by the website and its creator (See Berger and Ezzy 2004, 184; O'Horan 2005, 2; Dawson and Hennebry 2004, 157–160), and inviting curious non-Wiccans and potential converts to interact with Wiccans and Wiccan information.

My research also indicates that the capacity to have open discussion among members and non-members is an integral function for religious groups on the Internet—especially for those people who do not have an offline social counterpart—and can be a significant aspect of group identity (see Berger and Ezzy 2004, 180; Horsfall 2000, 187). I contend that including a range of interactive activities such as message boards, chat rooms, and invitations to join interactive prayer services and rituals—where people can share and discuss their beliefs, and where the religion in question can be presented as more accessible and welcoming—transforms a religious website into a community maintenance *and development* type of website.

The importance of this human-to-human interactive content, according to marketing and advertising research specialists, is that people are better able to "actively participate in the persuasion process by controlling the advertising message, amount of information, and order of presentation at any time, according to their needs and preferences" (Ko *et al.* 2005, 59). This in turn leads to greater receptivity to the message and has a "significantly positive effect" on the audience's attitude toward the website and its "product," therefore making the commodity, or religious belief and tradition, more likely to be accepted and evaluated positively (60–2).[15]

It is with these interactive and informative aspects of religious websites that persuasive writing can become proselytization, as it transforms "information" into "coercive advertising." In advocating the insider's perception of the group and its benefits, many websites attempt to persuade outsiders to adopt a similar understanding of the group and/or to join the group in question. For example, website use of interactive elements that cajole visitors to "click here" in order to pray because they "need" to "Know Jesus, Now!"—so that they can avoid the dire consequences of being a sinner (Howard 2005: 173, 181)—goes beyond merely providing information about Christianity to actively attempting to change the visitor's religious affiliation if they are an inactive or non-Christian.

Wiccan websites also utilize emotional and persuasive language in their attempts to convince others of the "right" way to think about Wicca and Paganism as religions. The author of "The Inner Sanctum" website writes: "Since long before The Burning Times, Witches have been persecuted and ridiculed. This site was designed to stop that attitude. Witches love... Witches *HARM NONE*" (www.witchway.net; emphasis in original). Anti-propaganda apologetics such as this are not intended for practicing Wiccans; rather, I argue that they are explicit attempts at a public relations strategy meant to defend the religion against perceived attacks, to market Wicca in its own words rather than those of its detractors, and to persuade outsiders to change their possibly negative opinions about Wicca. Hence, these should be considered as examples of online proselytization.

Audience motivations: ways of viewing religious websites

In order to attract visitors, it is evident that website creators actively consider their intended audiences when crafting their website content.[16] The range of audiences that visit any given religious website is ultimately unknown, but it is made up of at least four major groups: members of the religion or group, non-members who are curious about and/or amenable to the content, those who remain neutral, and those who are not amenable and/or in opposition to the particular message of the website. Although creators of religious websites might not intend their sites to become advertisements, websites nonetheless can have this effect on visitors (See Long and Hadden 1983, 6; Mayer 2000, 268; Helland 2004, 33). It is synergy between the website's aesthetics, its interactive aspects, its message, and the visitor's intent that allows for education and possible conversion to take place.

Motivation plays a key role in a visitor's choosing to interact with a particular website. According to Internet applications of the "uses and gratification" theory, an axiomatic advertising and marketing theory, people most often engage in Internet surfing in a goal-oriented way to satisfy their perceived needs, different motivations effect levels of interactivity, and interactivity leads to more positive attitudes toward the products being marketed on a particular website, which in turn leads to greater intent to consume the product offered on the website (Ko *et al.* 2005, 58, 60–62; Horsfall 2000, 180, 182). People who are actively seeking information will be more likely to accept and digest the information presented on a sophisticated, well-constructed website. Furthermore people seeking religious "truths" online will also be more likely to convert their beliefs based on a well-presented, persuasive, and interactive website (Dawson and Cowan 2004, 10; Horsfall 2000, 157).

The reality of online proselytism

Having discussed the major motivations for creating religious websites and the various means by which this is accomplished, I am now able to address the key questions of the essay: is proselytism an active component of cyberspace, can proselytism be practiced via the medium of the Internet, and if so, what is the possibility for Internet-mediated religious conversion?

Proselytism involves a variety of strategies: from using threats and force, to promising this-worldly benefits, to compelling people through coercive arguments and language. However, I contend that the major motivations for creating a religious website (to inform, to advertise, to attract, and to persuade) in combination with various marketing techniques (such as invitations, testimonials, interactive content, and persuasive language) produce growing evidence of proselytizing activities in cyberspace. Arguably, a large proportion of religious websites are forms of and forums for proselytizing, where the promotion of certain perspectives is meant to change peoples' perceptions and beliefs about the religion in question, and where persuasive language replaces the pressures of one-on-one contact common to traditional conversion techniques (see Varisco 2000, 4).

Although the idea of proselytization traditionally has implied face-to-face coercive interaction between the proselytizer and his/her "target," certain interactive aspects of the Internet such as chat rooms, bulletin boards, and mailing lists can function as human-to-human communication in lieu of face-to-face situations. Additionally, the use of persuasive language, aesthetics, and marketing techniques also has important implications for the ways that a curious visitor might be influenced to experience a particular website and the religion that it represents more positively, more completely, for a longer time, and as having more authority and legitimacy than previously thought.

According to Cecil Stalnaker, "[i]n authentic evangelism, the communication is entirely void of any coercive methods" (2002, 349). However, given the nature of publishing and print media that constitute cyberspace communication techniques, persuasion and coercion become easily enmeshed. For example, in instances of the "Sinner's Prayer" online, the language used to catch the attention of the website audience—in the hopes of convincing them not only to perform the prayer but through it to also become a Christian—goes beyond mere information and evangelism to include elements of proselytism (Howard 2005, 175, 181, 184). Additionally, in its online forms, the element of coercion is much more implicit and understated in many cases, as it comes hidden in the aesthetically-pleasing images, welcoming messages, autobiographical self-aggrandizement, and persuasive language that are present on websites, as discussed above.

Therefore, it must be concluded that the difference between information-dissemination, evangelism, and proselytism is not nearly as clear online as it might be in the offline, face-to-face world because one cannot always determine the intent of the website creator. Given the complex interplay between the motivations of the website creator and the audience members themselves that produces the range of perceptions about and interactions with any given website; I argue that both the author and the viewer play important roles in determining what constitutes proselytism or information-dissemination.

Another aspect of this discussion of the differences between offline proselytization and its online counterpart is that it is possible for individuals to provide much more thorough introductions to themselves and their religious groups on their websites compared with the relatively brief nature of face-to-face interactions. This might mitigate some of the coercive elements of interpersonal conversion attempts because the immediacy factor does not seem to be present to the same degree online. Many missionary groups do realize that a person may only visit their website once; they also accurately recognize that if the website is inviting and pleasing to visitors, they are more likely to return for further exploration and contact.

Due in part to this desire to attract new believers, the past decade has seen an exponential increase in the number of religious groups and actors using the Internet for advertising and proselytism. For example, in 1995, the Christian group Ecunet (The Ecumenical Network) hosted a conference on the theme of "Ministry in Cyberspace;" in 2000, the Southern Baptist Convention appointed its first online missionary devoted to finding ways to convert Christians via the Internet; and Mormons, Roman Catholics, Muslims, and Scientologists invest much money and time on their websites to attract visitors and promote their beliefs (Lature 1995; Anonymous 2001; Horsfall 2000, 173, 156–60; see also Campbell 2004, 109; Fernback 2002, 268; Howard 2005, 184; Nash 2002, 280; Senter 2002, 224; Varisco 2000, 4). As Horsfall recognizes, "Almost all of [religious] sites and pages have an evangelistic element, more or less prominently displayed according to the nature of the group. Each group, however subtly, is advertising a way of life and a religious practice to which they are inviting others to join" (2000, 173). In other words, religious websites regularly focus on outreach: for public relations, member interaction, information sharing, *and proselytization.*

Wicca: a closer examination

The example of Wicca is particularly useful for investigating some of the nuances of Internet-based proselytization, because Wiccan ideas about proselytization often contradict the attitudes present on Wiccan websites. Wiccans routinely claim on websites, in books, and in person that they do not proselytize and that they are not interested in converting others to Wicca. Various reasons for this stance include the belief that all religious paths are sacred and should be individually chosen and not forced upon another, the dislike of being proselytized themselves, the fact that many do not want to create converts because this necessitates teaching more students, and because they do not want to be associated with "cultic" activities such as proselytism. Peg Aloi writes in a review of a poorly-produced news item, "[if the reporter] had spent even a minute studying InterNet websites related to Paganism, [she] would have learned that Pagans do not indoctrinate, recruit, proselytize or preach; they do not, in other words, engage in cult mind-control activities" (2002; see also Ellwood 2003).

In fact, Wiccans so often argue that they do not proselytize or seek converts that an anti-proselytism rhetoric has become an informal tenet of the religion—one that is repeated on nearly every Wiccan website and in nearly every introductory book as part of their public relations strategy. However, according to my research, this maxim is inaccurate for a number of reasons. First, there are Wiccan groups that actively search for new members, including those who have had little or no previous experience with Wicca. Additionally, the vast numbers of Wiccan websites that attempt to attract visitors with introductory material on "how to become Wiccan" clearly indicate that advertising, proselytizing, and other examples of attempted conversion abound in cyberspace.

Second, there are many online forums where Wiccans attempt to generate interest in their beliefs, to solicit interaction, and to invite interested newcomers to communicate with existing Wiccans and Pagans.[17] Generally, the more experienced members will not actively attempt to convert newcomers, but they do present a welcoming atmosphere, answer questions, and are often happy and willing to help newcomers in their conversion process if asked (See Berger and Ezzy 2004, 179–80; Ellwood 2003; O'Horan 2005, 3; Pan 2005). In other words, Wiccan websites regularly function to make Wicca more accessible to outsiders.[18]

Third, many Wiccans actively attempt to change peoples' misperceptions and negative opinions about the religion, its beliefs, and its practices. This is accomplished through websites, books, Pagan Pride celebrations, media coverage, and interpersonal interactions. For example, after arguing against proselytism, Pagan author Taylor Ellwood (2003) writes: "Some of the media exposure is good because it stimulates interest in the occult, but even that exposure does not necessarily tell people the truth about the beliefs we hold." I question this sentiment because the desire to "stimulate interest" in Wicca seems to contradict his earlier anti-conversion polemic.

Subtle proselytization activities, such as Ellwood's example of "stimulating interest" and actively attempting to explain the "truth" about Wicca, often originate as a reaction against anti-Wiccan propaganda—in an attempt to counter negative views, to combat intolerance, and to gain legitimacy. A major reason for including introductory explanations about Wicca on Wiccan websites is to convince the mostly uninformed public to change some aspects of their previous beliefs and to change the cultural landscape in which those beliefs belong or proliferate. This tendency is not necessarily a conventional form of proselytization; however, the fact that many Wiccans are actively working to change the perceptions of Christians in particular does indicate implicit proselytism.

The reason for this is because Christian ideas about and criticisms of Wicca are firmly grounded in particular beliefs and interpretations of biblical text. In other words, Christian anti-Wiccan ideas can accurately be understood as specific "religious beliefs." Furthermore, I consider that for many Christians to suddenly, or gradually, accept the validity of Wicca as a legitimate religion requires a radical shift in certain religious beliefs, even if that shift is only away from a misinformed perspective. This radical shift is indicative of a type of religious conversion called "consolidation" because it begins to integrate two contradictory worldviews (see Snow and Machalek 1984, 169).

Although most Wiccans do not want to cause people from other religions to become Wiccan themselves, they often *do* want people from other religions, especially those religions that actively denigrate Wicca, to change their religiously-derived perceptions about Wicca and to accept it as a legitimate religious tradition worthy of respect. Some websites even go so far as to argue that certain Christians misunderstand and misuse the Bible when critiquing Wicca.[19] Therefore, it is my contention that the general Wiccan goal to change people's anti-Wiccan perspectives through public Pagan Pride celebrations and online Wiccan apologetics is a form of proselytization, because the practice amounts to significantly changing peoples' religious beliefs.

I am not arguing against Wiccans' desires to legitimize themselves in a society that often discriminates against them; I only highlight one interpretation of the implications of this practice. I also realize that changing people's perspectives happens regularly throughout all aspects of life—whether one tries to convince a friend of the benefits of one's preferred political party or the merits of one's favorite sports team. It seems though that where religious beliefs are concerned, conversion rhetoric takes on a heightened tone. Furthermore, Wiccan perspectives on proselytization are clearly beginning to evolve—especially as Wiccan apologetics develops. Although many Wiccans actively decry the idea of proselytization as a means of community growth, popular Wiccan author Lilith McLellan tellingly discusses in a recent book the "proper way" to "proselytize gently" when someone enquires about the religion (2002, 179).

In this regard, proselytization to convert others to Wiccan religious practices is not a major goal, yet proselytization meant to convert others into "believing" that Wicca is a real, legitimate, beneficial, well thought out, non-evil religion *is* a clearly stated major goal.[20] In fact, these practices directly relate to my definition of "proselytism" as the persuasive attempt to change another person's pre-existing religious beliefs and commitments.

To what end is conversion possible via the Internet?

As Barney Warf and John Grimes rightly argue, the "Internet is neither inherently oppressive nor automatically emancipatory; it is a terrain of contested philosophies and politics" (1997, 259). The Internet is definitely being used for advertising, for information-dissemination, for proselytization, and to disseminate religious propaganda. Recognizing the regularity with which one finds proselytization activities on religiously-oriented websites, one must also ask about the effectiveness of these strategies. I argue that two distinct varieties of conversion are present in online interactions: first, conversion to a religious tradition; and second, conversion (whether for good or ill) to certain perceptions of, beliefs about, or attitudes toward a specific religious tradition.

Regarding the possibility for Internet-mediated conversion, information and communication in cyberspace may facilitate conversion attempts, but there are a few important variables that need to be addressed. First, it seems that people who are actively seeking personal self-transformation, a new spiritual practice, or acceptance in a group are more likely to be amenable to undergoing the conversion process (Long and Hadden 1983, 6). For example, a new Wiccan named Jodie was seeking nature-related religious practices when she found Wicca. She told Helen A. Berger and Douglas Ezzy, "I actually felt 'Oh no, not witchcraft. It's evil.' [Laughs] But the more I researched the more [I felt comfortable with it]" (2004, 180–1). This is also a good representation of how well Wiccan apologetics works—Jodie's perceptions of Wicca were completely transformed from fear to acceptance through her interactions with Wiccan websites.

Second, a face-to-face social network remains integral to the conversion process if converts are expected to remain group members with long-term commitments (Dawson and Hennebry 2004, 153, 161; Long and Hadden 1983, 6; Mayer 2000, 254, 268; Snow and Machalek 1984, 180, 182–83). Seekers of religion or religious experience may be able to initiate contact with extant groups, but only a small percentage will have their first introduction to a new set of beliefs in cyberspace, and fewer still will become converts via, or primarily due to, information found on the Internet (Mayer 2000, 252–53; Dawson and Cowan 2004, 7; Berger and Ezzy 2004, 176). In other words, without sufficient personal interactions to supplement information gained on websites, and given the fact that potential converts exercise selectivity in their adoption and practice of beliefs and rituals, Internet-based conversions are unlikely to develop into long-lasting commitments (see Kao this volume; Horsfall 2000, 173–74).

Third, it seems that religious websites generally attract like-minded individuals or those seeking information about specific groups or religions. If web surfers are not motivated to seek religious information or religiously-themed products, they will be highly unlikely to interact with religious websites or religious advertising (Varisco 2000, 4). Even when a message intended for advertising or proselytization is encountered, if the viewer is not previously amenable to the message it generally will be overlooked or ignored.

With the ability to create religiously-oriented social support networks comes the capacity for religious conversion (Hadden and Cowan 2000, 19), yet most researchers have been skeptical about the ability of religious groups to convert others solely through Internet-based information and virtual communities. After examining recruitment efficiency, Jean-François Mayer and others conclude that, although proselytization occurs online, and may lead people to seek further information and face-to-face communication, there is little evidence to support early trepidations that the Internet is a powerful medium for creating and maintaining converts (Mayer 2000, 252, 268; see also Campbell 2004, 118; Dawson and Hennebry 2004, 153, 161; Horsfall 2000, 173–74, 180; Howard 2005, 172, 181; Long and Hadden 1983, 6; Snow and Machalek 1984, 178).[21] In fact, Howard's research indicates that Christian websites built for missionary purposes were only marginally successful (2005, 181). Rather than having many desired converts, most of the people who contacted the website creators professed to be Christians expressing admiration of the websites and reaffirmations of their own faith.

On the other hand, when we explore the phenomenon of proselytism aimed at changing peoples' ideas and beliefs about a religious tradition, such as with Jodie's example above, I find that this type of conversion is increasingly commonplace on the Internet. Exploring a variety of communication forums and online testimonials, researchers easily can find examples of how effectively online proselytization tactics—such as information-dissemination, advertising, and apologetics—actually attain their desired outcome. Persuasive language and other aspects of websites, such as the aesthetic quality and perceived authority of the creators, can and do influence audiences' perspectives about a religion or group.

In other words, whilst converting to a different religious tradition via the Internet is not as widespread as once anticipated, online conversion of perception and belief does seem to be relatively commonplace. Furthermore, as Horsfall recognizes:

> [w]hereas the Web material is unlikely to convince anyone who does not want to be convinced, it is a powerful resource for the novice. Potential believers can read and study religious material on-line, using it to help them make important decisions, which are likely to then be shared with others.
>
> (2000, 180).

In addition to providing information for newcomers, many religious groups actively proselytize using the Internet in the hopes of gaining converts. From Scientology to Wicca to the myriad forms of Christianity, these groups—and individuals associated with them—regularly create and maintain websites meant to elicit interest among visitors, to promote their own legitimacy, and ultimately to attract possible converts. This indicates that differences along the continuum from information-dissemination to advertising to proselytism are becoming increasingly blurred. It is my contention that the growth of online religious advertising and public education about particular religions by their members is actively engendering implicit *and* explicit forms of proselytizing. These public relations motivations, enacted through a variety of "persuasion engineering" techniques, marketing strategies, and apologetics meant to promote a sympathetic portrayal of the religious group and its legitimacy, while negating oppositional views, is an increasingly prevalent form of proselytic message, for which the Internet is now the central medium.

Notes

1. On a peripheral note, it would be interesting to reflect upon the similar functions of spam (mass, anonymous, advertising) e-mails in secular cyberspace. Special thanks to Dr. Hannah Sanders for our insightful discussions regarding the topic of this essay.

2. In a similar fashion, Douglas E. Cowan defines the related term "propaganda" as "a systematic, ideologically driven, action-oriented manipulation and dissemination of information, which is (a) designed for a specific target audience, and (b) intended to influence the beliefs and behaviors of that audience in a manner consonant with the aims and objectives of the propagandist" (Cowan 1999, 161–70 as quoted in Cowan 2004, 259). Using the idea of propaganda instead of proselytism, Jean-François Mayer argues that the concept of "*cyberspace propaganda wars*" is particularly useful and appropriate for understanding the dynamics of the struggle of religious movements to define themselves and relate to their audiences on the Internet (Mayer 2000, 250).

3. All of the websites mentioned throughout this essay were last accessed on November 1, 2005.

4. My research has found many information-only websites, but few that are created and maintained by religious organizations—the reasons for this will be discussed shortly. The best example of a non-religious informative website about religion is hosted by the Ontario Consultants on Religious Tolerance (www.religioustolerance.org), although it too has a specific agenda: to present the most objective, balanced views possible in order to promote religious tolerance (Robinson 2000). This website contains hundreds of well-researched articles on a wide variety of religious traditions and religious debates, and the writers work to provide both insider and outsider perspectives in their attempts to present objective discussions. Other sites such as beliefnet.com contain articles by practitioners, and these are not as objective or well-researched as those by the OCRT.

5. It must be noted that virtually anyone with a computer, Internet access, and the desire to share their beliefs could create and maintain a popular website; therefore, the veracity and accuracy of these websites should be viewed with suspicion (see Dawson and Cowan 2004, 2; Horsfall 2000, 179).

6. By "creator" I mean the person (or persons) who wrote and produced the website. I also use the term "author" to indicate this person when I refer to the composition of textual information as presented (published) on a website.

7. A Wiccan friend, who owns an online store for Wiccan and Pagan merchandise, has often expressed to me in conversation that she has numerous people write to her through her website asking many questions about Wicca, asking to join a Wiccan study group, and asking her to teach and initiate them into the Wiccan religion. Another good example is provided by one of Sara Horsfall's informants who explained that although his website is intended for information only, many people write to him asking to teach more about Catholicism and to help them in the conversion process (2000, 157).

8. For example, Shari Eicher, an 11th grade public school teacher in North Carolina, lost her job in 2000 after students were found looking at her group's Wiccan website on which were posted naked pictures of group members during a ritual celebration. Eicher was accused of advertising for her Wiccan group via this website and attempting to solicit converts (www. religioustolerance.org/news_00jan.htm; see also Long and Hadden 1983, 8).

9. The Witches' League for Public Awareness (www.celticcrow.com) and the Pagan Awareness League were begun as community outreach programs, and they initiated the first Pagan Pride events on September 19, 1998 (O'Horan 2005, 3). Pagan Pride events function as reaffirmations of belief and commitments to community for Wiccans and Pagans themselves, but also as missionary-style programs that increase public awareness, provide community outreach and public relations performance, educate non-members about Wicca and Paganism as religions, and attempt to change the negative perceptions of outsiders.

10. One site was a Pagan-owned store with Wiccan books and paraphernalia, but it did not contain information about Wicca or apologetic rhetoric. The search actually yielded 3,250,000 hits, of which I investigated the first forty. Of these forty, twenty were owned and run by Wiccans or Pagans, eleven were non-Wiccan stores or informational sites (such as Amazon.com and Religioustolerance.org), two links did not function, and seven were anti-Wiccan Christian websites.

11. Other examples include: In Defense of Wicca (www.holysmoke.org/wicca/wicca_defense.html), The Church and School of Wicca (www.wicca.org), and Amethyst's Wicca (www.angelfire.com/realm2/amethystbt). It must be noted that this is an understandable practice given the discrimination that many Wiccans face for practicing their marginalized and misunderstood religion.

12. Examples of self-promotion in the subtle attempt to claim authority and legitimacy include: providing autobiographical content about the length of one's affiliation with the group or religion, posting awards that the website has received, posting positive comments that have been sent to the site, and including visitor counters to show how many people have visited the site—a large number of visitors can indicate to an audience that many people view the site as legitimate and authoritative.

13. One of the most interesting aspects of website aesthetics is that technical ability to create a pleasing-looking website has nothing at all to do with the creator's actual expertise regarding the content of the website. A sophisticated, impressive website can positively

affect a group's legitimacy; however, the resulting authority associated with the website may be displaced (Horsfall 2000, 175; Mayer 2000, 253). For example, although the "Wiccan Ring" website (http://o.webring.com/hub?ring=wicca_ring) has a professional look and has 179 websites linked to it, the site also includes the following statement of purpose: "Dedicated to wiccans of all king [*sic*] and there [*sic*] websites, The wicca ring is always welcoming to new sites and wiccans looking for more info." This quote's misspellings, improper punctuation, and lack of capitalization are part of the original text and can indicate to readers a relative lack of maturity and authority that might outweigh other positive qualities.

14. Of my November 1, 2005 Google.com search, four of twenty websites included invitations to join a religious ritual and seven included invitations to join a Wiccan group or a training class; however, eighteen included invitations to explore the website and seventeen contained direct invitations to contact the website host with any questions that the visitor might have.

15. With this line of reasoning, I am not implying that all website creators are acutely aware of all aspects of their creations, yet they are aware, at least intuitively, of the attractive features of websites that they have visited.

16. However, I would postulate that many website creators do not actively think about or plan a strategy in creating their websites; they instead pattern their creations on the types of experiences that they themselves like to encounter on a website and on feedback from the interactive elements of their creations.

17. For example, see the "Children of Artemis" website at http://www.witchcraft.org/ and "WiccaNet: Home of Wicca and Wiccans on the Web" at http://wiccanet.us/CMS.

18. For example, see "Amethyst's Wicca" at http://www.angelfire.com/realm2/amethystbt, "Trellix WebBuilder" at http://www.fortunecity.com/greenfield/tigris/567, and "Children of Artemis" at http://www.witchcraft.org.

19. E.g., see http://www.holysmoke.org/wicca/wicca_defense.html [accessed 9/28/2005].

20. For example, Ryynänen (2000) claims that Wiccans should not proselytize, but they *should* provide ample evidence "to prove that your religion is as good as you say." This is a typical example of Wiccan anti-proselytism rhetoric that also includes the desire to convince others of the legitimacy Wiccan perspectives.

21. It should be noted that activities such as the performance and receipt of psychotherapy treatments via the Internet implies that conversion and the radical changing of ideas is entirely possible if the receiver of these ideas is either amenable to or predisposed to such changes (see Miller and Gergen 1998).

References

Aloi, Peg. 2002. Heaven's Gate 3. In Adult Pagan Essay Series on The Witches' Voice. http://www.witchvox.com/va/dt_va.html?a=usma&c=cases&id=4890 [Accessed on 9/28/2005].

Anonymous. 2001. Net Witness. *Your Church* 47(1): 9.

Arthur, Shawn. 2002. Technophilia and Nature Religion: the Growth of a Paradox. *Religion*, 32(4): 305–16.

Beardslee, William A. 1993. Poststructuralist Criticism. In *To Each Its Own Meaning: An Introduction to Biblical Criticisms and their Application*, ed. Steven L. McKenzie and Stephen R. Haynes, 221–36. Louisville, KY: Westminster/ John Knox Press.

Berger, Helen A. and Douglas Ezzy. 2004. The Internet as Virtual Spiritual Community: Teen Witches in the United States and Australia. In *Religion Online: Finding Faith on the Internet*, ed. Lorne L. Dawson and Douglas E. Cowan, 175–88. New York: Routledge.

Campbell, Heidi. 2004. "This Is My Church:" Seeing Internet and Club Culture as Spiritual Spaces. In *Religion Online: Finding Faith on the Internet*, ed. Lorne L. Dawson and Douglas E. Cowan, 107–21. New York: Routledge.

Cowan, Douglas E. 2004. Contested Spaces: Movement, Countermovement, and E-Space Propaganda. In *Religion Online: Finding Faith on the Internet*, ed. Lorne L. Dawson and Douglas E. Cowan, 255–71. New York: Routledge.

———. 2005. Online U-Topia: Cyberspace and the Mythology of Placelessness. *Journal for the Scientific Study of Religion* 44(3): 257–63.

Dawson, Lorne L. and Douglas E. Cowan. 2004. Introduction in *Religion Online: Finding Faith on the Internet*, ed. Lorne L. Dawson and Douglas E. Cowan, 1–16. New York: Routledge.

Dawson, Lorne L. and Jenna Hennebry. 2004. New Religions and the Internet: Recruiting in a New Public Space. In *Religion Online: Finding Faith on the Internet*, ed. Lorne L. Dawson and Douglas E. Cowan, 151–73. New York: Routledge.

Ellwood, Taylor. 2003. Our Spiritual Rights and Public Perception. In Adult Pagan Essay Series on The Witches' Voice. http://www.witchvox.com/va/dt_va.html?a=usoh&c= words&id=7539 [Accessed on 9/28/2005].

Fernback, Jan. 2002. Internet Ritual: A Case Study of the Construction of Computer-Mediated Neopagan Religious Meaning. In *Practicing Religion in the Age of the Media*, ed. Stewart M. Hoover and Lynn Schofield Clark, 254–75. New York: Columbia University Press.

Freedman, David H. 2005. The Future of Advertising is Here. *Inc. Magazine* 27(8): 70–77.

Griffiths, Paul J. 2002. Proselytizing for Tolerance: Part I. *First Things: A Monthly Journal of Religious and Public Life* 11: 30–34.

Hadden, Jeffrey K. and Douglas E. Cowan. 2000. The Promised Land or Electronic Chaos? Toward Understanding Religion on the Internet. In *Religion on the Internet: Research Prospects and Promises*, vol. 8, ed. Jeffrey K. Hadden and Douglas E. Cowan, 3–21. New York: Elsevier Science/JAI Press.

Harris, Grove. 2005. Pagan Involvement in the Interfaith Movement: Exclusion,

Dualities, and Contributions. *Crosscurrents* 55(1):66–76.

Helland, Christopher. 2004. Popular Religion and the World Wide Web: A Match Made in (Cyber) Heaven. In *Religion Online: Finding Faith on the Internet*, ed. Lorne L. Dawson and Douglas E. Cowan, 23–35. New York: Routledge.

Horsfall, Sara. 2000. How Religious Organizations Use the Internet: A Preliminary Inquiry. In *Religion on the Internet: Research Prospects and Promises*, vol. 8, ed. Jeffrey K. Hadden and Douglas E. Cowan, 153–82. New York: Elsevier Science.

Howard, Robert Glenn. 2005. A Theory of Vernacular Rhetoric: The Case of the "Sinner's Prayer" Online. *Folklore* 116: 172–88.

Kao, Grace Y. The Logic of Anti-Proselytization, Revisited. In *Proselytization Revisited: Rights Talk, Free Markets and Culture Wars*, ed. Rosalind I.J. Hackett, 77–108. London: Equinox.

Ko Hanjun, Chang-hoan Cho, and Marilyn S. Rogers. 2005. Internet Uses and Gratifications: A Structural Equation Model of Interactive Advertising. *Journal of Advertising* 34(2): 57–70.

Larsen, Elena. 2004. Cyberfaith: How Americans Pursue Religion Online. In *Religion Online: Finding Faith on the Internet*, ed. Lorne L. Dawson and Douglas E. Cowan, 17–20. New York: Routledge.

Lature, Dale. 1995. The Ecunet '95 Conference represented a kind of collage of the deepest influence on my life. http://theoblogical.org/dlature/united/ph2paper/wt2ecu95.html [accessed on 9/25/2005].

Lénárt-Cheng, Helga. 2003. Autobiography As Advertisement: Why Do Gertrude Stein's Sentences Get Under Our Skin? *New Literary History* 34: 117–31.

Lindholm, Tore, W. Cole Durham Jr., and Bahia G. Tahzib-Lie. 2004. Proselytism and Cultural Integrity. In *Facilitating Freedom of Religion or Belief: A Deskbook*, ed. Tore Lindholm, W. Cole Durham Jr., and Bahia G. Tahzib-Lie, 651–68. Oslo, Norway: Martinus Nijhoff.

Long, Theodore E. and Jeffrey K. Hadden. 1983. Religious Conversion and the Concept of Socialization: Integrating the Brainwashing and Drift Models. *Journal for the Scientific Study of Religion* 22(1): 1–14.

Lord, Andrew M. 2002. Virtual Communities and Mission. *Evangelical review of Theology* 26(3): 196–207.

Mayer, Jean-François. 2000. Religious Movements and the Internet: the New Frontier of Cult Controversies. In *Religion on the Internet: Research Prospects and Promises*, vol. 8, ed, Jeffrey K. Hadden and Douglas E. Cowan, 249–76. New York: Elsevier Science.

———. Conflicts of Proselytism: An Overview and Comparative Assessment. In *Proselytization Revisited: Rights Talk, Free Markets and Culture Wars*, ed. Rosalind I.J. Hackett, 35–52. London: Equinox.

McKnight, Edgar. 1993. Reader-Response Criticism. In *To Each Its Own Meaning: An Introduction to Biblical Criticisms and their Application*, ed. Steven L. McKenzie and Stephen R. Haynes, 197–220. Louisville, KY: Westminster/ John Knox Press.

McLelland, Lilith. 2002. *Out of the Shadows: Myths and Truths of Modern Wicca*. New York: Citadel Press.

Miller, John K. and Kenneth J. Gergen. 1998. Life on the Line: the Therapeutic Potentials of Computer-mediated Conversation. *Journal of Marital and Family Therapy* 24(2): 189–202.

Nash, David. 2002. Religious Sensibilities in the Age of the Internet: Freethought Culture and the Historical Context of Communication Media. In *Practicing Religion in the Age of the Media*, ed. Stewart M. Hoover and Lynn Schofield Clark, 276–90. New York: Columbia University Press.

O'Horan, Kevin. 2005. Pagans seek to inform and to connect. *Herald Tribune*, September 22. www.heraldtribune.com [Accessed 9/28/2005].

Pan. 2005. Our Foundations Won't Support Traditional Structures. In Adult Pagan Essay Series on The Witches' Voice. http://www.witchvox.com/va/dt_va.html?a=usga&c=words&id=8979 [Accessed 9/28/2005].

Patte, Daniel. 1993. Structural Criticism. In *To Each Its Own Meaning: An Introduction to Biblical Criticisms and their Application*, ed. Steven L. McKenzie and Stephen R. Haynes, 153–70. Louisville, KY: Westminster/John Knox Press.

Robinson, Bruce A. 2000. Evolution of a Religious Web Site Devoted to Tolerance. In *Religion on the Internet: Research Prospects and Promises*, vol. 8, ed. Jeffrey K. Hadden and Douglas E. Cowan, 309–23. New York: Elsevier Science.

Ryynänen, Otto. 2000. The Broom Closet–In or Out? In Adult Pagan Essay Series on The Witches' Voice. http://www.witchvox.com/va/dt_va.html?a=usxx&c=words&id=2685 [Accessed 9/28/2005].

Senter, Mark H., III. 2002. Napster, Moody Bible Institute and Christianity Online. *Evangelical Review of Theology* 26(3): 223–28.

Snow, David A. and Richard Machalek. 1984. The Sociology of Conversion. *Annual Review of Sociology* 10: 167–90.

Stalnaker, Cecil. 2002. Proselytism or Evangelism? *Evangelical Review of Theology* 26(4): 337–53.

Uzzell, Lawrence A. 2004. Don't Call it Proselytism. *First Things: A Monthly Journal of Religious and Public Life* 10: 14–16.

Varisco, Daniel Martin. 2000. Slamming Islam: Participant Webservation with a Web of Meanings to Boot. www.aaanet.org/mes/lectvar1.html [Accessed 9/19/2005].

Warf, Barney and John Grimes. 1997. Counterhegemonic Discourses and the Internet. *Geographical Review* 87(2): 259–74.

CHAPTER 18

You Can't Talk to an Empty Stomach: Faith-based Activism, Holistic Evangelism, and the Publicity of Evangelical Engagement

Omri Elisha

The political currency of faith-based welfare activism reflects remarkable cultural trends in American evangelicalism in recent decades, particularly with regard to how evangelical activists approach the issue of proselytism. In addition to major gains in congregational growth, political influence, and media exposure, contemporary born-again evangelicals enjoy high levels of socioeconomic and educational mobility. At least one outcome of this trend is a growing concern to practice evangelism in ways that conform to prevailing middle-class norms of social respectability and tact. Many evangelicals are sensitive to the fact that non-evangelicals view some of the most common forms of proselytizing—such as door-to-door witnessing (or "visitation evangelism")—with ridicule and scorn. They are conscious of negative stereotypes that portray their efforts to "save souls" as intolerant, naïve, and manipulative, even predatory. Although the provocative and impersonal methods of "spreading the gospel" that have long fueled such stereotypes continue to exist, modern evangelicals are increasingly moving toward new styles of evangelism that stress the importance of interpersonal relationships predicated on reciprocity, compassion, and trust.[1] In this light, it is easy to see why evangelicals in the post-welfare era have hailed the discourse of "faith-based initiatives" as a golden opportunity to advance the cause of Christian evangelism. Such initiatives (federal, state, and local) are viewed by many evangelicals as consistent with their key moral and theological tenets, and perhaps more importantly, they are seen as paving the way for proselytic practices that are holistic, philanthropic, and deemed socially acceptable.

In this essay I discuss *faith-based activism* as an emerging and controversial field of evangelical social engagement. The field is not strictly limited to the mobilization of tax revenues for religious charities, though this has been its most public face. My use of the term encompasses a wide range of evangelical practices, including church-based outreach ministries, Christian charities, philanthropies, and social service organizations, and community development initiatives. Faith-based activism also involves various levels of strategic discourse that are used to mobilize local churches to increase their participation in welfare projects. Such projects seek to improve the lives of poor and distressed people, while promoting moral and spiritual renewal in a broader sense as well. Through such efforts, faith-based activists are implicated in larger political and cultural efforts of the Christian Right to enhance the public profile of evangelical communities as arbiters of social welfare and moral governance.

Consensus around faith-based activism is far from uniform throughout the evangelical subculture. Theologically and politically conservative evangelicals, a powerful constituency of leaders and churchgoers, are known to express considerable ambivalence. In the eyes of many conservative evangelicals, who are predominantly white, too much social engagement at the expense of active proselytization is a potentially dangerous accommodation to secular humanism. However, since the implementation of federal welfare reform in the 1990s—a political triumph for the religious right—faith-based organizations have come to be seen as viable substitutions for the welfare state, and moderate as well as conservative evangelicals are seizing the cultural moment. The post-welfare public sphere has become saturated with distinctly evangelical models of civic responsibility, inspiring evangelicals to become more socially engaged and thus more public with their religiosity.

One of the main mobilization strategies of evangelical faith-based activists is to establish direct conceptual links between social engagement and evangelism. Coining concepts such as "servant evangelism" and "holistic ministry," evangelical activists seek to convince their fellow believers that effective proselytism can involve more than just preaching and verbal witnessing. They argue that elevating faith-based activism to the same ideological prominence normally reserved for rhetorical strategies of conversion would allow the evangelical community as a whole to have a deeper social, moral, and ultimately spiritual impact in the world, thereby embodying a fuller and theologically "authentic" adherence to the Word of God.

In what follows, I analyze the discourse and practices of faith-based activism at the literary, theological, and grassroots level, situating my analysis in the contemporary political-historical moment. I argue that, beyond the mere desire to bring nonbelievers into the kingdom of God, the cultural politics of faith-based activism is also linked to a diffuse but crucial aspect of evangelism, which I call cultural Christianization. Evangelical activists are engaged in cultural Christianization because their goal-oriented, apostolic practices are fundamentally (if often implicitly) geared toward transforming public culture into a space of missionary intervention. At least one implication of this for analyzing evangelical proselytism in the U.S. is that even while it is ostensibly driven by the singular motive to "save individual souls" before the Second Coming, the cultural practices attending Christian evangelism are also implicated in collective efforts to reconstitute civil society. This reconstitution involves elevating the publicity of evangelical orthodoxy, as well as seeking to create the conditions under which evangelical orthodoxy replaces secular liberalism as the prevailing norm of moral governance in American life.

Evangelical congregations are of course no strangers to the work of charity and social outreach. The biblical mandate to care for "the least of these" is as old as the church itself. Ministries to the poor, distressed, and disabled have always been a central aspect of Christian religiosity, and a wide variety of such ministries exist among American congregations today (Cnaan 2002). Partnerships between church and state have also been quite common in the welfare arena for many years. Long before it became politically meaningful to rally under the banner of faith-based initiatives, government agencies regularly outsourced social services to religious organizations, such as homeless shelters and rehabilitation programs. However, social ministries are regarded with skepticism by the more conservative elements of evangelicalism. Conservative evangelicals view traditional missionary activities as far more deserving of church resources, and many would rather not see their proselytizing efforts hampered in any way by the restrictions of taxpayer funding. Moreover, certain aspects of evangelical social engagement are, for conservative evangelicals, reminiscent of the secular humanism they associate with progressive politics and the liberalism of the Social Gospel, which they view with contempt.

The social conscience of evangelicals has re-awakened in recent years, apace with a steady rise in mobilization literature and para-church organizations that address social concerns and encourage evangelical pastors and congregations to take proactive roles with regard to community welfare. Dedicated advocates of faith-based activism remain a relative minority among evangelicals, but their voices are gradually gaining strength and reaching wider audiences. To the extent that their message of social engagement resonates for conservative evangelicals it is largely because they are able to couch their rhetoric solidly within a rubric of evangelism, one that deliberately brings together "Word" and "deeds" in a holistic approach to proselytism. Armed with conservative Protestant notions of biblical orthodoxy, a firmly Christ-centered view of salvation, and a strong emphasis on the experiential dimensions of religious conversion and piety, evangelical activists give equal weight to what they see as the prophetic virtues of Christianity's social teachings. In so doing, they promote a manner of evangelical social engagement that, while rarely conducive to radical social reform, transcends the moral individualism usually associated with evangelical theology, in favor of practices that carry broader implications and presuppose larger religious, political, and cultural transformations. Faith-based activism, like all missionary enterprises, seeks not just religious but social change in a most profound sense (cf. Beidelman 1982).

Political-historical context

The recent dismantling of the welfare state developed as a result of more than sixty years of conservative opposition to federal entitlement policies established under the New Deal in the 1930s and elaborated in the Great Society program of the 1960s (both under Democratic administrations). In the 1980s, President Ronald Reagan made drastic cuts in federal welfare spending, initiating a gradual withdrawal of the state from the business of welfare. Conservatives justified the shift in policy by inveighing against the bureaucratic evils of "big government" and accusing liberal do-gooders of "enabling" wastefulness and encouraging "welfare queens" (a pejorative and racially charged stereotype). With U.S. politics moving steadily toward neo-liberal reforms that included the privatization of welfare, conservative evangelicals—who had already become a political force to be reckoned with —were drawn to the cause. The evangelical base of the "new Christian Right" shared (and continues to share) strong affinities with conservative political movements that seek to promote free-market capitalism and its supposed moral virtues, including individual accountability and limited government. With a penchant for moral individualism, and nostalgia for an imagined national past free of the taint of secularism, conservative evangelicals had few qualms about their increasingly solid alliance with the Republican Party.

In the 1980s and 1990s, conservative reformers pushed federal regulations that allowed private nonprofits, especially faith-based organizations, to become "an integral and necessary part of the local service system's resource base and partners in the design and delivery of services" (Cnaan 1999, 15). The prospect of reforming federal welfare altogether was a burgeoning moral crusade that benefited from an impressive grassroots infrastructure of parachurch organizations and political action committees (PACs). Conservative Christian leaders recognized the welfare debate as a strategic battleground in the so-called "culture wars." Their public rhetoric deftly combined the language of democratic pluralism with uncompromising assertions that religious (read: Christian) charity organizations are inherently superior to state agencies and secular charities in the provision of social services.

Among the most vocal proponents of this viewpoint was Marvin Olasky, a conservative evangelical ideologue and publisher of the magazine *World*. In his influential book, *The Tragedy of American Compassion* (1992), Olasky argued that the history of American charity reveals that religious organizations are best suited to serve the welfare needs of local communities. Relying on a revisionist historical narrative, Olasky extols the virtues of private, community-based forms of caregiving that, prior to government intervention, were thriving and efficient because they were free to exercise "compassion" with unfettered authority and according to biblical standards of accountability and moral worth. By providing a means of articulating conservative objections to government welfare, *The Tragedy of American Compassion* played a crucial role leading up to the welfare reform in the 1990s.[2]

In 1996, Democratic President Bill Clinton signed the Personal Responsibility and Work Opportunity Reconciliation Act into law. This legislation drastically reduced federal welfare spending, imposed limits and restrictions on government aid in order to reduce the welfare rolls and encourage aid-seekers to find jobs, shifted regulatory control to state and local agencies, and facilitated increased privatization of social services. A controversial provision known as Charitable Choice (section 104) allows faith-based organizations to compete with secular organizations for federal grants. Charitable Choice, written into the bill by Senator John Ashcroft (a Pentecostal who later became U.S. Attorney General under President George W. Bush), provoked heated debates over the separation of church and state. Despite legal and ethical controversies surrounding Charitable Choice, politicians and religious leaders from across the ideological spectrum recognized that public opinion was gravitating around the idea that faith-based organizations might prove particularly effective for alleviating social problems such as poverty, unemployment, substance abuse, and risk activity among youth. In 2000, all of the major presidential candidates voiced unqualified support for the work of faith-based organizations.

Following the 2000 election, one of George W. Bush's first executive acts was to create the White House Office of Faith-Based and Community Initiatives. The new department established faith-based centers in five cabinet agencies (Departments of Education, Health and Human Services, Housing and Urban Development, Justice, and Labor) in order to channel public funds to faith-based organizations and facilitate collaboration between poli-cymakers and religious leaders in developing new policy proposals.[3] Bush, an evangelical himself, frequently credits the role of faith in his own recovery from alcoholism. His push to create a "level playing field" for faith-based and secular service providers to compete for federal grants is motivated in large part by his belief that religious agencies are often better suited to help the poor and needy. A number of prominent evangelical leaders and activists were closely involved in the implementation of Bush's faith-based initiatives (Sherman 2003, 158).

Despite popular approval for faith-based activism in principle, federal initiatives have met political resistance. First Amendment advocates remain opposed to Charitable Choice on the grounds that it violates the constitu-tional separation of church and state. Aside from questioning the constitu-tionality of state funds going to religious institutions—even if, as current law stipulates, the funds are never used for "inherently religious activities"—church-state separationists are particularly vigilant about federal legislative efforts to expand Charitable Choice to allow faith-based organizations to express their religious character more openly, particularly in terms of meth-odology and hiring standards. In the face of negative publicity and the threat of legal challenges to federally subsidized religious proselytization and job discrimination, Congress has yet to pass any of these legislative efforts.

Christian conservatives, despite general optimism, have been cautious in their support of federal faith-based initiatives, largely out of concern that federal restrictions will force faith-based organizations to modify the spiritual component of their work. Even staunch advocates like Marvin Olasky, who championed the expansion of Charitable Choice during the 2000 elections, have since urged religious leaders that public funding for faith-based organi-zations will be a "fatal compromise" if government officials will be allowed to influence or dictate "the form or frequency of preaching, teaching, and prayer in a faith-based grant program."[4] While such concerns reflect conservative anti-statist attitudes, they also highlight the degree to which evangelicals value the holistic approach to social service that sectarian faith-based organi-zations see as the core of their mission. For evangelical faith-based activists, altruistic ministries cannot be dissociated from the religious ideals that are believed to be the source of their efficacy.[5]

In 2002, President Bush issued an executive order dictating that faith-based organizations receiving government aid may openly express their religious character and use religious criteria in making hiring decisions. The order also stipulated that faith-based organizations cannot discriminate against clients on the basis of religious faith, and that any "inherently religious activities" must be voluntary and be held separately from the services funded by taxpayer dollars. While only partially satisfying the demands of conservatives, the executive order (which has yet to face any serious political or legal challenge) reflects a political climate favorable to government facilitation and non-intervention with regard to religious expression in public settings. The long-term implications are already evident. According to federal estimates from 2004 alone, faith-based organizations and church outreach ministries, including homeless shelters, health clinics, youth programs, and housing agencies, received over $2 billion in social service grants and state contracts.

The politics of faith-based activism are undoubtedly historically and culturally significant, despite ongoing discord and disappointment among religious leaders. From the point of view of many religious and community activists at the local level, federal faith-based initiatives have so far failed to live up to expectations. This is especially true for African-American activists, who were ardent supporters at first because they had the most to gain in terms of resources but remain frustrated by a lack of political support for their own grassroots programs. However, what is clear is that religious involvement in the business of welfare has regained its social prominence, which Christian conservatives believe was previously undermined by the welfare state. Evangelical activists, many of whom do not even agree with every policy aspect, are ideologically invested in the discourse that has emerged in religious and secular media as well as among political, philanthropic, and academic institutions about the social benefits of religious interventions in the welfare arena. Although studies have suggested that conservative evangelical churches are among the least likely to apply for government grants (Bartkowski and Regis 2003; Chaves 1999), survey research has also shown that support for government funding of church-based social services is relatively strong among evangelicals and other Christian conservatives (Wuthnow 2004, 291–96). Welfare privatization has opened up new spaces of discourse and ministry opportunities for evangelical activists, who are, by definition, implicated in proselytic ventures of one kind or another.

As they develop and promote new partnerships and styles of civic-religious engagement, evangelicals believe they are sowing the seeds of cultural Christianization in the fertile ground of an evolving neo-liberal public sphere. Increasingly, local and national coalitions are being formed around issues of social welfare, with faith-based organizations playing key roles and evangelicals, in many cases, leading the way. The cultural idiom of "faith" is, after all, a deeply rooted Protestant notion, and the principles that animate public discourse are more often than not flavored by its theological and sentimental import. Evangelicals may not be the only group with a vested interest in the politics of faith-based activism, but they are in the best position to reap the political and cultural benefits, particularly given the high public profile of evangelical faith-based organizations, coalitions, and ministries nationwide. The post-welfare era is a time of accelerated opportunity and innovation for evangelicals, who are always prepared to adapt the methods of evangelism to the changing winds.

Words and deeds

For fifteen months between 1999–2001, I conducted ethnographic fieldwork among socially engaged evangelicals in the suburbs of Knoxville, Tennessee. The subjects of my study were predominantly white evangelicals affiliated with locally prominent and theologically conservative megachurches. They included church pastors, outreach coordinators, faith-based ministry workers, lay mobilizers, and volunteers of varying levels of commitment. Few of these people would self-identify as "activists," but I describe them as such to highlight important shared characteristics among them, including goal-oriented dedication to social engagement and grassroots mobilization. They represent a small but increasingly influential movement in Knoxville (and elsewhere) of moderate and conservative evangelicals who have grown frustrated with separatism and social disengagement in their churches. They aspire toward a new kind of public religiosity, one that will lead congregations to commit greater human and financial resources to problems of social welfare, especially urban poverty, public education, healthcare, housing, and economic development.

With the exception of a few urban activists, few of the evangelicals in my study spoke about Charitable Choice, and they never seemed particularly concerned with the specifics of President Bush's faith-based initiatives. However, they clearly acknowledged that the federal government was "finally" stepping aside and allowing local communities and faith-based organizations to assume responsibility over social welfare. Coming from affluent megachurches, where human and material resources are plentiful, these evangelicals were not as interested in the availability of government aid as they were galvanized by the resurgence of religion out of the private and into the public sphere. Moreover, they were driven by a strong desire to overcome what they perceived as an atmosphere of apathy and indifference in their congregations with regard to the pressing needs of the social world beyond the sanctuary walls. From the perspective of pastors and activists, the biggest obstacle to effective outreach mobilization is middle-class complacency on the part of suburban churchgoers whom they claim are lured by materialism and status mobility rather than the radical demands of Christian piety (Elisha 2004). Activists seek to overcome such obstacles by constantly framing outreach mobilization within the idiom of evangelism, portraying social engagement not only as the right thing to do, but more importantly as an indispensable component in sustaining the vitality of the gospel message.

In 2000, an evangelical activist and former pastor named Paul Genero founded the Samaritans of Knoxville, a parachurch organization dedicated to building "bridges" between welfare needs and the resources of churches in the greater Knoxville area.[6] Aside from helping local faith-based organizations and social service agencies develop stronger ties with area churches (upon whom they are dependent for volunteers as well as financial donations), the Samaritans of Knoxville conducts mobilization workshops and provides educational resources for church pastors and outreach coordinators. The organization makes a special effort to assist and encourage lay activists in congregations where social outreach receives little attention and scant resources. Under Paul's leadership, the Samaritans of Knoxville attends to a broad range of social issues in the region, including domestic violence, care for the disabled and mentally ill, inner-city poverty, and homelessness. Paul sees himself as helping to bring about a "cultural transformation" in the region, one that he believes will result in greater numbers of Christians becoming willing "servants" of God in their communities.

Paul is a charismatic leader with an almost infectious enthusiasm for his work. It is perhaps fitting that, when offering spirited words of encouragement to his fellow activists, Paul often speaks of how local congregations will soon be "infected" with a radical desire to serve their community. Such metaphors are loaded with theological implications. In an interview, Paul described for me one of his favorite rhetorical devices for mobilization. It conveys with remarkable clarity the essence of a moral logic linking together altruistic deeds and evangelism.

> Let's look at it this way. If Jesus had come to this planet and put masking tape over his mouth, what would have been the implications of that? So the real question becomes, how important are his actions? You see him reaching out and touching the eyes of lepers —do you realize he violated every cleanliness law the Jews had when he did that? But by doing that he showed that God was serious about loving lepers, he *showed* that. Okay, so if he had masking tape over his mouth and went his whole life just touching, healing, loving people with his actions, then he would have shown us quite a bit about God. It's amazing, things that would have blown people's minds!

> But if he had come to this planet, moved the tape down and put it over his hands, so he could only talk, then the question becomes, how important were his words? Well, what his words do is they kind of tell the rest of the *story*. You know, I can learn so much about God from Jesus' actions that I never knew, but I can learn in addition so much about God from his words. You know, I can learn that he forgives sins. That's huge. His actions don't

tell me that. I can learn about heaven. His actions don't tell me that. See? So the reality is you need words *and* actions to get the whole gospel. And if you leave one out without the other you can see that it's a deficient gospel, it's a deficient message. When you do just deeds or you do just words, it's an incomplete message.

The imagery here is simple and straightforward. Paul Genero invites his listeners to imagine Jesus with masking tape alternately covering his mouth and binding his hands in order to stress the point that Jesus was in fact limited by no such constraints, that the fullness of Christ's divinity was revealed in words and deeds, and that his followers should, as the Bible says, "go and do likewise" (Luke 10:37). However, for evangelicals this ideal is not easy to put into practice, especially given the emphasis on "faith" over "works" in Protestant theology. The fear of violating the spirit of the Reformation by misidentifying "good works" as the means of salvation (an issue which conservative evangelicals see as the most crucial divide between themselves and Catholics) is felt most acutely in the evangelical community. This fear makes conservative evangelicals even more hesitant than they already are to become active in faith-based ministries. Those who are already active are careful to guard themselves, through prayer and group study, against the "deception" that righteousness and salvation might be achieved through good deeds. They warn one another against the tendency to perform acts of compassion purely out of some vague humanitarian ethic, sense of guilt, or desire to impress God. Paul Genero and other socially engaged evangelicals routinely remind anyone who will listen that "true" and "biblical" compassion is not a means to an end but rather an outgrowth of the "spiritual intimacy" that believers attain with God as a result of their justification by faith.[7]

Another source of tension for socially engaged evangelicals is the enduring influence of Christian fundamentalism among conservative congregations. Prior to their entry into the political realm, Christian fundamentalists were staunch political and cultural separatists. They commented upon the issues of the day but remained largely disengaged. The primary focus of their missionary zeal was defending biblical orthodoxy and gaining as many converts as possible before the Second Coming. Armed with the "culturally pessimistic" worldview of dispensational premillennialism, fundamentalists "had come to react against other facets of Christian life and work, such as social service and civic reform, as something done by their opponents, the liberal Social Gospelers" (Carpenter 1997, 78). There are many evangelicals today who reject the rigid separatism of the fundamentalists, but conservative evangelicals tend to share their disdain for liberal values and progressive politics. Evangelical teachings also reinforce a doctrinal emphasis on verbal and literary proselytization as preferred methods of evangelism, as opposed to social action. Furthermore, the importance of foreign missionary activity still far outweighs social outreach among conservative evangelical churches, limiting the resources available for outreach ministries, faith-based organizations, and other social initiatives. Studies have found that while theologically conservative evangelical churches are growing at a faster rate than their liberal mainline counterparts, they are "less likely than other churches to address, either politically or through community services, pressing social and economic problems," and more likely to "concentrate their energy on evangelism [i.e., proselytism and missions] or meeting the needs of congregational members" (Greenberg 2000, 389).

Evangelicalism is also rooted, however, in socially engaged revivalist traditions. The historic revivals of the nineteenth century that yielded a wide array of Christian missionary organizations and denominations also produced moral reform societies and voluntary associations promoting humanitarian concerns (Clydesdale 1990). Such enterprises were fueled by prophetic notions of human perfectibility and social uplift, and by the inspiration of leading revivalists such as Charles Grandison Finney who, while preaching the gospel in individualistic terms, viewed the social message of Christianity as an integral aspect of its redemptive power.

Socially engaged evangelicals aspire to renew this legacy through their efforts to promote holistic models of evangelism. They often quote the proverb, "Preach the gospel at all times—use words if necessary," commonly attributed to St. Francis of Assisi (although there is some question as to whether he actually coined it). This is a poignant statement, from an evangelical point of view, because it implies that qualities of human comportment matter as much, if not more, to successful evangelism as rhetoric and moral suasion. Such notions are familiar to all evangelicals, but nonetheless they remain difficult to implement on a practical level, especially since proselytism is often characterized by linguistic genres such as preaching and witnessing. How, then, do faith-based activists justify granting equal weight to words and deeds?

In their eagerness to become holistic evangelists, embodying Christian virtues of charity and compassion, socially engaged evangelicals spend a lot of time reading popular mobilization literature by renowned activists and theologians. Since most of the evangelicals that I studied in Knoxville are white suburbanites, often with very little previous exposure to the conditions of urban poverty or anti-poverty activism, they gravitate toward books written by white evangelical authors who entered the ministry field from social positions similar to their own (e.g., Bakke 1997; Lupton 1989; Sider 1999), and to a lesser extent books by black evangelical authors who have confronted social and economic struggles directly in their own lives (Perkins 1993). At once autobiographical, vocational, and theological, the books offer models for the framing of experience. Activist narratives provide a common language that merges the personal and theological, private and public, while outlining practical strategies for social engagement.

Ronald Sider, founder of Evangelicals for Social Action and author of numerous books including the bestselling *Rich Christians in an Age of Hunger* (1977), is a prominent advocate of "holistic ministry" (1999; Sider *et al.* 2002). For Sider, holistic evangelism "places spiritual nurture and social care on an equal footing from the start." He argues that evangelism is a process of "word and deed" focused on transforming nonbelievers into lifelong "disciples," rather that just converts, thus requiring that "verbal presentations of Christ's life, death, and resurrection" be combined with tangible acts of loving kindness and a sincere commitment among Christians to the principles of God's kingdom (2002, 64–67). In this scheme, biblical notions of social justice are included within the grand purview of evangelism, in addition to personalized virtues of compassion and repentance. Although Sider is conservative on hot-button "moral" issues such as abortion and homosexuality, his progressive views regarding social and economic justice have earned him the status of a "moderate" or "third-way" evangelical. Still, his influence is broad among conservative evangelicals who are involved in faith-based activism. His popularity is directly linked to the fact that his theology and sense of mission are explicitly and unapologetically "Christ-centered."

Sider notes that "holistic evangelism can take many forms," and he outlines several approaches for church strategists to adopt in reaching out to nonbelievers, including one he calls "service evangelism," or evangelism that occurs in the context of service provision (e.g. soup kitchens) or community development (e.g., Habitat for Humanity) (2002, 69). A similar approach is known as "servant evangelism," a term coined by Steve Sjogren, pastor of a Vineyard church in Cincinnati, Ohio. Sjogren defines servant evangelism as "demonstrating the kindness of God by offering to do some act of humble service with no strings attached" (1993, 17). In contrast to Sider's activist orientation, in which social reform is a factor of proselytic efficacy, Sjogren emphasizes "low risk/high grace" outreach activities such as free carwashes, health screenings, food delivery to shut-ins, collections for the poor, and giving away coffee, soda, and popsicles on street corners. While these activities are meant to be as unconditional as divine grace, they are also meant to create interpersonal bonds between believers and nonbelievers such that conversations may develop about Christian faith. Testimonial conversations are crucial, but the "acts of kindness" that precede them are paramount. In explaining the rationale behind a strategy of evangelism that relies on the efficacy of loving kindness, Sjogren writes: "The first 90 percent of bearing witness to God's love is 'precognitive.' The Holy Spirit is doing a deep work in the *heart* of the person being drawn to the Lord. It is not so much a matter of sharing *information* as sharing *love*" (1993, 17, author's emphases). While attributing agency to a divine rather than human source, this logic also privileges the role of affect over cognition in the process of conversion.

In his book, *Ministries of Mercy*, Timothy Keller, pastor of an evangelical megachurch in New York City called Redeemer Presbyterian Church, elaborates on what he sees as the church's clear directive from Jesus to meet the physical and economic needs of people in the world who are suffering or struggling to survive. He stresses that doing merciful deeds is the Christian's first responsibility, not merely because these are ways of solving people's problems but because acts of mercy are powerful expressions of the missionary imperative to proclaim God's kingdom to the world. By "feeding the hungry, comforting the suffering, [and] supporting the financially and physically weak," Christians make evident their capacities as agents of divine mercy, and in this way, Keller argues, "hearts can be softened to Christ" (Keller 1997, 55).

I cite these authors—Sider, Sjogren, and Keller—because they are among a select few who are frequently invoked as authoritative role models by evangelical activists in Knoxville and elsewhere in the U.S. Although the authors do not necessarily share identical views on theological and political issues, they collectively advocate a "word-and-deed" approach to evangelism, contributing to the emergence of a relatively coherent set of values and standards with regard to faith-based activism. A pivotal notion running throughout this discourse is that there is, or at least should be, a direct relationship between the practical immediacy of altruistic deeds, on the one hand, and the spiritual responsiveness on the part of nonbelievers to the power of the "faith" from which those deeds are said to emanate.

The softening of hearts mentioned by Keller (a ubiquitous trope in the poetics of evangelical conversion) refers, theologically speaking, to the breaking down of the willful resistance of "unbelief" so that new believers surrender themselves to "the Lordship of Christ." For this reaction to occur, it is assumed that the evangelizer must not only perform acts of kindness, but must be capable of doing so in such a way that he/she earns the trust and credibility of the recipient. From this point of view, the advantage of faith-based social services as avenues of Christian evangelism is that they are ready-made contexts for give and take, where the legitimacy of religious action is expected to be affirmed by those whose "felt needs" have been adequately served. Recipients of material and emotional support, in turn, are expected to become willing recipients of spiritual guidance. In this way, evangelicals believe, their "deepest need" will be served as well. It is significant that such moral expectations correspond to unequal power dynamics between service providers and recipients, but this issue is typically rationalized (if acknowledged at all) as a pitfall that one avoids by remaining attentive to one's motives, praying constantly, and sticking to "good theology."

In an interview I asked Kyle Anderson, an outreach coordinator at one of Knoxville's most popular suburban megachurches, how he deals with the question of evangelism in relation to social outreach. Without missing a beat, Kyle replied: "You can't talk to an empty stomach. Compassion has to come before the message." If we pursue Kyle's imagery further, the opposite of an empty stomach is one that has been fed, which is to say, one that is nourished. Nourishment figures prominently in various evangelical symbolic constructions; for example, when believers speak of the benefits of attending church services or Bible studies, they talk about "being fed" on the Word of God. Continuous indoctrination is seen as nourishing for the soul of the believer and a necessary precondition of righteousness and spiritual maturity. Kyle's statement carries this meaning and expands its implications by allowing nourishment in the literal or physiological sense to take on operative significance with regard to care for the poor, thus reaffirming the logic of holism (cf. Bartkowski and Regis 2003, 67). Food and compassion are understood as tangible manifestations of God's love (as is Jesus Christ, "the Word made flesh"), which in turn bestow legitimacy upon those who give/transmit them (the nourishers, acting on behalf/in place of Jesus). As Kyle explained to me, the intended outcome is that those who ingest/receive such nourishment are compelled to initiate the process of conversion (if they are not already believers, which I found evangelical caregivers often assume to be the case) by asking of their benefactors such questions as "Why do you care for me?" and "What is it about you that makes you so different from others?"

In short, nourished stomachs and softened hearts are means to a proselytic end, and this is a critical point with regard to how evangelicals approach faith-based activism. The popular vernacular of "faith-based" suggests that religious action can have religious motives that are separate from intrinsically religious ends, but for evangelicals this is not the case. At the same time, to suggest that converting individuals to Christianity is the sole objective of evangelical faith-based activism is an oversimplification that neglects broader reaching cultural goals and spiritual aspirations that also mobilize and shape the field.

Faith goes public

In evangelical theology, eternal salvation is achieved purely at the level of the individual. The experience of being "born again" is understood as a deeply personal interior conversion that is often described in terms of an unmediated spiritual intimacy between God and individual believers who become willing recipients of divine grace. Soteriological individualism is reinforced in most evangelical teachings and rituals. During baptism, for example, new converts are asked, "Have you accepted Jesus Christ as your *personal* Lord and Savior?" just before they are immersed in (or sprinkled with) the water that symbolizes the spiritual transformation. Evangelical political views and social attitudes are frequently influenced by such individualistic notions, suggesting that their import extends well beyond the realm of salvation.

However, we should be careful not to assume (as observers often do) that individualism is the only ideological framework through which evangelicals engage the world around them. I would argue that American evangelicals place equal emphasis on notions of religious intersubjectivity. Evangelicals are explicit in their belief that religious conversions are achieved most often through evangelism, a process of mediation that depends on social interactions of one kind or another. While it is true that evangelicals spend considerable time and energy cultivating individual piety, their religious identity is also oriented toward "redemptive relationships," a concept that contemporary evangelical pastors invoke when describing spiritually edifying social bonds. Redemptive relationships are defined as those that are clearly built upon cherished Christian values such as repentance, mercy, accountability, and love, and they may include relationships between pastors and churchgoers as well as relationships among like-minded believers within a congregation or church group. Evangelicals also hope to reproduce redemptive relationships in their interactions with nonbelievers, and they imagine that such an ideal is possible if, over the course of those interactions, they successfully communicate core Christian values, whether through their words or actions.

My point is that while evangelical faith, as a cultural construct, may be viewed as intensely personal, it is far from private. The very ethos of evangelism implicates the reborn, pious self, directly or indirectly, in modes of circulation by which the symbols, sentiments, beliefs and moral norms associated with evangelical faith are made known to others; in other words, they are made public. Among evangelists and evangelical activists, the publicity of faith is an object of conscious effort and relentless ambition. This brings us back to the issues of faith-based activism, which, like all forms of evangelism, seeks to promote a world of possibilities in which redemptive relationships and the religious ideals that sustain them abound.

It is understandable why evangelicals view faith-based activism, with its various religious, philanthropic, and political valences, as a productive field of engagement. On an individual level, faith-based ministries provide ample opportunities for evangelicals to proselytize to people in need using the techniques of holistic evangelism. In a broader sense, faith-based activism invites a whole range of institutional collaborations, partnerships, and coalitions that further the aims of cultural Christianization. The organizational and social networks that socially engaged evangelicals create as they develop outreach initiatives and mobilize resources in local communities propel them into the heart of public life, where they inevitably interact and compete with other civic associations and cultural institutions. Evangelical activists implicitly recognize faith-based activism as an avenue of *publicity*, by which I mean cultural prominence, political leverage, and media exposure. Publicity is achieved not only for evangelicals themselves but also the doctrines and moral norms that they seek to embody.

How do we interpret the publicity of faith-based activism in a nominally secular, pluralist democracy like the U.S.? A cross-cultural comparison is instructive. In a recent article, anthropologist Birgit Meyer (2004) analyzes the "increasing dissemination of Pentecostal signs" in the wake of democratization, economic liberalization, and the commercialization of popular media in Ghana. Meyer highlights the Ghanaian video-film industry as an example of "the convergence of Pentecostalism and popular culture in the newly constituted public realm," demonstrated by the fact that video-films are increasingly characterized by "pentecostally infused" aesthetics and plot-lines. She argues that the diffusion of a distinct cultural style associated with a particular mode of religiosity is one of the ways in which religions "go public," in the midst of social and political change. Meyer writes, "where the state has lost the power to control the media, and thus the production and circulation of images, there is a space for the expression of alternative imaginations" (2004, 105).

I want to argue along a similar vein that recent transformations in the U.S. public sphere—i.e., the reconfiguration of welfare and the growing political and popular appeal of faith-based activism—have created spaces for the expression of a distinctly evangelical "alternative imagination." This new "imagination" emerges particularly through organizational and social networks dedicated to the ideals of holistic evangelism. As the networks of evangelical engagement expand further into the realms of publicity once defined by the entitlement policies of the welfare state, they bring with them salient aspects of the ideological conservatism that characterizes much of American evangelicalism. Thus, while championing the virtues of charity, compassion, and community empowerment, evangelical faith-based activism tends to promote conservative social aesthetics that highlight ethics of individual responsibility rather than social justice, and support the politics of neo-liberalism rather than progressive economic reforms.

Maintaining a strong, positive public presence is a high priority among socially engaged evangelicals, one that they uphold in the name of advancing "the kingdom of God on Earth." Evangelical pastors and activists believe that "the church of Jesus Christ" is essentially better equipped to address the roots of social problems than any other institution, and that faith-based ministries in particular offer the added benefit of presenting a positive image of the church to the community. A proven reputation for mercy and compassion is considered "the best advertising a church can have" and "a dynamic witness" to the plausibility of the message of the gospel (Keller 1997, 211–12). This point is crucial for church pastors and activists at the local level, for whom ministries of social outreach are important sources of legitimacy and influence.

Pastor Tim, senior pastor of one of Knoxville's fastest growing megachurches, periodically gives sermons on the topic of social outreach, often linking it directly to issues of public perception and the prospects of "kingdom-building" in the city. "To others," he once preached, "Christians should look like people who are extravagantly loving each other, not like people who are getting all upset over prayer at football games, or Ten Commandments in offices. We should look like a community of little platoons that are known for loving each other, and for loving the poor." Pastor Tim explained to me that he preaches in this manner in order to broaden churchgoers' conceptions of evangelism and the role of the church in modern society. This rhetorical emphasis reflects deliberate efforts to divert attention away from negative stereotypes in mainstream culture associated with the reactionary politics of the Christian Right. While most evangelical pastors and activists share the same moral concerns that have motivated Christian political activism since the 1970s, there are those who clearly wish to capitalize on recent social trends in order to renew evangelical social consciousness at the grassroots and improve the public image of the church.

Of course, there is more at stake in faith-based activism than just image management and good public relations on the part of evangelical communities. After all, it would be short-sighted to assume that conservative evangelical values are gaining ground in civil society simply because evangelical leaders claim such a truth as imminently self-evident. Moreover, we must not subscribe too readily to the notion that the ideological interests of evangelicalism are so completely dominant that other "alternative imaginations" are precluded from making an impact in the welfare arena. However, when we take into account the considerable gains that socially engaged evangelicals have indeed achieved in cities and communities throughout the U.S., we begin to see that the revivalist optimism of evangelical pastors and activists is more than a matter of rhetoric. I want to argue that the popularity of faith-based activism since welfare reform has made it possible for evangelicals to pursue bold new strategies of philanthropic and civic engagement, including broad-reaching institutional partnerships and interdenominational alliances (some of which would once have been unimaginable). In practical terms, evangelical investments in social welfare and community development initiatives lay the foundations for networks of co-operation that, among other effects, are bound to increase the political and moral leverage of evangelical communities in regions nationwide.

During my fieldwork I found that socially engaged evangelicals, particularly those who were involved in the Samaritans of Knoxville, spent a great deal of energy cultivating partnerships with a range of local institutions, including commercial industries, charitable nonprofits, and government agencies, as well as area churches. Such efforts are necessary to ensure the viability of local faith-based initiatives, which often require churches to interact in good faith with intermediaries who can provide access to resources and service opportunities. Co-operative networks also make it easier for organizations like the Samaritans of Knoxville to consolidate resources and share information pertaining to social service provisions of various kinds.

Interdenominational co-operation is seen as equally crucial among evangelical activists because of practical demands, as well as the prospect of creating unity among Knoxville's diverse and fragmented evangelical congregations. The Samaritans of Knoxville currently claims an informal membership of 120 local churches, representing fifteen denominations. It is not, however, an ecumenical association in the sense of being inter*faith* (I observed no obvious efforts to include Catholics and non-Christians). Rather, the organization hopes to promote a united evangelical front, one that transcends long standing denominational rivalries and overcomes racial tensions that fall conspicuously along an urban-suburban divide. Finding common ground among disparate evangelical groups is no easy task, especially when they are divided by doctrinal disagreement and differences of opinion with regard to the appropriateness of churches functioning as vehicles of social action. However, evangelical activists foster dialogue and co-operation by maintaining a collective focus on a single point of inspiration: the desire to usher the greater Knoxville area into a spirit of religious revival through faith-based activism. Evangelism, in the most general sense, serves as their common cause, the object of their shared moral ambition.

In addition to forming new alliances within the evangelical community, the founding members of the Samaritans of Knoxville pursue relationships with various representatives from the civic community at large. In contrast to the tendency among evangelical congregations to initiate social outreach ministries with little or no input from outside experts (except those who share the same ideological viewpoint), the Samaritans of Knoxville seeks out the expertise of qualified professionals and social workers who, in turn, stand to benefit from improved relations with the evangelical community. When Paul Genero, the organization's founder, first set out to gather statistical and anecdotal information about pressing social concerns and existing social services in Knoxville, he treated this as an important network-building process in and of itself. Paul instructed his interns and volunteer researchers about how to conduct interviews with non-evangelical service providers and civic leaders, reminding his interviewers that some people "may be somewhat antagonistic towards churches, as some of them have been frustrated by perceived apathy towards social justice within the faith community." He added, "we want to tear down assumptions of Christian exclusivity and isolationism, and we want to establish rapport and show that we care because Christ cares." While Paul was careful to point out that "evangelism is not the reason for the interview" (meaning, the interviewer was not supposed to proselytize), his instructions on interview etiquette fed into a larger evangelistic project, insofar as building "rapport" with key members of the social services community is one of the strategies by which evangelical activists expand their spheres of influence.

Paul frequently invites people with specialized expertise in particular areas of social work to the organization's public workshops. These include representatives from homeless shelters, urban youth programs, healthcare providers, and refugee sponsorship organizations, some of which are openly religious while others are secular or municipal. They are invited to give informative and motivational presentations for the purpose of soliciting volunteers and donor support. Many outside representatives are evangelicals themselves (as is a fairly large portion of the local population), but some of them are not. Non-evangelicals who attend events held by the Samaritans of Knoxville do so with veiled ambivalence. On the one hand, I found that some non-evangelical social workers worry about evangelicals taking advantage of volunteer opportunities in order to proselytize vulnerable people who should be entitled to receive charitable aid without religious strings attached. On the other hand, they are eager to gain new supporters and allies, especially among white suburbanites who represent an economically and politically dominant social group. As it has become clear to social workers and urban grassroots organizers that Knoxville's suburban evangelicals are serious about their intentions to make an impact in the affairs of social welfare, it has become increasingly important for these civic actors to curry their favor, or at least develop close enough ties to avoid social service redundancies.

In the years since it was founded the Samaritans of Knoxville has made significant progress promoting faith-based activism among evangelical churches in Knoxville. They have helped churches improve their social outreach and facilitated the creation of co-operative initiatives such as food pantries, mentoring programs, inner-city missions, and health clinics. In the process, the organization is contributing to a gradual appreciation for holistic evangelism among conservative churchgoers. Pastors and churchgoers who become actively involved in faith-based ministries as volunteers and donors also come to realize that in order to maintain productive relations with non-evangelical institutions it may be necessary to make strategic accommodations with regard to proselytization. Faith-based activism is thus a potential catalyst for evangelical moderation insofar as the will to proselytize is refined and redirected through social practices that conform (or appear to conform) with broader cultural values.

At the same time, however, by cultivating wide-reaching co-operative networks dedicated to the philanthropic aims of faith-based activism, socially engaged evangelicals increase not only the publicity of evangelical religiosity in general but also the publicity of the particular moral norms of conservative evangelical patrons. In Knoxville, for example, the success of local faith-based initiatives relies to a large extent on financial and institutional support from white conservative evangelicals who are the region's dominant political and socio-economic group. As a result, the manner in which faith-based social services and outreach initiatives are practiced is partially determined by the ideological demands of the conservative elite, which downplay systemic social reform in favor of liberalized community development, privatized welfare, and a strong emphasis on individual accountability. On several occasions I observed grassroots activists from the inner city, who normally speak in terms of social justice and community empowerment, adopting a more evangelistic rhetorical tone when soliciting the support of suburban evangelical churches and organizations. Welfare activists talk about the "transformed lives" and "softened hearts" of welfare clients, evoking the conversionist language of evangelical revivalism, rather than dwelling on the systemic roots of poverty as they might do when speaking before liberal audiences. In this respect, faith-based activism has the potential to reinforce hegemonic conditions in particular social contexts. The field allows a dominant cultural style of evangelicalism to increase its already significant influence in American society.

Conclusion

In 2004, the National Association of Evangelicals (NAE), which represents 30 million Americans, formerly endorsed a document entitled "For the Health of the Nation: An Evangelical Call to Civic Responsibility." The document, drafted by a committee of prominent evangelical figures, including Ron Sider, lays out the principles of a biblically rooted approach to public engagement in order to mobilize American evangelicals to take greater interest in social issues and world affairs. Without specifying any programmatic initiatives, the document states that "the Lord calls the church to speak prophetically to society and work for the renewal and reform of its structures." It seeks to define the parameters of "Christian citizenship," including the degree to which Christians should influence public policy and their responsibilities to defend human rights, religious freedom, the "sanctity" of life and hetero-sexual marriage, and "justice and compassion for the poor and vulnerable."

This is certainly not the first statement of its kind in modern evangelical-ism, as the NAE and various other associations have periodically issued simi-lar proclamations in the decades since the rise of neo-evangelicalism in the mid-twentieth century. While intended as a means of inculcating consensus and promoting unity among evangelical communities, these statements are also intended as public demonstrations to the non-evangelical world that evangelicals, heralds of the "kingdom come," are equally concerned about the health and sustainability of the world as we know it, a world that they view as sinful but ultimately redeemable. What stands out about "For the Health of the Nation" compared to past statements is the total absence of any explicit references to proselytism or evangelism. The document goes on at length about how followers of Jesus must, as a matter of biblical orthodoxy, realize their calling to protect the well-being of society, especially the weak and vulnerable, and participate actively in the public square in order to defeat the "bias of aggressive secularism" in American life. There is no mention that such engagement is predicated upon the mandate of evangelism. Instead, evangelicals are urged to educate themselves on social issues and political processes, enter into dialogue with people with whom they may not at first see any common ground, and always approach public engagement "with hu-mility and with earnest prayer for divine guidance and wisdom."

Nonetheless, statements like these do not exist in a vacuum. They are intrinsically linked to religious discourses and practices on the ground that reinforce the centrality of evangelism in the evangelical moral imagination. If explicit references to evangelism are absent from the text, this does not pre-clude an underlying significance that, among evangelicals, is taken for grant-ed. The exclusion of any such references is a strategic maneuver, reflecting deliberate shifts in emphasis that evangelical activists believe will benefit the long-term publicity of evangelical engagement. Therefore, we can read "For the Health of the Nation," and the literary, theological, and ethnographic examples of faith-based activism that I have discussed throughout this essay, as historically constituted modes of religious activity that, by virtue of their cultural and political valences, are mobilized in the service of an enduring missionary imperative. They are illustrations of a renewed commitment to social engagement among evangelicals, including conservative evangelicals, even as they continue to rally behind divisive political issues such as abortion, same-sex marriage, the teaching of evolution in public schools, and federal support for stem-cell research.

Given the wide range of social concerns and methods of engagement, evangelicals have yet to achieve the level of consensus and unity that evangelical activists strive for. However, the principle of evangelism remains the focal point of organized activity across the evangelical subculture, despite variations in emphasis and interpretation. Whether evangelicals promote proselytism or holistic evangelism, their efforts are uniformly oriented toward the prospect of cultural Christianization, an ideal that is both missionary and revivalist in character, and which will likely benefit from new patterns of evangelical social engagement in the post-welfare era.

Notes

1. The Barna Research Group, a Christian research organization, conducted a survey in 2004 and found that most born-again Christians prefer to share their religious beliefs with nonbelievers in a dialogical rather than confrontational fashion, and always in the context of real human relationships. The growing assumption among born-agains (including evangelicals) appears to be that one cannot fully communicate what it means to be a Christian through casual encounters that only create discomfort and hostility.

2. Olasky's books are read widely among political and religious conservatives, and his personal influence in American politics remains strong. He was a close consultant to George W. Bush prior to his presidential run in 2000, and is credited with devising the platform of "compassionate conservatism," the cornerstone of that campaign.

3. The number of Centers for Faith-Based and Community Initiatives in the federal infrastructure soon increased to ten. In 2002, Bush added two centers the Department of Agriculture and the Agency for International Development. In 2004, he added centers in the Departments of Commerce and Veteran Affairs, and the Small Business Administration.

4. Editorial, Marvin Olasky, *World* Magazine, February 10, 2001.

5. Another objection voiced by a number of religious leaders regarding federal faith-based initiatives has to do with the availability of public funds for religious organizations like the Church of Scientology, Hare Krishnas, and Nation of Islam, which are considered to fall outside the "Judeo-Christian" mainstream. Christian Right activists Pat Robertson and Jerry Falwell, as well as the Anti-Defamation League, have been outspoken critics in this regard.

6. All individuals and organizations that appear in connection to my ethnographic fieldwork in Knoxville are referred to by pseudonyms in the interests of confidentiality.

7. "Justification by faith" is an essential Protestant doctrine. It states that redemption cannot be earned through calculation or merit, but only through faith in Jesus Christ, which is made available to the sinner by the Holy Spirit and through divine grace.

References

Bakke, Ray. 1997. *A Theology as Big as the City*. Downers Grove, IL: InterVarsity Press.

Bartkowski, John P. and Helen A. Regis. 2003. *Charitable Choices: Religion, Race, and Poverty in the Post-Welfare Era*. New York: New York University Press.

Beidelman, T.O. 1982. *Colonial Evangelism: A Socio-Historical Study of an East African Mission at the Grassroots*. Bloomington: Indiana University Press.

Carpenter, Joel A. 1997. *Revive Us Again: The Reawakening of American Fundamentalism*. New York: Oxford University Press.

Chaves, Mark. 1999. Religious Congregations and Welfare Reform: Who Will Take Advantage of Charitable Choice? *American Sociological Review* 64: 836–46.

Clydesdale, Timothy T. 1990. Soul-Winning and Social Work: Giving and Caring in the Evangelical Tradition. In *Faith and Philanthropy in America: Exploring the Role of Religion in America's Voluntary Sector*. ed. R. Wuthnow, and Virginia A. Hodgkinson, 187–209. San Francisco: Jossey-Bass Publishers.

Cnaan, Ram A., Robert J. Wineburg, and Stephanie C. Boddie. 1999. *The Newer Deal: Social Work and Religion in Partnership*. New York: Columbia University Press.

Cnaan, Ram A. 2002. *The Invisible Caring Hand: American Congregations and the Provision of Welfare*. New York: New York University Press.

Elisha, Omri. 2004. Sins of Our Soccer Moms: Servant Evangelism and the Spiritual Injuries of Class. In *Local Actions: Cultural Activism, Power, and Public Life in America*. ed. M. Checker and M. Fishman, 136–58. New York: Columbia University Press.

Greenberg, Anna. 2000. The Church and the Revitalization of Politics and Community. *Political Science Quarterly* 115(3): 377–94.

Keller, Timothy J. 1997. *Ministries of Mercy: The Call of the Jericho Road*. Phillipsburg, NJ: P and R Publishing.

Lupton, Robert D. 1989. *Theirs is the Kingdom: Celebrating the Gospel in Urban America*. San Francisco: Harper Collins.

Meyer, Birgit. 2004. "Praise the Lord:" Popular Cinema and Pentecostalite Style in Ghana's New Public Sphere. *American Ethnologist* 31(1): 92–110.

Olasky, Marvin. 1992. *The Tragedy of American Compassion*. Washington, DC: Regnery Publishing.

Perkins, John M. 1993. *Beyond Charity: The Call to Christian Community Development*. Grand Rapids, MI: Baker Books.

Sherman, Amy L. 2003. Evangelicals and Charitable Choice. In *A Public Faith: Evangelicals and Civic Engagement*. ed. M. Cromartie, 157–72. Lanham, MD: Rowman and Littlefield.

Sider, Ronald J. 1977. *Rich Christians in an Age of Hunger*. Downers Grove, IL:

Intervarsity Press.

— 1999. *Just Generosity: A New Vision for Overcoming Poverty in America.* Grand Rapids, MI: Baker Books.

Sider, Ronald J., Philip N. Olson and Heidi Rolland Unruh. 2002. *Churches That Make A Difference: Reaching Your Community with Good News and Good Works.* Grand Rapids, MI: Baker Books.

Sjogren, Steve. 1993. *Conspiracy of Kindness: A Refreshing New Approach to Sharing the Love of Jesus with Others.* Ann Arbor, MI: Vine Books.

Wuthnow, Robert. 2004. *Saving America?: Faith-Based Services and the Future of Civil Society.* Princeton, NJ: Princeton University Press.

CHAPTER 19

Proselytization: Closing Thoughts from a Sociologist

James T. Richardson

Introduction

This fine collection on the timely topic of proselytization offers much to students and scholars of religion from many fields, including the history of religions, comparative world religions, religious studies, the sociology, social psychology, and psychology of religion, as well as specific areas within some of those disciplines, especially studies of new and minority religions, studies of conversion and recruitment, and the effects of globalization on religion (and vice-versa: see Beckford 2003, 103–44). My comments will be made from the point of view of a sociologist/social psychologist of religion with a strong interest in how law affects religion and religious groups in modern societies.

Rosalind Hackett, the editor of this informative collection, offered some insightful comments in her introduction to the volume, noting that religious proselytization has become one of the more controversial topics in today's world. The free market of religious ideas that is supposed to exist in modern societies has not materialized. Instead, there is great concern in many nations about the issue of proselytization. Indeed, proselytization has become a flash-point in our contemporary world, even in some long-term democratic societies such as France and Belgium (Beckford 2004; Luca 2004; Fautré 2004; Duvert 2004). Other societies governed by more authoritarian regimes also have severe concerns about proselytization, particularly if those regimes espouse an ideology perceived to be challenged by religious proselytization

(Hanks 2004; Rahn this volume; Mayer this volume).

As Hackett notes, democratization and the growth of the human rights revolution have carried within themselves the seeds of this divisive controversy, as some have viewed these related movements as carte blanche to promote their religion using any means possible. Such unrestrained behavior, real or perceived, has led others to suggest necessary limits to religious freedom in a functioning democracy, and to emphasize the rights of privacy and cultural integrity as overwhelming the right to proselytize. Protective paternalism by governments has sometimes trumped personal religious freedom, in part because of vast differences among religious traditions under-girding societies in our world.[1]

Both the promotional and protective efforts seem contrary to the spirit of religious freedom that is supposed to pervade our modern and sophisticated world; hence the controversy that has developed concerning proselytization in a number of modern democracies. And in non-democratic societies, the very existence of religious groups can be viewed as a challenge, even if they are not overtly proselytizing in traditional ways. This is clearly shown by the initial reaction of Chinese political officials to the rise of the Falun Gong, which has transformed its adversity under the Chinese government into a unique method of proselytizing using modern media technologies (see Rahn's chapter, as well as Edelman and Richardson 2003, 2005).

Proselytization as process

Given the remarkable development of concerns about proselytization around the world, it is fitting to see a collection such as has been developed in this volume. The focus herein on the term *proselytization*, as opposed to a focus on conversion, is noteworthy. Discussions of conversion are often quite individualized, attending to attributes of the convert.[2] The proselytization perspective used herein turns attention, quite explicitly and in a somewhat neutral manner, to the *process* whereby groups and individuals seek to attract others to their own religious orientation.

This focus on process moves the inquiry into the fruitful realm of the sociological and social psychological, as attention is given to the manner in which methods of proselytizing are developed, executed, and received. Many of the case studies reported herein demonstrate well the organizational nature of proselytization, as well as the organizational elements involved in anti-proselytization efforts. Some religions engaged in proselytization can best be described as multi-national religious firms developing bureaucratic and efficient means of sharing their religion with others, which can mean use of modern communication technologies.[3]

These entrepreneurial organizational elements of proselytization need to be understood, as they may be essential to grasping the true nature of what is happening in the new global world of proselytization. The global competition among religious traditions has spawned some intriguing developments such as that discussed by Scott herein, who describes the world-wide proselytizing efforts of the huge and growing Dhammakaya Buddhist organization headquartered in Thailand.[4] Also, as Freston's examination of Brazilian Christian missionary activities in northern hemisphere nations and Kovalchuk's research on Korean Christian missionary efforts in the far east of the Russian Federation point out, there has been a significant shift occurring in the origins of many Christian-derived proselytizing efforts. Nowadays many missionaries are being sent from countries that were formerly the targets of mission activity. This global trend is new but could become a dominant theme in future decades. Balci's chapter concerning vigorous and creative Islamic proselytization coming out of Turkey also shows an aspect of the global picture of proselytizing that is often missing from scholarly discussions. The organization of anti-proselytizing by governments and dominant religious organizations attempting to stave off proselytizing groups also is worthy of study.[5]

Developing a more sociological perspective concerning the topic of proselytization also allows a better grasp of the distinction between individual, group, and collective or community rights, as well as an understanding that these three types of rights often collide. A community (nation) may seek to preserve itself in the face of efforts to recruit its individual citizens, which might mean normative developments and even laws being passed that limit individual or group freedoms, a growing trend in our world today.[6] Also, a nation may fear religious violence that could erupt as a result of proselytizing efforts by a religious tradition, such as is the case in Singapore (DeBernardi this volume).

A group, such as a family, may react strongly to the idea of a member leaving the group to affiliate with another group or organization, especially when that outside entity appears to espouse values that are at odds with the group (family) culture and values. Also, a family group or a minority religious organization may object strenuously to community (state) efforts to dictate what they can and cannot do concerning their religious beliefs and practices. Such problems are, of course, compounded greatly if there are racial and ethnic differences among and between the groups, a situation that can add greatly to the conflicts involved.[7] Hence the study of proselytization becomes ipso facto a study of inter and intra-group conflict, a topic well studied within sociology, but which can gain from the chapters in this collection.

Proselytization and social control

Proselytization research also is a study in social control and regulation of individual and group behaviors (see Richardson 2004). The chapters in this volume offer many examples of how governments attempt to exert control over religion and religious groups and practitioners. Kao's chapter herein carefully delineates various facets of one form of social control mechanism—anti-proselytization efforts by governments and other entities. Sometimes such efforts take on a definite anti-colonialist bent, as is shown in the Berkwitz chapter on efforts to adopt laws precluding proselytizing in Sri Lanka. Other times such efforts clearly demonstrate the collusion between governments and dominant religious traditions within a society, as is the case with Russia (See Kazmina [this volume] and also Shterin and Richardson 1998, 2000 on the Russian situation.) Also, social control may take the form of self-monitoring by religious groups, as demonstrated by the efforts briefly mentioned in the editor's introduction. (See article on this effort in *New York Times*, Aug. 16, 2007.)

Just as interesting as how governments and other organizational entities attempt to exert control over religion and religious groups are the responses to those efforts by the entities that are the focus of such efforts. Such reactions can "deform" religious groups and deter them from their original purpose and goals, and dramatically impact how the organization develops over time. Mayer's chapter discusses this aspect of anti-proselytization efforts. Another example of this is how the Jehovah's Witnesses have evolved into a different kind of organization based on efforts to defend themselves and promote their message through litigation, using the legal system in societies where that was possible (Côté and Richardson 2001).

Sometimes social control and regulation of religion take on a different connotation, as when governments try to mold religious groups to their purposes, and co-opt the religious groups to some extent. Elisha's chapter on the actions of the federal government in the United States attempting to shift many social welfare responsibilities to religious organizations clearly demonstrates this facet of regulation and control (also see Davis, 2001). Some religious groups are quite willing to participate in these efforts (Formicola and Segers 2002), but questions are raised about how this affects the religious group, as well as whether this is in effect supporting the establishment of official religions that become thereby arms of the state. Furnishing social services through selected religious groups reminds one of the implications of the term "rice Christians" that was applied to mass conversions in previous time through the use of food and other material goods. Such efforts seemed coercive and offensive to many in hindsight, and modern variants of this approach to proselytization may not fare any better in the venue of public opinion (see

Kao [this volume] for a thoughtful discussion of rice Christians).

Religious freedom

Before closing, a few remarks about the issue of religious freedom are in order. I recently published an article entitled "The Sociology of Religious Freedom" (Richardson, 2006) where I discussed structural and historical requisites in order for religious freedom to flourish. Needless to say, my treatment of the subject would have been more informed had I read this collection of papers beforehand. But, given this opportunity, I can perhaps make amends, and briefly apply some ideas from my earlier effort.

In the article I briefly summarized the history of the concept of religious freedom, noting its origins in religious conflict in western Europe, as strong states developed in part to maintain peace between warring religious factions. From this cauldron of conflict, the idea of religious freedom (and tolerance) has grown and spread around the world, developing first in full bloom in the fledging United States of America. There the well-known First Amendment compromise was struck to make certain that no one religious tradition could dominate others that held sway in parts of the new nation.

From this beginning the concept of religious freedom has spread globally, partly in response to growing pluralism,[8] and in an effort to keep peace among strongly held religious beliefs in increasingly pluralistic societies. That diffusion has not been modeled completely after the American experience, as the adoption of the idea has often not incorporated prohibitions against state-sponsored churches, and there have been limitations placed on individual and group religious freedom.[9] As noted in some of the chapters herein, the spread of the concept of individual religious freedom also has often been accompanied by certain ideas about how to organize societies, including especially economic institutions. Imperialism has been associated in the minds of many with Christian proselytizing efforts, and the proselytizing has been made more feasible with growing global acceptance of the concept of religious freedom. Thus religious freedom as a value has indeed become important in many areas and arenas, as evidenced by the inclusion of the language affirming religious freedom, albeit with some important limitations, in many international documents and in the constitutions of many nations.

My analysis of the structural requisites for religious freedom, which drew ideas from the sociology of religion and of law, did not speak to the important point made above about the association of religious freedom with certain political and economic ideas. However, it is worth noting that the analysis presented does offer possible insights into how proselytization is treated in the various societies discussed in Professor Hackett's very illuminating collection. For instance, how religious hierarchies are established by law or practice to regulate religious pluralism, and how those arrangements can either support or suppress religious freedom are worth attention. Also, trying to understand how legal systems deal with the concept of religious freedom is made clearer by incorporating theories from sociological studies of law that explain why some parties in legal actions win and others lose, as well as why religious issues end up in courts of law so often in many modern societies. Concepts such as pervasiveness and centrality of legal systems, as well as the importance of autonomy and independence of the judicial system are crucial to understanding how religious freedom operates in various societies in the modern world. Illustrations of all these concepts can be found in chapters within this collection, as can demonstrations of the importance of knowing about the relative social status of parties to legal actions involving religion, and the degree of intimacy among the parties and decision makers.

When minority religions win legal battles this demands explanation, and suggests that the values espoused within key institutions such as the judiciary and the media in a society strongly support religious freedom for minority religions, and that these values can be implemented by decision makers with impunity. It may also suggest that powerful "third party partisans" (Black and Baumgartner 1999) have come to the aid of the usually politically weak religious minority. Such partisans coming to the aid of religious groups embroiled in controversy is not just a concept referring to the action of NGOs, although those organizations can play a significant role in how religious freedom is implemented. In my analysis I characterized even the European Court of Human Rights as a key partisan on behalf of religious minorities under certain circumstances.[10] The globalization of the impact of major governmental organizations such as the United Nations and the ECHR is playing an important role in the interpretation of religious freedom in today's world.[11]

Just how continuing conflicts over proselytization in various societies will play out remains to be seen, of course. We could be involved in the beginnings of a major global and very destructive "clash of civilizations" to use Huntington's phrase. Or we could use key international bodies and a large dose of common sense to avoid such a fate. Whatever course is taken by leaders around the world, reading the entries in this collection will contribute to an understanding of the depth and breadth of the controversy, and perhaps some ways to handle such difficulties short of major violence.

Notes

1. See Claerhout and De Roover (this volume) for the provocative claim that any defense of proselytizing and conversion privileges Christianity and Islam at the expense of other religious traditions, and Sharma (2006) for a broader treatment of this issue.

2. Example of this focus can be found in the vast literature dealing with personality and personality change in religious converts (see for example, Paloutzian, Richardson, and Rambo (1999) and that entire issue of *Journal of Personality*. However, some work on conversion is quite process oriented in its thrust: see Bainbridge (1992), Tippett (1992), Kraft (1992), and Richardson (1992), all included in the fine volume, *Handbook of Religious Conversion,* edited by Newton Malony and Samuel Southard.

3. See discussions (this volume) by Kovalchuk, of Korean Christian missionaries operating in Russia; as well as Arthur's chapter on use of the internet by Wicca and other groups; Ukah's discussion of the "poster wars" among Nigerian proselytizing groups; and Scott's analysis of various approaches and use of technology by one of Thailand's major Buddhist groups, for examples.

4. The changes wrought in this particular branch of Buddhism by a decision to engage in the competitive global religious economy are dramatic, and demonstrate the impacts of societal context on religious traditions. On a smaller scale this contextual impact also was shown in Pilarzyk's (1983) study of how a new Hindu group in the United States was forced to incorporate proselytizing techniques in order to survive in the very competitive religious climate of that country.

5. See Kazmina's chapter herein on the actions of the Russian Orthodox Church in conjunction with the Russia political structure to curtail religious competition for instance.

6. See the broad-ranging comparative discussions in this volume by Meyer and by Kao, as well as chapter by Claerhout and De Roover, and Rao (2004) on such efforts in India, by Sharkey concerning Egypt, and by Mullins on the conflicts over proselytization in Japan.

7. See DeBernardi's chapter on the volatile situation in Singapore (this volume), as well as Hill (2004) and Tremlett (this volume) on conflicts in one region of the Philippines.

8. See Beckford's (2003, 73–102) thoughtful deconstruction of the term religious pluralism in which he notes that it has often meant diversity (itself a problematic term), but that it can also mean acceptance of various religious traditions, or, even more positively, the valuing of such religious variation in a society.

9. It is quite noteworthy that in the face of growing power from certain religious groups in America, a movement has developed promoting limitations on religious freedom in that country. See Hamilton (2005) for one well known articulation of this position that espouses the view that religious organizations should be subject to all facially neutral laws, and be granted few special privileges.

10. The ECHR did not render any decision finding a violation of religious freedom in a Member State until 1993 (Richardson 1995), but since then has made a number of decisions supportive of such rights, especially in former communist countries recently affiliated with the Council of Europe, as well as in Greece, where proselytizing is a criminal offense (Richardson and Garay 2004).

11. See Richardson (2007) for a social constructionist approach to understanding human rights, including religious freedom, and the role that major international organizations as well as some national governments are playing in promoting and defending these rights.

Also see Evans (2001) for a critical analysis of the role of the ECHR in this arena, as well as Gunn (2002) for a discussion of the activities of the Organization for Security and Co-Operation in Europe, and Sharma (2006) for a quite critical analysis of the entire concept of human rights.

References

Bainbridge, William. 1992. The sociology of conversion. In *Handbook of Religious Conversion,* ed. N. Malony and S. Southard, 178–91. Birmingham, AL: Religious Education Press.

Beckford, James A. 2003. *Social Theory and Religion*. Cambridge: Cambridge University Press.

———. 2004. Laicite, "dystopia," and the reaction to new religions in France. In *Regulating Religion,* ed. J. Richardson, 27–40. New York: Kluwer.

Black, Donald, and M.P. Baumgartner. 1999. Toward a theory of the third party. In *The Sociology of Right and Wrong,* ed. D. Black, 95–124. New York: Academic Press.

Côté, Pauline and James T. Richardson. 2001. Disciplined litigation, vigilante litigation, and deformation: Dramatic organizational change in Jehovah's Witnesses. *Journal for the Scientific Study of Religion* 40: 11–26.

Davis, Derek. 2001. President Bush's Office of Faith-Based and Community Initiatives: Boon or Boondoggle? *Journal of Church and State* 43: 411–22.

Duvert, Cyrill. 2004. Anti-cultism in the French Parliament. In *Regulating Religion,* ed. J. Richardson, 41–52. New York: Kluwer.

Edelman, Brian, and James T. Richardson (2003). Falun Gong and the law: Development of legal social control in China. *Nova Religio* 6: 312–31.

———. 2005. Imposed limitation on freedom of religion in China and the margin of appreciation doctrine. *Journal of Church and State* 47: 243-68.

Evans, Carolyn. 2001. *Freedom of Religion Under the European Convention on Human Rights*. Oxford: Oxford University Press.

Fautré, Willy. 2004. Belgium's anti-sect policy. In *Regulating Religion,* ed. J. Richardson, 113–26. New York: Kluwer.

Formicola, Jo, and Mary Segers. 2002. The Bush faith-based initiative: The Catholic response. *Journal of Church and State* 44: 693–716.

Gunn, Jeremy. 2002. The Organization for Security and Co-operation in Europe and the rights of religion and belief. In *Protecting the Human Rights and Religious Minorities in Eastern Europe,* ed. P. Danchin and E. Cole, 222-2?50. New York: Columbia University Press.

Hamilton, Marci. 2005. *God vs. the Gavel: Religion and the Rule of Law*. Cambridge: Cambridge University Press.

Hanks, Reuel. 2004. Religion and Law in Uzbekistan: Renaissance and repression in an authoritarian context. In *Regulating Religion,* ed. J. Richardson, 319–32). New York: Kluwer.

Hill, Michael. 2004. The rehabilitation and regulation of religion in Singapore. In *Regulating Religion,* ed. J. Richardson, 343–58. New York: Kluwer.

Kraft, Charles. 1992. Conversion in group settings. In *Handbook of Religious Conversion,* ed. N. Malony and S. Southard, 259–75). Birmingham, AL: Religious Education Press.

Luca, Nathalie. 2004. Is there a unique French policy of cults? A European perspective. In *Regulating Religion,* ed. J. Richardson, 53–72). New York: Kluwer.

Malony, Newton and Samuel Southard. 1992. *Handbook of Religious Conversion.* Birmingham, AL: Religious Education Press.

New York Times. 2007. Evangelicals join in interfaith effort to write rules for conversion. August 16, A5.

Paloutzian, Raymond F., James T. Richardson and Lewis R. Rambo. 1999. Religious Conversion and Personality Change. *Journal of Personality* 67(6): 1047–79.

Pilarzyk, Thomas. 1983. Conversion and alternation processes in the youth culture. In *The Brainwashing/Deprogramming Controversy,* ed. D. Bromley and J. Richardson, 51–72. New York: Edwin Mellen.

Rao, Badrinath. 2004. Religion, law, and minorities in India: Problems with judicial regulation. In *Regulating Religion,* ed. J. Richardson, 381–413). New York: Kluwer.

Richardson, James T. 1992. Conversion processes in the new religions. In *Handbook of Religious Conversion,* ed. N. Malony and S. Southard, 78–89). Birmingham, AL: Religious Education Press.

———. 1995. Minority religions, religious freedom, and the new pan-European political and judicial institutions. *Journal of Church and State* 37(2): 39–59.

———. 2004. *Regulating Religion: Case Studies from Around the Globe.* New York: Kluwer.

———. 2006. The sociology of religious freedom: A structural and socio-legal analysis. *Sociology of Religion* 67: 271–94.

———. 2007. Religion, law, and human rights. In *Religion in Global Perspective,* ed. Peter Beyer and Lori Beaman, 409–30. Boston: Brill.

Richardson, James T. and Alain Garay. 2004. The European Court of Human Rights and former communist states. In *Religion and Patterns of Social Transformation,* ed. D.M. Jerolimov, S. Zrinscak, and I. Borovik, 223–34). Zagreb: Institute of Social Research.

Sharma, Arvind. 2006. Are Human rights Western? New Delhi: Oxford University Press.

Shterin, Marat and James T. Richardson. 1998. Local laws restricting religion in Russia: Precursor's of Russia's new national law. *Journal of Church and State* 40: 319–42.

————. 2000. Effects of Western anti-cult movement in development of laws concerning religion in post-communist Russia. *Journal of Church and State* 42:
247–71.
Tippett, Alan. 1992. The cultural anthropology of conversion. In *Handbook of Religious Conversion,* ed. N. Malony and S. Southard, 192–208). Birmingham,
AL: Religious Education Press.

INDEX

10/40 window, 18, 253–254, 268–271, 273, 389–407

A

abortion, 99 n.9, 119, 125, 452
accountability, 15, 330, 434, 435, 442, 445, 450
activism, 3, 112, 446–451. See also Missionary activity; Missionization
activists
  animal rights, 87
  Buddhist, 46, 205, 218
  Christian, 40, 124
  cyber-, 19, 409–430
  faith–based, 431–454
  Hindu, 21 n.5, 24 n.37, 37, 41, 43, 47
  for indigenous rights, 41
  Islamist, 140
  Muslim, 38–40
  religious, 13, 49
  See also Missionary activity; Missionization
AD2000 and Beyond Movement, 271–277
Adventists, 390
advertisement, 242, 244, 327
  Pentecostal, 168–198
advertising
  in Nigeria, 16, 168–198, 415–420, 426 n.8
  See also Competition; Marketplace; Posters; Publicity
advocacy 85, 213, 216, 222, 225 n.9, 411
  secular, 85, 86, 87, 100 n.13
Afghanistan, 8
Africa, 6, 8, 10, 40, 62, 79, 88–89, 92, 95, 109, 113, 121, 127, 133
African Traditional Religions (ATR), 69, 88–90, 167, 190–191 n.31, 191–192 n.42
  See also Mutua, Makau

Afro-Brazilian religions, 127, 132
agency, 9, 11, 12, 20, 24 n.41, 36, 151, 182, 269, 310–311, 443
aid
  to children, 79–80
  and missionary outreach, 79–82
aid evangelism. See under Evangelism
Algeria, 144
America, 288
  See also United States
American Presbyterians, 16,139–161
Anglican Church, 267, 279 n.9, n.11
Angola, 39
An-Na'im, Abdullahi A., 1, 3, 21, 97, 155, 162
anthropologists, 2, 10–11, 43, 85, 111
Antioch, 253, 255, 257, 268
anti-abortion. See under Abortion
anti-colonialism. See under Colonialism
anti-conversion laws. See under Conversion
anti-proselytization. See under Proselytization
anti-sect policies, 89
apocalypticism, 310
apologetics
  online 19, 413, 423
  Islamic 414
  Wiccan 409–430
apostasy, 8, 16, 39, 61, 77, 89, 100 n.12, 110, 119, 134, 139, 140, 142, 153–156, 158 n.12, 161 n.40
Argentina, 41, 114
Asad, Talal, 20, 22 n.8, 24 n.40, n.41
Asia, 8, 10, 16, 17, 62, 79, 92, 95, 109, 114, 124, 127, 152, 248, 263, 267, 274, 288, 376
Assemblies of God, 398
Altai Republic, 389, 394–397
Aum Shinrikyo, 18, 321, 328, 330–331

Australia, 270
authenticity, 17, 116, 283, 288, 294–298
autobiography, 416
Azerbaijan, 366, 368, 380, 383, 384

B

Balagangadhara, S.N., 62, 63, 69, 70
Banahaw, Mount, 17, 283–284, 288,
    292–294, 296
Bangladesh, 44–45
Baptists, 390, 397
Bashkortostan, 371, 384
Beach, B.B., 7, 20 n.16, 233
Becket Fund for Religious Liberty, 216, 225
    n.7, n.9
Beckford, James, 461
Belgium, 455
Black Sunday, 289–290
blasphemy, 89
Bonk, Jonathan, 9, 23 n.29, 27
Bosnia, 125
brainwashing, 11–12, 144, 219
Brazil, 13, 15, 114–116, 266, 336 n.25, 457
broadcasting commissions,
    Nigeria, 170–175
Buckser, Andrew, 86
Buddhism, 18, 23 n.29, 53, 54, 55, 57,
    58, 59–60, 62, 63, 64, 65, 69, 113,
    199–229, 394, 395, 397, 398, 399, 402,
    404–405, 461 n.4
  in Japan, 322, 323, 324, 326, 328, 333
  Sinhala, 16, 199–229, 249 n.5
  Theravada, 231–252, 461, n.3, n.4
    and development, 237
    as missionary religion, 234–238
    monks, 232, 235–252
Buddhists, 255, 265, 269
Burkhanism, 394–395
Burundi, 114
Buryatia Republic, 397, 399

C

Cairo Declaration on Human Rights in
    Islam. *See under* Human rights
Cambodia, 270
Canada, 114
canonical territory. *See under* Orthodox Church

capitalism, 87, 285, 287, 434
  See also Market; Marketplace, of religion
captive audiences, 78, 82, 99 n.3
caste, 55, 56, 57, 59, 60, 62, 111
Catholic Church. *See* Roman Catholic Church
censorship, 147, 159 n.24, 303
Central America, 126
Central Asia and the Caucasus, 38
  See also under Islam
  reislamization of,
change of religion, 2, 3, 12, 15, 16, 19, 44,
    67, 68, 70, 85, 134, 145, 154, 168, 224,
    258, 340, 349, 352, 410
  See also Apostasy; Religious freedom; Con-
    version, religious reaffiliation
charismatics, 254, 265–266, 277
charismatic practices, 256
Charitable Choice, 435–436, 438
Chiapas (Mexico), 38
children, 36, 79–80, 89, 99 n.8
Chiluba, Frederick, 120
China, 17, 40, 254, 269, 301–320, 322,
    370, 391, 392–393, 394, 456
Chinese, 258, 259, 268
  Communist Party (CCP), 304, 309–312
  government, 301–320
  religions, 255, 264, 267
Cho, David Yonggi, 399–400
Christendom, 333, 390
Christian fiction, 256, 263
Christian freedom, 70
Christian militia, 125
Christian music, 256
Christian–Muslim relations, 8, 40, 119,
    139–161, 172
Christian Right, 24 n.42, 432, 434, 447,
    452 n.5
  See also Evangelicals
Christian theology, 53–76
  as dominant principle of religious freedom, 68
  secularization of, 69–70
Christianity, 10–11, 15, 21, 53–76, 78, 89,
    95, 109–137, 234, 460 n.1
  concept of freedom in, 70
  and conversion, 53–76
  as European religion, 9
  as global religion, 9

Indianization of, 72
influence on Turkish missionary movements, 365
in Japan, 322–324, 328
Orthodox. *See* Orthodox Church
as post-Western, 109–137
relations with Muslims, 40
rice Christians. *See under* Rice Christians
Russian, 339–364
shift in gravity in, 8–9, 15
world, 9
See also Christian theology
Christianization, 111–112, 128, 155, 345, 351
cultural, 19, 433, 437, 446, 452
Christians, 39, 40, 45, 48, 56, 97, 232, 440
church history, 7
Church of Jesus Christ of Latter-day Saints (Mormons), 78, 80, 84, 85, 98, 99 n.3, 327, 411
Church of Scientology. *See* Scientology
CIA, 41
Ciudad Mistica de Dios (CMD), 284, 291–394, 296, 297
civil religion, 323–324
civil society, 110, 113, 222, 325, 433, 447
global, *see* Global civil society
clashes, 40, 58, 61, 122, 147
See also Conflict; Clash of civilizations
clash of civilizations, 13, 15, 40, 458, 460
See also Huntington, Samuel
code of conduct for religious conversion, *See under* Conversion
coercion, 5, 419
Coleman, Simon, 265–266
colonialism, 2, 6, 10, 11, 48, 69, 79, 88, 111, 113, 124, 132, 155, 201–204, 219, 235, 236, 237, 257, 267, 274, 284, 287, 288, 297, 333 n.1
anti-colonialism, 2, 85, 291, 458
British, in Egypt, 139–161
neo-colonialism, 94
post-colonialism, 7, 20, 111, 113, 127, 132, 133, 257
competition
of ideas, 69
between religions, 2, 3, 12, 14, 16, 18, 19, 38, 40, 46, 53, 54, 57–62, 65, 73 n.2, 119, 131, 167–198, 345, 359, 410, 457, 461 n.5
See also Advertising; Religious rivalry
conflict, 1, 3, 9, 15, 18, 35–52, 53, 81, 111, 119, 328–329, 349–356, 395, 457, 459, 461 n.6
See also Competition; Clashes; Clash of civilization; Controversy; Cult controversies
ethnic, 80
religious, 35, 80, 328
controversy, 3, 16, 72, 123, 308, 312, 359, 455–456, 460
cult, 35, 41
headscarf. *See under* Headscarf
in Sri Lanka over Christian conversion, 199–229
in Thailand over agressive proselytization, 231–252
See also Conflict
conversion, 2, 3, 4, 9, 15, 16, 17, 20, 22 n.7, 24 n.33, 29, 36, 40, 46, 262, 265, 267, 274, 275, 292, 298, 305, 311, 327, 334 n.5, 340, 351, 384, 398, 405, 409, 412, 413, 418, 421, 422, 427 n.21, 432, 455, 456, 460 n.1, 461 n.2
anti-conversion laws, 16, 72, 91, 199–229
castes and sects as instances of, 57
as Christian, 3, 54–76
code of conduct for, 20–21
comparing Christian and Muslim, 9
as consolidation, 422
defining, 54–62, 212
European connotations of, 55
evangelical, 443–445
forced, 3, 98
experience of, 3, 86
internal, 58
Internet-mediated, 423–424
as Islamic, 55, 56
mass, 334 n.5, 458
methods, 210
Muslim, 142, 154, 155
narratives, 10
out-conversion, 141
joint declaration on Muslim-Christian, 8
politics of, 58, 59, 199–229

process, 24 n.40, 84, 421, 423, 426 n.7
and proselytizing, 21 n.5
as rational, 20
as reaffiliation, 172, 184, 185
reconversion, 41, 46–47, 91, 266
right to, 8, 23 n.19,
Russian to Catholicism, 332, 342, 350
as "sheep-stealing." *See* "sheep-stealing"
Sri Lanka, 199–229
unethical, 44
of vulnerable populations, 78
Western Christian understandings of, 53–76
See also Apostasy; *Da'wa*; Religious reaffiliation
conversionist religion, 19
convert, 49
Copts, 140, 141, 148, 149, 150, 154, 160 n.33
counter-missions, 46
crusade, 93, 94, 98, 119, 126, 157 n.4, 183, 192 n.45, 287, 342, 434
against Islam, 39
cult controversies. *See under* Controversy
cult deprogrammers, 78
cults, 24 n.33, 35, 41, 321, 336 n.26, 346–348, 420
cultural integrity, 68, 349, 398, 456
cultural universality of religion, 63
culture wars, 435

D

dalits, 62
da'wa, 8, 377, 383
decency, 4
decolonialization, 49, 147–149
See also Colonialism
defamation of Islam, 144–145
deliverance ministry, 17, 253, 266,
democracy, 1, 9, 13, 40, 62, 87, 100 n.16, 118, 121, 131, 347, 435, 446, 456
democratic sphere, 20
democratization, 118, 127, 446
democratizing impulse, 118
demonization, 3, 6, 7, 123, 127–128, 144, 204–205, 218, 225 n.9, 236, 260, 289, 293, 301–303
demon possession, 263–266
deregulation, 14, 170–175
Dhammakāya, 17, 231–252, 457

Dharmapala, Anagarika, 204–205, 235–238
dialogue, 7, 8, 14, 15, 22 n.22, 64, 79, 82, 97, 119, 130, 132, 149, 261, 277, 278 n.7, 288, 349, 351–356, 377, 395, 448, 451
diaspora, 131, 390, 393
disaster relief, 80
discourse. *See* Proselytizing discourse
discrimination, 4, 5, 6, 120, 121, 217, 426 n11, 436
dissemination
of information. *See under* Information
of message, 36
of religious ideas, 40

E

East African Revival, 127
East Asia, 17, 18, 234, 253
Eastern Europe, 7
education, 6, 18, 261, 277, 285, 324, 332, 418
in Central Asia, 365–387
lack of, 81
See also Schools
Egypt, 16, 39, 110, 139–161, 461 n.6
Emory Proselytism Project, 1, 339
England, 127
equality of religions, 71–72
ethnicity, 48, 88, 124, 125, 202–203, 221, 237, 255, 257, 270, 336 n.25, 339, 342, 345–347, 350, 353, 356, 390, 392, 457
See also Indigenous
Europe, 9, 14, 41, 48, 88, 90, 114, 115, 127, 234, 237, 256, 265, 270, 288, 302, 333 n.3, 342, 459
European Court of Human Rights, 22 n.14, 460, 461 n.10, 461–462 n.11
evangelical(s), 7, 11, 12, 16, 17, 19, 37, 41, 64, 88, 98, 109–137, 152, 200, 206, 209, 210, 211, 212, 213–215, 217, 218–220, 224 n.3, 225 n.6, 253–282
campaign for international religious freedom, 24 n.42
demographics of global movement, 112–114
National Association of (NAE), 450
politics, 124
and relationship to world culture, 110
in Russia, 343, 345, 349, 359
socially engaged, 431–454

from/in US/America, 38, 41, 49, 54,
  80–81, 93–95, 110
and violence, 124–127
evangelism, 9, 10, 19, 22 n.7, 82, 83, 88, 92,
  95, 97, 101 n.21, 110, 140, 145, 157 n.7,
  188, 201, 209, 215, 219, 232, 233, 256,
  268, 269, 271, 278 n.2, 333 n.1, 334 n.9,
  339, 346, 419, 433, 438–439, 443–444
aid, 8, 224 n.4
child, 404, fig.3
ethical, 215
false, 22 n.16, 23 n.18
holistic, 432, 434, 436, 441, 442, 444,
  446, 450, 452
prayer, 263–266, 271–273, 277
in relation to social engagement, 431–454
servant, 442
service, 442
strategies, 261–277, 438, 441, 443
street, 402, 403, fig.2
US, 431–454
World, 265, 271, 279 n.8
evangelists, 255, 262, 266, 323, 333 n.1
intolerant, 10
evangelistic malpractice, 7, 15, 77
evil
  problem of, 80
  religion, 333 n.3
exclusivity, 449
exclusivism, 18, 110, 328–329
exploitation, 81, 110

F
faith-based initiatives, 431
faith-based organizations, 78–82, 94, 99 n.9
Falun Gong (Falun Dafa), 17, 301–320, 456
  banned, 301–303, 312, 315 n.6
  "clarify the truth." 304, 307, 312,
    317–318 n.22
  Consummation, 304, 305, 306, 313–314,
    316 n.10
  cultivation, 302, 305
  disciples, 305, 306, 311, 312, 313, 315 n.6
  fa (law), 304
  Fa-rectification, 304–314
  practitioners, 304, 305, 312
  sentient beings, 304, 306, 313, 316 n.13

"validate the fa." 304
  See also Qigong
Far East (Russia), 355, 359, 389–407
fetullahci, 37, 365–384
  See also Gülen, Fetullah; nurcu; Nursi, Said
Finney, Charles Grandison, 441
folk religion, 295, 321
Foucault, Michel, 284–285
flashpoint, 455
France, 1, 35, 36, 48, 89, 90, 100 n.16, 336
  n.26, 455
  See also French government
free market. See Market.
Freemasonry, 267
free speech, 111
  See also Freedom of expression
freedom from religion, 145
freedom of expression, 4–5, 22 n.13
  See also Free speech
freedom of religion
  See Religious freedom
French government, 36
Full Gospel Business Men's Fellowship
  International, 13
fundamentalism, 12, 41, 122, 133, 249 n.3
fundraising, 39

G
Gandhi, Mahatma, 65
gender, 11, 119, 150
  See also Women
Germany, 343, 391
Ghana, 114, 446
Glazier, Stephen D., 85, 86
global Christian community, 112
global civil society, 109–110
global religious resurgence, 2, 9, 13
global South, 13, 15, 21, 109–137
globalization, 12, 13, 15, 20, 37, 48, 50,
  109–137, 221, 222, 232, 238–249, 333,
  391, 445, 460
  from below, 116
Graham, Reverend Franklin
  See also Samaritan's Purse
Great Commission, 253, 256
Greece, 44, 58, 87–91, 97, 461 n.10
group protection, 15, 78, 87, 89, 91, 96

See also Self-determination; Human rights,
　　group/collective
Guatemala, 114, 126
Guinea-Bissau, 114
Gülen, Fetullah, 18, 37, 38, 365–387
　See also *Fetullahci*; *Nurcu*; Nursi, Said
Gunn, T. Jeremy, 89, 90, 94

H

Haggai Institute, 13
Hakhasia Republic, 389, 397
Hare Krishnas, 452 n.5
hate speech, 45
headscarf, 36, 37, 89, 90, 100 n.16
　as propaganda, 36
　as provocation, 36
　as proselytism, 36
　See also Scarves, Islam
Hefner, Robert W., 19
Hindu(s), 18, 37, 45, 46, 47, 49, 50, 89,
　　255, 265, 269, 461 n.4
Hinduism/Hindu tradition, 53–76, 113,
　　128, 133, 200, 202, 203, 206, 220
Hindutva, 42, 54, 58, 59, 71, 72, 89, 90, 91
　See also Hinduism, Nationalism, Hindu
Hodgson, Dorothy, 10–11
Honohana, 321, 332, 336, n.19
humanitarian aid, 79–82, 92, 94, 95, 99
　　n.9, 211, 212, 217, 220, 222
　Christian, 8
　coupled with proselytism, 81, 92, 96
　links to military action, 95
　See also Aid evangelism; Rice Christians
human rights, 1–7, 13, 21, 22 n.9, 22 n.14,
　　44, 45, 307, 311, 313, 316 n.14, 359,
　　451, 456, 461 n.11, 462 n.11
　African Charter of Human and People's
　　Rights, 7
　Cairo Declaration on Human Rights in
　　Islam, 78
　European Court of Human Rights, 44,
　　153–155
　and foreign aid, 222
　group/collective, 45, 78, 211, 224, 232, 457
　indigenous, 6–7, 41, 88
　individual, 3, 45, 140, 457
　International Religious Freedom Act

　　(IRFA), 20, 94
　Islamic, 153–154, 161 n.38
　language/discourse of, 213, 223, 345–357
　right to self determination, 6–7, 88
　UN Draft Declaration on the Rights of
　　Indigenous Peoples, 6, 88
　universalism of, 21, 145
　Hmong, 41
　See also International Covenant of Civil
　　and Political Rights (ICCPR); Universal
　　Declaration of Human Rights; UN Dec-
　　laration on the Elimination of all Forms
　　of Intolerance and Discrimination Based
　　on Religion or Belief; Religious freedom
Huntington, Samuel, 13, 118, 134, 458
　See also Clash of Civilizations

I

International Covenant on Civil and Politi-
　　cal Rights (ICCPR), 6, 216
iconoclasm, 209, 267
identity, 11, 12, 16, 86, 87, 89, 125, 220,
　　313–314, 346, 350, 356, 366, 380, 383,
　　390, 391, 398, 401, 405, 445
　media, 174–175
　See also Religious identity
ideology, 20, 40, 60, 409, 445, 447, 455
idolatry, 68, 128, 266, 293
imperialism, 6, 10, 11, 15, 41, 48, 91, 95,
　　101 n.21, n.22, 110, 111, 139, 140,
　　141, 142, 151, 459
　anti-imperialism, 91–95
India, 1, 15, 21 n.5, 35, 37, 41, 46, 48,
　　53–76, 89, 111, 113, 114, 124, 134,
　　234, 254, 255, 269, 391
indigenous
　cultures, 9
　Hmong, 41
　India, 57, 91
　peoples, 6, 57, 79, 101 n.21, n.22, 237
　practices, 38
　religions, 6, 289
　　African, 69, 88–89, 127
　rights, 40
　See also Human rights, indigenous
individualism, 445
individualistic religious experience, 3

individualized religious choice, 140
Indonesia, 80, 99 n.8, 125, 258, 259, 391
inducements (material), 78, 79, 87, 88, 91
information
dissemination, 411, 423, 425
See also Misinformation
International Covenant on Civil and Political Rights (ICCPR), 6, 154, 155, 216
See also Human rights
International Religious Freedom Act (IRFA), 152–153, 214, 217
See also Human rights; Religious freedom
Internet. *See under* Media
interreligious tensions, 121
See also Conflict
intolerance, 110, 117, 125, 129, 131, 133, 421
See also Tolerance
invitations, 412, 416–417
Iran, 41
Iraq, 8, 39, 92, 94, 97
Islam, 8, 9, 15, 38, 39, 40, 42, 48, 53, 54, 58, 62, 63, 64, 65–69, 71, 72, 89, 90, 92, 93, 94, 97, 101 n.19, 112, 119, 121, 128, 133, 139–161, 167–168, 184, 233, 234, 254–255, 260, 268, 269, 278 n.3, n.4, 394, 395, 411, 460 n.1
Al Qaeda, 121
apostasy in, 110
in Central Asia and the Caucasus, 365–387
conversion to, 9
da'wa, 8, 377, 383
human rights, 78
See also Cairo Declaration on Human Rights in Islam *under* Human Rights
scarves in, 35
Muslim Brotherhood, 39–40
Nigerian, 167, 168
Qur'an/Koran, 71, 72
radical, 366
Shia, 371, 380
Sunni, 371, 380
in Turkey, 365–387
in Turkic states, 365–387
See also Muslims, Islamic revivalism; Islamism
Islamic law, 44, 80, 153, 154
See also Shari'a
Islamic revivalism, 40, 278 n.3

Islamism, 16, 93, 100 n.12, 120, 122, 133, 139, 140, 143, 147, 156
Israel, 54, 84, 97, 100 n.10, 115, 118, 125, 130, 259

J

Jainism, 53, 5, 57, 58, 62, 63, 64, 65, 69
Japan, 17–18, 127, 274, 321–338, 391, 461 n.6
Jathika Hela Urumaya (JHU), 200–201, 208–209, 217, 224 n.3, 225 n.11, 226 n.12
Jehovah's Witnesses, 87, 258, 321, 329, 332, 335 n.16, n.17
Jenkins, Philip, 9, 119
Jews, 80, 83–84, 91, 97, 98, 99 n.3, 100 n.10
Jubilee Campaign, 215–216
Judaism, 47, 49, 65, 233, 269

K

Kazakhstan, 366, 374, 379, 383, 387, 392, 394, 398–405
Keller, Timothy, 443
Knoxville, TN, 438–439, 441, 443, 444, 447, 448–450
Kokkinakis, 87–88, 97
Korea
South, 24 n.38, 37, 95, 112–114, 127, 210, 279 n.8, 322, 326, 329, 334–335 n.9, 356, 389–394, 396–406, 406 n.4, 457, 461 n.3
North, 152, 214
Koreans, 389–407
Kyrgyzstan, 366, 371, 374 fig.5, 383, 387

L

laicité, 90, 100 n.16
See also Secular advocacy; Secularism; Secularity; Secularization
laity, 326–335 n.13
language. *See* Proselytizing discourse
See also Hate speech
Latin America, 8, 12, 41, 95, 109, 113, 114, 152
Lausanne Committee for World Evangelism, 265
law, 2, 3, 13, 20, 24 n.42, 87, 88, 91, 92, 97, 121, 132, 142, 146,147, 150, 155, 160 n.27, 257–259, 278 n.3, 285, 322, 325, 330, 331, 332, 393, 435, 436, 455,

457, 459, 461 n.9, 460
on religion in Russia, 344, 345, 347–349,
    356, 357, 359 n.1
See also Conversion; Human rights; Islamic
    law; Legal systems; Shari'a
legal systems, 458
  centrality of, 460
  judicial autonomy in, 460
  pervasiveness of, 460
Lerner, Nathan, 3, 4, 45
liberalization, 14
liberals/liberalism, 49, 96
liberty, 36
  See also Religious freedom; Religious liberty
Li Hongzhi, 301–320
literature, Christian, 393, 433, 441–442
localization, 232, 238
Lord's Resistance Army, 121
Lutherans, 61, 343, 390, 397
Ludwig, Frieder, 40

M

majority religions, 5, 6
Malaysia, 254–255, 258, 259, 269, 274,
    278, 287
maps/mapping, 39
  See also Spiritual mapping
market
  free, 21, 322, 358, 434
  religious, 36, 50, 61, 326, 455
marketing, 16, 169, 242, 248, 276, 15–420
marketplace
  of religions, 69, 88, 167–198, 326
  of ideas, 6
marriage, 154, 178, 278 n.4, 329
  forced, 139
  intermarriage, 49
Martin, David, 113, 122
Marty, Martin, 36
Mauritius, 409
Mayer, Ann Elizabeth, 152–153, 159 n.21, 164
Mayer, Jean-Francois, 424, 425 n.3
media, 2, 11, 13, 14, 16, 17, 18, 20, 24
    n.35, 24 n.39, 111, 112, 123, 127, 128,
    131, 132, 238–249, 255, 301, 376, 392,
    393, 406, 456
  broadcast, 170, 173

billboard, 231, 238, 248
blogs, 14
cassette tapes, 315 n.4
cable TV, 312
chat rooms, 14
comic book, 413
and conflict, 301–320
coverage of new religious movements, 321
cyberspace, 410, 412, 418, 420
deregulation, 170–175
films, 256
flyers, 274, 276
hijacking, 312–313, 317–318 n.22
identity, 174–175
Internet, 19, 37, 38, 169, 239, 245,
    269, 270, 303, 316 n.16, 392, 395,
    409–430, 461 n.3
  See also Websites
magazines, 244
Muslim, 180
movies, 256
newspapers, 248, 308, 327, 329, 330, 350,
    367–369, 387, 396
  See also Press
in Nigeria, 168–198
pamphlets, 43, 209, 239, 242, 244, 250
    n.8, 270, 414
posters, 175–198, 261, 276
press, 41, 47, 147, 210, 244, 248, 304,
    306–310, 316 n.16, 327, 329–331,
    344, 348, 358, 395
  Egyptian Arabic, 144, 158 n.17
radio, 11, 169, 170, 173, 174, 239, 384
    n.1, 393
  Russian, 339, 340, 344, 348, 356, 358
satellite, 169, 178, 240, 312, 317 n.22
television, 184, 208, 238, 239, 241, 248,
    308, 313, 317 n.21, n.22, 330, 334
    n.9, 384 n.1
  Brazilian, 123
tracts, 143, 203, 261
video, 168, 169, 182, 185, 239, 246, 255,
    271, 315 n.4, 317 n.22, 446
website(s), 14, 37, 46, 240, 256, 270, 276,
    303, 308, 309, 312, 314 n.2, 315 n.4,
    316 n.15, 317 n.21, 387, 410–430
  See also Internet; Miracles, broadcasting

meditation, 233, 234, 238–247
megachurches, 44, 438
Meiji Constitution, 323
Mennonite Church, 343
merit-making, 239, 242–248
Meyer, Birgit, 446
Middle East, 14, 48, 92, 144, 152, 260, 269, 317 n.17
militancy
  religious, 21
militant-groups, 39, 218
militarism, 95
militia
  Christian, 125
millennial
  movement, 310
  revolt, 310
Minghui (Clearwisdom), 315 n.4, 317 n.21
minority religions, 4, 5, 13, 90, 149, 223, 255, 258, 348, 411, 413, 455, 457, 460
miracles, 178, 180, 187, 190 n.29, 244
  broadcasting, 170–175, 189 n.9
misinformation, 413
missiology, 7–9, 24 n.32
mission
  Christian, 9–10, 46
  comparison of Christian and Muslim, 8
  counter-missions, 46
  fields, 37
  global, 253
  Hindu, 47
  Muslim, 46
  Overland Missions, 39
  See also *Da'wa*; Schools, Christian
missionaries
  American, 16, 79–80, 87, 139–161, 326, 390
  British, 140, 142, 202, 203, 267
  and anthropologists, 10–11
  bans on foreign, 111, 146, 347–349
  Brazilian, 114–116, 127–130, 132–133
  Buddhist, 231–252
  Christian, 8, 37, 38, 40, 44, 49, 54, 71, 205, 206, 326, 457
  charged as coercive, 110
  criticism of foreign, 88
  definition of, 235
  Dutch, 202

European, 326, 333–334 n.3
from global South, 15, 109–137
fundamentalist, 41
Japanese, 332–333
Jesuit, 322, 334 n.5
Korean, 37, 38, 326, 334 n.7, n.9, 389–407, 402 fig. 1, 457
medical, 98
Muslim, 38, 40
Portuguese, 202
Protestant, 9, 129, 139, 277, 283, 345
Scandinavian, 390
short-term, 38, 394
Spanish, 38
and trade/business, 365–387, 405
Turkish Muslim, 365–387
See also Activists
missionary activity, 40, 45, 234, 349, 393, 457
and aid, 79–82
  to children, 79–80
Buddhist, 17, 334 n.4
categories of, 39, 45, 201
Catholic, 342
demographics of, 8–9, 23 n.24, 23 n.25
ethos of, 249
flows of, 19, 109–137, 333
in France, 35
as fundraising, 39
as impulse, 10
identity relating to, 381
of Japanese religions, 322–329
motives of, 151, 207–208, 356, 376–377, 433, 440
Pentecostal, 343
as propaganda, 39
as provocation, 36
reactions to, 10, 39, 41, 46, 49, 54, 398
of regions, 21, 53–76
regulation of, 140, 148–151, 154–156, 356, 358
right to engage in, 3
Russian Orthodox, 355–356
short-term, 8
as social outreach, 433
as threat to national interests 42
unintended consequences of, 10, 431–454
US, 94

See also Missionary field; "Missionary position;" Missionary space
missionary field, 7, 18, 23 n.26, 346, 359
  as targets of neo-conservative military ambition, 93
missionary opportunities and American foreign policy, 94
missionary outreach, 79, 84, 253
"missionary position," 10–11
missionary religion, 21, 50, 322, 324, 328, 329
  non-missionary religion 49
missionary space, 295, 433
missionization, 265–266
modernity, 17, 55, 180, 186, 232, 235, 237, 239, 285, 287
Moscow Patriarchate, 41
Mott, John, 142–143
Mormons. *See under* Church of Jesus Christ of Latter-day Saints
multiculturalism, 39, 221, 254, 256
Mumbai Manifesto, 47
  See also World Council of Elders of Ancient Traditions and Cultures
Murabitun, 38
music, 87, 124, 132, 184, 246, 255, 256, 262, 296, 382, 414
Muslim Brotherhood, 39, 143, 159 n.24
Muslim(s), 18, 23 n.19, 37–38, 62, 84, 90, 100 n.11, n.16, 119, 122, 124, 130, 139–161, 167–168, 191 n.41, 200, 241, 254–255, 258, 260, 341
  missionaries, 38–39
  relations with Christians, 40
  See also Islam
Mutua, Makau, 6–7, 69, 88–89, 90, 100 n.15

N

National Evangelists
  Japan, 323
national consciousness, 43
national interests, 42
nationalism, 2, 10, 15, 17, 134, 391
  Christian, 123
  Egypt, 16, 139–161
  Hindu, 44, 49, 59, 73, 134
  Japan, 323–324
  as mutual practice, 291–292

Philippines, 283–286, 289, 291–292, 297–298
  and religion, 122
  in Russia, 345–347, 356
    Russian Far East, 395
  in Sri Lanka, 16, 199–229
  in Thailand, 237, 248
  Turkish, 365–387
  US, 94
national security, 42, 44
Nattier, Jan, 310
Navayana Diksha, 59
neo-colonialism. *See under* Colonialism
neo-liberalism, 1, 446
Netherlands, the, 210
New Age, 17, 298
  religion, 191 n.31
New Christian Right, 94, 119, 122
  See also Evangelical(s), US
new religions
  in Brazil, 336 n.25
  in France, 336 n.26
  Japanese, 321–338
  See also New religious movements
new religious movements (NRMs), 12, 17, 78, 312, 321, 326
  media coverage of, 320
  See also New religions
NGOs, 9, 460
Nigeria, 13, 16, 24 n.38, 112, 114, 124, 127, 167–198
non-interference, 68, 71, 85
non-intervention, 96
non-proselytizing groups, 69, 73
non-recruitment, 15, 78, 83–87
North Africa, 134
North America, 114, 234, 256, 270, 302
Norway, 8, 23 n.19
nurcu, 374–387
Nursi, Said, 365, 372, 387

O

offline religion, 419
  See also Online religion
Olasky, Marvin, 435, 436, 543 n.2
Omar, Rashied, 8
online apologetics. *See under* Apologetics
online religion

comparison with offline religion, 14
See also Offline religion; Online religious communities
online religious communities, 19, 426 n.7, n.9, n.10, 418–423
Orthodox Church, 85, 100 n.17
  Russian, 18, 38, 88, 127, 339–364, 389, 390, 392, 394, 397, 398, 461 n.5
  conflict with Roman Catholic Church over proselytism, 349, 356
  canonical territory, 38, 353
  Romanian, 82
  Greek, 87, 88, 89, 91
Orthodoxy, 23 n.18, 61
  Coptic, 139
  Russian, 13
  See also Orthodox Church, Russian
orthopraxy, 61
Ottoman Empire, 141, 142, 365, 376
outreach, 256, 420
  social, 431–454
Overland Missions. *See under* Missions
Oyakhilome, Chris, 171, 177–178, 189 n.17, 191 n.35, n.37

P

Pacific, 95, 109, 112
paganism, 410, 414, 417, 420
Pagan Pride, 19, 413–414, 421, 426 n.9,
pagans/neo-pagans, 47, 91
Pakistan, 114
para-church agencies, 13
Paraguay, 114
pastoral power, 285
peace, 9, 45
Pentecostalism, 12, 122–124
  and advertisement/advertising, 167–198
  in Ghana, 446
  in Nigeria, 167–198
  New, 168–198
Pentecostals, 8, 13, 14, 18, 40, 41, 82, 88, 112, 113, 115, 116, 122–124, 126, 127, 131, 132, 343–344, 390, 391, 396, 397, 398, 399, 400, 404–405
  Nigeria, 16, 167–198
persecution, 65, 98, 133, 152, 202, 213–217, 219, 334, 341, 366, 380

of Falun Gong 308, 313, 315 n.8, 317 n.17, n.21, n.22
  literature, 311
persuasion, 7, 85, 262, 313, 417, 425
Peru, 124
Philippines, 17, 112, 114, 127, 283–300, 391, 461 n.5
  See also under Nationalism
pluralism, 117, 118, 122
  religious, 1, 4, 7, 15, 16, 21 n.2, 37, 57, 117, 118, 256, 278 n.4, 347, 348, 359, 435, 459, 460, 461 n.8
  anti-pluralism, 122
political dominance, 40
Portugal, 114, 133
post-colonialism. *See under* Colonialism
posters, 168–198
  See also Proselytizing, poster; Publicity
prayer, 253–282
  for nations, 268–271, 277
  journeys/walking, 263–265, 272, 273
  United Prayer Track, 271–277
Priest, Robert, 10–11
Presbyterians, 396
privacy rights, 456
problem of evil, 80
Prodromou, Elizabeth, 4
propaganda, 16, 36, 39, 175, 186, 298, 302, 305, 306, 308, 311, 341, 378, 414, 417, 421, 423–425, 425 n.2
  Christian missionary, 39
  countering, 414
propagation (of religion), 1, 40, 92, 68, 69
proselytic activity, 14, 15, 17, 20
proselytism
  anti-proselytism, 39, 44, 88, 91, 134, 410, 420, 427 n.20
  balancing free speech and, 111
  and blasphemy, 5
  in China, 40
  comparative studies of, 10
  conflict between Russian Orthodox and Roman Catholic Church over, 349, 356
  coupled with humanitarianism, 81, 92, 96
  as criminal offense, 87–89
  definition of, 2, 4, 5, 7, 22 n.7, 87, 172, 190 n.21, 233, 278 n.2, 352, 356, 409, 410, 422

freedom from, 96
headscarf as, 35–36
guise of, 265–266, 278 n.5
illegal, 373
improper, 5, 111, 352, 356
interplay of Christian, and American
    militarism, 95
and injury about religious feeling, 5
Islamic, 377, 380
  See also *Da'wa*
logic of, 15, 97
Orthodox reconceptualization of, 23 n.18
as persuasion, 262
proper, 5, 111
purpose of, 82–83
restrictions on, 18, 44, 89, 185, 352, 353,
    356, 456
secular questioning of, 49
as threat to Christian unity, 36, 49
Proselytism Project. *See* Emory Proselytism
    Project
proselytization
and accountability, 15
ambiguities in standard relating to, 3
anti-proselytization, 3, 15, 75–107, 109,
    232, 247–249, 357, 456, 457, 458
banning of, 43, 62, 72
as Christian, 459
and contradictions with human rights
    corpus, 6–7
definition of, 2, 22 n.8, 232–234, 249 n.3,
    333 n.1, 409, 422
downward trend in recognition of right to, 3
ethical, 5, 8, 15, 149, 215, 432
and exploitation, 81
and foreign aid, 207
"from above," 323, 334 n.5
"from below," 323, 334 n.4
and humanitarianism, 8
illegitimate, 45, 109
implicit, 415
as instrumentalist, 2
and intolerance and civil exclusion, 110
and intentionality, 5
Islamic, 62
Jewish rejection of, 83–84
legal grounding of, 167–172

legal solutions, 72
and market forces, 13
motivations for, 411–415
multidisciplinary study of, 7–12
online, 409–430
political economy of, 11–12
politics of, 20
and political discourse, 344
poster 16, 167–198
as process, 456–457
reactions against, 2, 15, 18, 21 n.6, 48,
    49, 50, 62, 82, 91, 139–161, 204,
    247–249, 311, 322, 331–332, 346,
    349–357, 431–432, 456
restrictions on, 3, 4, 5, 7, 274
and religious freedom/freedom of religion
    and belief, 1–7
and right to choose or change one's reli-
    gion, 3, 8
regulation of, 4, 5, 356
strategies, 5, 11, 13, 14, 18, 321,
    327–328, 335 n.14, 322, 365,
    375, 379–380, 389, 401–404, 432,
    440–444, 449–452, 452 n.1
theology of, 15
as threat to ancestral tradition, 73
unethical, 41, 44, 77, 82, 84, 88, 140,
    170–175, 247–249, 256, 330, 335
  Roman Catholic ban on, 7
in world politics, 16, 54, 57
See also Non-proselytizing groups;
    Proselytic activity; Tactics; Target(s);
    Unreached peoples
proselytizer(s), 14, 20, 40, 45, 49, 50, 77,
    78, 79, 81, 82, 85, 86, 87, 93, 96, 97
    n.99, 109, 110, 111, 123, 1132, 133,
    134, 210, 248, 328, 378, 406, 419
proselytizing discourse, 15, 16–17, 18, 19,
    21, 20, 97, 231–252, 283–300, 380,
    416–420, 422, 432, 439, 447, 450–451
as advertizing, 16, 167–198, 415–420
as countering misinformation, 409–430
differences between online and offline,
    419–420, 423–424
as information dissemination, 409–430
as social engagement, 431–454
Protestantism, 17, 58, 61, 85, 118, 200,

215, 218, 236, 250 n.13, 256–257, 263, 268, 283, 328, 342, 378, 390, 437, 441, 452 n.7
  as global religion, 118
  in Russia, 343, 345, 349
publicity, 171, 175, 181, 183, 184, 192 n.46, 288, 313, 433, 436, 445, 446, 450
  See also Advertising; Proselytizing, poster
public order, 4, 89, 154, 161 n.42
public recognition, 2

Q

qigong, 302, 314 n.3, n.4

R

Rambo, Lewis, 3, 77, 78, 82, 86, 93, 101 n.22, 172, 200 n.22
Rashtriya Swayamsevak Sangh (RSS), 42–43
rational choice theory, 12
reconversion. *See under* Conversion
recruitment, 12, 15
  activities, 321, 322, 326–333, 333 n.1, 335 n.10, 372, 381
  efficiency, 424
  of new members, 36, 173, 192 n.46, 381
  of youth, 259
  non-recruitment, 15, 78, 83–87, 96
  See also Proselytization, strategies
Redeemed Christian Church of God, 13, 168–169, 182, 192 n.43
registration, 240, 302, 348, 397
regulation, 12, 140, 170–175, 458
  See also Missionary activity, regulation of; Proselytism, restrictions on; Proselytiza-tion, banning of
relativism, 49
  See also Universalism
religious activism. *See* Activism; Activists
religious
  affiliation, 14
  choice, 146, 147, 155
  competition. *See* Competition between religions
  dress, 14
  emblems, 14, 35
  harmony, 254
  identity, 45

instruction, 81
persecution, 215–216
reaffiliation, 14
religious conversion. *See* Conversion
religious discourse. *See also See* Proselytizing discourse
  See also Hate speech; Religious hatred
religious freedom, 3, 7, 8, 13, 15, 16, 20, 22 n.11, 22 n.14, 24 n.37, n.42, 40, 41, 44, 45, 46, 47, 53, 54, 61, 62, 67–72, 88, 100 n.15, 118, 121, 123, 124, 127, 130, 173, 200 n.10, 201, 214–216, 391, 451, 456, 459–460, 461 n.11
  abuse of, by evangelists, 210
  Cairo Declaration on Human Rights in Islam, 78
  evangelical campaign for, 24 n.42
  as freedom from proselytization, 68
  as freedom from religion, 145
  in Egypt, 139–161
  as individual and universal, 145
  individualized conception of, 3
  inequity of, 69
  International Religious Freedom Act (IRFA), 152–153, 214, 217
  in Japan, 324, 325
  in Nigeria, 167, 168, 173
  restrictions on, US, 13, 461 n.9
  role of state and, 53, 88
  as rooted in Western agendas, 151
  in Russia, 340–341, 344–345, 347–349, 352, 357, 359
  as secularization of Christian theology, 68
  Singapore, 257–259
  in Sri Lanka, 199–229
  US Commission on International Reli-gious Freedom, 40, 154
  US support for, 152
  See also Change of religion; Human rights; Minority religions;
religious harmony (Singapore), 17, 257–261, 276
religious hatred, 3
religious liberty, 22 n.14, 67, 110, 117, 140, 141,145, 146, 147, 152, 157 n.2, 159 n.22, 172, 200, 223, 225 n.9, 214, 215, 216, 217
  See also Religious freedom

religious minorities. *See* Minority religions

religious pluralism. *See* Pluralism, religious

religious reaffiliation. *See under* Conversion, reaffiliation

religious rivalry, 57–64, 67, 69, 73 n.2
  See also Advertizing; Competition; Conflict

religious truth, 62, 64, 65, 66, 67, 68, 69, 70, 71

revivalism, 441, 447, 450
  Islamic, 40, 365–387

revivalist groups, 39, 48

rice Christians, 79, 99 n.6, 458–459

ritual
  rules, 57, 62, 82, 84, 168
  baptism, 83

rivalry between religions. *See* Religious rivalry

Rizal, José, 17, 283–294, 297

Robbins, Joel, 11

Robeck, Cecil, 7

Roman Catholic Church, 7, 10, 11, 13, 17, 22 n.15, 58, 61, 85, 98, 110, 112, 121, 200, 202, 215, 218, 220, 241, 259, 283, 286, 294–298, 322, 342–343, 345, 349–359, 395
  Second Vatican Council/Vatican II, 83, 352

Russia, 1, 13, 18, 54, 88, 90, 114, 339–364, 366, 370, 389–407, 457, 458, 461 n.3
  Asian region, 389–407
  Far East Region, 355, 359, 389–407
  indigenous populations of, 390, 392, 394–395, 398–405, 406 n.1
  Roman Catholic Church in, 342–343, 345, 349–359
  Russian Federation, 390

Russian Orthodox Church. *See* Orthodox Church, Russian

Rwanda, 125

S

Sakhalin Island, 392–394

salvation, 6, 256, 301–320
  religious goals, 303, 306, 311, 312, 314
  secular goals, 303, 311, 312, 314

Samaritan's Purse, 92–95, 99

Sanneh, Lamin, 9, 23 n.28, 111, 112, 120, 132, 152

Satan, 415

Satanism, 133

Saudi Arabia, 40, 92, 127, 153

school(s), 36, 78, 79, 147, 261, 323, 329
  American mission, in Egypt, 143
  Buddhist, 322
  Christian, 46, 143, 146, 148, 157 n.5, 158 n.19, 159 n.26, 160 n.27, 204, 205, 292
  Muslim, 144, 365–387
  Turkish, 18, 365–387
  See also Education

Scientology, Church of, 81, 85, 411, 424, 452 n.5

Second Vatican Council, 294–297

secular advocacy, 85–87

secular humanism, 432

secular liberalism, 433

secular nations, 40

secular notion of religious freedom, 15

secular objectives, 285

secular protest, 301–320

secular society, 333, 394

secular state, 18

secular translation of problem of conversion, 67

secularism, 4, 14, 58, 263, 434

secularists, 35, 36, 68, 71, 84

secularity, 36, 89, 122
  See also *Laïcité*

secularization, 14, 24 n.36, 68, 69, 70, 155, 284, 293, 354

security, 4, 20

separatism, 41

September 11, 2001, 8, 21, 130, 254, 260, 266

Shamanism, 394–395, 398, 399, 404, 405

Shari'a, 146, 168, 188 n.3
  See also Islamic law

Sharma, Arvind, 462 n.11

"sheep-stealing," 7, 82, 172, 185, 186, 187, 353

Shinto, 321–345

shuddhi, 46, 47

Siberia, 355, 359, 389–407

Sider, Ronald, 442, 450

Sikhism, 57

Singapore, 17, 21 n.5, 253–282, 457, 461 n.7

Sjogren, Steve, 442–443

social control, 12, 458

Social Gospel, 433, 440
social (in)equality, 58, 59, 60
social psychology, 455–456
sociologists, 2, 11, 16, 23, 24 n.33
sociology, 455–464
Soka Gakkai, 18, 238, 250 n.7, 321, 326, 328, 332, 333
Sona, Gangodawila, 206–208
South Africa, 45, 112, 114, 127, 128
South America, 41, 79, 270
South Asia, 113, 127, 234
South-East Asia, 234, 269
sovereignty, 41, 42, 96, 144, 148, 155, 221, 222, 237
  See also Nationalism; National security
Soviet Union, 41, 88, 365–366, 377, 380, 381
Soviet rule, 341
Spain, 114, 285, 286, 287
spiritual
  mapping, 253
  warfare, 123, 126, 253, 254, 263–266, 272, 276, 279 n.9
Sri Lanka, 16, 46, 54, 199–229, 458
Stahnke, Tad, 4–5, 22 n.13, 89, 91, 92, 111, 117, 223
state policy on proselytization, 2, 4, 5, 6, 14, 91, 118, 121
  in China, 301–320
  in Egypt, 139–161
  in Japan, 321–338
  as liberal and neutral, 53
  in Nigeria, 170–175
  in Russia, 339–364
  in Singapore, 253–282
  in Thailand, 237
  See also Missionary activity, regulation of; Nationalism; Proselytism, restrictions on; Proselytization, banning of
Stern, Jessica, 125
Sudan, 154
survival, 36, 48
Switzerland, 38
syncretism, 276

T

tactics, 15, 78, 84, 85, 96, 247
  See also Proselytization, strategies

Tajikistan, 37, 38
Tanzania, 40
Taoists, 255
target(s), 5, 7, 15, 45, 78, 84, 85, 96, 97, 172, 185, 248, 392, 425 n.2, 457
  See also Proselytization, strategies
Tatarstan, 366, 371
teblig, 377, 378
temsil, 378
territoriality, 126
territorial spirits, 263–276
terrorism, 1, 13, 121, 125, 308
Thailand, 17, 231–252, 391, 457, 491 n.3
Theravada. *See* Buddhism
third party partisans, 460
Third World, 114–116, 122, 133
Thomas, George, 11–13
Tiananmen Square, 304
Tocqueville, Alexis de, 117
tolerance, 71-72, 110, 111, 117, 129, 132, 203, 213, 260, 342, 379, 425 n.4, 459
  See also Intolerance; Toleration of religious difference
toleration of religious difference, 77, 119
tourism, 17, 298
tribal groups/peoples
  See Indigenous
tribulations, 305
truth. *See* Religious truth
tsunami, 1, 80, 81, 96
Tunisia, 153
Turkey, 1, 18, 37, 42, 253, 365–387, 457
Turkmenistan, 366, 370 fig. 3, 371, 373 fig. 4, 374, 383
Tuva Republic, 397, 398–405

U

UN Declaration on Rights of Indigenous Peoples, 88
UN Declaration on the Elimination of all Forms of Intolerance and Discrimination Based on Religion or Belief, 3
  See also Religious freedom
UN Special Rapporteur on Freedom of Religion or Belief, 3
Unification Church, 258, 321, 329–330, 334 n.9, 335–336 n.18

United Kingdom, 114, 129, 133, 170, 210, 413
United Nations, 3, 303, 460
United States, 13, 16, 19, 24 n.38, 40, 48, 54,
    61, 73, 80, 85, 87, 92–95, 100 n.18, 110,
    111, 114, 119, 143, 144, 150, 152, 210,
    214–216, 225 n.12, 285, 302, 303, 317
    n.17, 391, 411, 413, 431–454, 458, 461 n.4
Unitarian–Universalists, 47
Universal Church of the Kingdom of God
    (UCKG), 13, 115, 123, 127–129, 132, 133
Universal Declaration of Human Rights
    (UDHR), 69, 140, 147, 152, 153–155
    Article 18, 6
universalism, 21, 47, 49, 234, 351, 356, 359
    See also Relativism
universality of religion, 61, 62, 63, 72
universities, 35
unreached peoples, 39, 268–271, 394
UN Special Rapporteur on Freedom of
    Religion or Belief, 3
US Commission of International Religious
    Freedom. *See under* Religious freedom
Uzell, Lawrence A., 87, 409
Uzbekistan, 366, 368, 370, 374, 376, 379,
    381, 382, 383, 391, 392, 399

V

Van der Veer, Peter, 12 n.5, 19, 20
Van der Vyver, Johan, 3
Vietnam, 41
violence, 53, 73, 124–126, 129, 130, 224
    n.2, 261, 317 n.20, 330–331, 457, 460
Vishnu Hindu Parishad (VHP), 43, 46

W

Wagner, C. Peter, 258, 271–272, 279 n.9
Walls, Andrew F., 8–9, 23 n.28, 24 n.30,
    82, 85, 98, 101 n.22, 108 n.2, 113
war of civilizations, 39
    See also Clash of civilizations
war for souls, 1, 339
War on Terror/Terrorism, 8, 93
websites. *See under* Media
    See also Internet
welfare, 327, 334 n.8
    reform, 432, 434, 446, 19
    social, 277
Wessinger, Catherine, 38, 310, 314 n.1
West Africa, 2, 18, 126, 253
Wicca, 19, 409–430, 461 n.3
winning souls, 79–80
witchcraft, 127, 128
Witches' Voice, the, 412
witness, 22 n.7, 22 n.15, 82, 83, 149, 212,
    223, 233, 256, 268, 352, 354, 353, 447
witnessing, 2, 7, 329, 431, 432, 441, 443
Witte, John, 1, 2, 3, 4, 21 n.5, 22 n.22, 118
women, 9, 47, 158 n.18, 153, 178–180, 184,
    279 n.11, 294, 297, 327, 372, 396, 401
    See also Gender
World Council of Churches, 7, 22 n.15, 82, 111
World Council of Elders of Ancient Tradi-
    tions and Cultures, 47
    See also Mumbai Manifesto
world peace, 231–252
World Vision, 210–211, 224 n.4

Y

Yoido Full Gospel Church, 397, 398
youth, 355–356
Yugoslavia, 125

Z

Zambia, 120, 121, 329, 410